The Psychology of Human Sexuality

The Psychology of Human Sexuality

Justin J. Lehmiller, Ph.D.

Harvard University

WILEY Blackwell

This edition first published 2014
© 2014 John Wiley & Sons, Ltd

Registered Office
John Wiley & Sons, Ltd, The Atrium, Southern Gate, Chichester, West Sussex, PO19 8SQ, UK

Editorial Offices
350 Main Street, Malden, MA 02148-5020, USA
9600 Garsington Road, Oxford, OX4 2DQ, UK
The Atrium, Southern Gate, Chichester, West Sussex, PO19 8SQ, UK

For details of our global editorial offices, for customer services, and for information about how
to apply for permission to reuse the copyright material in this book please see our website at
www.wiley.com/wiley-blackwell.

Library of Congress Cataloging-in-Publication Data

Lehmiller, Justin J.
  The psychology of human sexuality / Justin J. Lehmiller.
     pages   cm
  Includes bibliographical references and index.
    ISBN 978-1-118-35133-8 (cloth) – ISBN 978-1-118-35121-5 (pbk.)   1. Sex (Psychology)
2. Sex (Biology)   I. Title.
  BF692.L435 2014
  155.3–dc23
                                    2013033147

A catalogue record for this book is available from the British Library.

Cover image: © James Cotier / Getty Images
Cover design by Simon Levy Design Associates

Set in 10.5/12.5pt Dante by SPi Publisher Services, Pondicherry, India
Printed and bound in Singapore by Markono Print Media Pte Ltd

2   2014

Contents

About the Author   xi
Foreplay   xii
Illustrations   xiv
Text Boxes   xx
Tables   xxii

1   **Theoretical Perspectives on Human Sexuality**   1
    Introduction   2
    What Drives Us to Have Sex?   2
        Psychological Influences   2
        Cultural and Societal Influences   3
        Biological and Evolutionary Influences   7
    Major Theoretical Perspectives on Human Sexuality   8
        Psychoanalytic Theory   8
        Cognitive-Behavioral and Learning Theories   11
        Exchange Theories   15
        Personality Theories   16
        Evolutionary Theory   19
    The Perspective of This Text   21
    Key Terms   23
    Discussion Questions   23
    References   23

2   **Sexology Research: History, Methods, and Ethics**   27
    Introduction   28
    A Brief History of Sexology   29
    Sexology as a Science   31
    Sample Selection   32
    Nonexperimental Research   34
        Surveys   34
        Direct Observation   38

Case Reports	42
Experimental Research	42
A Sample Sexperiment	43
Strengths and Limitations of the Experimental Method	43
A Note on Statistics	44
Means and Medians	44
Incidence and Prevalence	44
Correlation	44
Ethics in Sexology Research	45
Informed Consent	48
Debriefing	50
Confidentiality	51
Evaluating Sex Research	51
Key Terms	52
Discussion Questions	52
References	52

3   Human Sexual Anatomy — **55**

Introduction	56
Male Sexual Anatomy	56
A Historical and Cultural Overview of the Penis	56
External Anatomy	58
Internal Anatomy	59
Psychology of the Penis: Male Genital Concerns	64
Male Genital Health Issues	66
Female Sexual Anatomy	67
A Historical and Cultural Overview of the Vulva	67
External Anatomy	68
Internal Anatomy	73
Breasts	75
Psychology of the Breasts and Vulva: Female Bodily Concerns	77
Female Breast and Genital Health Issues	79
Moving Forward	82
Key Terms	82
Discussion Questions	83
References	83

4   Human Sexual Response: Understanding Arousal and Orgasm — **87**

Introduction	88
Factors That Influence Sexual Arousal	88
The Brain	88
The Senses	90
Hormones	97
Substances	100
The Sexual Response Cycle	103
The Masters and Johnson Model	103
Psychological Models of Sexual Response	108
Key Terms	111

Discussion Questions   111
References   111

5   Gender and Gender Identity   **115**
Introduction   116
Biological Influences on Gender Identity and Sexuality   117
Biological Sex Variations   120
Psychosocial Influences on Gender Identity and Sexuality   126
Social Interactions and Norms   126
Physical Environments   128
Media   129
Variations in Gender Expression   130
Transsexualism   130
Cross-Dressing   135
Other Identities   136
Just How Different Are Men and Women?   137
Sex Differences in Psychology   137
Sex Differences in Sexuality and Attitudes Toward Sex   138
Key Terms   139
Discussion Questions   140
References   140

6   Sexual Orientation   **144**
Introduction   145
Sexual Orientation: Definitions and Types   145
Measurement and Prevalence   146
Theories of Sexual Orientation   149
Early Psychological Theories   149
Biological and Hormonal Theories   149
Evolutionary Theories   151
Biopsychosocial Theories   152
Sex Differences in the Expression of Sexual Orientation   155
Sexual Orientation Attitudes   158
Prejudice Against Gay, Lesbian, and Bisexual Persons   158
Sexual Orientation in Psychological Perspective   162
Sexual Orientation Myths   164
Key Terms   167
Discussion Questions   167
References   168

7   The Laws of Attraction   **171**
Introduction   172
What Attracts Us To Other People?   173
Affective Influences   173
Propinquity   177
Similarity   177
Scarcity   180
Physiological Arousal   180

Neurochemical Factors   182
Physical Attractiveness   182
Attraction Processes among Gay Men and Lesbians   185
Why Are Men and Women Attracted to Different Characteristics?   185
Evolutionary Theory   186
Social Structural Perspectives   188
Key Terms   192
Discussion Questions   192
References   192

8   Intimate Relationships: Sex, Love, and Commitment   196
Introduction   197
Singlehood and Casual Relationships   197
Sexuality Among Singles   199
Hookups   199
Friends with Benefits   200
Singles' Sexual Outcomes   202
Love and Committed Relationships   203
The Nature of Love   203
The Nature of Commitment   208
Varieties of Loving and Committed Relationships   211
Why Do Some Relationships Succeed While Others Fail?   216
Characteristics of Good Relationships   216
The Dark Side of Relationships   220
Coping with Breakup   224
Key Terms   224
Discussion Questions   225
References   225

9   Sexual Behaviors   229
Introduction   230
Solitary Sexual Behaviors   230
Asexuality and Celibacy   230
Sexual Fantasy   232
Masturbation   235
Partnered Sexual Behaviors   240
Kissing   241
Touching   242
Oral Sex   243
Vaginal Intercourse   243
Anal Sex   244
Same-Sex Behaviors   245
Frequency and Benefits of Sex and Orgasm   248
Sexual Behavior in Psychological Perspective   249
Self-Regulation   249
Attachment Style   251
Mortality Salience   251
Key Terms   252

    Discussion Questions   252
    References   252

10 Sex Education, Contraception, and Pregnancy   255
    Introduction   256
    Sex Education   256
    Contraception   261
      History   262
      Types of Contraceptives   262
      Choosing the Right Contraceptive   270
    Pregnancy   272
      The Psychology of Trying to Have a Baby   272
      Psychological Changes During Pregnancy and After Birth   273
      Abortion   274
    Key Terms   275
    Discussion Questions   275
    References   276

11 Sexually Transmitted Infections and Safer-Sex Practices   279
    Introduction   280
    Sexually Transmitted Infections   280
      Bacterial Infections   281
      Viral Infections   284
      Other Infections   289
    Factors That Increase the Spread of STIs   290
      Biological   290
      Psychological   291
      Social and Environmental   292
    The Psychological Impact of STIs   293
      Implications for Romantic and Sexual Relationships   295
    Preventing Infection   296
    Key Terms   299
    Discussion Questions   299
    References   299

12 Sexual Dysfunction and Sex Therapy   302
    Introduction   303
    Causes of Sex Difficulties   303
      Biological   303
      Psychological   304
      Social   306
    Types of Sexual Dysfunction   308
      Desire Problems   308
      Arousal Problems   311
      Orgasm Problems   311
      Pain Disorders   312
    Sex Therapy   313
      Schools of Thought   313

Specific Treatments	318
Tips For Avoiding Sexual Difficulties	324
Key Terms	324
Discussion Questions	325
References	325

13   Variations in Sexual Behavior   **328**

Introduction	329
What are Paraphilias?	329
Types of Paraphilias	331
Fetishism	331
Transvestism	335
Sadomasochism	336
Voyeurism	338
Exhibitionism	339
Pedophilia	341
Other Paraphilias	341
Treatment of Paraphilic Disorders	345
Medical Therapies	346
Psychological Therapies	346
Social Skills Training	347
Effectiveness	347
Key Terms	348
Discussion Questions	348
References	348

14   Sex Laws, Sexual Victimization, and the Sexual Marketplace   **351**

Introduction	352
A Brief History of Sex Laws	352
Sexual Coercion and Violence	354
Sexual Assault	354
Child Sexual Abuse	357
Sexual Harassment	358
The Sexual Marketplace	360
Prostitution	360
Sex Trafficking	364
Pornography	365
Key Terms	374
Discussion Questions	374
References	374

Epilogue	378
Glossary	379
Index	391

About the Author

Justin J. Lehmiller (PhD, Purdue University) is a College Fellow in the Department of Psychology at Harvard University. He has been teaching college-level human sexuality courses for more than 8 years and is an accomplished educator. As a graduate student at Purdue, he received an award for outstanding teaching and, since serving on the faculty at Harvard, was awarded a Certificate of Teaching Excellence.

Dr. Lehmiller is also a prolific scholar, having published more than 25 pieces of scientific writing to date, including articles in some of the leading journals on sex and relationships, such as the *Journal of Sex Research* and the *Journal of Social and Personal Relationships*. He conducts research on topics including secret relationships, prejudice and stigma, sexual orientation, safer-sex practices, and friends with benefits. Dr. Lehmiller's credentials have made him an internationally recognized expert on sexuality. He is frequently interviewed by and has his research highlighted in news and media outlets, including *CNN.com, The Chicago Tribune, The Huffington Post, Men's Health*, and *The Sunday Times*. He writes a popular blog, *The Psychology of Human Sexuality*, that is updated several times per week and presents the latest research on sex and relationships in a way that is both educational and entertaining. Learn more about Dr. Lehmiller and follow his blog at www.lehmiller.com.

Foreplay

Sex. Almost everyone does it, but almost no one wants to talk about. It is quite the paradox when you consider how vital sex is to human life. Not only is it the act that propels our species forward, but it is also a way to bond with a romantic partner, a way to relieve the stress of daily life, not to mention an enjoyable way to pass the time. Of course, sex is not fun and games all of the time. For some people, sex can be a constant source of anxiety and insecurity, an awkward and embarrassing topic of discussion, not to mention a potential pathway to disease and death. Sex thus has both a light side and a dark side, and each deserves to be acknowledged.

The goal of this book is to give you a better understanding of the ins and outs of sex from a psychological perspective. There are many excellent books out there already that tackle this topic from a largely biological standpoint, and you could certainly learn a lot from reading those texts. However, most of those books give short shrift to the roles that psychology and the social and cultural context play in shaping human sexual behavior. I have used many of these books in previous courses I have taught and have found that students who were majoring in psychology or who took the course because it was advertised as *Psychology* of Human Sexuality were largely unsatisfied. In fact, the first few times I taught this class, my end-of-semester evaluations looked pretty similar: students commented on how much they loved and enjoyed the course, but wanted to know, *"Where's the psychology?"* Because I was unable to find a book that truly met the needs and desires of my students, I decided to write this one.

Of course, this book will not focus on psychology to the total exclusion of other factors, because that would ultimately do a disservice to readers by providing an utterly imbalanced perspective. I have therefore sought to put psychology front and center throughout, but also to give due consideration to biological, evolutionary, and sociocultural influences on sexuality where relevant. As some of you may recognize, this book mirrors the *biopsychosocial* perspective adopted in most health psychology textbooks.

When it comes to teaching a sexuality course, my philosphy is to be *sex-positive*. I have heard people define sex-positive in many different ways, but my personal definition involves: (1) adopting comprehensive and inclusive definitions of gender and sexual orientation, (2) rejecting narrow definitions about what constitutes sex (e.g., the view that only vaginal intercourse "counts"), (3) giving due consideration to the potential positive *and* negative consequences of being sexually active, (4) providing students with the information and tools they need to optimize their sexual health and to make healthy decisions, (5) promoting healthy and respectful sexual and romantic relationships, (6) recognizing that monogamy and marriage are not universal relationship goals and ideals, (7) understanding that not everyone is a sexual being and that a lack of sexual desire is not inherently dysfunctional, and (8) respecting people who have different views about sex. I kept this philosophy in mind when writing this book with the goal of making it as inclusive and respectful as possible for a diverse audience.

After reading this book, my hope is that you will have a better understanding of and appreciation for the amazing complexity of human sexuality, as well as the incredible variation that exists in sexual perspectives and behaviors. The ultimate goal is to enhance your psychological training and for you to be able to think and communicate about sex at a much deeper level in your everyday life, in both casual conversations and interactions with sexual and/or romantic partners.

Now let's talk about sex.

Illustrations

1.1 The ancient Greeks and Romans believed in gods and goddesses devoted to love and sex, such as Aphrodite. 5

1.2 Flamingos are just one of many animal species in which same-sex sexual behavior has been observed. 8

1.3 Sigmund Freud. 10

1.4 Pairing dirty talk or other stimuli with sexual activity may lead those stimuli to become sexually arousing in and of themselves. 12

1.5 There is no reliable evidence that therapies designed to change patients' sexual orientation actually work. 13

1.6 Both adolescents and adults imitate the activities they see depicted in sexually explicit material. 14

1.7 Sensation seekers tend to engage in activities that bring more thrills and excitement. 19

1.8 Evolutionary theory posits that heterosexual men are attracted to women whose bodies are shaped like an hourglass and who have long, silky hair because these are signs of good health and fertility. 20

1.9 The biopsychosocial model as applied to sexual health. 22

2.1 Alfred Kinsey. 30

2.2 A mercury-in-rubber penile strain gauge. 40

2.3 An early generation vaginal photoplethysmograph. 40

2.4 fMRI. 41

2.5 Although there may be a correlation between the stork population and the rate of human births, it would be erroneous to conclude that storks are responsible for delivering babies. Correlations do not imply cause-and-effect. 45

2.6 Laud Humphries studied men who have sex with men in public restrooms. Was it ethically appropriate for Humphries to deceive the men about his true identity and intentions? 46

2.7 At the beginning of any study on sex and sexuality, participants must be informed of their rights, the nature of the research, and the potential risks involved. 50

3.1 In recent history, the penis has largely been seen as vulgar and makes infrequent appearances even in artistic depictions of the male body. 57

3.2, 3.3, 3.4	The appearance of the penis and scrotum varies substantially across persons.	61
3.5	The male reproductive system.	63
3.6	Penis size is one of men's biggest body concerns. Some men pursue dangerous and untested treatments with the hope of enhancing the size of their genitals.	65
3.7	The appearance of the vulva can vary widely.	69
3.8	Some of the structures of the vulva, including the labia, clitoral hood, and introitus.	72
3.9	The female reproductive system.	74
3.10	Anatomy of the female breast.	76
3.11	Female dolls often have extreme and unrealistic bodily proportions, some of which would be nearly impossible to obtain in real life.	77
3.12	Research has found that breast self-exams are not as effective as doctors once believed. Thus, they are not a substitute for consulting with a physician.	82
4.1	The structures of the limbic system.	89
4.2	Physical touch is perhaps the strongest sexual sense.	91
4.3	Men have long been thought to be more visually stimulated than women, but recent research suggests that this may not be the case.	92
4.4	Other people's scents can turn us off or on; however, we may not always consciously recognize when this is happening.	93
4.5	Being on the pill can potentially impact the amount of money a woman can make from exotic dancing.	95
4.6	Why do female humans and animals vocalize more during sexual activity than their male counterparts?	97
4.7	Testosterone replacement is sometimes used as a treatment for low libido in both men and women.	98
4.8	Oxytocin (often referred to as the "cuddle drug") facilitates sexual and romantic bonding, but it may also play a role in generating sexual arousal.	100
4.9	Oysters are just one of many foods that have been thought to be an aphrodisiac.	101
5.1	Chaz Bono is a female-to-male transsexual.	116
5.2	Prenatal hormone exposure is theorized to alter brain structures that contribute to both our gender identity and sexual orientation.	119
5.3	World running champion Caster Semenya	122
5.4	Can you guess the sex of this child?	126
5.5	Teachers' expectations for their students' performance can influence academic achievement and later career interest in gender-stereotypic ways.	127
5.6	The physical environments that surround us as children cue us in as to what our interests and activities "should" be.	128
5.7	The most popular and iconic female characters in television and film, such as Snow White, tend to perpetuate stereotypical notions of how women are "supposed" to be.	130
5.8	There are a lot of misconceptions about transvestites and transsexuals. This stems at least in part from inconsistent and misleading media portrayals.	131
5.9	Drag queens are men who dress up as women for show.	136
5.10	Are men inherently more aggressive than women, or does society just promote and accept male aggression more than female aggression?	138

6.1   Kinsey's famous sexual orientation rating scale places sexuality on a continuum,
       which allows for varying degrees of heterosexuality and homosexuality
       (Kinsey et al., 1948).   146
6.2   The ratio of the second to fourth digit on the hand has been shown to predict
       sexual orientation in numerous studies.   151
6.3   The Exotic Becomes Erotic theory incorporates biological and environmental
       influences on sexual orientation (Bem, 1996).   153
6.4   Childhood gender nonconformity is one of the strongest predictors of adult
       homosexuality.   154
6.5   Research has found that women demonstrate signs of sexual arousal in response
       to a wider range of pornography than men.   156
6.6   Can our eyes reveal our sexual orientation? Research indicates that our pupils
       dilate in response to imagery that we find sexually arousing.   157
6.7   Overt displays of homophobia are common in many parts of the world.   159
6.8   Several prominent politicians, including former United States Senator
       Larry Craig, have been embroiled in gay sex scandals despite voting in favor
       of legislation restricting gay rights.   160
6.9   Despite a continued high prevalence of sexual prejudice, gay, lesbian,
       and bisexual persons have more ability today to live openly and freely
       than ever before.   162
6.10   Sexual orientation does not affect one's ability to develop and maintain
       a long-term, loving relationship   167
7.1   Psychologists have found that we form impressions of other people's
       attractiveness and personality in a matter of seconds.   173
7.2   Inducing positive affect is one of the keys to generating attraction.   176
7.3   Internet dating companies often attempt to match people based solely on
       measures of similarity.   179
7.4   In the Dutton and Aron (1976) study, men who walked across a high and shaky
       suspension bridge misattributed their arousal to the attractive research assistant
       instead of the nature of the situation.   181
7.5   Viewing pornography or other popular media featuring highly attractive people
       can produce a contrast effect in which the attractiveness of the average person
       is distorted.   183
7.6   Heterosexual men tend to rate women with long hair and a low waist-to-hip ratio
       as optimally attractive.   186
7.7   Schmitt and colleagues' (2003) research demonstrated a consistent sex difference
       in the number of sexual partners desired across many different cultures.   187
7.8, 7.9 When men and women imagine offers of casual sex from celebrities like
       Zac Efron and Mila Kunis, there is no sex difference in likelihood of accepting
       the offer.   190
7.10   The traditional sex difference in selectivity disappears when women approached
       men instead of the reverse.   191
8.1   Single people are typically viewed and treated quite negatively in modern
       society.   198
8.2   Friends with benefits frequently try to maintain an intimate and sexual
       relationship without developing romantic feelings.   202
8.3   Passionate love is characterized by high levels of sexual desire and activity. 205

8.4	Companionate love reflects a deep emotional connection that tends to be enduring.	205
8.5	Robert Sternberg (1988) theorizes that the "triangle" of love is composed of passion, intimacy, and commitment.	207
8.6	Making comparisons to couples that appear to be worse off (e.g., couples who fight all of the time) can make you feel better about your own relationship.	210
8.7	The degree to which same-sex relationships are socially accepted varies substantially across cultures.	212
8.8	An infinity symbol encased within a heart is often used to symbolize polyamory, or the idea that it is possible to love multiple persons simultaneously.	213
8.9	In collectivistic cultures such as India, the practice of arranged marriage is common: the needs of the family and community are given greater weight than the needs of the individual.	215
8.10	Communicating about sex appears to enhance sexual satisfaction.	217
8.11	For couples in good relationships, having sex can relieve feelings of stress.	218
8.12	Couples that violate societal or cultural expectations are subject to stigmatization, which may end up hurting the health of the couple members and their relationship.	222
8.13	Infidelity is one of the biggest causes of relationship turmoil, breakup, and divorce.	223
9.1	Sexual fantasies are very common in both men and women and serve a number of different purposes.	233
9.2, 9.3	The content of men's and women's sexual fantasies differs, and often in a way that is consistent with gender role stereotypes.	234
9.4	Sizes, and shapes, and colors, oh my!	237
9.5	John Harvey Kellogg.	239
9.6	For some individuals, kissing is one of the most pleasurable sexual activities there is.	241
9.7	Touch can be a sensual experience even if it is not focused on the genitals	242
9.8	Despite the widespread stereotype of "lesbian bed death," many female same-sex couples lead very active and satisfying sex lives.	246
9.9	Contrary to popular belief, kissing on the mouth is the most frequently reported sexual behavior among men who have sex with men.	247
9.10	Frequent sex increases the growth rate of neurons in rats. Are creatures that have more frequent sex smarter?	249
9.11	When our self-control resources are low, we may become more susceptible to cheating on a romantic partner.	250
10.1	Sex education courses often contain insufficient and, in some cases, inaccurate information about sex and sexuality.	257
10.2	Talking to kids about sex can be an awkward and embarrassing experience for some parents, but it is important to not let that stop the conversation.	260
10.3	Fertility awareness methods utilize a variety of techniques to advise women of their fertile periods, during which time they will either abstain from sex or use barriers.	264
10.4	Female condoms are less well-known and utilized than male condoms; however, both are desirable in that they provide at least some protection from STIs.	265
10.5	Combined hormonal methods of contraception come in a variety of forms and dosages to meet women's needs, such as the contraceptive patch.	266

10.6   An IUD sits inside the uterus like this and can remain in place and effective for up
to five years.   267
10.7   This chart depicts contraceptive use patterns among US women ages 15–44.
About 62 % of women of childbearing age actively use some form of
contraception.   268
10.8   Heterosexual women report greater attraction to masculine men like
Channing Tatum when they are ovulating compared to other stages
of the menstrual cycle.   270
10.9   Sterilization involves severing the fallopian tubes (female) or vas deferens (male)
in order to eliminate the possibility of conception.   271
10.10   Trying to have a child and the transition to parenthood are stressful events for
people of all sexes and sexualities – not just for heterosexual couples.   273
11.1   Historically, the US government sought to alert servicemen about the dangers
of STIs during times of war.   283
11.2   Many people fail to realize that "cold sores" and "fever blisters" are caused by
the herpes virus and that they are highly contagious through kissing and
oral sex.   286
11.3   Out of all world regions, Africa is disproportionately affected by the HIV / AIDS
epidemic.   287
11.4   One of the most persistent myths about STIs is that condoms provide an absolute
safety guarantee.   288
11.5   Anti-retroviral drug therapy significantly reduces the risk of HIV transmission
during sexual activity and childbirth, and may potentially serve as a preventive
agent for HIV-negative individuals who are at high risk of contracting the virus.   290
11.6   As people become more committed to one another, safe-sex practices tend to
drop off; however, that can create risk if one of the partners ends up cheating.   292
11.7   Both doctors and patients express some reluctance to talking about sex during
medical visits, which creates many missed opportunities for STI detection and
diagnosis.   294
11.8   Several websites now offer persons with a positive infection status the chance
to meet other partners of the same status.   295
11.9   If you do not have access to a dental dam, remember that you can create one
from an everyday latex condom.   298
12.1   Both prescription and non-prescription drugs and medications can contribute
to sexual problems.   305
12.2   Spectatoring and other distractions during sex can make it difficult to maintain
arousal and reach orgasm.   306
12.3   Golfer Tiger Woods is just one of many male celebrities who have sought
treatment for "sexual addiction" in recent years after it was revealed that he was
having an affair.   310
12.4   Sensate focus exercises focus on promoting relaxation, communication, and
intimacy. These exercises alone are often enough to resolve sexual difficulties.   314
12.5   In the 2012 film *The Sessions*, Helen Hunt portrayed a sex surrogate who helped
a disabled man discover his sexual potential.   316
12.6   One option for treating erectile dysfunction is a penis pump, which draws blood
into the penis through vacuum pressure.   320

12.7 Upon its release in the late 1990s, Viagra quickly became the fastest-selling prescription drug of all time and continues to be a popular ED treatment to this day. 320

12.8 One type of penile implant involves placing inflatable cylinders inside the cavernous bodies, which are attached to a fluid-filled reservoir in the pelvic cavity and a pumping mechanism placed inside the scrotum. 321

12.9 Botox has a number of unexpected but potentially useful applications including an ability to prevent facial wrinkles, stop excess sweating, and treat vaginismus. 323

13.1 Feet and toes are among the most common fetish objects. 332

13.2 Rachman (1966) classically conditioned a mild boot fetish in a group of male participants, thereby providing a clear demonstration of the role of learning in the development of paraphilias. 333

13.3 Transvestites dress as members of the other sex because they receive sexual arousal from it, not because they truly want to become members of the other sex. 335

13.4 Contrary to popular belief, most people who practice BDSM prefer to give or receive only very mild forms of pain. 337

13.5 As the name "peeping tom" implies, most voyeurs are men who become aroused by watching unsuspecting persons undress or have sex. 338

13.6 What turns the exhibitionist on is the shocked reaction of an unsuspecting stranger. Exposing oneself to willing others is not of particular interest to the true exhibitionist. 340

13.7 Frotteurists derive sexual arousal from rubbing up against unsuspecting strangers in crowded places. 342

13.8 Necrophiles often work in settings where they can easily access corpses. Homicidal necrophiles may kill in order to have access to a dead body, but such behavior is quite rare. 344

14.1 Many cultures and societies regulate the sexual behavior of consenting adults, which has resulted in some truly surprising sex laws. 353

14.2 Rohypnol ("roofies") tends to be the date rapist's drug of choice due to its fast-acting and powerful sedative effects. 356

14.3 The aftermath of sexual assault includes a variety of negative emotional responses, with the potential for post-traumatic stress. 357

14.4 Although many people think of the nature of sexual harassment as being cut and dried, such as unwanted physical touching, the reality is that harassment may constitute a wide range of verbal and physical acts. 359

14.5 When it comes to prostitution, women are most commonly the sellers and men the buyers; however, male prostitutes and female "johns" certainly exist. 361

14.6 In the state of Nevada, brothels are legal in a couple of counties. 362

14.7 Like pornography, erotica may depict explicit sexual activity. The difference is that erotica generally evokes themes of mutual consent, equality, and emotionality. 365

14.8 Despite the widespread belief that porn stars represent "damaged goods," research suggests that porn actresses feel just as positively about themselves as other women. 368

14.9 Not only do more men report having utilized porn than women, but men also tend to use it on a much more frequent basis. 369

14.10 Frequent pornography viewing may result in distorted views about what is normal when it comes to sex and the appearance of the human body. 372

Text Boxes

Digging Deeper

The *Digging Deeper* boxes are designed to reveal the science behind some of the most provocative and controversial topics in the field of human sexuality.

1.1	Can You Change Someone's Sexual Orientation through Operant Conditioning?	13
2.1	Do Sex Surveys Pose Harm to Student Participants?	49
3.1	Should Men be Circumcised?	60
3.2	Female Genital Cutting: What is it, and What Should Be Done about it?	70
3.3	Can Women Orgasm From Nipple Stimulation?	76
4.1	Do Birth Control Pills Make Exotic Dancers Less Appealing To Men?	95
5.1	Can Gender Really Be "Assigned" At Birth?	123
5.2	Cross-Dressing and Gender-Bending: Separating Science Fact from Fiction	131
6.1	Are Homophobic People Repressing Their Own Same-Sex Desires?	160
6.2	Are Bisexual People Aroused By Both Men and Women?	164
7.1	"Is It Hot In Here, Or Is It Just You?" Do Pick-up Lines Work?	174
7.2	Are Women Really the Choosier Sex?	190
8.1	Why is it Socially Stigmatized to be Single?	198
8.2	Are There Different Types of "Friends With Benefits?"	201
8.3	Does Having Sex Relieve Stress For Couples?	219
9.1	How Do Men's and Women's Sexual Fantasies Differ?	233
9.2	The History of Motorized Sex Toys	236
9.3	Do Gay Men's Sex Lives Match Up With the Stereotypes?	246
10.1	When and How Should You Talk to Your Kids About Sex in the Age of Internet Porn?	260
10.2	How Close Are We to Having a Male Version of "The Pill?"	271
11.1	Do Sexually Transmitted Infections Affect Women's Ability to Orgasm?	282
11.2	Six Myths About Sexually Transmitted Infections Debunked	287
12.1	Sex Surrogacy: The "Hands-On" Approach to Sex Therapy	316
12.2	How Long Should Sex Last and How Can I Last Longer in Bed?	322
13.1	Why Do People Have Fetishes?	332

13.2   A Top 10 List of Unusual Sexual Behaviors   342
14.1   A Top 10 List of Wacky Sex Laws   353
14.2   What Do Men and Women Focus on When They Watch Porn?   370
14.3   Five Misconceptions About Sex and the Human Body Spread By Porn   372

Your Sexuality

The *Your Sexuality* boxes are designed to engage readers with the chapter material. Readers are asked to reflect upon their own experiences and relationships, as well as to articulate their own unique perspectives on unsettled issues in the field.

1.1   Are You Erotophilic or Erotophobic?   18
2.1   Was the Tearoom Trade Study Ethically Acceptable?   47
3.1   Does the Sexual Double Standard Still Exist?   79
4.1   Faking Orgasms: Who Benefits More From a False Finish?   107
5.1   Where Do Transgendered and Intersexed Individuals Fit in a Gender Binary World?   135
6.1   What Percentage of the Population is Gay? It Depends How You Ask the Question   147
7.1   What Characteristics are Important to You in a Potential Partner?   172
8.1   What is Your "Love Style?"   209
9.1   The Dark Side of Sexual Fantasy   236
10.1   What Should School-Based Sex Education Look Like?   258
11.1   Should STI Vaccinations Be Mandated For Adolescents?   285
12.1   Is Sexual "Addiction" Real?   310
13.1   Perspectives on Zoophilia   345
14.1   Should Prostitution Be Legal?   363

Tables

1.1	Cross-cultural Variations in Human Sexual Behavior	4
1.2	Television Shows that have Pushed the Sexual Envelope	6
1.3	Summary of the Major Psychological Theories in the Study of Human Sexuality	9
1.4	The Big Five Personality Traits and their Association with Sexual Behavior	17
2.1	A Summary of Sexology Research Methods	32
2.2	Selected Findings from the NSSHB	38
4.1	Sexual Effects of Several Alleged Aphrodisiacs	102
4.2	Potential Variations in Female Sexual Response	109
4.3	Comparing Different Models of Sexual Response	110
5.1	Typical Sequence of Biological Sex Differentiation	118
5.2	Biological Sex Variations	121
5.3	Gendered Presentations of Men and Women in the Media	129
6.1	Comparing Sexual Identity and Same-sex Sexual Behavior across National US Sex Surveys	148
6.2	Countries with Laws that Prohibit Employment Discrimination on the Basis of Sexual Orientation	163
7.1	Examples of Best and Worst Pick-up Lines	175
7.2	Evidence of Assortative Mating: Percentage of Partners across Different Relationship Types Displaying Similarity in Age, Religious Background, and Education Level	178
7.3	Major Variables in Sexual Attraction	184
7.4	Percentage of Men and Women Accepting Requests for Offers of Casual Sex	188
8.1	Sternberg's Eight Varieties of Love	206
8.2	Countries that Recognize Same-sex Marriage	212
8.3	Likelihood that a First Marriage will last up to 20 years by Race of Partners in the US	220
9.1	Male and Female Sexual Behaviors across the Lifespan	231
9.2	Frequency of Masturbation by Age and Gender Groups	238
9.3	Frequency of Sexual Activity in the Past Year among Adults Age 18–59	248
10.1	Reasons Women Failed to Use Contraception Before an Unintended Pregnancy	258
10.2	Typical and Perfect Use Effectiveness Rates for Various Contraceptives	264

11.1   Incidence and Prevalence of Selected Curable STIs across World Regions   281
11.2   CDC Screening Recommendations for STIs   281
11.3   Guidelines for Proper Condom Use   297
12.1   Factors Associated with Risk of Sexual Dysfunction in the National Health and Social Life Survey   307
12.2   Prevalence of Various Forms of Sexual Dysfunction Across Different Life Stages   309
13.1   Types of Paraphilias   331
13.2   Prevalence of Selected Fetishes among Members of Online Fetish Communities   334
14.1   Number of Sexual Assaults in the US   355
14.2   Comparing Porn Actresses to a Matched Sample of Women who have Never Been in Porn   367

1
Theoretical Perspectives on Human Sexuality

©Piotr Marcinski/123RF.COM.

Chapter Outline

- Introduction   2
- What Drives Us to Have Sex?   2
  - Psychological Influences   2
  - Cultural and Societal Influences   3
  - Biological and Evolutionary Influences   7
- Major Theoretical Perspectives on Human Sexuality   8
  - Psychoanalytic Theory   8
  - Cognitive-Behavioral and Learning Theories   11
  - Exchange Theories   15
  - Personality Theories   16
  - Evolutionary Theory   19
- The Perspective of This Text   21

The Psychology of Human Sexuality, First Edition. Justin J. Lehmiller.
© 2014 John Wiley & Sons, Ltd. Published 2014 by John Wiley & Sons, Ltd.

Introduction

For centuries, societies around the world adopted the view that sex means just one thing: penis-in-vagina intercourse within the context of marriage for the purpose of procreation. Pursuing any other form of genital pleasure was not only viewed as sinful, but it could get you thrown in jail or, in some cases, put to death. In stark contrast to this view, the concept of sex in modern times has been significantly expanded, and sexual activity has become quite complex. For instance, "sex" now refers to a wide range of behaviors, including everything from mutual masturbation to oral, vaginal, and anal stimulation, not to mention things like "sexting" and phone sex. Sexual activity today is no longer legally or morally restricted to traditional heterosexual marriage either; sex occurs between unmarried romantic partners, "friends with benefits," and people of varying sexual orientations. Furthermore, sexual acts can serve a wide range of purposes, with procreation being just one possibility. People now see sex as a form of recreation, a way to express love or get closer to a partner, a way to celebrate special occasions, and (for some) a way to make money. In fact, in a recent study in which people were asked why they have sex, participants reported 237 distinct reasons for "getting it on" (Meston & Buss, 2007)! This immense variation in sexual activities, relationships, and motivations means that understanding sex in today's world is a complicated task. The goal of this chapter is to give you the theoretical foundation necessary for appreciating the complexities and intricacies of modern human sexuality from a psychologist's perspective.

As a starting point, it is useful to acknowledge that every single sexual act is the result of several powerful forces acting upon one or more persons. These forces include our individual psychology, our genetic background and evolved history, as well as the current social and cultural context in which we live. Some of these influences favor sexual activity, whereas others oppose it. Whether sex occurs at any given moment depends upon which forces are strongest at the time.

Let us consider in more detail some of these different forces and the ways they can impact human sexual decision making and behavior. Following that, we will consider some of the dominant theoretical perspectives used by psychologists in understanding human sexuality, before ultimately presenting the model that we will use to organize the remaining chapters in this book.

What Drives Us to Have Sex?

The forces that interact to produce sexual behavior can be lumped into three broad categories: psychological variables, cultural and societal factors, and biological and evolutionary influences. We will consider each of these in turn, providing specific examples of some of the ways they can shape human sexuality.

Psychological Influences

An enormous number of psychological factors can affect sexual behavior, including our mood states, level of cognitive alertness, our attitudes toward sex and relationships, behavioral expectancies, as well as associations learned through reinforcement. Some of these factors are transitory, meaning they can change from moment to moment, whereas others are relatively stable characteristics we carry with us throughout our lives. Regardless of their stability, each of these psychological variables can promote or inhibit sexual behavior.

For instance, personality is a relatively stable individual characteristic that may affect both the nature and frequency of our sexual activities (e.g., Markey & Markey, 2007; Miller et al., 2004). To illustrate this idea, just imagine the types of sexual situations that a very extraverted thrill seeker might get into compared to someone who is very introverted and likes to play it safe. Throughout this book, we will discuss many personality characteristics from the Big Five to sensation seeking to erotophilia that can have a profound influence on our sex lives (all of these personality characteristics will be defined later in this chapter).

Learned associations are another relatively stable characteristic that can affect sexual behavior (e.g., Plaud & Martini, 1999). Each of us associates something different with sex, based upon our prior learning experiences. When someone believes that sexual behavior will be helpful in some way (e.g., because that person was previously rewarded with social acceptance for engaging in this activity), sex is more likely to occur. In contrast, when someone expects that sexual behavior might be harmful (e.g., if one's perceived risk of contracting a sexually transmitted infection (STI) appears high or if one's previous sexual experiences have been bad), sex is less likely to occur.

Likewise, if someone has a negative attitude toward sex or toward a given partner, the odds of sexual activity decrease; in contrast, positive attitudes are likely to increase sexual activity, even in cases where that person might not necessarily be "in the mood" (e.g., someone who is tired might acquiesce to a partner's request for sex to make that partner happy, not because this individual is feeling particularly interested in sex).

Finally, mood states are important as well – and they provide an example of a psychological characteristic that varies from moment to moment in terms of the impact it has on sex. Another example along these lines would be level of cognitive distraction (Masters & Johnson, 1970). When someone is in a negative mood or is highly distracted, not only is that person likely less inclined to have sex, but the sex they do have will probably be less satisfying; positive mood states and low levels of distraction tend to generate an opposite pattern of effects.

It is important to note that all of the effects discussed above are bidirectional (i.e., attitudes and mood states shape sexual behavior, but sexual behavior also shapes our attitudes and mood states, thereby creating a feedback loop). Moreover, keep in mind that these are just a few of the many ways that psychology and sexuality can intersect. Later in this chapter, we will explore several important theories that provide evidence of other, additional psychological variables that can affect sexuality. These include classical and operant conditioning, observational learning, and social exchange, among others.

Cultural and Societal Influences

The cultural and societal context in which we live plays a large role in determining sexual behavior. Virtually all societies around the world regulate sexuality in one form or another (DeLamater, 1987), effectively establishing standards for what should be considered sexually "normal" and "deviant" among certain groups of people. However, there is huge variability in these standards. For instance, although most industrialized societies today have established a norm of sexual monogamy, there are other cultures that not only permit, but explicitly encourage a free exchange of sex partners, even within marriage (see Ryan & Jetha, 2010). Although it is true that some sexual views and practices are more widely shared than others across cultures, such as the promotion of marriage and the discouragement of **incest** (i.e., sexual activity among blood relatives; Gregersen,

Table 1.1   Cross-cultural Variations in Human Sexual Behavior
Sexual behavior with a member of the same sex is controversial in many parts of the world, but is punishable by death in Saudi Arabia, Pakistan, Iran, and Afghanistan (ILGA, 2013).
Among certain tribes in New Guinea, adolescent boys ingest the semen of older men because it is believed to promote strength and virility (Herdt, 1982).
In parts of South Asia, a third gender, *hijra*, is observed. Hijra consist of biological men who have had their genitalia removed in ritual castration. They are believed to possess special powers (Nanda, 2001).
Although kissing is a normal sexual behavior in most Western societies, it is viewed as disgusting among the Thonga of South Africa (Gregersen, 1996).
In some Asian and African countries, the practice of arranged marriage is relatively common. In such marriages, parents are responsible for selecting their child's future spouse (Malhotra, 1991).

1996), there do not appear to be many (if any) truly universal principles of sexuality. For a few provocative examples of how sexual practices vary cross-culturally, see Table 1.1.

One of the major factors that propels these cultural variations in sexuality is religion. As some evidence of the powerful role that religion exerts on people's views of sexuality, we will consider a few prominent historical examples. First, let us look back at the ancient Greeks and Romans, who shared a belief in multiple gods. Many of the most common myths and stories from these early times centered around the sexual exploits of those gods, which included everything from incest to sex with animals. These ancient peoples even had gods and goddesses devoted exclusively to sex, such as Aphrodite (Greek) and Venus (Roman). As a result, it is perhaps not surprising that the Greeks and Romans were a sexually active bunch and had relatively permissive attitudes toward practices such as homosexuality and bisexuality (Boswell, 1980). For instance, relatively common in ancient Greece was **pederasty**: an arrangement in which an older man would educate and mentor a male adolescent, who would have sex with him in return (Scanlon, 2005).

As a sharp contrast to the sexual permissiveness of the Greeks and Romans, consider the early Christians, who believed in a single deity and enforced a set of sharply defined rules that governed sexual behavior and the roles of men and women in society. Those who did not follow these rules were subject to severe punishment, both here on earth and (as they believed) in the afterlife. For example, one of the most prominent Christian scholars, St Paul, wrote extensively about the sinful nature of any form of sex outside of heterosexual marriage and praised the ideals of celibacy and chastity (i.e., remaining unmarried and sexually pure). St Augustine expanded upon these notions in his writings, but went even further in declaring that female submissiveness was part of God's plan. As part of this, he considered the only "natural" sexual position to be one in which the man was on top of the women (Wiesner-Hanks, 2000). Given these strict rules for sexual and gender roles and the harsh punishments for violating them, sexuality became very restricted in Christian countries, and these effects can still be felt today.

Most other early religions viewed sex in similar terms (i.e., as a sinful activity that should only exist within the confines of marriage) and promoted gender roles characterized by male dominance and female submissiveness. However, the extremity of these views varied. For instance, according to Islam, a religion that spread throughout the Middle East and Asia a few centuries after the birth of Christianity, intercourse within marriage is seen as a religious deed and is viewed

Figure 1.1 The ancient Greeks and Romans believed in gods and goddesses devoted to love and sex, such as Aphrodite, from whom aphrodisiacs got their name. ©perseomedusa/123RF.COM.

positively. In fact, it is seen as a higher state than remaining single and celibate, which is quite a departure from the writings of Christian scholars such as St Paul. Despite promoting a slightly more permissive view in this regard, Muslims are in many ways more restrictive when it comes to gender. For example, in a high proportion of Muslim societies past and present, female modesty in clothing is mandated, and women have very few rights – they may not even be permitted to leave their homes unless accompanied by their husband or a male relative.

Taoism (a belief system with its origins in ancient China) offers another somewhat more permissive view when it comes to sex. For example, according to Taoist beliefs, sexual inter-course serves to balance the opposing forces of *yin* and *yang*, with *yin* representing female energy and *yang* representing male energy. Sex is thus held in very high regard, and is seen as serving a number of important functions beyond reproduction. However, this belief system was largely replaced by much more sexually conservative views with the rise of Confucianism about a thousand years ago. As a result of this shift, China continues to hold relatively conservative views of sex to this day.

Of course, religion is not the only cultural force acting upon sexuality. Science and the popular media play very large roles as well. We will discuss the role of science in detail in the next chapter, and the ways in which the emergence of a scientific enterprise devoted exclusively to sexuality has impacted sexual attitudes and behaviors. We will focus here on the role of the media, which in today's world includes television and movies, songs, advertisements, newspapers, magazines, as well as the Internet. Because of the media's omnipresence in our everyday lives, it has multiple opportunities to affect us in very visual and dramatic ways.

Since its invention, television has gradually come to include more and more sexual content, albeit with a bit of social resistance along the way. Believe it or not, it was once considered contro-versial for a television program to include an interracial couple (such as on the 1970s program *The Jeffersons*) or a single, pregnant woman who decides to have a baby on her own (such as on the 1990s program *Murphy Brown*). These things are pretty tame by today's standards, especially when you consider that programmers are now talking about showing full-frontal nudity and group sex scenes on prime time cable (Strauss, 2010). For a sampling of some of the ways that television

Table 1.2	Television Shows that have Pushed the Sexual Envelope	
Show title	*Basic premise*	*Selected sexual content*
Californication	Tells the story of Hank Moody, a middle-aged novelist who has problems with sex, drugs, and booze.	Hank has a sexual relationship with a 16-year old girl. Hank has a dream about receiving oral sex from a nun in church.
Glee	Follows the lives of several high school students in Lima, Ohio who belong to the school's glee club.	Two young teen couples, one gay (Blaine and Kurt) and one heterosexual (Rachel and Finn), lose their virginity in one episode. (This may sound tame compared to the other shows, but was controversial because it aired on network TV instead of cable.)
The L-Word	Follows the lives of several lesbian, bisexual, and transgendered women living in Los Angeles, California.	Full-frontal female nudity present in many episodes, along with explicit simulations of various sexual activities between women. Nikki has sex with her girlfriend, Jenny, while wearing a strap-on penis.
Queer as Folk	Follows the lives of five gay men living in Pittsburgh, Pennsylvania.	Full-frontal male nudity present in many episodes, along with explicit simulations of oral and anal sex between men. A male high-school student, Justin, carries on a sexual relationship with a significantly older man (Brian).
Sex and the City	Follows the lives of four very sexually active, mostly heterosexual women living in New York City.	Samantha experiments with bisexuality and discovers female ejaculation. Miranda receives anilingus (oral stimulation of the anus) from a male partner.

shows have pushed the sexual envelope in recent years, see Table 1.2. Of course, television's evolution in this regard was not in isolation. Popular songs, music videos, and video games have become more explicit over time as well. Proponents of social learning theory (a topic we will discuss later in this chapter) argue that these sexualized media depictions have contributed to some profound changes in sexual attitudes and behaviors over the past few decades.

However, TVs, stereos, and game consoles are not the only forms of media we are exposed to – our computers and phones matter too, and there is no denying that our constant access to the Internet has forever changed our sex lives. For one thing, a vast selection of sexual information and pornography is now available for free at the click of a button. Thus, people can readily obtain sexually explicit material that they might otherwise be unable to get, and they can avoid potential embarrassment by doing it in the privacy of their own homes. However, the Internet has done much more than that. It has also opened up the world of online dating and hookups, not to mention sexual self-expression through webcams and mobile phones via "cyber sex" and "sexting" (i.e., sending sexually explicit images via text message). Sexting in particular has become very common and controversial. For example, one study of high school students found that 18.3 % of male students and 17.3% of female students had sexted images of themselves, and about twice as many were the recipients of a sext by others (Strassberg, McKinnon, Sustaita, & Rullo, 2013). Although such photos are often meant for just one other person's eyes, these images are sometimes circulated publicly after breakups ("revenge porn"), which can create significant distress and embarrassment. In addition, many adolescents fail to realize that it is a criminal act to take and distribute sexual photos of anyone under the age of 18 (see chapter 14), which means sexting can generate legal troubles. We will elaborate on the complex effects of the media on sexual behavior throughout this book when we begin talking about sexual education, risky sexual behavior, and pornography.

Biological and Evolutionary Influences

The other major forces affecting human sexual behavior are biological and evolutionary factors. Biological factors refer primarily to an individual's genetic makeup and hormone levels. In recent years, genetics have been linked to sexuality in several ways. For instance, research has increasingly shown that homosexuality appears to be driven, at least in part, by a variety of hereditary factors, an issue we will return to in chapter 6 (e.g., Dawood, Bailey, & Martin, 2009). Likewise, the gender roles adopted by men and women seem to be influenced by the sex hormones they were exposed to while developing in the womb (Beltz, Swanson, & Berenbaum, 2011). For example, individuals with congenital adrenal hyperplasia (CAH) are exposed to a higher than usual level of "male" sex hormones (i.e., androgens) in utero. As adults, women with CAH tend to have much more masculine interests (e.g., technology) than women without CAH. In contrast, when a male fetus is insensitive to "male" sex hormones in utero, a more feminine gender identity and role tend to emerge later in life. Findings such as these demonstrate how biology can profoundly influence us in ways that we are completely unaware of.

Evolutionary factors have also been proposed to play a role in human sexuality. In making a case for this, researchers have looked at how human sexual behavior compares to that of other animal species. To the extent that our species and others around us evolved from common ancestors, we should expect to see similarities with other species in the ways we behave sexually. The results of this research suggest that, by and large, there is little that is unique about humans' sexual activities. For instance, same-sex sexual activity has been documented in hundreds of animal species, from fruit flies to flamingos (Bagemihl, 1999). Likewise, oral sex (Tan et al., 2009) and masturbation (Bagemihl, 1999) occur in other species as well. Humans cannot even stake a claim to being the only species that has sex for pleasure, or mates face to face! Thus, although there are certainly major differences in culture, society, intelligence, and communication between us and other species, there are numerous similarities when it comes to our sexual behaviors.

Human sexuality is thus a complex phenomenon with many contributing factors, from the psychological to social to the biological. Although the goal of this text is to primarily provide you with a psychological understanding of sexual attitudes and behaviors, we will also address and acknowledge the important roles played by these other factors.

Figure 1.2   Flamingos are just one of many animal species in which same-sex sexual behavior has been observed. ©smileus/123RF.COM.

Major Theoretical Perspectives on Human Sexuality

At this point, we will turn our attention to some of the major theoretical perspectives on human sexual behavior. We will focus exclusively on theories put forth by psychologists. However, please be aware that many different theories exist in other fields of study, such as sociology and anthropology; by no means is this a comprehensive list of all possible theories of sexual behavior. In this section, theories will be addressed in approximate chronological order from oldest to newest in order to give you some appreciation of how psychological perspectives have changed over time. As you will see, different psychologists may evaluate a given sexual act in very different terms, depending upon their theoretical orientation. Also, please note that none of these perspectives is necessarily better than any of the others because each provides some unique insight into the diversity of sexual behaviors and attitudes that exist. For a handy summary of the main idea(s) behind each theory, see Table 1.3.

Psychoanalytic Theory

Psychoanalytic theory is the oldest perspective on sexuality in the field and is credited to Sigmund Freud. Freud believed that human behavior was driven by two factors: sex and death. He termed our sexual and life instincts **libido** (a term that is still in use today, even outside of the psychoanalytic tradition), and our death instinct, *thanatos*.

Freud believed that personality consisted of three distinct parts. First is the **id**, which is the most basic part of the personality and contains the libido. The id operates according to the *pleasure principle*, meaning it seeks to obtain gratification and fulfillment of its needs. Second is the **ego**, which exists to keep a check on the id. The ego operates under the *reality principle*, meaning it tries to satisfy the id's desires in a way that is rational and avoids self-destruction. The last portion of personality is the **superego**, which can be thought of as our conscience. The superego tries to persuade the ego to do not what is realistic, but what is moral.

Table 1.3	Summary of the Major Psychological Theories in the Study of Human Sexuality
Theory	*Main point(s)*
Psychoanalytic theory	Personality structure consisting of the id, ego, and superego drives behavior. Sexual abnormalities arise when individuals become fixated during one of the psychosexual stages of development.
Classical conditioning	Repeated pairing of a neutral stimulus with one that produces a specific behavior will eventually lead the neutral stimulus to elicit the same behavior.
Operant conditioning	Reinforced behaviors increase in frequency; punished behaviors decrease. Reinforcement is more effective than punishment.
Social/Observational learning	Behavior can be learned through observation of others (e.g., peers, parents) or through media exposure, including pornography.
Exchange perspectives	Exchange of resources is fundamental to social relationships. Behavior is driven by perceived costs and benefits derived from trades occurring between partners.
Personality theories	Relatively stable individual traits generate consistent patterns of behavior across situations. Big Five, erotophobia-erotophilia, sensation seeking, and sociosexuality are major personality traits associated with sexual behavior.
Evolutionary theory	Human beings are motivated to produce as many of their own offspring as possible. We have evolved preferences for physical and psychological traits and characteristics in sexual partners that promote reproductive success.
Biopsychosocial model	Biological, psychological, and social factors interact to produce variations in sexual orientations and behaviors. The mind and body are fundamentally intertwined. Sexual health is not just the absence of biological dysfunction; it runs on a continuum with varying degrees of sexual illness and wellness.

These personality aspects work together to produce behavior across all situations, sexual and otherwise. To consider just one example, imagine that you meet a friend's spouse for the first time and find that person to be very attractive. Your id would probably be telling you to screw the consequences and start flirting right now. At the same time, your ego would probably step in and tell you to at least wait until your friend goes to the bathroom so that you do not start a major fight. However, the superego would ultimately chime in and tell you to forget about the whole thing because you do not want to hurt your friend or become a "home-wrecker."

Figure 1.3   Freud made numerous contributions to the study of sexuality from a psychological perspective, including his theorized personality structure consisting of the id, ego, and superego. ©basphoto/123RF.COM.

In addition to this personality structure, Freud also proposed an elaborate theory of psycho-sexual development. The basic idea is that all children pass through a series of five stages in which different parts of the body serve as a source of pleasure: oral, anal, phallic, latent, and genital. To the extent that a child does not pass through all of the stages in their expected order, that child can become "fixated," which leads to a lifelong urge to gratify the relevant body part from that stage (e.g., someone fixated in the oral stage might wind up constantly chewing on pens or fingernails as an adult). Perhaps the most well-known aspect of Freud's psychosexual theory was the notion of the *Oedipus complex* in boys (i.e., sexual desire for one's mother and hatred for one's father), as well as *penis envy* and the *Electra complex* in girls (i.e., psychological traumatization due to the lack of a penis and sexual desire for one's father, respectively).

Although certain aspects of Freudian theory are fascinating and provocative, it has long since been rejected, on numerous grounds. For one thing, much of what Freud proposed could not be tested scientifically because most of his work was based on case reports of his clinical patients (we will dis-cuss the limitations of this research method in detail in chapter 2). Also, if you have ever taken a course in psychology of women or psychology of gender, you are probably well aware that many of Freud's theories and writings smack of sexism, especially the idea of penis envy, which suggests that women will always be "incomplete" because they lack penises. In addition, consider that Freud frequently argued that women who achieve orgasm through clitoral stimulation are not as "mature" as women who can achieve orgasm through vaginal intercourse alone. There is no rational or scientific basis for such a claim. Despite the obvious biases and problems inherent in Freud's work, we still owe a great debt to him for getting the field of psychology to recognize the importance of studying sexuality.

Cognitive-Behavioral and Learning Theories

Psychoanalytic theory and its emphasis on unconscious factors that influence behavior fell out of favor with psychologists in the early part of the twentieth century, when a new school of thought known as behaviorism emerged. The focus shifted from studying the unknowable unconscious to an empirical investigation of overt behavior. Initially, most behaviorists adopted a rather extreme view that it was impossible to scientifically measure mental processes, thereby leaving observable behavior as psychologists' only unit of analysis. However, the field later backed away from this radical view, and began to acknowledge and addresses the vital role that cognitive processes play in producing behavior. Central to the behaviorism movement was the idea that behaviors are learned from experience. Also, through this learning process, appropriate behaviors can come to replace previously learned behaviors that are ineffective or maladaptive. The major types of learning that emerged from this movement are classical conditioning, operant conditioning, and social (observational) learning. Each of these perspectives is still relevant to psychologists' understanding of sexual attitudes and behaviors today and you will see them referenced repeatedly throughout this book.

Classical Conditioning

The first and perhaps most well-known learning theory that emerged from behaviorism is **classical conditioning**. Every student of psychology is familiar with Pavlov's (1927) famous experiments in which he was able to induce salivation in dogs by the simple ringing of a bell. Pavlov accomplished this by repeatedly pairing the bell with the presentation of meat powder. To demonstrate its applicability to human sexuality, let's walk through the steps involved in classical conditioning with a relevant example. First, we must identify a specific stimulus that produces a specific behavior. For example, when someone has their genitals gently touched or stroked, it will typically produce sexual arousal. Next, the original stimulus must be paired with a new stimulus that does not cause that same behavior. For instance, dirty talk (e.g., "Let me be your personal sex toy. Use me any way you want tonight!") is something that is not inherently sexually arousing to everyone. So let us imagine that while someone's genitals are being touched, that person's partner starts talking dirty. If these two stimuli are paired together frequently enough, each one will eventually be capable of eliciting the same behavior independently. Thus, in our example, both genital touching and dirty talk will eventually lead that person to experience sexual arousal, even in cases where dirty talk is not accompanied by any genital touch. Classical conditioning has been implicated as one of the major psychological roots of many sexual behaviors, including fetishes (an issue we will return to in chapter 13). Conditioning of this nature can also be useful in the treatment of sexual difficulties (see chapter 12).

Operant Conditioning

Of course, classical conditioning is limited in that it cannot provide a complete understanding of all behavior, sexual or otherwise. Not every behavior is cued by a stimulus that appears immediately before it. Psychologists quickly recognized the need to explore other types of learning and the result was **operant conditioning**, initially proposed by B.F. Skinner (1938). The main idea behind operant conditioning is that when behaviors are *reinforced* (i.e., when they are rewarded or lead to pleasurable consequences), they tend to be repeated; in contrast, when behaviors are *punished* (i.e., when the consequences are unpleasant or undesirable), they tend to occur with less frequency. In order for this form of learning to occur, the reinforcement/punishment must

Figure 1.4   Pairing dirty talk or other stimuli with sexual activity may lead those stimuli to become sexually arousing in and of themselves. ©Vojtech VIK/123RF.COM

follow the behavior immediately and consistently, otherwise the association will not be learned. As a general rule, reinforcements are generally more effective than punishments in shaping behavior.

Operant conditioning is very applicable to the study of sex because sex is not only a behavior than can be increased or decreased through reinforcement and punishment, but it is also a reinforcing variable that can increase or decrease the frequency of other, nonsexual behaviors. Demonstrating the former role, people who typically experience pleasurable consequences from sex (e.g., bonding with or getting closer to a partner) will likely have sex more frequently; those who find sex to be punishing (e.g., because of pain or embarrassment caused by a sexual dysfunction) will likely have sex with less frequency. Demonstrating the latter role, an individual may use sex as a way of reinforcing desirable behaviors in a partner, such as enticing someone to do more housework with the prospect of a having sex more often (incidentally, research has found that people who do more housework have sex more frequently, so there might be something to this idea! (Gager & Yabiku, 2010)). For more on the use of operant conditioning as applied to sexual behavior, see the Digging Deeper 1.1 box.

Social/Observational Learning

Operant conditioning is incapable of providing a complete understanding of human behavior because some of our behaviors develop independently of direct reinforcement and punishment. The perspective of those who adopt a **social or observational learning** approach is that some behavioral tendencies are acquired through simple observation of others' activities. If we see others rewarded for engaging in certain behaviors, we tend to imitate them; if we see others experience negative outcomes as a result of engaging in certain behaviors, we typically avoid those behaviors.

Perhaps the most well-known example of social learning in the field of psychology is Albert Bandura's classic Bobo doll experiments (Bandura, Ross, & Ross, 1962). In these studies,

Digging Deeper 1.1   Can You Change Someone's Sexual Orientation through Operant Conditioning?

A small number of therapists have attempted to use operant conditioning principles to change the sexuality of some of their clients from homosexual to heterosexual through a controversial process known as **reparative therapy**. This is often accomplished by having the therapist subject clients to physical punishment upon their exposure to homoerotic stimuli (note that the use of punishments to change behavior is sometimes referred to as *aversive conditioning*). For example, the therapist might present a gay or lesbian client with erotic photos of members of the same sex and pair that with electric shocks to the genitals. Alternatively, a therapist might ask a client to wear a rubber band on the wrist all day long and snap it every time the client has a sexual thought about a member of the same sex. Are such "treatments" effective at changing someone's sexuality?

Figure 1.5   There is no reliable evidence that therapies designed to change patients' sexual orientation actually work. In fact, the evidence suggests that they may do more harm than good. ©milosb/123RF.COM.

There is no scientific evidence published in reputable, peer-reviewed journals indicating that reparative therapy works. In fact, the weight of the published research suggests that it is psychologically harmful to those who undergo this treatment (Halderman, 2003). The use of conditioning principles to change one's sexual orientation is not even warranted in the first place, given that homosexuality is not a psychological disorder. A listing for homosexuality is not included in either the *Diagnostic and Statistical Manual of Mental Disorders* (DSM-5) or the *International Statistical Classification of Diseases and Related Health Problems* (ICD), both of which are considered the definitive guides for diagnosing psychological disorders. In addition, the American Psychological Association, the American Psychiatric Association, and the World Health Organization have long held the position that homosexuality is not a disorder. Thus, reparative therapy is perhaps the most prominent example of the misuse and abuse of psychological theory in the context of sexuality.

Figure 1.6 Both adolescents and adults imitate the activities they see depicted in sexually explicit material. ©wrangel/123RF.COM.

Bandura and his research associates examined how exposure to violent media affects children's aggressive tendencies. What they found was that children who watched a video of an adult acting aggressively toward an inflatable Bobo doll (e.g., hitting it with a hammer, throwing it across the room) ended up terrorizing the Bobo doll when given an opportunity; kids who watched a control video of an adult sitting quietly exhibited far less aggression toward the Bobo doll.

The social learning perspective has obvious and important implications for the development of sexual behavior. For example, if high school students see others receive a popularity boost for becoming sexually active, those students may become inclined to do the same. This perspective also speaks to the especially powerful role that the media and pornography can have on our sexuality. The sexual depictions that appear in popular music, films, television shows, advertisements, and the Internet may shape our views of what is and is not appropriate sexual behavior. To the extent that the media depicts positive sexual role models (e.g., people who practice safe sex and communicate about their sexual history), this is not inherently bad. However, if the media depicts poor sexual examples (e.g., people who have multiple sexual partners and fail to use protection), this can be incredibly dangerous. As it turns out, most media depictions of sex portray it in quite risky and unrealistic terms. For example, an analysis of sexual content in the most popular movies released between 1983 and 2003 found that most sex acts depicted (70%) occurred among people who had just met (Gunasekera, Chapman, & Campbell, 2005). Moreover, almost every scene (98%) failed to address the topic of contraception, and virtually none of these sexual acts resulted in negative consequences (e.g., unintended pregnancies, STIs, etc.). Given these findings, it is perhaps not surprising that longitudinal research has revealed that the more sexual content adolescents are exposed to in popular films, the earlier they start having sex, the more sexual partners they accumulate, and the less likely they are to practice safe sex (O'Hara et al., 2012). Of course, the media is not the sole contributing factor, and other explanations are possible for these effects, such as a lack of parental supervision and involvement (for more on the limitations of correlational research, see chapter 2).

A related concern is that a growing number of adolescents are turning to pornography to determine what "normal" sexual behavior is because they are not getting this information anywhere else (Bowater, 2011). However, there is nothing "normal" about what is depicted in most pornography. Not only do most porn actors and actresses have very atypical bodies (sometimes from extreme dieting and/or plastic surgery), but their sexual activities and practices do not mirror reality either (we will return to this issue in chapter 14 when we cover pornography in greater detail). Thus, there are potential dangers in having porn serve as one's primary source of sex education and social comparison.

Despite their inherent value and intuitive appeal, none of the learning theories discussed above tell us the entire story when it comes to sexual behavior. For example, these theories have been criticized for being oversimplified and depersonalized (i.e., they do not take into account idiosyncratic features of the individual, such as personality or mood states), and for failing to address important biological and hormonal influences on behavior.

Exchange Theories

Exchange theories offer another psychological explanation of human behavior, and primarily help us to understand how social relationships are formed, maintained, and terminated. Specifically, the main idea advanced by the social exchange perspective is that the way we feel about a given relationship and behave toward our partner depends upon the type of outcomes we receive in return for what we have put into the relationship (Homans, 1961; Thibaut & Kelley, 1959). Thus, relationships are fundamentally about exchanges between the parties involved, and those trades can involve sex, money, time, or anything else you can think of. When our exchanges yield high rewards and low costs, we act so as to maintain our relationship; however, when the costs begin to exceed the benefits, we are likely to end things and move on.

To determine whether our outcomes are good, we hold them up to some **comparison level** (i.e., the standard by which we judge our relationships). For example, we may compare the outcomes we are receiving in our current relationship to those that we received in the past. What we are looking for is a cost-benefit ratio that is favorable relative to our comparison level. Whether the ratio is perceived as favorable depends largely upon whether the exchange is *equitable*, or whether the distribution of outcomes is fair (i.e., are you getting what you deserve? (Walster, Walster, & Berscheid, 1978)).

Social exchange theorists have proposed that sex is a fairly common resource traded in heterosexual relationships, with women more likely to be the "sellers" and men more likely to be the "buyers" of it (Baumeister & Vohs, 2004). The theory is that female sexuality has much more "value" than male sexuality, thereby enabling women to obtain more resources in exchange for sex than men. Female sexuality is more valuable because it is in demand, given that there are lots of men who are interested in and are looking for sex at any given time. Also, because women are less interested in having casual sex with multiple partners than are men, female sexuality is in limited supply. Several research findings lend support to this proposition. First, and perhaps most obvious, prostitution is a more common and profitable activity for women. Second, women are significantly more likely to view their virginity as a "gift" that is given to someone special than are men (by contrast, men tend to see their virginity as something stigmatizing that they need to get rid of; Carpenter, 2001). *However, none of this should be taken to mean that all or even most women go around trading their bodies to the highest bidder!* The point of this theory is simply to suggest that in cases where sex is traded in a heterosexual social exchange, it is more likely to be offered by a woman than it is by a man.

The social exchange view of relationships and sexuality has its own problems, of course. For one thing, not all relationship behavior is motivated by a perceived cost–benefit analysis – sometimes people act altruistically, seeking to help another person without expecting anything in return. In fact, research indicates that willingness to sacrifice one's own self-interest for the sake of one's partner is a sign of a very healthy and high-functioning relationship (Van Lange et al., 1997).

Personality Theories

After the rejection of psychoanalytic theory, most psychological research focused solely on the study of behavior, because it was both observable and measurable. However, this emphasis on behavior gradually subsided and cognitive process started coming back into favor, which can be seen happening in both the social learning and exchange perspectives. This ultimately paved the way for a rebirth of **personality psychology**, or the study of relatively stable, intrapsychic factors that generate consistent patterns of behavior. In other words, personality refers to something enduring that resides within an individual, which leads that person to respond to specific stimuli in a certain way. In developing and validating these theories of personality, psychologists moved away from clinical case reports (the basis for Freud's work) and began applying the scientific method. Over the years, psychologists have identified numerous personality factors that are important for understanding sexuality.

For example, you probably learned about the **Big Five** personality factors in some of your other psychology courses (McCrae & Costa, 1987). The idea behind the Big Five is that we can gain a reasonably good understanding of an individual's personality by looking at that person's standing on five distinct factors: *openness to experience, conscientiousness, extraversion, agreeableness,* and *neuroticism.* For a brief definition of each of these traits and how they relate to sexual behavior, see Table 1.4. Of the five factors, extraversion and agreeableness have been the most consistently related to sexual behavior.

Beyond the Big Five, research has uncovered a number of additional personality traits that have implications for sexual behavior. For example, **erotophilia** and **erotophobia** refer to two ends of a personality continuum that comprises how individuals approach sex (Fisher, White, Byrne, & Kelley, 1988). Erotophilia refers to a tendency to exhibit strong, *positive* emotions and attitudes toward sex; erotophobia refers to a tendency to exhibit strong, *negative* emotions and attitudes toward sex. For example, someone who scores high on the trait of erotophilia would likely agree with statements such as "engaging in group sex is an entertaining idea," and "masturbation can be an exciting experience." In contrast, people who score high on erotophobia would likely agree with statements such as "if people thought I was interested in oral sex, I would be embarrassed," and "it would be emotionally upsetting to me to see someone exposing themselves publicly" (all of these statements are items on the actual Erotophilia–Erotophobia scale). These personality traits may have important implications for sexual behavior. For example, among women, greater erotophobia is linked to less sexual satisfaction (Hurlbert, Apt, & Rabehl, 1993) and less consistent contraception use (Kelly, Smeaton, Byrne, Przybyla, & Fisher, 1987). To see where you fall on the dimensions of erotophilia and erotophobia, check out the Your Sexuality 1.1 box.

Another personality trait relevant to sexual behavior is **sensation seeking**, which refers to a tendency to pursue thrilling and risky activities (Zuckerman, Eysenck, & Eysenck, 1978). Some research has suggested a biological basis for this trait, such that sensation seekers look for excitement as a means of compensating for lower levels of certain brain chemicals, with the prime candidate being the neurotransmitter *dopamine* (Geen, 1997). Dopamine is part of the brain's "reward

Table 1.4   The Big Five Personality Traits and their Association with Sexual Behavior

Personality trait	Definition (McCrae & Costa, 1987)	Noted relations to sexual behavior
Openness to experience	Desire for new and varied experiences. Inventive and curious.	High openness is related to lower sexual anxiety (Heaven et al., 2003); however, most other studies have failed to find an association between openness and sexual behavior.
Conscientiousness	Dependable and responsible. Self-disciplined. Tendency to plan behavior rather than act spontaneously.	Low conscientiousness is linked to having unprotected sex (Hoyle, Fefjar, & Miller, 2000) and combining alcohol and drugs with sex (Miller et al., 2004).
Agreeableness	Caring and compassionate about other people. Generally friendly and helpful.	Low agreeableness is linked to having casual sex with someone other than one's romantic partner and combining drugs and alcohol with sex (Hoyle, Fefjar, & Miller, 2000; Miller et al., 2004) Both high and low levels of interpersonal warmth are linked to having more sexual partners (Markey & Markey, 2007).
Extraversion	Desire to interact with other people. Self-confident and sociable.	High extraversion is linked to having more sexual partners (Miller et al., 2004; Schenk & Pfrang, 1986) and sexual risk taking (Turchik et al., 2010). Interpersonal assertiveness and dominance are linked to having more sexual partners (Markey and Markey, 2007).
Neuroticism	Characterized by feelings of anxiety and insecurity. Emotional instability.	High neuroticism is linked to risky and unprotected sex (Trobst et al., 2002). Most other studies have shown no relation to sexual behavior.

Note: Research on the association between the Big Five personality factors and sexual behavior has not produced entirely consistent results across studies, particularly in the cases of openness to experience and neuroticism. Thus, caution is warranted in drawing too many conclusions about the role of these two personality traits in sexual behavior.

pathway," meaning that release of this chemical makes us feel good. Persons who are less sensitive to the effects of dopamine may need to continually engage in thrilling activities in order to achieve the same psychological "highs" as everyone else. Consistent with this idea, research has found that a specific variation of the dopamine D4 receptor gene that leaves individuals with fewer dopamine receptors is linked to engaging in a variety of sensation-seeking behaviors, such as taking financial risks, substance use, and committing infidelity (Garcia et al., 2010). More generally, research has consistently found that sensation seekers tend to take a lot of sexual risks, including having much

Your Sexuality 1.1   Are You Erotophilic or Erotophobic?

Below is a subset of items from the erotophilia–erotophobia scale. Please indicate how much you agree with each statement on a scale ranging from 1 (strongly disagree) to 7 (strongly agree).

1. I think it would be very entertaining to look at hardcore pornography.
2. Pornography is obviously filthy and people should not try to describe it as anything else.
3. Masturbation can be an exciting experience.
4. If people thought I was interested in oral sex, I would be embarrassed.
5. Engaging in group sex is an entertaining idea.
6. Almost all pornographic material is nauseating.
7. It would be emotionally upsetting to me to see someone exposing themselves publicly.
8. Touching my genitals would probably be an arousing experience.
9. I do not enjoy daydreaming about sexual matters.
10. Swimming in the nude with someone else would be an exciting experience.

Add up your scores for items 1, 3, 5, 8, and 10 (erotophilic items). Then add up your scores for items 2, 4, 6, 7, and 9 (erotophobic items). Which of the two scores is higher? Is there a big difference between them? Are your scores consistent with how you view your own sexuality? Please note that there are no correct or incorrect answers to any of these questions. It is not necessarily "better" to be erotophilic or erotophobic.

Note: Adapted from Fisher et al. (1988). The wording of some items has been modified from the original scale and scoring criteria have changed to fit the abbreviated version presented here.

larger numbers of sexual partners and a greater frequency of unprotected sex (Gullette & Lyons, 2005). Perhaps not surprisingly, sensation seekers also tend to contract more STIs (Ripa, Hansen, Mortensen, Sanders, & Reinisch, 2001).

One other personality trait that is particularly relevant here is **sociosexuality**, which refers to a person's willingness to have sex in the absence of commitment and without an emotional connection to one's partner (Gangestad & Simpson, 1990). Persons with what is known as a *restricted sociosexual orientation* require feelings of closeness to a partner before having sex and tend to seek out more long-term relationships (e.g., they would agree with statements such as "I would have to be closely attached to someone before I could feel comfortable and fully enjoy having sex"); in contrast, persons with an *unrestricted sociosexual orientation* do not need to establish such an emotional connection first and tend to seek more short-term relationships (e.g., they would agree with statements such as "sex without love is OK"; Simpson & Gangestad, 1991). The more unrestricted a person's sociosexual orientation is, the more frequently they have sex and the more sexual partners they accumulate. In addition, research has found that having an unrestricted orientation is linked to greater impulsivity, as well as a higher likelihood of having unprotected sex (Seal & Agostinelli, 1994). On a side note, popular media portrayals might lead one to assume that there is a huge difference between men and women in sociosexuality, with

Figure 1.7 Sensation seekers tend to engage in activities that bring more thrills and excitement, such as seeking multiple partners, perhaps because their brains require greater stimulation in order to achieve pleasure. Image Copyright altafulla, 2013. Used under license from Shutterstock.com.

men tending toward unrestricted and women tending toward restricted. While there a hint of truth to this, it is important to note that there is far more variability within the sexes than between them (Simpson & Gangestad, 1991). What this means is that whereas men are more interested in casual sex *on average*, this is not true for all men. It also means that there are some women who are more interested in casual sex than some men. This is but one of many reminders throughout this book that it is not wise to assume anyone's sexual interests and practices based solely upon their sexual or gender identity.

The personality perspective is appealing to many psychologists who study sexual behavior, but it has its own limitations. For one thing, some of the scales used to measure personality appear to measure attitudes more than enduring traits or characteristics (e.g., erotphilia–erotophobia). This calls into question whether we are measuring personality or something else (e.g., learned associations based upon past experience). In addition, it seems to be the case that some personality effects may be accounted for by genetics (e.g., consider our discussion of the role of the D4 receptor gene in sensation seeking; Garcia et al., 2010). Thus, is the key factor here really one's personality or one's biological makeup?

Evolutionary Theory

One of the more recent theoretical developments applicable to the study of human sexuality comes from **evolutionary psychology**. The idea of evolution itself is certainly not new (Darwin's *On the Origin of Species* was actually published in 1859), but the study of psychological traits as evolved adaptions has only become a major area of research in the past three or four decades. Because evolution-based studies of human sexuality have undergone explosive growth in recent years, evolutionary psychology will be covered extensively in this book. At this point, however, we will simply summarize some of the major highlights and findings of this theoretical perspective.

One of the main ideas promoted by evolutionary psychologists is that human beings have an inherent motivation to produce as many of their own offspring as possible. To assist us in achieving this goal, it is thought that we have gradually developed preferences for specific physical and psychological characteristics in our romantic and sexual partners that are likely to result in successful reproduction. In other words, the reason you find certain traits to be attractive and "sexy" in another person is a result of thousands of years of selection pressures pushing humans to gravitate toward partners who are genetically fit and who are likely to have the best reproductive potential. For example, heterosexual men today tend to be attracted to young, "hourglass"-shaped women with long, silky hair (Hinsz, Matz, & Patience, 2001; Singh, 1993). Each of the characteristics signifies a woman who is healthy and capable of making babies. Specifically, younger women are more fertile, women with "hourglass" figures have an easier time delivering children, and long, silky hair indicates good physical health. It is theorized that our early ancestors recognized the value associated with such traits (either consciously or unconsciously) and developed preferences for them, thereby laying the seeds for what we in the modern era deem attractive.

Another key component of evolutionary psychology is the idea that men and women have developed different approaches to mating. From the perspective of **sexual strategies theory** (Buss & Schmitt, 1993), these differences evolved because the *parental investment* required to produce a child (i.e., the amount of time and bodily effort expended) differs across the sexes. Specifically, the investment required by men to make a baby is relatively small – some of them can do their part in under a minute! As a result, in order to maximize their chances of reproductive success, it is in men's best interest to be sexually active and sleep with a lot of fertile

Figure 1.8   Evolutionary theory posits that heterosexual men are attracted to women whose bodies are shaped like an hourglass and who have long, silky hair because these are signs of good health and fertility. ©Vitaly Valua/123RF.COM.

women. This helps to explain modern man's well-documented desire for many sexual partners and his disproportionate attention to physical appearance. In contrast, the investment required to make a baby is huge for women – pregnancy lasts nine months and after that, the child needs to be taken care of until it is self-sufficient. Thus, to maximize reproductive success, it is in women's best interests to look for men who are going to stick around and provide the resources necessary to help raise any children conceived. This may explain modern woman's well-documented tendency to desire reliable men with high social status and good jobs. Numerous studies have found support for these sex differences in mating preferences (e.g., Okami & Shackelford, 2001).

While fascinating and heavily researched, the evolutionary perspective is not free of problems or controversy. For example, evolutionary psychology has always struggled to explain why variations in sexual orientation exist. If human beings are inherently motivated to reproduce, why would anyone be anything other than heterosexual? Additionally, recent research suggests that most of the noted sex differences in attraction and mating preferences have been overstated and that many of these differences can be reduced in size or eliminated completely when certain social factors are taken into account, such as the fact that women are judged more harshly than men for being sexually active (Conley, Moors, Matsick, Ziegler, & Valentine, 2011). Finally, some have argued that evolution-based interpretations of human sexuality are fundamentally flawed and that modern mating preferences have little, and perhaps nothing, to do with parental investment and an inherently "selfish" drive to propagate one's genes, such as in the perspective offered by the book *Sex at Dawn* (Ryan & Jetha, 2010), which we will consider in chapter 7.

The Perspective of This Text

As you probably noticed above, psychological theories of sexuality largely fall into one of two camps (DeLamater & Hyde, 1998). On the one hand, we have so-called "essentialist" theories, which view sexuality as an essential aspect of humans, rooted in evolution and biology. Such theories look to factors including hormones, genetics, evolved processes, or innate characteristics for the answers to their questions. On the other hand, we have so-called "social constructionist" theories, which view sexuality largely as a product of socialization and cultural influences. Such theories argue that our sexuality is not "hardwired" and, instead, is largely learned.

My perspective is that taking a singular approach to the study of sexuality would be both misleading and unfulfilling. It is clear that human sexuality is determined by multiple factors. In addition, despite a vast range of theories designed to explain our sexual attitudes and behaviors, at best, each one offers only a partial explanation. In order to address this issue and to create a unifying theme and perspective to organize the remainder of this book, we will adopt a **biopsychosocial perspective**.

If you have ever taken a course in health psychology, you are probably familiar with the biopsychosocial model, which proposes that one's health status is the result of a complex interaction of biological, psychological, and social factors (Engel, 1977). For example, a health psychologist might view coronary heart disease as the product of not just biological (e.g., cholesterol and blood pressure levels) and genetic factors (e.g., family history of heart problems), but also psychological traits (e.g., Type A personality pattern) and social variables (e.g., occupational and marital stress). The objective of this textbook is to view sexual health and behavior through a similar lens. For

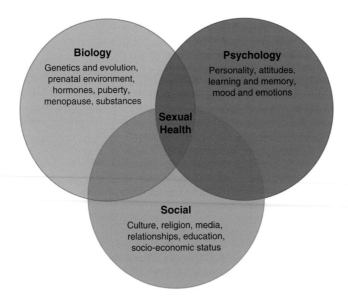

Figure 1.9   The biopsychosocial model as applied to sexual health.

instance, if we want to understand why a given woman has difficulty achieving orgasm, we need to consider possible explanations at the biological (e.g., is intercourse painful due to the presence of a sexually transmitted infection or a lack of lubrication?), psychological (e.g., is she depressed or under a lot of stress?), and social levels (e.g., is there a lot of conflict in her relationship?).

Although the biopsychosocial approach is not often discussed in relation to sexuality, it is extremely applicable to this area. As discussed at length earlier, sexual behavior is a consequence of multiple disparate forces acting upon a person. Some of these forces are internal and specific to the individual, whereas others are broad, external factors that affect everyone in a given culture or society. Moreover, some of these factors are under our complete conscious control, while we are victims of circumstance to others. Some of these factors are certainly more important than others in helping us to understand human sexuality, and the relative importance of these factors can vary considerably across individuals and across the lifespan. However, the biopsychosocial perspective acknowledges this complexity and allows us to look at sexuality as a product of the whole person, with the mind and body being fundamentally and intimately interconnected.

One unique advantage of adopting a biopsychosocial perspective is that it allows us to put sexual health on a continuum, running from wellness to illness (just as health psychologists do with the more general concept of "health"). Thus, rather than seeing sexual health as simply the absence of disease or dysfunction, we can view it as having different degrees of wellness and illness. Individuals may move back and forth on this continuum from exhibiting healthy to unhealthy sexuality depending upon the unique biological, psychological, and social forces acting upon them at the time. For instance, imagine that someone were to experience an episode of clinical depression. The resulting emotional state and lack of energy might seriously undermine that person's sex life, pushing them toward the unhealthy end of the continuum. However, after undergoing treatment and making some major life changes, their sex life might improve back to the point that it was before and possibly even exceed the previous level. The strength of looking at sexuality on such a continuum is that it offers a much more holistic approach where we consider the entire person, rather than just looking for a specific sexual problem. Thus, having an optimum state of sexual health is a function of possessing physical, psychological, *and* social well-being – it is so much more than just being free of physical dysfunction and disease.

Another important implication of this model and its focus on the mind–body connection is that psychology can be viewed not only as a factor that causes or drives sexual behavior, but also as a product of sexual behavior. In other words, not only do our emotions, cognitions, and behaviors affect our sex lives, but our sex lives have a direct impact on our psychology.

Throughout the remainder of this book, we will consider sexuality from a biopsychosocial perspective. However, because this is inherently a psychological textbook, psychology will have a more prominent, front and center role than some of the other factors. This will allow you to see how the study of sex is approached in the field of psychology and emphasize how the material connects to other psychology courses, while still acknowledging the irreducible complexity of human sexuality.

Key Terms

incest
pederasty
libido
id
ego
superego
classical conditioning
operant conditioning

reparative therapy
social or observational
  learning
comparison level
exchange theories
personality psychology
the big five
erotophilia

erotophobia
sensation seeking
sociosexuality
evolutionary psychology
sexual strategies
  theory
biopsychosocial
  perspective

Discussion Questions: What is Your Perspective on Sex?

- We know that biological, psychological, and social factors all contribute to human sexual behavior; however, do you see one of these factors as being relatively more important than the others? Why?
- Does sexual content in television and film truly affect people's sexual behavior, or does it simply reflect contemporary sexual practices?
- Some research has suggested that as gender equality has increased, men's and women's mating preferences have become more similar. What does this mean for our understanding of evolution-based accounts of human sexuality?

References

Bagemihl, B. (1999). *Biological exuberance: Animal homosexuality and natural diversity*. New York: St. Martin's Press.

Bandura, A., Ross, D., & Ross, S.A. (1961). Transmission of aggression through imitation of aggressive models. *Journal of Abnormal and Social Psychology*, *63*, 575–582. DOI:10.1037/h0045925.

Baumeister, R.F., & Vohs, K.D. (2004). Sexual economics: Sex as female resource for social exchange in heterosexual interactions. *Personality and Social Psychology Review*, 8, 339–363. DOI:10.1207/s15327957pspr0804_2.

Beltz, A.M., Swanson, J.L., & Berenbaum, S.A. (2011). Gendered occupational interests: Prenatal androgen effects on psychological orientation to Things versus People. *Hormones and Behavior*, 60, 313–317. DOI:10.1016/j.yhbeh.2011.06.002.

Boswell, J. (1980). *Christianity, social tolerance, and homosexuality: Gay people in Western Europe from the beginning of the Christian era to the fourteenth century*. Chicago: The University of Chicago Press.

Bowater, D. (2011). Pornography is replacing sex education. *The Daily Telegraph*. Retrieved from http://www.telegraph.co.uk/education/educationnews/8961010/Pornography-is-replacing-sex-education.html (accessed August 16, 2013).

Buss, D.M., & Schmitt, D.P. (1993). Sexual strategies theory: A contextual evolutionary analysis of human mating. *Psychological Review*, 100, 204–232. DOI:10.1037/0033-295X.100.2.204.

Carpenter, L.M. (2001). The ambiguity of "having sex": The subjective experience of virginity loss in the United States. *Journal of Sex Research*, 38, 127–140. DOI:10.1080/00224490109552080.

Conley, T.D., Moors, A.C., Matsick, J.L., Ziegler, A., & Valentine, B.A. (2011). Women, men, and the bedroom: Methodological and conceptual insights that narrow, reframe, and eliminate gender differences in sexuality. *Current Directions in Psychological Science*, 20, 296–300. DOI:10.1177/0963721411418467.

Dawood, K., Bailey, J.M., & Martin, N.G. (2009). Genetic and environmental influences on sexual orientation. In Y. Kim (Ed.), *Handbook of behavioral genetics* (pp. 269–280). New York: Springer.

DeLamater, J. (1987). A sociological perspective. In J.H. Geer & W.T. O'Donohue (Eds.), *Theories of human sexuality* (pp. 237–256). New York: Plenum.

DeLamater, J. D., & Hyde, J. S. (1998). Essentialism vs. social constructionism in the study of human sexuality. *Journal of Sex Research*, 35, 10–18. DOI:10.1080/00224499809551913.

Engel, G.L. (1977). The need for a new medical model: A challenge for biomedicine. *Science*, 196, 129–136. DOI:10.1126/science.847460.

Fisher, W.A., White, L.A., Byrne, D., & Kelley K. (1988). Erotophobia–erotophilia as a dimension of personality. *Journal of Sex Research*, 25, 123–151. DOI:10.1080/00224498809551448.

Gager, C.T., & Yabiku, S.T. (2010). Who has the time? The relationship between household labor time and sexual frequency. *Journal of Family Issues*, 31, 135–163. DOI:10.1177/0192513X09348753.

Gangestad, S.W., & Simpson, J.A. (1990). Toward an evolutionary history of female sociosexual variation. *Journal of Personality*, 58, 69–96. DOI:10.1111/j.1467-6494.1990.tb00908.x

Garcia, J.R., MacKillop, J., Aller, E.L., Merriwether, A.M., Wilson, D.S., & Lum, JK. (2010). Associations between dopamine D4 receptor gene variation with both infidelity and sexual promiscuity. *PLoS ONE* 5(11): e14162. DOI:10.1371/journal.pone.0014162

Geen, R.G. (1997). Psychophysiological approaches to personality. In J. Hogan, J. Johnson, & S. Briggs (Eds.), *Handbook of personality psychology* (pp. 387–416). San Diego, CA: Academic Press.

Gregersen, E. (1996). *The world of human sexuality: Behaviors, customs, and beliefs*. New York: Irvington.

Gullette, D.L., & Lyons, M.A. (2005). Sexual sensation seeking, compulsivity, and HIV risk behaviors in college students. *Journal of Community Health Nursing*, 22, 47–60. DOI:10.1207/s15327655jchn2201_5.

Gunasekera, H., Chapman, S., & Campbell, S. (2005). Sex and drugs in popular movies: An analysis of the top 200 films. *Journal of the Royal Society of Medicine*, 98, 464–470.

Halderman, D.C. (2003). Gay rights, patient rights: The implications of sexual orientation conversion therapy. *Professional Psychology: Research and Practice*, 33, 260–264. DOI:10.1037//0735-7028.33.3.260.

Heaven, P.C.L., Crocker, D., Edwards, B., Preston, N., Ward, R., & Woodbridge, N. (2003). Personality and sex. *Personality and Individual Differences*, 35, 411–419. DOI:10.1016/S0191-8869(02)00203-9.

Herdt, G.H. (1982). *Rituals of manhood: Male initiation in Papua New Guinea*. Berkeley: University of California Press.

Hinsz, V.B., Matz, D.C., & Patience, R.A. (2001). Does women's hair signal reproductive potential? *Journal of Experimental Social Psychology*, 37, 166–172. DOI:10.1006/jesp.2000.1450.

Homans, G.C. (1961). *Social behavior and its elementary forms*. New York: Harcourt, Brace, and World.

Hoyle, R.H., Fejfar, M.C., & Miller, J.D. (2000). Personality and sexual risk taking: A quantitative review. *Journal of Personality, 68*, 1203–1231. DOI:10.1111/1467-6494.00132.

Hurlbert, D.F., Apt, C., & Rabehl, S.M. (1993). Key variables to understanding female sexual satisfaction: An examination of women in nondistressed marriages. *Journal of Sex & Marital Therapy, 19*, 154–165. DOI:10.1080/00926239308404899.

ILGA (2013). *Lesbian and Gay Rights in the World*. Retrieved from http://old.ilga.org/Statehomophobia/ILGA_map_2013_A4.pdf (accessed September 2, 2013).

Kelley, K., Smeaton, G., Byrne, D., Przybyla, D.P.J., & Fisher, W.A. (1987). Sexual attitudes and contraception among females across five college samples. *Human Relations, 40*, 237–253. DOI:10.1177/001872678704000404.

Malhotra, A. (1991). Gender and changing generational relations: Spouse choice in Indonesia. *Demography, 28*, 549–570.

Markey, P. M., & Markey, C. N. (2007). The interpersonal meaning of sexual promiscuity. *Journal of Research in Personality, 41*, 1199–1212. DOI:10.1016/j.jrp.2007.02.004.

Masters, W., & Johnson, V. (1970). *Human sexual inadequacy*. Boston: Little, Brown.

McCrae, R.R., & Costa, P.T. (1987). Validation of the five-factor model of personality across instruments and observers. *Journal of Personality and Social Psychology, 52*, 81–90. DOI:10.1037/0022-3514.52.1.81.

Meston, C. M., & Buss, D. M. (2007). Why humans have sex. *Archives of Sexual Behavior, 36*, 477–507. DOI:10.1007/s10508-007-9175-2.

Miller, J.D., Lynam, D., Zimmerman, R.S., Logan, T.K., Leukefeld, C., & Clayton, R. (2004). The utility of the Five Factor Model in understanding risky sexual behavior. *Personality and Individual Differences, 36*, 1611–1626. DOI:10.1016/j.paid.2003.06.009.

Nanda, S. (2001). *Gender diversity: Crosscultural variations*. Prospect Heights, IL: Waveland Press.

O'Hara, R.E., Gibbons, F.X., Gerrard, M., Li, Z., & Sargent, J.D. (2012). Greater exposure to sexual content in movies predicts earlier sexual debut and increased sexual risk taking. *Psychological Science, 23*, 984–993. DOI:10.1177/0956797611435529.

Okami, P., & Schackelford, T.K. (2001). Human sex differences in sexual psychology and behavior. *Annual Review of Sex Research, 12*, 186–241.

Pavlov, I.P. (1927). *Conditioned reflexes*. Oxford: Oxford University Press.

Plaud, J.J., & Martini, J.R. (1999). The respondent conditioning of male sexual arousal. *Behavior Modification, 23*, 254–268. DOI:10.1177/0145445599232004.

Ripa, C.P.L., Hansen, H.S., Mortensen, E.L., Sanders, S.A., & Reinisch, J.M. (2001). A Danish version of the Sensation Seeking Scale and its relation to a broad spectrum of behavioral and psychological characteristics. *Personality and Individual Differences, 30*, 1371–1386. DOI:10.1016/S0191-8869(00)00119-7.

Ryan, C., & Jetha, C. (2010). *Sex at dawn: How we mate, why we stray, and what it means for modern relationships*. New York: HarperCollins.

Scanlon, T.F. (2005). The dispersion of pederasty and the athletic revolution in sixth-century BC Greece. *Journal of Homosexuality, 49*, 63–85. DOI:10.1300/J082v49n03_03.

Schenk, J., & Pfrang, H. (1986). Extraversion, neuroticism, and sexual behavior: Interrelationships in a sample of young men. *Archives of Sexual Behavior, 15*, 449–455. DOI:10.1007/BF01542309.

Seal, D.W., & Agostinelli, G. (1994). Individual differences associated with high-risk sexual behaviour: Implications for intervention programmes. *AIDS Care, 6*, 393–397. DOI:10.1080/09540129408258653.

Simpson, J.A., & Gangestad, S.W. (1991). Individual differences in sociosexuality: Evidence for convergent and discriminant validity. *Journal of Personality and Social Psychology, 60*, 870–883. DOI:10.1037/0022-3514.60.6.870.

Singh, D. (1993). Adaptive significance of female physical attractiveness: Role of waist-to-hip ratio. *Journal of Personality and Social Psychology, 65*, 293–293. DOI:10.1037/0022-3514.65.2.293.

Skinner, B.F. (1938). *The behavior of organisms: An experimental analysis*. New York: Macmillan.

Strassberg, D.S., McKinnon, R.K., Sustaíta, M.A., & Rullo, J. (2013). Sexting by high school students: An exploratory and descriptive study. *Archives of Sexual Behavior, 42*, 15–21. DOI:10.1007/s10508-012-9969-8.

Strauss, G. (2010). Sex on TV: It's increasingly uncut – and unavoidable. *USA Today*. Retrieved from http://www.usatoday.com/life/television/news/2010-01-20-sexcov20_CV_N.htm (accessed August 16, 2013).

Tan, M., Jones, G., Zhu, G., Ye, J., Hong, T., Zhou, S., ... Zhang, L. (2009). Fellatio by fruit bats prolongs copulation time. *PLoS ONE*, 4(10), 1–5. DOI:10.1371/journal.pone.0007595.

Thibaut, J.W., & Kelley, H.H. (1959). *The social psychology of groups*. New York: John Wiley & Sons.

Trobst, K K., Herbst, J.H., Masters, H.L., & Costa, P.T. (2002). Personality pathways to unsafe sex: Personality, condom use, and HIV risk behaviors. *Journal of Research in Personality*, 36, 117–133. DOI:10.1006/jrpe.2001.2334.

Turchik, J.A., Garske, J.P., Probst, D.R., & Irvin, C.R. (2010). Personality, sexuality, and substance use as predictors of sexual risk taking in college students. *Journal of Sex Research*, 47, 411–419. DOI:10.1080/00224490903161621.

Van Lange, P.A., Rusbult, C.E., Drigotas, S.M., Arriaga, X.B., Witcher, B.S., & Cox, C L. (1997). Willingness to sacrifice in close relationships. *Journal of Personality and Social Psychology*, 72, 1373–1395.

Walster, E., Walster, W., & Berscheid, E. (1978). *Equity: Theory and research*. Boston: Allyn & Bacon.

Wiesner-Hanks, M. (2000). *Christianity and sexuality in the early modern world*. London: Routledge.

Zuckerman, M., Eysenck, S.B., & Eysenck, H.J. (1978). Sensation seeking in England and America: Cross-cultural, age, and sex comparisons. *Journal of Consulting and Clinical Psychology*, 46, 139–149.

2

Sexology Research: History, Methods, and Ethics

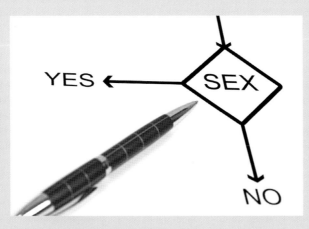

©fuzzbones/123RF.COM.

Chapter Outline

- Introduction   28
- A Brief History of Sexology   29
- Sexology as a Science   31
- Sample Selection   32
- Nonexperimental Research   34
  - Surveys   34
  - Direct Observation   38
  - Case Reports   42
- Experimental Research   42
  - A Sample Sexperiment   43
  - Strengths and Limitations of the Experimental Method   43
- A Note on Statistics   44
  - Means and Medians   44
  - Incidence and Prevalence   44
  - Correlation   44
- Ethics in Sexology Research   45
  - Informed Consent   48
  - Debriefing   50
  - Confidentiality   51
- Evaluating Sex Research   51

The Psychology of Human Sexuality, First Edition. Justin J. Lehmiller.
© 2014 John Wiley & Sons, Ltd. Published 2014 by John Wiley & Sons, Ltd.

Introduction

It is admittedly the most important subject in life. It is admittedly the thing that causes the most shipwrecks in the happiness of men and women. And yet our scientific knowledge is so meager... Those of us who try to salvage some of the shipwrecks need to have a thousand questions answered before we can guide other human beings intelligently. And we want them answered not by our mothers and grandmothers, not by priests and clergymen in the interest of middle-class mores, nor by general practitioners, not even by Freudians; we... want them answered by scientifically-trained students of sex.

John B. Watson (as cited in Magoun, 1981, p. 374)

The above quote comes from the writings of John B. Watson, one of the preeminent psychologists of the twentieth century. Perhaps you know him from some of your other psychology courses as the founder of the *behaviorism* movement, or from his research on Little Albert (a young boy in whom Watson classically conditioned a fear of white rats). However, it is probably safe to assume that none of these other courses taught you about Watson's interest in human sexuality. Not only was he very vocal about the need for sex to be studied scientifically, but he practiced what he preached. Watson was actually one of the first psychologists to study sex in a laboratory setting, even going so far as to develop scientific instruments that could record human sexual responses (Magoun, 1981). Watson allegedly served as his own subject, as did his mistress, Rosalie Rayner (whom, as some of you may recall, assisted Watson in his research with Little Albert). Being the good scientist that he was, Watson took detailed notes on all of his "sexperiments." However, that may have ultimately been his undoing. When Watson's wife and the university at which he was working discovered his sexual exploits with Rayner, he lost both his marriage and job (McConnell, 1974).

Even though it was not politically popular at the time and may have "shipwrecked" his personal and professional life, Watson was willing to acknowledge the important role of sex in human life and the relative dearth of scientific knowledge on the subject. We owe a great debt to Watson and several like-minded researchers who followed, including Alfred Kinsey, William Masters, and Virginia Johnson, all of whom were willing to stand against the prevailing social norms and values of their time and declare sex a worthy topic of scientific inquiry.

The result of these early researchers' efforts is the modern field of **sexology**, the scientific study of sex. Although sexology is a relatively young field, it has a rich, fascinating, and somewhat scandalous history (including some wife-swapping scientists who filmed each other's sexual exploits! For good and obvious reasons, that would be considered a research no-no today.) However, before we delve into those details, let me first paint a better picture of the field of sexology for you. The goal of sexology is to increase our understanding of all aspects of human sexuality, including everything from why different sexual orientations exist, to the frequency of specific sexual practices across cultures, to the motivations behind rape and other sex crimes, to therapies that can treat sexual problems. Given the broad array of topics studied within this field, sexologists necessarily consist of a diverse group of scientists who employ a wide range of research methodologies; these scientists include psychologists, sociologists, anthropologists, biologists, and many others.

In this chapter, we will consider what it is that makes sexology a science, detail some of the major methodological tools utilized in this field, and highlight the unique ethical issues and difficulties associated with the study of sex. Before we do, let us first consider the evolution of sexology as a field and how we got where we are today.

A Brief History of Sexology

In some ways, the study of sex dates back as early as the ancient Greeks (Haeberle, 1983). Some of the most prominent figures of that period, including Hippocrates, Aristotle, and Plato, wrote and theorized about a variety of topics pertaining to sex. However, the scientific study of sex as we know it today did not begin to take shape until the mid-nineteenth century, when several physicians, such as Heinrich Kaan and Richard von Krafft-Ebing, began publishing books on sexual behavior. These books signified a radical shift in perspective because rather than viewing sexual "aberrations" and dysfunctions as moral failings (as most cultures and societies had for centuries), they reconceptualized them as medical and mental issues.

This medicalization of sexuality began to pick up steam and psychology took center stage at the turn of the twentieth century, when Sigmund Freud began the psychoanalytic movement. Psychoanalytic theory increased momentum for the idea that a true understanding of sexual behavior rests with an in-depth exploration of human psychology. However, the Freudian approach, which largely relied upon case studies of highly unusual clinical patients (a research method we will discuss later in this chapter), was not satisfying to those who wanted the study of human sexuality to be grounded in science and experimentation. To meet this need, researchers began to move sex into the laboratory.

Those who attempted scientific studies of sex in the pioneer days faced numerous challenges. For one thing, the prevailing attitudes of society were still negative, if not outright hostile, toward any open discussion of sex. As a result, few scientists were willing to risk their careers to even speak publicly about this topic, let alone research it (John Watson was clearly an exception). Those researchers who did were confronted with funding agencies that were unwilling to back their work, a significant segment of the population that was either too embarrassed or too offended to participate in their studies, and publishers who rejected their articles outright, especially if the researchers were studying "deviant" sexual behaviors (e.g., masturbation, homosexuality). Even research on topics that many people would consider mundane today (e.g., people's attitudes toward sex outside of marriage) sparked public outcry and those who dared to study them risked ending their careers (Magoun, 1981). Early sex research thus necessitated some degree of secrecy. However, this heightened level of secrecy combined with a lack of formal oversight, led to some ethical lapses that arguably threatened some researchers' reputations and the legitimacy of their work.

The scientific study of human sexuality remained almost completely underground until the 1940s and 50s when Dr. Alfred Kinsey entered the limelight. Kinsey's interest in the study of sex came about after he began teaching a college-level marriage course and, in the process, discovered that our scientific knowledge of sex was incredibly narrow and rife with inaccuracies. It was this glaring problem that eventually spurred Kinsey and his team of colleagues to travel across the United States and interview thousands of Americans regarding their sexual lives (we will discuss the specifics of his methods later in this chapter). Kinsey, who received his graduate training in biology, published two books based upon the results of his research (*Sexual Behavior in the Human Male* and *Sexual Behavior in the Human Female*). Both were national bestsellers and made Kinsey an instant celebrity; however, they were also very risqué for the time and resulted in controversy and scandal. Not only did the FBI begin compiling a dossier on Kinsey and his associates, but his work resulted in a congressional investigation of the Rockefeller Foundation, the source of Kinsey's research funding.

Figure 2.1   Alfred Kinsey was a pioneer in the field of sex research and conducted some of the most well-known and highly cited sex research of all time. Photograph by William Dellenback and provided by The Kinsey Institute for Research in Sex, Gender, and Reproduction.

Although Kinsey was most famous for the sex interviews he conducted, it is no big secret that he (like many early sexologists) had a strong interest in studying sex from a more biological standpoint. Specifically, Kinsey wanted to observe systematically how the body reacts to sexual stimulation. Given the harsh public criticism he endured after the publication of his first book, Kinsey realized that if wanted to study the mechanics of sexual response, he would need to do it rather discreetly. Thus, it was in the attic of Kinsey's house that his lesser-known observational studies of sex took place. Kinsey and his research associates filmed each other while engaging in various sexual activities, sometimes with their wives, and sometimes with each other's wives (for a more colorful description of some of the activities they filmed, I encourage you to read the first chapter of *Bonk: The Curious Coupling of Science and Sex* by Mary Roach. It provides an informative, albeit cheeky look at Kinsey's life and work).

Certainly, we owe a lot to Kinsey for his systematic and enlightening studies of sex; however, it seems fair to say that he became a little too personally "involved" in his work toward the end. It was around this time (in the 1950s and 60s) that the husband and wife team of William Masters and Virginia Johnson came along and brought a renewed sense of objectivity to the study of sex. Masters (a gynecologist) and Johnson (a student of psychology and aspiring country singer) sought to conduct the most elaborate and scientifically-grounded observational research on sex to date. All of their work was conducted in a laboratory setting with the latest technology and with the utmost professionalism (we will discuss the details of their methods later in this chapter). Masters and Johnson observed thousands of complete sexual responses in both men and women and published several influential books based upon their findings, with *Human Sexual Response* being perhaps the most well-known. Despite their best efforts at keeping things on the up-and-up, Masters and Johnson's work did not escape controversy. For example, as part of their research, they interviewed prostitutes, filmed individuals and couples as they engaged in sexual activity, and even created a sex toy with a built-in camera that allowed them to observe the physical changes that happen inside the vagina during sexual arousal and orgasm. In light of this, and society's negative attitudes toward sex at the time, it is perhaps not surprising that many people considered their work immoral. In fact, part of the reason Masters and Johnson (and Kinsey too, for that matter) published their work in book format was because most academic journals deemed their research "pornographic."

The popularity of Masters and Johnson's books, coupled with the sexual revolution of the 1960s and 70s, moved the study of human sexuality further into the open. Since then, societal and cultural attitudes toward sex have gradually become more progressive and sexuality research has come to achieve greater levels of acceptance. *Gradually* is the key word here, though. Just consider that it was not until the 1990s that the first nationally representative survey of sexual behavior was conducted in the United States! Even today, despite the fact that there are several academic journals that exclusively publish sex research, and the popular media frequently highlights this work, the legitimacy of sexuality research is still questioned. For example, there are some politicians who regularly threaten to rescind federal grant funding from research projects that focus on sexuality or relationships, even though those projects have already been deemed worthy of study by a panel of scientific experts. Studies of sexual and gender minorities, prostitutes, and the sex lives of older adults are particularly prone to political criticism as topics that are "inappropriate" for government grants. Thus, sexuality research still has its detractors, and probably always will.

The struggle to find sex a place within science may have cost some researchers their careers and ruffled the feathers of more than a few politicians, but the benefits gained by these research endeavors have far outweighed the costs. It is through this research that we have begun to correct a multitude of myths and misconceptions about sex and the human body, reset our expectations about what is "normal" when it comes to sexual attitudes and behaviors, and discovered how to prevent and treat various sex and relationship problems. You will read more about these and other benefits of sex research as you progress through this book, but keep in mind that sexology is still a very young field of science and much remains that we do not yet know.

Sexology as a Science

In most regards, sexology operates in a similar way to any other field of science. The only real difference is that sexologists use some unique technologies and, of course, have more fun! Thus, the basic building blocks of research that you learned in other science classes still apply (e.g., the scientific method, the principles and values that scientists must uphold). For this reason, we will not review the fundamentals of how a science operates. Instead, we will focus primarily on understanding the specific research methods and techniques employed in the field of sexology and consider when such methods are appropriate for use. As you will soon discover, sometimes it is impossible or unethical to use certain methods in answering some research questions. We will divide our discussion of research techniques

Table 2.1 A Summary of Sexology Research Methods

Research method	Definition	Strengths	Limitations
Survey	A large number of participants report on their own sexual attitudes and practices via an interview or questionnaire.	Quick and easy way of collecting data. Several modes of administration.	Nonresponse. Self-selection. Social desirability and other response biases. Writing a good survey requires skill and effort.
Direct Observation	Researchers observe participants and record what they see.	Less chance of response biases. Observations can be preserved on film.	Self-selection. Reactivity.
Case Report	One participant or a small group of participants is studied in great detail.	In-depth information is provided about an unusual case.	Limited generalizability. Often rely upon subjective self-reports.
Experiment	Researchers manipulate or change one variable (the independent variable) in order to see what effect this has on a measurable outcome (the dependent variable).	Precise control of variables. Ability to infer cause and effect.	Not possible or ethical to implement for all research questions. Several threats to external validity.

into two sections: nonexperimental approaches (which include surveys, direct observation, and case reports) and the experimental method. Table 2.1 provides a concise summary of these different methodologies. Before detailing these methods, we will briefly cover the basics of sample selection, because the value and importance of any scientific study of sexuality (whether experimental or nonexperimental) depends upon the nature of the research participants. Without a good sample, it may be impossible to know how meaningful the findings really are and to what extent they might apply to the rest of the population.

Sample Selection

In sexology research, we typically gather data from a very small group of individuals and use that information to draw conclusions about a much larger group of people. In order to accomplish this, researchers must first identify their *target population*, or the group of people about whom they wish to learn. For example, assume a sexologist is interested in determining whether there is a link between taking birth control pills and sexual satisfaction. This researcher might identify their target population as pre-menopausal, sexually active, heterosexual women. It would not be sufficient to simply state that "women" are the target population in this case, because the researcher is not interested in learning about *all* women – only those women who might be taking "the pill" in order to prevent pregnancy.

Once the target population is specified, researchers choose a *sample*, or a smaller group of people who will actually participate in the study. A sample is chosen because it is not practical to study every single member of the target population. In our example, just think about how many millions (if not billions) of pre-menopausal, sexually active, heterosexual women there are in the world and what an impossible task it would be to survey all of them.

There are two main types of samples researchers can recruit: convenience samples and random samples. **Convenience samples** consist of those individuals who are most readily accessible for research purposes. Because a large number of sexologists work in university settings, convenience samples often consist exclusively of undergraduate students. Thus, in our example study of birth control and sexual satisfaction, we might recruit a group of sexually active, female students enrolled in introductory psychology courses to participate.

The advantage of this type of sampling is that we can complete our study quickly and easily without spending any money, given that psychology students are sometimes required to participate in studies in exchange for course credit. However, there are numerous drawbacks, with the main concern being whether the sample is *representative* enough of the target population to allow us to draw conclusions. College samples have a notoriously limited demographic composition. Not only are they more highly educated than average, but they tend to be very young, mostly White, and most of them are from the United States (Gosling, Vazire, Srivastava, & John, 2004). Thus, we must be very cautious about the generalizations we make from college samples, especially if we are at all concerned about how the variables we are studying might be affected by age, race, culture, and education – and when we are talking about sexual attitudes and behaviors, these are extremely important factors to take into account!

To get around the limitations of convenience sampling, researchers sometimes turn to **random selection**. This sampling procedure involves identifying all members of the target population and contacting a subset of them at random to participate. In this process, each member of the population has an equal chance of being selected to take part in the study. For example, if a sexologist were interested in studying attitudes toward legalizing prostitution among likely voters in their city, they might get a list of all registered voters and contact 500 of them at random about being in the study. When the randomization procedure is implemented appropriately, it typically results in a sample that is reflective of the broader population from which it was drawn.

If random selection is so much better than convenience sampling, how come sexologists do not use it all of the time? The reason is because random selection is much more challenging to implement. It is difficult to get people outside the university community to participate unless you have some incentive to offer. As previously mentioned, convenience samples with college students often involve no financial cost because participants typically receive course credit as compensation.

Throughout this book, we will reference the results of national studies employing random selection whenever possible in an attempt to provide the most definitive information. However, keep in mind that sexology, like most other fields of science, relies heavily on studies that employ convenience samples, which means that much of our knowledge base is limited and may not necessarily be reflective of or generalizable to all sexual and gender minority groups.

Nonexperimental Research

Nonexperimental research methods allow us to describe people's thoughts, feelings, and behaviors in a systematic manner with as much objectivity as possible. In studies of this nature, researchers do not directly manipulate or change any variables; rather, they simply make observations and note which variables seem to go together. In this section, we will discuss three types of nonexperimental research. As we address each method, we will consider the nature of the information it can provide about human sexuality, as well as detail its unique strengths and limitations.

Surveys

The vast majority of our knowledge on human sexuality comes from **survey research**, in which people are simply asked to report on their own sexual attitudes and practices. There are multiple modes of survey administration, including face-to-face interviews, questionnaires administered over the phone or online, as well as the increasingly antiquated pencil-and-paper format. Surveys are ideal for researchers who want to consider general trends in attitudes and behaviors across a relatively large group of people.

Strengths and Limitations of Surveys

The primary advantage of the survey method is that data can be collected quickly and easily from large numbers of people. The advent of online research has made these advantages even more apparent, enabling sexologists to conduct research 24 hours per day all over the world! In addition, online surveys have opened up a new and much more diverse audience than the typical college student subject pool, with online samples typically yielding more variation in age, socioeconomic status, and geographic location (Gosling et al., 2004). Online surveys also offer enhanced anonymity and privacy to participants. As we will see later in this section, anonymity is extremely important for gathering accurate data about people's sex lives.

Another advantage of this method is that there are multiple methods of administration, and researchers can choose the one that best fits their budget and needs. For example, if you wanted to survey people about whether they have ever cheated on their romantic partner, an anonymous online survey might be your best bet to ensure honest responding. In comparison, if you wanted to find out how people first learned about sex and what that experience was like for them, a face-to-face interview might be most appropriate. Interviews provide much greater depth of information than surveys and are advantageous in that they can be adapted to each interviewee. For instance, both the interviewer and interviewee can seek clarification if they find anything to be confusing or unclear.

Of course, the survey method has some notable limitations. First, no matter how much effort you put into identifying the right sample, not everyone you contact will want to participate in your study. This problem is known as **nonresponse**, and it has always been a major issue in sex research (Wiederman, 2001). There are many reasons individuals might refuse to participate, which can include anything from lack of time or interest to discomfort with the research topic. Nonresponse ultimately hurts the representativeness of your sample because those who refused to participate may be different in some way from those who agreed to take part in the study. For example, to the extent that people who opt out of sexuality surveys are more likely be virgins, have more conservative religious or political backgrounds, or have unusual sexual interests or desires, researchers' ability to make accurate generalizations about their findings is dramatically reduced.

The flip side of this problem is an issue known as **self-selection**. This is a broad term that refers to all of the ways that research volunteers differ from nonvolunteers. For example, in published research on sexuality and relationships, it is often the case that women far outnumber men (e.g., Lehmiller & Agnew, 2006; Lehmiller, VanderDrift, & Kelly, 2011). Likewise, those who sign up to participate in sexuality studies tend to be more sexually experienced and have more favorable attitudes about sex than those who do not (Plaud, Gaither, Hegstad, Rowan, & Devitt, 1999). Again, this reduces our ability to make inferences about target populations.

Response biases and self-presentational concerns are another factor complicating sexuality surveys. These biases encompass everything from whether subjects are accurately remembering the past, are lying, or are misrepresenting themselves. Perhaps the largest concern here is **socially desirable responding**, or the tendency for subjects to present themselves in the most favorable light possible. This is a concern in all psychological survey research, but it is especially problematic in studies of sexuality (Meston, Heiman, Trapnell, & Paulhus, 1998). Divulging one's sexual history can be embarrassing or threatening, especially when it is unclear who might eventually see or hear about this information. In order to cope with this uncertainty and maintain a positive sense of self, research participants may intentionally skip questions when they are afraid answering would make them look bad, or they may respond in a way that makes them look good, even if it is not the truth. As one example of socially desirable responding, consider that female participants completing sex surveys report less sexual experience (e.g., less masturbation and less exposure to pornography) when they believe their responses might become known to others compared to when they are assured anonymity (Alexander & Fisher, 2003). Thus, when women are concerned that their sexual history might become public knowledge, they are inclined to present themselves in a way that society is more likely to approve of. Assuring participants that their responses will remain anonymous and confidential helps to address this problem, but no safeguards can completely eliminate all tendencies toward socially desirable responding.

Finally, it is important to recognize that the overall quality of a survey depends upon the quality of the individual questions and how they are organized. Writing high-quality survey questions is not as easy as it sounds. For one thing, you must ensure that your word choices are appropriate and understandable for your audience. For instance, if you were conducting a survey of sexual behaviors among inner-city adolescents, it would be ill-advised to ask them whether they have ever given or received *fellatio* or *cunnilingus*. Although these are technically the correct terms for oral stimulation of the penis and vulva respectively, they are very clinical and some adolescents may not know what they mean. With such an audience, slang terms such as *blowjob* or *eating out* may be more appropriate.

Researchers must also take great care to avoid the use of leading and double-barreled questions. *Leading questions* direct participants to a specific answer. For example: "Most Americans believe that abortion should be legal. Do you support a woman's right to choose?" A question like this pressures participants to respond in a certain way. To avoid such bias, the question should instead be phrased more generally, such as: "Do you favor or oppose legalized abortion?" *Double-barreled questions* inquire about multiple things, thereby muddling responses. For instance: "Do you consider yourself to be experienced and knowledgeable about sex?" Participants may not know how to respond to such a question because sexual experience and knowledge are completely different things. Two separate questions should be asked instead.

In addition, it is vital to consider the order in which you ask the questions in your survey. For example, public opinion polls regarding legal recognition of same-sex relationships have found that Americans' support for legalizing civil unions is higher when they are first asked their opinions on same-sex marriage, but lower if opinions on marriage are assessed later in the survey (Moore & Carroll, 2004). It appears that people's support for same-sex civil unions depends upon whether they think about them in reference to same-sex marriage (and when compared to marriage, civil unions seem to be viewed as a more acceptable alternative to many people). As you can see, sexologists must think very carefully about how they put all aspects of their surveys together.

Examples of Major Sex Surveys

Given their importance to the field of sexology, a few of the most influential sex surveys ever conducted are discussed below. These surveys are useful to consider not only for historical purposes, but also because they further highlight the strong and weak points of utilizing this method.

The Kinsey reports.   Perhaps the most famous sexuality surveys ever conducted are those of Alfred Kinsey, a former professor at Indiana University. Kinsey's goal was to provide the first comprehensive examination of men's and women's sexual behavior in the United States. In his bestselling and highly controversial books, he and his research team detailed the results of their interviews with 5,300 men and 5,940 women. Although people of different racial backgrounds were initially interviewed, only data from White participants were included in the final publications because Kinsey felt that his racial minority samples were of inadequate size to draw conclusions. Moreover, although his sampling efforts were admirable and ambitious for the time, his participants were disproportionately young, well-educated, Protestant, and from larger cities.

Whereas Kinsey's sampling methods have long been criticized for their lack of diversity, his actual data-collection techniques have always been well respected. Kinsey collected most of his data during face-to-face interview sessions that followed a very careful and elaborate protocol. This involved working hard to establish a rapport with interviewees as a means of putting them at ease, building in checks for false responding, and only allowing a select group of highly trained researchers to conduct the interviews.

Kinsey's research reports shocked the American public because they suggested that masturbation, homosexual behavior, extramarital sex, and many other historically "deviant" sexual activities were occurring with much greater frequency than anyone ever thought possible. For instance, Kinsey found that most men (92%) and women (62%) had masturbated before, that a significant number of men (37%) and women (13%) reported at least one sexual experience with a member of the same sex, and that the vast majority of men (69%) reported having at least one sexual experience with a prostitute (Kinsey, Pomeroy, & Martin, 1948; Kinsey, Pomeroy, Martin, & Gebhard, 1953)! Even today, many of you are probably surprised by some of these numbers. However, it is important to note that although some of Kinsey's findings have held up in subsequent research (e.g., his findings about masturbation), others have not (e.g., his findings about the prevalence of same-sex activity). Thus, Kinsey's findings must be interpreted in light of his sampling limitations (e.g., restricted geographic diversity) and the time in which they were conducted. In order to understand sexuality in today's world, it is necessary to consult more recent research efforts.

The National Health and Social Life Survey.   For the better part of the past two decades, the National Health and Social Life Survey (NHSLS; Laumann, Gagnon, Michael, & Michaels, 1994) has been considered the definitive survey of sexual attitudes and behaviors in the United States, and for good reason. It was the first attempt to conduct a comprehensive survey of Americans' sexual practices since Kinsey's work in the 1940s. The NHSLS originally came about in response to the AIDS crisis that emerged in the 1980s. In the wake of this devastating disease, the US government recognized that our scientific knowledge of sexuality was extremely limited and this lack of information was hampering efforts to stop the spread of AIDS.

A team of researchers at the University of Chicago was initially granted enough government funding to conduct a national survey of 20,000 people. However, this financial support was later revoked by a conservative congress that felt taxpayer money should not be spent studying sex. The research team was not deterred and went to private sources in order to secure funding that would allow them to complete their project. They did not raise enough money to carry out the study as originally intended, but they achieved enough to finish the project on a smaller scale. In the end, a representative sample of 3,432 individuals across the US was surveyed. Participants ranged in age from 18 to 59 and exhibited some variability in terms of race, with the two largest racial minority groups (African Americans and Hispanics) well-represented.

The study involved a mix of face-to-face interviews and pencil-and-paper questionnaires. Interviews were conducted first in order to obtain more in-depth and detailed information from interviewees, but also because it was believed that starting with an interview would yield a higher compliance rate than starting with a written survey (and they were right – nearly four out of five people contacted for the study were willing to participate!). The interviewees then filled out a written questionnaire that addressed more personal topics (e.g., questions about masturbation), which they returned in a sealed envelope. This was done in order to provide them with more privacy on the most sensitive matters.

Upon their release, the results of the NHSLS provoked controversy, but not in the way that Kinsey's studies did. For one thing, the NHSLS suggested that Americans were *more sexually conservative* than previously thought! For example, most people reported having sex only a few times each month. Likewise, one in five men and nearly one in three women reported having had only one sexual partner in their lifetime. Furthermore, the reported prevalence of same-sex activity was much lower than Kinsey's estimates.

Since its publication, the NHSLS has been lauded by the scientific community for the quality of its sample and research design. Of course, it is not without its limitations. For example, older adults and some racial minority groups, including Asian Americans and Native Americans, were not adequately reflected in the sample. In addition, given that the survey was carried out a few decades ago, the NHSLS may not be an accurate account of the sexual practices of Americans today.

The National Survey of Sexual Health and Behavior.   American sexuality has changed dramatically since the NHSLS. For instance, Viagra and other medications for sexual dysfunction have been introduced, online dating and hooking up have become increasingly common, and societal attitudes toward homosexuality have become more accepting. In order to keep up with such changes and to address the problem of the aging NHSLS dataset, the National Survey of Sexual Health and Behavior (NSSHB; Herbenick et al., 2010) was conducted.

The NSSHB is the largest and most diverse nationally representative survey of sexuality ever completed, with a sample consisting of 5,865 adolescents and adults ages 14 to 94 living in the United States. The project was carried out by researchers at the Center for Sexual Health Promotion at Indiana University (the same university where Alfred Kinsey spent most of his career). Participants for this study were initially recruited by mail or phone, which yielded a high response rate of 82% for adults. However, recruiting adolescent participants (one of the unique strengths of this survey) was more challenging, because it was necessary to seek parental permission first. Only 62% of parents contacted were willing to let their children under age 18 participate, which is revealing of Americans' attitudes toward adolescent sexuality (a topic we will return to in chapter 10).

Table 2.2   Selected Findings from the NSSHB
Among adults, 7% of women and 8% of men identified as gay, lesbian, or bisexual.
85% of men and 64% of women reported reaching orgasm during their most recent sexual experience.
Among participants who were single, only one in three acts of vaginal intercourse involved condom use.
Black and Hispanic men were more likely to use condoms during intercourse than White men.
Adolescents reported being more likely to use condoms during intercourse than adults over age 40.
Sex means a lot of different things to Americans. Adults reported a total of 41 different ways of "getting busy" during their most recent sexual encounter.
When adults have sex, they do not just have intercourse – they typically engage in multiple sexual activities during each sexual event, which may include oral sex, anal sex, mutual masturbation, and other activities.

Source: The National Survey of Sexual Health and Behavior, http://www.nationalsexstudy.indiana.edu/

Unlike the previous sex surveys discussed in this chapter, the NSSHB did not involve face-to-face interviews. Instead, all data were collected entirely over the Internet. For people who wanted to participate but did not have Internet access, it was provided for them by the researchers. The first results from the NSSHB were published in 2010 in the *Journal of Sexual Medicine* and were greeted with relatively little controversy, which suggests attitudes toward sex have come a long way since Kinsey. A summary of some of the major findings from the NSSHB can be seen in Table 2.2. In later chapters, we will explore additional results from this and some of the other surveys mentioned above.

Other prominent sex surveys.   Several large scale sexuality surveys have been conducted outside of the United States. The results of national sex surveys in Britain (e.g., Johnson et al., 2001) and Australia (e.g., Rissel Richters, Grulich, de Visser, & Smith, 2003) reveal trends that are similar in many ways to those observed in the United States. For example, across most Western countries, sex surveys reveal that men report having more sexual partners than women. In addition, the age of first intercourse appears to have decreased in recent years.

National sex surveys in non-Western countries are more difficult to come by, due to cultural differences in the acceptability of talking about sex publicly. However, the few surveys that have been administered have enlightened us considerably with respect to the role that culture and society play in shaping sexual behavior. For example, a national sex survey in China revealed that most people do not begin having sex until their early to mid-20s, compared to ages 16 or 17 in many Western countries (Parish, Laumann, & Mojola, 2007). Likewise, Chinese men and women typically get married very quickly (i.e., within a year or two) after they begin having premarital sex, whereas Westerners often wait a decade or more between when they first have sex and when they get married.

Direct Observation

Although sex surveys are perhaps the most common research method in the field of sexology, they are far from perfect. This is largely because surveys require participants to report their own behavior, and they may or may not provide accurate descriptions. The reasons for this may be unintentional (e.g., memory loss) or intentional (e.g., socially desirable responding). To get around this issue, sexologists sometimes turn to a seemingly more objective research technique: **direct observation**. This is exactly what it sounds like – rather than having subjects describe their own behavior, researchers watch them with their own eyes and record what they see. Although observing the subject directly may result in a more accurate account of behavior, this method is not commonly utilized in sexology for many reasons, which we discuss below.

Strengths and Limitations of Direct Observation

The major strength of direct observation is that it takes a number of response biases out of the picture by eliminating participants' subjective reports of their own behavior. Another benefit is that observations can be filmed, thereby allowing researchers to go back in case they missed something or want to look at the behaviors in a different way.

However, there are obvious drawbacks. First and foremost, think for a moment about whether you would be willing to have sex on camera or in front of a researcher, while various pieces of recording equipment are attached to your genitalia. Many of you would probably be reluctant to agree to this. Thus, self-selection is a big concern with studies of this nature, perhaps because it is only the exhibitionists among us who are willing to participate in such research. As support for this idea, a survey of 485 college undergraduates found that only 15% said they would be willing to participate in an observational study of sexual arousal (Plaud et al., 1999). Another major concern is **reactivity**, which refers to the idea that research participants sometimes alter their behavior when they know others are watching. How might people alter their sexual behavior when others are present or if they know they are being filmed? It probably depends upon the person, with some people acting more inhibited than usual, and others getting especially excited. Finally, observational studies are expensive to conduct and often require a lot of special equipment and technology that can be hard to come by (see below – "Technologies Used in Observational Sex Research" – for more on this).

The Research of Masters and Johnson

The most famous and well-known example of observational research in sexology is the work of William Masters and Virginia Johnson. The data reported in their book *Human Sexual Response* came from laboratory studies of 694 men and women, who ranged in age from 18 to 89. Subjects consisted mostly of White, highly educated students from the local community in St Louis, Missouri. Efforts were made to screen out exhibitionists and individuals with emotional problems during the recruitment process. Although the sample was far from representative of the US population, Masters and Johnson deserve some credit for finding such a large number of people willing to participate in their research, especially given that they were conducting their work in a time and setting that was not overly enthusiastic about sexual science.

Masters and Johnson sought to understand exactly how men's and women's bodies respond to sexual stimulation. To do so, they had subjects engage in sexual activities in their lab, including masturbation, sexual intercourse, and simulated intercourse, all while various pieces of technology recorded the changes that happened to their bodies (e.g., changes in muscle tension and blood flow). In case you are curious, the simulated intercourse trials refer to instances in which female participants were stimulated with an "artificial coition machine" (i.e., the sex toy with a built in camera previously mentioned). It was essentially a motorized dildo that had a remote control women could use to adjust the speed and depth of thrusting. Did this really happen in Missouri? In the 1960s? It sure did! After engaging in sexual activity, participants were thoroughly interviewed, which provided an extra level of depth to the data obtained.

The results of Masters and Johnson's research were greeted with much controversy, but they provided a wealth of information and new insights into human sexuality. It is also important to note that the data they collected on the bodily changes that accompany sexual arousal appear to be consistent across diverse groups of people, despite their aforementioned sampling limitations. As a result, you will see their research findings presented throughout this book.

Technologies Used in Observational Sex Research

Masters and Johnson were among the first sex researchers to use electronic devices for studying sexual arousal. Variations of these devices are still in use today and are frequently mentioned in published reports of both observational and experimental sex studies. Below are some of the most common technologies used in sexuality research today.

To measure male sexual arousal, a device called a **penile strain gauge** is often employed. It consists of a small circular tube that is placed around the base of the penis, just like a "cock ring." Attached to this tube are wires that connect to a recording device. The strain gauge works by measuring changes in penile circumference. In other words, as blood flows into the penis, leading it to increase in size, the machine records this—and it is very sensitive to even the tiniest changes in size. To avoid potential embarrassment and maintain privacy, male participants in sex studies usually attach this device to themselves.

To measure female sexual arousal, a **vaginal photoplethysmograph** is usually employed. This device consists of a small, acrylic rod that is inserted into the vagina (again, this is something subjects can introduce to their bodies in private). Like the penile strain gauge, wires are attached that connect it with a recording instrument. The photoplethysmograph works by giving off light, and then measuring how much of that light is reflected back from the vaginal walls. When women are sexually aroused, the vaginal walls fill with blood, which decreases the amount of reflected

Figure 2.2 A mercury-in-rubber penile strain gauge. The loop at the end of the wires is placed around the base of the penis and measures changes in penile circumference. © Sarah Sudhoff.

Figure 2.3 An early generation vaginal photoplethysmograph. The acrylic rod is placed inside the vagina to measure changes in vaginal blood volume. © Sarah Sudhoff.

light. Clearly, the strain gauge and photoplethysmograph operate very differently; however, they are similar in that they both measure sexual arousal in terms of increased blood flow to the genital region. Other devices for measuring female sexual arousal have been developed, including the labial photoplethysmograph (Prause, Cerny, & Janssen, 2005) and the clitoral photoplethysmograph (Gerritsen et al., 2009), but they have not yet achieved widespread use. Although these and other tools for measuring physiological arousal are increasingly used, they are not without controversy. One concern is that while a person's genitals may show signs of arousal, the individual may not feel aroused psychologically. Thus, it is not always clear what these measures are telling us.

One other technology frequently used in studies of sexual arousal in men and women is *functional magnetic resonance imaging (fMRI)*. With fMRI scans, we can see what areas of the brain respond when individuals are turned on or experience orgasm. For example, fMRI scans of men and women viewing erotic videos have revealed some similarities and some differences in the way that the sexes' brains operate (Karama et al., 2002). Specifically, while viewing erotic stimuli, both men and women show increased activation of the amygdala; in contrast, men show significant activation of the hypothalamus, whereas women do not. Both the amygdala and hypothalamus are part of the limbic system, a part of the brain that helps regulate sexual behavior (more on this in chapter 4). Such findings can not only help us to better understand differences in how men and women experience sex psychologically, but they can also potentially help us to better understand cases of sexual dysfunction (e.g., a brain scan of a person with arousal difficulties could help to identify whether there is a neurological basis for the problem based upon the pattern of activation observed).

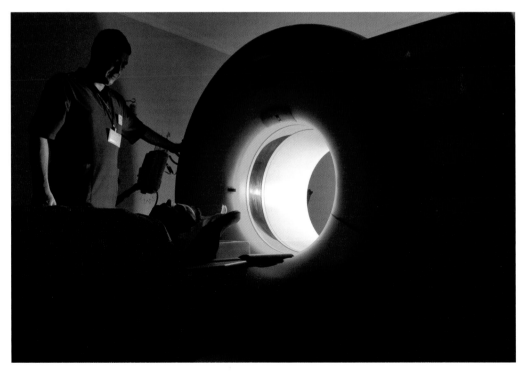

Figure 2.4 fMRI and other neuroimaging techniques are increasingly being used in sex research to explore differences in how people process sex-related stimuli and to identify neurological and physiological causes of sexual dysfunction. ©Levent Konuk/123RF.COM.

Case Reports

The final method of nonexperimental research we will consider is the **case report**. Researchers who utilize this method study either one participant or a small group of participants in great depth and detail. In general, the subject selected for a report of this nature is unusual in some way. For example, a sexologist might perform a case study on someone with a sexual dysfunction, someone who has a rare sexual desire (e.g., a fetish), or a prostitute.

Case reports were a reasonably common method of data collection among early sex researchers, particularly Sigmund Freud (some of you may recall his famous case reports of Anna O. and Little Hans from your other psychology courses). Such studies still appear in the sexology literature today, but they are primarily conducted by those who have clinical or medical training (e.g., clinical psychologists or psychiatrists). We will consider the findings of a couple of relevant case reports in chapter 4.

Strengths and Limitations of Case Reports

The major benefit of case reports is that they provide great depth of information about an unusual subject. If a similar subject is encountered in the future, the case report can provide a very valuable source of information for guiding therapeutic intervention (e.g., if the subject suffered from a sexual problem, a therapist could review the report to see what treatments worked and what did not).

However, case reports are of inherently limited value from the standpoint that they sample either a single individual or a very small group of people who are not representative of the broader population. Thus, generalizing the findings of case studies to larger groups of people is difficult, if not impossible. In addition, case reports rely heavily on participants' subjective reports of the past, which are subject to the same self-presentational issues and responses biases that affect survey research.

Experimental Research

Up until this point, all of the research designs we have considered are *correlational*. In other words, surveys, direct observation, and case reports can tell us what sexuality variables are related to one another, but they cannot tell us anything about the *causes* of sexual behavior. The only way sexologists can establish cause and effect is to conduct an **experiment**. In an experiment, researchers manipulate or change one variable in order to see what effect this has on a measurable outcome. As you have probably learned in other courses, the manipulated variable is known as the *independent variable*, while the measured outcome is known as the *dependent variable*. Thus, the independent variable is presumed to be the cause of any changes in the dependent variable.

In order to make inferences about cause and effect in an experiment, researchers must hold all factors constant other than the independent variable. If other factors change alongside the independent variable (this is known as *confounding*), it becomes impossible to determine why the results turned out the way they did. One of the most vital methods of protecting the integrity of an experiment is to ensure participants are *randomly assigned* to different experimental conditions. In other words, the level of the independent variable a participant receives (e.g., placebo vs. active drug) should be determined at random. Random assignment helps to ensure that the groups of participants you are comparing have a similar composition, thereby preventing third variables (e.g., group differences in attitudes or demographic composition) from serving as alternative explanations for the findings.

A Sample Sexperiment

To give you a better idea of how the experimental method is employed in sexology, let us consider a study conducted by Galliot and Baumeister (2007). The idea behind this study was to examine the link between self-control and sexual behavior. To give you a little theoretical background, research shows that human beings have a limited capacity for self-control (Baumeister, Bratslavsky, Muraven, & Tice, 1998). That is, no matter how strong we are, sometimes our willpower gives out and we subsequently find it difficult to curb our impulses (e.g., just think about the last time you tried dieting. How long were you able to hold out before you gorged on junk food?). Self-control can thus be thought of as a muscle, such that when we use it too much, it gets tired and leads us to act in uncontrollable ways. What Galliot and Baumeister wanted to do was see whether depletion of self-control affects how people behave sexually.

To test this idea, college students in romantic relationships brought their partner to the lab. The independent variable was a self-control manipulation, such that couples were randomly assigned to either expend their self-control abilities or not. This was accomplished by having each couple watch a silent video that depicted a woman talking. At the bottom of the screen, words would flash for a few seconds at a time. Half of the couples were asked to refrain from looking at the words (the *depletion condition*), whereas the other half were given no such instructions (the *no-depletion condition*). The thought here is that consciously avoiding the words on the screen requires effort, thereby depleting self-control reserves for those participants.

The dependent variable was the extent of the couple's sexual behavior after watching the video. Specifically, couples were given a private room and were asked to express some type of physical intimacy with their partner (they could do anything as long as it was consensual). Afterward, participants filled out a questionnaire in which they reported the extent of their sexual behavior.

Results indicated that participants in the depletion condition "kissed open-mouthed for prolonged periods of time, groped and caressed each other… and even removed articles of clothing so as to expose themselves" (pp. 182–183). However, these findings only held for couples who were sexually inexperienced. It is thought that sexually inexperienced couples may have been more depleted to begin with because they must engage in more sexual self-control on a daily basis. As a result, they may have experienced double depletion.

Strengths and Limitations of the Experimental Method

The major strength of experiments is the ability to control variables precisely, thereby allowing us to make claims about causality. Thus, if we find differences in the dependent variable across conditions, we may be able to infer that they were caused by the independent variable. No other research method allows us to draw such conclusions.

Unfortunately, however, experiments are not always a viable option for sexology studies because certain research questions do not lend themselves readily to this method. Sometimes it is impossible or unethical to manipulate a variable of interest. For example, if we wanted to study the impact of parental divorce on children's academic performance, we could not randomly assign some couples to get divorced and some to stay together! To address that topic, we would have to take a nonexperimental approach. Another limitation of experiments is that people may act differently in a laboratory setting than they do in the real world, thereby threatening *external validity* (i.e., the ability to generalize the findings beyond the lab). For instance, subjects may purposely alter their behavior because they like/dislike the experimenter or because they have guessed the purpose of the study.

A Note on Statistics

As we go forward in this book, we will discuss the results of several sexuality studies, both experimental and nonexperimental. To understand the results of these studies, it is important for you to have knowledge of some basic statistical concepts. We will review these briefly here, but please do not be intimidated! You do not need to have a strong statistical background to comprehend this information.

Means and Medians

In sexuality research, we often want to speak in terms of what the average person does, rather than focus on the extremes (although we will certainly cover our fair share of extremes in chapter 13, when we discuss sexual behavior variations). In statistical terms, the **mean** refers to the average value of all of the scores in a dataset. Sometimes it is also useful to consider the **median**, which is the middle score in a distribution.

However, please do not confuse the terms mean and median with "normal." When it comes to sexual behavior, it is important to keep in mind that there is huge variability. As a result, "normal" does not represent a single value, but rather a large range of values. Thus, please do not fall into the habit of comparing yourself to every single average presented in this book and make judgments about your own normalcy. Chances are that even if you seem pretty far from average, you would still be considered normal.

Incidence and Prevalence

When we begin to talk about sexual dysfunction and disease, we will frequently use the terms incidence and prevalence. **Incidence** refers to the rate at which new cases of a problem or disease occur. It is usually expressed as the number of new cases that appeared in a given time (e.g., one year) divided by the total size of the population. Thus, incidence is useful for helping us to understand how quickly a problem is spreading. In contrast, **prevalence** is a broader measure of the total number of people who are currently afflicted with a given problem or disease. It is often expressed in terms of the number of people per 100,000 who have it. Thus, prevalence helps us to understand the overall scope of the issue.

Correlation

The last statistical concept you should know is **correlation**, a concept we briefly introduced earlier. Correlation refers to the statistical association between two variables (i.e., the degree to which two variables are related). A correlation can be negative, positive, or zero. Negative correlations refer to cases where two variables move in opposite directions (i.e., as one variable increases, the other decreases). For example, the frequency of condom use is negatively correlated with likelihood of contracting a sexually transmitted infection, such that as condom use goes up, infection risk goes down. Positive correlations refer to cases where two variables move in the same direction (i.e., both variables increase together and decrease together). For instance, the number of sexual partners you have is positively correlated with the risk of contracting a sexually transmitted infection, such that as number of partners increases, so does infection risk. Finally, a correlation of zero

Figure 2.5   Although there may be a correlation between the stork population and the rate of human births, it would be erroneous to conclude that storks are responsible for delivering babies. Correlations do not imply cause-and-effect. ©James Steidl/123RF.COM.

occurs when two variables have no relationship whatsoever. One example of this would be the size of a woman's breasts and the amount of breast milk she produces. This may surprise you, but women with larger breasts do not necessarily produce more milk (we will address the reason for this in the next chapter when we cover sexual anatomy).

Please keep in mind that correlations are useful for summarizing patterns in data, but they tell us nothing about cause and effect. Thus, just because two variables are correlated does not mean that one is causing the other. As one example of this, consider that a strong, positive correlation has been found between the stork population and the birth rate in several European countries (Matthews, 2000). As children, some of you probably learned that storks delivered human babies—and this correlation would seem to support that theory, right? Wrong. This is but one of many examples of a *spurious correlation* (i.e., an association that exists due to some third factor that links the variables together—in this case, what was happening is that as the human population increased, so did the number of houses, and more houses provided more roofs for storks to build nests). Thus, whenever we talk about variables being correlated, keep in mind that we do not necessarily know why that association exists.

Ethics in Sexology Research

To round out our discussion of the scientific study of sex, let us consider research ethics. Ethics is something that should be at the forefront of any researcher's mind, whether that researcher studies sexuality or not. Historically, however, this has not always been the case. For example, in your other psychology courses, you probably discussed the potential ethical violations associated with Stanley Milgram's classic studies on obedience to authority (Milgram, 1963) and the Stanford

Figure 2.6   Laud Humphries studied men who have sex with men in public restrooms. Was it ethically appropriate for Humphries to deceive the men about his true identity and intentions? ©mrosica/123RF.COM.

Prison Experiment (Haney, Banks, & Zimbardo, 1973). Sexology has had its own ethically questionable moments in the past, and these have served to shape the field's modern-day approach to research ethics. Before we consider the ethical principles that sexologists must uphold, let us first look back at some of the most controversial sex studies ever conducted so that you can better appreciate why these ethical requirements are in place.

First, let us consider Laud Humphreys' (1970) *Tearoom Trade Study*. Humphreys was a sociologist who wanted to understand why some men are motivated to have anonymous sexual encounters with other men in public restrooms. Before we go on, I should note that in the 1970s, the bathrooms where men would meet up for this purpose were known colloquially as "tearooms," hence the name of this study (by the way, the Russian Tea Room in New York City is actually a pretty fancy and exclusive restaurant, not an actual *tearoom*). At that time, a lot of men were being arrested for tearoom sex all across the United States. Humphreys believed that attempting to understand who these men were and what motivated them to engage in this behavior would be of inherent value to society.

In carrying out his research, Humphreys visited a number of tearooms, where he volunteered to be the "lookout" for men who wanted to have a quick sexual encounter in a stall. His job was to cough or otherwise signal the men in the stall if police were coming. As if this behavior were not questionable enough for a scientist, Humphreys sometimes followed these tearoom visitors back to their cars and surreptitiously recorded their license plate numbers. One year later, he used this information to track the men down. Specifically, he showed up at their homes unannounced (disguised, of course, so that he would not be recognized) and proceeded to interview them to learn more about their lives, supposedly as part of a completely unrelated study.

Humphreys' results were interesting and influential from the standpoint that they disproved a number of stereotypes about the typical tearoom patron. For example, more than half of the men were actually married to *women* and, aside from the occasional tearoom rendezvous, many of them appeared to be in model marriages. Furthermore, after Humphreys' research was published, police departments began to devote less attention and resources to investigating and prosecuting tearoom sex, which many would view as a positive outcome (e.g., some would argue that limited police resources should be spent preventing and punishing nonconsensual sex crimes, such as sexual assault, rather than regulating the sexual activities of consenting adults). However, it is clear that Humphreys deceived those who took part in his research. In fact, many of the subjects were not even aware that they were taking part in a study. Humphreys also invaded his subjects' privacy in more than one way. Do you think the ends justified the means in this study? Visit the Your Sexuality 2.1 box and weigh in with your perspective.

If you thought the Humphreys study was ethically dubious, you might want to brace yourself for our discussion of the *Tuskegee Syphilis Study* (for a more in-depth account of this study, see Jones, 1992). This study was conducted by the United States Public Health Service from the 1930s until the 1970s. The goal of this research was to track the normal progression of syphilis among a group of 399 low-income, African American men from Tuskegee, Alabama (hence the name of

---

Your Sexuality 2.1   Was the Tearoom Trade Study Ethically Acceptable?

Opinions on Laud Humphreys' Tearoom Trade study vary widely, with some arguing that the study was entirely too unethical to have ever been carried out, and others arguing that the methods were relatively harmless and that the study did more good than anything. Below are some of the most common arguments on both sides of the issue. Which do you find most persuasive? Why? What other arguments can you come up with that support your perspective?

- CON: Subjects did not provide their consent to participate. If they would have known they were being observed, many subjects might have chosen not to participate.
  PRO: Tearoom activities were illegal at the time. Requiring written informed consent would have created a permanent record linking the subjects to the research, which could have put them at risk for later identification and arrest.
- CON: Subjects had a right to privacy in the bathroom and in their homes.
  PRO: Public bathrooms are by definition "public," meaning that they do not inherently offer privacy from researchers or nonresearchers. In addition, subjects were engaging in sexual behavior in public, which suggests that they did not necessarily mind if anyone else observed. In terms of privacy in the home, unannounced door-to-door solicitations for product sales, political canvassers, and census takers are a commonplace occurrence.
- CON: Humphreys was observing what was, at the time, an illegal behavior. By collecting data on these subjects and recording their license plate numbers, he was putting them at risk of arrest if his data fell into the wrong hands.
  PRO: Humphreys went to great lengths to maintain the anonymity of his participants, including keeping any potentially identifying information in a safe-deposit box 1,000 miles away from the research site. In addition, by studying this population, it ended up reducing the social stigma associated with same-sex sexual behavior.

the study). All of the men already had syphilis, but none were told they had it. Instead, participants were told that they had "bad blood" and would receive free medical treatment for their condition along with meals in exchange for their participation in the study.

If these researchers had simply been tracking patients with an incurable disease to see what happened, that would be one thing. However, a cure for syphilis, penicillin, was developed in the 1940s and was intentionally withheld from the men. Even more egregious than just withholding treatment, the men were told that they would lose their benefits if they sought treatment elsewhere for their "bad blood." Researchers also went out of their way to inform local doctors that they were not to provide these patients with antibiotics! By the time this study became public knowledge, it was too late for these men; they had suffered irreparable physical harm and many had died as a result of the disease (we will discuss the debilitating effects of untreated sexually transmitted diseases in more detail in chapter 11). In the end, not only were the participants seriously deceived, but they experienced substantial physical harm and some died as a result. There is no justifying that under any circumstances. To add insult to injury, the US government did not even issue a public apology for this horrendous study until the 1990s.

The ethics of both the Tearoom Trade and Tuskegee Syphilis Studies are no doubt questionable, and each was conducted in a time where there was less oversight of scientific research and where fewer policies were in place to prevent physical and psychological mistreatment of research participants. In the early 1970s, these studies came to light (right around the same time as the controversial Milgram studies and the Stanford Prison Experiment). Ethical concerns in psychology and sexology had reached a boiling point and more strict research regulations were put into place. As a result, modern sexology research is subject to much higher levels of scrutiny and must meet certain ethical standards before it can be carried out. However, it is possible that we may have overcorrected because we now subject even very minor and routine sex surveys to extremely high levels of scrutiny, even though they pose little risk of harm to participants (for more on this idea, see the Digging Deeper 2.1 box).

The specific ethical guidelines followed by sexologists vary somewhat depending upon their field of study, the requirements of their university's ethics board, the organization that funds their work, as well as local and federal laws. However, there are several general principles all sexologists must uphold, including the requirements of informed consent, debriefing, and confidentiality, all of which apply in psychological research more broadly.

Informed Consent

Before beginning any research study, participants must provide their **informed consent**. This means that individuals must be told up front the nature of the study, their rights as a research participant, and the potential risks and rewards associated with their involvement. With this information in mind, individuals must make a conscious decision as to whether they want to participate, free from pressure or coercion.

During the informed consent process, researchers cannot withhold significant information about the study. Does this mean that **deception** (i.e., intentionally withholding certain information from subjects or misleading them) is never ethically permissible? Certain types of deception are acceptable and appropriate, especially if they are necessary to ensure the validity of your data. For example, during informed consent, you do not have to explicitly tell subjects the hypothesis you are testing and the true purpose of your study. However, you cannot withhold or lie about

Digging Deeper 2.1   Do Sex Surveys Pose Harm to Student Participants?

Ever since the pioneering work of Alfred Kinsey, there has been a persistent concern that asking people questions about sex on surveys is too personal and is likely to make them feel distressed and uncomfortable. Although there may have been some validity to this concern several decades ago, times have changed. We now live in a world where people talk about sex more freely than ever before and sex is represented everywhere in the media. So should ethics review boards scrutinize sex studies more than other types of research?

In a study by Yeater, Miller, Rinehart, and Nason (2012), 504 college student participants were randomly assigned to complete one of two surveys. Half of the participants were given a survey that inquired about their own sexual attitudes and experiences, including traumatic events they have endured. The survey items they completed were deliberately chosen because they were thought to have the highest potential to cause distress. These participants were asked hundreds of questions about topics such as rape, masturbation, childhood sexual abuse, body image, sexual history, and so forth. The other half of the participants completed a very general psychological survey, which included tests of vocabulary, abstract thinking, and analogies.

The results indicated that completing the sex survey did not increase reports of negative emotions among participants – in fact, negative emotions *decreased* among participants, regardless of which survey they completed! Participants who completed the sex survey also reported feeling less mentally taxed and believed that they benefitted more from having participated in the study than those who completed the cognitive tests. In addition, both surveys were rated as being less stressful than many normal, everyday stressors that everyone occasionally experiences (e.g., getting a paper cut, waiting in line, spilling your coffee, etc.).

The researchers also looked specifically at women who had a previous history of sexual victimization because there is a commonly held belief among ethics review boards that such women are especially susceptible to distress in research of this nature. However, women who were previously victimized did not report feeling any worse at the end of the study no matter which survey they completed.

This research indicates that sex surveys clearly fall in the category of **minimal risk** – that is, they are unlikely to cause more harm to someone than might ordinarily be experienced in everyday life or when completing other, more general psychological tests. Of course, there are some limitations of this study, given that participants were undergraduate students from just one university in the United States. Further research with more diverse samples would be advisable before making sweeping recommendations. For now, however, it would at least appear reasonable to conclude that American college students probably are not as sensitive about sex as ethics boards have made them out to be.

Note: Reprinted with permission from *The Psychology of Human Sexuality* blog (www.lehmiller.com).

Figure 2.7   At the beginning of any study on sex and sexuality, participants must be informed of their rights, the nature of the research, and the potential risks involved. This usually entails obtaining a written or electronic signature. ©gajus/123RF.COM.

something that could potentially affect a subject's decision to participate. For example, if you planned to expose subjects to violent pornography in order to see how it affects their acceptance of violence toward women, it would *not* be ethically permissible to tell subjects that they will simply be "watching some videos and answering some questions." The informed consent process would need to make clear that subjects may be viewing sexually explicit materials and answering questions about their personal views.

Debriefing

At the end of any study, participants must receive a thorough **debriefing**. This means that after completing all study requirements, participants must be told the true purpose of the research and be informed of any deception that took place. In other words, researchers must give subjects all of the information they did not receive up front in order to ensure that they do not walk away with any misconceptions. This is especially important in any instances in which participants are intentionally misled about facts or information.

For example, consider the following study by Dana Bramel (1963). Male college student participants were hooked up to a machine that measured galvanic skin response (GSR). Subjects were told that GSR was a reliable indicator of one's sexual arousal and that, when aroused, the needle on the measurement instrument would move higher. Participants were then shown photographs of men who varied in their degree of attractiveness and how much clothing they were wearing. Unbeknownst to the subject, the machine was rigged, such that the experimenter was controlling the movement of the needle! Regardless of participants' own sexual orientation, many of them saw the machine register very high levels of arousal in response to the photos of attractive and semi-nude men. Thus, some men were falsely led to believe that they possessed "latent homosexuality." The value of debriefing should be apparent from a study like this. It would not be ethically acceptable to simply allow these participants to walk away from this study without correcting such misinformation. Subjects should never leave a research study harboring false impressions or feeling any kind of stress or anxiety.

Confidentiality

One additional ethical requirement of sexology research is maintaining **confidentiality**, or protecting the privacy of your research subjects. In sexuality studies, keeping confidentiality is vital for several reasons. First, sexologists sometimes collect very personal information from their subjects, and this information could potentially damage people's lives if it got out. For example, I have conducted research on people who keep their romantic relationships secret (Lehmiller, 2009). Although there are many reasons someone might hide a relationship, one that frequently comes up is that the individual is having an affair. No matter what my personal feelings are about this, I must keep the identities of my participants private. I have no legal obligation to report known or suspected adultery to the authorities, and releasing participants' identities could create emotional distress, conflict, and breakup. Second, if research participants are not assured confidentiality, they will be less likely to respond honestly and accurately, thereby undermining the validity of the data. For example, in my study of secret relationships you can bet that people would not have told me about their affairs if they thought I might publicly divulge that information or contact their partner.

On a side note, researchers may need to break confidentiality on very rare occasions if it is required by law. For example, if a developmental psychologist studying children or adolescents discovered that a participant was the victim of sexual abuse, that scientist would have a legal duty to report this information to the authorities, even though it means violating a research subject's trust.

Evaluating Sex Research

As we close out this chapter, I hope you have come to appreciate the science of sexology. Researchers in this field take great care in designing each and every study by giving ample consideration to how they select their participants, how they phrase and order their questions, as well as how they manipulate and measure their variables. Keep this in mind any time you see sex surveys or research reports about sex in the popular media. For example, many men's and women's magazines (e.g., *Playboy*, *Men's Health*, *Cosmopolitan*, *Glamour*) regularly report the results of reader sex surveys. Likewise, many major news websites have a daily "quick poll," in which a single question (sometimes pertaining to sexual matters) is asked of visitors. People who do not have a strong research background may look at these results and accept them as fact, or at least ascribe some importance to them. After reading this chapter, however, you should be aware that such "research" requires scrutiny. Specifically, you should always ask:

- Who conducted the study and why? Do they have the training and credentials necessary to conduct research of this nature? Also, are they truly seeking to increase our understanding of human sexuality, or do they simply want to sell you a product?

- What are the characteristics of the sample? To whom can we generalize these results? Be wary of research reports that provide no information or only very limited information about the sample.
- Were the survey questions high-quality and free from bias?
- Are the results consistent with what you learned in this book?

In summary, when it comes to learning about human sexuality, we need to carefully consider the source of our information. John Watson said it best when he argued that we deserve to have our questions answered not by those who are pushing a social or moral agenda, but "by scientifically-trained students of sex."

Key Terms

sexology	reactivity	prevalence
survey research	penile strain gauge	correlation
convenience samples	vaginal photoplethysmograph	minimal risk
random selection	case report	informed consent
nonresponse	experiment	deception
self-selection	mean	debriefing
socially desirable responding	median	confidentiality
direct observation	incidence	

Discussion Questions: What is Your Perspective on Sex?

- In your own view, how big of an issue is self-selection in the scientific study of sex? What are some ways in which sex researchers can reduce this problem?
- A researcher is interested in studying the effects of exposure to pornography on heterosexual men's attitudes toward women. What type of study design would you use to address this research question and what are the strengths and limitations of your chosen method?
- Would it be possible to carry out the Tearoom Trade Study in a way that meets modern ethical requirements of informed consent, debriefing, and confidentiality? Do you think it is permissible to breach ethical guidelines in order to study a particular research topic? Why or why not?

References

Alexander, M.G., & Fisher, T.D. (2003). Truth and consequences: Using the bogus pipeline to examine sex differences in self-reported sexuality. *Journal of Sex Research, 40,* 27–35. DOI:10.1080/00224490309552164.
Baumeister, R.F., Bratslavsky, E., Muraven, M., & Tice, D.M. (1998). Ego depletion: Is the active self a limited resource? *Journal of Personality and Social Psychology, 74,* 1252–1265. DOI:10.1037/0022-3514.74.5.1252.

Bramel, D.A., (1963). Selection of a target for defensive projection. *Journal of Abnormal and Social Psychology, 66*, 318–324. DOI:10.1037/h0044935.

Gailliot, M.T., & Baumeister, R.F. (2007). Self-regulation and sexual restraint: Dispositionally and temporarily poor self-regulatory abilities contribute to failures at restraining sexual behavior. *Personality and Social Psychology Bulletin, 33*, 173–186. DOI:10.1177/0146167206293472.

Gerritsen, J., Van Der Made, F., Bloemers, J., Van Ham, D., Kleiverda, G., Everaerd, W., ... Tuiten, A. (2009). The clitoral photoplethysmograph: A new way of assessing genital arousal in women. *Journal of Sexual Medicine, 6*, 1678–1687. DOI:10.1111/j.1743-6109.2009.01228.x.

Gosling, S.D., Vazire, S., Srivastava, S., & John, O.P. (2004). Should we trust web-based studies? *American Psychologist, 59*, 93–104. DOI:10.1037/0003-066X.59.2.93.

Haeberle, E.J. (1983). *The birth of sexology: A brief history in documents.* Retrieved from http://www.iub.edu/~kinsey/resources/sexology.html (accessed August 26, 2013).

Haney, C., Banks, W.C., & Zimbardo, P.G. (1973). Interpersonal dynamics in a simulated prison. *International Journal of Criminology and Penology, 1*, 69–97. DOI:10.1037/h0076835.

Herbenick, D., Reece, M., Schick, V., Sanders, S.A., Dodge, B., & Fortenberry, J.D. (2010). Sexual behavior in the United States: Results from a national probability sample of men and women ages 14–94. *Journal of Sexual Medicine, 7*(Suppl. 5), 255–265. DOI:10.1111/j.1743-6109.2010.02012.x.

Humphreys, L. (1970). *Tearoom trade: A study of homosexual encounters in public places.* London: Duckworth.

Johnson, A.M., Mercer, C.H., Erens, B., Copas, A.J., McManus, S., Wellings, K., ... Field, J. (2001). Sexual behavior in Britain: Partnerships, practices, and HIV risk behaviours. *The Lancet, 358*, 1835–1842. DOI:10.1016/S0140-6736(01)06883-0.

Jones, J.H. (1992). *Bad blood: The Tuskegee syphilis experiment.* New York: The Free Press.

Karama, S., Lecours, A.R., Leroux, J.M., Bourgouin, P., Beaudoin, G., Joubert, S., & Beauregard, M. (2002). Areas of brain activation in males and females during viewing of erotic film excerpts. *Human Brain Mapping, 16*, 1–13. DOI:10.1002/hbm.10014.

Kinsey, A., Pomeroy, W.B., & Martin, C.E. (1948). *Sexual behavior in the human male.* Philadelphia: Saunders.

Kinsey, A., Pomeroy, W.B., Martin, C.E., & Gebhard, P. (1953). *Sexual behavior in the human female.* Philadelphia: Saunders.

Laumann, E.O., Gagnon, J., Michael, R., & Michaels, S. (1994). *The social organization of sexuality: Sexual practices in the United States.* Chicago: University of Chicago Press.

Lehmiller, J.J. (2009). Secret romantic relationships: Consequences for personal and relational well-being. *Personality and Social Psychology Bulletin, 35*, 1452–1466. DOI:10.1177/0146167209342594.

Lehmiller, J.J., & Agnew, C.R. (2006). Marginalized relationships: The impact of social disapproval on romantic relationship commitment. *Personality and Social Psychology Bulletin, 32*, 40–51. DOI:10.1177/0146167205278710.

Lehmiller, J.J., VanderDrift, L.E., & Kelly J.R. (2011). Sex differences in approaching friends with benefits relationships. *Journal of Sex Research, 48*, 275–284. DOI:10.1080/00224491003721694.

Magoun, H.W. (1981). John B. Watson and the study of human sexual behavior. *Journal of Sex Research, 17*, 368–378. DOI:10.1080/00224498109551127.

Matthews, R. (2000). Storks deliver babies (p = 0.008). *Teaching Statistics, 22*, 36–38. DOI:10.1111/1467-9639.00013.

McConnell, J.V. (1974). *Understanding human behavior.* New York: Holt, Rinehart & Winston.

Meston, C.M., Heiman, J.R., Trapnell, P.D., & Paulhus, D L. (1998). Socially desirable responding and sexuality self-reports. *Journal of Sex Research, 35*, 148–157. DOI:10.1080/00224499809551928

Milgram, S. (1963). Behavioral study of obedience. *Journal of Abnormal and Social Psychology, 67*, 371–378. DOI:10.1037/h0040525.

Moore, D.W., & Carroll, J. (2004). *Support for gay marriage/civil unions edges upward: Public remains divided on constitutional amendment to ban gay marriage.* Retrieved from http://www.gallup.com/poll/11689/support-gay-marriagecivil-unions-edges-upward.aspx (accessed August 26, 2013).

Parish, W.L., Laumann, E.O., & Mojola, S.A. (2007). Sexual behavior in China: Trends and comparisons. *Population and Development Review, 33*, 729–756. DOI:10.1111/j.1728-4457.2007.00195.x.

Plaud, J.J., Gaither, G.A., Hegstad, H.J., Rowan, L., & Devitt, M.K. (1999). Volunteer bias in human psycho-physiological sexual research: To whom do our research results apply? *Journal of Sex Research, 36*, 171–179. DOI:10.1080/00224499909551982.

Prause, N., Cerny, J., & Janssen, E. (2005). The labial photoplethysmograph: A new instrument for assessing genital hemodynamic changes in women. *Journal of Sexual Medicine, 2*, 58–65. DOI:10.1111/j.1743-6109.2005.20106.x.

Rissel, C.E., Richters, J., Grulich, A.E., de Visser, R.O., & Smith, A.M.A. (2003). Sex in Australia: First experiences of vaginal intercourse and oral sex among a representative sample of adults. *Australian and New Zealand Journal of Public Health, 25*, 78–83. DOI:10.1111/j.1467-842X.2003.tb00800.x.

Wiederman, M. (2001). *Understanding sexuality research*. Belmont, CA: Wadsworth.

Yeater, E., Miller, G., Rinehart, J., & Nason, E. (2012). Trauma and sex surveys meet minimal risk standards: Implications for institutional review boards. *Psychological Science, 23*, 780–787. DOI:10.1177/0956797611435131.

3

Human Sexual Anatomy

© Jeff Thrower, 2013. Used under license from Shutterstock.com.

Chapter Outline

- Introduction   56
- Male Sexual Anatomy   56
  - A Historical and Cultural Overview of the Penis   56
  - External Anatomy   58
  - Internal Anatomy   59
  - Psychology of the Penis: Male Genital Concerns   64
  - Male Genital Health Issues   66
- Female Sexual Anatomy   67
  - A Historical and Cultural Overview of the Vulva   67
  - External Anatomy   68
  - Internal Anatomy   73
  - Breasts   75
  - Psychology of the Breasts and Vulva: Female Bodily Concerns   77
  - Female Breast and Genital Health Issues   79
- Moving Forward   82

The Psychology of Human Sexuality, First Edition. Justin J. Lehmiller.
© 2014 John Wiley & Sons, Ltd. Published 2014 by John Wiley & Sons, Ltd.

Introduction

"What's the average penis size?"
"Is it possible for a woman to have an orgasm during intercourse without clitoral stimulation?"
"Does penis size really affect your partner's pleasure?
"Is female ejaculation real?"

The above questions were submitted to me by college students taking my human sexuality course, but not just once – these questions have come up semester after semester. As a result, I have come to realize that most students taking this course never learned what they really want and need to know about their bodies and their sexuality. The goal of the current chapter is to address this fundamental need.

You may be wondering why you are reading an entire chapter about human anatomy in a psychology textbook, but I can assure you that there are several good reasons for it. For one thing, many people are unfamiliar with the exact names and locations of certain portions of their genitalia. To the extent that this lack of information prevents you from knowing what is and is not normal, that can create a number of problems. For instance, if you do not know how things are supposed to look or function, you will be unable to identify potential health threats. Likewise, lacking knowledge about your own physique can cause unnecessary anxiety about body image, which can feed into sexual dysfunction and relationship problems. Lacking knowledge about your partner's body can lead to similar issues by reducing sexual satisfaction and decreasing the odds that your partner will reach orgasm. As we will see in chapter 12, one of the first steps involved in many forms of sex therapy is giving the client(s) specific information, often consisting of the anatomy lesson you will get in this chapter. This alone is sometimes enough to solve certain sexual problems. Thus, learning about anatomy has definite psychological importance because it can help you to feel better about yourself, enhance the quality of your sex life, and potentially prevent future problems from developing in your sexual relationships.

We will begin by covering genital anatomy in men, followed by women. However, as we discuss anatomy, please keep in mind that not everyone who has a penis necessarily identifies as a man and not everyone with a vulva necessarily identifies as a woman. One's gender identity (i.e., one's psychological sense of being male or female) does not necessarily match one's genital anatomy. Also, keep in mind that not every person has a penis or a vulva. For example, intersexed individuals may have genitals that appear to be a mix of male and female genital structures. We will return to these points in chapter 5 when we discuss gender issues in more detail. For the time being, however, we will describe genital anatomy in terms of how things typically appear and function in most *biological* men and women.

Male Sexual Anatomy

A Historical and Cultural Overview of the Penis

Humans have been obsessed with the penis for thousands of years. However, the nature of phallic attitudes has varied considerably. At times, the penis has been celebrated and openly displayed as a symbol of fertility. This view was perhaps best exemplified by the ancient Romans,

Figure 3.1 In recent history, the penis has largely been seen as vulgar and makes infrequent appearances even in artistic depictions of the male body. Image Copyright Dragonfly Studio, 2013. Used under license from Shutterstock.com.

who surrounded themselves with artistic representations of penises in their everyday life. For instance, it was once considered a sign of prestige for Roman boys to wear a tiny replica of an erect penis around their neck known as a *fascinum* (on a side note, the word "fascinating" is derived from fascinum. Thus, when we say that something is "fascinating," we are actually likening it to the wonders and intrigue of nothing other than the penis!) At other times, however, the penis has been seen as vulgar, and every effort has been made to hide it from view. This has been the case throughout much of recent history. The penis certainly has no place in the modern media (e.g., when was the last time you saw a penis on primetime TV?), and it makes only infrequent appearances in the world of art. In fact, it is not uncommon to see artistic representations of the penis painted over in pictures or broken off of sculptures so as to keep any semblance of the penis out of public view.

Given that much of the modern world is anti-penis, most of us know relatively little about it, including how it works and how it is "supposed" to look. This has led to a lot of penile misconceptions and misinformation. For instance, many people think that the penis consists of muscles and/or bone, when in reality it is composed mostly of fibrous tissue and blood vessels. Thus, despite the fact that an erection is often referred to as a "boner," there are no bones in the human penis. In contrast, some other species, such as chipmunks and dogs, do have a penis bone (known as the *baculum*), which assists during sexual intercourse. Another thing people frequently get wrong when it comes to the human penis is that they assume it is supposed to be extremely large, like the ones they may have seen in porn videos. Many people also assume that bigger is better when it comes to penises, such that men who are more well-endowed are more sexually satisfied and better able to please their partners. However, as we will see later in this chapter, this is not necessarily the case.

External Anatomy

With the preceding in mind, let us begin our discussion of the external sexual anatomy of biological men. The penis consists of three parts: the root, shaft, and glans. The root is the completely internal portion of the penis that serves to anchor it to the pubic bones. The shaft and glans are the external portions of the penis that are visible to the naked eye. The shaft (in its non-aroused state) is loose and pendulous, and is usually covered with hair at the base. The glans (head) sits at the end of the shaft and contains the urethral opening (meatus). The glans is the most sensitive portion of the penis, containing the largest concentration of nerve endings.

At the base of the glans is the *corona* ("crown"), which is the distinctive ridge encircling the head. The flared shape of the glans and the surrounding corona is theorized to have evolved that way as a potential "semen displacement device" (Gallup et al., 2003). That is, the unique shape of the penis combined with the thrusting action of intercourse may exist to enable men to remove any semen deposited in the female reproductive tract by other men before depositing their own. In fact, research by Dr. Gordon Gallup and colleagues in which they simulated intercourse with artificial penises, ejaculate, and vaginas found that just one thrust of their mock penis was enough to displace more than 90% of any previously deposited "ejaculate." They tested a variety of alternative "penises" that did not have the same features (i.e., penises without a flared glans and corona), but found that they were far less effective at semen displacement. Of course, we cannot say for sure why the head of the penis has the shape that it does, and Gallup's theory has been disputed by others. For example, Bowman (2013) argues that because sperm travel into the uterus very quickly, and any sperm remaining outside the uterus will not live long in the acidity of the vagina anyway, semen displacement is unlikely to have significant effects on conception likelihood. Bowman's argument is that the penile glans is instead optimized for absorption of chemicals in the vaginal secretions, such as oxytocin (see chapter 4), which helps facilitate bonding between partners. Some scientists think that such bonding is adaptive in that it helps facilitate the survival of any offspring produced.

Covering the corona and glans is the **foreskin** (prepuce), a loose and retractable layer of skin that can be thought of as a sheath for the head of the penis. Not all men have foreskin because it is sometimes removed during infancy in a procedure known as **circumcision**. For men who retain their foreskin into adulthood, it requires proper care and attention. Specifically, it is important for the foreskin to be gently pulled back and cleansed with some regularity to prevent the buildup of *smegma*, a smelly, cheese-like substance that consists of an accumulation of glandular secretions and dead skin cells.

In the United States, just over half of all male infants today are circumcised, although the percentage of parents opting for this procedure has decreased dramatically in recent years (Centers for Disease Control and Prevention, 2011). Circumcision rates in other countries around the world vary, with the highest rates in the Middle East and the lowest rates in Europe. There are vast differences in opinion on this procedure, which has made it a subject of hot debate. See the Digging Deeper 3.1 box for a discussion of some of the oft cited pros and cons of male circumcision. It is also worth pointing out that foreskin cutting may take other forms in different cultures. For instance, in some Polynesian cultures, a procedure known as a **superincision** (sometimes called a *dorsal slit*) is performed, in which a lengthwise slit is made in the upper portion of the foreskin (Diamond, 2004). This reveals the glans of the penis without necessarily removing the foreskin.

Removal or cutting of foreskin is obviously one major factor that affects the external appearance of the penis. However, penises also vary substantially in terms of several other features, including the presence or absence of pubic hair, degree of curvature, and overall length. First, pubic hair naturally varies from man to man in terms of density, color, and coarseness. Of course, some men opt to trim and, in some cases, completely shave off their pubic hair for a variety of reasons (e.g., some men prefer the sensation of no hair, while others think it makes their genitals look larger). Second, with respect to curvature, it is normal for penises to not be perfectly straight and instead curve slightly to one side or the other. In cases where there is a severe curvature (known as **Peyronie's disease**, caused by a build-up of scar tissue), intercourse may be difficult and painful. However, surgical intervention can correct this. Third, penile length can vary considerably. In a flaccid (i.e., non-erect) penis, the average length is 3.5 inches (approximately 9 centimeters); in an erect penis, the average length approaches 6 inches (approximately 15 centimeters; Templer, 2002). Keep in mind that these are just averages and that, if anything, they may be overestimates of penis size because (1) men tend to exaggerate the size of their own penis in self-report studies and (2) observational studies have a selection bias such that they are disproportionately likely to sample men who are more comfortable with their bodies and, therefore, likely have larger than average penises. It is also important to note that smaller flaccid penises tend to grow more than larger flaccid penises during erection. Thus, some men are "growers," while others are "showers." One final note about penis size is that some studies have suggested that there are racial differences, and that those differences are consistent with popular stereotypes, with men of African descent tending to be above average and men of Asian descent tending to be below average (Lynn, 2013). However, these data are based almost exclusively upon self-reports of men from nonrepresentative Internet samples, which means that a hefty dose of caution is in order when considering these findings. The question of racial differences in penis size is one that remains controversial and is far from settled.

Aside from the penis, the other major external portion of male sexual anatomy is the *scrotum*. The scrotum is a pouch of skin hanging behind the penis that houses the testicles. The scrotum is sparsely covered in hair (although, as previously mentioned, some men opt to shave it off) and usually hangs loosely. However, in colder temperature and during sexual excitation, the scrotum elevates closer to the body. Like the penis, scrotal appearance varies from man to man, particularly in terms of size and symmetry. It is difficult to say what the average scrotal size is because most studies have measured only the size of the penis. With respect to appearance, it is perfectly normal for men to have an asymmetrical scrotum where one side hangs lower than the other. Specifically, the left testicle tends to hang lower than the right, generally because the spermatic cord (which suspends the testicles inside the scrotum) it typically longer on the left side.

Internal Anatomy

We begin our discussion of the internal workings of the penis by considering the makeup of the shaft and glans. The shaft is composed of three long cylinders, all of which fill with blood during sexual arousal, thereby creating an erection. Two of these cylinders are known as the **cavernous bodies** (*corpora cavernosa*) and run right next to each other on the upper portion of the penis. Sitting below the cavernous bodies is the smaller **spongy body** (*corpus*

Digging Deeper 3.1   Should Men be Circumcised?

Circumcision used to be performed on virtually all infant boys in the United States. However, this practice has become increasingly controversial and the number of US parents opting to subject their male children to it has dropped to 55–57% (Centers for Disease Control and Prevention, 2011). Many parents have asked me whether circumcision is a good idea. Although there are strong arguments for and against it, no scientific consensus exists.

One argument in favor of circumcision is that it serves religious and cultural purposes. For instance, this procedure is commonplace in the Jewish religion, where it has a basis in scripture and is performed during a *bris* eight days after birth. Circumcision is frequently practiced in Islamic cultures as well, although it is typically performed at puberty as a rite of passage instead of during infancy. The other major argument on this side is that circumcision provides hygienic and health benefits. For example, circumcision is a medical treatment for a condition known as *phimosis*, in which one's foreskin is too tight and is not easily retracted, thereby creating painful erections. In addition, circumcision is linked to a reduced risk of contracting sexually transmitted infections, including HIV. The thought here is that the foreskin contains certain cells that are highly susceptible to infection, and by removing them, it may cut off that route to disease transmission. Just consider that a clinical trial in African in which adult men were either circumcised or not (voluntarily, of course) had to be called off because the observed rate of contracting HIV was so much lower among newly circumcised men that ethical concerns were raised about withholding circumcision from men who still had their foreskin (Roehr, 2007)! Other studies have shown that circumcision is linked to a reduced risk of contracting the human papilloma virus (HPV; Larke, Thomas, Dos Santos Silva, & Weiss, 2011a) and syphilis (Weiss, Thomas, Munabi, & Hayes, 2006), as well as a lower likelihood of developing penile cancer (Larke, Thomas, Dos Santos Silva, & Weiss, 2011b). This research, combined with a low rate of side effects and no evidence of reduced sexual satisfaction, have resulted in significant support for circumcision within the medical community.

On the other hand, some argue that circumcision should never be performed unless there is a true medical need and that routine circumcision amounts to nothing more than male genital cutting/mutilation. One common argument on this side is that everyone has the right to an intact body, and that extends to the sexual organs (Hammond, 1999). As a result, some see it as cruel to irreversibly modify another person's body, especially when they cannot consent to the procedure themselves. Likewise, others have focused on the pain and trauma that circumcision is likely to cause to male infants, given that anesthetics are not always used (particularly when the procedure occurs as part of a religious ritual). Some have argued against the religious practice of circumcision, suggesting that it is an affront to try and improve upon God's creation. Yet one additional argument is that if delaying circumcision until adulthood can still yield health benefits, such as reducing HIV risk (Roehr, 2007), why not let men decide whether they want the procedure when they become adults and can evaluate the pros and cons themselves?

As you can see, there are compelling arguments on both sides of this issue that make it difficult to state whether circumcision is categorically good or bad. The important thing is to educate yourself about the different perspectives and come to your own conclusions.

Note: Reprinted with permission from *The Psychology of Human Sexuality* blog (www.lehmiller.com).

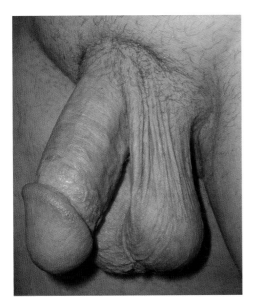

Figure 3.2 The appearance of the penis and scrotum varies substantially across persons. Source: stnu (Own work) [CC-BY-SA-2.0 (http://creativecommons.org/licenses/by-sa/2.0)], via Wikimedia Commons.

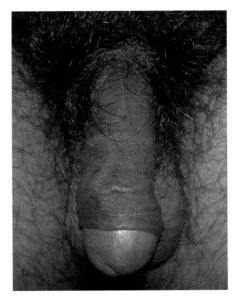

Figure 3.3 Source: Ramjet (Own work) [CC-BY- SA-3.0 (http://creativecommons.org/licenses/by-sa/3.0)], via Wikimedia Commons.

Figure 3.4 Source: Krittika (Own work) [CC-BY-SA -3.0 (http://creativecommons.org/licenses/by-sa/3.0)], via Wikimedia Commons.

spongiosum), which encases the *urethra* (i.e., the tube that carries urine and semen out of the body) and expands to become the glans.

At the base of the penis is a complex musculature. The muscles here are used primarily to eject semen from the body during ejaculation. These muscles can be strengthened by doing Kegel exercises, and men who practice these exercises enough tend to report more ejaculatory control and better orgasms. Because of these benefits, Kegel exercises are sometimes used as a treatment for premature ejaculation (LaPera & Nicastro, 1996). These exercises are easy enough to do (if you have a penis you can even do them while you read this book, if you like). The muscles you are looking to strengthen are the ones you would use to stop the flow of urine midstream. Once you know which muscles to exercise, you simply start by squeezing and releasing them rapidly several times. When you are comfortable doing a lot of repetitions, add in some "long Kegels," where you squeeze the muscles for a few seconds before releasing them. After a few weeks of daily exercise, the benefits are likely to start kicking in.

Inside the scrotum are the **testes**, or male gonads, which are suspended by the spermatic cord. Most men have two testes that are usually similar in size, with each serving two functions: (1) production of sex hormones (largely testosterone) and (2) production of sperm. On an interesting side note, there are some who argue that testicle size (like the distinct shape of the penis) is an evolutionary adaptation, such that the testes tend to be larger in societies that have historically had more "sperm competition" (see Ryan & Jetha, 2010). In other words, in societies where men tend to clash over access to mates, testicle size may be larger in order to enable more sperm production and, hence, the potential for intravaginal sperm wars when multiple men have had sex with the same woman. We cannot definitively say why any differences in testicle size might exist across people of different races and ethnicities; however, we will consider some additional evidence for sperm competition theory at the end of this section.

Returning to testicular functions, sperm production begins inside the testes in a series of tightly coiled tubes known as the **seminiferous tubules**. This is where the manufacturing of sperm occurs. Sperm production begins at puberty (a developmental stage known as *spermarche*) and continues through old age. The **interstitial cells**, which sit in between the seminiferous tubules, carry out the testes' other job: production of sex hormones. These cells secrete hormones directly into the bloodstream.

In order for healthy sperm production to occur inside the testes, a constant temperature must be maintained. The testes sit outside of the body and maintain the ideal temperature for sperm health, which is slightly below a man's normal body temperature. However, in order to account for the rapid temperature changes we experience throughout the day, the testes are capable of moving closer or further from the body via the **cremaster muscle**. In warmer temperature, the muscle relaxes, letting the testes fall further from the body; in colder temperature, the muscle contracts, drawing the testes in and generating "shrinkage." Because this temperature regulation is so vital for sperm health, men who have undescended testes (or in medical terms, *cryptorchidism*) are infertile.

After sperm are produced in the seminiferous tubules, they proceed to the **epididymis**, where they are stored for several weeks to allow them time to mature. The epididymis is shaped like a crescent moon and sits on the top and back of each testicle. Eventually, sperm are carried away from the epididymis via the **vas deferens**. Because the vas deferens is what transports sperm from the testes, this is the tube that is cut during a *vasectomy* (a procedure we will cover in more detail in chapter 10). The vas deferens exits the scrotum through the spermatic cord, goes up into the abdomen, and loops around the bladder before joining up with the prostate.

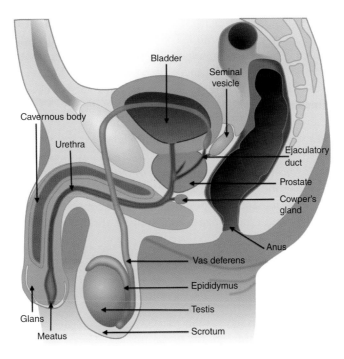

Figure 3.5 The male reproductive system. Source: Tsaitgaist (Derivative work) [CC-BY-SA-3.0 (http://creativecommons. org/licenses/by-sa/3.0)], via Wikimedia Commons.

The portion of the prostate where the vas deferens enters is known as the *ejaculatory duct*, which empties into the urethra. In the ejaculatory duct, sperm from the vas deferens mix with secretions from the seminal vesicles and the prostate to create **semen**. The **seminal vesicles** are two small glands that empty into the ejaculatory duct. They produce the bulk of the seminal fluid (60–70% of the volume) by secreting an alkaline, sugary substance that appears designed to enable nutrition and survival of sperm (Gonzales, 2001). Once sperm come into contact with these secretions, they gain the ability to move on their own.

The remaining portion of the seminal fluid (30–40%) is produced by the **prostate gland**. The prostatic secretions are also very alkaline, which aids sperm survival in the acidity of the male urethra and the female reproductive tract. The prostate gland, which sits just below the bladder, is sometimes referred to as the male equivalent of the G-spot, because some men have reported that prostate stimulation results in very intense orgasms. The prostate gland can be stimulated gently through rectal insertion, or by pressing on the *perineum* (the strip of skin that runs between the scrotum and the anus).

Where the ejaculatory duct empties into the urethra, there are the two small **Cowper's glands** (*bulbourethral glands*). As a man becomes sexually aroused, these glands release a small amount of fluid that will appear as a drop or two on the glans prior to ejaculation. This pre-ejaculate is thought to alkalinize the urethra, making it more hospitable for sperm to travel through. Although this secretion is not semen, it can potentially contain active sperm. As a result, even if a heterosexual couple stops sexual intercourse before the man ejaculates, it is theoretically possible for a pregnancy to occur and for sexual infections to be transmitted.

During ejaculation, semen is released from the body via contractions of the urethra and the muscles at the base of the penis. The amount of semen expelled varies from man to man and depends upon a number of factors (e.g., a longer duration of sexual activity will typically produce more semen); however, it consists of one or two teaspoons of fluid on average. Each ejaculate contains hundreds of millions of sperm. Given that a single sperm cell is necessary to fertilize an egg, the huge number of sperm produced is yet another theorized evolutionary adaptation (i.e., men may have evolved a tendency to produce sperm in such large quantities as a way of competing with other men's sperm in the female reproductive tract; Baker & Bellis, 1993). The concept of human sperm competition is a controversial and unsettled subject, but researchers have produced some provocative evidence in support of this idea. For example, in one study, male participants who viewed erotic images depicting two men with one woman (a scenario suggestive of sperm competition) subsequently produced ejaculate containing more active sperm than male participants who viewed erotic images consisting of three women together (Kilgallon & Simmons, 2005).

Psychology of the Penis: Male Genital Concerns

Perhaps the biggest concern men have about their genitals is the size of their penis. Although survey studies have reported that the majority of gay (65%) and heterosexual men (55%) sampled were satisfied with their penis size, there was a substantial minority who wished they could change it (Grov, Parsons, & Bimbi, 2010; Lever, Frederick, & Peplau, 2006). Among the latter, there was an almost unanimous desire to be larger; less than 1.5% of men of both sexualities wished their penis was smaller. Many of those men who were unhappy with their penis size were of average or above average size to begin with. So why do they want to change? Probably because we are surrounded by constant media messages telling us that "bigger is better" and "size matters." In addition, the penises that appear in most porn videos are much larger than average, and measuring up to them is enough to make almost any guy feel inadequate. Unfortunately, most men fail to recognize just how rare those gigantic porn penises actually are. In fact, researchers estimate that only about 2.5% of men have penises larger than 6.9 inches (17.5 centimeters; Lever et al., 2006).

As a result of the pressure to be big, many guys have gone to great lengths to try and increase the size of their penis, including everything from the pursuit of penile augmentation surgeries to the use of "natural male enhancement," stretching devices, and vacuum pumps. It is important to note that none of these techniques have been subject to rigorous scientific testing and, thus, it is not clear whether any provide the benefits frequently touted on the Internet and in popular men's magazines. In fact, these methods can be quite dangerous and carry the risk of potentially serious side effects. For example, penile augmentation surgery (also known as *phalloplasty*) usually involves cutting the ligaments that attach the penis to the pubic bone (which theoretically increases length by letting more of the penis hang outside of the body) and/or adding tissue grafts or fat injections to the penile shaft (the goal of which is to increase penile "girth" or circumference). Many men who have undergone phalloplasty have been disfigured and have required follow-up surgery to correct some of the complications, which frequently include scarring, penile lumps, and an erection that points down instead of up (Alter, 1997; Dillon, Chama, & Honig, 2008).

Figure 3.6 Penis size is one of men's biggest body concerns. Some men pursue dangerous and untested treatments with the hope of enhancing the size of their genitals. Image Copyright minemero, 2013. Used under license from Shutterstock.com.

So what is all the fuss about? Does penile size really matter? Yes and no. First, men with larger penises typically report better body image (Lever et al., 2006) and greater psychosocial adjustment (Grov et al., 2010). Thus, having a larger penis may make men feel better about themselves. Some guys appear to let this go to their head, though, because well-endowed men also tend to be more narcissistic (i.e., self-obsessed; Moskowitz, Rieger, & Seal, 2009). In addition, having a bigger penis does not necessarily translate into a greater ability to please a sexual partner. For example, as you will see when we cover female sexual anatomy, most of the nerve endings in the female genital area are on the outside of the body, not inside of it. Thus, a penis capable of deeper penetration does not necessarily result in a more pleasurable experience for women. Consistent with this, the vast majority of heterosexual women (85%) report being satisfied with the size of their partner's penis (Lever et al., 2006). Likewise, in a study that surveyed women about penis length and sexual pleasure, most women (66.3%) reported that size made no difference in their own pleasure or that shorter than average penises were more pleasurable than longer penises (Costa, Miller, & Brody, 2012). Thus, women certainly do not seem to be clamoring for larger male genitals. Of course, there are some women who prefer larger penises and who find them to be more sexually pleasing; however, the majority of women appear to be content with their partners' penis just the way it is, and most of those penises are of average size.

How does penis size play out with respect to sexual satisfaction in gay male relationships? Unfortunately, we do not have enough empirical data to address whether gay men are typically content with their partners' penis size and the implications this might have for sexual pleasure and enjoyment. However, I would theorize a similar pattern such that most gay men would be satisfied with their partners' size and, furthermore, that penis size would not necessarily affect likelihood of orgasm. I should also add that regardless of whether a man's partner is male or female, smaller penises may be preferred to larger penises for certain sexual activities (e.g., anal sex).

Although size concerns are largely confined to the length and width of the penis, there are some men who are dissatisfied with the size of their scrotum. Among the men who believe their scrotum is too small, a growing number of them have resorted to self-injecting saline solution into their scrotums in order to temporarily increase its size (Summers, 2003). There are also some men who do this because they enjoy the feeling of a distended scrotum and find it to be sexually pleasurable (i.e., it has a *fetish* quality to it). The fluid is usually absorbed by the body within a few days, after which time the genitals return to their normal appearance. However, this procedure is very risky and can result in serious complications (e.g., it could result in sterility if the testes themselves were injected or an embolism should air be injected into a vein). Indeed, there are several care reports in the literature of men who have wound up in the emergency room after engaging in some variation of this practice. As a result, no matter what you read on websites about "scrotal infusion" or "scrotal inflation" being harmless, it should be avoided. Among the men who believe their scrotum is too large or too droopy, some doctors are performing scrotum reduction surgery (CBS News, 2012). Thus, male genital modification is certainly not confined to the penis!

It is important to note that male genital concerns vary considerably across cultures. Thus, not every culture is equally obsessed large penises, and some cultures have their own unique genital concerns. Two such concerns that are practically nonexistent in the modern Western world are dhat and koro (Bhugra, Popelyuk, & McMullen, 2010). **Dhat**, which is found almost exclusively on the Indian subcontinent, is anxiety that stems from a fear of semen loss. Persons with dhat believe that semen is made from blood, and that it takes a significant amount of blood to make even a very small amount of semen. As a result, semen is seen as a very precious and vital bodily fluid, and loss of it (e.g., through masturbation, nocturnal emissions, etc.) creates anxiety and depression. In contrast, **koro** (found most commonly in southeast Asia) is a fear that the penis is shrinking and retracting inside the body, which creates anxiety and panic. It is thought that the term "koro" is derived from the Japanese word for "tortoise."

Male Genital Health Issues

It is important for men to take proper care of their genitals because not only are they delicate, but they are a common site of infection and other potential health problems. First, regular genital cleansing can prevent the buildup of smegma in uncircumcised men. Some in the medical community have also argued that washing one's genitals before and after sex may reduce the likelihood of transmitting certain infections, but research in that area has been mixed and, make no mistake, regular washing is in no way a substitute for safer sex practices (i.e., condom or other barrier use). Second, regular self-exams of the penis and scrotum can reveal signs of sexually transmitted infections and cancers. We will talk more about potential infection signs you should look for in chapter 11 when we cover sexually transmitted diseases in detail. With respect to signs of cancer, check for any kinds of bumps or masses on each of the testicles once per month. You can do this by rolling each testicle gently between your thumb and forefinger.

The surface should feel smooth, except for the epididymis, which hangs over the back of each testicle. Be sure to check for any sores or growths on the penile shaft and glans as well. Any time you detect one of these things, it is important to get it checked out by a doctor, even if you are not experiencing any pain. Many of the early signs and symptoms of testicular and penile cancer are completely painless, but can progress into major problems and potentially become deadly if left untreated. Fortunately, survival rates for both of these cancers are high if caught and treated early.

Lastly, it is important to be careful with the penis during sexual activity. For example, although you know there are no bones in the human penis, you should be aware that it is still possible to fracture an erect penis during sexual activity (Yapanoglu et al., 2009). What happens in such cases is a rupturing of the cavernous bodies due to some type of blunt trauma (e.g., attempting very forceful intercourse and missing one's target). Penile fractures are usually reported as being very painful and they have the potential to result in deformity and sexual dysfunction. However, if treated appropriately, normal functioning may return. It is also important for men to take great care when inserting their penis into any type of sex toy or (I wish I did not have to say this) household appliance. With respect to sex toys, be careful with "cock rings." These are circular pieces of rubber or metal that tightly grip the base of the penis, with the goal of generating longer-lasting and fuller erections. If you use one of these rings, it is advisable not to wear it for more than thirty minutes at a time, otherwise it can cause death of penile tissue and lead to permanent erectile difficulties. Thus, do not put it on before you head out to the bar for the evening or fall asleep wearing it. With respect to household appliances, please watch where you put your penis! Over the years, I have read news stories about men putting their penises in everything from swimming pool suction pumps to vacuum cleaners, and these stories often do not have happy endings, ranging from embarrassing rescues from the local fire department to penile decapitation. Ouch.

Female Sexual Anatomy

A Historical and Cultural Overview of the Vulva

Throughout history, attitudes toward the vulva have varied just as much as attitudes toward the penis. In the earliest of times, the vulva was seen as the source of life and was prized above all other fertility symbols (Blackledge, 2003). In fact, the penis did not even become a fertility symbol until long after the vulva, because early societies did not necessarily see a direct link between the penis and childbirth. Thus, artistic representations of the female body and genitalia were common and celebrated. More recently, however, the vulva has been seen as both dirty and pornographic – something that should be hidden. This idea is reflected in the fact that in the Western world, the female genitals are often referred to as the *pudendum*, which comes from the Latin word *pudere*, literally meaning "to be ashamed." Also, like the penis, the vulva has no place in the modern media. It is certainly not visually depicted, and the only time it is even alluded to is in advertisements for "feminine hygiene products," which perpetuate the idea that the female genitals are unclean.

Because our world is rather anti-vulva, most people (both men and women) know relatively little about it. For instance, most of us do not know how the vulva is "supposed" to look because it is something we see so rarely. Not only does this generate unnecessary anxiety for a lot of women who wonder whether they look normal, but this lack of familiarity with the female genitalia creates confusion for women and their sexual partners because they often have no idea what the different structures are and how they function. This also contributes to misinformation about female sexuality, such as the idea that all women "should" experience orgasm from vaginal penetration. As we will see later in this chapter, however, vaginal penetration is not the primary means by which most women reach orgasm.

External Anatomy

With this information in mind, let us discuss external sexual anatomy in biological women. The collective term that encompasses all of the external genital structures is the **vulva**. The vulva thus includes everything from the pubic hair to the labia to the vaginal opening. You may or may not realize this, but vulvas (like penises) comes in all different shapes and sizes and its appearance is incredibly variable from one woman to the next.

One of the most prominent parts of the vulva is the **mons veneris** (*mons pubis*). This is the pad of fatty tissue that covers the front portion of the pubic bones. The mons contains many nerve endings, which makes compression of this tissue sexually pleasurable. The primary purpose of the mons is to protect the internal genital structures during sexual activity. Although the mons is typically covered with pubic hair in adulthood, Western women are increasingly opting to have this hair partially or wholly removed through shaving, waxing, and/or laser treatments, usually because they feel it improves the aesthetic appearance of their genitals or makes them feel "sexier." Research finds that women who remove some or all of their pubic hair report having more sex than women who go au naturel (Herbenick, Schick, Reece, Sanders, & Fortenberry, 2010); however, we do not know if that is because women who shave are simply more sexually active, or if shaving begets more sex.

Next, we have the labia. The **labia majora** (outer lips) are folds of tissue usually covered with pubic hair that begin at the mons and extend downward, encasing most of the remaining genital structures. The **labia minora** (inner lips) are hairless folds of tissue situated between the outer lips that serve to protect the vaginal and urethral openings. The labia are richly endowed with nerve endings and blood vessels. As a result, they are very responsive to stimulation and they swell and deepen in color during sexual arousal. The labia may take on incredibly different appearance from one woman to the next, with wide variation in how prominent and symmetrical the lips are. Some women are concerned about the appearance of their labia, at least partly because we typically only see "perfectly" shaped and proportioned labia in pornography. In fact, research has found that in the last few decades, the labia minora have almost become invisible among *Playboy* centerfold models (Schick, Rima, & Calabrese, 2010). As a result, labial reduction surgery has become increasingly common. However, a recent study of women undergoing this procedure found that all of the women actually had normal sized labia to begin with (Crouch, Deans, Michala, Liao, & Creighton, 2011)! Thus, just as it is important for men to avoid comparing their penises to those that they see in porn, women should refrain from making the same comparisons with their vulvas.

Just below the mons, the inner lips join to form the **prepuce** (clitoral hood). The prepuce is akin to the male foreskin and provides a loose covering over the clitoris. As we discussed in our section on male anatomy, it is important for men to thoroughly cleanse their foreskin to

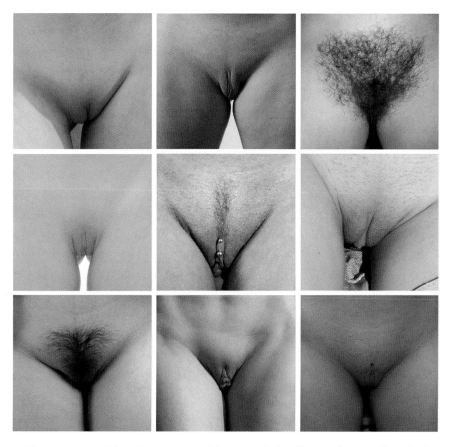

Figure 3.7 The appearance of the vulva can vary widely. Source: badiya bhosda, ich, Irmgardh, Mikael Haggstrom, Timasia, Peter Klashorst, Schamlippen, and Piercelot (Derivative work) [CC-BY-SA-3.0 (http://creativecommons.org/licenses/by-sa/3.0)], via Wikimedia Commons.

avoid the buildup of smegma. It is equally important for women to gently wash under the prepuce for the same reason.

The **clitoris** can be likened to the male penis in the sense that it is composed of a glans, a shaft containing two cavernous bodies, and crura that anchor it to the pubic bone (O'Connell, Sanjeevan, & Hutson, 2005). The glans may be seen by gently retracting the clitoral hood, whereas the shaft and crura are completely internal. Because the clitoris contains erectile tissue, it increases in size during sexual arousal. Thus, women technically get erections too (although they are not quite as prominent as men's tend to be). As with all features of the vulva, the size of the clitoris can vary widely across women.

The clitoris is unique in the sense that its sole purpose is to provide sexual pleasure – there is no other organ in the human body (male or female) like it. Although relatively small in size, the clitoris contains about as many nerve endings as a penis and is therefore a major source of sexual pleasure. Given this information, it should come as no surprise that the most common means by which women reach orgasm is through clitoral stimulation, not vaginal penetration (Fugl-Meyer, Oberg, Lundberg, Lewin, & Fugl-Meyer, 2006). Some research suggests that women who experience orgasm during vaginal intercourse are the beneficiaries of an anatomic variation in which their clitoris is closer to their vaginal opening than usual (Wallen & Lloyd, 2011). Specifically, when the distance between these structures is one inch (2.5 centimeters) or less, the clitoris is likely to receive more friction during sexual activity. For women who have a larger distance between the clitoris and vagina, they may find it easier to orgasm during intercourse by trying different sexual positions or different pelvic movements that enhance clitoral contact.

Because of the unique role the clitoris plays in producing female sexual pleasure, it has become one of the most controversial aspects of female genitalia. In fact, in some cultures, the clitoris is surgically removed for a variety of social and religious reasons. For a more in-depth discussion of this topic, see the Digging Deeper 3.2 box.

Digging Deeper 3.2   Female Genital Cutting: What is it, and What Should Be Done about it?

Female genital cutting (FGC) involves permanently damaging or removing portions of a woman's external genitals when it is not medically necessary. FGC has been practiced in many parts of the world for centuries, but today is most commonly performed in Africa and the Middle East, where millions of women have undergone some variation of it. FGC is done for a variety of reasons, with one of the most common being to ensure that a woman remains a virgin until marriage. In other cases, FGC is practiced as an initiation rite to adulthood, as a way of aesthetically "improving" the appearance of the genitals, and as a means of preventing women from becoming "over-sexed."

FGC is usually performed on young girls who have not gone through puberty (although age varies across cultures, ranging from infancy to adulthood) and involves cutting the genital tissues with sharp objects, such as knives, scissors, or broken glass. The least invasive form, *sunna*, involves removing or creating a slit in the prepuce. Alternatively, a *clitoridectomy* may be performed, in which the clitoris is completely removed. A few cultures opt for the even more extreme practice of *infibulation*, in which both the clitoris and labia are removed. In this case, the remains of the labia are stitched together and the girl's legs are bound for a few weeks to allow the tissues to heal. All that remains is a tiny opening to permit the exit of urine and menstrual blood.

Regardless of how FGC is performed, it usually occurs in unsanitary conditions and anesthetic is rarely administered. Thus, not only is there a high risk of infection, but it is incredibly painful. There is also a high likelihood of complications, especially for women undergoing infibulation. Potential problems include difficulty urinating, painful intercourse (it may take weeks or months for the opening to stretch to the point where intercourse is possible, and sometimes it never is), as well as childbirth dangers.

Most Western cultures have outlawed the practice, viewing FGC as inhumane and deeming it a form of genital "mutilation." Westerners typically consider FGC an unnecessary threat to women's health that permanently impairs female sexual pleasure and functioning.

However, in the 28 cultures where FGC is currently practiced, it is rarely questioned (at least publicly), even by women. In fact, many women say they want the procedure because it is a requirement for marriage, which is usually the only path for a woman in these cultures. The resistance to ending FGC stems from the fact that this tradition dates back centuries and has become part of the cultural psyche about how to properly raise a girl.

On a side note, FGC is often referred to as "female circumcision." However, it is unwise to equate this procedure with male circumcision because FGC is far riskier and much more invasive. Also, *FGC is a way that many societies attempt to control women's sexuality.* This stands in stark contrast to male circumcision, which is generally not intended to affect men's sexual behavior (although there was a time in recent history in which boys were sometimes circumcised as a means of discouraging masturbation). Certainly, there are some parallels between these practices (e.g., both are frequently performed on infants who cannot consent, they are often practiced as part of a cultural ritual), but they are hardly the same thing.

The controversy over FGC is unlikely to be resolved any time soon because those challenging this practice face a number of ethical and legal dilemmas. For example, what authority do we have to tell another culture that it must abandon its traditions? Also, some of the most common arguments against FGC are that women are socially pressured into it, that it is medically unnecessary, and that it creates health risks; however, can we not level similar arguments against many forms of cosmetic bodily modification performed on Western women (e.g., breast augmentation, "vaginal rejuvenation," labial reduction)? I do *not* wish to imply that FGC and these other procedures are equivalent, because they are not, especially in terms of the risks they carry, whether the procedure is voluntary, and whether it is performed on adults or children. I am simply stating that drawing a line between which forms of bodily modification are acceptable and which are not is harder than it sounds.

Note: Reprinted with permission from *The Psychology of Human Sexuality* blog (www.lehmiller.com). To learn more about FGC, please consult Momoh (2005).

Continuing our discussion of the vulva, within the labia minora is a region known as the *vestibule*, which houses the openings to the urethra and the vagina. The meatus (i.e., the urethral opening) is located between the clitoris and vaginal opening and has excretory functions. The **introitus** (i.e., the vaginal opening) is situated between the urethral opening and the anus. On either side of the introitus are the **Bartholin's glands**, which secrete a drop or two of fluid during sexual arousal, perhaps to create a genital scent; however, scientists do not necessarily agree on the precise function of the Bartholin's secretion. The introitus is partly covered by a thin piece of tissue known as the **hymen**. The hymen usually remains intact until a woman's first intercourse, although it sometimes breaks sooner as a result of nonsexual activity. When the hymen initially breaks, it may be accompanied by light bleeding and some pain, but it is usually not a traumatic experience, especially among women who practice stretching it out prior to their first sexual experience.

The thickness and appearance of the hymen varies across women. In fact, some women's hymens are so thick that they are difficult to break during intercourse and, on rare occasions, the

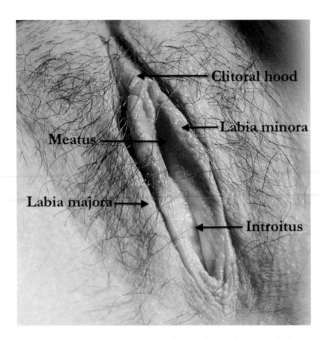

Figure 3.8   In this photo you can see some of the structures of the vulva, including the labia, clitoral hood, and introitus. Source: Bobisbob (en.wikipedia) [CC-BY-SA-3.0 (http://creativecommons.org/licenses/by-sa/3.0)], via Wikimedia Commons.

hymen may close off the entire vaginal opening, not even allowing menstrual blood to flow out. In these cases, medical intervention is usually necessary to allow intercourse and to prevent women's sexual partners from mistaking the meatus for the introitus, which I am sorry to say has happened in at least a few documented cases in the medical literature. Unfortunately, when neither partner has particularly good knowledge of female sexual anatomy and the only obvious orifice on the vulva is the urethral opening, some people have treated it as the entrance to the vagina.

While the hymen serves no true medical function, the fact that it may signal a woman's virginity status has caused many societies to place great social value on this tiny piece of tissue. For instance, in some African and Middle Eastern cultures, a woman is not eligible for marriage unless her hymen is intact. Women may be required to undergo pelvic exams prior to marriage in order to verify their virginity, or they may be required to produce a blood-stained sheet after their wedding night as proof that they lost their virginity to their new husband (Roberts, 2006). Given the great social pressure to be a demonstrable virgin at marriage, many women are undergoing "revirginiza-tion" surgery (also known as *hymenoplasty*) to reconstruct broken hymens. In this procedure, the original hymen is sutured back together, or a new hymen is fashioned out of other vaginal tissue. Upon request, a gelatin capsule containing artificial blood may be inserted to create the appear-ance of bleeding at her next intercourse. Among women who have had this procedure, they typi-cally report being very satisfied with the outcome (Logmans, Verhoeff, Raap, Creighton, & van Lent, 1998). On a side note, there are some women in the Western world who are getting "revirgi-nized" for a completely different set of reasons. Most commonly, it is because they want to physi-cally and psychologically recreate their first sexual experience (e.g., perhaps they regretted who they had sex with the first time and want to try it again with someone they care more about).

The final portion of the vulva is the **perineum**, an area of skin that runs between the introitus and the anus. During childbirth, an *episiotomy* is sometimes performed, in which an incision is made into the perineum to expand the size of the birth canal. This procedure reduces vaginal tearing and can make childbirth easier when the baby is larger than average or when a mother has undergone certain forms of female genital cutting (see the Digging Deeper 3.2 box).

Internal Anatomy

Beneath the vulva are several important structures, including the *pelvic floor muscles*, a complex, crisscrossed set of muscles that contract involuntarily when a woman reaches orgasm. These muscles can be strengthened through Kegel exercises, and women who do them experience numerous benefits (Beji, Yalcin, & Erkan, 2003). These exercises were first developed in the 1950s by Dr. Arnold Kegel as a way of helping women who suffer from incontinence problems after childbirth. Kegel and others found that these exercises are indeed an effective means of regaining urinary control, but they have the added benefit of increasing women's genital sensation during sexual intercourse. These exercises are easy enough to do and the steps involved are similar to the Kegel exercises men do to strengthen the muscles at the base of the penis. To begin, locate the muscles used to stop the flow of urine midstream. Once familiar with the muscles, simply start by squeezing them, holding for several seconds, and then releasing. After several repetitions, move onto squeezing and releasing the muscles rapidly a few times. These exercises must be done a few times per day for several weeks before the benefits start to become noticeable.

Next, let us consider the structure of the **vagina**, which is the canal that extends from the introitus to the uterus. The vagina expands in size and changes in shape during sexual intercourse and childbirth. The interior lining of the vagina (the vaginal mucosa) is a mucous membrane through which a lubricating substance is secreted during arousal. Some women produce less of this natural lubrication than others, which can make intercourse painful; however, artificial lubricants offer an inexpensive and practical solution. Surrounding the mucosa are layers of muscle and fibrous tissue that aid in expansion and contraction. Contrary to popular belief, most of the nerve endings in the vagina are concentrated around the introitus. The inner portions of the vagina have far fewer nerves, which means that a longer penis will not necessarily provide a heterosexual woman with more pleasurable stimulation.

On each side of the vagina near the introitus are the **vestibular bulbs**. They consist of spongy tissue (similar to the tissue in men responsible for penile erections) and expand in size during sexual arousal, causing the vulva to extend outward.

Deeper within the vagina is the **Grafenberg spot** (or G-spot), another controversial portion of female sexual anatomy. The location of the G-spot is most commonly described as being a couple of inches inside the vagina on the front wall (i.e., just underneath the mons veneris) and can be stimulated by inserting two fingers into the vagina and making the "come here" motion. Many women have reported that stimulation of this area results in very intense orgasms, sometimes accompanied by an ejaculation of fluid (known colloquially as "squirting"). The source of this fluid is often identified as the *Skene's glands* (or "female prostate," given the tissue's similarity to the male prostate), which surround the urethra. That said, a recent review of the scientific literature failed to provide conclusive evidence that the G-spot is a distinct anatomical structure (Kilchevsky, Vardi, Lowenstein, & Gruenwald, 2012). Not all women seem to have a G-spot, and studies trying to pinpoint the location of the G-spot have not provided consistent results (leading

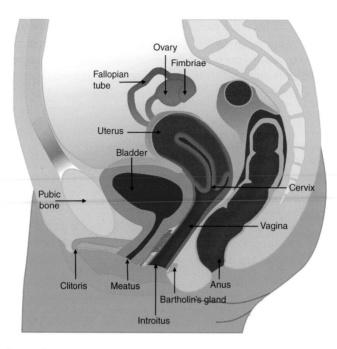

Figure 3.9   The female reproductive system. Source: Tsaitgaist (Derivative work) [CC-BY-SA-3.0 (http://creativecommons. org/licenses/by-sa/3.0)], via Wikimedia Commons.

some scientists to refer to the G-spot as a "gynecological UFO"—it has many sightings, but no confirmation of its existence). This does not mean that there is no such thing as the G-spot; rather, what some scientists are arguing is that the area people typically think of as the G-spot is actually the internal portion of the clitoris, which falls in the same general region and is highly sensitive to stimulation.

At the end of the vagina is the **cervix**, which is the lower end of the uterus. The opening of the cervix (the *os*) permits sperm to enter and menstrual fluid to exit. The cervix secretes mucus that has different effects depending upon the stage of the menstrual cycle a woman is in. This mucus assists the entry of sperm during fertile periods, but blocks sperm during the rest of the cycle. A woman who is very comfortable and familiar with her body can test the consistency of her cervical mucus to figure out where she is in her cycle and whether conception is likely to occur (see chapter 10 to learn more about this as a method of birth control). On a side note, the cervix may be a source of sexual pleasure for some women, with research indicating that cervical stimulation activates the same area of the brain as vaginal and clitoral stimulation (Komisaruk, Wise, Frangos, Liu, Allen, & Brody, 2011).

The **uterus** is a muscular organ suspended by ligaments in the pelvic cavity. Its primary purpose is to protect and nourish the fetus as it develops during pregnancy. The innermost lining of the uterus is the *endometrium*, which builds up and sheds during each menstrual cycle. Surrounding the endometrium are layers of muscle (the *myometrium*) and fibrous tissue (the *perimetrium*) that enable the uterus to change greatly in size during pregnancy. The uterus of a woman who has given birth will be much larger compared to a woman who has never been pregnant.

At the upper end of the uterus, a **fallopian tube** extends out on each side. This tube carries eggs from the ovaries to the uterus. At the end of the fallopian tubes are *fimbriae*, which are fingerlike projections that "catch" eggs and direct them into the tubes. Once inside the fallopian tube, an egg moves slowly toward the uterus via tiny hairs (*cilia*). It is in the upper portion of the tube near the fimbriae where fertilization is most likely to occur. When an egg is fertilized, it must implant itself in the uterine wall in order to generate a successful pregnancy. Occasionally, a fertilized egg will implant in the fallopian tube before it reaches the uterus, which creates a dangerous situation known as *ectopic pregnancy*. Pregnant women who experience severe abdominal pain, vaginal bleeding, and/or shoulder pain should consult a physician to check for ectopic pregnancy. If left untreated, it is potentially deadly.

Finally, we have the **ovaries**, or female gonads, which have two primary functions: (1) production of sex hormones (namely estrogen and progesterone), which play an important role in regulating the menstrual cycle, and (2) production and release of eggs (*ova*). During ovulation (i.e., the fertile period of a woman's menstrual cycle), either the left or right ovary will release an egg. Throughout her lifetime, a woman releases somewhere between 300 and 500 eggs (Macklon & Fauser, 1999).

Breasts

The breasts are not technically part of a woman's sexual anatomy (they are considered *secondary sex characteristics*, or physical indicators of sexual maturity); however, they are important to discuss because they have roles in both sexual pleasure and reproduction. Externally, breasts are composed of a **nipple** through which maternal milk can be released. The nipple is surrounded by a round, darkened area known as the **areola**. Both the nipple and areola contain many nerve endings, making them sensitive to touch. In fact, some women's nipples are so sensitive that they can achieve orgasm through nipple stimulation alone (Levin, 2006)! See the Digging Deeper 3.3 box for more on this.

Internally, breasts are composed of fatty tissue and mammary glands. What determines the size of a woman's natural breasts is the amount of fatty tissue. All women have approximately the same number of *mammary glands*, the structures that generate maternal milk. Thus, women with larger breasts do not necessarily produce more milk during lactation. It is also important to note that larger breasts do not necessarily contain more nerve endings. In fact, smaller breasts may be more erotically sensitive than larger breasts because they have the same number of nerve endings in a much denser concentration. Women with smaller breasts may therefore find more intense and forceful forms of stimulation (e.g., biting) unpleasant.

Breast appearance varies considerably across women. Not only are there huge differences in size and shape, which have only been exacerbated by the increasingly popular trend of surgical augmentation, but the look of the nipple and areola varies too. For instance, some areolas are much larger than others, and some nipples point outward, while others are inverted.

On a side note, some scientists have theorized that the appearance of the breasts has evolutionary significance (just like the size and shape of the male penis). The thought here, known as *genital echo theory*, proposes that women developed larger and more pendulous breasts after humans began walking upright as a way of mimicking the appearance of the buttocks, which used to be the biggest visual source of excitement for men (Fisher, 1992). In other words, women's main fertility symbol moved from the back to the front when we stood up.

Digging Deeper 3.3   Can Women Orgasm From Nipple Stimulation?

Some women have reported that they can achieve an orgasm simply by having their breasts and nipples stimulated (Levin, 2006). The idea of a woman experiencing orgasm without any genital touching whatsoever might seem perplexing, but research suggests there is a sound biological basis for it.

Komisaruk and colleagues (2011) sought to determine what areas of the brain are active in response to stimulation of different parts of the female body. Female participants were asked to lie inside an fMRI machine and alternate between stimulating the clitoris, vagina, cervix, and nipple. An experimenter instructed the women to "comfortably" stimulate one of those body parts for 30 seconds, then rest for 30 seconds before repeating the process with a different part of the body. All participants were asked to stimulate themselves in the exact same way to keep the results as constant as possible (e.g., when it came to nipple stimulation, women were asked to use their right hand to "tap the left nipple rhythmically").

The researchers discovered that stimulation of the nipple activated an area of the brain known as the *genital sensory cortex*. This is the same brain region activated by stimulation of the clitoris, vagina, and cervix. What this means is that *women's brains seem to process nipple and genital stimulation in the same way*. In light of this, it is not at all surprising that many women are aroused by having their nipples touched and that, for some, this may be enough to lead to orgasm.

If I may offer one note of caution, keep in mind that when it comes to nipple stimulation, there is good touching and bad touching. The nipple is a highly sensitive part of the body, which means that more aggressive handling (e.g., twisting) can potentially be unpleasant. As always, it is best to communicate with your partner about what is and is not pleasurable.

Note: Reprinted with permission from *Science of Relationships* (www.scienceofrelationships.com).

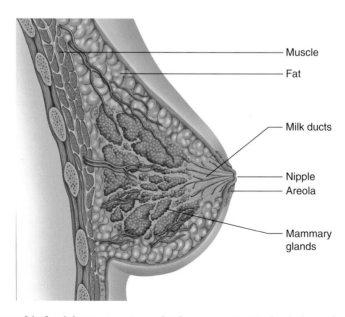

Figure 3.10   Anatomy of the female breast. Image Copyright Alex Luengo, 2013. Used under license from Shutterstock.com.

Psychology of the Breasts and Vulva: Female Bodily Concerns

One of women's biggest concerns about their bodies is the size of their breasts. In fact, research has found that only a minority of women (30%) reported being satisfied with the appearance of their chest (Frederick, Peplau, & Lever, 2008). Of the 70% who were dissatisfied, most of these women were worried that their breasts were either too small (28%) or too droopy (33%). Only a small number of women (9%) wished they could reduce the size of their breasts. Across all stages of the lifespan, most women expressed some form of breast dissatisfaction. The only thing that appeared to change with age is the nature of women's concerns. Specifically, younger women were more concerned being larger, whereas older women were concerned with being less droopy. Why are women so concerned with the appearance of their chests? It is likely the product of social learning. From a very young age, women are bombarded with messages that big breasts are better. For instance, Barbie dolls are a popular toy among young girls, but the bodies of these dolls (which typically have exaggerated breasts, tiny waists, and wide hips) are far from realistic. In fact, it is estimated that only 1 in 100,000 women have bodies that match Barbie's extreme proportions (Norton, Olds, Olive, & Dank, 1996)! Also, a large number of the female celebrities young girls look up to have had their breasts surgically enhanced, which further reinforces the notion that breasts are "supposed" to be huge and that they make women more popular, attractive, and likeable.

Given the immense pressure on women to have large chests, it should come as no surprise that breast augmentation surgery has become perhaps the most popular form of cosmetic surgery in

Figure 3.11 Female dolls often have extreme and unrealistic bodily proportions, some of which would be nearly impossible to obtain in real life. Source: Daniel Kruczynski (Own work) [CC-BY-SA-2.0 (http://creativecommons.org/licenses/by-sa/2.0)], via Wikimedia Commons.

the world. In 2012, more than 286,000 women had their breasts enlarged in the US alone (Lewis, 2013). Breast augmentation involves surgically inserting implants into the chest that consist of either saline or silicone encased in rubber shells. As with any form of surgery, breast augmentation carries a number of risks, including hardening of the breasts, changes in breast and nipple sensitivity, deformity, and implant rupture (Food and Drug Administration, 2012). Breast implants also have the potential to impair a woman's ability to breast feed. Overall, breast augmentation is probably safer than penile augmentation surgery, given that surgical breast enhancement has been around a lot longer and has been the subject of more scientific study. However, any woman considering breast implants should carefully weigh the risks before deciding whether to go forward.

Should women be so obsessed with how their breasts look? It may comfort some of you to know that, at least in heterosexual relationships, the majority of men (56%) reported being satisfied with the size and shape of their female partners' chests (Frederick et al., 2008). Of course, that still makes for a substantial minority of men who report some form of dissatisfaction. If we compare these results to the previously discussed study of penis size (Lever et al., 2006), it appears that men tend to judge women's bodies more harshly than women judge men's bodies. In some ways, this is not particularly surprising because most societies unfairly hold women to higher standards of beauty than they do men.

In addition to breast concerns, many women are worried about the appearance of their vulva. For instance, as previously discussed, many women are concerned that their labia are too large or asymmetrical and have thus undergone labial reduction surgery. In addition, some women believe that their vaginas are too large or too loose. It is a myth that women's vaginas become "looser" as a result of frequent sexual activity, so do not let anyone convince you otherwise; however, some degree of looseness may occur with older age and following vaginal delivery of children. Among those women who believe they are too loose, some are pursuing "vaginal rejuvenation" surgery, which is advertised to tighten the vagina. There are also a growing number of women who are concerned about their lack of ability to achieve orgasm during vaginal intercourse and will try almost anything to make it happen. Some of these women have sought out "G-spot amplification," in which collagen is injected into their supposed G-spot. Women should be especially wary of these procedures. For one thing, if scientists cannot agree on the location of the G-spot or whether it even exists (Kilchevsky et al., 2012), how can one possibly "amplify" it? More importantly, these procedures that attempt to sell women "designer vaginas" have not been subject to scientific scrutiny, which means we do not even know whether they are safe or effective (American Congress of Obstetricians and Gynecologists, 2007). Any claims to the contrary are simply deceptive marketing. It is therefore advisable to be extremely cautious about these and any of the other new genital surgeries.

All of the female breast and genital procedures discussed in this chapter (breast augmentation, revirginization, labial reduction, vaginal rejuvenation, G-spot amplification, and female genital cutting) are evidence that societies and cultures around the world consider the female body and women's sexuality to be highly malleable. There are many more cosmetic procedures available for women than there are for men, and women are much more likely to be socially pressured into undergoing these surgeries. This is but one small piece of evidence that there is a *sexual double standard*, in which men's and women's bodies and sexualities are evaluated very differently, with women being subject to the harshest criticism. For more on the nature and scope of the sexual double standard, check out the Your Sexuality 3.1 box.

Your Sexuality 3.1   Does the Sexual Double Standard Still Exist?

Researchers have recorded evidence of a sexual double standard dating back several decades. However, recent research has produced conflicting findings, with some studies finding support for the typical double standard, others showing no effect, and some even showing a *reverse* double standard (i.e., that men are judged more harshly than women in certain cases; Milhausen & Herold, 1999). So is the notion that women's bodies and sexual behaviors are subject to greater scrutiny than men's actually on the wane? Answer each of the questions below and see what your own experiences would suggest about the nature of modern day sexual attitudes.

- Culture and society dictate what the "ideal" male and female body looks like; however, are men and women penalized to the same extent for falling short of these ideals? Do they experience the same degree of pressure to have their body look a certain way in order to find a sexual and/or romantic partner?
- What names or labels would most people apply to a woman who frequently engages in one-night stands? What names or labels would most people apply to a man who engages in the same behavior? How did the number and nature of the labels you generated differ between groups?
- Would you encourage a heterosexual male friend to date a woman who you knew had ten previous sexual partners? Would you encourage a heterosexual female friend to date a man who you knew had ten previous sexual partners?
- Is a woman who has sex on the first date potential "marriage material?" What about a man who does the same thing?
- Imagine someone doing a "walk of shame." What is the sex of the first person who pops into your head?
- How would society evaluate a woman who carries condoms in her purse? How would society evaluate a man who carries condoms in his pocket?

Female Breast and Genital Health Issues

The Menstrual Cycle

A healthy woman of reproductive age will likely have an established menstrual cycle. This cycle is regulated by a complex interplay of hormones that produces a number of effects in the ovaries and uterus. There are four phases of this cycle: the follicular phase, ovulation, the luteal phase, and menstruation. Of most interest to us in this book because of their effects on female psychology are ovulation and menstruation. During **ovulation**, a mature egg is released by one of the ovaries. As we will discuss in chapter 10, ovulation produces a number of important changes in women's sexual behavior, including everything from how she dresses to the types of partners she finds attractive. The other stage of interest, **menstruation**, is when the endometrial lining of the uterus, which has built up in anticipation of pregnancy, sheds if conception does not occur, thereby producing a bloody discharge (often referred to as a "period"). On average, a complete menstrual cycle lasts 28 days, although there is significant variability across women in terms of cycle length and at what point ovulation occurs. There is also a lot of variation in the age at which a woman experiences her first menstruation (*menarche*) and when menstruation permanently ceases (*menopause*).

Most women experience at least some physical and psychological effects during each menstrual cycle. On a psychological level, changes in mood are common. This is often chalked up to **premenstrual syndrome (PMS)**, a very general term that encompasses all of the emotional changes and physical discomfort a woman might experience prior to getting her period. In more severe cases, the term **premenstrual dysphoric disorder (PMDD)** is sometimes used, which is an actual diagnostic category in the DSM-5. Specifically, PMDD is diagnosable when a woman presents with at least five of the symptoms specified by the DSM (e.g., marked changes in mood, difficulty sleeping, concentration problems, physical symptoms) and is experiencing personal distress or interference in daily life as a result.

In the medical literature, hundreds of symptoms of PMS have been identified (e.g., depression, irritability; O'Brien, Wyatt, & Dimmock, 2000), and studies suggest that as many as 80% of women report at least some of them (Stanton, Lobel, Sears, & DeLuca, 2002). However, one might reasonably wonder what use there is in defining this term so broadly as to apply to almost all women and, if that is the case, why we call it a "syndrome," which sounds like a problem. In fact, some argue that we are medicalizing and pathologizing normal female experience by using terms like PMS and PMDD. It is important to keep in mind that the psychological changes that women experience during menstruation are usually small on average and the wild mood swings depicted on television sitcoms are exaggerations.

Two of the most common menstrual cycle problems are dysmenorrhea and amenorrhea. **Dysmenorrhea** refers to painful menstruation. The most common symptom is cramping, but other women experience nausea, headaches, disorientation, and fatigue. *Primary dysmenorrhea* is diagnosed when the body produces too many *prostaglandins*, a substance that causes very intense contractions of the uterus. *Secondary dysmenorrhea* is diagnosed when a pre-existing medical condition creates painful menstruation. Perhaps the most common cause of secondary dysmenorrhea is **endometriosis**, a condition in which a woman has endometrial cells outside of her uterus, often on the ovaries or fallopian tubes. These cells respond the same way as the endometrial cells inside the uterus (i.e., they build up and then shed during the menstrual cycle). If left untreated, endometriosis can permanently damage reproductive structures, resulting in infertility.

Amenorrhea occurs when menstruation is absent and may take two forms. *Primary amenorrhea* is when an adolescent girl fails to menstruate by age 16, often because of a congenital malformation of the uterus, an imbalance of hormones, or as a result of being intersexed (i.e., not fitting the biological definitions of female or male; a topic we will return to in chapter 5). *Secondary amenorrhea* is when a woman who has already had a least one period experiences an interruption in her menstrual cycle. This type of amenorrhea occurs naturally during pregnancy, but is also normal among women who have recently stopped using birth control pills and among older women who are approaching menopause. It is also common among girls who are very athletic as well as girls who have anorexia.

Gynecological Health Issues

Just as proper genital health care is important for men, it is vital for women to take good care of their vulvas. First, maintaining good genital hygiene by bathing regularly can prevent the build-up of smegma and reduce the likelihood of urinary and vaginal infections. Thus, it is advisable for a woman and her partner to wash their hands and genitals prior to sexual activity. Again, this is not a substitute for safer sex – it is simply an extra precaution. A woman's genital cleansing routine should not include douching, though. *Douching* (i.e., rinsing the vaginal canal with liquids) can actually make vaginal infections more likely by changing the natural pH and bacteria balance. Second, women should perform regular self-exams of their genitals to look for changes that might indicate potential health issues (e.g., redness, unusual discharge). However, before you start looking for problems, begin by spending some time just getting acquainted with your genitalia under normal circumstances. You need this baseline so that you will know in the future what is normal for your body and what is not.

It is also important for women to have regular gynecological exams from a physician, because a physician can observe things that a woman cannot do on her own. In particular, physicians can perform *Pap tests*, a procedure in which a scraping of cells is taken from the cervix to test for cancer. Cervical cancer is one of the most common types of cancer in women, but if it is caught and treated early, the survival rate is very high (Mayr, Small, & Gaffney, 2011). Because one of the most common causes of cervical cancer is a sexually transmitted infection, HPV, it is especially important for sexually active women to get regular Pap tests. Specifically, the current recommendation is that women over age 21 get tested once every three years (U.S. Preventive Services Task Force, 2012). Until recently, the medical community recommended annual testing, but they now believe testing at less frequent intervals is likely just as effective. Pap tests may be simultaneously combined with a test for HPV, which is the preferred strategy.

Breast Issues

Breast cancer is the second most common and second most deadly type of cancer in women. The chance of an American woman developing breast cancer in her lifetime is approximately 1 out of 8, and her chance of dying from it is approximately 1 out of 36 (American Cancer Society, 2012). There appears to be a strong genetic component to breast cancer, which means that a woman's risk of developing it is higher to the extent that she has close female relatives who have had this type of cancer.

Although women are frequently told that they should do self-exams as part of the cancer screening process, research indicates that they are not all that effective at reducing death rates (Gaskie & Nashelsky, 2005). By the time a lump can be felt, it is often too late to do anything about it if it is a malignant cancer. Likewise, most of the lumps detected by women end up being benign cysts or fibroadenomas, which result in a lot of unnecessary healthcare utilization. Thus, while there may be some value to performing self-exams on occasion to become familiar with one's own body, they are by no means a substitute for regular clinical exams.

Mammography is the primary clinical technique for detecting breast cancer; it involves taking an X-ray of each breast. The traditional recommendation is that women over the age of 40 should get an annual mammogram; however, a recent US government task force argued that mammograms should instead be conducted biennially starting at age 50 and that regular breast cancer screenings should only begin before that if warranted by individual patient circumstances (e.g., previous family history of breast cancer; U.S. Preventive Services Task Force, 2009). The reason for this recommendation change is that administering mammograms routinely to women under age 50 is unlikely to provide a large benefit and there is a risk that repeated exposure to radiation from mammograms may itself cause cancer. This recommendation has proved controversial and the medical community remains split on it.

Figure 3.12   Research has found that breast self-exams are not as effective as doctors once believed. Thus, they are not a substitute for consulting with a physician. Source: Public domain image, via Wikimedia Commons.

Moving Forward

By this point, I hope I have successfully made the case that there is psychological value to learning about sexual anatomy, and that a lack of knowledge about your own body or that of your partner could have a wide range of implications. That said, you will want to keep in mind everything you have learned here about the human body because going forward in this text, you need to understand the basics of genital anatomy in order to appreciate our upcoming discussions of sexual arousal and response (chapter 4), biological sex variations (chapter 5), sexual behaviors (chapter 8), contraception and pregnancy (chapter 10), as well as sexual problems and sex therapy (chapter 12).

Key Terms

foreskin	seminiferous tubules	prostate gland
circumcision	interstitial cells	Cowper's glands
superincision	cremaster muscle	dhat
Peyronie's disease	epididymis	koro
cavernous bodies	vas deferens	vulva
spongy body	semen	mons veneris
testes	seminal vesicles	labia majora

labia minora

prepuce

clitoris

female genital cutting

introitus

Bartholin's glands

hymen

perineum

vagina

vestibular bulbs

Grafenberg spot

cervix

uterus

fallopian tube

ovaries

nipple

areola

ovulation

menstruation

premenstrual syndrome (PMS)

premenstrual dysphoric disorder (PMDD)

dysmenorrhea

endometriosis

amenorrhea

Discussion Questions: What is Your Perspective on Sex?

- How is pornography changing our perceptions and standards of physical attractiveness? Do producers of pornography select actors and actresses who conform to contemporary standards of beauty? If so, what effect does this have on our perceptions of the human body?
- Some scientists believe routine male circumcision would significantly reduce rates of sexually transmitted infections among men and their sexual partners, thereby lowering healthcare costs by billions of dollars over time. However, others argue that everyone has a right to an intact body and that circumcision causes pain, trauma, and potentially serious side effects. What is your view on this issue?
- Should penile augmentation, vaginal rejuvenation, and other such medical procedures be legal or illegal? Do individuals have a right or pursue experimental genital surgeries for which the benefits are unclear and the risks are very high?

References

Alter, G. (1997). Reconstruction of deformities resulting from penile enlargement surgery. *The Journal of Urology, 158,* 2153–2157.

American Cancer Society (2012). *How many women get breast cancer?* retrieved from http://www.cancer.org/Cancer/BreastCancer/OverviewGuide/breast-cancer-overview-key-statistics (accessed August 28, 2013).

American Congress of Obstetricians and Gynecologists (2007). *Vaginal "rejuvenation" and cosmetic vaginal procedures.* Retrieved from http://www.acog.org/Resources_And_Publications/Committee_Opinions/Committee_on_Gynecologic_Practice/Vaginal_Rejuvenation_and_Cosmetic_Vaginal_Procedures (accessed August 28, 2013).

Baker, R.R., & Bellis, M.A. (1993). Human sperm competition: Ejaculate adjustment by males and the function of masturbation. *Animal Behaviour, 46,* 861–885. DOI:10.1006/anbe.1993.1271.

Beji, N.K., Yalcin, O., & Erkan, H.A. (2003). The effect of pelvic floor training on sexual function of treated patients. *International Urogynecology Journal, 14,* 234–238. DOI:10.1007/s00192-003-1071-2.

Bhugra, D., Popelyuk, D., & McMullen, I. (2010). Paraphilias across cultures: contexts and controversies. *Journal of Sex Research, 47,* 242–256. DOI:10.1080/00224491003699833.

Blackledge, C. (2003). *The story of V: Opening Pandora's box.* London: Weidenfeld & Nicolson.

Bowman, E.A. (2013). Sperm competition and the absorption of neuropeptides by the prepuce. *Archives of Sexual Behavior, 42,* 701–702. DOI:10.1007/s10508-013-0086-0.

CBS News (2012). 14 most shocking beauty treatments. Retrieved from http://www.cbsnews.com/2300-204_162-10004213-5.html (accessed August 28, 2013).

Centers for Disease Control and Prevention (2011). *Trends in in-hospital newborn male circumcision – United States, 1999–2010*. Retrieved from http://www.cdc.gov/mmwr/preview/mmwrhtml/mm6034a4.htm?s_cid=mm6034a4_w (accessed August 28, 2013).

Costa, R., Miller, G.F., & Brody, S. (2012). Women who prefer longer penises are more likely to have vaginal orgasms (but not clitoral orgasms): Implications for an evolutionary theory of vaginal orgasm. *Journal of Sexual Medicine, 9*, 3079–3088. DOI:10.1111/j.1743-6109.2012.02917.x.

Crouch, N.S., Deans, R., Michala, L., Liao, L.M., & Creighton, S.M. (2011). Clinical characteristics of well women seeking labial reduction surgery: A prospective study. *International Journal of Obstetrics and Gynaecology, 118*, 1507–1510. DOI:10.1111/j.1471-0528.2011.03088.x.

Diamond, M. (2004). Sexual behavior in pre contact Hawai'i: A sexological ethnography. *Revista Española del Pacifico, 16*, 37–58.

Dillon, B.E., Chama, N.B., & Honig, S.C. (2008). Penile size and penile enlargement surgery: A review. *International Journal of Impotence Research, 20*, 519–529. DOI:10.1038/ijir.2008.14

Fisher, H.E. (1992). *Anatomy of love*. New York: Fawcett Columbine.

Food and Drug Administration (2012). *Risks of breast implants*. Retrieved from http://www.fda.gov/MedicalDevices/ProductsandMedicalProcedures/ImplantsandProsthetics/BreastImplants/ucm064106.htm (accessed August 28, 2013).

Frederick, D A., Peplau, L.A., & Lever, J. (2008). The Barbie mystique: Satisfaction with breast size and shape across the lifespan. *International Journal of Sexual Health, 20*, 200–211. DOI:10.1080/19317610802240170.

Fugl-Meyer, K.S., Oberg, K., Lundberg, P.O., Lewin, B., & Fugl-Meyer, A. (2006). On orgasm, sexual techniques, and erotic perceptions in 18- to 74-year-old Swedish women. *Journal of Sexual Medicine, 3*, 56–68. DOI:10.1111/j.1743–6109.2005.00170.x.

Gallup, G.G., Burch, R.L., Zappieri, M.L., Parvez, R.A., Stockwell, M.L., & Davis, J.A. (2003). The human penis as a semen displacement device. *Evolution and Human Behavior, 24*, 277–289. DOI:10.1016/S1090-5138(03)00016-3.

Gaskie, S., & Nashelsky, J. (2005). Are breast self-exams or clinical exams effective for screening breast cancer? *The Journal of Family Practice, 54*, 803–804.

Gonzales, G.F. (2001). Function of seminal vesicles and their role on male fertility. *Asian Journal of Andrology, 3*, 251–258. DOI:10.1038/aja.2008.47.

Grov, C., Parsons, J.T., & Bimbi, D.S. (2010). The association between penis size and sexual health among men who have sex with men. *Archives of Sexual Behavior, 39*, 788–797. DOI:10.1007/s10508-008-9439-5.

Hammond, T. (1999). A preliminary poll of men circumcised in infancy or childhood. *British Journal of Urology International, 83*(Suppl. 1), 85–92. DOI:10.1046/j.1464-410x.1999.0830s1085.x.

Herbenick, D., Schick, V., Reece, M., Sanders, S., & Fortenberry, J. D. (2010). Pubic hair removal among women in the United States: Prevalence, methods, and characteristics. *Journal of Sexual Medicine, 7*, 3322–3330. DOI:10.1111/j.1743-6109.2010.01935.x.

Kilchevsky, A., Vardi, Y., Lowenstein, L., & Gruenwald, I. (2012). Is the female G-spot truly a distinct anatomic entity? *Journal of Sexual Medicine, 9*, 719–726. DOI:10.1111/j.1743-6109.2011.02623.x.

Kilgallon, S.J., & Simmons, L.W. (2005). Image content influences men's semen quality. *Biology Letters, 22*, 253–255. DOI:10.1098/rsbl.2005.0324.

Komisaruk, B.R., Wise, N., Frangos, E., Liu, W.C., Allen, K., & Brody, S. (2011). Women's clitoris, vagina, and cervix mapped on the sensory cortex: fMRI evidence. *Journal of Sexual Medicine, 8*, 2822–2830. DOI:10.1111/j.1743-6109.2011.02388.x.

LaPera, G., & Nicastro, A. (1996). A new treatment for premature ejaculation: The rehabilitation of the pelvic floor. *Journal of Sex & Marital Therapy, 22*, 22–26. DOI:10.1080/00926239608405302.

Larke, N., Thomas, S.L., Dos Santos Silva, I., & Weiss, H.A. (2011a). Male circumcision and human papillomavirus infection in men: A systematic review and meta-analysis. *Journal of Infectious Diseases, 204*, 1375–90. DOI:10.1093/infdis/jir523.

Larke, N.L., Thomas, S.L., Dos Santos Silva, I., & Weiss, H.A. (2011b). Male circumcision and penile cancer: A systematic review and meta-analysis. *Cancer Causes Control, 22*, 1097–110. DOI:10.1007/s10552-011-9785-9.

Lever, J., Frederick, D.A., & Peplau, L.A. (2006). Does size matter? Men's and women's views on penis size across the lifespan. *Psychology of Men and Masculinity, 7*, 129–143. DOI:10.1037/1524-9220.7.3.129.

Levin, R.J. (2006). The breast/nipple/areola complex and human sexuality. *Sexual & Relationship Therapy, 21*, 237–249. DOI:10.1080/14681990600674674.

Lewis, R. (2013).Money quick tips: The costs of cosmetic surgery. *USA Today*. Retrieved from http://www.usatoday.com/story/money/personalfinance/2013/05/18/money-quick-tips-cosmetic-plastic-surgery-costs/2194647/ (accessed August 28, 2013).

Logmans, A., Verhoeff, A., Raap, R.B., Creighton, F., & van Lent, M. (1998). Should doctors reconstruct the vaginal introitus of adolescent girls to mimic the virginal state? *British Medical Journal, 316*, 459–460.

Lynn, R. (2013). Rushton's r–K life history theory of race differences in penis length and circumference examined in 113 populations. *Personality and Individual Differences, 55*, 261–266. DOI:10.1016/j.paid.2012.02.016.

Macklon, N.S., & Fauser, B.C.J.M. (1999). Aspects of ovarian follicle development throughout life. *Hormone Research, 52*, 161–170. DOI:10.1159/000023456.

Masters, W.H., & Johnson, V.E. (1966). *Human sexual response*. Boston: Little, Brown.

Mayr, N.A., Small, W., & Gaffney, D.K. (2011). Cervical cancer. In J. J. Lu & L. W. Brady (Eds.) *Decision Making in Radiation Oncology*. New York: Springer.

Milhausen, R.R., & Herold, E.S. (1999). Does the sexual double standard still exist? Perceptions of university women. *Journal of Sex Research, 36*, 361–368. DOI:10.1080/00224499909552008.

Momoh, C. (2005). *Female genital mutilation*. Milton Keynes: Radcliffe Publishing.

Moskowitz, D.A., Rieger, G., & Seal, D.W. (2009). Narcissism, self-evaluations, and partner preferences among men who have sex with men. *Personality and Individual Differences, 46*, 725–728. DOI:10.1016/j.paid.2009.01.033.

Norton, K.I., Olds, T.S., Olive, S., & Dank, S. (1996). Ken and Barbie at life size. *Sex Roles, 34*, 287–294. DOI:10.1007/BF01544300.

O'Brien, P.M., Wyatt, K., & Dimmock, P. (2000). Premenstrual syndrome is real and treatable. *Practitioner, 244*, 185–195.

O'Connell, H.E., Sanjeevan, K.V., & Hutson, J.M. (2005). Anatomy of the clitoris. *The Journal of Urology, 174*, 1189–1195. DOI:10.1097/01.ju.0000173639.38898.cd.

Roberts, H. (2006). Reconstructing virginity in Guatemala. *The Lancet, 367*, 1227–1228. DOI:10.1016/S0140-6736(06)68522-X.

Roehr, B. (2007). Dramatic drop in HIV infections halts circumcision trials. *British Medical Journal, 334*, 11. DOI:10.1136/bmj.39073.473634.DB.

Ryan, C., & Jetha, C. (2010). *Sex at dawn: How we mate, why we stray, and what it means for modern relationships*. New York: HarperCollins.

Schick, V.R., Rima, B.N., & Calabrese, S.K. (2010). E vulva lution: The portrayal of women's external genitalia and physique across time and the current Barbie doll ideals. *Journal of Sex Research, 48*, 74–81. DOI:10.1080/00224490903308404.

Stanton, A.L., Lobel, M., Sears, S., & DeLuca, R.S. (2002). Psychosocial aspects of selected issues in women's reproductive health: Current status and future directions. *Journal of Consulting and Clinical Psychology, 70*, 751–770. DOI:10.1037/0022-006X.70.3.751.

Summers, J.A. (2003). A complication of an unusual sexual practice. *Southern Medical Journal, 96*, 716–717.

Templer, D.I. (2002). *Is size important?* Pittsburgh, PA: CeShore.

U.S. Preventive Services Task Force (2009). *Screening for breast cancer.* Retrieved from http://www.uspreven tiveservicestaskforce.org/uspstf/uspsbrca.htm (accessed August 28, 2013).

U.S. Preventive Services Task Force (2012). *Screening for cervical cancer: U.S. preventive services task force recommendation statement.* Retrieved from http://www.uspreventiveservicestaskforce.org/uspstf11/cervcancer/ cervcancerrs.htm (accessed August 28, 2013).

Wallen, K., & Lloyd, E.A. (2011). Female sexual arousal: Genital anatomy and orgasm in intercourse. *Hormones and Behavior, 59,* 780–792. DOI:10.1016/j.yhbeh.2010.12.004.

Weiss, H.A., Thomas, S.L., Munabi, S.K., & Hayes, R.J. (2006). Male circumcision and risk of syphilis, chancroid, and genital herpes: A systematic review and meta-analysis. *Sexually Transmitted Infections, 82,* 101–9. DOI:10.1136/sti.2005.017442.

Yapanoglu, T., Aksoy, Y., Adanur, S., Kabadayi, B., Ozturk, G., & Ozbey, I. (2009). Seventeen years' experience of penile fracture: Conservative vs. surgical treatment. *Journal of Sexual Medicine, 6,* 2058–2063. DOI:10.1111/j.1743-6109.2009.01296.x.

4

Human Sexual Response: Understanding Arousal and Orgasm

Image Copyright Hasloo Group Production Studio, 2013. Used under license from Shutterstock.com.

Chapter Outline

- Introduction   88
- Factors That Influence Sexual Arousal   88
  - The Brain   88
  - The Senses   90
  - Hormones   97
  - Substances   100
- The Sexual Response Cycle   103
  - The Masters and Johnson Model   103
  - Psychological Models of Sexual Response   108

The Psychology of Human Sexuality, First Edition. Justin J. Lehmiller.
© 2014 John Wiley & Sons, Ltd. Published 2014 by John Wiley & Sons, Ltd.

Introduction

If you have ever looked at the magazines sitting beside the checkout line at the grocery store, you have probably noticed that at least half of them feature stories about "how to turn him on" or "what you need to know to drive her wild." To be perfectly honest, these stories are usually garbage: they are not based upon sound scientific research, they are not written by experts, and they tend to reinforce gender stereotypes. Such articles drive psychologists crazy, and not in a good way.

The purpose of this chapter is to tell you what you really need to know about the topic of sexual arousal. We will explore the biological, psychological, and social factors that lead to arousal and consider the accompanying changes that occur in the male and female body during sexual activity. Knowledge of the factors that generate arousal and an appreciation of how the body normally reacts to sexual stimuli are both vital for understanding the basis of sexual difficulties and the ways in which a sex therapist might go about treating them (chapter 12 will cover sexual dysfunction and therapy in detail). This information is also important for understanding similarities and differences in male and female sexuality. This chapter will give you far more valuable insight than you could get from any magazine at the supermarket and will hopefully serve as a valuable reference guide for you in the future.

Factors That Influence Sexual Arousal

Is your brain really your biggest sex organ? It most certainly is! Sexual arousal is contingent upon the way your brain perceives a given sexual stimulus. It does not matter whether the most sensitive parts of your body are being touched, or how little clothing the person in front of you is wearing, because if your brain does not interpret that stimulus as arousing, you are unlikely to have a sexual response. We will therefore begin our discussion of sexual arousal with the brain and our senses, and subsequently consider the myriad other factors that can affect arousal, including hormones and substances.

The Brain

The brain is the control center for sexual arousal. Through cognitions, mood states, and fantasies, we are able to turn ourselves off and on, independent of any sensory input. However, the degree of control a person has, as well as the way that person responds to sexual stimuli, varies considerably between individuals. For example, emotions such as depression and anger can make sexual arousal difficult in some people, but pose little problem for others. Likewise, some people may not notice any sounds while they are having sex, but others may find the same noise so distracting that it kills the mood.

In this section, we will consider the sections of the brain that are most important for arousal. First is the **limbic system**, a set of structures deep within the brain that exerts a profound influence on both animal and human sexual behavior. The limbic system is composed of several important elements, including the hypothalamus (which controls autonomic processes and sexual responses), hippocampus (which assists in learning and memory), and amygdala (which plays a role in emotion regulation and the processing of social information). As early as the 1950s, scientists identified the limbic system as the "pleasure center" of the brain through studies of rats

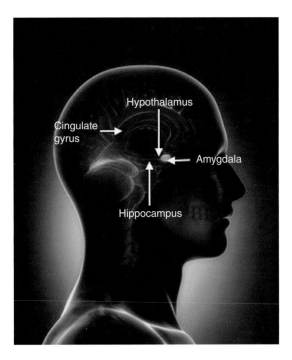

Figure 4.1 In this picture, you can see the approximate locations of the structures of the limbic system depicted. ©Peter Lecko/123RF.COM.

(Liebowitz, 1983). In one of these studies, rats had tiny electrodes implanted into their brains through which they were able to administer a small electric jolt to their own limbic system by pressing on a lever. Scientists soon observed those rats pressing the lever hundreds of times per hour! Subsequent research on human participants revealed similar effects and, believe it or not, humans pressed the lever even more frequently than did the rats (Heath, 1972)! In addition, subjective reports from human patients indicate that electrical stimulation of the limbic system is highly pleasurable and can sometimes generate orgasmic responses.

The role of the limbic system in sexual arousal has been further established in recent years by functional magnetic resonance imaging (fMRI). Through fMRI scanning, we can see what areas of the brain "light up" (i.e., become neurologically active) when we experience arousal. For example, in studies of individuals exposed to erotic films during an fMRI scan, male and female participants showed significant activation of the amygdala (Karama et al., 2002) and, at least for men, activation of the hypothalamus as well (Arnow et al., 2002). Other neuroimaging studies have reported similar results (e.g., Ferretti et al., 2005). Of all of the limbic structures, the hypothalamus appears to be one of the most important for normal sexual functioning, particularly in the males of most species. Destruction or chemical inactivation of certain portions of the hypothalamus (especially a region known as the medial preoptic area, or MPOA) results in a significant decrease in sexual behavior (Hurtazo, Paredes, & Agmo, 2008), whereas electrical stimulation to this same area generally increases such behavior (Rodriguez-Manzo, Pellicer, Larsson, & Fernandez-Guasti, 2000).

Beyond the limbic system, the **cerebral cortex** also plays an important role in sexual arousal. The cerebral cortex is the outer layer of the brain, and it is this region that controls our thoughts, memories, imagination, and use of language. Given that it controls such a large number of mental processes, it is plain to see that the cerebral cortex can be used to either facilitate or inhibit sexual arousal in a variety of ways. Among the many sexual functions of the cerebral cortex is sexual fantasy, a topic we will return to in chapter 9.

One other important way the brain influences sexual arousal is through the production of *neurotransmitters*, substances that transmit signals between nerve cells. Perhaps the two most potent neurotransmitters that affect sexual arousal are dopamine and serotonin. The presence of **dopamine** has the effect of enhancing sexual arousal and increasing sexual behavior. As some evidence of this, women who have taken drugs that reduce dopamine levels (e.g., certain antipsychotics) often report difficulties achieving orgasm (Shen & Sata, 1990). In contrast, women who have taken drugs that increase dopamine levels (e.g., the antidepressant bupropion) typically report more sexual arousal and greater ability to reach orgasm (Segraves, Clayton, Croft, Wolf, & Warnock, 2004).

The sexual effects of **serotonin** are the opposite of dopamine. The presence of serotonin tends to reduce sexual arousal and inhibit orgasm. This probably does not come as a surprise to anyone who has seen advertisements for Prozac or any other antidepressant in the class of *selective serotonin reuptake inhibitors* (SSRI). These ads frequently mention potential sexual side effects of taking SSRIs, such as low libido. Indeed, research has found that patients taking SSRIs typically report lower levels of arousal and delayed orgasm (Serretti & Chiesa, 2009). Thus, while keeping higher levels of serotonin in the brain may be good for one's mood, it can be bad for one's sex life. On an interesting side note, these inhibitory side effects of serotonin may be desirable in some patients, particularly for persons who typically reach orgasm too quickly (an issue we will return to in chapter 12).

The Senses

Another way the brain contributes to sexual arousal is by interpreting sensory input from our skin, eyes, nose, ears, and mouth. The way our brains interpret sensory information is complex and takes into account psychological and social factors, including prior learning experience and cultural values. As input comes in, the brain also releases different types of neurotransmitters that can either facilitate or inhibit arousal. Given all of the factors at play here, it should be easy to understand why a given stimulus may be perceived as sexual by some people but not by others.

We will begin by discussing touch, which is an important source of sexual stimulation for most people. However, as we discuss the remaining senses, you will see much wider variability in response and preference emerging.

Touch

Touch is usually an integral part of sexual arousal and pleasure, regardless of whether an individual is engaging in solo or partnered sexual activity. However, the type and nature of touch that is sexually pleasing can be quite different from one person to the next, due to biological, psychological, and sociocultural factors. Of course, most people find it arousing when one of their **primary erogenous zones** is touched. Primary erogenous zones are portions of the body where nerve endings are present in large quantities, such as the genitals, perineum, nipples, lips, and inner thigh. Type of touch is very important, though. Some people prefer lighter touch (e.g.,

Figure 4.2 Physical touch is perhaps the strongest sexual sense, although the type and nature of touch that is considered desirable varies across persons. ©Frenk And Danielle Kaufmann / 123RF.COM.

gentle kissing and stroking of the nipple), whereas others prefer to be more aggressively handled (e.g., having their nipples clamped and twisted). The key is for partners to discuss with each other what does and does not feel good. Do not leave it up to your partner to guess, because some people are poor guessers!

Sometimes, people enjoy having portions of the body other than their primary erogenous zones touched during sexual activity. These body parts are known as **secondary erogenous zones**, or regions of the body that have taken on sexual significance as a result of conditioning. For instance, if you were to have the back of your knee caressed and licked during sexual activity, this body part might eventually come to be its own erogenous zone. Secondary erogenous zones may take on heightened importance for persons with physical disabilities (e.g., spinal cord injuries that impair genital response). For such individuals, these erogenous zones can be one way of maintaining an active sex life.

Vision

Reflecting on the value that our society places on physical attractiveness and the immense popularity of sexually explicit films, magazines, and websites, it should come as no surprise that for many people, vision is almost as important as touch in generating sexual arousal. However, the types of visual stimuli that generate arousal vary across persons and cultures. Broadly speaking, cultures and societies shape individual preferences by dictating what is and is not sexually attractive (e.g., in the Western world, the popular media typically depicts the "ideal" woman as having an hourglass figure and the "ideal" man as being tall and muscular). Of course, those individual preferences are further refined as a result of our own learning and experience and, in some cases, people's preferences may barely resemble the cultural standard.

There is a widely held belief that men are more strongly aroused by visual stimuli than are women and, on the surface, research seems to support this idea. For example, when shown a variety of pornographic video clips, male participants consistently report experiencing more

Figure 4.3   Men have long been thought to be more visually stimulated than women, but recent research suggests that this may not be the case after all. Image Copyright Jiang Dao Hua, 2013. Used under license from Shutterstock.com.

sexual arousal than female participants on subjective self-reports (e.g., Koukounas & McCabe, 1997). However, when sexual arousal is assessed by physiological indicators (i.e., penile strain gauges and vaginal photoplethysmographs), this sex difference starts to disappear: both men and women show significant arousal in response to visual erotic stimuli. In fact, these physiological measures reveal that women actually show more arousal than men to certain kinds of sexual stimuli (Chivers, Rieger, Latty, & Bailey, 2004). For example, whereas heterosexual men show significant genital arousal only in response to porn featuring women in some way, heterosexual women show strong levels of genital arousal in response to all kinds of porn, regardless of whether it features lesbians, gay men, or heterosexual couples. Compared to men, women thus seem to be turned on by a wider range of visual stimuli, an indicator that they may have greater *erotic plasticity* than men (more on this in chapter 6).

You may be wondering what accounts for the disconnect between the subjective and the physiological reports of sexual arousal in women in response to visual stimuli. We cannot say for sure, but there is likely a cultural explanation here. As mentioned in the previous chapter, there is a sexual double standard in many modern cultures, in which women are evaluated more negatively than men for pursuing and enjoying sexual activity. It could be that social pressure either consciously or unconsciously leads women to report lower levels of sexual interest and arousal than men. An alternative possibility is that male sexual arousal (i.e., erection and pre-ejaculate) is more obvious or is easier to detect and interpret than female sexual arousal (i.e., clitoral blood flow and vaginal lubrication).

Smell

Our sense of smell can contribute to sexual arousal in two ways: consciously or unconsciously. Sometimes we breathe in a scent and consciously think "her perfume smells lovely," or "his feet reek like moldy cheese," and these thoughts either put us in or out of the mood. Other times, however, a scent can affect our brain and behavior in ways we do not realize.

Figure 4.4   Other people's scents can turn us off or on; however, we may not always consciously recognize when this is happening. ©Imagehit International Ltd/123RF.COM.

Conscious effects are determined by our prior learning experiences and cultural standards. For example, if you previously dated a man you found very sexy and who happened to wear Abercrombie and Fitch cologne every day, you might come to think of that scent as being very sexually pleasing and get turned on any time you catch a whiff of someone wearing that cologne in the future. Thus, the scents you have learned to associate with sex (a la classical conditioning processes) can become powerful triggers of future arousal. However, keep in mind that these need not be artificial scents – some people find natural body odors sexually pleasing, and this is where cultural values and standards come into play. In cultures that do not mask body scents, a person's own odors or the "smell of sex" may be considered the ultimate turn on. In societies that value covering up any natural bodily scents through deodorants, perfumes, mouthwashes, and soaps, those scents will be preferred and "natural" scents may be considered a turn off. However, there is a double standard when it comes to masking body scents, in that there is a huge market for "feminine hygiene products" designed to cleanse the female genitals, while similar products for men are not nearly as ubiquitous.

In terms of unconscious effects of smell, a growing amount of research suggests that **pheromones** affect humans. Pheromones are chemicals secreted by the body that play a role in sexual communication. Anyone who has ever been to a zoo knows that pheromones affect animals, because when the female of a given species is "in heat," all of the nearby males start going crazy. As scientific evidence of this, when male apes and monkeys are exposed to pheromones from the urine of females of their species, the males experience increases in testosterone and exhibit more frequent erections (Snowdon, Ziegler, Schultz-Darken, & Ferris, 2006). As you will see below, human pheromones seem to exist, but the effects do not appear to be quite as dramatic, perhaps because we have a less developed sense of smell than most other animal species.

The portion of the olfactory (i.e., smell) system that processes pheromones in animals is the **vomeronasal organ (VNO)**. We know this because in cases where the VNO has been removed or surgically damaged, sexual behaviors tend to drop off quickly, which further highlights the important role of smell in animal sexuality (Wysocki & Lepri, 1991). Research has found that humans also possess a VNO and that this structure is responsive to pheromones (Monti-Bloch, Jennings-White, & Berliner, 1998).The primary source of human pheromones are the apocrine (i.e., sweat) glands in the armpits and pubic region, although scientists are now able to manufacture synthetic versions of human pheromones in the lab, which some companies are bottling and selling.

What evidence do we have that pheromones affect human sexual behavior? The earliest support for this idea came from research by Martha McClintock (1971) who found that female college students who lived together in close quarters exhibited *menstrual synchrony*. That is, the women eventually started to get their periods around the same time, which was thought to stem from women's exposure to each other's pheromones. This was demonstrated more convincingly in a subsequent study in which female participants had the sweat of another woman regularly applied to their upper lip several times per week for four months. (The things people will do for science!) Over time, the women who received the sweat applications showed more menstrual synchrony than control subjects (Preti et al., 1986).

Even more convincing are two placebo-controlled studies in which men (Cutler, Friedmann, & McCoy, 1998) and women (McCoy & Pitino, 2002) were randomly assigned to wear either synthetic pheromones or a non-pheromone, placebo solution on a daily basis for several weeks. During this time period, participants regularly reported on their sexual activities. For both male and female participants, those who wore pheromones reported having more sex than those who wore the placebo.

Naturally, you might wonder whether these pheromone effects are specific to heterosexual individuals, or if they might also have effects in gays and lesbians. There is some fascinating research suggesting that people of all sexual orientations pick up on pheromones. For instance, in one study, participants were asked to rate the pleasantness of armpit sweat collected from heterosexual and homosexual men and women (Martins et al., 2005). Without knowing the source of the odors, heterosexual men and women least preferred the odors of gay men, while gay men least preferred the odors of heterosexual men. Pheromones may thus represent a subtle way of helping us to identify compatible sexual partners.

It is important to emphasize that the effects of pheromones on sexual behavior are often completely unconscious (McClintock, 2000). That is, we do not have to consciously perceive a scent in order for it to change our behavior, which means that pheromones may be driving our sexuality more than we possibly know. For more information on the potential sexual effects of pheromones, see the Digging Deeper 4.1 box.

On a side note, what happens when someone's sense of smell is not working? Research on isolated congenital anosmia (ICA), a condition in which a person lacks a sense of smell from the time of birth, has revealed that men with ICA report fewer sexual partners as adults than men with a functional sense of smell (Croy, Bojanowski, & Hummel, 2013). To the extent that ICA prevents men from picking up on pheromones, that could explain the lower number of partners; however, this effect may also be attributable to the fact that the lack of a sense of smell may make people feel more socially insecure because they are unable to determine if they have unpleasant body odor or bad breath.

Digging Deeper 4.1   Do Birth Control Pills Make Exotic Dancers Less Appealing To Men?

Most women know that being on "the pill" may have sexual side effects, such as decreased libido and reduced sexual enjoyment. However, the sexual side effects of oral contraceptives do not stop there. In fact, being on the pill can potentially impact the amount of money a woman can make from a night of exotic dancing!

In a titillating study (pun intended) of professional female lap dancers, researchers found that *naturally cycling women* (i.e., women who were not taking a hormonal contraceptive) experienced an increase in tips when they were ovulating; women on the pill did not show a similar peak in their earnings at any time of the month (Miller, Tybur, & Jordan, 2007). This difference translated to real money too – naturally cycling women earned an average of just over $354 per shift while ovulating, compared to a more modest $200 per shift for women on the pill.

Figure 4.5   Being on the pill can potentially impact the amount of money a woman can make from exotic dancing. ©Stanislav Perov/123RF.COM.

However, we cannot definitively say why some of these women made more money than others. Did ovulating lap dancers alter their behavior in ways that made them more attractive and tip-worthy? Or were their male customers able to detect when the dancers were ovulating, and this made them more willing to part with their cash? It is probably a bit of both. For instance, research shows that ovulating women tend to dress sexier and show more skin (Haselton, Mortezaie, Pillsworth, Bleske-Rechek, & Frederick, 2007). So, perhaps the ovulating dancers chose to wear more sensual or revealing outfits (or no outfits at all!). The answer may also be a function of pheromones. Research shows that men experience a bigger increase in testosterone levels after sniffing shirts worn by ovulating women than after sniffing shirts worn by nonovulating women (Miller & Maner, 2010), suggesting that men may subconsciously pick up on female ovulation through their noses. Thus, the amount that men tip an exotic dancer may not only depend upon her looks, but how she smells.

Either way, whatever it is that leads ovulating dancers to receive bigger tips appears to be wiped out when women are on the pill.

Note: Reprinted with permission from *Science of Relationships* (www.scienceofrelationships.com).

Hearing

The role of sound in sexual arousal is perhaps the most variable of all of the senses. Many people like to hear their partners moan and groan, others enjoy "dirty talk" or listening to music, and some prefer no sound at all when they are between the sheets (or where ever it is that they like to have sex). These individual preferences for sound are often established through learning (e.g., if a partner repeatedly talks dirty to you when you are aroused, or if you watch porn with a lot of raunchy language while masturbating, you may come to prefer this kind of sound during future sexual activity).

Making sounds during sex can be helpful for letting your partner know what does and does not feel good. Thus, you can use it to enhance your own sexual experience. However, sounds can also be used to facilitate your partner's sexual response. In fact, research has found that, among heterosexual couples, men perceive the sounds that women make during sex (known scientifically as **female copulatory vocalizations**) to be very sexually arousing and these noises help to facilitate men's orgasms (Levin, 2006). Women seem to know this because they consciously report vocalizing during sex in order to increase a male partner's enjoyment and help him climax faster (Brewer & Hendrie, 2011).

On an interesting side note, researchers have found that the females of most species are much more vocal than the males during sexual activity (Hamilton & Arrowood, 1978). We do not know why females make more noise, but some scientists have suggested that this finding is evidence of a nonmonogamous approach to mating among both humans and primates, whereby the female "announces" her sexual availability to other potential suitors (Ryan & Jetha, 2010).

Taste

Taste can affect sexual arousal, although its effects can be somewhat hard to separate from those of smell because these two senses are highly intertwined. For example, you have probably found that food does not have nearly as much flavor when you have a stuffy nose, because your sense of smell is diminished. As with smell and hearing, taste can be very specific to the individual in terms

Figure 4.6   Why do female humans and animals vocalize more during sexual activity than their male counterparts? ©Yuri Arcurs/123RF.COM.

of what is sexually pleasing. For example, some people enjoy the taste of natural bodily secretions (e.g., semen, vaginal fluids), whereas others find them to be a turn off. In fact, some people insist on covering up any natural bodily tastes through the use of flavored lubricants, mouthwashes, and mints. Taste can also contribute to arousal to the extent that people incorporate food with sex. If you try this, just be careful not to condition yourself to experience arousal every time you eat!

Hormones

In addition to the brain and sensory processes, several hormones play an important role in sexual arousal. In particular, we will consider the effects of testosterone and oxytocin. Although estrogen is a sex hormone that plays some role in female sexual functioning (e.g., estrogen helps maintain the thickness of the vaginal walls and is important for vaginal lubrication), most research to date has failed to establish a consistent effect of this hormone on male or female sexual arousal and, thus, it is not discussed further in this chapter.

Testosterone

Testosterone is a steroid hormone secreted by both the gonads and the adrenal glands. Many people think of testosterone as a "male" sex hormone; however, this could not be further from the truth. Both men and women produce testosterone, and it has a number of important effects in each sex. The majority of the testosterone is produced in the testes and ovaries, with a much smaller amount released by the adrenal glands. Although men produce more testosterone than women, women do not need the same amount as men for normal functioning because women's bodies are more sensitive to it (Bancroft, 2002).

As we will discuss in the next chapter, the presence or absence of testosterone prenatally affects internal and external development of the genital structures. In addition, prenatal exposure has important effects on how the brain is organized. Testosterone is thus vital during certain critical periods in order for typical sexual development to proceed. When testosterone levels are unusually high or low during these critical periods, the result can be variations in gender identity, sexual orientation, and degree of psychological masculinity and femininity. We will explore these effects in more detail in chapters 5 and 6.

Our primary concern in this chapter is with the effects of circulating levels of testosterone on people's sexual behaviors in adolescence and adulthood (i.e., testosterone's *activating effects*). Testosterone has clear effects on men's levels of sexual desire and their sexual behaviors. For example, men who have had their testes (i.e., their primary source of testosterone) removed through **castration** (known in medical terms as *orchidectomy*) typically experience a loss of libido and have a more difficult time achieving erections (e.g., Shabsigh, 1997). Not all castrated men experience these effects, though; at least a few of them retain some degree of sexual interest and behavior afterward. Such findings indicate that while testosterone production by the testes has important sexual effects in most men, it is not the sole factor influencing sexual behavior.

Additional evidence for the important role of testosterone in male sexual arousal comes from studies of men with **hypogonadism**, a physical condition in which testosterone production is diminished. This may occur as a result of a specific disease process, or as a natural result of aging (although there is no true "male menopause," men usually experience a gradual decrease in the production of sex hormones with age). Regardless of the reason, men with lower levels of testosterone typically have less sexual desire (Hintikka et al., 2009). These effects can be reversed through *testosterone replacement therapy*, in which supplementary testosterone is administered (Wang et al., 1996). This has become an increasingly common treatment for low libido in both men and women, although the potential long-term health implications and side effects are not well-understood yet. Incidentally, low testosterone is linked to depression in middle-aged men, but it is not clear whether

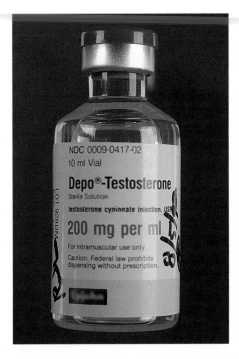

Figure 4.7   Testosterone replacement is sometimes used as a treatment for low libido in both men and women. Source: Public domain image, via Wikimedia Commons.

there is a direct effect of low testosterone on mood, or whether the decrease in sexual functioning is the cause of depression in such cases (Hintikka et al., 2009).

Testosterone is also related to sexual desire in women. For instance, women who have their ovaries (i.e., their primary source of testosterone) removed through an **oophorectomy** frequently experience low libido and difficulties becoming sexually aroused (McPherson et al., 2005). However, testosterone replacement therapy reverses these effects, increasing both sexual desire and activity (Simon et al., 2005). Likewise, older women who have gone through menopause naturally appear able to restore lost sexual desire through supplementary testosterone (Spark, 2002). In short, a certain amount of testosterone is vital for achieving sexual desire in both men and women; however, the necessary amount varies considerably from person to person.

Physical and Chemical Castration as Treatments for Sex Offenders
Because testosterone plays such an important role in generating sexual arousal and behavior, many legal systems around the world have contemplated instituting treatments that would reduce testosterone levels in convicted sex offenders with the hope of decreasing the likelihood of convicts committing future crimes. Physical castration is obviously a drastic and controversial step, and public opinion about it is very polarized. Some people see castration as cruel and unusual, while others think it is a fitting punishment for sex crimes. Physical castration for sex offenders is relatively rare these days and is generally only performed on a voluntary basis. For example, in Germany, the Czech Republic, and certain parts of the United States, convicted sex offenders can voluntarily seek castration as a means of bargaining for reduced sentences (BBC News Europe, 2012; Sealey, 2012).

Lately, the trend has been to offer chemical castration instead of or as an alternative to physical castration. **Chemical castration** involves administering anti-androgen drugs that block the production of testosterone. One of the most commonly used drugs of this nature is Depo-Provera. While some countries offer chemical castration on a voluntary basis (e.g., the United States and several European nations), others, such as South Korea (Woo-young, 2011), have enacted laws that force convicted sex offenders to take these drugs. Chemical castration is controversial, with some people questioning whether it is a violation of human rights and others worried about its effectiveness, because both physical and chemical castration do not always have predictable results when it comes to sexual behavior. As a result, castration should not necessarily be the only treatment considered for sex offenders. We will consider other options in chapter 13.

Oxytocin
Oxytocin is a neuropeptide hormone manufactured in the brain that has a wide range of effects on human sexual behavior. Perhaps its best known function is to assist in the release of milk during breastfeeding. However, oxytocin is increasingly being recognized as playing a vital role in developing bonds between romantic and sexual partners because it is released during physical intimacy (we will return to this topic in chapter 7 when we discuss sexual attraction). For this reason, oxytocin is sometimes referred to in the popular media as the "love hormone" or "cuddle drug."

In addition to helping generate bonds and attraction, oxytocin plays at least some role in sexual arousal. For example, research on male rats has found that oxytocin injections produce erections (Gimpl & Fahrenholz, 2001). Likewise, a few recent case studies of humans have found that oxytocin administered via a nasal spray produced unexpected increases in sexual desire and activity. In one study, a woman was given oxytocin to assist in breastfeeding (Anderson-Hunt & Dennerstein,

Figure 4.8   Oxytocin (often referred to as the "cuddle drug") facilitates sexual and romantic bonding, but it may also play a role in generating sexual arousal. Image Copyright sam100, 2013. Used under license from Shutterstock.com.

1994), and in another study, a man with Asperger's syndrome (a former DSM diagnosis in which social interaction abilities are impaired) was given oxytocin to improve his social functioning (MacDonald & Feifel, 2012). In both cases, the changes in sexuality were dramatic. However, these sexual effects disappeared once the hormone treatments stopped. Although these results are far from conclusive (recall the limitations of case studies discussed in chapter 2) and more research on this topic is needed, these findings suggest that oxytocin is involved in sexual arousal and that it could potentially be used as a treatment for individuals who experience low libido.

Substances

One other set of factors that affects sexual arousal are the substances that we put into our bodies (e.g., food, drinks, drugs). Substances vary in terms of whether they have inhibiting or facilitating sexual effects. Some substances are **aphrodisiacs**, which increase sexual desire and behavior, while others are **anaphrodisiacs**, which reduce sexual arousal and activity. Substances also very in terms of whether their effects are mediated by physiology or psychology. In other words, some substances have a direct effect on arousal by affecting hormone and neurotransmitter levels, while other substances only change people's behavior because of the **placebo effect**. Placebo effects occur when people strongly believe that something they are taking will have an effect on them, even if the substance or treatment is biologically inert. When the belief is strong enough, people often end up showing the expected change in behavior. For example, research has found that when depressed patients take a sugar pill that they believe is an actual medication designed to improve their mood, their symptoms improve 75% as much as people who take genuine antidepressant medication (Kirsch & Sapirstein, 1998)! Placebo effects are rampant when it comes to aphrodisiacs because people are often highly motivated to believe they can restore lost desire or enhance their sexual potency by taking a substance or changing their diet.

Figure 4.9   Oysters are just one of many foods that have been thought to be an aphrodisiac. However, any sexual effects of such foods are likely a result of faith and the power of suggestion. ©Fedor Kondratenko/123RF.COM.

Aphrodisiacs

For centuries, people have believed that various foods possess aphrodisiac qualities. The common theme uniting the most popular foods of this nature is that they bear a striking resemblance to the penis. You can test this out by doing a quick online search for "aphrodisiacs." You will soon be able to compile a long list of food products with reported sexual effects that includes bananas, cucumbers, carrots, and asparagus. Also featuring prominently will be foods that resemble the vulva, such as oysters, open figs, and peaches.

Beyond this, animal horns and penises are highly sought after in some Asian cultures because they are thought to enhance sexual potency and virility if consumed (Harding, 2006). While horns are usually ground up or powdered, penises can be served in a variety of ways. You can have a penis pickled, in a soup, or even served as fondue (I kid you not!). One of the rarest delicacies of this nature is tiger penis. Tiger parts have long been popular in traditional Chinese medicine and are thought to have medicinal benefits. Although tigers are an endangered species, and trading their parts is illegal in many parts of the world, they are still pursued because of their supposed health benefits, and people will pay exorbitant sums to get them. In fact, some restaurants in China charge as much as $6,000 for a tiger penis dinner (Harding, 2006)!

Do any of these foods actually enhance sexual desire? Although many people swear by them, we do not have scientific evidence that consumption of these foods in typical quantities generates physiological arousal effects. Thus, any reported sexual influences of such foods are likely attributable to the placebo effect.

Table 4.1 Sexual Effects of Several Alleged Aphrodisiacs	
Substance	*Sexual effects*
Alcohol	Through both a reduction in inhibitions and expectancy effects, alcohol can be a mild aphrodisiac in small doses. In larger quantities, alcohol has a depressant effect on arousal and orgasm in men and women.
Ecstasy (MDMA)	Users report enhanced desire and more intense orgasms, but also erectile difficulties and delays in achieving orgasm.
Marijuana	About half of users report increased libido and greater sexual pleasure; the other half do not.
Poppers (amyl nitrate)	Users who inhale poppers report more intense orgasms, but some men experience temporary erectile difficulties.
Viagra	Creates a capacity for erection in men. Linked to the release of oxytocin in male rats; unknown if similar hormonal effects occur in humans.

Beyond food, alcohol and drugs have often been considered aphrodisiacs as well. Some of these substances can affect sexual arousal physiologically and psychologically; however, understanding the sexual effects of drugs is complicated because different drugs have different effects, and the amount of the drug consumed matters greatly (for a summary of the sexual effects of various drugs, see Table 4.1). We will begin with alcohol, which is indeed an aphrodisiac, but only when it is consumed in small quantities. Alcohol not only reduces our inhibitions, but it can also create expectancy effects, whereby we come to believe that consuming alcohol will put us "in the mood" or make us feel more sexual (Cooper, 2010). If you have ever taken a course in social psychology, you can think of expectancy effects as a *self-fulfilling prophecy* (i.e., if we believe that some outcome is likely, we will work consciously and unconsciously to make it a reality). However, when alcohol is consumed in very large quantities it has a depressing effect on sexual arousal and makes it more difficult for both men and women to achieve orgasm. Chronic alcohol abuse can also contribute to sexual dysfunction. We will explore the sexual effects of alcohol use in more detail later in this book when we discuss sexual difficulties (chapter 12) and sexually transmitted infections (chapter 11).

Aside from alcohol, people sometimes turn to other drugs (some legal and others illegal) to enhance their sexual experience, including Ecstasy, "poppers," marijuana, and Viagra. First, Ecstasy (the popular name of methylenedioxymethamphetamine or MDMA): this is a popular club drug that seems to enhance sexual desire and produce more intense orgasms in recreational users (Zemishlany, Aizenberg, & Weizman, 2001). At the same time, however, it is linked to reports of erectile difficulties in a large number of men and often delays male and female orgasm. Second, "poppers" (amyl nitrate): this is an inhalant that users have reported as intensifying the experience of orgasm (Everett, 1972). "Poppers" have been used in the club scene for decades, particularly by people who practice anal sex (because it supposedly enhances pleasure from this activity). Common side effects for users include headaches, nausea, and temporary loss of erection (Wood, 1983). Third, marijuana: this is a widely used drug that does not have consistent sexual effects on those who consume it. For example, in one study of recreational marijuana users in Canada, about half of the participants reported that marijuana increased libido and enhanced sexual pleasure, while the other half reported no such effects (Osborne & Fogel, 2008). In other research, a majority of men reported that marijuana enhanced their sexual stamina (Shamloul & Bella, 2011); however, it is unclear whether the drug had that effect or if it simply affected men's perception of time.

We do not fully understand why any of these drugs have the sexual effects they do, but at least part of the reason is likely attributable to neurochemical changes (indeed, many of these drugs have been linked to increased dopamine release) and, just as with alcohol, expectancy effects probably play a role. As you can see from this discussion, there appear to be at least some aphrodisiac-like properties of many recreational drugs, but the effects are not necessarily consistent across persons and are often counterbalanced by negative effects on sexual response.

One other drug we should mention here is the erectile dysfunction medication Viagra, which is available by prescription only. A growing number of men are taking Viagra or one of its sister medications (e.g., Cialis, Levitra) recreationally because they believe it will increase their sexual pleasure. The primary effect of the drug (which we will discuss in more detail in chapter 12) is to create the capacity for an erection. Contrary to popular belief, Viagra does not give men an automatic erection – sexual stimulation is still required. Traditionally, the medical community has not viewed Viagra as an aphrodisiac because there was no evidence that it increased sexual desire. However, recent research has found that Viagra stimulates the release of oxytocin in the brains of male rats (Zhang, Klyachko, & Jackson, 2007). If subsequent research confirms that Viagra leads to the release of more oxytocin in humans, we may one day see it discussed as an aphrodisiac.

Anaphrodisiacs

In recent years, some scientists have shifted their focus from identifying substances that increase sexual desire to those that curb it. Why would anyone want a lower sex drive? There is medical and political interest in uncovering safe and effective anaphrodisiacs that could potentially be used to stop rapists and other sex offenders from committing future crimes, but also to help reduce sexual desire in people with *hypersexuality* (i.e., "excessive" sexual behavior). Right now, the most promising anaphrodisiacs available for dealing with such issues are Depo-Provera and SSRIs. Drugs like these can successfully lower sexual desire by reducing levels of testosterone (Depo-Provera) or enhancing the amount of serotonin in the brain (SSRIs).

The Sexual Response Cycle

Now that you have an understanding of the factors that affect sexual arousal, let us turn to the topic of sexual response and consider the internal and external bodily processes that occur once sexual arousal begins.

The Masters and Johnson Model

The most widely known and discussed model of human sexual response was developed by Masters and Johnson (1966). As the basis for their model, they observed more than 10,000 complete sexual cycles of men and women and found that sexual arousal and response followed a predictable pattern. There are certainly many individual differences when it comes to sex and sexuality, but with respect to patterns of physical responding, human beings are more similar than you might expect.

Masters and Johnson specified four phases in their model: *excitement*, *plateau*, *orgasm*, and *resolution*. In reality, it may be hard to pinpoint exactly when one phase ends and another begins, so you should not think of these as four truly separate phases – rather, these phases are labeled to help simplify and explain the numerous processes that occur in the body during sexual activity. Please keep in mind that although many of Masters and Johnson's observations have held up over time, some have not, which means that their model is not universally accepted. After detailing this model, we will address its limitations and consider a few alternative models.

Excitement

The **excitement** phase marks the start of sexual arousal and is characterized by two physiological processes that begin here and are carried through the remaining phases. First, **vasocongestion** refers to an increase in blood flow to bodily tissues (in this case, the genital tissues). The most obvious physical manifestation of this in men is erection of the penis, which occurs as the cavernous and spongy bodies fill with blood. In women, the clitoris, labia, and uterus become engorged and increase in size. Across the sexes, these physical changes ebb and flow throughout the excitement phase (e.g., a man's penis may vacillate between partially and fully erect) depending upon the level of stimulation. Second, **myotonia** refers to the voluntary and involuntary tensing and contracting of muscles both in the genital region and throughout the rest of the body.

Other physical changes that occur during excitement include increases in heart and breathing rate, as well as the *sex flush*, the increasingly reddish appearance of the chest and torso during arousal. The sex flush does not occur in everyone and often appears more prominently in women than it does in men. Additional changes that men experience include a tightening of the scrotal skin and elevation of the testes closer to the penis. In women, the vagina expands in length and the vaginal walls begin to lubricate.

The trigger for sexual excitement and the length of this phase varies widely across persons and situations, lasting from a few moments to a few hours. In some cases, excitement may be preceded by physical stimulation from the self (e.g., masturbation) or from a partner (e.g., kissing). Alternatively, excitement may be the result of a visual stimulus (e.g., pornography), a substance (e.g., an aphrodisiac), or a cognitive process (e.g., sexual fantasy). Excitement is thus a biopsychosocial event.

Plateau

As excitement continues, an individual enters the **plateau** phase, during which sexual tensions continue to mount. The plateau phase is really an extension of the excitement phase, and is characterized by vasocongestion and myotonia becoming more pronounced. Several sexual scientists have argued that discussing excitement and plateau as two separate events is unnecessary (e.g., Levin & Riley, 2007), which is why some textbook authors combine their descriptions of these phases.

In men, the major bodily changes that occur during this stage include a complete erection, fully engorged and elevated testes, and the secretion of pre-ejaculate by the Cowper's gland. In women, the major changes include swelling of the nipples and areola, complete expansion and lengthening of the vagina, retraction of the clitoris into the body, and the development of the **orgasmic platform**, which refers to the increased swelling of the outer third of the vagina. In addition, both men and women experience continued increases in heart and breathing rates and a deepening of the sex flush. Overall, the plateau phase can last anywhere from a few seconds to a few minutes depending upon the individual and the situation. However, prolonging this phase (known colloquially as "edging") may enhance the pleasure of a subsequent orgasm.

Orgasm

If appropriate sexual stimulation continues, an individual may experience **orgasm**, during which the muscles around the genitals make a series of brief, rhythmic contractions. In men, orgasm usually (although not always) coincides with ejaculation, which occurs when the accumulated secretions of the vas deferens, seminal vesicles, and prostate gland are released into the urethra and expelled from the body. In women, the orgasmic platform and uterus contract several times, and this may or may not be accompanied by an expulsion of fluid (as discussed in chapter 3). Bodily changes during orgasm are not limited to the genitals, though. Other changes that may occur include increases in heart rate and breathing rate, as well as various forms of myotonia, including facial grimaces (i.e., the "O" face) and contractions of muscles in other parts of the body (e.g., the toes or fingers may curl). For men, orgasm pretty consistently follows the plateau phase. In fact, it is rare for men *not* to experience orgasm during sexual activity. In comparison, many women do not regularly reach climax, especially when vaginal intercourse is the only form of stimulation (Fugl-Meyer, Oberg, Lundberg, & Lewin, 2006).

When orgasm occurs, it is quite brief, lasting just a few seconds in most cases. Male and female orgasms are similar in length, although there is significant variability both within and between persons, with orgasms varying in intensity, number of contractions, and duration. Even though orgasms are quite brief, those few seconds are usually extremely pleasurable to both men and women. In fact, research suggests that the psychological experience of orgasm is virtually identical across the sexes. Several studies have been conducted in which participants have been asked to guess whether written descriptions of what an orgasm feels like were provided by men or by women (Vance & Wagner, 1976; Wiest, 1977). Regardless of whether the judges in these studies were college students or clinical psychologists, participants were unable to reliably determine which descriptions were written by which sex, indicating that orgasms appear to be processed by the brain similarly among men and women.

Theories of orgasm.   It should be pretty obvious why men experience orgasm. By typically co-occurring with ejaculation and the release of semen, orgasm helps to make sexual reproduction become possible. Thus, the male orgasm has a vital biological function. What about the female orgasm? It is not necessary for a woman to climax in order to get pregnant, so what purpose does the female orgasm serve? This question has been a topic of debate among sexual scientists for decades.

The earliest theories of female orgasm suggested that it served as a "sperm retention mechanism." The thought is that because some amount of sperm is naturally ejected from the vagina after intercourse, orgasm might serve the purpose of retaining as much sperm as possible. There are two main arguments for how this might occur. One is that orgasm increases the likelihood that a woman will fall asleep after sex, and as a result of lying down, sperm loss will be minimized (Levin, 1981). The other main argument is that the female orgasm induces a "blow–suck" mechanism in which the uterine contractions draw sperm further inside the reproductive tract (Fox, Wolff, & Baker, 1970). (By the way, "blow–suck" is a technical term used in an actual research paper, so you can stop snickering!)

Some research has found support for the sperm retention idea. For example, in one study, researchers asked a sample of women to collect "flowback" (i.e., ejaculate that seeps out after sex), which was then analyzed by the researchers for sperm content (Baker & Bellis, 1993). They found that when women experienced orgasm just before or after her male partner, her flowback contained less sperm than when women did not orgasm at all or had an orgasm well before their partner. Studies like this, although admirable for their creativity, are fraught with some important problems. For instance, how do we know that women collected all of their flowback and did it consistently? We also have no idea how much sperm was initially released in each ejaculation to draw firm conclusions about how much sperm was retained.

The sperm retention evidence is thus not entirely convincing. In addition, this perspective has been criticized on the grounds that if the female orgasm is so adaptive for reproduction, why does it take women so much longer to climax than men, and why do so few women regularly achieve orgasm during vaginal penetration alone? Another evolutionary theory that attempts to account for the fact that the female orgasm does not happen consistently is the *mate-choice hypothesis*, which argues that the female orgasm is only likely to occur with those men who are the most genetically fit, or who represent the best long-term prospects (Puts, Dawood, & Welling, 2012). The theory is that by reserving orgasm only for the highest-quality mates, orgasm then becomes a reinforcing variable that encourages continued copulation with those partners, thereby promoting reproductive success. This might help to explain the fact that women in long-term relationships report having far more orgasms than single women (see chapter 8). Perhaps women are more likely to persist in relationships with those partners who give them the most orgasms.

One alternative to these evolutionary theories suggests that women's climaxes may not serve any biological purpose and may instead be a byproduct of the fact that the male orgasm is so heavily favored by our biology (Lloyd, 2005). To understand this idea, consider that everyone looks the same when they are initially developing in the womb. During the first two months of development, our genital structures are undifferentiated and can potentially develop toward the male or female form depending upon the hormones we are exposed to (see chapter 5). Because everyone's genitals develop from the same tissues and because nerve structures are laid out in such a way as to ensure orgasm if a male develops, the female orgasm may simply by a byproduct of that, much like the male nipple is a byproduct of the fact that women require nipples for breastfeeding. Proponents of this theory thus argue that the female orgasm is nothing but a "fantastic bonus" for women.

Sex differences in orgasm.   Aside from their theorized purpose, male and female orgasms differ in a number of other ways. First, men are more likely to achieve orgasm than women, especially during vaginal intercourse. Second, some researchers have suggested that whereas men seem to have just one type of orgasm, women's orgasms vary considerably in terms of bodily location, intensity, and whether there is an emotional aspect to it (e.g., Hite, 1976). For example, as discussed in chapter 3, some women achieve orgasm during vaginal insertion, while others require clitoral or G-spot stimulation, and yet others require nipple stimulation. Moreover, researchers have found that women have both "good sex" and "not-as-good-sex" orgasms, which have very different physical and psychological components (King, Belsky, Mah, & Binik, 2011).

Third, women are often able to achieve multiple orgasms (i.e., having two or more orgasms in rapid succession), while this ability has rarely been documented among men. For instance, a study of over 800 female college graduates found that approximately 43% reported having had multiple orgasms (Darling, Davidson, & Jennings, 1991). The reason women seem more capable of this is likely attributable to the fact that men usually experience a **refractory period** after orgasm, whereas women typically do not. The refractory period is a span of time after climax during which no additional orgasms are possible, regardless of whether sexual stimulation continues. We do not know why the refractory period usually occurs in men, but it is thought to have its basis in neurological and hormonal changes that occur in the body following orgasm, particularly release of the hormone *prolactin* (Kruger et al., 2003). The length of this period can last anywhere from a few minutes to a few days, depending upon a range of factors such as age and sexual desire. Although women are usually biologically capable of achieving additional orgasms with continued stimulation, some may be unaware of this or may not desire it.

One other way that male and female orgasms differ is that women are more likely to fake orgasms than are men. Studies have found that between one-half and two-thirds of women have "faked it" at one time or another (Wiederman, 1997), while the percentage of men who admit having done so is much lower (Muehlenhard & Shippee, 2010). Why do women fake orgasms so frequently? Women report a variety of reasons, with some research suggesting that at least some women fake orgasms as part of a "mate retention strategy" to keep their partners from cheating (Kaighobadi, Shackelford, & Weekes-Shackelford, 2012). In this research, the women who were the most likely to fake orgasms were also the most likely to fear that their partners would be sexually unfaithful. Could faking orgasms really help keep your partner around? Theoretically, it is possible. As previously discussed, men tend to find women's moaning and groaning sexually exciting and this may even enhance men's own orgasms (Levin, 2006). Thus, if a man does not know he is being deceived and his pleasure and excitement is enhanced by his partner's false finishes, faking may indeed reduce the likelihood that he will stray. To learn more about faking orgasms and to reflect on your own views on this issue, see the Your Sexuality 4.1 box.

Your Sexuality 4.1   Faking Orgasms: Who Benefits More From a False Finish?

According to Meg Ryan's character in *When Harry Met Sally*, "Most women at one time or another have faked it." By "it" she was referring to the seemingly elusive female orgasm. And she was right – studies consistently show that most women have faked a climax at some point (Wiederman, 1997). What may surprise you is that men fake orgasms at least some of the time too. In fact, one study found that one in four male college students admitted pretending to orgasm at least once (Muehlenhard & Shippee, 2010). It makes sense that men fake it less often than women, given that men are much more likely to reach orgasm in the first place and because men produce more physical "evidence" when it happens, making it harder to fool a sexual partner.

So why would someone pretend to climax? People report a variety of reasons for faking it, from the understandable (e.g., lack of sexual experience) to the unfortunate (e.g., lack of attraction to one's partner). However, when it comes to discussing motivations for faking, it is important to recognize that men and women are similar in some ways, but very different in others.

For instance, the sexes are equally likely to report having had a false finish because they felt an actual orgasm was unlikely to happen (e.g., they were overly intoxicated or it was just taking too long). In comparison, men are more inclined to say they faked it because they just wanted sex to end (e.g., they were tired), whereas women are more inclined to say they did so because they wanted to improve a partner's self-esteem or avoid hurt feelings.

To sum it up, both men and women fake it, but women do it more often and frequently see it as a way to protect their partners from getting hurt. When men fake it, they are more likely to see it as a way to exit an undesirable or uncomfortable situation. Thus, no matter who fakes it, the resulting "show" would appear to benefit men (or their egos) more than it does women.

What do you think about fake orgasms? Have you ever or would you ever "fake it?" Do you think faking can potentially be a good thing in some cases, or would honest communication always be preferable? If one of your partners had faked an orgasm with you, would you want to know?

Note: Reprinted with permission from *Science of Relationships* (www.scienceofrelationships.com).

The aforementioned differences in likelihood of orgasm and ability to achieve multiple orgasms have the effect of generating substantial variation in how the typical male and female sexual response cycle plays out. Whereas men's responses tend to follow the sequential pattern of excitement, plateau, orgasm, and resolution, women's responses have the potential to be far more variable. Table 4.2 provides an overview of some of the different patterns that may emerge in women's sexual response.

Resolution

The last phase of the sexual response cycle is **resolution**, which occurs once all stimulation stops. Resolution involves the return of the genitals to their nonaroused state (e.g., the penis becomes flaccid again, the orgasmic platform disappears, heart rate and breathing rate slow). Resolution can follow any of the previous phases (i.e., you do not necessarily have to achieve orgasm to enter resolution). The length of this phase can take anywhere from a few minutes to a few hours, but it typically occurs more quickly in older adults than it does in younger persons (Nusbaum, Lenahan, & Sadovsky, 2005). Behaviors during the resolution phase vary. Some people relax or sleep, some express intimacy, and others may head out of the bedroom to work or walk the dog. Contrary to popular belief, there is no scientific evidence to support the stereotype that men typically fall asleep immediately after sex while women stay awake wanting to cuddle. In fact, research finds that men and women are equally likely to report being the first one to fall asleep after sex (Kruger & Hughes, 2011)!

Psychological Models of Sexual Response

As previously noted, the Masters and Johnson model of sexual response is not universally accepted. One of the most common criticisms of it is that it is purely biological, giving no consideration to the psychological aspects of sexual arousal and response. For example, how does sexual desire factor into this equation? In this section, we will consider two theories that have attempted to incorporate psychology into the Masters and Johnson approach.

The Triphasic Model of Sexual Response

Noted sex therapist and author Helen Singer Kaplan (1974) introduced a three-stage model of sexual response that streamlined the Masters and Johnson model, while adding a psychological component. Kaplan also reconfigured the model so as to make it more applicable to the treatment of sexual disorders.

The first stage in Kaplan's model is *sexual desire*. Kaplan reasoned that sexual response is not likely to occur unless someone wants to have sex – in other words, something needs to precede excitement. Sexual desire is the most novel part of Kaplan's theory because it is psychological in nature. Desire is a product of many psychological factors, including emotions, stress, prior learning experiences, body image, and so forth. Of course, biological factors (e.g., hormones) play a role in desire as well, but psychology has at least as large of an effect on the drive to pursue sexual activity.

Following desire is *excitement*. In this phase of the model, Kaplan simply combined the excitement and plateau phases of the Masters and Johnson model because she saw little to distinguish between them, especially from the perspective of treating sexual problems. The final phase of this model is *orgasm*. Kaplan's discussion of sexual response stopped here because people rarely experience problems during the resolution phase, which makes it of little interest to sex therapists.

Table 4.2 Potential Variations in Female Sexual Response

Variation	Sexual response pattern						
Four-Phase Pattern (Typical Male Pattern)	Excitement	Plateau	Orgasm	Resolution			
Prolonged Plateau, No Orgasm	Excitement	Plateau	Resolution				
Multiple Orgasm (Variation 1)	Excitement	Plateau	Orgasm	Resolution to Plateau	Orgasm	Final Resolution	
Multiple Orgasm (Variation 2)	Excitement	Plateau	Orgasm	Resolution to Plateau	Orgasm	Resolution to Plateau	Orgasm	Final Resolution

Note: In the multiple orgasm variations, additional orgasm are achieved most quickly when the resolution phase only lasts long enough to return arousal back to plateau levels. If arousal dips back to excitement levels, producing additional orgasms will require greater stimulation.

Kaplan's view was that sexual problems could occur at any stage of the model and that problems in one stage do not necessarily translate to problems in other stages. For example, although one might have *hypoactive sexual desire disorder* (i.e., low levels of sexual desire), one may still be able to have a physical sexual response. Identifying the stage at which the problem occurs is necessary for understanding and treating cases of sexual dysfunction because different parts of the brain and body are involved at each stage.

Although Kaplan's model has been a popular alternative to the Masters and Johnson approach, it is not without its detractors. Perhaps its most controversial aspect is the emphasis on sexual desire. Even in someone who is free of sexual dysfunction, desire is not a necessary precursor for sexual response (e.g., desire may develop after sexual activity has begun).

The Erotic Stimulus Pathway Theory

Building upon the work of both Masters and Johnson and Kaplan, psychiatrist David Reed proposed the Erotic Stimulus Pathway Theory (Keesling, 2004). There are four stages in this model: *seduction*, *sensations*, *surrender*, and *reflection*. The first phase, *seduction*, is akin to the desire stage of Kaplan's model and refers to the set of processes that stimulate sexual activity. In this case, however, desire is viewed as stemming from the behaviors we employ to attract (or "seduce") other people. This can include spending a lot of time on one's personal appearance or flirting with someone. Seduction ultimately gives way to *sensations*, a phase that roughly corresponds to what Masters and Johnson termed excitement and plateau. Here, the five senses (vision, touch, hearing, smell, and taste) and our sexual fantasies combine to create a heightened sense of arousal that makes us want to continue sexual activity. In these first two phases, psychological factors are seen as propelling physiological responses.

Ultimately, we reach the peak of arousal and give into (or *surrender*) to orgasm; however, our ability to give up control affects this response. Some people may have a more difficult time "letting go" than others (e.g., they may feel vulnerable or distracted). Following this is the *reflection* phase, during which we psychologically reinterpret our sexual experiences and give them meaning. Depending upon the individual, that person may attach a positive or negative meaning to the event, which will affect the likelihood of pursuing this partner specifically and sexual activity more generally in the future.

As you can see, although this model shares some degree of overlap with the other models (for a summary of all three models, see Table 4.3), it may have swung too far in the opposite direction, because it focuses almost exclusively on the role of psychology and cognitive factors, while giving little attention to physical responses. Going forward in this book, we will not necessarily emphasize one of these models over the other, but rather we will pay attention to the unique points and perspectives that each has to offer. As you will see throughout this text, it is almost never the case

Table 4.3   Comparing Different Models of Sexual Response

Researcher(s)	*Stages of sexual response*			
William Masters and Virginia Johnson	Excitement	Plateau	Orgasm	Resolution
Helen Singer Kaplan	Desire	Excitement	Orgasm	
David Reed	Seduction	Sensations	Surrender	Reflection

that one perspective is "correct" and the others are wrong; rather, different theories seem to explain different pieces of the puzzle.

Key Terms

limbic system
cerebral cortex
dopamine
serotonin
primary erogenous zones
secondary erogenous zones
female copulatory
   vocalizations
pheromones

vomeronasal organ (VNO)
testosterone
castration
hypogonadism
oophorectomy
chemical castration
oxytocin
aphrodisiacs
anaphrodisiacs

placebo effect
excitement
vasocongestion
myotonia
plateau
orgasmic platform
orgasm
refractory period
resolution

Discussion Questions: What is Your Perspective on Sex?

- Should chemical castration be mandated for sex offenders to reduce the likelihood that they will commit crimes in the future? Explain your answer.
- Have you ever tried an aphrodisiac? Did it work as you expected? Why do you think it turned out the way that it did?
- What is your strongest sexual sense? Why do you think this is the case (e.g., biological or evolved predisposition, social learning)?

References

Anderson-Hunt, M., & Dennerstein, L. (1994). Increased female sexual response after oxytocin. *British Medical Journal, 309*, 929. DOI:10.1136/bmj.309.6959.929.

Arnow, B.A., Desmond, J.E., Banner, L.L., Glover, G.H., Solomon, A., Polan, M.L., ... Atlas, S.W. (2002). Brain activation and sexual arousal in healthy, heterosexual males. *Brain, 125*, 1014–1023. DOI:10.1093/brain/awf108.

Baker, R.R., & Bellis, M.A. (1993). Human sperm competition: Ejaculate manipulation by females and a function for the female orgasm. *Animal Behavior, 46*, 887–909. DOI:10.1007/978-0-387-28039-4_11.

Bancroft, J. (2002). The medicalization of female sexual dysfunction: The need for caution. *Archives of Sexual Behavior, 31*, 451–455. DOI:10.1023/A:1019800426980.

BBC News Europe (2012) Germany urged to end sex offender castration. Retrieved from http://www.bbc.co.uk/news/world-europe-17124604 (accessed September 1, 2013).

Brewer, G., & Hendrie, C.A. (2011). Evidence to suggest that copulatory vocalizations in women are not a reflexive consequence of orgasm. *Archives of Sexual Behavior, 40*, 559–564. DOI:10.1007/s10508-010-9632-1.

Chivers, M.L., Rieger, G., Latty, E., & Bailey, J.M. (2004). A sex difference in the specificity of sexual arousal. *Psychological Science, 15*, 736–744. DOI:10.1111/j.0956-7976.2004.00750.x.

Cooper, M.L. (2006). Does drinking promote risky sexual behavior? A complex answer to a simple question. *Current Directions in Psychological Science, 15*, 19–23. DOI:10.1111/j.0963-7214.2006.00385.x.

Croy, I., Bojanowski, V., & Hummel, T. (2013). Men without a sense of smell exhibit a strongly reduced number of sexual relationships, women exhibit reduced partnership security – A reanalysis of previously published data. *Biological Psychology, 92*, 292–294. DOI:10.1016/j.biopsycho.2012.11.008.

Cutler, W.B., Friedmann, E., & McCoy, N.L. (1998). Pheromonal influences on sociosexual behaviour in men. *Archives of Sexual Behavior, 27*, 1–13. DOI: 10.1023/A:1018637907321.

Darling, C.A., Davidson, J.K., & Jennings, D.A. (1991). The female sexual response revisited: Understanding the multiorgasmic experience in women. *Archives of Sexual Behavior, 20*, 527–540. DOI:10.1007/BF01550952.

Everett, G.M. (1972). Effects of amyl nitrite ("poppers") on sexual experience. *Medical Aspects of Human Sexuality, 6*, 146–151.

Ferretti, A., Caulo, M., Del Gratta, C., Matteo, R.D., Merla, A., Montorsi, F., … Romani, G.L. (2005). Dynamics of male sexual arousal: Distinct components of brain activation revealed by fMRI. *NeuroImage, 26*, 1086–1096. DOI:10.1016/j.neuroimage.2005.03.025.

Fox, C.A., Wolff, H.S., & Baker, J.A. (1970). Measurement of intra-vaginal and intra-uterine pressures during human coitus by radio-telemetry. *Journal of Reproduction and Fertility, 22*, 243–251. DOI:10.1530/jrf.0.0220243.

Fugl-Meyer, K., Oberg, K., Lundberg, P., & Lewin, B. (2006). On orgasm, sexual techniques, and erotic perceptions in 18- to 74-year-old Swedish women. *Journal of Sexual Medicine, 3*, 56–68. DOI:10.1111/j.1743-6109.2005.00170.x.

Gimpl, G., & Fahrenholz, F. (2001). The oxytocin receptor system: Structure, function, and regulation. *Physiological Reviews, 81*, 629–683.

Hamilton, J., & Arrowood, P.C. (1978). Copulatory vocalizations of chacma baboons (*Papio ursinus*), gibbons (*Hylobates hoolock*), and humans. *Science, 200*, 1405–1409. DOI:10.1126/science.663622.

Harding, A. (2006). Beijing's penis emporium. *BBC News*. Retrieved from: http://news.bbc.co.uk/2/hi/programmes/from_our_own_correspondent/5371500.stm (accessed September 1, 2013).

Haselton, M.G., Mortezaie, M., Pillsworth, E.G., Bleske-Rechek, A., & Frederick, D.A. (2007) Ovulatory shifts in human female ornamentation: Near ovulation, women dress to impress. *Hormones and Behavior, 51*, 40–45. DOI:10.1016/j.yhbeh.2006.07.007.

Heath, R.G. (1972). Pleasure and brain activity in man. *Journal of Nervous and Mental Disease, 154*, 3–18.

Hintikka, J., Niskanen, L., Koivumaa-Honkanen, H., Tolmunen, T., Honkalampi, K., Lehto, S.M., & Viinamaki, H. (2009). Hypogonadism, decreased sexual desire, and long-term depression in middle-aged men. *Journal of Sexual Medicine, 6*, 2049–2057. DOI:10.1111/j.1743-6109.2009.01299.x.

Hite, S. (1976). *The Hite Report: A nationwide survey of female sexuality*. London: Bloomsbury.

Hurtazo, H.A., Paredes, R.G., & Agmo, A. (2008). Inactivation of the medial preoptic area/anterior hypothalamus by lidocaine reduces male sexual behavior and sexual incentive motivation in male rats. *Neuroscience, 152*, 331–337. DOI:10.1016/j.neuroscience.2007.10.063.

Kaighobadi, F., Shackelford, T.K., & Weekes-Shackelford, V.A. (2012). Do women pretend orgasm to retain a mate? *Archives of Sexual Behavior, 41*, 1121–1125. DOI:10.1007/s10508-011-9874-6.

Kaplan, H.S. (1974). *The new sex therapy*. New York: Brunner/Mazel.

Karama, S., Lecours, A.R., Leroux, J.M., Bourgouin, P., Beaudoin, G., Joubert, S., & Beauregard, M. (2002). Areas of brain activation in males and females during viewing of erotic film excerpts. *Human Brain Mapping, 16*, 1–13. DOI:10.1002/hbm.10014.

Keesling, B. (2004). *Sexual pleasure: Reaching new heights of sexual arousal and intimacy*. Alameda, CA: Hunter House.

King, R., Belsky, J., Mah, K., & Binik, Y. (2011). Are there different types of female orgasm? *Archives of Sexual Behavior, 40*, 865–875. DOI:10.1007/s10508-010-9639-7.

Kirsch, I., & Sapirstein, G. (1998). Listening to Prozac but hearing placebo: A meta-analysis of antidepressant medication. *Prevention & Treatment, 1*, Article 0002a. DOI:10.1037/1522-3736.1.1.12a .

Koukounas, E., & McCabe, M. (1997). Sexual and emotional variables influencing sexual response to erotica. *Behaviour Research and Therapy, 35*, 221–230. DOI:10.1016/S0005-7967(96)00097-6.

Kruger, D.J., & Hughes, S.M. (2011). Tendencies to fall asleep first after sex are associated with greater partner desires for bonding and affection. *Journal of Social, Evolutionary, and Cultural Psychology, 5*, 239–247.

Kruger, T.H., Haake, P., Haverkamp, J., Kramer, M., Exton, M.S., Saller, B., … Schedlowski, M. (2003). Effects of acute prolactin manipulation on sexual drive and function in males. *Journal of Endocrinology, 179*, 357–365. DOI:10.1677/joe.0.1790357.

Levin, R.J. (1981). The female orgasm: A current appraisal. *Journal of Psychosomatic Research, 25*, 119–133.

Levin, R.J., & Riley, I. (2007). The physiology of human sexual function. *Psychiatry, 6*, 90–94. DOI:10.1016/j.mppsy.2007.01.004.

Levin, R.J., (2006). Vocalised sounds and human sex. *Sexual and Relationship Therapy, 21*, 99–107. DOI:10.1080/14681990500438014.

Liebowitz, M.R. (1983). *The chemistry of love*. Boston.MA: Little, Brown, & Co.

Lloyd, E. (2005). *The case of female orgasm: Bias in the science of evolution*. Cambridge, MA: Harvard University Press.

MacDonald, K., & Feifel, D. (2012). Dramatic improvement in sexual function induced by intranasal oxytocin. *Journal of Sexual Medicine, 9*, 1407–1410. DOI:10.1111/j.1743-6109.2012.02703.x.

Martins, Y., Preti, G., Crabtree, C.R., Runyan, T., Vainius, A.A., & Wysocki, C.J. (2005). Preference for human body odors is influenced by gender and sexual orientation. *Psychological Science, 16*, 694–701. DOI:10.1111/j.1467-9280.2005.01598.x.

Masters, W.H., & Johnson, V.E. (1966). *Human sexual response*. Boston, MA: Little, Brown.

McClintock, M.K. (1971). Menstrual synchrony and suppression. *Nature, 229*, 244–245. DOI:10.1038/229244a0.

McClintock, M.K. (2000). Human pheromones: Primers, releasers, signalers, or modulators? In K. Wallen & J. Schneider (Eds.), *Reproduction in context* (pp. 355–420). Cambridge, MA: MIT Press.

McCoy, N.L, & Pitino, L. (2002). Pheromonal influences on sociosexual behaviour in young women. *Physiological Behavior, 75*, 367–375. DOI:10.1016/S0031-9384(01)00675-8.

McPherson, K., Herbert, A., Judge, A., Clarke, A., Bridgman, S., Maresh, M., & Overton, C. (2005). Psychosexual health 5 years after hysterectomy: population-based comparison with endometrial ablation for dysfunctional uterine bleeding. *Health Expectations, 8*, 234–243. DOI:10.1111/j.1369-7625.2005.00338.x.

Miller, G., Tybur, J.M., & Jordan, B.D. (2007). Ovulatory cycle effects on tip earnings by lap dancers: Economic evidence for human estrus? *Evolution and Human Behavior, 28*, 375–381. DOI:10.1016/j.evolhumbehav.2007.06.002.

Miller, S.L., & Maner, J.K. (2010). Scent of a woman: Men's testosterone responses to olfactory ovulation cues. *Psychological Science, 21*, 276–283. DOI:10.1177/0956797609357733.

Monti-Bloch, L., Jennings-White, C., & Berliner, D.L. (1998). The human vomeronasal system: A review. *Annals of the New York Academy of Sciences, 855*, 373–389. DOI:10.1111/j.1749-6632.1998.tb10595.x.

Muehlenhard, C.L., & Shippee, S.K. (2010). Men's and women's reports of pretending orgasm. *Journal of Sex Research, 47*, 552–567. DOI:10.1080/00224490903171794.

Nusbaum, M.R., Lenahan, P., & Sadovsky, R. (2005). Sexual health in aging men and women: Addressing the physiologic and psychological sexual changes that occur with age. *Geriatrics, 60*, 18–23.

Osborne, G.B., & Fogel, C. (2008). Understanding the motivations for recreational marijuana use among Canadians. *Substance Use and Misuse, 43*, 539–572. DOI:10.1080/10826080701884911.

Preti, G., Cutler, W.B., Garcia, C.R., Krieger, A., Huggins, G.R., Lawley, H.J. (1986). Human axillary secretions influence women's menstrual cycles: The role of donor extracts of females. *Hormones and Behavior, 20*, 474–482. DOI:10.1016/0018-506X(86)90009-7.

Puts, D.A., Dawood, K., & Welling, L.L.M. (2012). Why women have orgasms: An evolutionary analysis. *Archives of Sexual Behavior, 41*, 1127–1143. DOI:10.1007/s10508-012-9967-x.

Rodriguez-Manzo, G., Pellicer, F., Larsson, K., & Fernandez-Guasti, A. (2000). Stimulation of the medial preoptic area facilitates sexual behavior but does not reverse sexual satiation. *Behavioral Neuroscience, 114*, 553–560. DOI:10.1037/0735-7044.114.3.553.

Ryan, C., & Jetha, C. (2010). *Sex at dawn: How we mate, why we stray, and what it means for modern relationships*. New York: HarperCollins.

Sealey, G. (2012). Some sex offenders opt for castration. *ABC News*. Retrieved from http://abcnews.go.com/US/story?id=93947&page=1#.T8aQoII8WSp (accessed August 31, 2013).

Segraves, R.T., Clayton, A., Croft, H., Wolf, A., & Warnock, J. (2004). Bupropion sustained release for the treatment of hypoactive sexual desire disorder in premenopausal women. *Journal of Clinical Psychopharmacology, 24,* 339–343. DOI:10.1080/009262301750257155.

Serretti, A., & Chiesa, A. (2009). Treatment-emergent sexual dysfunction related to antidepressants: A meta-analysis. *Journal of Clinical Psychopharmacology, 29,* 259–266. DOI:10.1097/JCP.0b013e3181a5233f.

Shabsigh, R. (1997). The effects of testosterone on the cavernous tissue and erectile function. *World Journal of Urology, 15,* 21–26. DOI:10.1007/BF01275152.

Shamloul, R., & Bella, A. J. (2011). Impact of cannabis use on male sexual health. *The Journal of Sexual Medicine, 8,* 971–975. DOI:10.1111/j.1743-6109.2010.02198.x.

Shen, W.W., & Sata, L.S. (1990). Inhibited female orgasm resulting from psychotropic drugs: A five-year, updated, clinical review. *Journal of Reproductive Medicine, 35,* 11–14.

Simon, J., Braunstein, G., Nachtigall, L., Utian, W., Katz, M., Miller, S., … Davis, S. (2005). Testosterone patch increases sexual activity and desire in surgically menopausal women with hypoactive sexual desire disorder. *Journal of Clinical Endocrinology and Metabolism, 90,* 5226–5233. DOI:10.1210/jc.2004-1747.

Snowdon, C.T., Ziegler, T.E., Schultz-Darken, N.J., & Ferris, C.F. (2006). Social odours, sexual arousal, and pairbonding in primates. *Philosophical Transactions of the Royal Society B, 361,* 2079–2089. DOI:10.1098/rstb.2006.1932.

Spark, R.F. (2002). Dehydroepiandrosterone: A springboard hormone for female sexuality. *Fertility and Sterility, 77,* 19–25. DOI:10.1016/S0015-0282(02)02987-4.

Vance, E.B., & Wagner, N.N. (1976). Written descriptions of orgasm: A study of sex differences. *Archives of Sexual Behavior, 5,* 87–98. DOI:10.1007/BF01542242.

Wang, C., Eyre, D.R., Clark, R., Kleinberg, D., Newman, C., Iranmanesh, A., … Swerdloff, R.S. (1996). Sublingual testosterone replacement improves muscle mass and strength, decreases bone resorption, and increases bone formation markers in hypogonadal men – A clinical research center study. *Journal of Clinical Endocrinology and Metabolism, 81,* 3654–3662.

Wiederman, M.W. (1997). Pretending orgasm during sexual intercourse: Correlates in a sample of young adult women. *Journal of Sex & Marital Therapy, 23,* 131–135. DOI:10.1080/00926239708405314.

Wiest, W. (1977). Semantic differential profiles of orgasm and other experiences among men and women. *Sex Roles, 3,* 399–403. DOI:10.1007/BF00289562.

Wood, R.W. (1983). The acute toxicity of nitrate inhalants. Retrieved from: http://hdl.handle.net/1802/1150 (accessed August 31, 2013).

Woo-young, L. (2011). Pedophiles to be chemically castrated. *The Korea Herald*. Retrieved from: http://view.koreaherald.com/kh/view.php?ud=20110724000341&cpv=0 (accessed August 31, 2013).

Wysocki, C.J., & Lepri, J.J. (1991). Consequences of removing the vomeronasal organ. *Journal of Steroid Biochemistry and Molecular Biology, 39,* 661–669. DOI:10.1016/0960-0760(91)90265-7.

Zemishlany, Z., Aizenberg, D., & Weizman, A. (2001). Subjective effects of MDMA ('ecstasy') on human sexual function. *European Psychiatry, 16,* 127–130. DOI:10.1016/S0924-9338(01)00550-8.

Zhang, Z., Klyachko, V., & Jackson, M.B. (2007). Blockade of phosphodiesterase Type 5 enhances rat neuro-hypophysial excitability and electrically evoked oxytocin release. *Journal of Physiology, 584,* 137–147. DOI:10.1113/jphysiol.2007.139303.

5

Gender and Gender Identity

©Benoit Chartron/123RF.COM.

Chapter Outline

- Introduction   116
- Biological Influences on Gender Identity and Sexuality   117
  - Biological Sex Variations   120
- Psychosocial Influences on Gender Identity and Sexuality   126
  - Social Interactions and Norms   126
  - Physical Environments   128
  - Media   129
- Variations in Gender Expression   130
  - Transsexualism   130
  - Cross-Dressing   135
  - Other Identities   136
- Just How Different Are Men and Women?   137
  - Sex Differences in Psychology   137
  - Sex Differences in Sexuality and Attitudes Toward Sex   138

The Psychology of Human Sexuality, First Edition. Justin J. Lehmiller.
© 2014 John Wiley & Sons, Ltd. Published 2014 by John Wiley & Sons, Ltd.

Introduction

Gender is between your ears and not between your legs.

Chaz Bono

If you were asked to name just one characteristic that is essential in order for someone to be considered a man, what would be it? If you were asked the same question with respect to what makes someone a woman, what would you say then? I pose these questions to the students in my human sexuality course each semester and, invariably, the vast majority of them come up with the same two answers: men have penises and women have vaginas. The remaining students usually focus on other physical or biological differences (e.g., the presence of testicles vs. ovaries, production of testosterone vs. estrogen, etc.). Thus, most college students I have encountered seem to believe that what makes you male or female is what you have between your legs. While that is certainly part of the story, there is a lot more to it than that and the goal of this chapter is to get you to think differently about what makes someone a man or a woman and to recognize that not everyone fits neatly into one of these two categories.

Before we begin, it is useful to distinguish between the terms sex and gender. Although many people use these words interchangeably, it is important to recognize that they have very different

Figure 5.1   Chaz Bono is a female-to-male transsexual who received international media scrutiny upon announcing that he was transitioning into a man. Chaz and others like him are an important reminder than not everyone fits neatly into a two-category gender system. Image Copyright s_bukley, 2013. Used under license from Shutterstock.com.

meanings and refer to separate aspects of the self. **Sex** is the term we use to categorize whether someone is biologically male or female. There are three different dimensions of sex we will discuss momentarily: chromosomes, gonads, and hormones. In contrast, **gender** is a psychosocial term that encapsulates all of the psychological, cultural, and social characteristics we think of as belonging to men and women. Thus, gender refers to our set of expectations about what makes someone masculine or feminine.

Related to the concept of gender are three other important terms that will come up repeatedly throughout this chapter and later in the book: gender identity, gender roles, and gender stereotypes.

Gender identity refers to an individual's own psychological perception of being male or female. Although people's gender identity is usually consistent with their biological sex, this is not always the case. Thus, someone with a biological sex of male could identify as female and vice versa. This is a form of *transgenderism*, a concept we will discuss at length later in this chapter.

Gender roles refer to a set of cultural norms or rules that dictate how people of a specific sex "should" behave. Gender roles create a set of expectations for the things that men and women are supposed to believe and how they are supposed to act.

Closely related to gender roles are **gender stereotypes**, which refer to overgeneralized beliefs about the qualities and characteristics of men and women. Stereotypes about gender fall along several dimensions, including psychological traits, role behaviors, and occupations (Deaux & Lewis, 1984).

With these terms in mind, we will turn our focus to the development of gender identity. Specifically, we will discuss biological, psychological, and social factors that affect how we come to know our own gender. Following that, we will discuss variations in gender expression and finish by addressing just how different men and women actually are.

On a side note, we will use terms such as "male body" and "female body" throughout this chapter to refer to the overall set of physical characteristics that distinguish biological males from biological females. However, as mentioned above, not everyone who has a "male body" identifies as male, just as not everyone who has a "female body" identifies as female. Thus, keep in mind the very important distinction between these biological and psychological aspects of sexuality.

Biological Influences on Gender Identity and Sexuality

Our biological sex is a function of three separate components: our chromosomes, gonads, and hormone levels. These factors work together to differentiate the bodies and brains of biological males and females. See Table 5.1 for a summary of the typical sequence of biological events that occurs in each sex. **Chromosomal sex** refers to the specific combination of sex chromosomes contained within our genes. Chromosomal sex is determined at the moment of conception (i.e., when a sperm cell fertilizes an egg). Typically, egg cells carry a single X-chromosome, while sperm cells carry either a single X- or Y-chromosome. If the resulting combination is XX, fetal development will proceed toward the female form; if the resulting combination is XY, development will proceed toward the male form.

Gonadal sex refers to the specific gonads (i.e., ovaries vs. testes) present within the body. The gonads begin to develop in response to genetic signals approximately six weeks after conception.

Table 5.1 Typical Sequence of Biological Sex Differentiation		
Level of sex differentiation	*Male*	*Female*
Chromosomal sex	XY	XX
Gonadal sex	Testes	Ovaries
Hormonal sex	Androgens	Estrogens
Sexual anatomy	Fully developed penis and scrotum, as well as their corresponding internal reproductive structures	Fully developed vulva, as well as its corresponding internal reproductive structures
Sexually dimorphic brain	Larger preoptic area and bed nucleus of the stria terminalis (BNST)	Smaller preoptic area and bed nucleus of the stria terminalis (BNST)

Once developed, the gonads begin releasing sex hormones. **Hormonal sex** refers to the major class of hormones released by the gonads: *estrogens* (primarily released by the ovaries) or *androgens* (primarily released by the testes). As mentioned in chapter 4, men and women both produce a certain amount of each of these sex hormones, but the female body produces far more estrogens, while the male body produces far more androgens. As a fetus is developing, it is the presence or absence of these hormones that differentiates the internal and external sexual structures of the male and female body.

In addition to influencing development of the internal and external genital structures, hormones have a profound effect on how our brains develop in utero. Specifically, hormones can masculinize or feminize the brain before birth in such a way that it creates lifelong effects on our gender identity and sexual behavior. Compelling evidence demonstrating some of these effects comes from studies of rats, which have shown that changing early hormone exposure affects adult rats' sexual interests and behavior. Scientists have tested this by castrating male rat pups immediately after birth and exposing female rat pups to testosterone immediately after birth. This is equivalent to changing hormone exposure prenatally in humans, because rats are born at a much earlier stage of development than we are. Researchers have found that castrated male rats tend to show feminine sexual behavior through their lives (Beach, Noble, & Orndoff, 1969). Specifically, when mounted by an intact (i.e., noncastrated) male rat, a castrated male rat will exhibit **lordosis**, a sexual posture that occurs naturally in female rats in which the back curves upward to assist in copulation. This effect persists even if the castrated rat is given testosterone injections later in life; however, if testosterone is administered within the first week after castration, lordosis behavior is unlikely to develop.

What about the female rats who are given testosterone injections? They typically exhibit masculine behavior throughout their lives (Whalen & Rezek, 1974). That is, testosterone-injected females will attempt to mount other rats, and when they themselves are mounted, they do *not* exhibit lordosis; in fact, these rats seem rather indifferent to such sexual advances. Taken together, these findings indicate that, at least in animal studies, there appears to be a critical period of development during which hormones "wire" the brain for sexual behavior.

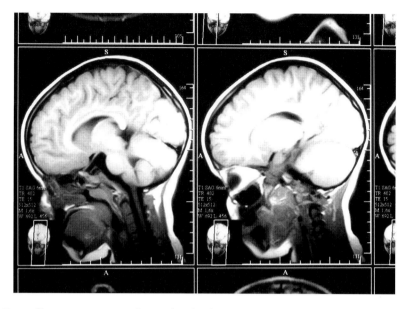

Figure 5.2 Prenatal hormone exposure is theorized to alter brain structures that contribute to both our gender identity and sexual orientation. ©Natalia Merzlyakova / 123RF.COM.

One especially important area of the brain that appears to be affected by prenatal hormone exposure is the **hypothalamus**. As discussed in the preceding chapter, the hypothalamus is a portion of the limbic system located deep within the brain that plays an important role in regulating sexual behavior, among many other things. One portion of the hypothalamus in which there are reliable sex differences is the *preoptic area* (POA), which tends to be larger in adult men than adult women (Hofman & Swaab, 1989). Rat studies have found that the POA controls copulatory behavior (Balthazart & Ball, 2007) and that it undergoes a critical period, such that testosterone injections only affect its size until the fifth day after birth; injections beyond that have no effect on POA size (Rhees, Shryne, & Gorski, 1990). Another portion of the hypothalamus that differs between men and women is the *bed nucleus of the stria terminalis* (BNST). The BNST tends to be larger in men (Allen & Gorski, 1990), perhaps also as a result of specific hormone exposure at certain stages of development. Research in humans suggests that size of the BNST is related to gender identity. Specifically, the number of neurons present in the BNST of male-to-female transsexuals more closely resembles the number found in biological females than biological males, while the size of the BNST of female-to-male transsexuals more closely resembles biological males than biological females (Kruijver et al., 2000). This suggests that early hormonal exposure may potentially organize the brain toward a specific gender.

As you can see, chromosomes, gonads, and hormones are all linked to the development of our sexual and gender identities. In order to develop typical male and female bodies, brains, and behaviors, all of these factors must work together and build on each other in a very specific sequence. If anything falls out of that sequence, the end result can be very different. What happens when things do not unfold according to the typical male or female schedule? The result is intersexuality.

Biological Sex Variations

Although most people think of biological sex as having two categories (i.e., male and female), the reality is that sex is much more complex. There are several variations on sex because some people are born with bodies and genitals that do not appear completely male or female, but rather have features of both. A person who possesses both male and female biological traits is **intersexed**. Although you may hear some intersexed individuals referred to as *hermaphrodites*, that term is generally not used anymore because it is considered outdated, offensive, and inaccurate. You may also see other sexuality texts refer to intersexed individuals as having "ambiguous" genitalia because their genitals appear to be somewhere in between a penis and a vagina; however, keep in mind that any ambiguity is on the part of the perceiver. To intersexed persons, there is nothing "ambiguous" about what is between their legs.

Being intersexed is more common than most people realize. The prevalence of specific sex variations differs, but overall, intersexed individuals represent approximately 2% of live births (Blackless et al., 2000). So much of what we know about the impact of biology on gender and sexuality comes from research on these individuals because they can tell us what effect chromosomes, gonads, and hormones likely have in relation to gender identity and sexual expression. We will consider some of the most common sex variations in this section and discuss what they have told psychologists about the origin of gender. See Table 5.2 for a summary of these sex variations.

Klinefelter's Syndrome

Klinefelter's syndrome is one of the most common sex variations, occurring once in every 1,000 male births (Blackless et al., 2000). It results when a Y-carrying sperm fertilizes an egg that possesses two X-chromosomes. Although they possess both the typical male (XY) and female (XX) chromosome combinations, individuals with Klinefelter's syndrome are anatomically male in terms of their genital appearance, but their testes are usually smaller than average and sperm production tends to be very low. In addition, their bodies often have feminized features, including increased breast tissue and a rounded body shape (Bock, 1993).

With respect to gender, individuals with Klinefelter's syndrome tend to identify as male, although some adopt other identities (Intersex Society of North America, 2012). In terms of sexuality, same-gender attraction is no more common among Klinefelter's males than it is among biological (i.e., XY) males; however, overall interest in sex tends to be low (Bock, 1993). Testosterone injections can enhance sexual desire and increase masculinization of the body among those who wish to pursue hormone treatment (Bock, 1993).

Turner's Syndrome

Turner's syndrome is a less common sexual variation in which an individual is born with a single X chromosome. In such cases, the second sex chromosome is missing or damaged. Individuals with Turner's syndrome have a feminine body appearance, although they tend to be shorter than average and typically have little breast development (Morgan, 2007). External genitals appear feminine, but internally the ovaries are underdeveloped and may only appear as streaks of tissue, which means that menstruation does not occur at puberty and sexual reproduction is not possible (i.e., they are infertile; Morgan, 2007).

Individuals with Turner's syndrome usually identify as female and tend to have feminine interests (Boman, Mollet, & Albertsson-Wikland, 1998). Just like Klinefelter's syndrome, Turner's syndrome

Table 5.2 Biological Sex Variations

Type of variation	Brief description	Gender identity	Sexuality
Klinefelter's syndrome	XXY chromosome combination. Anatomic male with some female features. Low interest in sex.	Usually male	Same-gender attraction no more common than it is among biological (i.e., XY) males
Turner's syndrome	Single X-chromosome. Feminine body and genital appearance, but no functioning internal reproductive structures. Sex life depends on when puberty is induced by physician.	Female	Not linked to same-gender attraction
Complete androgen insensitivity syndrome	XY male insensitive to androgens. Feminine genital appearance. Usually not detected until puberty.	Female	Most are attracted to men
Partial androgen insensitivity syndrome	XY male who does not respond completely to androgens. Genitals appear to be a mix of male and female structures.	Can be male or female	Sexual attraction is variable
5-Alpha-reductase deficiency	XY male unable to convert testosterone to DHT. Possesses testes, but has feminized genital appearance until puberty.	Usually female during childhood, male starting at puberty	Most are attracted to women
Congenital adrenal hyperplasia	XX female with adrenal glands that produce excessive androgens. Masculinized genital appearance. Can also occur in XY males, but they are similar to unaffected males in most regards.	Usually female with masculine interests	Most are attracted to men, but prevalence of same-gender attraction is high

is not linked to same-gender attraction. Many of these women go on to lead active sex lives; however, the age at which puberty is induced via hormone injections (a necessity because no ovaries are present) has an important effect on how their sexuality develops, and it is important that physicians do not delay its induction too long (Carel et al., 2006).

Androgen Insensitivity Syndrome

Androgen Insensitivity Syndrome (AIS) occurs when a biologically male fetus is insensitive to the production of its own androgens. As a result, despite possessing the XY chromosome combination, testes, and high levels of masculinizing hormones, the end result is a body and genitals that have a feminine appearance. AIS can be either *complete* or *partial* (Androgen Insensitivity Syndrome, 2010). In cases of complete AIS, the child appears to be a typical female at birth and has a shallow vagina. A diagnosis of AIS is generally not made until adolescence when there is a failure to menstruate, although it may be detected earlier if an undescended testicle appears as a mass in the groin or abdomen. Individuals with complete AIS are usually raised as girls and almost always adopt a female gender identity (Mazur, 2005). As adults, most become sexually active and the vast majority report sexual attraction to men (Wisniewski et al., 2000). On a side note, you may have noticed that I have avoided talking about heterosexuality and homosexuality in relation to being intersexed because such labels are difficult to apply in these cases. For example, a person with complete AIS is technically a biological male with a (usually) female gender

Figure 5.3   World running champion Caster Semenya became the focus of significant media attention after it was discovered that she has androgen insensitivity syndrome. Some people argued that she should not be allowed to complete as a woman because she is technically a chromosomal male. Intersex issues and sports have since become a huge source of controversy. Do we use biology, psychology, or both in making decisions about whether someone should compete against men or against women? Source: Chell Hill (Own work) [CC-BY-SA-3.0 (http://creativecommons.org/licenses/by-sa/3.0)], via Wikimedia Commons.

identity. So if that person is exclusively attracted to men, does that make this individual gay or heterosexual? In such cases, it is best to allow the individual to report their own sexual identity rather than to arbitrarily designate one.

Partial AIS usually results in an incomplete masculinization of the genitalia. Consequently, a child with partial AIS may possess genitals that are not clearly identifiable as male or female. In some cases, a penis does clearly develop, but the urethral opening may appear on the underside of the penis near the corona rather than at the tip of the glans (a physical variation known as *hypospadias*; Androgen Insensitivity Syndrome, 2010). Doctors and parents are often confused about how to raise children with partial AIS. A gender is usually "assigned" to the child and in some cases, the child's genitals may be surgically altered to remove any perceived "ambiguity." For an in-depth discussion of treatment guidelines for intersexed children, see the Digging Deeper 5.1 box. Gender

Digging Deeper 5.1   Can Gender Really Be "Assigned" At Birth?

A few decades ago, psychologist John Money advanced his *theory of gender neutrality*. His idea was that with respect to gender, everyone is initially a blank slate. In Money's own words: "It seems that every child is born with some predisposition to go both ways. Which way it will finally go is determined by its environment" (Brewington, 2006). Money put this theory to the test when he was contacted by a very concerned mother who did not know what to do after her son's penis was destroyed during a circumcision that went horribly wrong.

Money advised the parents to raise their little boy, Bruce, as a girl. On Money's advice, Bruce was castrated, renamed "Brenda," and given female sex hormones during adolescence. Money recommended that sex reassignment surgery be performed at a later age to create a vagina. Dr. Money followed the case for years afterward and personally met with Brenda annually to evaluate her progress. According to Money's reports published in leading sex journals, Brenda's transition was a smashing success and the theory of gender neutrality had been supported. However, the facts of the case did not match what Money claimed.

In reality, Brenda did not see herself as a girl. She did not want to wear dresses and she preferred to play with boys. She felt depressed and confused, had a hard time fitting in, and later became suicidal. As a teenager, Brenda rebelled against the hormone treatments and refused the surgery to complete her transition. At that point, her parents told her the truth about what had happened. Shortly thereafter, Brenda adopted a male gender identity, started calling himself David, and eventually underwent surgery to become the man he felt he was always supposed to be.

The Brenda/David story is fascinating on multiple levels, but the main thing it tells us is that gender is not something that we can simply assign at birth. In David's case, not only did his doctors and parents try to "teach" him a specific gender, but they modified his genitals and gave him hormone treatments. This was not enough to override his feeling that he was supposed to be a man, suggesting that gender identity is likely "wired" in our brains before birth.

This case, combined with a number of other studies suggesting a neurological basis for gender identity (e.g., Kruijver et al., 2000), has fundamentally changed the way physicians and families are dealing with intersexed children. Traditionally, when a child was born with genitals that were not clearly male or female, the doctors and parents would "pick" a gender and perform genital-altering surgery to make the child's body a match for their assigned sex (Bomalaski, 2005). This is problematic because many intersexed individuals switch away from their assigned gender identity later in life and are upset to learn that their genitals were irreversibly altered without their consent. Numerous cases like this have led to a growing movement for intersex rights.

Biologist Milton Diamond (the whistle-blower in the Brenda/David case) has been at the forefront of this movement and has put forth a set of treatment recommendations for intersexed children (Diamond & Sigmundson, 1997). His approach starts by considering these cases sexual "differences" or "variations" instead of "disorders" because there is nothing inherently pathological about being intersexed and there is no reason an intersexed person cannot live a completely normal life. Diamond recommends avoiding genital-altering surgery in infancy, especially if the sole purpose is cosmetic and is not medically necessary. He also recommends providing ongoing counseling and support for intersexed children and their parents, communicating openly and honestly, avoiding secrecy, as well as refraining from creating any stigma or shame about the issue.

For more information on the intersex movement and treatment guidelines, check out the Intersex Society of North America website (www.isna.org).

Note: Reprinted with permission from *The Psychology of Human Sexuality* blog (www.lehmiller.com).

identity and sexuality is more variable in cases of partial AIS. For example, while it is possible to identify as male and be attracted to women (Gooren & Cohen-Kettenis, 1991), other identities and patterns of attraction are possible.

5-Alpha-Reductase Deficiency

Related to AIS is **5-alpha-reductase deficiency** (**5αRD**). This occurs when a biologically male fetus is unable to convert testosterone into dihydrotestosterone (DHT) due to insufficient levels of the 5-alpha reductase enzyme. DHT is necessary for the development of male external genital structures. Thus, without DHT (or with levels lower than usual), the end result is a feminized genital appearance. Depending upon the amount of feminization, external appearance may be completely female, a mix of male and female structures, or incomplete male. Regardless of external appearance, however, male gonads are present internally.

In most cases, babies with 5αRD are raised as girls and adopt a female gender identity during childhood. However, upon reaching puberty, testosterone production ramps up and their bodies start to become more masculine. Specifically, the testes usually descend, the genital structures begin to grow into a small penis, and male secondary sex characteristics develop (e.g., chest and facial hair, deepening of the voice, etc.). At this point, most individuals with 5αRD switch from a female to male gender identity (Mendonca et al., 1996). Those who switch to a male identity are usually sexually interested in women (Imperato-McGinley, Peterson, Gautier, & Sturla, 1979). Men with 5αRD may be capable of penetrative intercourse and produce viable sperm, but this varies across persons.

Congenital Adrenal Hyperplasia

Congenital adrenal hyperplasia (CAH) occurs when a person's adrenal glands produce excessive amounts of androgens from before birth throughout the individual's life. This can happen in both men and women. In affected men, physical and psychological development follows the typical male pattern. However, affected women become more masculine both physically and psychologically. At birth, a female child with CAH will have genitals that appear to be either partially or (in some cases) completely masculine, although internally, female gonads are present.

Most biological females with CAH end up adopting a female gender identity; however, they tend to have interests that are more typical for men (Meyer-Bahlburg, Dolezal, Baker, Ehrhardt, & New, 2006). For example, they express more interest in working with things (e.g., in areas like technology) than in working with people (Beltz, Swanson, & Berenbaum, 2011). In terms of sexuality, most females with CAH report attraction to men, but some studies have found higher rates of same-gender attraction and bisexual orientations (Meyer-Bahlburg, Dolezal, Baker, & New, 2008).

What Do These Biological Sex Variations Tell Us About Gender Identity?

Together, all of these sexual variations tell us that biology and genetics play an undisputable role in the development of both gender identity and sexuality. First, it should be clear that when biological events do not follow the typical male or female pattern, it is not always easy to predict the identity a person will adopt later in life. Second, out of all of the potential biological variables, prenatal sex hormone exposure may be the most important of all. For example, in both 5αRD and AIS, we have biological males with XY chromosomes and testes whose bodies do not get the full effect of androgen exposure. However, one of these cases usually results in a female identity (AIS) and the other in a male identity (5αRD). This is perhaps because in AIS, the entire body (including the brain) is not responsive to androgens, which means the brain never has an opportunity to become masculinized. In contrast, in 5αRD, the lack of DHT prevents external genital masculinization, but does not necessarily preclude masculinization of the brain. Thus, it may be the impact of hormones on the brain that explains why these sexual variations typically result in different gender identities. CAH also highlights the important role that prenatal hormones may play in organizing the brain toward a certain gender by showing that greater androgen exposure in women is linked to more masculine interests.

At the same time, however, these sexual variations also do not tell the entire story. For example, in the case of Turner's syndrome, we see that a female gender identity can develop in the absence of a second sex chromosome, ovaries, and female sex hormones. Likewise, in the case of 5αRD, it would appear that a female gender identity can be learned at least temporarily during childhood. Thus, there would certainly seem to be room for psychosocial factors to contribute to the development of gender.

Psychosocial Influences on Gender Identity and Sexuality

Take a look at infant pictured on this page. Can you guess this baby's biological sex? If you are like most of my students, about half of you probably guessed male and the other half guessed female. In the absence of physical and environmental cues that "announce" a child's sex (e.g., wearing the color pink versus the color blue), it is difficult to answer this question with any degree of certainty. As you will see below, there are a vast number of social factors that teach us about our gender identity and gender role at a very young age. These same factors then encourage us to conform to a very specific set of gendered expectations throughout our lives.

Social Interactions and Norms

Social interactions are among the first things to shape our perceptions of gender, and interactions with our parents in particular are among the most influential. A child's gender is seemingly very important to parents, given how "it's a boy" and "it's a girl" is often announced and celebrated before a child ever even comes into the world. If you have taken a course in developmental psychology, you probably already know that from the moment a child is born, the way parents interact with that child is completely different depending upon whether it is a boy or a girl. As some particularly compelling evidence of this, dozens of studies have been conducted in which adult men and women were given the opportunity to interact with an infant that was presented as either male or female (for a review of the research in this area, see Stern & Karraker, 1989). In reality, all adults were interacting with the same infant. Researchers found that infants presented as male and female were often (but not always) treated differently,

Figure 5.4   Can you guess the sex of this child? It is much harder to predict an infant's sex when they are not surrounded by gendered social cues. ©Paul Hakimata/123RF.COM.

and these differences usually fell along very sex-stereotypic lines. For example, adults verbalized more and engaged in more nurturing play when the child was perceived to be a girl compared to a boy. Likewise, adults tended to choose dolls and other feminine toys when playing with girls, but trucks and tools when playing with boys. Thus, the simple knowledge of a child's sex appears to prompt a set of beliefs about gender-appropriate behaviors and traits that can creep into social interactions, sometimes completely outside of conscious awareness (Rubin, Provenzano, & Luria, 1974). This may lead children to engage in gender-stereotypic behavior through a **self-fulfilling prophecy** in which parents' expectations elicit and reinforce gendered behavior, effectively making gender stereotypes come true. Of course, in an age where more mothers are in the workplace and more fathers are becoming stay-at-home dads, things are changing somewhat, and there are certainly many parents who make a concerted effort not to teach their kids strict gender roles. However, gendered expectations for children persist, and they are often conveyed subconsciously.

Beyond parents, social interactions that occur in school with peers and teachers further reinforce these ideas about gender. For example, gender-segregated play begins very quickly in childhood and continues through adolescence. This means that boys typically play with other boys, and girls with other girls. Children who violate this norm are often looked down upon and have a hard time fitting in (as we saw in the Brenda/David case described in the Digging Deeper 5.1 box). Research shows that the more time children spend in sex-segregated play, the more gender-typed their behaviors become (e.g., girls playing "house" and boys playing superhero games; Martin & Fabes, 2001).

Teachers play a vital role in reinforcing societal and cultural gender expectations among students. For example, teachers tend to be more tolerant of bad behavior in boys than in girls, and they tend to give boys more attention (Leaper & Friedman, 2007). Teachers also harbor stereotypes about the academic abilities of the sexes, such as believing that math comes easier to boys

Figure 5.5 Teachers' expectations for their students' performance can influence academic achievement and later career interest in gender-stereotypic ways. Image Copyright michaeljung, 2013. Used under license from Shutterstock.com.

(Riegle-Crumb & Humphries, 2012). This can have important implications for students' academic outcomes and ultimately their chosen career paths. Research has found that teachers' beliefs about their students' abilities subtly and unintentionally affects how well students do in school (e.g., some students may be given more time and attention than others; Rosenthal & Jacobson, 1968). This is essentially another self-fulfilling prophecy taking place. Also, to the extent that teachers subtly encourage mathematical and science abilities in their male students but not in female students, it may lead fewer women to pursue careers in these areas because they do not have the opportunity to develop their skills to the same level. Teacher expectations may contribute to *stereotype threat* as well, in which reminding women about the stereotype that females are not as good at math creates anxiety that distracts them and contributes to worse performance on mathematical tests (Spencer, Steele, & Quinn, 1998).

Socialization within religious contexts further reinforces gender role beliefs. The writings and teachings of many religious traditions propagate themes of male dominance and female submissiveness. Likewise, many religions do not permit women to serve as clergy or in leadership roles, which can send a very visible and powerful statement that men are the ones in charge. Consistent with this idea, research finds that religiosity is typically a strong predictor of holding traditional gender-role attitudes (e.g., Morgan, 1987).

Physical Environments

The physical environment in which we grow up can have a profound influence on our gender role beliefs. For instance, what is your earliest memory of what your bedroom looked like as a child? If you do not remember, try to track down a picture of your room and see what sort of gendered cues it contained. Probably, many of you will find that your room was blue (if you are male) or

Figure 5.6   The physical environments that surround us as children cue us in as to what our interests and activities "should" be. ©HONGQI ZHANG / 123RF.COM.

Table 5.3   Gendered Presentations of Men and Women in the Media
An analysis of G-rated films released between 1990 and 2005 revealed that only 28% of speaking characters were female (this included both real life and animated characters). Likewise, 83% of narrators in these films were male.
An analysis of films across all rating categories released between 1990 and 2006 found that women were more likely to be presented as parents and as part of a committed relationship compared to men. This same analysis found that women were more than five times as likely to be depicted in sexy and revealing attire than men. Together, these results suggest that women are usually only presented in either a very traditional or highly sexual manner.
An analysis of female leads from 13 of the most popular G-rated films released between 1937 and 2006 found that all of the women were valued and praised for being beautiful and that their primary focus was finding love.
An analysis of 1,034 TV shows spanning 12 different networks airing in 2005 found that male characters outnumbered female characters two to one in children's programming. In addition, female characters were more than four times as likely as male characters to be dressed in a sexy fashion.

Source: Smith (2008).

pink (if you are female). You will probably also see that the clothes you wore and the selection of toys at your disposal was fairly typical for your gender. Speaking of toys, check out the toy section the next time you are in a big store. You will likely notice that the store has made it glaringly obvious which aisles are meant for boys and which are meant for girls. As a child walking down the toy aisle designated for your gender, you are told in a not-so-subtle way what your likes and interests "should" be. At the same time, these toy aisles put pressure on parents to select gender-appropriate gifts for their children.

Media

Last but not least, the media plays a part in conveying gender role information to children. By the time most students graduate from high school, they will have spent more hours watching TV than they spent at school (American Academy of Child & Adolescent Psychiatry, 2011). When you factor in time spent on the Internet, at the movies, playing video games, and listening to music, there is simply no comparison for the amount of influence the media has. When it comes to sex and gender, the media tends to present men and women in highly gender-stereotyped ways. As just a few examples of this, see Table 5.3 for a look at what some of the research on this topic has found. These stereotypical portrayals do not go unnoticed by children and adolescents either. For example, studies have found that holding more traditional gender-role beliefs is associated with more frequent watching of music videos (Ward, Hansbrough, & Walker, 2005) and toy commercials in children and adolescents (Pike & Jennings, 2005).

   As you can see, gender-role information and expectations are conveyed to us from the moment we come into being through a number of different sources. Repeated exposure to these ideas leads

Figure 5.7   The most popular and iconic female characters in television and film, such as Snow White, tend to perpetuate stereotypical notions of how women are "supposed" to be. Source: H. Michael Miley (Own work) [CC-BY-SA-2.0 (http://creativecommons.org/licenses/by-sa/2.0)], via Wikimedia Commons.

us to internalize these gendered beliefs, which then become self-perpetuating. However, despite the amount of pressure exerted by these sources to conform to a specific gender identity and role, not everyone follows their socially prescribed role. This often happens for intersexed individuals, but it also happens for persons who are transgendered.

Variations in Gender Expression

The general term for someone whose behaviors or physical appearance is not consistent with societal gender roles is **transgender**. In other words, a transgendered person does not conform to ideas of what men and women are "supposed" to be. Transgender is a broad umbrella term that encompasses different forms of gender role nonconformity. In this section, we will consider two of the most common transgender variants: transsexualism and cross-dressing (i.e., transvestism). In my experience teaching about human sexuality, I have found that students frequently confuse the terms transsexual and transvestite, so before you go any further, check out the Digging Deeper 5.2 box for a more in-depth understanding of these terms.

Transsexualism

A **transsexual** is someone whose gender identity does not match their biological sex. The clinical term for this is **gender dysphoria**, which refers to unhappiness and discomfort that stems from an incongruence between one's physical sex and one's psychological gender identity. Thus, a male-to-female (MTF) transsexual is someone who is born male but perceives herself as female, whereas a female-to-male (FTM) transsexual is born female but perceives himself as male.

Digging Deeper 5.2   Cross-Dressing and Gender-Bending: Separating Science Fact from Fiction

Every year, particularly on Halloween, people descend upon movie theaters to catch midnight screenings of *The Rocky Horror Picture Show*. This film tells the story of Dr. Frank-N-Furter, a mad scientist and self-described "sweet transvestite" from the planet Transsexual. Throughout the film, Frank dresses as a woman and has sex with anything (human, alien, or creature) that moves. The film is definitely an experience, to say the least. However, as a psychologist, I cannot help but wonder what kind of impressions this movie leaves on audiences when it comes to the subject of transgenderism. Do viewers walk away thinking transvestites and transsexuals are one and the same? Do they think transvestites are willing to have sex with anyone or anything? Let us set the record straight on these important questions.

Figure 5.8   There are a lot of misconceptions about transvestites and transsexuals. This stems at least in part from inconsistent and misleading media portrayals. ©jackmalipan/123RF.COM.

First of all, and this is a key point, a transvestite engages in cross-dressing for purposes of sexual arousal, but does not wish to change sexes (Langstrom & Zucker, 2005). In other words, transvestites dress as members of the other sex because it turns them on. While some dress entirely as the other sex, others wear only a single piece of the other sex's clothing (e.g., a male transvestite might wear just panties or a bra). Transvestism is often (although not always) a type of *fetish*, where a certain object or action is necessary in order to "give yourself over to absolute pleasure" (if I may borrow a line from *Rocky Horror*).

In comparison, transsexuals do not cross-dress because they find it arousing; rather, transsexuals feel as though they are trapped in the body of the "wrong" sex (Cole, O'Boyle, Emory, & Meyer, 1997). It is for this reason that transsexuals sometimes undergo sexual reassignment to change their body's appearance to a form consistent with their psychological identity. If I may borrow one more line from *Rocky Horror*, Dr. Frank-N-Furter's advice to a transsexual would probably be: "Don't dream it, be it."

What about the characteristics of the average transvestite? Most people assume that the majority of transvestites are men – and they are. People also assume that most transvestites are gay, or at the very least, bisexual, but this is not the case at all. In fact, *most transvestites are heterosexual, married men* (Doctor & Prince, 1997). Moreover, most of these men hide their transvestic tendencies from the rest of the world. Transvestites typically engage in this behavior in private and do not cross-dress when they go to work or to the bar. This tends to be a private, momentary activity that is accompanied by immediate sexual gratification. In fact, transvestites are often so secretive about their behaviors that they do not even let their romantic partners know about them.

That said, feel free to enjoy a late-night screening of *The Rocky Horror Picture Show*, but keep in mind that most of what this film has to say about human sexuality is a matter of science fiction.

Note: Reprinted with permission from *Science of Relationships* (www.scienceofrelationships.com).

Up through the DSM-IV-TR (American Psychiatric Association, 2000), an entry called *gender identity disorder* (GID) was listed. In the DSM-5, published in 2013, although the diagnostic criteria remained similar, the GID name was replaced with "gender dysphoria," which is now diagnosed according to the following criteria:

- Incongruity between one's expressed gender and one's physical characteristics.
- A desire to get rid of one's primary and secondary sex characteristics, and to have the primary and secondary sex characteristics of the other sex.
- A desire to be the other sex and be treated as such.
- A belief that one's feelings and behaviors are typical of the other sex.
- Clinically significant distress or impairment in addition to feelings of incongruence. Gender dysphoria is not considered a clinical problem unless the patient is distressed.

Although transsexualism is no longer called a "disorder," the fact that a diagnostic label still exists is highly controversial among professionals in the field and transsexuals themselves (Mayer-Bahlburg, 2010). For one thing, many people believe that including transsexualism in the DSM serves to stigmatize this community. Additionally, the primary treatments for GID are sex reassignment surgery (in adults) and puberty-blocking drugs (in adolescents). However, these are not psychiatric treatments, and this, some have argued, calls into question whether this should even be thought of as a psychological disorder (McHugh, 2004). Moreover, many transsexual persons are not distressed because of their identity, and being transsexual does not necessarily prevent one from leading a normal life. On the other hand, some argue that a diagnostic category is valuable in that it offers the opportunity for health insurance coverage for treatment, guides research in the area, and prevents transsexuals from being misdiagnosed with other labels (Mayer-Bahlburg, 2010).

We do not have a good sense of how common transsexualism is, because relatively little research has explored this topic and many transsexuals attempt to keep their identity hidden as a result of widespread prejudice and discrimination. What little research does exist suggests that transsexualism is less common than intersexuality and that MTF transsexuals far outnumber FTM transsexuals (De Cuypere et al., 2007; Veale, 2008).

The origin of transsexualism is not well understood, but current research suggests that it has a neurological basis and may be tied to prenatal hormone exposure (Kruijver et al., 2000). Transsexualism is not linked to any kind of chromosomal or physical anomalies, nor is it linked to general psychopathology. We also know that most transsexuals begin identifying with the other sex at a very young age, usually well before any feelings of sexual attraction develop.

Studies have typically found that a majority of FTM transsexuals report attraction to women (Chivers & Bailey, 2000), while a majority of MTF transsexuals report attraction to men (Rehman, Lazer, Benet, Schaefer, & Melman, 1999). Thus, most transsexuals appear to be attracted to people who match their biological sex, not people who match their gender identity. However, keep in mind that the transsexual community is incredibly diverse, and patterns of sexual attraction and sexuality labels vary widely. This means that FTM and MTF transsexuals can be attracted to men or to women, they can be bisexual, they can have sexual interests outside of the traditional gender binary, or they can be asexual (i.e., lacking in sexual interest). Most transsexuals define their sexual orientation in relation to their gender identity and not their biological sex. This means that a MTF who is attracted to men would likely think of herself as heterosexual, while a FTM who is attracted to men would likely consider himself gay.

Options for Transsexual Adults
As mentioned in the preceding section, the primary treatments offered to transsexuals are not psychiatric in nature. In fact, providing psychotherapy alone as a way of relieving the distress that many transsexuals experience is generally ineffective. As a result of significant medical advances, biological alterations are increasingly being pursued by transsexuals to bring their body in line with their gender identity.

For transsexual adults, the primary way of accomplishing this is through **sex reassignment surgery**. Contrary to popular belief, it is not possible to simply walk into a doctor's office and ask for sex reassignment. There is usually a lengthy prequalification process that consists of (1) psychological evaluations and interviews to determine the individual's motivations and identify potential conflicts; (2) a transition period of up to one year where the patient lives as a member of the other sex for all intents and purposes; and (3) hormone therapy to begin adjusting the patient's body to more closely match the desired sex (e.g., MTF transsexuals would be given estrogen to reduce body hair and stimulate breast growth, while FTM transsexuals would be given testosterone to increase growth of body and facial hair and halt menstruation). Genital surgery is only performed after all of the preceding criteria have been met.

For MTF transsexuals, the main surgical process involves removing the penis and scrotum and reusing the skin to create a functional vagina with labia (**vaginoplasty**). In this surgery, the urethra is rerouted to permit urination as a biological female would experience it. Surgical procedures such as breast implants, Adam's apple reduction, and voice box operations (to raise voice pitch) may also be performed, depending upon the patient's wishes.

For FTM transsexuals, the surgical process usually includes a complete *hysterectomy* (i.e., removal of the ovaries, fallopian tubes, and uterus) and *mastectomy* (i.e., removal of the breasts). Genital reassignment can be accomplished in one of two ways. One possibility is a **metoidioplasty**, in which the clitoris is turned into an erectile phallus (Perovic & Djordjevic, 2003). Specifically, the clitoris is straightened and lengthened, moved slightly to approximate the location of a typical male penis, and the urethra is routed through it. Because the clitoris is homologous to the penis and contains actual erectile tissue, the result is a phallus capable of erection through sexual stimulation. However, the size of the phallus may not be sufficient for penetrative intercourse because it is only a few centimeters long. If a larger phallus is desired, a **phalloplasty** may be performed instead in which skin taken from other parts of the body is transplanted to the genital area to create a functional penis with the urethra running through it. Although the end result is much larger with a phalloplasty, these phalluses are not capable of erection on their own because they contain no erectile tissue. As a result, a penile implant must be inserted (for more on penile implants, see chapter 12). In both metoidioplasty and phalloplasty, the labia are usually sutured together to create a scrotum, and testicular implants may be inserted.

In both FTM and MTF surgeries, the original sensory pathways in the genital region are retained and reused as much as possible to maximize the ability to be sexually responsive afterward. Indeed, orgasm is often possible after such surgeries (Lawrence, 2005; Lief & Hubschman, 1993). However, the ability to orgasm usually declines among MTF transsexuals, but increases among FTM transsexuals. One caveat to this is that FTM transsexuals given metoidioplasty tend to have more orgasmic capacity afterward than those given phalloplasty, because metoidioplasty retains more of the original nerve pathways.

The outcomes of sex reassignment surgery are generally favorable. Genital surgeries can produce results that are not only functional, but appear very physically accurate, which helps to explain why levels of satisfaction are generally very high post-surgery (Lief & Hubschman, 1993). Even in cases where orgasmic capacity is lost or declines, sexual satisfaction is usually still higher after surgery than it was before.

Options for Transsexual Children

Transsexuality is increasingly being recognized in children by parents and doctors alike. For transsexual children who have not yet gone through puberty, there has been a growing trend to administer *puberty-blocking drugs*, medications that halt the development of secondary sex characteristics (Spiegel, 2008). In FTM boys, these drugs inhibit breast development, increase height and muscularity, and prevent menstruation. In MTF girls, these drugs inhibit growth of facial and body hair, restrict growth of the Adam's apple, and maintain a higher pitch voice. In effect, these drugs prevent bodily changes that can be difficult to adjust surgically once puberty has taken place. Puberty blockers are taken until about age 16, when the individual begins taking hormones of the desired sex. If desired, genital surgery can follow once the individual reaches adulthood. This treatment approach is new, with puberty blockers having been administered only since 2004. It is also highly controversial, with some questioning whether children can truly comprehend the effects of these drugs, which produce physical changes that cannot easily be undone.

Attitudes Toward Transsexualism

In most parts of the world, sex is viewed as a binary construct. That is, people tend to think that you can be either male *or* female, with nothing in between. Generally speaking, if you have a penis you are expected to be a man, whereas if you have a vulva you are expected to be a woman. Visit the Your Sexuality 5.1 box to consider just a few of the many ways that society not-so-subtly tells you how to behave based upon your genital anatomy. Persons who violate these social norms are typically

Your Sexuality 5.1   Where Do Transgendered and Intersexed Individuals Fit in a Gender Binary World?

Most societies fail to accept or accommodate people who do not fit neatly into the male or female category. Just think about it – many things in this world are divided into men's versus women's. Consider the following examples:

- Almost all public restrooms, as well as locker rooms at gyms and fitness clubs, are labeled "Men" or "Women."
- Most school and professional sporting leagues, not to mention the Olympics, are divided into male-only and female-only categories.
- Clothing stores sell clothes for men/guys or clothes for women/ladies. Very few items are explicitly labeled "unisex."
- Toy stores do not explicitly label their aisles "boy" or "girl," but it is usually obvious which toys are "meant" for which sex based upon their location and the surrounding color scheme.

What other examples can you think of where society presumes that everyone is part of the gender binary? Can you imagine how stressful and challenging it might be to fall outside of this binary worldview, especially when it comes to something as simple as using the bathroom in a public setting?

marginalized. Prejudice against transsexuals (known as **transphobia**) is very common. Transphobia is strongly correlated with *homophobia* (i.e., prejudice against nonheterosexuals), but people feel more negatively about transsexuals than they do about gay men, lesbians, and bisexuals (Norton & Herek, 2013). In addition, men tend to be more transphobic and homophobic than women. Due to the widespread prevalence of transphobia, many transsexuals attempt to keep their identity secret.

That said, some cultures adopt a much broader view of gender and are more accepting of persons who do not fit neatly into the gender binary. One example of this would be the **two-spirit** phenomenon documented in dozens of Native American tribes (Jacobs, Thomas, & Lang, 1997). The idea behind two-spirit is that both male and female spirits are presumed to occupy a single person's body. Historically, two-spirits were respected in their tribes and in many cases were revered and held important social positions; however, this has changed somewhat as Christian values have crept into many tribes and displaced traditional beliefs (Murg, 2011). Aside from the two-spirit concept in North America, third genders exist in many other parts of the world, including India, Pakistan, and Indonesia.

Cross-Dressing

Another subtype of transgenderism is cross-dressing. **Cross-dressing** is a broad term that refers to the act of wearing clothing typically associated with the other sex. One variant of cross-dressing is **transvestism**, which refers to the act of obtaining sexual gratification from wearing clothing of the other sex (for more on transvestism, see the Digging Deeper 5.2 box and chapter 13). However, not everyone who cross-dresses does so because it is a turn-on. Thus, keep in mind that while the

Figure 5.9 Drag queens are men who dress up as women for show. Unlike male-to-female transsexuals, drag queens do not truly wish to change their sex. ©Karen Struthers/123RF.COM.

terms "cross-dresser" and "transvestite" are overlapping, they are not synonymous. Also, please note that the term "transvestite" is considered offensive in some parts of the transgender community. The use of this term in this book is not meant to be offensive in any way and is only used to distinguish the subtype of cross-dressers who experience arousal as a function of their behavior.

Aside from sexual arousal, some cross-dressers engage in this behavior for performance art. Examples of this would be *drag kings* (women who dress as men) and *drag queens* (men who dress as women), people who cross-dress primarily for entertainment or as a career. On a side note, although cross-dressing of this nature often seems to coincide with being gay or bisexual, this is not always the case. Heterosexuals can and do participate in drag.

Other Identities

Transgendered persons may adopt a number of other identities beyond those already mentioned, although somewhat less is known about these identities from a scientific standpoint. For example, *androgynous* persons possess both masculine and feminine psychological characteristics simultaneously (please note that this does not necessarily imply being intersexed). *Bigendered* persons change their gender role behavior depending upon the context, moving fluidly between a more masculine and feminine role. *Genderqueer* individuals think of themselves outside of binary gender classifications, such as individuals who think of themselves as having a third gender or as being genderless. Being genderless is sometimes referred to as *asexuality*, although this term is used more commonly to represent a lack of interest in partnered sex (see chapter 6). As you can see, transgender is a broad term that encompasses a multitude of perspectives on gender.

Just How Different Are Men and Women?

To round out this chapter, let us consider one of the most controversial topics in this area: sex differences. Most of you are probably well aware of the stereotype (and very popular book of the same name) "Men are from Mars, Women are from Venus." Stories about sex differences appear frequently in the popular media, from front page headlines, to relationship advice columns, to self-help books. The media is pushing the idea that men and women want fundamentally different things when it comes to sex and relationships, and also that men and women use completely different language to communicate. These ideas are selling to the tune of millions of books and billions of dollars. But is this really true? Are men and women so different as to suggest that they are from different planets? Although people have staked out very different positions on this topic, a review of research in this area makes it clear that the Mars/Venus analogy is a hyperbole. The reality is that while there are indisputably *some* differences between men and women, these differences are often smaller than we have been led to believe, and sociocultural factors offer a very plausible explanation for many of them. In other words, men and women are not from different planets, but they are certainly socialized very differently. Below, we will examine the degree to which men and women differ in several aspects of their psychology and sexuality and consider some of the explanations that have been offered for the differences observed.

Sex Differences in Psychology

Researchers have examined how men and women differ in many ways, including their personality, level of aggression, and communication style. With respect to personality, many studies have compared men and women in the context of The Big Five personality factors of *openness to experience, conscientiousness, extraversion, agreeableness,* and *neuroticism.* To review the definitions of these traits, see Table 1.4 in chapter 1. Generally speaking, research has yielded sex differences that are either inconsistent or very small for extraversion, openness to experience, and conscientiousness; in contrast, larger and more reliable sex differences have emerged with respect to agreeableness and neuroticism (Costa, Terracciano, & McCrae, 2001; Feingold, 1994). Thus, the main areas men and women seem to differ in terms of personality concern the fact that women tend to be (1) more trusting and compliant, and (2) experience more anxiety and negative affect than men. Although we cannot say for sure why these personality differences exist, the fact that sex differences in the Big Five vary considerably across cultures (Schmitt, Realo, Voracek, & Allik, 2008) suggests that such differences are a product of culture and society, not genetics.

With respect to aggression, there has been a longstanding assumption that men are more aggressive than women in almost all ways, and most early research in social psychology seemed to support this idea. However, recent work has found that there are sex differences in certain types of aggression. Specifically, men are more inclined than women to aggress in very direct and physical ways, while women are more inclined than men to aggress in more indirect and verbal ways (e.g., by spreading rumors or gossip; Hess & Hagen, 2006). In addition, when you take into account *provocation* (i.e., when someone incites another person to become aggressive, such as through taunting), sex differences in aggression become much smaller (Bettencourt & Miller, 1996). At least part of the reason that men are more aggressive overall is that they are provoked more often. Together, these findings suggest that men may not be genetically predisposed to be more

Figure 5.10   Are men inherently more aggressive than women, or does society just promote and accept male aggression more than female aggression? ©Cathy Yeulet/123RF.COM.

aggressive than women; rather, it may be that society expects men and women to act out their aggression in very different ways and allows men more opportunities to be aggressive.

Lastly, in terms of communication style, studies have found differences in terms of how men and women communicate verbally and nonverbally. For instance, men tend to interrupt their conversation partners more than women; however, the degree to which this difference is observed varies across different social situations, which suggests that this is a situational effect rather than a stable individual difference between men and women (Anderson & Leaper, 1998). As another example, women tend to be better at men in decoding the emotion behind facial expressions (Hall & Matsumoto, 2004). Although there are numerous other studies suggesting that women have a greater ability to decode nonverbal cues such as this, it is not clear whether women are "hardwired" to pick up on others' emotions or if this is simply a reflection of the fact that we expect women to be more sensitive to other people's feelings than men.

Sex Differences in Sexuality and Attitudes Toward Sex

Research has also examined how men and women differ with respect to their attitudes toward sex, their sexual behaviors, and their sexuality. For instance, men have more favorable attitudes toward "hooking-up" and are more willing to have sex with someone they have just met (Petersen & Hyde, 2010). In terms of sexual behaviors, a few of the biggest areas men and women differ include frequency of masturbation and use of pornography. Perhaps not surprisingly, men masturbate more, and utilize far more porn, than women (Petersen & Hyde, 2010).

In addition, men report having a higher sex drive and more daily thoughts about sex (Fisher, Moore, & Pittenger, 2012). However, there is no truth to the common stereotype that men think about sex every seven seconds. Just think about it: if the average guy is awake for 16 hours and thinks about sex every 7 seconds, he would have 8,228 sexy thoughts per day! The reality is that when asked to tally their daily thoughts about sex, men average 34 sexual thoughts per day, or about twice per hour (Fisher et al., 2012). In contrast, women average about 19 sexual thoughts per day, or just over once per hour.

We will come back to these and a number of other sex differences throughout the book; however, as they come up, keep in mind that there are many possible explanations for them and they are not necessarily a function of men having a stronger libido than women, as many people assume. For instance, the evolutionary perspective argues that men and women have evolved distinct mating strategies due to differences in the parental investment required to create a child (i.e., it is more work for women than it is for men). One implication of this is that men should have more permissive attitudes toward casual sex than women because it is more reproductively advantageous for men to have multiple partners. In contrast, the sociocultural perspective argues that most sex differences are a reflection of patriarchal gender roles and a sexual double standard that inhibits female sexuality. As some evidence of this, survey research has found that women report having had more sexual partners when they think their answers will be anonymous compared to when they think their answers might become known to others (Alexander & Fisher, 2003). Not only does this finding highlight the important role of psychosocial factors on women's reported sexual attitudes and behaviors, but it tells us that some sex differences may be overstated due to social pressure on women to underreport their true sexual experiences. We will revisit some of the competing explanations for sex differences in sexual attitudes and behaviors in chapter 7.

One other important area men and women seem to differ is in their sexuality. Specifically, research suggests that women have more *erotic plasticity* than men. That is, female sexuality is more flexible and responsive to social and cultural factors than male sexuality. Evidence for this comes from a variety of studies indicating that (1) women become physiologically aroused to a wider range of sexual targets (Chivers, Rieger, Latty, & Bailey, 2004), (2) women are more likely to report a bisexual orientation (Chandra, Mosher, & Copen, 2011), (3) women's sexual identity is more likely to change over time (Diamond, 2008), and (4) women are far less likely to develop fetishes or become fixated on one specific sexual object. Why is this the case? As with all of the other sex differences discussed above, it is not entirely clear. However, the evidence seems to point to differences in how sexuality is organized in the brains of men and women. In the following chapter, we will begin our discussion of sexual orientation paying specific attention to how it is expressed differently in men and women and considering some of the possible reasons why.

Key Terms

sex	chromosomal sex	intersexed
gender	gonadal sex	Klinefelter's syndrome
gender identity	hormonal sex	Turner's syndrome
gender roles	lordosis	androgen insensitivity
gender stereotypes	hypothalamus	syndrome (AIS)

5-alpha-reductase
   deficiency (5αRD)
congenital adrenal
   hyperplasia (CAH)
self-fulfilling
   prophecy

transgender
transsexual
gender dysphoria
sex reassignment
   surgery
vaginoplasty

metoidioplasty
phalloplasty
transphobia
two-spirit
cross-dressing
transvestism

Discussion Questions: What is Your Perspective on Sex?

- In competitive and professional sports, should participants be grouped according to biological sex or gender identity? Is it ever necessary for sports to categorize participants based on sex and gender?
- Are puberty-blocking drugs an appropriate treatment for children experiencing gender dysphoria? Why or why not?
- Do you think that most sex differences in attitudes and personality are a function of biological differences between men and women or a result of different social interactions and expectations?

References

Alexander, M.G., & Fisher, T.D. (2003). Truth and consequences: Using the bogus pipeline to examine sex differences in self-reported sexuality. *Journal of Sex Research, 40*, 27–35. DOI:10.1080/00224490309552164.

Allen, L.S., & Gorski, R.A. (1990). *Sex difference in the bed nucleus of the stria terminalis of the human brain. Journal of Comparative Neurology, 302*, 697–706. DOI:10.1002/cne.903020402.

American Academy of Child & Adolescent Psychiatry (2011). *Children and watching TV.* Retrieved from http://www.aacap.org/cs/root/facts_for_families/children_and_watching_tv (accessed September 1, 2013).

American Psychiatric Association (2000). *Diagnostic and statistical manual of mental disorders* (4th ed., text rev.). Washington, DC: Author.

Anderson, K.J., & Leaper, C. (1998). Meta-analyses of gender effects on conversational interruption: Who, what, when, where, and how. *Sex Roles, 39*, 225–252. DOI:10.1023/A:1018802521676.

Androgen Insensitivity Syndrome (2010). *A.D.A.M. Medical Encyclopedia.* Retrieved from http://www.ncbi.nlm.nih.gov/pubmedhealth/PMH0002163/ (accessed September 1, 2013).

Balthazart J., & Ball, G.F. (2007). Topography in the preoptic region: Differential regulation of appetitive and consummatory male sexual behaviors. *Frontiers in Neuroendocrinology, 28*, 161–178. DOI:10.1016/j.yfrne.2007.05.003.

Beach, F.A., Noble, R.G., & Orndoff, R.K. (1969). Effects of perinatal androgen treatment on responses of male rats to gonadal hormones in adulthood. *Journal of Comparative and Physiological Psychology, 68*, 490–497. DOI:10.1037/h0027658.

Beltz, A.M., Swanson, J.L., & Berenbaum, S.A. (2011). Gendered occupational interests: Prenatal androgen effects on psychological orientation to Things versus People. *Hormones and Behavior, 60*, 313–317. DOI:10.1016/j.yhbeh.2011.06.002.

Bettencourt, B.A., & Miller, N. (1996). Gender differences in aggression as a function of provocation: A meta-analysis. *Psychological Bulletin, 119*, 422–427. DOI:10.1037/0033-2909.119.3.422.

Blackless, M., Charuvastra, A., Derryck, A., Fausto-Sterling, A., Lauzanne, K., & Lee, E. (2000). How sexually dimorphic are we? Review and synthesis. *American Journal of Human Biology, 12*, 151–166. DOI:10.1002/ajhb.10122.

Bock, R. (1993). *Understanding Klinefelter syndrome: A guide for XXY males and their families*. NIH Publication No. 93-3202. Retrieved from http://www.clevelandclinic.org/health/health-info/docs/0800/0852.asp (accessed September 1, 2013).

Bomalaski, M.D. (2005). A practical approach to intersex. *Urological Nursing, 25*, 11–18.

Boman, U.W., Mollet, A., & Albertsson-Wikland, K. (1998). Psychological aspects of Turner syndrome. *Journal of Psychosomatic Obstetrics & Gynecology, 19*, 1–18. DOI:10.3109/01674829809044216.

Brewington, K. (2006). Hopkins pioneer in gender identity: Dr. John Money 1921–2006. *The Baltimore Sun*. Retrieved from http://articles.baltimoresun.com/2006-07-09/news/0607090031_1_gender-johns-hopkins-john-money (accessed September 1, 2013).

Carel, J.C., Elie, C., Ecosse, E., Tauber, M., Leger, J., Cabrol, S., … Coste, J. (2006). Self-esteem and social adjustment in young women with Turner syndrome – influence of pubertal management and sexuality: population-based cohort study. *Journal of Clinical Endocrinology and Metabolism, 91*, 2972–2979. DOI:10.1210/jc.2005-2652.

Chandra, A., Mosher, W.D., & Copen, C. (2011). Sexual behavior, sexual attraction, and sexual identity in the United States: Data from the 2006–2008 National Survey of Family Growth. *National Health Statistics Reports, 36*, 1–36.

Chivers, M.L., & Bailey, J.M. (2000). Sexual orientation of female-to-male transsexuals: A comparison of homosexual and nonhomosexual types. *Archives of Sexual Behavior, 29*, 259–278. DOI:10.1023/A:1001915530479.

Chivers, M.L., Rieger, G., Latty, E., & Bailey, J.M. (2004). A sex difference in the specificity of sexual arousal. *Psychological Science, 15*, 736–744. DOI:10.1111/j.0956-7976.2004.00750.x.

Cole, C., O'Boyle, M., Emory, L., & Meyer, W. (1997). Comorbidity of gender dysphoria and other major psychiatric diagnoses. *Archives of Sexual Behavior, 26*, 13–26. DOI:10.1023/A:1024517302481.

Costa, P.T., Terracciano, A., & McCrae, R.R. (2001). Gender differences in personality traits across cultures: Robust and surprising findings. *Journal of Personality and Social Psychology, 81*, 322–331. DOI:10.1037//0022-3514.81.2.322.

De Cuypere, G., Van Hemelrijck, M., Michel, A., Carael, B., Heylens, G., Rubens, R., … Monstrey, S. (2007). Prevalence and demography of transsexualism in Belgium. *European Psychiatry, 22*, 137–141. DOI:10.1016/j.eurpsy.2006.10.002.

Deaux, K., & Lewis, L.L. (1984). Structure of gender stereotypes: Interrelationships among components and gender label. *Journal of Personality and Social Psychology, 46*, 991–1004. DOI:10.1037/0022-3514.46.5.991.

Diamond, L. (2008). *Sexual fluidity: Understanding women's love and desire*. Cambridge, MA: Harvard University Press.

Diamond, M., & Sigmundson, H.K. (1997). Management of intersexuality. Guidelines for dealing with persons with ambiguous genitalia. *Archives of Pediatric and Adolescent Medicine, 151*, 1046–1050.

Doctor, R., & Prince, V. (1997). Transvestism: A survey of 1,032 cross-dressers. *Archives of Sexual Behavior, 26*, 589–605. DOI:10.1023/A:1024572209266.

Feingold, A. (1994). Gender differences in personality: A meta-analysis. *Psychological Bulletin, 116*, 429–456. DOI:10.1037/0033-2909.116.3.429.

Fisher, T.D., Moore, Z.T., & Pittenger, M. (2012). Sex on the brain?: An examination of frequency of sexual cognitions as a function of gender, erotophilia, and social desirability. *Journal of Sex Research, 49*, 69–77. DOI:10.1080/00224499.2011.565429.

Gooren, L., & Cohen-Kettenis, P.T. (1991). Development of male gender identity/role and a sexual orientation towards women in a 46,XY subject with an incomplete form of the androgen insensitivity syndrome. *Archives of Sexual Behavior, 20*, 459–470. 10.1007/BF01542408.

Hall, J.A., & Matsumoto, D. (2004). Gender differences in judgments of multiple emotions from facial expressions. *Emotion, 4*, 201–206. DOI:10.1037/1528-3542.4.2.201.

Hess, N.H., & Hagen, E.H. (2006). Sex differences in indirect aggression: Psychological evidence from young adults. *Evolution and Human Behavior, 27*, 231–245. DOI:10.1016/j.evolhumbehav.2005.11.001.

Hofman, M.A., & Swaab, D.F. (1989). The sexually dimorphic nucleus of the preoptic area in the human brain: A comparative morphometric study. *Journal of Anatomy, 164*, 55–72.

Imperato-McGinley, J., Peterson, R.E., Gautier, T., & Sturla, E. (1979). Androgens and the evolution of male-gender identity among male pseudohermaphrodites with 5-alpha-reductase deficiency. *New England Journal of Medicine, 300*, 1233–1237.

Intersex Society of North America (2012). *Klinefelter syndrome.* Retrieved from http://www.isna.org/faq/conditions/klinefelter (accessed September 1, 2013).

Jacobs, S.E., Thomas, W., & Lang, S. (1997). *Two-spirit people: Native American gender identity, sexuality, and spirituality.* Chicago: University of Illinois Press.

Kruijver, F.P.M., Zhou, J.N., Pool, C.W., Hofman, M.A., Gooren, L.J.G., & Swaab, D.F. (2000). Male-to-female transsexuals have female neuron numbers in a limbic nucleus. *Journal of Clinical Endocrinology & Metabolism, 85*, 2034–2041. DOI:10.1210/jc.85.5.2034.

Langstrom, N., & Zucker, K. (2005). Transvestic fetishism in the general population: Prevalence and correlates. *Journal of Sex and Marital Therapy, 31*, 87–95.

Lawrence, A.A. (2005). Sexuality before and after male-to-female sex reassignment surgery. *Archives of Sexual Behavior, 34*, 147–166. DOI:10.1007/s10508-005-1793-y.

Leaper, C., & Friedman, C.K. (2007). The socialization of gender. In J. Grusec & P. Hastings (Eds.), *Handbook of socialization: Theory and research* (pp. 561–587). New York: Guilford Press.

Lief, H.I., & Hubschman, L. (1993). Orgasm in the postoperative transsexual. *Archives of Sexual Behavior, 22*, 145–155. DOI:10.1007/BF01542363.

Martin, C.L., & Fabes, R.A. (2001). The stability and consequences of young children's same-sex peer interactions. *Developmental Psychology, 37*, 431–446. DOI:10.1037/0012-1649.37.3.431.

Mazur, T. (2005). Gender dysphoria and gender change in androgen insensitivity or micropenis. *Archives of Sexual Behavior, 34*, 411–421. DOI:10.1007/s10508-005-4341-x.

McHugh, P. (2004). Surgical sex. *First Things: The Journal of Religion, Culture and Public Life, 147*, 34–38.

Mendonca, B.B., Inacio, M., Costa, E.M.F., Arnhold, I.J.P., Silva, F.A.Q., Nicolau, W., … Wilson, J.D. (1996). Male pseudohermaphroditism due to steroid 5alpha-reductase 2 deficiency. Diagnosis, psychological evaluation, and management. *Medicine, 75*, 64–76.

Meyer-Bahlburg, H.F. (2010). From mental disorder to iatrogenic hypogonadism – Dilemmas in conceptualizing gender identity variants as psychiatric conditions. *Archives of Sexual Behavior, 39*, 461–476. DOI:10.1007/s10508-009-9532-4.

Meyer-Bahlburg, H.F., Dolezal, C., Baker, S.W., & New, M.I. (2008). Sexual orientation in women with classical or non-classical congenital adrenal hyperplasia as a function of degree of prenatal androgen excess. *Archives of Sexual Behavior, 37*, 85–99. DOI:10.1007/s10508-007-9265-1.

Meyer-Bahlburg, H.F., Dolezal, C., Baker, S.W., Ehrhardt, A.A., & New, M.I. (2006). Gender development in women with congenital adrenal hyperplasia as a function of disorder severity. *Archives of Sexual Behavior, 35*, 667–684. DOI:10.1007/s10508-006-9068-9.

Morgan, M.Y. (1987). The impact of religion on gender-role attitudes. *Psychology of Women Quarterly, 11*, 301–310. DOI:10.1111/j.1471-6402.1987.tb00905.x.

Morgan, T. (2007). Turner syndrome: Diagnosis and management. *American Family Physician, 76*, 405–410.

Murg, W. (2011). Momentum mounts to again embrace two-spirits. *Indian Country Today Media Network.* Retrieved from http://indiancountrytodaymedianetwork.com/2011/06/06/momentum-mounts-to-again-embrace-two-spirits-35837 (accessed September 1, 2013).

Norton, A.T., & Herek, G.M. (2013). Heterosexuals' attitudes toward transgender people: Findings from a national probability sample of U. S. adults. *Sex Roles, 68*, 738–753. DOI:10.1007/s11199-011-0110-6.

Perovic, S.V., & Djordjevic, M.L. (2003). Metoidioplasty: A variant of phalloplasty in female transsexuals. *British Journal of Urology International, 92*, 981–985. DOI:10.1111/j.1464-410X.2003.04524.x.

Petersen, J.L., & Hyde, J.S. (2010). A meta-analytic review of research on gender differences in sexuality. *Psychological Bulletin, 136,* 21–38. DOI:10.1037/a0017504.

Pike, J.J., & Jennings, N.A. (2005). The effects of commercials on children's perceptions of gender appropriate toy use. *Sex Roles, 52,* 83–91. DOI:10.1007/s11199-005-1195-6.

Rehman, J., Lazer, S., Benet, A., Schaefer, L., & Melman, A. (1999). The reported sex and surgery satisfactions of 28 postoperative male-to-female transsexual patients. *Archives of Sexual Behavior, 28,* 71–89. DOI: 10.1023/A:1018745706354.

Rhees, R.W., Shryne, J.E., & Gorski, R.A. (1990). Termination of the hormone-sensitive period for differentiation of the sexually dimorphic nucleus of the preoptic area in male and female rats. *Developmental Brain Research, 52,* 17–23. DOI:10.1016/0165-3806(90)90217-M.

Riegle-Crumb, C., & Humphries, M. (2012). Exploring bias in math teachers' perceptions of students' ability by gender and race/ethnicity. *Gender & Society, 26,* 290–322. DOI:10.1177/0891243211434614.

Rosenthal, R., & Jacobson, L. (1968). Pygmalion in the classroom. *The Urban Review, 3,* 16–20. DOI:10.1007/BF02322211.

Rubin, J., Provenzano, R., & Luria, Z. (1974). The eye of the beholder: Parents' views on sex of newborns. *American Journal of Orthopsychiatry, 44,* 512–519. DOI:10.1111/j.1939-0025.1974.tb00905.x.

Schmitt, D.P., Realo, A., Voracek, M., & Allik, J. (2008). Why can't a man be more like a woman? Sex differences in Big Five personality traits across 55 cultures. *Journal of Personality and Social Psychology, 94,* 168–182. DOI:10.1037/0022-3514.94.1.168.

Smith, S.L. (2008). *Gender stereotypes: An analysis of popular films and TV.* Retrieved from http://www.seejane.org/downloads/GDIGM_Gender_Stereotypes.pdf (accessed September 1, 2013).

Spencer, S.J., Steele, C.M., & Quinn, D.M. (1998). Stereotype threat and women's math performance. *Journal of Experimental Social Psychology, 35,* 4–28. DOI:10.1006/jesp.1998.1373.

Spiegel, A. (2008). Parents consider treatment to delay son's puberty: New therapy would buy time to resolve gender crisis. *NPR.* Retrieved from http://www.npr.org/templates/story/story.php?storyId=90273278 (accessed September 1, 2013).

Stern, M., & Karraker, K.H. (1989). Sex stereotyping of infants: A review of gender labeling studies. *Sex Roles, 20,* 501–522. DOI:10.1007/BF00288198.

Veale, J.F. (2008). Prevalence of transsexualism among New Zealand passport holders. *Australian & New Zealand Journal of Psychiatry, 42,* 887–899. DOI:10.1080/00048670802345490.

Ward, L.M., Hansbrough, E., & Walker, E. (2005). Contributions of music video exposure to black adolescents' gender and sexual schemas. *Journal of Adolescent Research, 20,* 143–166. DOI:10.1177/0743558404271135.

Whalen, R.E., & Rezek, D.L. (1974). Inhibition of lordosis in female rats by subcutaneous implants of testosterone, androstenedione or dihydrotestosterone in infancy. *Hormones and Behavior, 5,* 125–128. DOI:10.1016/0018-506X(74)90035-X.

Wisniewski, A.B., Migeon, C.J., Meyer-Bahlburg, H.F.L., Gearhart, J.P., Berkovitz, G.D., Brown, T.R., & Money, J. (2000). Complete androgen insensitivity syndrome: Long-term medical, surgical, and psychosexual outcome. *The Journal of Clinical Endocrinology & Metabolism, 85,* 2664–2669. DOI:10.1210/jc.85.8.2664.

6

Sexual Orientation

©William Perugini, 2013. Used under license from Shutterstock.com.

Chapter Outline

- Introduction   145
- Sexual Orientation: Definitions and Types   145
- Measurement and Prevalence   146
- Theories of Sexual Orientation   149
  - Early Psychological Theories   149
  - Biological and Hormonal Theories   149
  - Evolutionary Theories   151
  - Biopsychosocial Theories   152
- Sex Differences in the Expression of Sexual Orientation   155
- Sexual Orientation Attitudes   158
  - Prejudice Against Gay, Lesbian, and Bisexual Persons   158
  - Sexual Orientation in Psychological Perspective   162
- Sexual Orientation Myths   164

The Psychology of Human Sexuality, First Edition. Justin J. Lehmiller.
© 2014 John Wiley & Sons, Ltd. Published 2014 by John Wiley & Sons, Ltd.

Introduction

"Is it true that all women are inherently bisexual?"
"When a guy says he's bisexual, does that mean he's secretly gay?"
"Why are all gay men so effeminate?"
"Are gay and lesbian parents more likely to raise gay children?"
"How do gay people determine which one will be the 'husband' and which one will be the 'wife' in their relationship?"

I have been asked these questions and numerous variations on them countless times. It is clear from their nature that there is a fundamental lack of knowledge about variations in sexual orientation and what it really means to be gay, lesbian, or bisexual. These questions also highlight some of the most common stereotypes that exist about sexual minorities, and many people fail to realize just how hurtful and offensive these stereotypes can be. The purpose of this chapter is to provide a scientifically based understanding of sexual orientation that will dispel some of the most widespread myths and misconceptions about homosexuality and bisexuality.

Sexual Orientation: Definitions and Types

Most textbook chapters on sexual orientation begin by providing a definition. Before we do that, however, it is important to acknowledge that there is no universally agreed-upon definition of this concept. Some people view sexual orientation as a matter of sexual attraction (i.e., who do you find sexually desirable?). Others view it as a matter of sexual behavior (i.e., who do you have sex with?). Yet others view it as a matter of psychological identity and labels (i.e., do you identify as gay, straight, bisexual, or something else?). Scientists adopt different definitions to suit their research purposes. For example, researchers in medicine and public health often focus on behavior and tend not to concern themselves with matters of identity because they want to understand infection risk. In contrast, researchers in psychology tend to focus more on attraction and identity because they are more concerned with how sexuality is perceived and psychologically experienced. These variable definitions have the effect of making the literature on sexual orientation difficult to decipher at times. For instance, as you will see in the next section, the way you define "sexual orientation" significantly affects prevalence estimates (e.g., consider that far more people have engaged in same-sex behavior than identify as gay or bisexual). Thus, when talking about sexual orientation, it is important to look at it through a broad lens that takes into account attraction, behavior, *and* identity, and recognizes that these factors may express themselves very differently in different individuals. For purposes of this textbook, we will therefore define **sexual orientation** as the unique pattern of sexual and romantic desire, behavior, and identity that each person expresses.

Sexual orientation can take many different forms. Many people tend to think of it as comprising just three categories: *heterosexual* (interest in members of the other sex), *homosexual* (interest in members of the same sex), and *bisexual* (interest in men and women). However, sexual orientation is perhaps best viewed as existing on a continuum, because sexuality can be quite complex and people rarely fit neatly into a narrowly defined set of categories. The idea of a sexual orientation continuum was first described by Alfred Kinsey (Kinsey, Pomeroy, & Martin, 1948) and can be seen in Figure 6.1. The classic **Kinsey Scale** ranges from 0 (defined as an exclusive pattern of heterosexual attraction and behavior) to 6 (defined as an exclusive pattern of homosexual attraction and

(0) Exclusively heterosexual	(1) Mostly heterosexual, incidentally homosexual	(2) Mostly heterosexual with significant homosexual experience	(3) Equally heterosexual & homosexual	(4) Mostly homosexual with significant heterosexual experience	(5) Mostly homosexual, incidentally heterosexual	(6) Exclusively homosexual

Figure 6.1   Kinsey's famous sexual orientation rating scale places sexuality on a continuum, which allows for varying degrees of heterosexuality and homosexuality (Kinsey et al., 1948).

behavior), with 3 representing equal levels of heterosexuality and homosexuality. The remaining numbers reflect varying degrees of bisexuality. One advantage of looking at sexuality on a continuum such as this is that it provides a more accurate method of categorization that accounts for individual variability. In addition, the continuum does not imply that individuals will always have the same "number" for their entire lives – it allows for the possibility that some people's pattern of attraction, behavior, and identity may change over time, and, indeed, this does happen.

While the Kinsey Scale is widely used even today, some would argue that it is incomplete because it does not encompass all possible sexualities. For example, where would someone who is asexual fit in? **Asexuality** refers to individuals who have no interest in partnered sexual activity. Kinsey and most other sex researchers have seemingly assumed that everyone experiences at least some degree of sexual attraction, but that is not necessarily the case. Likewise, where does pansexuality fall on this continuum? **Pansexuality** encompasses attraction to members of all sexes and gender identities. It is broader than bisexuality, which implies that one can only be attracted to biological males and females. As we learned in the previous chapter, this binary view of gender necessarily excludes some people.

Asexuality and pansexuality are mentioned here as just two examples of sexual orientation variations that may not be captured by current measurement methods. Keep in mind that other sexualities can and do exist. Unfortunately, however, very little research has explored such alternative sexualities. Because almost all research on nonheterosexual orientations in psychology has focused on homosexuality and bisexuality, and this book is empirically based, those are the sexual orientations we will focus on for the remainder of this chapter.

Measurement and Prevalence

Every time I teach a course on sexuality I ask my students to tell me what percentage of the population they think is gay or lesbian. There is always a range of answers, but the most common estimate is typically 10%, and the students who cite it usually present it as a statement of fact. However, the oft cited 10% statistic was derived from Alfred Kinsey's work, in which he found that 10% of the men in his sample were predominately gay (i.e., they scored a 5 or higher on the Kinsey Scale; Kinsey et al., 1948). For comparison purposes, the corresponding number for women was 3% (Kinsey, Pomeroy, Martin, & Gebhard, 1953). As we discussed in chapter 2, though, Kinsey did not include a nationally representative sample. In fact, he oversampled from the gay community by recruiting a lot of his participants in gay bars. Thus, Kinsey's estimates may not be reliable.

More recent research based upon nationally representative samples has yielded somewhat smaller numbers, although it is important to keep in mind that the results are not directly comparable across studies due to differences in how sexual orientation has been defined and measured.

Your Sexuality 6.1   What Percentage of the Population is Gay?
It Depends How You Ask the Question

The question of sexual orientation prevalence has vexed social scientists for decades. There is not one simple statistic researchers can point to because scientists cannot agree upon a universal definition of sexual orientation. As mentioned at the outset of this chapter, it is difficult to fit everyone into neat, non-overlapping categories. As some evidence of the challenges faced by researchers in this area, please answer each of the questions below.

1. With which sexual orientation label do you identify? _____
2. Are you currently attracted to anyone of the same sex? _____
3. Have you ever been attracted to anyone of the same sex? _____
4. Are you currently involved in a same-sex relationship? _____
5. Have you ever been involved in a same-sex relationship? _____
6. Have you ever engaged in sexual behavior with a member of the same sex (e.g., kissing, masturbation, oral sex, etc.)? _____
7. Have you ever had a sexual dream or fantasy involving a member of the same sex? _____
8. Do you connect better intimately or emotionally with members of the same sex? _____

Were your answers to questions 2–8 perfectly consistent with the label that you specified in the first question? For some people, their answers are consistent, whereas for others there is a lot of variability. Labels do not always match up with behaviors, and neither behaviors nor labels necessarily remain constant over time. If you were designing a survey and could only ask about sexual orientation using one question, how would you ask it? Why?

Before we review the exact numbers, visit the Your Sexuality 6.1 box to think about your own sexual orientation and how you would measure this construct if you were conducting a sex survey.

In the National Health and Social Life Survey, 2.8% of men and 1.4% of women identified themselves as gay, lesbian, or bisexual (Laumann, Gagnon, Michael, & Michaels, 1994). In this same study, however, the percentage who ever had same-sex contact after age 18 (5.0% of men and 4.0% of women) or who reported feelings of attraction to a member of the same sex (6.0% of men and 5.5% of women) was a bit higher. Why is there such a discrepancy between sexual identity and sexual behavior? Because identities and behaviors do not overlap as well as people assume. Not everyone who has sex with persons of the same sex identifies as gay. For example, research has found that men can be heterosexually identified, yet occasionally have sex with other men (i.e., they do it on the "down-low"; Reback & Larkins, 2013). Likewise, research has found that some women experience sexual fluidity, a concept we will discuss later in this chapter. As you can see, the way researchers operationalize sexual orientation has major implications for the results obtained, with lower numbers typically observed when sexual orientation is assessed in terms of self-identity and higher numbers when it is assessed in terms of behavior.

Table 6.1 Comparing Sexual Identity and Same-sex Sexual Behavior across National US Sex Surveys				
	National Survey of Family Growth, 2002	National Survey of Family Growth, 2006–2008	National Health and Nutrition Examination Survey, 2007–2008	National Survey of Sexual Health and Behavior, 2009
Age range	18–44	18–44	20–44	14–94
Female				
Ever had sex with same-sex partner?	11.2	12.5	7.1	—
Sexual Identity				
Homosexual	1.3	1.1	1.5	0.9
Bisexual	2.8	3.5	4.9	3.6
Something else	3.8	0.6	0.8	2.3
Male				
Ever had sex with same-sex partner?	5.6	5.1	6.8	—
Sexual Identity				
Homosexual	2.3	1.7	2.0	4.2
Bisexual	1.8	1.1	1.3	2.6
Something else	3.9	0.2	0.3	1.0

Note: "Something else" may indicate that individuals are questioning their identity or have adopted a different label (e.g., queer).
— indicates data not available.
This table was adapted from data presented in Chandra, Mosher, & Copen (2011).

The most recently available sexual orientation data from a representative US sample comes from the National Survey of Sexual Health and Behavior, which reported that 7.8% of men and 6.8% of women identified as non-heterosexual (Herbenick et al., 2010). Specifically, among men, 4.2% identified as gay, 2.6% as bisexual, and 1.0% as something else. Among women, the numbers were 0.9%, 3.6%, and 2.3%, respectively. For additional data derived from recent national US sex surveys looking at both sexual identity and behavior, see Table 6.1. It is worth mentioning that national survey data from other countries has yielded similar estimates. For example, in England, 5.3% of men and 5.6% of women identify as something other than heterosexual (Hayes et al., 2012). Thus, regardless of data source, it should be clear that even when we consider all non-heterosexual identities together, the resulting number is reliably less than 10%. However, keep in mind that any estimates of prevalence need to be taken with a grain of salt, given that some people may not be willing to reveal their true sexual identity in survey research because they are not comfortable with it or do not wish to be "outed." The numbers presented here simply reflect our best available data.

Theories of Sexual Orientation

The origin of sexual orientation is one that is fraught with myths and misconceptions. For example, some people have argued that homosexuality and bisexuality reflect a conscious choice. However, there are no data to support the idea that most people choose their sexuality (American Psychological Association, 2012). Also, if you accept the notion that homosexuality and bisexuality are a matter of choice, then heterosexuality must also be a matter of choice. If that is the case, why does it sound so absurd to ask someone who is heterosexual questions like "Why did you decide to be heterosexual?" or "How old were you when you made the decision to become straight?" Likewise, there are no data to support the idea that homosexuality is socially "caught" or transmitted or that it is the result of a person just not having had a good heterosexual experience yet (Bell, 1981). With this in mind, let us review research and theory offered by psychologists on the origin of sexual orientation.

Early Psychological Theories

Sigmund Freud (1949) provided one of the first psychological perspectives on the development of sexual orientation. According to Freud, all human beings are **polymorphously perverse**. By this, he meant that humans can derive sexual pleasure from almost anything. One implication of this is that when it comes to sexual attraction, everyone is inherently bisexual, possessing the capacity to develop attraction to men or to women. However, he theorized that normal progression through the psychosexual stages of development would typically result in a pattern of heterosexual attraction, thereby making bisexuality a latent characteristic in most people. Freud argued that homosexuality could stem from several factors, including fixation while passing through certain stages or from having heterosexual experiences that are distressing. Subsequent research found little support for many of Freud's ideas, though, particularly the notion that bad heterosexual experiences may result in homosexuality.

Biological and Hormonal Theories

Modern research on the origin of sexual orientation has largely taken a biological perspective, with the goal of finding physical or genetic markers associated with non-heterosexuality. Over the past two decades, several studies have provided support for the idea that sexual orientation is at least partially rooted in our biology.

First, several studies have reported differences in brain structure between persons with heterosexual and homosexual orientations. For instance, Simon LeVay (1991) reported that the third *interstitial nucleus of the anterior hypothalamus* (INAH3) in heterosexual men was more than twice the size of the INAH3 in homosexual men. For homosexual men, their INAH3 was very similar in size to the corresponding structure in heterosexual women. Although compelling, LeVay's work had a major shortcoming, which was that he made his discovery through post-mortem dissections in which he had to infer subjects' sexual orientation based upon their medical records. Thus, subjects' sexuality was not necessarily known with certainty, meaning some participants may have been miscategorized. In addition, almost all of the men he categorized as homosexual had died of AIDS, making it unclear whether the size of their INAH3 was a product of their sexuality or of a disease process.

More recent studies building upon these limitations continue to support LeVay's contention that sexuality may be rooted in the size and structure of our brains. For instance, a study that utilized brain-imaging technology on live patients found that participants' self-reported sexual orientation was associated with brain symmetry and the number of nerve connections in the amygdala (Savic & Lindstrom, 2008). Specifically, this study found that gay men's brains looked more like those of heterosexual women in that they tended to be more symmetrical (i.e., the left and right hemispheres were of similar size) and possessed a greater concentration of nerve connections in the left side of the amygdala. In contrast, lesbian's brains looked more like those of heterosexual men in that they tended to be asymmetrical (i.e., one hemisphere was bigger than the other) and possessed more nerve connections in the right side of the amygdala.

In addition to brain symmetry, facial symmetry (i.e., the degree to which the left and right sides of the face are identical) is related to sexual orientation (Hughes & Bremme, 2011). Specifically, heterosexual individuals (both male and female) tend to have more symmetrical faces than gay men and lesbians. This same research revealed that facial symmetry was highly correlated with "gaydar," or people's ability to correctly guess others' sexual orientation simply by looking at them. This suggests that symmetry may be one cue we use to infer the sexuality of others; however, this is likely subconscious (i.e., people probably are not thinking "he's pretty asymmetrical, so I'd guess he's gay") and/or it may be correlated with a number of other physical cues that have been shown to relate to the accuracy of sexual orientation judgments (e.g., movement, speech patterns; Rieger, Linsenmeier, Gygax, Garcia, & Bailey, 2010).

Some research suggests that our sexual orientation may be revealed by our hands. For instance, persons with a homosexual orientation are significantly more likely to be left-handed than their heterosexual counterparts (Lalumiere, Blanchard, & Zucker, 2000). In addition, both gay men and lesbians tend to exhibit sex-atypical finger-length ratios (Williams et al., 2000). The finger-length ratio typically observed in heterosexual individuals is as follows: among women, the index finger (second digit) is usually the same length as the ring finger (fourth digit), whereas in men, the index finger is usually a little shorter than the ring finger. Studies indicate that lesbians tend to exhibit the more masculine pattern (i.e., shorter index finger relative to ring finger), whereas gay men (but only gay men with two or more older brothers) tend to show an even more exaggerated masculine pattern. You may think the caveat about older brothers is odd and that the researchers were grasping at straws there, but it is consistent with other research finding that the more older brothers a man has, the more likely he is to be gay. In fact, studies have found that for each extra brother a man has, his odds of being gay increase by 33% (Blanchard & Bogaert, 1996). Why? The prevailing theory is something changes inside the mother's body with each successive son (e.g., her body may be creating antibodies to male proteins that affect all of the following sons). Thus, it makes sense that the exaggerated finger-length pattern only emerged among gay men with a greater number of older male siblings because these two factors may be related in some way.

One final piece of evidence suggesting a biological basis for sexual orientation is twin studies. In general, research has found that the more genetic material two people share, the more likely they are to have the same sexual orientation. Thus, most twin studies have found that the concordance rate for homosexuality is higher for identical twins (who share 100% of their DNA) than it is for fraternal twins (who share about 50% of their DNA; Hershberger, 2001). In other words, identical twins are more likely to have the same sexual orientation than are fraternal twins or non-twin siblings.

The primary explanation for most of the above effects centers around prenatal hormone exposure. One theory is that both gay men and lesbians are exposed to higher than usual levels of androgens in utero. Such an explanation makes sense in light of the finger-length ratio studies; however, it

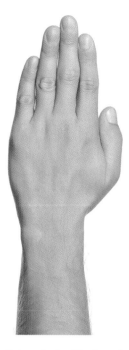

Figure 6.2 The ratio of the second to fourth digit on the hand has been shown to predict sexual orientation in numerous studies. This image depicts the typical male finger length pattern, with the second digit being shorter than the fourth. Image Copyright DenisNata, 2013. Used under license from Shutterstock.com.

would seem to have trouble accounting for the studies indicating that gay men's brains tend to look more like those of heterosexual women than those of heterosexual men. This is not to say that this explanation is inherently wrong, but rather it may be that there are different genetic paths to homosexuality (i.e., for some it may be a matter of hormones, for others it may be due to genes, etc.). As some support for this idea, keep in mind that none of above findings applies in every single case. For instance, not all identical twins share the same sexual orientation, some gay men are the first-born in their families, some lesbians show the more feminine finger length pattern, and so on. There are numerous exceptions to *all* of the effects documented above, which tells us that sexuality is complex and likely multi-determined. The results of this research simply reveal that biology seems to play *some* role in the development of sexual orientation, but it is not necessarily the only factor.

Evolutionary Theories

As discussed in Chapter 1, evolutionary theory would appear to have a hard time explaining the prevalence of homosexuality, given that same-sex behavior does not enhance one's chances of reproductive success. Nonetheless, others have argued that homosexuality may be adaptive in a non-obvious way. For instance, what has come to be known as the "gay uncle" hypothesis was advanced several decades ago and proposes that people who do not necessarily produce their own genetic offspring may enhance the survival of their family's genes by providing resources to their relatives' children (Mayr, 1982). The viability of this hypothesis is questionable, given how homosexuality has long been a socially stigmatized behavior. If it were an adaptive behavior in the sense of this hypothesis, one might expect homosexuality to be socially revered rather than marginalized.

A more recent evolutionary explanation suggests that male homosexuality may be a byproduct of high female fertility (Camperio-Ciani, Corna, & Capiluppi, 2004). Specifically, some studies have found that gay men's female relatives on their mothers' side tend to have significantly more offspring than heterosexual men's maternal female relatives. No such effect has been found for paternal relatives. The results of such research tell us that greater female fertility is associated with a higher likelihood of having gay children. Some have argued that enhanced fertility would more than compensate for the fact that not all children in that genetic pool end up producing offspring of their own. If this is indeed true, it would provide a plausible evolution-based account for why homosexuality, at least in men, has persisted across time.

Evolutionary accounts of female same-sex behavior are harder to come by, but one such explanation is the *alloparenting hypothesis* (Kuhle & Radtke, 2012). This hypothesis specifies that women have evolved a "flexible" sexuality that can shift between attraction to men and attraction to women. It is thought that such flexibility was adaptive for our female ancestors, because when the father of their children was out of the picture (e.g., he died) or did not make an adequate parenting contribution (e.g., he defected to another relationship), one way of securing the help and resources necessary to successfully raise their children was to start a relationship with another woman. Of course, this hypothesis is limited in that it cannot provide an explanation for female same-sex behavior that occurs outside the context of child-rearing.

Biopsychosocial Theories

The last set of theories we will consider view sexual orientation through a biopsychosocial lens, acknowledging that a number of complex and diverse forces act upon human beings to create different sexualities. These theories posit that homosexuality is a product of more than just a "gay gene," and that genetics create certain predispositions that may only come out under certain environmental conditions. In this section, we consider Daryl Bem's Exotic Becomes Erotic theory and Lisa Diamond's work on sexual fluidity.

Exotic Becomes Erotic

Social psychologist Daryl Bem (1996) proposes that individuals are not born with a certain sexual orientation; rather, he theorizes that we are born with a temperament that predisposes us to prefer some activities over others. Generally speaking, our temperaments lead to preferences for behaviors that are typical for our sex (i.e., boys tend to like male-typical activities such as competitive sports, whereas girls tend to like female-typical activities such as cooperative play). As a result, most of us engage in *gender conformity* as children. However, some children's temperaments lead them to prefer activities typically associated with the other sex. These children engage in *gender nonconformity*.

Regardless of whether they are conformers or nonconformers, kids tend to seek out playmates who enjoy the same activities. The result of this is that gender-conforming kids will begin to see themselves as different from children of the other sex, while gender-nonconforming kids will start to feel different from children of the same sex. In other words, we come to see those who engage in different activities as *exotic*. Bem theorizes that these feelings of difference evoke nonsexual physiological arousal whenever a child is near peers from whom that child feels different. During

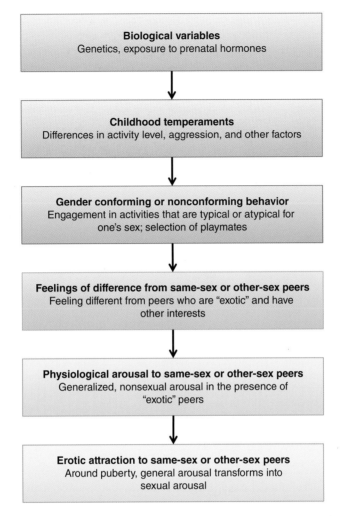

Figure 6.3 The Exotic Becomes Erotic theory incorporates biological and environmental influences on sexual orientation (Bem, 1996).

puberty, when sexual feelings begin to develop, that physiological arousal eventually transforms into sexual arousal. Hence, the **exotic becomes erotic**.

Bem's theory has received a lot of praise for the way it seamlessly links biological and environmental influences. There is also a lot of support for the model in the sense that childhood gender nonconformity is indeed one of the stronger predictors of adult homosexuality (Bailey & Zucker, 1995). As evidence linking childhood behavior to adult sexuality, consider a study in which heterosexual and homosexual men and women were asked to supply childhood home videos (Rieger, Linsenmeier, Gygax, & Bailey, 2008). Research participants then rated the videos on the degree of gender nonconformity expressed. Results indicated that "prehomosexual" children were rated as significantly more gender-nonconforming than "preheterosexual" children.

Nonetheless, the validity of this model has been questioned on numerous grounds. For one thing, some have argued that it does not apply equally well to men and women (Peplau, Garnets,

Figure 6.4 Childhood gender nonconformity is one of the strongest predictors of adult homosexuality. However, keep in mind that there is wide individual variability. Some nonconformers will become heterosexual and some conformers will become homosexual. ©auremar/123RF.COM.

Spalding, Conley, & Veniegas, 1998). As we will discuss in the next section, sexual orientation may develop and express itself differently across the sexes and perhaps a single theory cannot account for this. In addition, Bem's model would appear to imply that if you can change the nature of a child's behavior, you may be able to influence that child's sexual orientation; however, most psychologists doubt this would be possible (LeVay, 2010).

Sexual Fluidity

Developmental psychologist Lisa Diamond (2008a,b) offers a rather different perspective on the origin of sexual orientation. In her work, she argues that sexual orientation may have a stronger biological component in men than in women. Specifically, she adopts the view men are more likely to be "hardwired" for attraction to one sex, whereas women's sexuality is less likely to be focused on one specific category. The result is that women are more likely to experience variations in their patterns of sexual attraction and behavior than are men.

As some evidence for this view, consider a longitudinal study conducted by Diamond (2008a) in which she studied 100 women for nearly 10 years. All of her participants had experienced at least some amount of same-sex attraction in the past and considered their sexuality to be bisexual, lesbian, or unlabeled at the start of the study. Diamond found that about two-thirds of these women changed their sexual orientation label at least once during that 10-year period, and these changes went in all possible directions (i.e., some went from lesbian to bisexual, some from bisexual to heterosexual, some from unlabeled to lesbian, etc.). These changes often coincided with who their specific sexual or romantic partner was at the time. Diamond termed this pattern of behavior **sexual fluidity** and described it as the ability to adapt sexual and romantic attraction toward a specific person instead of an overall gender category. Although Diamond's research would appear to suggest that sexual fluidity is a phenomenon unique to women, a national US survey in which participants were tracked for a 10-year period found that about one-half of the men with a bisexual identity evidenced some identity change over the course of the study (Mock & Eibach, 2012). Of course, the sample in this particular study was very small (only 34 participants identified as bisexual at the start of the study), but it suggests that for at least a small number of men, sexual fluidity may be possible and that being male does not necessarily mean having a rigid and unchanging sexuality.

Diamond's perspective is similar to Bem's Exotic Becomes Erotic theory in that it suggests that biology creates a sexual capacity that is influenced by social and environmental factors. It is perhaps best to view Diamond's work as a complement to Bem's rather than as an alternative because each may be better suited to helping us understand the nature of sexual orientation in different sexes.

Of course, it is important to keep in mind that this perspective, like all of the others covered in this section, is inherently limited. For instance, although two-thirds of the women in Diamond's research evidenced sexual fluidity, she was not dealing with a representative sample. Thus, it would not be wise to assume that all or even most women have a fluid sexuality, and it is not at all clear why some women have it and others do not. In short, if you were hoping for a simple, clear answer as to why variations in sexual orientation exist, I am afraid such an answer does not exist. In all likelihood, sexuality is a product of multiple factors and there may be several routes to any given sexual orientation.

Sex Differences in the Expression of Sexual Orientation

As mentioned above, sexual fluidity is one way the sexual orientation of men and women differs, and it is part of a much broader literature suggesting that women seem to have more **erotic plasticity** than do men. Erotic plasticity is defined as the degree to which a person's sex drive and sexual behavior is "flexible" and responsive to cultural and situational pressures (Baumeister, 2000).

In the seminal paper describing this phenomenon, Baumeister (2000) details evidence throughout the history of sex research indicating that (1) women's sexual behavior fluctuates and varies more across time than does men's, (2) culture, education, and religion appear to have a stronger effect on female sexuality than on male sexuality, and (3) there is a greater discrepancy between sexual attitudes and behaviors for women than there is for men.

Let us review some specific research examples cited by Baumeister in support of these points. With respect to women's greater individual variability, consider that contrary to popular belief and media depictions, women are more likely to engage in same-sex activity while in prison than are men (Gagnon & Simon, 1968). Likewise, among married "swingers" (i.e., couples who swap or exchange sexual partners) same-sex activity is common among wives, but extremely rare among husbands (Bartell, 1970). In terms of women's greater susceptibility to social influence, consider that Catholic nuns are more successful at maintaining vows of celibacy than are male priests (Murphy, 1992) and that female adolescents show more similarity in sexual attitudes and behaviors to their parents than do male adolescents (Thornton & Camburn, 1987). Finally, regarding greater inconsistency in women's sexual attitudes and behaviors, research has found that women are far more likely than men to engage in sexual activity when they do not have the desire for it (O'Sullivan & Allgeier, 1998).

Figure 6.5   Research has found that women demonstrate signs of sexual arousal in response to a wider range of pornography than men. Image Copyright Dewayne Flowers, 2013. Used under license from Shutterstock.com.

Recent research has found additional evidence supporting the idea that women's sexuality is more flexible and adaptable than men's. For instance, if you recall from chapter 4, we discussed a study by Chivers, Rieger, Latty, and Bailey (2004) demonstrating that while heterosexual men only exhibited significant genital arousal in response to porn featuring women, heterosexual women exhibited strong levels of genital arousal in response to all kinds of porn, irrespective of whether it featured lesbians, gay men, or heterosexual couples. An almost identical pattern of results was reported by Rieger and Savin-Williams (2012), who assessed pupil dilation in response to sexually arousing stimuli. Pupil dilation is an automatic response that occurs when we see an interesting stimulus. In this study, gay and heterosexual men only showed dilation in response to images of their desired sex; in contrast, heterosexual women showed dilation in response to both male *and* female sexual imagery.

Similar conclusions could be drawn from research into the male and female sex drive. Across three studies involving over 3,600 participants, Lippa (2006) found that for heterosexual women, a high sex drive was correlated with reporting greater attraction to both men and women. In contrast, for gay and heterosexual men, a higher sex drive was correlated with increased attraction only to their desired sex. One interesting caveat to Lippa's (2006) sex-drive study and Rieger and Savin-Williams' (2012) pupil-dilation study is that in both cases, lesbians' patterns did not match those of heterosexual women. Specifically, lesbians' data tended to look more like those

Figure 6.6 Can our eyes reveal our sexual orientation? Research indicates that our pupils dilate in response to imagery that we find sexually arousing. ©Svetlana Vitkovskaya/123RF.COM.

of heterosexual men (i.e., they only evidenced high levels of attraction toward their desired sex). This suggests that lesbians may not demonstrate the same degree of erotic plasticity as heterosexual women.

As two additional pieces of evidence suggesting that women's sexuality tends to be variable whereas men's tends to be more category-specific, consider the fact that *fetishes* (i.e., cases where sexual arousal is dependent upon the presence of a specific object) occur with some frequency in men, but are almost unheard of in women. Likewise, as you can see in Table 6.1, men are more likely to identify as homosexual, whereas women are more likely to identify as bisexual or "something else." This same table also reveals that the prevalence of same-sex activity tends to be higher among women than it is among men.

When considered together, all of this evidence suggests that sexual orientation is organized differently in the brains of men and women, such that men are more likely to "orient" on a specific target, whereas women tend to possess more flexibility. Please note that this should not be taken to mean that "all women are inherently bisexual" or that "bisexuality does not exist in men." As with all research on sexuality, we can only speak in terms of general trends – there are few, perhaps no, truly universal principles that apply to *everyone* of a specific group. Thus, if you are a heterosexual man whose ultimate fantasy is for your girlfriend to be bisexual, you should not automatically conclude that all you need to do to make your dreams come true is give your girlfriend a little nudge in that direction. While women appear to have more erotic plasticity than men, the degree of "flexibility" varies considerably and some women may not have any flexibility at all (as evidenced by some of the lesbian data reported above).

Sexual Orientation Attitudes

In numerous societies throughout history, people who engaged in any form of same-sex behavior were looked down upon. Of course, attitudes have fluctuated across time and culture (e.g., homosexuality and bisexuality were more socially accepted among the ancient Greeks and Romans), but for the most part, they have been negative. In this section, we will explore modern attitudes toward non-heterosexuals, including the different forms of prejudice that exist and the way the field of psychology views sexual orientation.

Prejudice Against Gay, Lesbian, and Bisexual Persons

Sexual prejudice is the general term used to describe all forms of prejudice that stem from an individual's actual or perceived sexual orientation (Herek, 2000). This could include bias toward persons of any sexuality, including heterosexuals. However, such prejudice is most frequently directed against gay, lesbian, and bisexual individuals.

Prejudice specific to gays and lesbians is known more commonly as **homophobia**. This term suggests that sexual prejudice stems from an irrational fear (i.e., a true *phobia*) of homosexual persons. However, antigay prejudice is usually construed more broadly as consisting of a constellation of negative attitudes, with fear being just one such attitude. Related to homophobia is **heterosexism**, or the assumption that everyone is heterosexual and that attraction to the other sex is normative. Many people would assume that homophobia and heterosexism are perfectly correlated, but that is not the case. It is possible for an individual to be heterosexist without necessarily being homophobic. For instance, a non-homophobic person may still assume that anyone who wears a wedding ring is married to someone of the other sex because that person may have been culturally conditioned to view marriage as a heterosexual institution.

Prejudice specific to bisexuals is known as **biphobia**. Again, while it may take the form of a true phobia for some, this type of prejudice can have its basis in a number of other emotions (e.g., anger, resentment). A related form of bias is **monosexism**, or the belief that exclusive attraction to one sex is the norm. It is important to recognize that heterosexuals are not the only ones who can be biphobic and monosexist – gays and lesbians can hold these biases as well.

Prejudice against non-heterosexuals is common. For instance, a 2013 Gallup poll found that two in five Americans believe that sexual activity among persons of the same sex is wrong (Newport & Himelfarb, 2013). Of course, it is important to recognize that these attitudes have shifted considerably in the past few years. In fact, just one decade before that 2013 poll, the vast majority of

Figure 6.7   Overt displays of homophobia are common in many parts of the world. Constant encounters with prejudice of this nature have adverse effects on the gay and lesbian community. Source: EwS (Own work) [CC-BY-SA-2.0 (http://creativecommons.org/licenses/by-sa/2.0)], via Wikimedia Commons.

Americans held negative views. It is also worth noting that these attitudes vary considerably cross-culturally, with more tolerance in the Western world and less throughout much of Africa and Asia, where laws criminalizing same-sex behavior still exist in some countries. For instance, sexual activity with a member of the same sex is a crime punishable by death in Sudan, Iran, Saudi Arabia, and Yemen (ILGA, 2013a).

Although homophobia and biphobia are common, some research suggests that biphobia may be even more prevalent. For instance, in one national US survey, participants were asked to rate how they felt about various groups of people (including racial, religious, political, and sexual minority groups) using a *feeling thermometer* (Herek, 2002). The thermometer ranged from 0 to 100, with higher ratings indicating "warmer" (i.e., more positive) feelings. Bisexual men and women were the second-lowest-rated group, appearing below gays and lesbians. The only group rated lower than bisexuals was injection drug users.

Despite the prevalence of homophobia and biphobia, gay and bisexual persons tend to have more ability to "come out" and live their lives openly today than at any other time in recent history. For instance, a growing number of countries have passed laws protecting the rights of sexual minorities in housing and employment. Moreover, some of these countries offer legal recognition for same-sex couples in the form of marriages, civil unions, or domestic partnerships. In addition, there are numerous organizations worldwide that offer support to the gay and bisexual communities and provide a voice for them in ongoing political debates.

Origins of Sexual Prejudice

Where do homophobia and biphobia come from? There are likely many contributing factors. For example, research has found that the holding of strong religious beliefs is one of the most potent predictors of sexual prejudice (Herek & Capitanio, 1996). This is perhaps not surprising in light of how many religions throughout the world hold the view that sexual behavior with someone of the same sex is always morally wrong. This research also reveals that lower levels of education, older age, and having little contact with gays and lesbians are associated with greater sexual prejudice. Another contributing factor is a fear of one's own same-sex attraction. Consistent with this idea, research has found that homophobic men who identify as heterosexual demonstrate significantly greater sexual arousal in response to gay pornography than their non-homophobic, heterosexual counterparts (Adams, Wright, & Lohr, 1996). For more on how homophobia may stem from one's own homosexuality, see the Digging Deeper 6.1 box.

Digging Deeper 6.1   Are Homophobic People Repressing Their Own Same-Sex Desires?

The idea that homophobia stems from fears of one's own homosexuality has received a lot of public validation in recent years. From evangelical preacher Ted Haggard, to former United States Senator Larry Craig, to psychologist George Reckers (one of the leading proponents of "reparative therapy"), some of those who have been fighting hardest against LGBT rights have wound up embroiled in gay sex scandals of their own. Naturally, many of us wonder why. A fascinating set of studies suggests that this type of hypocrisy may be traced back to the way these individuals were raised by their parents (Weinstein, Ryan, DeHaan, Przybylski, & Legate, 2012).

Figure 6.8   Several prominent politicians, including former United States Senator Larry Craig, have been embroiled in gay sex scandals despite voting in favor of legislation restricting gay rights. This tells us that homophobia may partly stem from discomfort with one's own same-sex attraction. Source: Public domain image, via Wikimedia Commons.

The theory is that when parents fail to provide support for their children's sense of independence, those children become susceptible to developing a discrepancy between their true identity and the identity they express to the rest of the world. That is, when parents try to control their children's opinions, beliefs, and behaviors or make their love contingent upon their children acting a certain way, children may start behaving in a way that is consistent with their parents' desires, even though it may be opposite from their true feelings. This is especially likely to happen in children whose feelings of self-worth are dependent upon parental approval, as opposed to children who could not care less about what their parents think of them. Thus, if a gay person is raised by parents who believe that homosexuality is unacceptable, that individual might repress any same-sex desires and express the homophobic attitudes that are likely to earn parental love and approval. This might lay the foundation for a lifelong pattern of being outwardly homophobic and denying one's own homosexuality as a way of gaining social acceptance.

Support for this idea was obtained in a set of four studies conducted by Weinstein and colleagues (2012). Participants were male and female college students in the United States and Germany. Results indicated that people whose parents (especially their fathers) discouraged independence were the most likely to have a discrepancy between their explicit and implicit sexual identities (i.e., they identified as straight, but showed unconscious attraction toward members of the same-sex). Individuals with these identity discrepancies also expressed the most hostility toward homosexuality and were the most likely to support public policies that discriminate against gays and lesbians (e.g., policies prohibiting same-sex couples from marrying or adopting children).

These studies suggest that parenting styles and internal conflict may play an even larger role in the development of homophobia than previously thought. They also provide us with insight into some of the psychological factors that may underlie the hypocrisy evident in recent cases of anti-gay religious and political figures caught in gay sex scandals, not to mention the motivations behind anti-gay bullying and hate crimes more broadly. Of course, it is important to keep in mind that homophobia does not necessarily have to develop this way and not everyone who is homophobic has repressed same-sex attraction. While this research represents a fascinating and important piece of the puzzle, it is certainly not the last word on the origin of anti-gay prejudice.

Note: Reprinted with permission from *The Psychology of Human Sexuality* blog (www.lehmiller.com).

Another factor in sexual prejudice is biological sex. Research has reliably found that heterosexual men tend to be more homophobic and biphobic than heterosexual women (Herek, 2002). Although heterosexual men are more negative overall, their attitudes toward sexual minority men tends to be more negative than their attitudes toward sexual minority women.

Consequences of Sexual Prejudice

Sexual prejudice has a wide range of effects on the gay, lesbian, and bisexual population. For instance, sexual minorities are frequently the victims of violent crimes and vandalism as a result of their sexuality. Specifically, one out of three gay men and one out of eight lesbians has been the

Figure 6.9 Despite a continued high prevalence of sexual prejudice, gay, lesbian, and bisexual persons have more ability today to live openly and freely than ever before. Source: Rama (Own work) [CC-BY-SA-2.0 France (http://creativecommons.org/licenses/by-sa/2.0/fr/deed.en)], via Wikimedia Commons.

victim of a property crime or personal violence due to their sexual orientation (Herek, 2008). Criminal acts that target people because of their actual or perceived sexuality are usually referred to as *hate crimes*, and these can be extremely serious. In recent years, international attention has been drawn to several cases where individuals have been horrifically beaten, tortured, or even killed solely because they were not heterosexual.

In addition to more physical forms of victimization, sexual minorities frequently experience harassment and bullying, intimidation, and discrimination (for a list of countries worldwide that have anti-discrimination policies covering sexual orientation, see Table 6.2). This takes an important toll on the overall physical and psychological well-being of gay, lesbian, and bisexual persons. Frequent experiences with prejudice are stressful, and if you have ever taken a course in health psychology, you are probably well aware of the detrimental effects of chronic stress on our bodies and brains. As just one example, research on gay men has found that experiencing more sexuality-related stressors (e.g., discrimination) is linked to greater symptoms of psychological distress, substance use, and riskier sexual behaviors (Hatzenbuehler, Nolen-Hoeksema, & Erickson, 2008). Numerous other studies have demonstrated similar effects. Thus, it is important to keep in mind that any time you hear about sexual minorities having elevated rates of psychopathology or drug use, we are likely talking about the consequences of differential experiences with stress.

Sexual Orientation in Psychological Perspective

For most of the twentieth century, the prevailing view of homosexuality in the field of psychology was that it was a mental illness. In fact, until 1974, homosexuality was listed as a disorder in the DSM. One of the major reasons behind this diagnostic change was the pioneering research of

Table 6.2 Countries with Laws that Prohibit Employment Discrimination on the Basis of Sexual Orientation

National laws	Some local laws, but no national law
Albania	Argentina
Bosnia and Herzegovina	Australia
Canada	Brazil
Chile	Japan
Columbia	Paraguay
Croatia	United States
European Union (All 27 Nations)	
French Guiana	
Georgia	
Greenland	
Israel	
Kosovo	
Macedonia	
Mexico	
Montenegro	
Mozambique	
New Zealand	
Norway	
Serbia	
South Africa	
Switzerland	
Venezuela	

Source: ILGA (2013b).

psychologist Evelyn Hooker. In her most famous study, she gave psychological tests such as the Thematic Apperception Test and the Rorschach Test to a sample of heterosexual and homosexual men (Hooker, 1957). She then presented the results to a panel of psychological experts and asked them to identify which results came from heterosexual men and which came from homosexual men. This study revealed that there was no discernible difference in psychological adjustment among men of different sexualities. Hooker's work, combined with Alfred Kinsey's research suggesting that same-sex activity is quite common, culminated in the field of psychology re-evaluating its stance on sexual orientation.

Since the 1970s, the psychological community has viewed homosexuality and bisexuality as natural human variations that do not require any type of "cure" or treatment. In fact, the American Psychological Association encourages **gay affirmative therapy** for clients who are gay or lesbian. The goal of this approach is to get patients to accept their sexuality, not to change their identity, pattern of attraction, or behavior. Treatment focuses on helping the client cope with any stress or stigma they experience as a result of their sexual identity.

A handful of therapists continue to deviate from this and practice *reparative therapy* (also known as conversion therapy). As discussed in chapter 1, this practice involves active attempts at changing a person's sexual orientation, largely through the use of operant conditioning principles. However, there is no evidence that this works and, in fact, it appears to cause more harm than anything (Halderman, 2003).

Sexual Orientation Myths

To finish this chapter, let us set the record straight on some of the most common myths and stereotypes that exist on the topics of homosexuality and bisexuality.

MYTH: Men cannot truly be bisexual.   Contrary to the popular stereotype that bisexual men are just guys who are not ready to come out of the closet yet, research has found evidence of "true" male bisexuality (i.e., strong physiological and psychological arousal in response to both men and women). For more on this research, see the Digging Deeper 6.2 box.

Digging Deeper 6.2   Are Bisexual People Aroused By Both Men and Women?

"I'm not even sure bisexuality exists. I think it's just a layover on the way to gaytown."
– Carrie Bradshaw (*Sex and the City*)

Many of you are familiar with the popular stereotype of bisexual people as closeted gays who are not ready to admit it to the world. Proponents of this stereotype were seemingly validated by a 2005 study published in *Psychological Science*, which found that most men who identified as bisexual exhibited stronger genital arousal in response to male pornographic imagery than female pornographic imagery (Rieger, Chivers, & Bailey, 2005). However, a more recent study published in *Biological Psychology* disputes this finding and presents convincing evidence that "true" bisexuality (i.e., strong attraction to both men and women) exists (Rosenthal, Sylva, Safron, & Bailey, 2011).

Both of these studies employed identical methods. In each case, a sample of self-described heterosexual, homosexual, and bisexual men was recruited. All participants were exposed to a series of videos that alternated between non-sexual content, man-on-man pornography, and woman-on-woman pornography. While watching these videos, male participants were hooked up to a device that measured changes in penile size (i.e., a penile strain gauge). The only difference between the studies was in how bisexual participants were recruited. In the original Rieger and colleagues (2005) report, bisexual participants were selected based upon their self-reported sexual orientation (i.e., the only criterion was that they had to identify as bisexual). In the more recent Rosenthal and colleagues (2011) report, bisexual participants were selected *only if they confirmed a history of sexual and romantic relationships with members of both sexes*. This was to help ensure that participants' sexual identities and behaviors were consistent.

The results for heterosexual and homosexual participants were consistent across studies and were exactly what you would expect (i.e., genital arousal was strongest when exposed to pornographic imagery featuring members of their desired sex). The findings for bisexual men were more surprising, and each study reported a completely different pattern of results. In the original report, bisexual participants' genital arousal was almost always stronger in response to men (same sex) than to women (other sex), consistent with the stereotype that bisexuals are just "latent homosexuals." However, in the more recent study, most bisexual men exhibited high levels of genital arousal in response to both male and female pornography, providing evidence of true bisexuality. Bisexual men did not necessarily show *equally* strong arousal to both sexes, but they showed high levels of arousal in each case.

Combined, these studies tell us that bisexuality is a complex identity that means different things to different people, and that the way researchers define it has implications for the kinds of results they obtain. For some people, bisexuality represents strong attraction toward both men and women. For others, a bisexual identity may signify openness to new experiences, confusion or discomfort with one's sexuality, or a number of other things. Although much more research is needed on this topic (especially research that includes male *and* female participants), these findings provide evidence that bisexuality is a distinct sexual orientation that should not be dismissed.

Note: Reprinted with permission from *The Psychology of Human Sexuality* blog (www.lehmiller.com).

MYTH: *All gay men are effeminate and all lesbians are masculine.* While gender nonconformity is indeed associated with homosexuality, behavioral characteristics and appearance vary considerably across both gay men and lesbians. While it is certainly true that *some* gay men are effeminate, there are also a lot of macho gay men. Likewise, *some* lesbians are masculine or "butch," but others are extremely feminine. The reality is that the gay and lesbian community is enormously diverse, which means that traits and characteristics can vary greatly from one person to the next. As some evidence of this, consider the fact that studies of "gaydar" have found that it is far from perfect (Rieger et al., 2010), and that not everyone who identifies as gay displays gender nonconformity (Rieger et al., 2008).

MYTH: *In a gay relationship, someone must play the "husband" and someone must play the "wife".* Despite popular media depictions that almost universally portray gay couples in this way, there are not assigned roles in a gay relationship. The reality is that partners in gay and lesbian relationships tend to share responsibilities equally rather than conforming to traditional gender roles (Kurdek, 1998).

MYTH: Gay parents tend to raise gay children.   As previously mentioned, there is no empirical support for the idea that homosexuality is socially transmitted. As a result, it is perhaps not surprising that children of gay parents are no more likely to be gay than children of heterosexual parents (Fitzgerald, 1999). Besides, if sexual orientation was purely a learned behavior, then why do so many heterosexual parents produce gay children?

MYTH: Homosexuality is correlated with pedophilia.   There is no scientific link between homo-sexuality and sexual interest in children. For instance, consider a study by Freund, Watson, and Rienzo (1989) in which adult heterosexual and homosexual men were exposed to sexually suggestive photos of male and female individuals at various ages (as children, adolescents, and adults). The men were hooked up to penile strain gauges in order to measure arousal. Results indicated that gay men did not respond any more to images of male children than heterosexual men responded to images of female children. These findings, combined with other studies suggesting that it is rare for child molesters to be gay or lesbian indicates that there is nothing to even remotely back up this idea.

MYTH: All gay men are promiscuous and are incapable of having long-term relationships.   This is perhaps the most common stereotype about gay men, but the truth of the matter is that it is a wild exaggeration. First, consider that gay and heterosexual men report having equally high sex drives (Lippa, 2006). Thus, gay men do not necessarily have stronger libidos than their heterosexual counterparts. But do they have more partners? Research has found that gay men have a higher average number of partners (Laumann et al., 1994). However, a closer look at these data reveals that this average is thrown off by a small number of gay men who reported an exceptionally large number of partners. Instead, if you consider the median (which is not susceptible to the same distortion as an average), homosexual men report having just one more partner than heterosexual men do. Thus, the idea that *all* gay men are sleeping around at a substantially elevated rate is not supported by research. Also, to the extent that some gay men indeed accumulate more partners, it can probably be explained by the fact that it is easier to find a willing male partner than a willing female partner due to differential interest in casual sex. If women expressed greater interest in casual sex (or if society permitted them to do so without penalty), heterosexual men would likely have just as many partners as gay men. It is also worth noting that gay men are perfectly capable of having long-term, satisfying relationships. Sexuality makes no difference in one's ability to have a functional relationship.

MYTH: Bisexual people cannot be faithful.   Some people believe that a bisexual person cannot remain in an exclusive, monogamous relationship for long because a bisexual individual will ultimately become dissatisfied and desire a partner of the other sex. However, bisexuals can indeed be content with monogamy. For example, in Lisa Diamond's (2008a) longitudinal study of sexual fluidity, she found that 89% of the women who identified as bisexual wound up in long-term, monogamous relationships.

MYTH: Most people who have HIV are gay or bisexual men.   In the United States, this statement is technically true. Most new infections are currently attributable to gay and bisexual men (Centers for Disease Control and Prevention, 2012). However, if you look beyond the US, this is not true at all. In other parts of the world, particularly in Africa, where HIV is most prevalent, the vast

Figure 6.10   Sexual orientation does not affect one's ability to develop and maintain a long-term, loving relationship. Image Copyright Kobby Dagan, 2013. Used under license from Shutterstock.com.

majority of people infected are heterosexuals, and about half of them are women. Thus, while this statement may be true in some places, it is far from accurate when looking at the overall picture for this disease.

Key Terms

sexual orientation	exotic becomes erotic	heterosexism
Kinsey scale	sexual fluidity	biphobia
asexuality	erotic plasticity	monosexism
pansexuality	sexual prejudice	gay affirmative therapy
polymorphously perverse	homophobia	

Discussion Questions: What is Your Perspective on Sex?

- What do you make of Freud's notion that human beings are "polymorphously perverse?" Do you think we all have an inherent tendency toward bisexuality and that exposure to different environmental factors can bring out different sexualities? Does this remind you of other theoretical perspectives we discussed?

- What are some examples of heterosexism and monosexism you have observed in your own life?
- Proponents of "reparative therapy" often argue that if it is legitimate to help persons with gender dysphoria change their sex, it should also be legitimate to help someone who is distressed about their sexual orientation to change that aspect of the self. What is your response to this argument?

References

Adams, H.E., Wright, L.W., & Lohr, B.A. (1996). Is homophobia associated with homosexual arousal? *Journal of Abnormal Psychology, 105,* 440–445. DOI:10.1037/0021-843X.105.3.440.

American Psychological Association (2012). *Sexual orientation and homosexuality.* Retrieved from http://www.apa.org/helpcenter/sexual-orientation.aspx (accessed September 1, 2013).

Bailey, J.M., & Zucker, K.J. (1995). Childhood sex-typed behavior and sexual orientation: A conceptual analysis and quantitative review. *Developmental Psychology, 31,* 43–55. DOI:10.1037/0012-1649.31.1.43.

Bartell, G.D. (1970). Group sex among the mid-Americans. *Journal of Sex Research, 6,* 113–130. DOI:10.1080/00224497009550655.

Baumeister, R.F. (2000). Gender differences in erotic plasticity: The female sex drive as socially flexible and responsive. *Psychological Bulletin, 126,* 347–374. DOI:10.1037//0033-2909.126.3.347.

Bell, A.P., Weinberg, M.S., & Hammersmith, S.K. (1981). *Sexual preference: Its development in men and women.* Bloomington: Indiana University Press.

Bem, D.J. (1996). Exotic becomes erotic: A developmental theory of sexual orientation. *Psychological Review, 103,* 320–335. DOI:10.1037/0033-295X.103.2.320.

Blanchard, R., & Bogaert, A. F. (1996). Homosexuality in men and number of older brothers. *The American Journal of Psychiatry, 153,* 27–31.

Camperio-Ciani, A., Corna, F., & Capiluppi, C. (2004). Evidence for maternally inherited factors favouring male homosexuality and promoting female fecundity. *Proceedings of the Royal Society B: Biological Sciences, 271,* 2217–2221. DOI:10.1098/rspb.2004.2872.

Centers for Disease Control and Prevention (2012). *HIV/AIDS Statistics and Surveillance.* Retrieved from http://www.cdc.gov/hiv/topics/surveillance/basic.htm (accessed September 2, 2013).

Chandra, A., Mosher, W.D., & Copen, C. (2011). Sexual behavior, sexual attraction, and sexual identity in the United States: Data from the 2006–2008 National Survey of Family Growth. *National Health Statistics Reports, 36,* 1–36.

Chivers, M.L., Rieger, G., Latty, E., & Bailey, J.M. (2004). A sex difference in the specificity of sexual arousal. *Psychological Science, 15,* 736–744. DOI:10.1111/j.0956-7976.2004.00750.x.

Diamond, L., (2008a). Female bisexuality from adolescence to adulthood: Results from a 10-year longitudinal study. *Developmental Psychology, 44,* 5–14. DOI:10.1037/0012-1649.44.1.5.

Diamond, L. (2008b). *Sexual Fluidity: Understanding Women's Love and Desire.* Cambridge, MA: Harvard University Press.

Fitzgerald, B. (1999). Children of lesbian and gay parents: A review of the literature. *Marriage and Family Review, 29,* 57–75. DOI:10.1300/J002v29n01_05.

Freud, S. (1949). *Three essays on the theory of sexuality* (1st English edition). London: Imago Publishing Company.

Freund, K., Watson, R., & Rienzo, D. (1989). Heterosexuality, homosexuality, and erotic age preference. *Journal of Sex Research, 26,* 107–117. DOI:10.1080/00224498909551494.

Gagnon, J.H., & Simon, W. (1968). The social meaning of prison homosexuality. *Federal Probation, 32,* 28–29.

Halderman, D.C. (2003). Gay rights, patient rights: The implications of sexual orientation conversion therapy. *Professional Psychology: Research and Practice, 33,* 260–264. DOI:10.1037//0735-7028.33.3.260.

Hatzenbuehler, M.L., Nolen-Hoeksema, S., & Erickson, S.J. (2008). Minority stress predictors of HIV risk behavior, substance use, and depressive symptoms: Results from a prospective study of bereaved gay men. *Health Psychology, 27,* 455–462. DOI:10.1037/0278-6133.27.4.455.

Hayes, J., Chakraborty, A.T., McManus, S., Bebbington, P., Brugha, T., Nicholson, S., & King, M. (2012). Prevalence of same-sex behavior and orientation in England: Results from a national survey. *Archives of Sexual Behavior, 41*, 631–639. DOI:10.1007/s10508-011-9856-8.

Herbenick, D., Reece, M., Schick, V., Sanders, S.A., Dodge, B., & Fortenberry, J.D. (2010). Sexual behavior in the United States: Results from a national probability sample of men and women ages 14–94. *Journal of Sexual Medicine, 7*(Suppl. 5), 255–265. DOI:10.1111/j.1743-6109.2010.02012.x.

Herek, G.M. (2000). The psychology of sexual prejudice. *Current Directions in Psychological Science, 9*, 19–22. DOI:10.1111/1467-8721.00051.

Herek, G.M. (2002). Heterosexuals' attitudes toward bisexual men and women in the United States. *Journal of Sex Research, 39*, 264–274. DOI:10.1080/00224490209552150.

Herek, G.M. (2008). Hate crimes and stigma-related experiences among sexual minority adults in the United States: Prevalence estimates from a national probability sample. *Journal of Interpersonal Violence, 24*, 54–74. DOI:10.1177/0886260508316477.

Herek, G.M., & Capitanio, J. (1996). "Some of my best friends": Intergroup contact, concealable stigma, and heterosexuals' attitudes toward gay men and lesbians. *Personality and Social Psychology Bulletin, 22*, 412–424. DOI:10.1177/0146167296224007.

Hershberger, S.L. (2001). Biological factors in the development of sexual orientation. In A. R. D'Augelli & C. J. Patterson (Eds.) *Lesbian, Gay, and Bisexual Identities and Youth: Psychological Perspectives* (pp. 27–51). New York: Oxford University Press.

Hooker, E. (1957). The adjustment of the male overt homosexual. *Journal of Projective Techniques, 21*, 18–31. DOI:10.1080/08853126.1957.10380742.

Hughes, S.M., & Bremme, R. (2011). The effects of facial symmetry and sexually-dimorphic facial proportions on assessments of sexual orientation. *Journal of Social, Evolutionary, and Cultural Psychology, 5*, 214–230.

ILGA (2013a). *Lesbian and gay rights in the world.* Retrieved from http://old.ilga.org/Statehomophobia/ILGA_map_2013_A4.pdf (accessed September 2, 2013).

ILGA (2013b). Laws prohibiting discrimination on grounds of sexual orientation (in employment). Retrieved from http://ilga.org (accessed September 2, 2013).

Kinsey, A., Pomeroy, W.B., & Martin, C. E. (1948). *Sexual behavior in the human male.* Philadelphia: Saunders.

Kinsey, A., Pomeroy, W.B., Martin, C.E., & Gebhard, P. (1953). *Sexual behavior in the human female.* Philadelphia: Saunders.

Kuhle, B. X., & Radtke, S. (2012). Born both ways: The alloparenting hypothesis for sexual fluidity in women. *Evolutionary Psychology, 11*, 304–323.

Kurdek, L.A. (1998). Relationship outcomes and their predictors: Longitudinal evidence from heterosexual married, gay cohabiting, and lesbian cohabiting couples. *Journal of Marriage and Family, 60*, 553–568.

Lalumiere, M.L., Blanchard, R., & Zucker, K.J. (2000). Sexual orientation and handedness in men and women: A meta-analysis. *Psychological Bulletin, 126*, 575–592. DOI:10.1037/0033-2909.126.4.575.

Laumann, E.O., Gagnon, J., Michael, R., & Michaels, S. (1994). *The social organization of sexuality: Sexual practices in the United States.* Chicago: University of Chicago Press.

LeVay, S. (1991). A difference in hypothalamic structure between homosexual and heterosexual men. *Science, 253*, 1034–1037. DOI:10.1126/science.1887219.

LeVay, S. (2010). *Gay, straight, and the reason why: The science of sexual orientation.* New York: Oxford University Press.

Lippa, R.A. (2006). Is high sex drive associated with increased sexual attraction to both sexes? *Psychological Science, 17*, 46–52. DOI:10.1111/j.1467-9280.2005.01663.x.

Mayr, E. (1982). *The growth of biological thought: Diversity, evolution, and inheritance.* Cambridge, MA: Harvard University Press.

Mock, S.E., & Eibach, R.P. (2012). Stability and change in sexual orientation identity over a 10-year period in adulthood. *Archives of Sexual Behavior, 41*, 641–648. DOI: 10.1007/s10508-011-9761-1.

Murphy, S. (1992). *A delicate dance: Sexuality, celibacy, and relationships among Catholic clergy and religious.* New York: Crossroad.

Newport, F., & Himelfarb, I. (2013). *In U.S., record-high say gay, lesbian relations morally OK*. Retrieved from http://www.gallup.com/poll/162689/record-high-say-gay-lesbian-relations-morally.aspx (accessed September 2, 2013).

O'Sullivan, L.P., & Allgeier, E.R. (1998). Feigning sexual desire: Consenting to unwanted sexual activity in heterosexual dating relationships. *Journal of Sex Research*, *35*, 234–243. DOI:10.1080/00224499809551938

Peplau, L.A., Garnets, L.D., Spalding, L.R., Conley, T.D., & Veniegas, R.C. (1998). A critique of Bem's "exotic becomes erotic" theory of sexual orientation. *Psychological Review*, *105*, 387–394. DOI:10.1037/0033-295X.105.2.387.

Reback, C.J., & Larkins, S. (2013). HIV risk behaviors among a sample of heterosexually identified men who occasionally have sex with another male and/or a transwoman. *Journal of Sex Research*, *50*, 151–163. DOI:10.1080/00224499.2011.632101.

Rieger, G., & Savin-Williams, R.C. (2012). The eyes have it: Sex and sexual orientation differences in pupil dilation patterns. *PLoS ONE 7*(8): e40256. DOI:10.1371/journal.pone.0040256.

Rieger, G., Chivers, M.L., & Bailey, J.M. (2005). Sexual arousal patterns of bisexual men. *Psychological Science*, *16*, 579–584. DOI:10.2307/2137286.

Rieger, G., Linsenmeier, J.A.W., Gygax, L., & Bailey, J.M. (2008). Sexual orientation and childhood gender nonconformity: Evidence from home videos. *Developmental Psychology*, *44*, 46–58. DOI:10.1037/0012-1649.44.1.46.

Rieger, G., Linsenmeier, J.A.W., Gygax, L., Garcia, S., & Bailey, J.M. (2010). Dissecting "gaydar": Accuracy and the role of masculinity–femininity. *Archives of Sexual Behavior*, *39*, 124–140. DOI:10.1007/s10508-008-9405-2.

Rosenthal, A.M., Sylva, D., Safron, A., & Bailey, J.M. (2011). Sexual arousal patterns of bisexual men revisited. *Biological Psychology*, *88*, 112–115. DOI:10.1016/j.biopsycho.2011.06.015.

Savic, I., & Lindstrom, P. (2008). PET and MRI show differences in cerebral asymmetry and functional connectivity between homo- and heterosexual subjects. *Proceedings of the National Academy of Sciences*, *105*, 9403–9408. DOI:10.1073/pnas.0801566105.

Thornton, A., & Camburn, D. (1987). The influence of the family on premarital attitudes and behavior. *Demography*, *24*, 323–340.

Weinstein, N., Ryan, W.S., DeHaan, C.R., Przybylski, A.K., & Legate, N. (2012). Parental autonomy support and discrepancies between implicit and explicit sexual identities: Dynamics of self-acceptance and defense. *Journal of Personality and Social Psychology*, *102*, 815–832. DOI:10.1037/a0026854.

Williams, T.J., Pepitone, M.E., Christensen, S.E., Cooke, B.M., Huberman, A.D., Breedlove, N.J., … Breedlove, S.M. (2000). Finger length ratios and sexual orientation: Measuring people's finger patterns may reveal some surprising information. *Nature*, *404*, 455–456. DOI:10.1038/35006555.

7

The Laws of Attraction

©vgstudio/123RF.COM.

Chapter Outline

- Introduction   172
- What Attracts Us To Other People?   173
  - Affective Influences   173
  - Propinquity   177
  - Similarity   177
  - Scarcity   180
  - Physiological Arousal   180
  - Neurochemical Factors   182
  - Physical Attractiveness   182
- Attraction Processes among Gay Men and Lesbians   185
- Why Are Men and Women Attracted to Different Characteristics?   185
  - Evolutionary Theory   186
  - Social Structural Perspectives   188

The Psychology of Human Sexuality, First Edition. Justin J. Lehmiller.
© 2014 John Wiley & Sons, Ltd. Published 2014 by John Wiley & Sons, Ltd.

Introduction

Every time I give a lecture on attraction, I begin by asking students to think about the most recent person they went on a date with. I then ask for a few volunteers to tell me where they first met that person and what their initial attraction was based on. A similar set of answers almost invariably emerges, with the most common meeting places being school, work, the gym, or one of the local bars. As for what stimulated the initial attraction, the responses usually fall along the lines of "she was good-looking," "he was so nice and friendly," and "we just had so much in common." Sound familiar? It should. As you will see in this chapter, psychologists have identified a basic set of principles that fuel sexual attraction. Although most of us tend to be drawn to the same set of things in our partners, there are some important differences based upon sexual orientation, not to mention notable differences between men and women. Sex differences in attraction have become one of the hottest and most contentious areas of research in psychology in recent years. As a result, we will spend some time exploring these differences and the theories that have been proposed to account for them. Before we begin our review of the relevant research on attraction, please take a moment to reflect on some of the characteristics you find attractive in others by checking out the Your Sexuality 7.1 box.

Your Sexuality 7.1   What Characteristics are Important to You in a Potential Partner?

On a scale ranging from 0 (not at all) to 7 (very willing), please rate how willing you would be to marry someone under each of the following circumstances:

_____ the person is five or more years older than you.
_____ the person is five or more years younger than you.
_____ the person is more highly educated than you.
_____ the person has a lower level of education than you.
_____ the person is unlikely to keep a steady job.
_____ the person is not good-looking.
_____ the person earns more money than you.
_____ the person earns less money than you.

Sprecher and colleagues (1994) administered these same questions to a nationally representative sample of individuals in the United States and found a number of important sex differences. Women were more willing than men to marry someone with the following characteristics: older, not good-looking, more highly educated, and higher earning potential. Men were more willing than women to marry someone with these characteristics: younger, less educated, less likely to hold a steady job, and lower earning potential. Did your responses follow the typical male pattern or the typical female pattern, or did you fall somewhere in between? What reasons can you think of for why men and women might value different characteristics in their partners?

What Attracts Us To Other People?

How much time do you need before you know whether you like someone? Social psychologists have discovered that we form first impressions very quickly. In fact, judgments of likeability and attractiveness can be formed in just a fraction of a second. For instance, in a study by Willis and Todorov (2006), participants were randomly assigned to view a photograph of another person for less than a second or for as long as they wanted. Afterward, participants were asked to rate that person's likeability, attractiveness, and personality. Results indicated that impressions formed from brief exposure to the target were highly correlated with impressions formed from unlimited exposure. Studies like this suggest that we may be able to tell almost immediately whether we are going to like someone. While fascinating, research of this nature provides an oversimplified view of how attraction works because when it comes to starting sexual and romantic relationships, we take into account more than what we learn at first glance. That first look is very important, but thankfully, it is not everything. As you will see below, biological, psychological, and social factors each play a unique role in stimulating attraction. You will also see that attraction to another person is not always immediate and sometimes builds gradually over time.

Affective Influences

Our emotional states have both direct and indirect influences on who we are attracted to. In terms of direct effects, experiencing positive affect usually leads us to evaluate others positively; experiencing negative affect typically leads to negative evaluations (Forgas & Bower, 1987). Thus, when someone makes us feel good or says something nice to us, we tend to like

Figure 7.1 Psychologists have found that we form impressions of other people's attractiveness and personality in a matter of seconds. ©Yuri Arcurs/123RF.COM.

that person more, whereas when someone makes us feel bad or says something mean to us, we tend to like that person less. As a result, if you are looking for the right pick-up line to use the next time you meet someone attractive, it would be advisable to stick to compliments or things that will make the other person feel good and to avoid flippant remarks, crude jokes, **negging** (i.e., pointing out something negative about another person as a means of catching that person's attention), or any other lines that have the potential to generate negative affect. Although there are a lot of pick-up artists out there who swear by negging (some even offer workshops that teach others how to do it!), do not be fooled – the way to a person's heart generally does not include saying anything that could be construed as belittlement. To learn more about research on effective opening lines and to see some specific examples, check out the Digging Deeper 7.1 box.

Digging Deeper 7.1   "Is It Hot In Here, Or Is It Just You?" Do Pick-up Lines Work?

When you see someone attractive that you desperately want to meet, how do you break the ice? Many of us opt for a simple "hi" or "hello," others offer a dance or a drink, and some choose to lead with an awesomely bad pick-up line (e.g., "Did you wash your pants with Windex? Because I can really see myself in them!"). Which of these approaches is most likely to succeed? Although no technique works 100% of the time, given that every person and situation is different, research suggests that your best bet is to be direct and be yourself, but steer clear of crude and sexually suggestive pick-up lines.

In one of my favorite psychological studies of all time, heterosexual male and female college students were asked to generate some pick-up lines that the other sex might use on them and to evaluate which lines they thought would be most likely to succeed (Kleinke, Meeker, & Staneski, 1986). Results indicated that three separate categories of pick-up lines emerged: *cute/flippant* (e.g., "Isn't it cold? Let's make some body heat"), *innocuous approach* (e.g., "Have you seen any good movies lately?"), and *direct approach* (e.g., "Hi. I like you."). Overall, both men and women preferred the innocuous and direct lines over the cute/flippant lines. However, women disliked cute/flippant remarks significantly more than men. To give you a better sense of how participants perceived opening lines, see Table 7.1 for a sampling of some of the best and worst lines used by women and men, respectively.

If cute/flippant pick-up lines are perceived as so undesirable by women, why do so many men insist on using them? We cannot say for sure, but some researchers have suggested that this may be a strategy some men use to advertise their sexual interest or to zero in on women who are sexually available (Bale, Morrison, & Caryl, 2006). As you can see in Table 7.1, there was not 100% agreement on whether any of the lines were good or bad. In fact, there was a small but significant number of women who liked the cute/flippant lines. Thus, although men who use these lines will probably have a low hit rate overall, guys may still end up getting lucky if they use them enough. Think about it this way: flippant pick-up lines produce a *variable ratio schedule* of reinforcement (i.e., the rewards are unpredictable), just like a slot machine in a casino. As some of you may know from personal experience, variable reinforcement

Table 7.1 Examples of Best and Worst Pick-up Lines

Lines used by women on men		Lines used by men on women	
Best pick-up lines		Best pick-up lines	
Line	*Percentage of participants rating line as good*	*Line*	*Percentage of participants rating line as good*
"Since we're both sitting alone, would you care to join me?"	71.6%	"Do you want to dance?"	63.6%
"Hi."	58.9%	"Hi."	60%
"I'm having trouble getting my car started. Will you give me a hand?"	57.1%	"I haven't been here before. What's good on the menu?"	58.2%
"I don't have anyone to introduce me, but I'd really like to get to know you."	54.6%	"I'm a little embarrassed about this, but I'd really like to meet you."	56.4%
"Can you give me directions to…" (anywhere)	47.8%	"You have really nice…" (hair, eyes, etc.)	50.4%
Worst pick-up lines		Worst pick-up lines	
Line	*Percentage of participants rating line as bad*	*Line*	*Percentage of participants rating line as bad*
"It's been a long time since I had a boyfriend."	81.6%	"Bet I can outdrink you."	89.3%
"Didn't we meet in a previous life?"	81.3%	"Is that really your hair?"	89%
"Hey baby, you've got a gorgeous chassis. Mind if I look under the hood?"	79.5%	"Did you notice me throwing that football? Good arm, huh?"	88.2%
"I'm easy. Are you?"	79.2%	"You remind me of a woman I used to date."	86.8%
"What's your sign?"	78.8%	"I play the field and I think I just hit a home run with you."	84.7%

Source: Kleinke, Meeker, and Staneski (1986).

schedules can be very effective at shaping behavior. Thus, even though cutesy pick-up lines may yield infrequent "jackpots," that may be enough to keep some guys coming back for more.

What is the take-home message from all of this? If you are really interested in meeting someone, a simple "hello" or a nice compliment is likely to open far more doors than some sexual innuendo.

Note: Reprinted with permission from *The Psychology of Human Sexuality* blog (www.lehmiller.com).

Beyond the rather intuitive direct effects of affect on attraction, research has found that we indirectly transfer our existing emotional states onto new people we meet. Thus, if you already happen to be feeling good when you meet someone for the first time, you may like that person more even though they have absolutely nothing to do with your positive mood (Berry & Hansen, 1996). Consistent with this idea, priming studies have shown that when participants are subliminally exposed to a pleasant stimulus (e.g., a photo of an adorable kitten), they evaluate strangers more positively than when they are first exposed to an unpleasant stimulus (e.g., a picture featuring a bucket of snakes; Krosnick, Betz, Jussim, & Lynn, 1992). You can think of these effects

Figure 7.2   Inducing positive affect is one of the keys to generating attraction. As such, it is a good idea to avoid raunchy jokes, flippant comments, and other remarks that have the potential to generate negative emotions. ©Scott Griessel/123RF.COM.

as a form of classical conditioning. That is, when a neutral stimulus is paired with something positive, we like it more, but when that same neutral stimulus is paired with something negative, we like it less.

Propinquity

The **propinquity effect** (sometimes known as the proximity effect) refers to the fact that the closer two people are physically, the greater the odds that they will meet and an attraction will develop between them (Festinger, Schachter, & Back, 1950). This means that people are more likely to start relationships with persons who are geographically near, including classmates, co-workers, and people who frequent the same businesses or belong to the same organizations.

The driving force behind the propinquity effect is repeated exposure. If you have ever taken a social psychology course, you probably learned about the **mere exposure effect**, which specifies that the more familiar we become with a given stimulus, the more we tend to like it (Zajonc, 1968). For example, perhaps you have had the experience where you heard a new song for the first time and your immediate reaction was pretty ho-hum – no strong impression either way. However, after several more listens to that same song, perhaps you found that it grew on you and maybe it even became one of your favorites. The idea is the same with sexual and romantic attraction. That is, when we meet someone new, we may not be quite sure what to make of that person; however, the more we continue to see that person (whether it is over the course of a long evening or a more extended period of time), the more we come to like that individual. The one caveat to this idea is that for mere exposure to work, your initial impression of another person must be close to neutral. If your initial reaction is strongly negative, repeated exposure will not necessarily improve that. In fact, it may make you like that person even less!

Repeated exposure increases liking in and of itself. However, it can have a couple of other effects on attraction. For one thing, when we see another person going to the same places we tend to frequent (assuming it is not in a creepy, stalker-like way), it suggests to us that they may have similar interests. In addition, our comfort with the other person also increases because repeated exposure tells us that this person is unlikely to represent any threat or danger to us.

Similarity

Most sexuality and relationships textbooks tout similarity as a driving force in romantic attraction, claiming that "birds of a feather flock together." Claims like this make a lot of intuitive sense from both an empirical and theoretical standpoint. For instance, we have a mountain of studies indicating that sexual and romantic partners are largely similar to one another on everything from their demographic profiles to their attitudes, and this holds regardless of whether we are talking about one-night stands or long-term lovers. This preference for similarity extends much further than you might imagine, though. In fact, we even appear to select partners who have similar intellectual capabilities and who are approximately of the same level of physical attractiveness (Berscheid, Dion, Walster, & Walster, 1971). This tendency for people to match with partners who are similar to them on a variety of dimensions is known scientifically as **assortative mating**. Table 7.2 summarizes some evidence of assortative mating.

Psychologists have proposed a number of explanations to account for this preference for similarity, such as **social comparison theory** (Festinger, 1954), which holds that we are driven to obtain accurate evaluations of the self. As such, we constantly compare our attitudes and beliefs to other

Table 7.2   Evidence of Assortative Mating: Percentage of Partners across Different Relationship Types Displaying Similarity in Age, Religious Background, and Education Level

	Relationship type		
Type of similarity	Married partners	Cohabiting partners	Short-term partners
Similarity in age (i.e., partners within 5 years of one another	78%	75%	83%
Similarity in religious background (i.e., having the same affiliation)	72%	53%	60%
Similarity in education level (i.e., being no more than one degree category apart)	82%	87%	87%

Note: Adapted with permission from Laumann, Gagnon, Michael, and Michaels (1994).

people in order to see how we stack up. However, we are biased to view the self positively, which means that we try to make comparisons that enhance our self-image. One consequence of this is that we actively seek to surround ourselves with people who hold similar beliefs and attitudes because it validates our own worldview and raises our self-esteem.

Given the prevalence of partner similarity across so many domains, many scientists have concluded that similarity is a necessary prerequisite for relationship success. A few psychologists have even tried to cash in on this conclusion. For instance, the online dating company eHarmony promises to match users based on the "29 Dimensions of Compatibility," which their website claims is "proven to predict happier, healthier long-term relationships" (eHarmony, 2012). The basic premise of eHarmony and many other dating websites (e.g., PerfectMatch, Chemistry) is that given the strong tendency toward assortative mating, all you need to do is put together the most similar couples possible and everyone should live happily ever after. But are relationships really that simple? As it turns out, similarity is a very poor predictor of relationship success. For example, in a meta-analysis of 313 studies of similarity in partners' personality, the researchers concluded that while actual similarity is indeed associated with attraction in lab-based studies, there is no significant link between actual similarity and satisfaction in existing relationships (Montoya, Horton, & Kirchner, 2008). Thus, while we do seem initially drawn to people who are similar to us, it turns out that the factors that initially attract us to someone are not necessarily the same factors that promote relationship stability and success. If this is the case, why are eHarmony and other such websites able to claim high success rates? Perhaps because there are inherent selection biases and expectancy effects in the world of online dating (e.g., maybe these websites attract people who are highly motivated to find a match, and who ultimately do so via a self-fulfilling prophecy).

Interracial and Interreligious Relationships

Although there is a lot of evidence for assortative mating, it is clear that not everyone selects sexual and romantic partners who are similar to them in most ways. In fact, the tendency to pair with demographically *dissimilar* partners appears to have increased in recent years. For example,

Figure 7.3 Internet dating companies often attempt to match people based solely on measures of similarity. Although we tend to be attracted to similar others, similarity does not guarantee relationship success. ©Gunnar Pippel/123RF.COM.

national US surveys and census data indicate that the rate of interracial marriage among heterosexuals is now at an all-time high of around 9%, a number that has almost tripled since the 1980s (Gates, 2012; Wang, 2012). Likewise, as seen in Table 7.2, the NHSLS (a study conducted in the early 1990s) found that 28% of heterosexual married couples were from different religious backgrounds. In comparison, a more recent national US survey put that number at 38% (Rosenfeld & Thomas, 2012). Thus, it is clear that couples today are more likely to be marrying outside of their race and faith.

There is likely a social psychological explanation behind these trends. For example, consider that in the US, interracial marriage (also known as *intermarriage*) was illegal throughout much of the country until a landmark Supreme Court ruling in the case of *Loving v. Virginia* in 1967. At that point in time, just 20% of Americans approved of intermarriage, and it was not until 1991 that more Americans approved than disapproved of couples marrying outside of their race for the first time (Carroll, 2007). Now, the vast majority of Americans approve of intermarriage, but some resistance remains. A review of public opinion polls has revealed similar trends in Americans' attitudes toward interreligious marriages over time (Riley, 2013). Thus, historically, there has been a lot of normative pressure against becoming sexually and/or romantically involved with outgroup members; however, as societal attitudes have changed and those pressures have lessened, certain forms of assortative mating have begun to diminish. Of course, there are likely numerous factors contributing to this change, including the increased racial and ethnic diversity of the US and a decline in Western religiosity. Although interracial and interreligious relationships are undeniably becoming more common, it remains more likely than not for people in the modern world to match with similar partners.

Scarcity

Ain't it funny, ain't it strange, the way a man's opinions change when he starts to face that lonely night.

Lyrics from the song *Don't the Girls All Get Prettier at Closing Time* by Mickey Gilley

People who work in marketing know that one of the keys to getting consumers to spend money on a product is to create an illusion of scarcity. In other words, if your product appears to be available in limited quantities or for a short time only, its desirability increases. A similar principle applies when it comes to finding sexual and romantic partners: when a person's availability decreases, their attractiveness increases. As some evidence of this, consider a classic study conducted by Jamie Pennebaker and colleagues (1979) in which men and women in a bar were approached at different hours of the evening and asked to rate the attractiveness of patrons of the other sex. Specifically, the bar closed at 12:30 a.m. and participants were either approached at 9:00 p.m., 10:30 p.m., or 12:00 midnight on the same evening. Participants' perceptions of attractiveness increased as the evening went on for both male and female participants. Thus, as the window of opportunity for going home with someone narrowed, perceptions of others' attractiveness went up. A subsequent study replicated this effect, but found that it only held for people who were single, not for people who were already in a committed relationship (Madey et al., 1996). Of course, these effects might also be partly a function of "beer goggles" (i.e., perhaps as people get more intoxicated, their standards of attractiveness lessen).

Perhaps more convincing evidence of the role of scarcity comes from research by Jonason and Li (2013), who found that "playing hard to get" increases one's desirability as a potential romantic partner. In one of their studies, heterosexual college students were given a series of dating profiles that differed only in the likelihood that the person would go out with someone they had just met. Specifically, each dating target was described as having either low, intermediate, or high availability. Afterward, participants were asked what kind of restaurant they would consider taking this person to (fast food, casual, or fine dining), as well as the amount of money they would be willing to spend on that person's dinner. Both men and women were willing to take the low-availability target to a fancier restaurant and spend more money on that person compared to the other targets. Specifically, the low-availability target was worth $44.45 on average, compared to $34.99 and $33.10 for the intermediate and high availability targets, respectively. These findings provide further support for the idea that scarcity increases perceived desirability of prospective partners and encourages people to expend more resources on them.

Physiological Arousal

There is a long-standing body of research in social psychology demonstrating that meeting a new person when one is already physiologically aroused increases the likelihood of developing an attraction toward that person. For instance, in a famous study conducted by Donald Dutton and Art Aron (1974), an attractive female research assistant approached men who happened to be walking alone across either a high and shaky suspension bridge that was very anxiety-inducing or a much lower and more stable bridge that was not scary at all. The female assistant asked each man to fill out a questionnaire while on the middle of the bridge, which included writing a brief narrative about a picture. After completing the survey, the assistant provided her name and number to the participant and told him to give her a call that evening if he wanted to learn more about the study.

Figure 7.4 In the Dutton and Aron (1976) study, men who walked across a high and shaky suspension bridge misattributed their arousal to the attractive research assistant instead of the nature of the situation. ©Harris Shiffman / 123RF.COM.

Results indicated that the men who encountered the assistant on the shaky bridge included much more sexual and romantic content in the stories they wrote. In addition, they were significantly more likely to call the number they had been given. This is just one of many studies indicating a positive association between generalized physiological arousal and attraction. For instance, another study found the same basic effect by having guys exercise for a few minutes prior to rating the attractiveness of a female confederate (White & Knight, 1984). In that study, men who exercised found the woman more attractive than guys who did not get their heart rates up. Recall how at the beginning of this chapter, I mentioned that students often tell me that they first met their partner at the gym? Does it now make more sense why fitness clubs are a common meeting place? Physiological arousal plus propinquity can be a potent combination.

How do we explain this pattern of results? The likely mechanism is a **misattribution of physiological arousal**. For misattribution of arousal to take place, the true source of the arousal must be ambiguous, meaning it cannot be entirely clear to the individual what is responsible for it. Such ambiguity may lead the aroused person to incorrectly label the source (e.g., in the Dutton and Aron study, participants mistook their fear of heights for attraction to the research assistant). Of course, keep in mind that this effect only occurs when there are competing explanations for the arousal. If there is nobody else around (or if nobody around is even remotely attractive), the true source of arousal is likely to be identified.

If there is a take-home message from this line of research, it would be that dinner and a movie might not be the best recipe for a successful first date after all (unless you choose a particularly suspenseful movie!). Instead, you might suggest something more physically active (e.g., biking, ice-skating, rock-climbing, or for the extremely adventurous, skydiving).

Neurochemical Factors

Beyond physiological arousal, there are several other biological factors that play a role in initial attraction. One such factor is the effect of pheromones. As previously discussed in chapter 4., studies have found that participants assigned to wear synthetic pheromones subsequently engaged in more sexual activity than participants who wore a placebo solution (e.g., McCoy & Pitino, 2002). This suggests that sexual attraction and behavior are at least partly determined by our sense of smell.

Neurotransmitters and hormones may also impact perceptions of attractiveness. For instance, we know from our discussion of sexual arousal in chapter 4 that dopamine and serotonin have facilitating and inhibiting effects on sexual arousal, respectively. This tells us that the relative amount of each of these neurotransmitters in our brain when we meet someone new may have a profound impact on whether we develop an attraction toward that person. Another way to think about this is that your brain chemicals affect your general level of interest in sex at any given moment, which in turn affects whether you are actively looking for partners and how you evaluate new people you meet.

With respect to hormones, there is a natural release of oxytocin during physical contact with another person, which may facilitate attraction toward a specific target by increasing feelings of bondedness. Research has also found that people in new romantic relationships (less than 6 months in duration) have higher levels of oxytocin than single people and, further, the higher the partners' levels of oxytocin, the more positive and affectionate they are around one another (Schneiderman, Zagoory-Sharon, Leckman, & Feldman, 2012). Thus, not only does oxytocin contribute to initial attraction, but it may also help sustain attraction over time by promoting reciprocal positive interactions.

Physical Attractiveness

Finally, and perhaps not surprisingly, **physical attractiveness** (the degree to which we perceive another person as beautiful or handsome) plays an important role in initial attraction. Perceptions of physical attractiveness can be based upon multiple factors, such as a person's age, height, eye color, hairstyle, manner of dress, and so on; however, different people may place more or less emphasis on each of these factors when it comes to making their own judgments of attractiveness as a result of personal preferences. In addition, the relative value individuals ascribe to physical attractiveness overall varies according to personality. For example, people with an unrestricted sociosexual orientation think a partner's physical beauty is more important than those with a restricted orientation (Wilbur & Campbell, 2010). Attractiveness judgments are not entirely a matter of personal preference and personality, though. Research indicates that perceptions of attractiveness are also subject to social influence (Graziano, Jensen-Campbell, Shebilske, & Lundgren, 1993; Sprecher, 1989). For instance, Sprecher (1989) found that the perceived desirability of a prospective romantic target was affected by how other people viewed that target. Specifically, targets were seen as more attractive when participants' peers had ostensibly rated those targets as being more attractive; participants were less attracted to targets when peer evaluations were negative.

Perceptions of attractiveness are also context-dependent, meaning that we evaluate a person's beauty in reference to other nearby people. For instance, imagine a person of slightly above-average

Figure 7.5 Viewing pornography or other popular media featuring highly attractive people can produce a contrast effect in which the attractiveness of the average person is distorted. ©scyther5 / 123RF.COM.

looks standing next to a group of supermodels. That person would probably not appear to be very good looking because there is a major **contrast effect** happening. A contrast effect refers to the idea that perceptions of average can be thrown off by the presence of a few outliers. Contrast effects have implications not only for initial attraction, but also for how we perceive our long-term partners. For instance, in one study, some participants were shown photos of highly attractive people prior to evaluating the attractiveness of a stranger. Participants who viewed the photos rated the stranger as less attractive than those who did not see those same images beforehand (Kenrick, Montello, Gutierres, & Trost, 1993). In a related study, after viewing a series of *Playboy* centerfolds, heterosexual married men rated their wives as less attractive compared to men who had viewed images of abstract art instead (Kenrick & Gutierres, 1980). As you can see, attractiveness is a complex judgment that not only depends upon individual preferences and personality, but also social influence and social comparison processes.

Despite the old saying "don't judge a book by its cover," almost all of us forget this when it comes to starting relationships. There are several reasons for this. One is that attractive people are stereotyped very positively – specifically, we see them as being more likeable, interesting, competent, and successful (Dion, Pak, & Dion, 1990). In other words, most of us subscribe to the heuristic that "what is beautiful is good." Another reason people place so much emphasis on physical attractiveness is that it may be a potential indicator of a person's health and fertility. We will come back to this idea in the next section when we discuss evolutionary theory.

Whatever the reason, attractiveness is usually most important early in a relationship and declines in importance over time. This is probably a good thing because many of us are not fortunate enough to get better looking with age! In addition, attractiveness is something that tends to be valued more by men than by women. This should *not* be taken to mean that attractiveness is unimportant to women: most women still care very much about finding an attractive partner. The difference is that women rate this characteristic as a little less important than do men. As some evidence of this, consider the results of an online study by Lippa (2007) of over 100,000 men and women representing 53 different countries around the world. Participants were given a list of 23 different traits in a potential relationship partner that they had to rank order in terms of desirability. Among men, the top three traits in order of importance were intelligence, "good looks," and humor. Among women, the top three traits were humor, intelligence, and honesty. "Good looks" came in at number eight on the women's list. Thus, good looks are certainly still important to women, but all else equal, there are a few other characteristics they value above it compared to men.

Physical attractiveness is just one of several characteristics that men and women evaluate differently in the area of attraction. Other studies have found that the sexes also differ in terms of preferences for partner age, earning potential, and educational background (Okami & Shackelford, 2001; Sprecher, Sullivan, & Hatfield, 1994). Specifically, men tend to prefer younger partners and are more comfortable with a partner who has less earning potential and a lower level of education (although this does not mean men want partners with *low* education – just that men are comfortable dating someone who has a little less education); in contrast, women tend to prefer older partners and desire someone with better financial prospects and a higher level of education. Thus, while there is a lot that the sexes have in common with regard to what drives attraction, they diverge in some important ways.

For a summary of the major factors influencing who we find attractive, see Table 7.3.

Table 7.3 Major Variables in Sexual Attraction	
Variable	*Description*
Affect/mood	We like people who make us feel good. We like someone more when we are in a positive mood, even if the other person has nothing to do with our current mood state.
Propinquity	We are more likely to develop an attraction to people in close geographic proximity.
Similarity	We tend to be attracted to persons who are similar to us. Similarity is not a sufficient condition for relationship success.
Scarcity	When the opportunity to meet partners is limited, others' perceived attractiveness increases. Potential romantic partners are more desirable when they are less available.
Physiological arousal	Meeting someone new when we are already physiologically aroused increases the chances of attraction.
Neurotransmitters and hormones	Higher levels of dopamine and oxytocin enhance attraction.
Physical attractiveness	We are more attracted to people we perceive as beautiful or handsome. Both men and women value attractiveness, but men report valuing this characteristic slightly more than women.

Attraction Processes among Gay Men and Lesbians

Are the factors that influence sexual attraction different for gay men and lesbians than for heterosexual persons? Research suggests that there are many similarities. For example, when asked how important a partner's physical appearance is, lesbian and heterosexual women do not differ from one another, nor do gay and heterosexual men (Bailey, Gaulin, Agyei, & Gladue, 1994). Likewise, gay and heterosexual men are very similar to one another in expressing a preference for younger sexual partners (Kenrick, Keefe, Bryan, & Brown, 1995). In addition, there is no theoretical reason or empirical evidence to suggest that affective influences, scarcity, physiological arousal, and neurochemical processes would have different effects on attraction across persons of varying sexualities.

At the same time, however, there appear to be some important differences. For example, although there is a lot of evidence that heterosexual persons tend to be attracted to partners who are similar to them, this effect does not appear to be quite as strong among gays and lesbians. Kurdek and Schmitt (1987) found that relationship partners' levels of education and income were positively correlated among heterosexual couples who were living together, but this was not the case for gay and lesbian partners. Likewise, 2010 US Census data revealed that 20.6% of same-sex couples were either interracial or interethnic, whereas only 9.5% of different-sex married couples were involved in such relationships (Gates, 2012). Other research has found that same-sex couples are more likely to come from different religious backgrounds than heterosexual married couples (Rosenfeld & Thomas, 2012). Together, all of these findings suggest that demographic differences appear to be more common among same-sex couples than among heterosexual couples. We cannot say for sure why this is the case, but it may be because people who are attracted to members of the same sex are working from a smaller *field of eligibles* (i.e., a smaller pool of potential dating prospects) than their heterosexual counterparts and, therefore, may not have as much choice when it comes to selecting partners based upon similarity or other characteristics.

Propinquity may also play a lesser role in attraction among gays and lesbians than among heterosexuals. A smaller dating pool combined with social stigma that causes many gays and lesbians to live their lives "in the closet" can make it more challenging for them to meet potential sexual and romantic partners in day-to-day life. As a result, gays and lesbians are much more likely to search for partners online than are heterosexuals. As some evidence of this, data from a nationally representative US survey of how couples meet found that 41% of same-sex couples reported having met online, compared to 17% of different-sex couples (Rosenfeld & Thomas, 2012). This is not to say that propinquity plays no role in attraction for gays and lesbians, just that it may not have as many opportunities to do so.

Why Are Men and Women Attracted to Different Characteristics?

The above-noted sex differences in preferences for physical attractiveness, age, and social status have been documented repeatedly using different types of samples across diverse cultures. How do we explain these pervasive sex differences? The explanation that has received the most attention is evolutionary theory; however, it is also the most controversial. In this section, we will review the basics of evolutionary theory and the evidence supporting it, but we will also consider some alternative perspectives.

Evolutionary Theory

You may recall from chapter 1 that the main idea behind *evolutionary theory* is that many of our behavioral tendencies reflect evolved adaptations. In other words, we have tendencies to behave in very specific ways because those actions were adaptive for the survival of our ancestors. It is theorized that humans today have a number of these behavioral tendencies that are not necessarily relevant for survival in the modern world, but instead represent remnants of our evolved history. Many of these behavioral tendencies center around sexual behavior, because evolutionary psychologists believe that after basic survival, our next-strongest motivation is to reproduce as much as we can to ensure that our genetic material is carried on to future generations. To that end, humans are thought to have evolved preferences for certain characteristics in our partners that are ultimately designed to enhance reproductive success.

From the evolutionary perspective, the observed sex differences in partner preferences reflect strategies for coping with the reality of unequal **parental investment** (i.e., the fact that it does not take nearly as much effort for men as it does for women to make a baby; Buss & Schmitt, 1993). Men's best strategy for passing along their genes is to have a lot of short-term sexual encounters with healthy and fertile women. But how can men tell which women are likely to be healthy and fertile? By paying attention to physical signs that indicate sexual maturity and good health. These include youth, a low waist-to-hip ratio (i.e., a waist that is smaller than the hips), facial and bodily symmetry (i.e., identical left and right sides), and long, shiny hair. Evolutionary psychologists

Figure 7.6   Heterosexual men tend to rate women with long hair and a low waist-to-hip ratio as optimally attractive. Evolutionary psychologists theorize that attending to such features was adaptive for our ancestors by promoting reproductive success. ©phartisan / 123RF.COM.

argue that men have become attuned to focus on appearance more than anything else because it is the most useful cue for enhancing their reproductive success.

For women, however, having a large number of short-term encounters is a riskier bet because she could potentially wind up pregnant by a man who turns out to be an absentee father. Women's best strategy is thus to pursue sex in the context of long-term relationships with men who are reliable and can provide protection and resources for her and any offspring produced. As a result, women should prefer somewhat older men, who have had the opportunity to acquire more resources. Physical appearance is presumably less important to women because most men are almost always fertile, producing sperm from puberty until the day they die. As a result, male appearance is not quite as informative for women in matters of reproduction. The one exception to this is that women show a preference for masculine-looking guys with chiseled faces when they are near ovulation (Jones et al., 2008). Masculine facial features are linked to having a stronger immune system. Thus, it may potentially confer evolutionary benefits on their offspring if women seek out more "manly" men when they are most fertile (see chapter 10 for more on this).

There is a significant amount of evidence indicating that, even in modern times, men seem oriented toward having numerous casual encounters with good-looking women, whereas women seem oriented toward long-term encounters with high status men. As some support for this idea, when men are asked how many sexual partners they would like to have in the future, they typically report much higher numbers than women, and this is true regardless of whether "the future" is specified as a month, a year, or their entire lifetime (Schmitt et al., 2003). To give you a sense of the magnitude of this difference and its seemingly universal nature, see Figure 7.7.

Likewise, consider a study by Clark and Hatfield (1989) in which male and female research assistants propositioned college undergraduates of the other sex who they deemed to be moderately attractive while walking around campus. The assistant would say to the student, "I have been noticing you around campus. I find you to be very attractive." Afterward, they randomly asked one

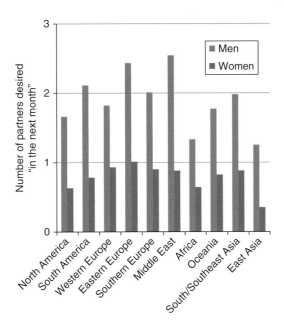

Figure 7.7 Schmitt and colleagues' (2003) research demonstrated a consistent sex difference in the number of sexual partners desired across many different cultures.

Table 7.4 Percentage of Men and Women Accepting Requests for Offers of Casual Sex			
Study 1	Request type		
Sex of person approached	*Date*	*Apartment*	*Bed*
Male	50%	69%	75%
Female	56%	6%	0%
Study 2	Request type		
Sex of person approached	*Date*	*Apartment*	*Bed*
Male	50%	69%	69%
Female	50%	0%	0%

Source: Clark & Hatfield (1989).

of the following three questions: "Will you go on a date with me tonight?" "Will you go back to my apartment with me tonight?" or "Will you go to bed with me tonight?" Once the participant provided an answer, he or she was debriefed and had no further contact with the research assistant. The results of this study are depicted in Table 7.4. As you can see in this table, men and women responded to these requests very differently. Specifically, when the question implied a higher likelihood of casual sex, men were more likely to accept the offer, whereas women were more likely to decline it.

Despite a rapidly growing body of evidence supporting evolutionary theory, not everyone is convinced of it. For instance, while a lot of research has found differences in men's and women's *ideal* mate preferences, what they *actually* do does not quite match up. In a speed-dating study where participants were asked to evaluate the characteristics of real-life romantic targets, no sex differences were observed in the value placed upon physical attractiveness and status (Eastwick & Finkel, 2008). If we assume that what people do in the real world is a more valid test of evolutionary theory's predictions than survey studies inquiring about what people would do in hypothetical situations, there are some legitimate questions to be raised about a lot of the evidence supporting this view. Another frequent criticism is that evolutionary theory has some difficulty explaining variations in sexual orientation. As discussed in chapter 6, some have argued that homosexuality may persist in the human population because it is adaptive in a nonobvious way. However, arguments such as this only serve to feed a broader criticism of evolutionary theory, which is that it is possible to develop theories to explain the adaptive nature of virtually every human trait, yet very challenging to conduct adequate tests of these theories.

Social Structural Perspectives

Of course, evolutionary theory is not the only perspective that offers an explanation for why men and women desire different features in their partners and display differences in their sexual behavior. In this section, we review two theories that distance themselves from the evolutionary account and instead emphasize the impact of the social structure.

Sociocultural Theory

Many scholars argue that modern sex differences in attraction and mating strategies may have more to do with social and cultural conditioning than anything else (Eagly & Wood, 1999). The

sociocultural perspective acknowledges that biological and evolved factors play *some* role (e.g., physical differences between men and women may influence the roles to which the sexes were initially assigned); however, these theorists hold that psychological sex differences are largely, if not exclusively, a response to the social structure. Thus, this theory holds that as the social structure changes, so should the magnitude and direction of sex differences. Consistent with this idea, research has found that in societies where there is more gender equality, men's and women's partner preferences are more similar (Zentner & Mitura, 2012). However, even in the most equal of countries, the traditionally observed sex differences still appear to some degree, perhaps because no country has yet to achieve full gender equality in all ways.

As additional evidence for the sociocultural view, several experimental studies have found that the typical sex differences in attraction and sexual behavior become much smaller or disappear entirely when social and cultural variables are manipulated. For instance, recall that Clark and Hatfield (1989) reported a huge difference between men and women in willingness to accept an offer of casual sex. Two decades after this study, Conley (2011) asked male and female participants about their likelihood of accepting an offer of casual sex from a very attractive famous person and found no sex difference in likelihood of saying yes. Conley argues that Clark and Hatfield's methods underestimated women's interest in casual sex because male strangers who ask for sex are perceived as having low sexual capabilities and as a threat to personal safety. In contrast, women's interest in casual sex is higher with a male celebrity because that person is more of a known quantity. Likewise, recall that several studies have found that men typically report desiring and having much higher numbers of sexual partners than women. Does this reflect a true sex difference in desires and behaviors, or is this simply an artifact of female underreporting and male overreporting of sexual behavior in an attempt to conform to traditional gender roles? Research has found some support for the latter explanation. In a classic study by Alexander and Fisher (2003) that employed the **bogus pipeline technique**, half of the participants were hooked up to a lie-detector machine and falsely convinced that it could detect the truth in an attempt to ensure greater honesty in responding. Afterward, these participants were asked about their sexual history. The other half of the participants answered the same set of questions, but they were not attached to the machine. When participants were *not* hooked up to the lie-detector, men reported more partners than women; however, in the lie-detector condition, there was no sex difference in number of partners reported. For more empirical evidence supporting the social structural account of sex differences, see the Digging Deeper 7.2 box.

Together, the results of all these studies provide a compelling alternative explanation as to why sex differences in attraction and sexual behavior exist. However, the sociocultural view is not without its limitations. For instance, while people who adopt this view do not dispute that evolution has created certain physical differences between the sexes, they simultaneously appear to argue that psychological characteristics are immune from evolutionary pressures. Given how fundamentally interconnected the mind and body are, some psychologists feel that such a view takes us backwards by essentially espousing a mind–body dualism a la René Descartes (Friedman, Bleske, & Scheyd, 2000). Another common criticism of sociocultural theory is that we already have fairly clear evidence that some psychological sex differences have a biological basis. For instance, recall our discussion of congenital adrenal hyperplasia (CAH) in chapter 5. Genetic females with CAH typically develop more masculine interests (Meyer-Bahlburg, Dolezal, Baker, Ehrhardt, & New, 2006). If sex differences were purely a product of socialization factors, why would women with CAH have such different interests from women without CAH? Such findings suggest that it is certainly conceivable that evolution and biology could be contributing factors when it comes to psychological sex differences.

Figures 7.8 and 7.9   When men and women imagine offers of casual sex from celebrities like Zac Efron and Mila Kunis, there is no sex difference in likelihood of accepting the offer. This suggests that women are actually just as interested in casual relationships as men in some cases. Zac Efron Image Copyright s_bukley, 2013. Used under license from Shutterstock.com. Mila Kunis Image Copyright Helga Esteb, 2013. Used under license from Shutterstock.com.

Digging Deeper 7.2   Are Women Really the Choosier Sex?

Conventional wisdom tells us that women tend to be "choosier" than men when it comes to selecting sexual and romantic partners, and there is plenty of scientific evidence to back up this idea. Evolutionary psychologists argue that because producing a child requires a significantly greater investment of one's body and time for women than it does for men, it is in women's best interests to be more selective about their partners to ensure they do not end up pregnant by someone who might skip town or settle down with a different mate (Buss & Schmitt, 1993). But is female choosiness an inevitable fact of life in the heterosexual mating marketplace?

The traditional heterosexual dating script dictates that men should approach women, not the other way around. As a result, women are approached more frequently than men. Thus, if women are the ones constantly being put in the position of having to choose, it should come as no surprise that they tend to be more selective. What would happen if the roles were reversed? If women were the ones doing the approaching, would men suddenly become choosier?

Figure 7.10 The traditional sex difference in selectivity disappears when women approached men instead of the reverse. ©Michał Nowosielski / 123RF.COM.

This idea was tested in a speed-dating study by Finkel and Eastwick (2009). For those of you who are not familiar with speed-dating, the basic idea is that a large number of single people come together in one place and then proceed to pair off for several brief mini-dates. Specifically, people usually rotate from table to table for a series of short (i.e., 2- or 3-minute) conversations with complete strangers. In one speed-dating event, each person involved may have 20 or more of these brief "dates." Based only upon these encounters, speed daters later decide who (if anyone) they would like to take on a real date afterward. In this particular study, the researchers manipulated who got up at the end of each encounter to move to the next table (i.e., who was doing the approaching). Half of the time it was the men; the other half of the time it was the women.

When the men were approaching women, it was business as usual in the sense that women were significantly choosier than men. *However, when women were the ones approaching men, this sex difference in selectivity disappeared completely!* The sex difference did not reverse itself (i.e., we did not see men become *more* selective than women). Instead, men and women became equally selective.

These findings suggest that choosiness may not be an innate part of female psychology, but rather a product of a highly gendered society that dictates who should be the initiator of sexual and romantic encounters. Although these findings do not necessarily rule out the evolutionary explanation, they do suggest the provocative possibility that women may only be the choosier sex because that is the way we expect them to be, not because that is the way they are by nature.

Note: Reprinted with permission from *The Psychology of Human Sexuality* blog (www.lehmiller.com).

Other Views

Another alternative to the evolutionary account is the perspective offered in the book *Sex at Dawn* (Ryan & Jetha, 2010), which suggests that evolution-based interpretations of human sexuality are fundamentally flawed and that our mating preferences have nothing to do with parental invest-ment and a "selfish" drive to spread one's genes. The primary argument in *Sex at Dawn* is that modern mating preferences and gender roles are a result of moving from hunter-gatherer societies to agricultural societies. In the days of hunter-gatherers, societies were communal, sharing food, child-care responsibilities, as well as sexual partners. When agriculture developed, however, per-sonal property and political systems began to emerge. In addition, agriculture limited the food supply for the first time. As a result of these dramatic changes, human motivations and relation-ships are thought to have dramatically changed, resulting in the sex differences we see today. Although the narrative presented in *Sex at Dawn* is provocative, the data upon which this book was based are primarily correlational and anecdotal, and in some cases, the strength of the data is over-stated. Thus, this view is not necessarily more conclusive than any others. In short, we lack a definitive explanation as to why men and women prefer different characteristics in their partners, and perhaps we always will.

Key Terms

negging
propinquity effect
mere exposure effect
assortative mating

social comparison theory
misattribution of
    physiological arousal
physical attractiveness

contrast effect
parental investment
sociocultural perspective
bogus pipeline technique

Discussion Questions: What is Your Perspective on Sex?

* What are the most and least effective pick-up lines you have ever heard? Do they fit with exist-ing research on this topic?
* Have you ever tried online dating? If so, have you found that what attracts you to someone online is similar to or different from what attracts you to someone you meet in person?
* Which explanation for sex differences in attraction do you find more convincing: evolutionary theory or the sociocultural perspective? Why?

References

Alexander, M.G., & Fisher, T.D. (2003). Truth and consequences: Using the bogus pipeline to examine sex differences in self-reported sexuality. *Journal of Sex Research, 40*, 27–35. DOI:10.1080/00224490309552164.

Bailey, J., Gaulin, S., Agyei, Y., & Gladue, B.A. (1994). Effects of gender and sexual orientation on evolution-arily relevant aspects of human mating psychology. *Journal of Personality and Social Psychology, 66*, 1081–1093. DOI:10.1037/0022-3514.66.6.1081.

Bale, C., Morrison, R., & Caryl, P. (2006). Chat-up lines as male sexual displays. *Personality and Individual Differences, 40*, 655–664. DOI:10.1016/j.paid.2005.07.016.

Berry, D.S., & Hansen, J. (1996). Positive affect, negative affect, and social interaction. *Journal of Personality and Social Psychology, 71*, 796–809. DOI:10.1037/0022-3514.71.4.796.

Berscheid, E., Dion, K., Walster, E., & Walster, G.W. (1971). Physical attractiveness and dating choice: A test of the matching hypothesis. *Journal of Experimental Social Psychology, 7*, 173–189. DOI:10.1016/0022-1031(71)90065-5.

Buss, D.M., & Schmitt, D.P. (1993). Sexual Strategies Theory: An evolutionary perspective on human mating. *Psychological Review, 100*, 204–232. DOI:10.1037/0033-295X.100.2.204.

Carroll, J. (2007). Most Americans approve of interracial marriages. *Gallup*. Retrieved from http://www.gallup.com/poll/28417/most-americans-approve-interracial-marriages.aspx (accessed September 3, 2013).

Clark, R.D., & Hatfield, E. (1989). Gender differences in receptivity to sexual offers. *Journal of Psychology & Human Sexuality, 2*, 39–55. DOI:10.1300/J056v02n01_04.

Conley, T.D. (2011). Perceived proposer personality characteristics and gender differences in acceptance of casual sex offers. *Journal of Personality and Social Psychology, 100*, 309–329. DOI:10.1037/a0022152.

Dion, K.K., Pak, A.W., & Dion, K.L. (1990). Stereotyping physical attractiveness: A sociocultural perspective. *Journal of Cross-Cultural Psychology, 21*, 158–179. DOI:10.1177/0022022190212002.

Dutton, D.G., & Aron, A.P. (1974). Some evidence for heightened sexual attraction under conditions of high anxiety. *Journal of Personality and Social Psychology, 30*, 510–517. DOI:10.1037/h0037031.

Eagly, A.H., & Wood, W. (1999). The origins of sex differences in human behavior: Evolved dispositions versus social roles. *American Psychologist, 54*, 408–423. DOI:10.1037/0003-066X.54.6.408.

Eastwick, P.W., & Finkel, E.J. (2008). Sex differences in mate preferences revisited: Do people know what they initially desire in a romantic partner? *Journal of Personality and Social Psychology, 94*, 245–264. DOI:10.1037/0022-3514.94.2.245.

eHarmony (2012). eHarmony is more than traditional dating sites. Retrieved from http://www.eharmony.com/why/ (accessed September 3, 2013).

Festinger, L. (1954). A theory of social comparison processes. *Human Relations, 7*, 117–140. DOI: 10.1177/001872675400700202.

Festinger, L., Schachter, S., & Back, K. (1950). The spatial ecology of group formation. In L. Festinger, S. Schachter, & K. Back (Eds.), *Social pressure in informal groups*1(pp. 41–161) Palo Alto, CA: Stanford University Press.

Finkel, E.J., & Eastwick, P.W. (2009). Arbitrary social norms influence sex differences in romantic selectivity. *Psychological Science, 20*, 1290–1295. DOI:10.1111/j.1467-9280.2009.02439.x.

Forgas, J.P., & Bower, G.H. (1987). Mood effects on person-perception judgments. *Journal of Personality and Social Psychology, 53*, 53–60. DOI:10.1037/0022-3514.53.1.53.

Friedman, B.X., Bleske, A.L., & Scheyd, G.J. (2000). Incompatible with evolutionary theorizing. *American Psychologist, 55*, 1059–1060. DOI:10.1037/0003-066X.55.9.1059.

Gates, G. J. (2012). Same-sex couples in Census 2010: Race and ethnicity. The Williams Institute. Retrieved from http://williamsinstitute.law.ucla.edu/wp-content/uploads/Gates-CouplesRaceEthnicity-April-2012.pdf (accessed September 3, 2013).

Graziano, W.G., Jensen-Campbell, L., Shebilske, L., & Lundgren, S. (1993). Social influence, sex differences, and judgments of beauty: Putting the "interpersonal" back in interpersonal attraction. *Journal of Personality & Social Psychology, 65*, 522–531. DOI:10.1037/0022-3514.65.3.522.

Jonason, P. K., & Li, N. P. (2013). Playing hard-to-get: Manipulating one's perceived availability as a mate. *European Journal of Personality, 27*, 458–469. DOI:10.1002/per.1881.

Jones, B.C., DeBruine, L.M., Perrett, D.I., Little, A.C., Feinberg, D.R., & Smith, M. (2008). Effects of menstrual cycle phase on face preferences. *Archives of Sexual Behavior, 37*, 78–84. DOI:10.1007/s10508-007-9268-y.

Kenrick, D.T., & Gutierres, S.E. (1980). Contrast effects and judgments of physical attractiveness: When beauty becomes a social problem. *Journal of Personality and Social Psychology, 38*, 131–140. DOI:10.1037/0022-3514.38.1.131.

Kenrick, D.T., Keefe, R.C., Bryan, A., Barr, A., & Brown, S. (1995). Age preferences and mate choice among homosexuals and heterosexuals: A case for modular psychological mechanisms. *Journal of Personality and Social Psychology, 69,* 1166–1172. DOI:10.1037/0022-3514.69.6.1166.

Kenrick, D.T., Montello, D.R., Gutierres, S.E., & Trost, M.R. (1993). Effects of physical attractiveness on affect and perceptual judgments: When social comparison overrides social reinforcement. *Personality and Social Psychology Bulletin, 19,* 195–199. DOI:10.1177/0146167293192008.

Kleinke, C., Meeker, F., & Staneski, R. (1986). Preference for opening lines: Comparing ratings by men and women. *Sex Roles, 15,* 585–600. DOI:10.1007/bf00288216.

Krosnick, J.A., Betz, A.L., Jussim, L.J., & Lynn, A.R. (1992). Subliminal conditioning of attitudes. *Personality and Social Psychology Bulletin, 18,* 152–162. DOI:10.1177/0146167292182006.

Kurdek, L.A., & Schmitt, J.P. (1987). Partner homogamy in married, heterosexual cohabiting, gay, and lesbian couples. *Journal of Sex Research, 23,* 212–232. DOI:10.1080/00224498709551358.

Laumann, E.O., Gagnon, J., Michael, R., & Michaels, S. (1994). *The social organization of sexuality: Sexual practices in the United States.* Chicago: University of Chicago Press.

Lippa, R.A. (2007). The preferred traits of mates in a cross-national study of heterosexual and homosexual men and women: An examination of biological and cultural influences. *Archives of Sexual Behavior, 36,* 193–208. DOI:10.1007/s10508-006-9151-2.

Madey, S.F., Simo, M., Dillworth, D., Kemper, D., Toczynski, A., & Perella, A. (1996). They do get more attractive at closing time, but only when you are not in a relationship. *Basic & Applied Social Psychology, 18,* 387–393.

McCoy, N.L, & Pitino, L. (2002). Pheromonal influences on sociosexual behaviour in young women. *Physiological Behavior, 75,* 367–375. DOI:10.1016/S0031-9384(01)00675-8.

Meyer-Bahlburg, H.F., Dolezal, C., Baker, S.W., Ehrhardt, A.A., & New, M.I. (2006). Gender development in women with congenital adrenal hyperplasia as a function of disorder severity. *Archives of Sexual Behavior, 35,* 667–684. DOI:10.1007/s10508-006-9068-9.

Montoya, R., Horton, R.S., & Kirchner, J. (2008). Is actual similarity necessary for attraction? A meta-analysis of actual and perceived similarity. *Journal of Social and Personal Relationships, 25,* 889–922. DOI: 10.1177/0265407508096700.

Okami, P., & Schackelford, T.K. (2001). Human sex differences in sexual psychology and behavior. *Annual Review of Sex Research, 12,* 186–241.

Pennebaker, J., Dyer, M., Caulkins, R., Litowitz, D., Ackreman, P.L., Anderson, D.B., & McGraw, K.M. (1979). Don't the girls get prettier at closing time: A country and western application to psychology. *Personality and Social Psychology Bulletin, 5,* 122–125. DOI:10.1177/014616727900500127.

Riley, N. S. (2013). *'Til faith do us part: The rise of interfaith marriage and the future of American religion, family, and society.* New York: Oxford University Press.

Rosenfeld, M.J., & Thomas, R.J. (2012). Searching for a mate: The rise of the internet as a social intermediary. *American Sociological Review, 77,* 523–547. DOI:10.1177/0003122412448050.

Ryan, C., & Jetha, C. (2010). *Sex at dawn: How we mate, why we stray, and what it means for modern relationships.* New York: HarperCollins.

Schmitt, D.P. (2003). Universal sex differences in the desire for sexual variety: Tests from 52 nations, 6 continents, and 13 islands. *Journal of Personality and Social Psychology, 85,* 85–104. DOI:10.1037/0022-3514.85.1.85.

Schneiderman, I., Zagoory-Sharon, O., Leckman, J.F., & Feldman, R. (2012). Oxytocin during the initial stages of romantic attachment: Relations to couples' interactive reciprocity. *Psychoneuroendocrinology, 37,* 1277–1285. DOI:10.1016/j.psyneuen.2011.12.021.

Sprecher, S. (1989). The importance to males and females of physical attractiveness, earning potential and expressiveness in initial attraction. *Sex Roles: A Journal of Research, 21,* 591–607. DOI:10.1007/BF00289173.

Sprecher, S., Sullivan, Q., & Hatfield, E. (1994). Mate selection preferences: Gender differences examined in a national sample. *Journal of Personality and Social Psychology, 66,* 1074–1080. DOI:10.1037/0022-3514.66.6.1074.

Wang, W. (2012). The rise of intermarriage: Rates, characteristics vary by race and gender. Retrieved from http://www.pewsocialtrends.org/2012/02/16/the-rise-of-intermarriage/?src=prc-headline (accessed September 3, 2013).

White, G.L., & Kight, T.D. (1984). Misattribution of arousal and attraction: Effects of salience of explanations for arousal. *Journal of Experimental Social Psychology*, *20*, 55–64. DOI:10.1016/0022-1031(84)90012-X.

Wilbur, C.J., & Campbell, L. (2010). What do women want? An interactionist account of women's mate preferences. *Personality and Individual Differences*, *49*, 749–754. DOI:10.1016/j.paid.2010.06.020.

Willis, J., & Todorov, A. (2006). First impressions: Making up your mind after a 100-ms exposure to a face. *Psychological Science*, *17*, 592–598. DOI:10.1111/j.1467-9280.2006.01750.x.

Zajonc, R.B. (1968). Attitudinal effects of mere exposure. *Journal of Personality and Social Psychology*, *9*(2, Pt.2), 1–27. DOI:10.1037/h0025848.

Zentner, M., & Mitura, K. (2012). Stepping out of the caveman's shadow: Nations' gender gap predicts degree of sex differentiation in mate preferences. *Psychological Science*, *23*, 1176–85. DOI:10.1177/0956797612441004.

8

Intimate Relationships: Sex, Love, and Commitment

©privilege, 2013. Used under license from Shutterstock.com

Chapter Outline

- Introduction   197
- Singlehood and Casual Relationships   197
  - Sexuality Among Singles   199
  - Hookups   199
  - Friends with Benefits   200
  - Singles' Sexual Outcomes   202
- Love and Committed Relationships   203
  - The Nature of Love   203
  - The Nature of Commitment   208
  - Varieties of Loving and Committed Relationships   211
- Why Do Some Relationships Succeed While Others Fail?   216
  - Characteristics of Good Relationships   216
  - The Dark Side of Relationships   220
  - Coping with Breakup   224

The Psychology of Human Sexuality, First Edition. Justin J. Lehmiller.
© 2014 John Wiley & Sons, Ltd. Published 2014 by John Wiley & Sons, Ltd.

Introduction

Intimate relationships are a central aspect of human life. Psychologists theorize that this stems from a **need to belong**, or a near-universal human desire to develop and maintain social ties (Baumeister & Leary, 1995). The need to belong is very powerful, and developing strong social bonds is vital to our physical and psychological well-being. Relationships with family, friends, and various social groups help to fulfill this need; however, our sexual and romantic relationships are at least as central (and some might argue even more central) to meeting our deep-seated needs and desires for social connection. As some evidence of this, research has found that having a high quality romantic relationship enhances personal health and longevity; in contrast, people who are alone or who lose their partners not only tend to be in worse health, but they tend to die sooner (Kiecolt-Glaser & Newton, 2001).

Although the drive to pursue intimate relationships is ubiquitous, the number and nature of relationships necessary to fulfill one's belongingness needs varies across persons. Some individuals prefer a series of relatively transient relationships that focus on sex and physical intimacy, whereas others prefer a single, stable relationship that emphasizes emotional intimacy. As a result, intimate relationships take many different forms in adult life. One of the primary goals of this chapter is to explore the various types of sexual and romantic relationships that individuals pursue in the modern world and the degree to which they meet people's needs. In addition, we will consider the topics of sex, love, and commitment and the role that each of these factors plays across different types of relationships. Finally, we will address both the positive and negative aspects of intimate relationships and the things you can do to enhance the quality of your own personal relationships.

We begin by exploring variability in relationship type and status. We will talk first about single living and relationships that focus on casual sex and then move on to discuss loving and committed relationships.

Singlehood and Casual Relationships

Living single has become increasingly common among adults over the past few decades. In fact, census data indicate that 27% of adult Americans are currently living single, a number that has increased by two-thirds since the 1970s (United States Census Bureau, 2010). On a side note, the Census Bureau defines "single" as someone who is unmarried and living alone. We will adopt the same definition for purposes of this chapter, meaning that singles can be involved in relationships, just not cohabiting or legally recognized relationships. Despite this increase in prevalence, perceptions of singles remain largely negative. There is a widely held belief that singles are lonely and that living life outside the context of a marital relationship is inherently unsatisfying (DePaulo & Morris, 2006; for more on this, see the Digging Deeper 8.1 box). However, this is not necessarily the case in reality. While some people find singlehood deeply depressing, there are others who enjoy the freedom and independence it provides and can meet their sexual and intimate needs through casual sex and dating. Thus, being single does not necessarily mean someone is socially detached or inherently lonely. Below we explore just how varied the nature of singlehood is.

Digging Deeper 8.1   Why is it Socially Stigmatized to be Single?

If you are single, after graduation there isn't one occasion where people celebrate you... Hallmark doesn't make a "Congratulations, you didn't marry the wrong guy" card. And where's the flatware for going on vacation alone?

Carrie Bradshaw (Sex and the City)

Despite the fact that the marriage rate is in decline, most people continue to view the institution positively and think of marriage as the ideal relationship state (Thornton & Young-DeMarco, 2001). Just look at how much money people are willing to spend on weddings and how it remains a social custom to shower people with gifts when they get engaged or married. In contrast, people who are single or divorced are rarely (if ever) celebrated for their relationship status.

Figure 8.1   Single people are typically viewed and treated quite negatively in modern society. ©joseelias/123RF. COM.

Being single is viewed as a "deficit" identity (Reynolds, Wetherell, & Taylor, 2007), meaning that singles are perceived as incomplete because of their lack of a relationship. As if that were not bad enough, singles are blamed for this perceived "deficiency." For instance, in one survey of college undergraduates, participants were asked to identify the most common characteristics associated with people who are married or single (DePaulo & Morris, 2006). Whereas married people were described in a very positive light (e.g., as nice, honest, and mature), singles were typically described in very harsh and negative terms, including lonely, immature, and ugly.

As a result of these negative stereotypes, people seem to feel that *singlism* (the scientific term for prejudice against singles) is justified. In fact, people think it is more legitimate to discriminate against singles than it is to discriminate against people based upon other personal characteristics (e.g., race, gender, sexual orientation). Consistent with this idea, in one study, participants were asked to evaluate a set of property rental applications and to select the applicant they would prefer to have as a tenant (Morris, Sinclair, & DePaulo, 2007). Participants overwhelmingly chose married couples over single people and happily stated that they based their decision largely upon the applicants' marital status. Thus, people do not even feel ashamed or embarrassed to admit holding this bias. This may stem, in part, from the fact that this kind of discrimination is legal in many parts of the United States and a number of other countries.

In short, as long as people continue to put marriage and other long-term, committed relationships on a pedestal, we can expect that those who are unattached will continue to be "singled out."

Note: Reprinted with permission from *The Psychology of Human Sexuality* blog (www.lehmiller.com).

Sexuality Among Singles

Single persons run the gamut of sexual activity, with some being fully or partially *celibate* (i.e., intentionally abstaining from partnered sexual activity), and others having frequent sexual contact with one or more partners. Believe it or not, people can be satisfied no matter where they fall on this spectrum. I know some of you may be asking yourselves how someone can really be happy without sex, but this idea is not as far-fetched as it may sound. For instance, in chapter 6, we discussed the notion of *asexuality*, a sexual orientation in which an individual simply has no desire for sexual contact with others. Approximately 1% of the population is thought to be asexual (Boaert, 2004), and for such individuals, a lack of sexual activity is not problematic at all. Likewise, for individuals who have decided to practice celibacy, some may find the lack of physical intimacy distressing; however, others may discover the experience is positive because it provides opportunities for self-reflection and development. Thus, singles do not necessarily have to be sexually active in order to be happy and they can potentially meet their belongingness needs through nonsexual relationships.

That said, most singles are sexually active and these individuals can pursue many different types of sexual relationships in order to meet their needs and desires. Below, we consider just a few of their relationship possibilities.

Hookups

Singles sometimes engage in **hookups**, or one-time sexual encounters among persons who do not know each other on a deep level (Paul & Hayes, 2002). Such encounters, also known as "one-night stands," tend to emerge after an evening at the bar or after a party. Indeed, research finds that hookups are strongly associated with alcohol use (Paul, McManus, & Hayes, 2000). After a hookup, there is usually no expectation that any kind of relationship will develop, although it is not unheard of for casual sex to precipitate love.

People vary considerably in the frequency with which they hook-up with others. For instance, in a study of college students, the self-reported number of hookups over the course of a year ranged anywhere from 0 to 65 (Paul et al., 2000)! Thus, some people hook-up far more often than others. In this same study, researchers found that 78% of male and female students had hooked up before, and among those who had done it at least once, the average number of hookups was 10.8. However, it is worth noting that hookups comprise a wide range of sexual activities and that sexual intercourse may or may not occur in a given encounter. In fact, most of the hookups reported in this study involved sexual activities other than intercourse.

Although a high percentage of both men and women report having hookups, research has found an important sex differences in how those experiences are perceived. Specifically, men (84%) are more likely to report having enjoyed their hookups than are women (54%; Campbell, 2008). Women are more inclined to report regretting their experiences, perhaps because women are judged more harshly than men for sex outside of a committed relationship.

Friends with Benefits

In contrast to the one-time nature of most hookups, singles also have the option of pursuing an ongoing sexual relationship with the same person. One of the most common such relationships is **"friends with benefits"** (FWBs). FWBs are usually defined as people who have a rather typical friendship, aside from the fact that they occasionally have sex (e.g., Bisson & Levine, 2009). However, research indicates that the term "friends with benefits" does not mean just one thing. In fact, there may be as many as seven distinct types of FWBs depending upon the motivations and intentions of the partners involved. See the Digging Deeper 8.2 box for more on this.

Studies of college students have reliably found that approximately half of the participants sampled reported having had one or more FWBs in the past (Bisson & Levine, 2009) and, like hookups, there is an association between alcohol consumption and sexual contact with a FWB (Owen & Fincham, 2011). However, these relationships are by no means limited to inebriated college students. In fact, Internet studies have found that adults in their 50s and 60s have these relationships too and, furthermore, that FWBs span a wide range of demographic groups (Lehmiller, VanderDrift, & Kelly, 2011).

It should come as no surprise that the most commonly reported reason for beginning a FWB relationship is regular access to sex. However, according to a study by Lehmiller and colleagues (2011), men are more likely than women to cite sex as their primary motivation for having a FWB, whereas women are more likely than men to cite "emotional connection" as their primary motivation. The sexes also diverged when it came to how they hoped their relationship would develop over time. By and large, men wanted to remain FWBs as long as possible, whereas most women hoped their relationship would ultimately revert back to a friendship or evolve into a romance. In fact, 43.3% of women in FWBs expressed hope that their FWB would eventually turn into a "real" relationship (by comparison, only 23.7% of men desired the same outcome). Thus, men may see FWBs as a relationship end-state, whereas women may see them as a means of beginning a more interdependent and committed type of relationship (VanderDrift, Lehmiller, & Kelly, 2012). Do such relationship transitions ever happen? Yes, and perhaps more often than you might think. A study of college student dating relationships revealed that approximately 1 in 5 participants reported being FWBs before they became romantic partners (Owen & Fincham, 2012). This study found that whereas partners who were FWBs before they became lovers were somewhat less satisfied with

Digging Deeper 8.2 Are There Different Types of "Friends With Benefits?"

"Friends with Benefits" (FWBs) are usually thought of as relationships in which two good friends decide to become sexually involved. This is how they are most often depicted in the popular media, such as in the films *No Strings Attached* and *Friends with Benefits*. However, research suggests that FWBs are much more complicated than this and do not necessarily represent just one thing. In fact, according to a study by Mongeau and colleagues (2013) there may be as many as seven distinct types of FWBs!

In this study, 177 heterosexual college students were asked to define what a "friends with benefits relationship" means to them in their own words. Researchers analyzed the content of these definitions and uncovered the following varieties of FWBs:

1. *True Friends* This most closely matches what people think of as a traditional FWB (i.e., close friends who happen to have an ongoing sexual relationship). This was the single most common type of FWB participants reported having personal experience with.

2. *Just Sex* This one is exactly what it sounds like: a sexual relationship that offers little more than the occasional roll in the hay. There is no true friendship in this case – it is all about the "benefits."

3. *Network Opportunism* In this setup, the partners share a common network of friends and hang out sometimes. However, they are not necessarily good friends and mostly hang out in situations where alcohol is being consumed. The partners tend to serve as "safeties" or "backups" for each other on occasions when neither person has found another sexual partner for the evening.

4. *Successful Transition In* These are cases where people reported intentionally using a FWB as a way of starting a true romance and succeeded in making the switch.

5. *Unintentional Transition In* These are cases where people reported accidentally or unintentionally going from being FWBs to romantic partners. Whoops! This is how things often seem to end up in the movies: media depictions suggest that FWBs can only go on so long before people start having romantic feelings for each other.

6. *Failed Transition In* This is a situation in which people reported that either one or both partners wanted to turn their FWB into a true romance, but failed to make a successful conversion.

7. *Transition Out* In these cases, people reported that they broke up with a romantic partner, but then became FWBs for at least a while after (i.e., they had "ex-sex").

As you probably noticed when reading about these different types of FWBs, there is only one thing they all have in common: sex. Other than that, they are quite distinct in terms of the amount of emphasis placed on the friendship, frequency of interaction, and what the partners want.

Please keep in mind that this research is limited in that it primarily examined heterosexual college students. Thus, we do not know whether the same variation in FWBs exists among people of different sexual orientations and ages. Although we still have much to learn about FWBs, it seems safe to conclude that this type of relationship is much more complicated than many of us ever thought!

Note: Reprinted with permission from *The Psychology of Human Sexuality* blog (www.lehmiller.com).

Figure 8.2 Friends with benefits frequently try to maintain an intimate and sexual relationship without developing romantic feelings; however, they are not always successful in doing so. ©vgstudio/123RF.COM.

their relationships, they were no more likely to break up over time than were romantic partners without prior FWB experience.

Singles' Sexual Outcomes

Hookups and FWBs are just two of the potential relationship options available to singles. Beyond this, singles may also be actively dating or pursuing a committed relationship. Dating relationships can either be exclusive (i.e., monogamous) or nonexclusive (i.e., nonmonogamous). Persons who pursue a pattern of entering and exiting sexually exclusive relationships are known as **serial monogamists**. It is worth noting that whereas some singles may only pursue one type of relationship at a time (e.g., hookups *or* dating), others may pursue multiple types of relationships simultaneously (e.g., dating someone but having a FWB at the same time). Consequently, the sex lives of singles are highly variable.

Although being single comprises a wide range of relationship states, one thing is clear: on average, singles tend to be less sexually satisfied than people who are married or involved in more committed relationships. Despite the glamorous nature of singlehood depicted in television shows such as *Sex in the City*, singles report less frequent sexual activity and lower levels of sexual satisfaction compared to their married counterparts (Laumann, Gagnon, Michael, & Michaels, 1994). In addition, single women are less likely to reach orgasm with casual partners than with committed partners. As some evidence of this, one survey of over 14,000 female college students found that just 11% of women reported orgasming during their most recent hookup if they had no previous sexual experience with that partner (Armstrong, England, & Fogarty, 2012). Among women in romantic relationships of at least six months duration, that number was 67%. What accounts for this "orgasm gap?" One reason is because sexual activities that increase the odds of female orgasm (e.g., cunnilingus) are more likely to occur in committed relationships than in casual encounters. In addition, long-term partners learn how to please each other better. Some have also argued that there is a sexual script that values male pleasure over female pleasure in the context of hookups.

Beyond this, research has found that FWBs tend to be less satisfied and have lower levels of sexual communication than people involved in committed romantic relationships (Lehmiller, VanderDrift, & Kelly, 2013). However, all of this should not be taken to mean that singles are inherently *dissatisfied* with the sex they are having or with the quality of their relationships; rather, it appears that singles are satisfied overall, but just not quite as satisfied as people in more committed relationships. Moreover, getting married is not necessarily the solution for persons who have an unsatisfying sex life because *sexless marriages* certainly exist. Maintaining high levels of sexual activity and satisfaction in marriage requires work, a topic we will return to at the end of this chapter.

One final note about singles is that some of their sexual behaviors pose important health risks. In particular, research finds that people who engage in hookups (Paul et al., 2000) and FWBs (Lehmiller et al., 2013) have far from perfect condom use and seem to have a higher than average number of sexual partners. Such behavior, coupled with increased alcohol use and (potentially) impaired decision-making (Owen & Fincham, 2011; Paul et al., 2000), poses a significant risk in terms of contracting and spreading sexually transmitted infections and could potentially result in unintended pregnancies. Serial monogamists face a similar risk because they often hold the mistaken belief that monogamous people do not need to use protection (Misovich, Fisher, & Fisher, 1997). The issue here is that serial monogamists often jump from one relationship to the next (sometimes very quickly) without being tested for infections in between, and while they may use condoms at first, this behavior rapidly drops off in a new relationship as the partners come to trust each other (Critelli & Suire, 1998), thereby creating infection vulnerability. Thus, it is important for singles of all stripes to recognize the need for consistency in safer-sex practices and to avoid falling prey to false feelings of security.

Love and Committed Relationships

At the other end of the relationship spectrum, we have loving and committed relationships. These are relationships where there is usually some sexual component, but also a very deep emotional and intimate aspect to the relationship. Let us begin by defining what psychologists mean by the terms "love" and "commitment" and consider some of the major theoretical perspectives. These theories will provide the necessary backdrop for understanding when and why relationships succeed or fail. After we describe these theories, we will discuss just how diverse loving and committed relationships can be.

The Nature of Love

Everyone thinks they know what love is, but in actuality, it is difficult to pinpoint a singular definition of this concept that all of us would agree with, because love is very subjective and means different things to different people. For instance, some people view love as an emotion and describe it in terms of how they feel when they are around someone else. In contrast, other people define love as a behavior and describe it in terms of the things they would do or the sacrifices they would make for another person. Given this variability in definition and meaning, we will define **love** very broadly for purposes of this chapter as a special set of cognitions, emotions, and behaviors observed in an intimate relationship. Thus, love is something that influences how we think, act, and feel toward another person.

Psychologists typically discuss love as consisting of two distinct subtypes: passionate and companionate (Hendrick & Hendrick, 2003). Each type of love encompasses a unique set of feelings, thoughts, and behaviors.

Passionate Love

Passionate love is an all-consuming psychological and physiological state. At the cognitive level, it is characterized by an almost obsessive preoccupation with the other person (i.e., you cannot stop thinking about your loved one), as well as an overly idealized view of your partner in which you fail to recognize and acknowledge that person's flaws. Emotionally, it is characterized by an intense sexual attraction, as well as frequent feelings of excitement and ecstasy in the partner's presence; however, when separated, feelings of sadness can be extremely intense. In addition, at the physical level, it is characterized by elevated heart rate, sweating, "butterflies" in the stomach, blushing, and other general signs of heightened arousal. While all of these feelings may be very strong in the early stages of a loving relationship, their intensity tends to decrease over time.

As you may have found in your own life, passionate love is something that usually develops before you know your partner very well. During this time, potential warning flags might emerge, but because our feelings for the other person are so intense, they lead us to overlook the other person's faults and to ignore potential relationship problems. As a result, this type of love has very little in the way of logic behind it. It is partly for this reason that passionate love tends to be a rather brief, transitory state that may only last for a period of weeks or months.

One of the keys to relationship success is to recognize that those early butterflies usually do not go on forever, which means it is generally advisable to avoid getting swept away and rushing into marriage because those initial feelings of passion do not guarantee long-term relationship success. Such relationships work out sometimes, but they often do not. As a personal example, from the day my parents met until they got married was less than six months and they are still together today; however, I have a close relative who followed an almost identical path to marriage and was divorced within a year. Some amount of disillusionment inevitably sets in as passion begins to subside, which forces couples to shift the foundation of their relationship to something more stable. The quote below from the book *Captain Corelli's Mandolin* captures this idea far more eloquently than I possibly can.

> Love is a temporary madness. It erupts like an earthquake and then subsides. And when it subsides you have to make a decision. You have to work out whether your roots have become so entwined together that it is inconceivable that you should ever part. Because this is what love is. Love is not breathlessness, it is not excitement, it is not the promulgation of promises of eternal passion. That is just being "in love" which any of us can convince ourselves we are. Love itself is what is left over when being in love has burned away, and this is both an art and a fortunate accident.

Companionate Love

Companionate love is much deeper and is not nearly as intense as passionate love. Companionate love is characterized by a strong emotional attachment and commitment to another person. Unlike passionate love, companionate love is based on the full knowledge and appreciation of another person's character. Thus, rather than overlook your partner's faults, you consciously recognize that your partner is imperfect (as we all are) and learn to tolerate any shortcomings. Companionate love is also characterized by a desire to make the relationship work despite any difficulties that might arise, as well as a willingness to sacrifice self-interest for the betterment of the relationship.

People who experience companionate love can and do still have sex, although it may not be as frequent or as intense as it is in a passionate love relationship. However, higher levels of trust and mutual concern for one another's needs could potentially improve sexual communication and satisfaction and allow partners to explore their sexual fantasies.

Companionate love obviously does not build up overnight; rather, it develops gradually as you get to know each other. As a result, it tends to be much more enduring. This is the type of love that can last for decades.

Relationships often begin with passionate love, and then either dissolve or transition into companionate love. There is no exact timetable for when this occurs, but the usual time course is somewhere between 6 and 30 months after the start of the relationship (Hatfield & Walster, 2002). On a side note, whereas the typical pattern is to go from passionate to companionate, the reverse can happen as well (i.e., when good friends become lovers), but this is far less common.

Figure 8.3 Passionate love is characterized by high levels of sexual desire and activity. ©Yuri Arcurs/123RF.COM.

Figure 8.4 Companionate love reflects a deep emotional connection that tends to be enduring. ©Alexey Kuznetsov/123RF.COM.

Robert Sternberg's Triangular Theory

This distinction between passionate and companionate love and the transition that occurs between them was expanded upon in one of the most well-known theories of love, Robert Sternberg's (1986) *Triangular Theory*. The idea behind this theory is that love consists of three distinct components. First, we have **passion**, the motivational dimension. Passion encompasses physical attraction and sexual desire, and it is what distinguishes romantic love from the love that we might feel toward our family and friends. Second is **intimacy**, the emotional dimension. Intimacy refers to our sense of bondedness and emotional connection with another person. Please note that in the context of this theory, "intimacy" does not refer to physical closeness; rather, it refers to emotional closeness (e.g., sharing personal information, giving and receiving support). Finally, we have **commitment**, the cognitive dimension. Commitment refers to our conscious decision to maintain a relationship over time, for better or for worse.

Consistent with our previous discussion of passionate love, Sternberg believes that passion tends to build up quickly, reach a peak, and then gradually decline. To compensate for the loss of passion, intimacy and commitment may come in, and when they do, the relationship is likely to survive. If no such compensation occurs, however, the relationship will dissolve rather quickly.

The Triangular Theory posits that passion, intimacy, and commitment exist to varying degrees in a given relationship. Depending upon the unique combination of components, we can experience a number of different forms of love. Specifically, this theory specifies eight varieties of love, which can be seen in Table 8.1. One of the nice things about this theory is that it helps to explain why there is so much variability in how people define love. In addition, it provides a conceptual basis for distinguishing between the kinds of love we feel for romantic partners and for other people in our lives (e.g., friends and family). In this theory, the ideal form of romantic love

Table 8.1   Sternberg's Eight Varieties of Love

Type of love	Passion?	Intimacy?	Commitment?	Example
Nonlove	No	No	No	Acquaintances
Liking	No	Yes	No	Close friends
Infatuation	Yes	No	No	Crushes
Empty love	No	No	Yes	Some arranged marriages
Fatuous love	Yes	No	Yes	Long-distance relationships
Romantic love	Yes	Yes	No	Friends with benefits
Companionate love	No	Yes	Yes	Long-term, happy couples
Consummate love	Yes	Yes	Yes	"Epic" romances

Source: Sternberg (1988).

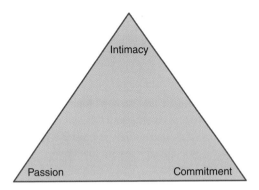

Figure 8.5   Robert Sternberg (1988) theorizes that the "triangle" of love is composed of passion, intimacy, and commitment.

is known as **consummate love**, in which passion, intimacy, and commitment are present simulta-neously. This is the kind of love we all dream of, but it is extremely difficult to achieve and maintain.

Sternberg's theory is called the Triangular Theory for a reason. Specifically, Sternberg views each person as having a unique *love triangle* (and no, this is not the type of love triangle you might see on a soap opera where three people are in love, but not all of those feelings are reciprocated). Your love triangle (see Figure 8.5) is the relative amount of passion, intimacy, and commitment you have in your relationship. However, within a given relationship, the partners' triangles may or may not overlap very well because the overall size of the triangle and each of the angles may be different (e.g., one person may be more committed or passionate than the other). The better the match between two people's triangles, the more satisfied they are likely to be together.

John Lee's Styles of Loving
An alternative perspective on love was provided by John Lee (1977). Whereas Sternberg focused on describing certain types of love, Lee's emphasis was on individual differences in how people approach love. Specifically, Lee argues that people can have one of six "love styles":

1. The *Romantic* love style is characterized by being hopelessly romantic (as depicted in films such as *Pretty Woman* and *The Notebook*). These are people who have a tendency to take great pleasure in their partner's physical appearance and often fall in love "at first sight."
2. The *Altruistic* love style is characterized by selflessness and unconditional love. Such persons are generous, self-sacrificing, and faithful.
3. The *Pragmatic* love style refers to a very rational and practical approach to love, in which peo-ple look for partners who are likely to be compatible. Sometimes known as the "shopping list" love style, the emphasis here is not on finding passion so much as the best life partner.
4. The *Game-Playing* love style emphasizes a more casual and uncommitted approach to love. Game players take great delight in the act of seduction and view marriage as the ultimate trap. Such individuals may not be fazed by a break-up, and they may not think twice about commit-ting infidelity.
5. The *Companionate* love style is an approach to love that begins with friendship and eventually transitions into a very peaceful, affectionate, and enduring form of love. These are people who want their lover to be their best friend.

6.   The *Possessive* love style (or as I call it, the *Fatal Attraction* approach) is characterized by very intense, obsessive love relationships in which it is very easy to reach emotional highs *and* lows. Such individuals can be insecure, jealous, and unstable, and they tend to see sex as a form of emotional reassurance.

In Lee's view, no single love style is "better" or "worse" than any of the others. Instead, what matters when it comes to relationship success is the match between the partners' approaches. As you might imagine, major mismatches (e.g., game-players paired with possessives) are unlikely to be successful. Research has revealed sex differences in love styles (Hendrick & Hendrick, 1986). College-age men are more likely to adopt the game-playing and romantic approaches, whereas women are more likely to adopt the pragmatic, possessive, and companionate styles. Such findings could be interpreted as evidence of evolutionary theorists' contention that men tend to be more focused on looks and casual relationships, whereas women are more focused on finding a long-term, reliable partner. What is your love style? Visit the Your Sexuality 8.1 box to find out.

The Nature of Commitment

As discussed in the context of the Triangular Theory, *commitment* is often defined as an individual's conscious decision to stick with a given partner over time. However, whereas Sternberg conceptualized commitment as a subcomponent of love, other psychologists have defined commitment as a separate, but overlapping construct. This makes sense because while love and commitment do have a lot in common, it remains possible to have one without the other. Another major distinction is that whereas love is a multi-faceted concept that has cognitive, emotional, and behavioral components, commitment is often viewed as a unitary cognitive construct. As a result, it is useful to consider love and commitment separately.

In this section, we will discuss commitment in the context of the *Investment Model* (Rusbult, 1980), which is one of the most well-known and widely utilized theories of relationship commitment in the field of psychology. This model is based heavily on the principles of exchange theory (see Chapter 1).

The Investment Model

From the perspective of the Investment Model, commitment is usually measured as one's intention to persist in a given relationship over time (Rusbult, Martz, & Agnew, 1998). This intention is viewed as a product of three related factors: satisfaction level, quality of alternatives, and investment size. **Satisfaction** refers to an individual's subjective evaluation of a relationship. Are things going well, or are they going poorly? In order to make this determination, we consider the overall ratio of good to bad things in the relationship and evaluate it relative to some *comparison level* that can help to establish whether we are getting what we think we deserve. That is, we think about whether our relationship outcomes are better or worse than those we have received in past relationships or those that our friends are receiving in their relationships. To the extent that we can make *downward social comparisons* (i.e., comparing ourselves to people who are worse off), the more satisfied we are, and the more committed we tend to be.

Quality of alternatives refers to your perception of how desirable all of the other people in your dating pool currently are. Thus, we also have a *comparison level for alternatives*, in which we compare the outcomes in our current relationship to those we think we could be getting with someone else (e.g., could you be having more or better sex with another person?). Quality of alternatives

Your Sexuality 8.1   What is Your "Love Style?"

How do you typically approach love? To figure out your own love style, please indicate how much you agree or disagree with each of the following statements while thinking about your current romantic relationship or the most recent person with whom you were romantically involved. Please use a response scale ranging from 1 (strongly disagree) to 7 (strongly agree).

Love Style A
_____ My partner and I were attracted to each other immediately after we first met.
_____ My partner fits my ideal standards for physical beauty/handsomeness.
_____ My partner and I have the right physical chemistry between us.

Love Style B
_____ I try to keep my partner a little uncertain about my commitment to him/her.
_____ I believe that what my partner does not know about me won't hurt him/her.
_____ When my partner gets too dependent on me, I want to back off a little.

Love Style C
_____ I expect to always be friends with my partner.
_____ Our love is really a deep friendship, not a mysterious, mystical emotion.
_____ Our friendship merged gradually into love over time.

Love Style D
_____ I considered what my partner was going to become in life before I committed myself to him/her.
_____ In choosing my partner, I believe it was best to love someone with a similar background.
_____ A main consideration in choosing my partner was how he/she would reflect on my family.

Love Style E
_____ When things are not right with my partner and me, my stomach gets upset.
_____ Sometimes I get so excited about being in love with my partner that I cannot sleep.
_____ I cannot relax if I suspect that my partner is with someone else.

Love Style F
_____ I would rather suffer myself than let my partner suffer.
_____ Whatever I own is my partners to use as he/she chooses.
_____ I am usually willing to sacrifice my own wishes to let my partner achieve his/hers.

Now go through and tally your scores for each section. Please note that love style A = romantic, B = game-playing, C = companionate, D = pragmatic, E = possessive, and F = altruistic. Which scores are your highest and lowest? Is this consistent with how you have approached romantic and sexual relationships in general, or do you tend to act differently with different partners? Please keep in mind that there are no "right" or "wrong" answers to any of the above questions and that no single love style is better than another.

Source of love style statements: Hendrick, Hendrick, & Dicke. *Journal of Social and Personal Relationships*, *15*, 147–159, copyright © 1998 by Clyde Hendrick, Susan S. Hendrick, and Amy Dicke. Reprinted by Permission of SAGE.

Figure 8.6   Making comparisons to couples that appear to be worse off (e.g., couples who fight all of the time) can make you feel better about your own relationship. ©Cathy Yeulet/123RF.COM.

also encompasses different relationship states with your current partner, meaning that we might also consider whether it would be more desirable to be friends or FWBs with our current partner rather than romantic lovers. The more desirable all of these other options appear, the less committed we are.

Finally, **investments** refer to everything we have put into our relationship over time that would be lost or decreased in value were our current relationship to end. Investments can be tangible (e.g., material objects, money) or intangible (e.g., shared memories, time and effort) in nature. As more investments are made, couples become tied together because starting a new relationship could mean losing certain things (e.g., homes, cars, custody of children) and dealing with a number of complications (e.g., figuring out which friends you get to keep). Thus, the more invested a couple is, the more committed they tend to be.

There is a vast amount of research showing that people are most committed when they are highly satisfied, perceive few alternatives, and have many investments (Le & Agnew, 2003). In addition, commitment strengthens a relationship by encouraging pro-relationship behavior (e.g., willingness to sacrifice your own interest for the sake of your partner; Van Lange et al., 1997). This, in turn, makes it more likely that the relationship will remain intact over time.

This model has been used to explain commitment across many types of relationships, including same-sex and heterosexual couples (Le & Agnew, 2003; Lehmiller 2010), but also more casual types of relationships, such as FWBs (VanderDrift et al., 2012). One final note about the Investment Model is that, in general, satisfaction tends to be the strongest predictor of commitment (Le & Agnew, 2003). However, some factors may be more or less important in certain relationships. For instance, women in abusive relationships often report being committed to their partners not because they are satisfied, but because they do not believe they have anywhere else to go (i.e., they may have very poor alternatives; Rusbult & Martz, 1995). Thus, this model is particularly valuable from the standpoint that it can help us to understand why people remain in both good *and* bad relationships.

Varieties of Loving and Committed Relationships

When asked to generate a real-life example of a loving and committed relationship, more often than not, people will point to some heterosexual married couple they know. The reason for this is because heterosexuality (Herek, 2000), monogamy (Conley, Moors, Matsick, & Ziegler, 2013), and marriage (Thornton & Young-DeMarco, 2001) tend to be held up as the ideal relationship characteristics. However, relationships are far more diverse than this. Below, we consider just a few dimensions on which loving and committed relationships vary and explore some of the characteristics associated with those relationships. Specifically, we will consider relationships that differ in terms of sexual orientation, views on monogamy, and decision to cohabit or get married.

Heterosexual vs. Same-Sex

Although same-sex couples can be found in most cultures and societies throughout the world, acceptance of these relationships varies considerably. Some cultures are more tolerant and offer government-sanctioned relationship recognition to same-sex partners; however, the legal name applied to such relationships (marriage, civil union, or domestic partnership) and the rights that go along with those relationship labels differ. Currently, relatively few societies offer full marriage equality to people of all sexualities. For a list of countries that recognize same-sex marriage, see Table 8.2.

There are a number of common myths and misconceptions about gay and lesbian couples. For instance, as noted in Chapter 6, same-sex couples do not typically adopt strict roles of "husband" and "wife"; rather, they are more inclined to establish equality and power-sharing (Kurdek, 1998). There is also a common assumption that gay and heterosexual relationships operate in fundamentally different ways, but the reality is that they are far more similar than they are different (Kurdek, 2004). Moreover, gay and lesbian couples tend to be just as satisfied with and committed to their partners as heterosexual couples, which indicates that overall relationship health and quality is similar across sexualities (Lehmiller & Agnew, 2006). That said, some research has found that same-sex couples tend to break up more frequently than different-sex couples (Kurdek, 1998); however, part of the reason for this likely stems from the fact that same-sex couples are less likely to have the option of legal marriage (Lehmiller, 2010). The lack of institutional and social support for gay relationships coupled with a less complicated exit strategy (i.e., no need for a messy divorce) would appear to be plausible explanations for the higher breakup rate.

Monogamous vs. Nonmonogamous

In the modern Western world, monogamous relationships are the norm, and they tend to be viewed very positively. In fact, research has found that a *halo effect* surrounds monogamy, with people perceiving that this practice promotes not only strong commitment, but also health and other benefits; in contrast, nonmonogamy is socially stigmatized, and people who practice it are viewed in a very negative light (Conley et al., 2013). Although no nationally representative surveys have attempted to assess the prevalence of monogamy and nonmonogamy, survey data utilizing convenience samples has found that about 4% of participants practice some form of **consensual nonmonogamy** (i.e., they have an explicit agreement with their partner that the pursuit of sexual and/or romantic relationships with other people is acceptable; see Conley et al., 2013). Please

Figure 8.7 The degree to which same-sex relationships are socially accepted varies substantially across cultures. ©Darren Baker/123RF.COM.

Table 8.2 Countries that Recognize Same-sex Marriage		
Same-sex marriage performed nationwide	*Same-sex marriage legal in parts of the country*	*Same-sex marriages performed elsewhere are recognized*
Argentina	Mexico	Israel
Belgium	United States	
Brazil		
Canada		
Denmark		
France		
Iceland		
The Netherlands		
New Zealand		
Norway		
Portugal		
South Africa		
Spain		
Sweden		
Uruguay		

Figure 8.8   An infinity symbol encased within a heart is often used to symbolize polyamory, or the idea that it is possible to love multiple persons simultaneously. Source: Ratatosk (Own work) [CC-BY-SA-2.0 Germany (http://creativecommons. org/licenses/by-sa/2.0/de/deed.en)], via Wikimedia Commons.

note that consensual nonmonogamy is distinct from infidelity, and that people who practice consensual nonmonogamy do not necessarily endorse or approve of cheating. In fact, consensual nonmonogamy is sometimes referred to as "ethical nonmonogamy," because the people who practice it are usually strong proponents of being open and honest with all parties involved.

Consensual non-monogamy can take many forms, including open relationships, swinging, polygamy, and polyamory. **Open relationships** refer to couples who have a relational "home base" with one another, but have the ability to pursue other intimate relationships at the same time. The way open relationships work varies. Some couples require full disclosure of any outside sexual activities, and others adopt a "don't ask, don't tell" policy. Some couples only "play together" (e.g., by having the occasional threesome or "fourgy"), while others may pursue outside relationships on their own, which may be one-time sexual encounters, ongoing FWBs, or perhaps something even more intimate. Related to this is **swinging** (formerly known as "wife swapping"), a sexual practice in which married couples swap partners for an afternoon or evening. This may occur in sex clubs, at private parties, or through online arrangements.

Polygamy refers to a form of marriage featuring multiple spouses. Scientists have reported that polygamy is permissible in 84% of human cultures; in most of those cultures, however, only a small minority of individuals practice it (Fisher, 1992). There are two variants of polygamy: *polygyny*, an arrangement in which one man has multiple wives, and *polyandry*, an arrangement in which one woman has multiple husbands. Polygyny tends to be the more common variation, although both forms are explicitly outlawed in the US and in a number of other countries. Both polygyny and polyandry have been argued to be evolutionarily adaptive practices at times. In polygyny, the potential evolutionary benefits for men are obvious: multiple female partners ensure a greater number of offspring carrying a man's genes. In polyandry, the proposed evolutionary benefits include protection against having just one partner who could potentially have a gene defect, as well as promoting sperm competition (i.e., survival of the fittest) in the fertilization of ova (for a review of these and other theories, see Cornell & Tregenza, 2007).

Finally, we have **polyamory**, which refers to the practice of having multiple sexual and/or romantic partners simultaneously. It is distinct from polygamy in the sense that someone who is polyamorous may or may not be married. It is also distinct from swinging and open relationships in the sense that within polyamory, the emphasis is generally not on recreational sex so much as on building intimate relationships. Polyamory is a term that means different things to different people. Some people consider it to be a type of relationship, whereas others categorize it as a *relationship orientation* (kind of like a sexual orientation). The one thing that is clear across all of the different definitions and views of polyamory is that being polyamorous means believing that exclusivity of both an intimate and sexual nature is not a necessary precursor to love and commitment.

Consensual nonmonogamy and its various permutations have been largely overlooked in psychological research. As a result, relatively little is known about them and how they compare to monogamous relationships. What little research exists suggests that people in nonmonogamous relationships tend to be sexually satisfied. For instance, a national US survey of 1,092 swingers found that they reported being happier in their marriages than couples in traditional marriages (Bergstrand & Blevins Williams, 2000). This same study revealed that the majority of swingers (62.2%) said that swinging *improved* their relationships; the remainder said it had no effect (35.6%) or that it made them less happy (1.7%). Of course, this is not to say that swinging would necessarily be good for all couples, and it could be that there was a major selection effect in this study (e.g., perhaps people who swing are less jealous than average, or perhaps when swinging has a negative effect it leads to a speedy divorce).

Although many people argue that monogamy is inherently "safe" and nonmonogamy is "unsafe," this may not be accurate. While nonmonogamous individuals may accumulate a greater number of lifetime sexual partners because they have more opportunity and more partners mean a higher risk of sexual infections (Levinson, Jaccard, & Beamer, 1995), the sexual health disparity between monogamous and nonmonogamous individuals is not likely to be as wide as it first seems. For one thing, monogamy is not 100% safe because people cheat, and as we will see later in this chapter, cheating is far from a rarity. Compounding the problem of cheating is that when it occurs, condom use tends to be low. In fact, people in monogamous relationships who cheat are less likely to use condoms than people who practice consensual nonmonogamy (Conley, Moors, Ziegler, & Karathanasis, 2012). Also, as noted earlier in this chapter, people who practice serial monogamy increase their infection risk each time they move on to a new partner because the transition between partners is often quick and the period of practicing safer-sex may be very short (Misovich et al., 1997). Thus, while monogamy is safe *in theory*, it may not be as safe as it is assumed to be in practice.

Married vs. Cohabiting

One other dimension on which loving and committed relationships vary is in the partners' decision to get married or to live together without a formal legal bond (i.e., to cohabit). Marriage is an institution that exists in most, but not all societies to serve purposes ranging from the practical (e.g., defining inheritance rights) to the romantic (e.g., achieving personal happiness and fulfillment). However, the precise function of marriage differs widely across cultures. For instance, in some Eastern cultures (e.g., India and China), the practice of **arranged marriage** is common, in which two sets of parents will join their children for pragmatic reasons (e.g., shared religion, reputation, consolidation of wealth). The children may have no or only limited say in who their partner will be. In contrast, the more individualistic cultures of the West consider marriage more a matter of individual choice, and religion may or may not factor into it at all.

Figure 8.9   In collectivistic cultures such as India, the practice of arranged marriage is common: the needs of the family and community are given greater weight than the needs of the individual. ©Deborah Kolb/123RF.COM.

Worldwide, the marriage rate has declined in recent years, whereas the number of couples who cohabit or seek to define their relationships in other ways has increased (Cohn, Passel, Wang, & Livingston, 2011). Part of the reason for this is because marriage is no longer viewed as a permanent (i.e., "till death do us part") institution. Given the high divorce rate and the fact that dissolving a marriage can be unpleasant, expensive, and time-consuming, people are increasingly opting to cohabit before marriage as a "trial period" or because they wish to create legal bonds that are more easily broken in the event the relationship crumbles. For instance, many heterosexual couples in France are opting for civil unions over marriages because civil unions (originally designed for France's same-sex couples) offer many of the same rights and privileges of full marriage, but can be entered and exited far more easily (Sayare & de la Baume, 2010).

Is the trend away from marriage and toward cohabitation and less restrictive legal arrange-ments a good thing? It depends which outcome variables you consider because each relationship type has its own set of advantages and disadvantages. For instances, couples who cohabit tend to have more equality in their relationships and are less likely to subscribe to the traditional gender role beliefs of male breadwinners and female housewives compared to those who are married (Blackwell & Lichter, 2000). Cohabitation also makes it easier to end the relationship because no divorce is typically required (unless you live in a state or country that offers *common-law marriage*, in which a couple that lives together for a set amount of time is automatically viewed as married in the eyes of the government; however, this is rare). Of course, the downside of cohabitation is that it offers fewer legal rights and protections to the partners (e.g., if one partner passes away, the surviving partner is not necessarily entitled to the entire estate and, even if it is inherited, a steep tax bill may be due, unlike married couples). In addition, couples who cohabit before marriage report lower marital quality (Jose, O'Leary, & Moyer, 2010). Although it was previously thought that cohabiting with someone before marriage increased risk of divorce, it now appears that a higher likelihood of divorce only occurs among individuals who have had prior experience moving in and out with multiple partners. This makes sense because if someone has dissolved several marital-like relationships in the past, they will likely have fewer hesitations about ending an actual marriage.

Regardless of whether a couple cohabits or gets married, one advantage offered by both relationship arrangements is enhanced health. Specifically, research has found that people who are in long-term relationships tend to have better physical and psychological health than those who are single (Musick & Bumpass, 2012). It was originally thought that these health benefits were unique to marriage, but more recent studies have found that the effects extend to cohabiting partners as well. The one caveat to this is that the health effects of being partnered are typically much greater for men than they are for women (Kiecolt-Glaser & Newton, 2001). We cannot say exactly why, but it likely has something to do with the fact that women typically have many sources of social and emotional support outside of their primary romantic relationship whereas men often do not.

Why Do Some Relationships Succeed While Others Fail?

To round out this chapter, we will discuss some of the characteristics associated with good relationships, and those that are linked to relationship difficulties.

Characteristics of Good Relationships

What can you do to enhance the quality of your own sexual and romantic relationships? Psychologists have identified several features of high-functioning relationships. Attempting to model these attributes in your own relationship may enhance satisfaction for both you and your partner(s).

Positive Communication
Psychologist John Gottman has studied married couples extensively and has found that the way couples communicate during conflict situations is a potent predictor of relationship success. In one of his most well-known studies, Gottman (1994) videotaped hundreds of married couples discussing a problem area in their relationship. These couples were then tracked over time to see which ones stayed together. The strongest predictor of whether a given relationship succeeded or failed was the ratio of positive to negative comments that emerged during the interaction. Specifically, those couples who expressed at least five positive comments for every one negative comment were the most likely to survive; couples who expressed negative comments more frequently often headed to an early divorce. This research revealed a few other important communication patterns. For instance, breakup rates were higher among couples who engaged in more defensive behaviors (e.g., making excuses or failing to take responsibility) and when male partners engaged in **stonewalling** (i.e., appearing indifferent or showing no emotional response to their female partner's concerns). Although this research focused on married heterosexual couples, Gottman's work on same-sex couples has yielded similar findings about the importance of positive communication (Gottman et al., 2003).

Figure 8.10   Communicating about sex appears to enhance sexual satisfaction. ©Dmitriy Shironosov/123RF.COM.

Healthy Sexuality

Positive communication during conflict is one important factor in relationship health, but it is just as important for that positive communication to carry over into the bedroom, because partners who communicate more about sex in general and during the act itself tend to be more sexually satisfied (Babin, 2013). This is not particularly surprising, because people who are comfortable talking about sex are more likely to give their partners direction, discuss their sexual fantasies, and inquire about their partners' needs. The keys to effective sexual communication are (1) listening to your partner's needs and concerns (perhaps even by repeating their concerns back in your own words or asking clarifying questions to ensure that you have understood), (2) expressing your own needs and concerns in very clear and unambiguous language (i.e., do not leave any room for guess-work), and (3) keeping the conversation positive and non-judgmental (i.e., do not just point out what your partner is doing wrong – make sure to tell them what they are doing right!). Also, keep in mind that not all sexual communication has to be in the form of words. Panting, moaning, and groaning can help convey your sexual likes and dislikes as well.

In addition, couples should continue having sex with a frequency that is desirable to both partners. Sexual activity provides an array of benefits both to the individuals involved and to their relationship, but chief among them is that sex appears to have a stress-relieving effect for couples that live together (Ein-Dor, & Hirschberger, 2012). To learn more about this research, see the Digging Deeper 8.3 box. How much sex is necessary for optimal relationship functioning? There is no "correct" frequency with which a couple is "supposed" to have sex, because the amount of sex desired differs widely across relationships. Different people have different sex drives, with some desiring sex all of the time and others hardly desiring it at all. Thus, what makes one couple happy might be seen as too little or too much by others. The key is to find a sexual frequency that meets both partners' needs. Of course, this is easier said than done, and in cases where there is a large discrepancy between partners' sexual desire, sex therapy may be the answer (see chapter 12). Consensual nonmonogamy may be a viable option for some couples too.

That said, finding the right frequency is easier if both partners possess **sexual communal strength**. This can be thought of as a willingness to satisfy your partner's sexual needs, even

Figure 8.11   For couples in good relationships, having sex can relieve feelings of stress. ©Frenk And Danielle Kaufmann/123RF.COM.

when they do not necessarily align with your own personal desires (Muise, Impett, Logan, & Desmarais, 2013). Having sexual communal strength may mean occasionally consenting to sex even when you are not quite in the mood, or perhaps indulging one of your partner's sexual fantasies even though it is not as big of a turn-on for you. This is *not* to say that you should start doing things that make you feel uncomfortable in order to keep your relationship alive; rather, think of this as mutual compromise designed to help one another achieve sexual satisfaction.

One question students often have about starting and maintaining a healthy sexual relationship is when a couple "should" have sex. The popular media suggests that having sex too early is problematic (e.g., your partner may not respect you or think of you as "relationship material"), but that waiting too long is equally bad (e.g., if you save yourself for marriage, you may discover that you are sexually incompatible with your partner). The truth is that there is no "right" or "correct" time to start having sex because each person and each relationship is different. The key is to do it when both of you are ready and feel comfortable, whether that is your first date or your wedding night. Consistent with this idea, research has found that there is no meaningful difference in relationship satisfaction between heterosexual couples who had sex early on and those who delayed. For example, Willoughby, Carroll, and Busby (2013) found a difference in relationship quality of just one-tenth of one point on a 5-point scale in a study comparing couples who had sex sooner to those who waited, which tells us that the timing of sex is not as important as the popular media makes it out to be.

Self-Expansion

One final characteristic of high-functioning relationships is fulfillment of both partners' needs for self-expansion. According to **self-expansion theory**, human beings have a fundamental need to "expand" or grow the self over time (Aron & Aron, 1986). This is accomplished by continually engaging in activities that are exciting and novel, as well as by developing new relationships. In

Digging Deeper 8.3   Does Having Sex Relieve Stress For Couples?

Makes me feel so fine, helps me relieve my mind, sexual healing baby, it's good for me.
                                                                Marvin Gaye

The idea that sex can relieve stress for couples is pervasive in popular culture. For example, many of you have probably heard the classic song *Sexual Healing* by Marvin Gaye. Many of you have probably also seen television shows and movies that feature storylines about the wonders of "makeup sex" following a couple's argument (which, according to Jerry Seinfeld, is the second best type of sex you can have after "conjugal visit sex"). So is there any truth to this idea? Is sex really a stress-reliever? According to research, yes – but only for couples who are in satisfying relationships to begin with (Ein-Dor, & Hirschberger, 2012).

In this study, 75 heterosexual men and women who were living with a romantic partner completed a sex diary for 18 consecutive days. Participants filled out their diary alone each night in which they reported on the amount of stress they had experienced in the past 24 hours (i.e., how many stressful events occurred and how stressful each one was) and indicated whether they had sexual intercourse with their partner that day.

Experiencing a high level of stress increased the likelihood of having intercourse the following day. In addition, when sex followed a particularly high-stress day, it reduced reports of stress on the following day; when a high-stress day was not followed by sex, there was not as much of a decrease in stress the next day. To put it more simply, when couples had sex, they felt less stress afterward than they did before. However, it is important to point out that this finding held only for couples who reported that their relationship was satisfying at the start of the study; for couples who were dissatisfied with their relationship, there was no stress-reducing effect of sex.

This research is limited in that it only examined heterosexual couples and only considered the potential stress relief associated with vaginal intercourse. Thus, it is not clear whether the same benefits would apply in same-sex couples or in couples who engage in other types of sexual activities. However, these results suggest that sex does have the potential to heal us from stress, but only if we are involved in a good relationship.

Note: Reprinted with permission from *The Psychology of Human Sexuality* blog (www.lehmiller.com).

---

fact, just being in a relationship provides some degree of expansion because, over time, the self will start to incorporate certain characteristics of the partner (i.e., we start to associate our partners' traits with ourselves; Aron & Aron, 1996). However, to meet one's self-expansion needs over the long run, couple members need to regularly share self-expanding experiences. That is, couples need to continually visit new places and try exciting and different things. When romantic partners fall into a routine of staying at home and watching TV every night, they fail to meet their expansion needs and run the risk of the relationship going stale. Consistent with this idea, research on long-term married couples has found that those who engage in the most novel and exciting activities together report having the most intense feelings of love for one another (O'Leary et al., 2012). This suggests that perhaps we should not resign ourselves to the idea that passion inevitably dies; rather, we may be able to keep it alive through self-expansion.

The Dark Side of Relationships

Not all relationships last. The divorce rate is about as high today as it has ever been, owing to reduced pressure to get married at a young age and a reduction in the stigma associated with ending a marriage. Only about half of all first marriages in the US last 20 years or longer (Copen, Daniels, Vespa, & Mosher, 2012), and cohabiting relationships tend to have an even shorter shelf-life. Table 8.3 gives a breakdown of the number of divorces occurring at various points in time and how this differs across partner race. Two things are worth noting about these data. First, marital longevity is related to racial background. We cannot say exactly why, but many variables could be at play, including socioeconomic factors and differences in mainstream acculturation. Second, the observed peak in divorce rates that occurs after two decades makes sense because for couples who had children right after getting married, this would be about the time that the kids have grown up and moved out of the house.

As a means of coping with the high prevalence of divorce, legislators in Mexico and other countries are considering granting "temporary" marriage licenses that would allow individuals to have a marital trial period before making a longer term commitment (Ng, 2011). Whether that will ever catch on remains to be seen, but it is just another symptom of the fact that relationships are not guaranteed to last. Why do so many relationship end? Below, we consider just a few of the many factors that contribute to breakups and divorces.

Social Disapproval

Not every relationship is socially accepted. As previously mentioned, same-sex couples and people in nonmonogamous relationships face widespread social stigma, but they are far from the only ones. Any relationship that deviates from the cultural prototype may be socially devalued. In many societies, this means that couples in which the partners differ from one another in terms of race, ethnicity, religion, social class, or age may lack approval for their relationship from their family, friends, and society at large. Such disapproval can take a toll on the partners. Research has found that the more disapproval a couple perceives, the less committed the partners tend to be (Lehmiller & Agnew, 2006) and the more likely they are to break up (Lehmiller & Agnew, 2007). Not only that, but involvement in a marginalized relationship is associated with worse physical and psychological health outcomes (Lehmiller, 2012). This makes sense because being the target of prejudice (whether it is directed at your race, gender, sexuality, or relationship status) is stressful, and if you have ever taken a health psychology course, you have probably learned just how much wear and

Table 8.3	Likelihood that a First Marriage will last up to 20 years by Race of Partners in the US			
	Duration of first marriage			
Race of Couple	*5 years*	*10 years*	*15 years*	*20 years*
Asian	91%	83%	78%	69%
Hispanic	84%	73%	64%	54%
White	80%	68%	61%	53%
Black	72%	56%	45%	37%

Source: Copen, Daniels, Vespa, & Mosher (2012).

tear chronic stress can put on an individual's well-being. Thus, lacking relationship acceptance and approval may be destructive to both the health of the partners and their romance.

Insecurity and Jealousy

Another factor that can generate relationship difficulties is a feeling of insecurity and/or jealousy. Some of us have a chronic tendency to experience these feelings as a result of our **attachment style** (Hazan & Shaver, 1987). Attachment styles refer to patterns of approaching and developing relationships with others. These patterns at least partially develop out of our early experiences with primary caregivers. Attachment styles tend to be relatively stable across time, but they can change to a degree as a result of new experiences and relationships (Simpson et al., 2003). *Securely attached* individuals have an easy time getting close to other people and do not worry about being abandoned by their partners. They are highly trusting and are confident that their partners will be there for them when it really counts. People who are *anxiously attached* worry that their partners may not want to get as close as they would like. They fear that their partner does not love them and may leave and, consequently, tend to be quite jealous. *Avoidantly attached* individuals are not overly comfortable with intimacy and do not wish to become dependent on others. They recognize that their partner will probably leave at some point, but this does not worry them because they see love and relationships as temporary. Most people are securely attached, and it should come as no surprise that their relationships tend to last the longest, whereas individuals with an anxious or avoidant attachment style tend to break up sooner on average (Duemmler & Kobak, 2001).

When jealousy emerges in a relationship, there tends to be large sex differences in how it is experienced. Men are typically more jealous about the prospect of their partner becoming *physically* involved with someone else, whereas women are usually more jealous about the prospect of their partner becoming *emotionally* involved with someone else (Buss, Larsen, Westen, & Semmelroth, 1992). This difference is most commonly explained in terms of evolutionary theory. The idea is that men have evolved a tendency to worry about sexual infidelity because there is **paternity uncertainty** (i.e., men cannot easily tell whether a pregnant women is carrying their child) and they want to avoid expending their resources on children who are not biologically theirs. In contrast, women are thought to have evolved a tendency to worry about emotional infidelity in order to reduce the risk of being abandoned by the father of their children. Consistent with the paternity uncertainly explanation, gay men tend to be more concerned with emotional infidelity than sexual infidelity (the same holds for lesbians; Carpenter, 2012). Thus, among men who do not have to worry about paternity issues, sexual infidelity appears to be less of a concern.

Of course, this is not the only possible explanation, and the research in this area is far from conclusive. For example, consider that virtually all of this research is based upon asking people whether they find physical *or* emotional infidelity more upsetting. This is a false dichotomy because, for many people, emotional infidelity (e.g., falling in love with someone else) also implies physical infidelity. In addition, if the evolutionary perspective is correct, one might assume that sexual jealousy would be greater when a heterosexual man's wife gets pregnant by a random stranger as opposed to his brother because if his wife is carrying his brother's child, it will at least share some of his genes. In reality, however, the opposite is true – men are more upset when their wives cheat with other relatives.

Regardless of where our feelings of jealousy come from, it is clear that jealousy has a wide range of negative effects on our relationships. Not only does jealousy often contribute to conflict and breakup, but it is also frequently implicated in relationship violence. In fact, research on men who have been sent to jail for domestic violence has revealed that jealousy was pervasive in almost

Figure 8.12   Couples that violate societal or cultural expectations are subject to stigmatization, which may end up hurting the health of the couple members and their relationship. ©Graham Oliver/123RF.COM.

all of these men's relationships and was the most frequently reported factor contributing to their violent actions (Nemeth et al., 2012).

Cheating

Last but not least, cheating is one of the most common causes of relationship turmoil and breakup. In fact, infidelity it is the most frequently cited reason for divorce (Amato & Previti, 2003). Please note that by "cheating" and "infidelity," I am referring to instances of **nonconsensual nonmonogamy** (i.e., cases in which a romantic partner violates a spoken or unspoken agreement to be sexually exclusive). As mentioned above, this is not the same as consensual nonmonogamy (e.g., swinging, polyamory, etc.), wherein the partners have agreed to some amount of outside sexual contact.

How common is cheating? Unfortunately, that is a difficult question to answer because prevalence estimates depend upon the type of relationship (e.g., dating vs. married), the timeframe assessed (e.g., in your current relationship vs. your entire life), and how "infidelity" is defined (i.e., physical vs. emotional). The definitional issue is perhaps the most vexing. As some evidence of just how widely people's definitions of cheating vary, consider a study in which college student participants were provided with a checklist of 27 interpersonal behaviors and were asked to rate the likelihood that each one represented cheating if someone in a relationship performed that behavior with someone who was not their current partner (Kruger et al., 2013). The behaviors included sexual interactions (e.g., intercourse, taking a shower together), emotional interactions (e.g., sharing secrets), and casual interactions (e.g., loaning someone $5, brief hugs). Interestingly, there was no universal consensus that any one behavior was definitely cheating or definitely not cheating! Researchers also found that participants' behavioral ratings depended upon both their

Figure 8.13 Infidelity is one of the biggest causes of relationship turmoil, breakup, and divorce. ©Konrad Bak/123RF.COM.

sex and their attachment style. Specifically, women were more likely than men to rate emotional interactions as cheating, and persons who were anxiously attached were more likely to label casual interactions as cheating than were securely attached individuals.

Given this vast variability in definitions, it is perhaps not surprising that a meta-analysis of 31 studies of infidelity revealed that the number of participants who reported cheating ranged anywhere from 1.2 to 85.5% depending upon how cheating was operationalized (Luo, Cartun, & Snider, 2010)! The 85.5% figure comes from a study in which college students were asked whether they had ever flirted with someone else while in a romantic relationship; estimates of sexual infidelity tend to be lower. The aforementioned meta-analysis (which focused mostly on data from the US and other Western cultures) revealed that among college students, most studies put the number who have committed sexual infidelity at one in two or one in three, and among married couples, it is more like one in four or one in five. However, there is significant cross-cultural variability, with much lower rates of infidelity in some cultures (e.g., the Philippines) and much higher rates in others (e.g., Cameroon) (Zhang, Parish, Huang, & Pan, 2012). Regardless of definition, type of relationship, and culture, one thing is clear with respect to cheating: men do it more than women (or at least men admit to doing it more than women).

Given the relatively high prevalence of cheating and the devastating effects it can have on a relationship, some scholars have questioned whether an expectation of lifelong monogamy and fidelity is even realistic for human beings and if perhaps destigmatizing consensual nonmonogamy could eliminate a lot of heartache and improve people's relationships (Ryan & Jetha, 2010). At the same time, evolutionary psychology would seem to be suggesting that monogamy has some adaptive value in the long run (i.e., it helps men to avoid being *cuckolded*, or having a partner who is pregnant with another man's child, and ensures male investment in any offspring produced). Also, if humans were designed for nonmonogamy, then why do they engage in so much mate-guarding behavior (e.g., checking up on each other) and become so jealous when their partners' eyes wander?

The question of whether human beings are "meant" to be monogamous or nonmonogamous remains a topic of scholarly debate. However, if I may offer one small piece of insight, I believe that the question of what we were "meant" to be is counterproductive and that it would be wrong to argue that *all* humans have a monogamous or nonmonogamous orientation. The fact of the matter is that monogamy works very well for some, but not for others. For example, research on same-sex couples has found that among people with moderate to high levels of attachment anxiety, having a monogamy agreement is linked to *higher* relationship satisfaction and commitment; however, for persons with low attachment anxiety, having a monogamy agreement is unrelated to how they feel about their relationship (Mohr, Selterman, & Fassinger, 2013). Thus, while monogamy may be a good idea for some people, it does not necessarily provide universal benefits. One key to a successful relationship is to find someone who shares your sexual values, not to impose a set of sexual expectations on another person.

Coping with Breakup

No matter what the cause, relationship breakups can be incredibly upsetting. After a breakup, it is common to feel depressed, to have lower self-esteem, to have difficulty concentrating, and to experience a range of other negative emotions and cognitions (Perilloux & Buss, 2008). In order to deal with these aftereffects, people adopt various coping strategies, with some of them being more effective than others. For example, a study of college students revealed that the most frequently reported methods of coping were to simply talk about their breakup and to try and remain friends with their ex-partner (Perilloux & Buss, 2008). Research suggests that *active coping strategies* (i.e., attempts to confront the problem) such as these are typically linked to better psychosocial adjustment following any type of relationship stressor (Seiffge-Krenke, 2011). Passive and avoidant forms of coping (e.g., drowning one's sorrows in alcohol, or socially withdrawing) are generally less adaptive.

Another way that some people cope is to see the end of their relationship as an opportunity for personal growth. For example, following a breakup, people frequently report learning things about themselves (e.g., what they do and do not want in a partner), skills for navigating relationships in the future (e.g., better communication), and a renewed focus on other aspects of their lives (e.g., greater appreciation for one's friends and family; Tashiro & Frazier, 2003). By dealing with your emotions head-on and searching for the silver lining in the breakup, you may find that you are able to move on with your life sooner.

Key Terms

need to belong

singlism

hookups

friends with benefits

serial monogamists

love

passionate love

companionate love

passion

intimacy

commitment

consummate love

satisfaction

quality of alternatives

investments

consensual
   nonmonogamy

open relationships

swinging

polygamy

polyamory

arranged marriage

stonewalling

sexual communal
   strength

self-expansion theory

attachment style

paternity uncertainty

nonconsensual
   nonmonogamy

Discussion Questions: What is Your Perspective on Sex?

- Is it possible for "friends with benefits" to maintain a "no strings attached" relationship or is it inevitable that one or both partners will end up developing feelings for each other?
- What role does sexual passion plays in relationship success? How much does it matter to you in the context of a long-term romantic relationship?
- What is your "cheating threshold?" That is, where do you draw the line in terms of what constitutes cheating? Fantasizing? Flirting? Cybersex? Watching pornography? Kissing? Something else?

References

Amato, P.R., & Previti, D. (2003). People's reasons for divorcing: Gender, social class, the life course, and adjustment. *Journal of Family Issues, 24*, 602–626. DOI:10.1177/0192513X03024005002.

Armstrong, E. A., England, P., & Fogarty, A. C. K. (2012). Accounting for women's orgasm and sexual enjoyment in college hookups and relationships. *American Sociological Review, 77*, 435–462. DOI:10.1177/0003122412445802.

Aron, A., & Aron, E.N. (1986). *Love and the expansion of self: Understanding attraction and satisfaction.* New York: Hemisphere/Harper & Row.

Aron, E.N., & Aron, A. (1996). Love and the expansion of the self: The state of the model. *Personal Relationships, 3*, 45–58. DOI:10.1111/j.1475-6811.1996.tb00103.x.

Babin, E.A. (2013). An examination of predictors of nonverbal and verbal communication of pleasure during sex and sexual satisfaction. *Journal of Social and Personal Relationships, 30*, 270–292. DOI:10.1177/0265407512454523.

Baumeister, R.F., & Leary, M.R. (1995). The need to belong: Desire for interpersonal attachments as a fundamental human motivation. *Psychological Bulletin, 117*, 497–529. DOI:10.1037/0033-2909.117.3.497.

Bergstrand, C., & Blevins Williams, J. (2000). Today's alternative marriage styles: The case of swingers. *Electronic Journal of Human Sexuality.* Retrieved from http://www.ejhs.org/volume3/swing/body.htm (accessed September 3, 2013).

Bisson, M.A., & Levine, T.R. (2009). Negotiating a friends with benefits relationship. *Archives of Sexual Behavior, 38*, 66–73. DOI:10.1007/s10508-007-9211-2.

Blackwell, D.L., & Lichter, D.T. (2000). Mate selection among married and cohabiting couples. *Journal of Family Issues, 21*, 275–302. DOI:10.1177/019251300021003001.

Boaert, A.F. (2004). Asexuality: Prevalence and associated factors in a national probability sample. *Journal of Sex Research, 41*, 279–287. DOI:10.1080/00224490409552235.

Buss, D.M., Larsen, R.J., Westen, D., & Semmelroth, J. (1992). Sex differences in jealousy: Evolution, physiology, and psychology. *Psychological Science, 3*, 251–255. DOI:10.1111/j.1467-9280.1992.tb00038.x.

Campbell, A. (2008). The morning after the night before: Affective reactions to one-night stands among mated and unmated women and men. *Human Nature, 19*, 157–173. DOI:10.1007/s12110-008-9036-2.

Carpenter, C. J. (2012). Meta-analysis of sex differences in responses to sexual versus emotional infidelity: Men and women are more similar than different. *Psychology of Women Quarterly, 36*, 24–37. DOI:10.1177/0361684311414537.

Cohn, D., Passel, J., Wang, W., & Livingston, G. (2011). Barely half of U.S. adults are married – A record low. *Pew Research Center.* Retrieved from http://www.pewsocialtrends.org/2011/12/14/barely-half-of-u-s-adults-are-married-a-record-low/ (accessed September 3, 2013).

Conley, T.D, Moors, A.C, Ziegler, A., & Karathanasis, C. (2012). Unfaithful individuals are less likely to practice safer sex than openly nonmonogamous individuals. *Journal of Sexual Medicine, 9*, 1559–1565. DOI:10.1111/j.1743-6109.2012.02712.x.

Conley, T.D., Moors, A.C., Matsick, J.L., & Ziegler, A. (2013). The fewer the merrier? Assessing stigma surrounding non-normative romantic relationships. *Analyses of Social Issues and Public Policy.* Advance online publication. DOI:10.1111/j.1530-2415.2012.01286.x.

Copen, C.E., Daniels, K., Vespa, J., & Mosher, W.D. (2012). First marriages in the United States: Data from the 2006–2010 National Survey of Family Growth. *National Health Statistics Reports, 49*, 1–22.

Cornell, S.J., & Tregenza, T. (2007). A new theory for the evolution of polyandry as a means of inbreeding avoidance. *Proceedings of the Royal Society B: Biological Sciences, 274*, 2873–2879. DOI:10.1098/rspb.2007.0926

Critelli, J.W., & Suire, D.M. (1998). Obstacles to condom use: The combination of other forms of birth control and short-term monogamy. *Journal of American College Health, 46*, 215–219. DOI:10.1080/07448489809600225.

DePaulo, B.M., & Morris, W.L. (2006). The unrecognized stereotyping and discrimination against singles. *Current Directions in Psychological Science, 15*, 251–254. DOI:10.1111/j.1467-8721.2006.00446.x.

Duemmler, S.L., & Kobak, R. (2001). The development of commitment and attachment in dating relationships: Attachment security as relationship construct. *Journal of Adolescence, 24*, 401–415. DOI:10.1006/jado.2001.0406.

Ein-Dor, T., & Hirschberger, G. (2012). Sexual healing: Daily diary evidence that sex relieves stress for men and women in satisfying relationships. *Journal of Social and Personal Relationships, 29*, 126–139. DOI:10.1177/0265407511431185.

Fisher, H.E. (1992). *Anatomy of love.* New York: Fawcett Columbine.

Gottman, J. (1994). *What predicts divorce? The relationship between marital processes and marital outcomes.* Hillsdale, NJ: Lawrence Erlbaum.

Gottman, J., Levenson, R., Swanson, C., Swanson, K., Tyson, R., & Yoshimoto, D. (2003). Observing gay, lesbian and heterosexual couples' relationships: Mathematical modeling of conflict interaction. *Journal of Homosexuality, 45*, 65–91. DOI:10.1300/J082v45n01_04.

Hatfield, E. & Walster, W.G. (2002). *A new look at love.* Lanham, MD: University Press of America.

Hazan, C., & Shaver, P. (1987). Romantic love conceptualized as an attachment process. *Journal of Personality and Social Psychology, 52*, 511–524. DOI:10.1037/0022-3514.52.3.511.

Hendrick, C., & Hendrick, S.S. (1986). A theory and method of love. *Journal of Personality and Social Psychology, 50*, 392–402. DOI:10.1037/0022-3514.50.2.392.

Hendrick, C., & Hendrick, S.S. (2003). Romantic love: Measuring cupid's arrow. In S. J. Lopez & C. R. Snyder (Eds.), *Positive psychological assessment: A handbook of models and measures* (pp. 235–249). Washington, DC: American Psychological Association.

Hendrick, C., Hendrick, S.S., & Dicke, A. (1998). The Love Attitudes Scale: Short form. *Journal of Social and Personal Relationships, 15*, 147–159. DOI:10.1177/0265407598152001.

Herek, G.M. (2000). The psychology of sexual prejudice. *Current Directions in Psychological Science, 9*, 19–22. DOI:10.1111/1467-8721.00051.

Jose, A., Daniel O'Leary, K.K., & Moyer, A. (2010). Does premarital cohabitation predict subsequent marital stability and marital quality? A meta-analysis. *Journal of Marriage and Family, 72*, 105–116. DOI:10.1111/j.1741-3737.2009.00686.x.

Kiecolt-Glaser, J.K., & Newton, T.L. (2001). Marriage and health: His and hers. *Psychological Bulletin, 127*, 472–503. DOI:10.1037/0033-2909.127.4.472.

Kruger, D. J., Fisher, M. L., Edelstein, R. S., Chopik, W. J., Fitzgerald, C. J., & Strout, S. L. (2013). Was that cheating? Perceptions vary by sex, attachment anxiety, and behavior. *Evolutionary Psychology, 11*, 159–171.

Kurdek, L.A. (1998). Relationship outcomes and their predictors: Longitudinal evidence from heterosexual married, gay cohabiting, and lesbian cohabiting couples. *Journal of Marriage and Family, 60*, 553–568.

Kurdek, L.A. (2004). Are gay and lesbian cohabiting couples really different from heterosexual married couples? *Journal of Marriage and Family, 66*, 880–900. DOI:10.1111/j.0022-2445.2004.00060.x.

Laumann, E.O., Gagnon, J., Michael, R., & Michaels, S. (1994). *The social organization of sexuality: Sexual practices in the United States*. Chicago: University of Chicago Press.

Le, B., & Agnew, C.R. (2003). Commitment and its theorized determinants: A meta-analysis of the investment model. *Personal Relationships, 10*, 37–57. DOI:10.1111/1475-6811.00035.

Lee, J. A. (1977). A typology of styles of loving. *Personality and Social Psychology Bulletin, 3*, 173–182. DOI:10.1177/014616727700300204.

Lehmiller, J.J. (2010). Differences in relationship investments between gay and heterosexual men. *Personal Relationships, 17*, 81–96. DOI:10.1111/j.1475-6811.2010.01254.x.

Lehmiller, J.J. (2012). Perceived marginalization and its association with physical and psychological health. *Journal of Social and Personal Relationships, 29*, 451–469. DOI:10.1177/0265407511431187.

Lehmiller, J.J., & Agnew, C.R. (2006). Marginalized relationships: The impact of social disapproval on romantic relationship commitment. *Personality and Social Psychology Bulletin, 32*, 40–51. DOI:10.1177/0146167205278710.

Lehmiller, J.J., & Agnew, C.R. (2007). Perceived marginalization and the prediction of romantic relationship stability. *Journal of Marriage and Family, 69*, 1036–1049. DOI:10.1111/j.1741-3737.2007.00429.x.

Lehmiller, J.J., VanderDrift, L.E., & Kelly, J.R. (2011). Sex differences in approaching friends with benefits relationships. *Journal of Sex Research, 48*, 275–284. DOI:10.1080/00224491003721694.

Lehmiller, J.J., VanderDrift, L.E., & Kelly, J.R. (2013). Sexual communication, satisfaction, and condom use behavior in friends with benefits and romantic partners. *Journal of Sex Research*. Advance online publication. DOI:10.1080/00224499.2012.719167.

Levinson, R., Jaccard, J., & Beamer, L. (1995). Older adolescents' engagement in casual sex: Impact of risk perception and psychosocial motivations. *Journal of Youth and Adolescence, 24*, 349–364. DOI:10.1007/BF01537601.

Luo, S., Cartun, M.A., & Snider, A.G. (2010). Assessing extradyadic behavior: A review, a new measure, and two new models. *Personality and Individual Differences, 49*, 155–163. DOI:10.1016/j.paid.2010.03.033.

Misovich, S.J., Fisher, J.D., & Fisher, W.A. (1997). Close relationships and elevated HIV risk behavior: Evidence and possible underlying psychological processes. *Review of General Psychology, 1*, 72–107. DOI:10.1037/1089-2680.1.1.72.

Mohr, J. J., Selterman, D., & Fassinger, R. E. (2013). Romantic attachment and relationship functioning in same-sex couples. *Journal of Counseling Psychology, 60*, 72–82. DOI:10.1037/a0030994.

Mongeau, P.A., Knight, K., Williams, J., Eden, J., & Shaw, C. (2013). Identifying and explicating variation among friends with benefits relationships. *Journal of Sex Research, 50*, 37–47. DOI:10.1080/00224499.2011.619282.

Morris, W.L., Sinclair, S., & DePaulo, B.M. (2007). No shelter for singles: The perceived legitimacy of marital status discrimination. *Group Processes and Intergroup Relations, 10*, 457–470. DOI:10.1177/1368430207081535.

Muise, A., Impett, E.A., Kogan, A., & Desmarais, S. (20132). Keeping the spark alive: Being motivated to meet a partner's sexual needs sustains sexual desire in long-term romantic relationships. *Social Psychological and Personality Science, 4*, 267–273. DOI:10.1177/1948550612457185.

Musick, K., & Bumpass, L. (2012). Reexamining the case for marriage: Union formation and changes in well-being. *Journal of Marriage and Family, 74*, 1–18. DOI:10.1111/j.1741-3737.2011.00873.x.

Nemeth, J.M., Bonomi, A.E., Lee, M.A., & Ludwin, J.M. (2012). Sexual infidelity as trigger for intimate partner violence. *Journal of Women's Health, 21*, 942–949. DOI:10.1089/jwh.2011.3328.

Ng, C. (2011). Mexico City considers temporary marriage licenses. *ABC News*. Retrieved from http://abcnews.go.com/blogs/headlines/2011/09/mexico-city-considers-temporary-marriage-licenses/ (accessed September 3, 2013).

O'Leary, K. D., Acevedo, B. P., Aron, A., Huddy, L., & Mashek, D. (2012). Is long-term love more than a rare phenomenon? If so, what are its correlates? *Social Psychological and Personality Science, 3*, 241–249. DOI:10.1177/1948550611417015.

Owen, J., & Fincham, F.D. (2011). Effects of gender and psychosocial factors on 'friends with benefits' relationships among young adults. *Archives of Sexual Behavior, 40*, 311–320. DOI:10.1007/s10508-010-9611-6.

Owen, J., & Fincham, F.D. (2012). Friends with benefits relationships as a start to exclusive romantic relationships. *Journal of Social and Personal Relationships, 29*, 982–996. DOI:10.1177/0265407512448275.

Paul, E.L., & Hayes, K.A. (2002). The causalities of "casual" sex: A qualitative exploration of the phenomenology of college students' hookups. *Journal of Social and Personal Relationships, 19*, 639–661. DOI:10.1177/0265407502195006.

Paul, E.L., McManus, B., & Hayes, A. (2000). "Hookups": Characteristics and correlates of college students' spontaneous and anonymous sexual experiences. *Journal of Sex Research, 37*, 76–88. DOI:10.1080/00224490009552023.

Perilloux, C., & Buss, D. M. (2008). Breakup up romantic relationships: Costs experienced and coping strategies deployed. *Evolutionary Psychology, 6*, 164–181.

Reynolds, J., Wetherell, M., & Taylor, S. (2007). Choice and chance: Negotiating agency in narratives of singleness. *The Sociological Review, 55*, 331–351. DOI:10.1111/j.1467-954X.2007.00708.x.

Rusbult, C.E. (1980). Commitment and satisfaction in romantic associations: A test of the investment model. *Journal of Experimental Social Psychology, 16*, 172–186. DOI:10.1016/0022-1031(80)90007-4.

Rusbult, C.E., & Martz, J.M. (1995). Remaining in an abusive relationship: An investment model analysis of nonvoluntary dependence. *Personality and Social Psychology Bulletin, 21*, 558–571. DOI:10.1177/0146167295216002.

Rusbult, C.E., Martz, J.M., & Agnew, C.R. (1998). The Investment Model Scale: Measuring commitment level, satisfaction level, quality of alternatives, and investment size. *Personal Relationships, 5*, 357–391. DOI:10.1111/j.1475-6811.1998.tb00177.x.

Ryan, C., & Jetha, C. (2010). *Sex at dawn: How we mate, why we stray, and what it means for modern relationships.* New York: HarperCollins.

Sayare, S., & de la Baume, M. (2010). In France, civil unions gain favor over marriage. *The New York Times.* Retrieved from http://www.nytimes.com/2010/12/16/world/europe/16france.html?pagewanted=all&_r=0 (accessed September 3, 2013).

Seiffge-Krenke, I. (2011). Coping with relationship stressors: A decade review. *Journal of Research on Adolescence, 21*, 196–210. DOI:10.1111/j.1532-7795.2010.00723.x.

Simpson, J.A., Rholes, W., Campbell, L., & Wilson, C.L. (2003). Changes in attachment orientations across the transitions to parenthood. *Journal of Experimental Social Psychology, 39*, 317–331. DOI:10.1016/S0022-1031(03)00030-1.

Sternberg, R.J. (1986). A triangular theory of love. *Psychological Review, 93*, 119–135. DOI:10.1037/0033-295X.93.2.119.

Tashiro, T.Y., & Frazier, P. (2003). "I'll never be in a relationship like that again": Personal growth following romantic relationship breakups. *Personal Relationships, 10*, 113–128. DOI:10.1111/1475-6811.00039.

Thornton, A., & Young-DeMarco, L. (2001). Four decades of attitudes toward family issues in the United States: The 1960s through the 1990s. *Journal of Marriage and the Family, 63*, 1009–1037. DOI: 10.1111/j.1741-3737.2001.01009.x.

United States Census Bureau (2010). America's families and living arrangements: 2010. Retrieved from http://www.census.gov/population/www/socdemo/hh-fam/cps2010.html (accessed September 3, 2013).

Van Lange, P.M., Rusbult, C.E., Drigotas, S.M., Arriaga, X.B., Witcher, B.S., & Cox, C.L. (1997). Willingness to sacrifice in close relationships. *Journal of Personality and Social Psychology, 72*, 1373–1395. DOI:10.1037/0022-3514.72.6.1373.

VanderDrift, L.E., Lehmiller, J.J., & Kelly, J.R. (2012). Commitment in friends with benefits relationships: Implications for relational and safe-sex outcomes. *Personal Relationships, 19*, 1–13. DOI:10.1111/ j.1475-6811.2010.01324.x.

Willoughby, B. J., Carroll, J. S., & Busby, D. M. (2013). Differing relationship outcomes when sex happens before, on, or after first dates. *The Journal of Sex Research.* Advance online publication. DOI: 10.1080/00224499.2012.714012.

Zhang, N., Parish, W.L., Huang, Y., & Pan, S. (2012). Sexual infidelity in China: Prevalence and gender-specific correlates. *Archives of Sexual Behavior, 41*, 861–873. DOI:10.1007/s10508-012-9930-x.

9

Sexual Behaviors

©ginasanders/123RF.COM.

Chapter Outline

- Introduction   230
- Solitary Sexual Behaviors   230
  - Asexuality and Celibacy   230
  - Sexual Fantasy   232
  - Masturbation   235
- Partnered Sexual Behaviors   240
  - Kissing   241
  - Touching   242
  - Oral Sex   243
  - Vaginal Intercourse   243
  - Anal Sex   244
  - Same-Sex Behaviors   245
- Frequency and Benefits of Sex and Orgasm   248
- Sexual Behavior in Psychological Perspective   249
  - Self-Regulation   249
  - Attachment Style   251
  - Mortality Salience   251

The Psychology of Human Sexuality, First Edition. Justin J. Lehmiller.
© 2014 John Wiley & Sons, Ltd. Published 2014 by John Wiley & Sons, Ltd.

Introduction

What does it mean to be "sexually active?" It is difficult to say because everyone has different ideas about what "counts" as sex and how frequently you need to do it in order to be considered "active." As you will soon see, human sexual practices are incredibly diverse, ranging from abstinence to anything goes. As some evidence of this wide variability in sexual behavior, consider that the National Survey of Sexual Health and Behavior (NSSHB) revealed that Americans reported 41 different combinations of sex acts during their most recent sexual encounter (Herbenick et al., 2010). The NSSHB also revealed that the prevalence of specific sexual acts varied considerably across sex, age, relationship status, and numerous other demographic variables. For a sampling of just a few of the ways that sexual activities differ across individuals, check out Table 9.1. Please pay particular attention to the finding that sexual activity persists across the lifespan. At least some participants in each age group reported practicing each activity, which tells us that there is no definitive end point to our sex lives. Although it is true that the frequency of sexual activity often decreases as we age (more on this in chapter 12), the stereotype that older adults do not desire or engage in sexual activity is patently false.

This chapter will shed light on some of the most common forms of sexual expression. We will consider both the prevalence of each behavior and the different forms each can take. Before we delve into the details, please recall that sexual behavior is a biopsychosocial event: as discussed in chapter 1, everything from hormones, to evolved traits, to cultural standards, to our current mood state affect both our general level of interest in sex and our specific sexual practices. That said, our psychology has a particularly profound influence on sexual behavior, affecting when and how it is expressed. As a result, we will explore the role of psychology in greater depth toward the end of this chapter.

Solitary Sexual Behaviors

We will begin our discussion of sexual practices by focusing on sexual thoughts and behaviors at the individual level.

Asexuality and Celibacy

Some individuals are not sexually active for a part of their life or for their entire life for reasons that vary widely. For instance, as discussed in previous chapters, some people are *asexual*, meaning they have a general lack of desire for partnered sexual activity. Asexual persons may still masturbate, but some do not engage in any type of sexual behavior whatsoever (Bogaert, 2013). Contrary to popular belief, many asexual individuals still desire relationships and intimacy (e.g., cuddling), and some even go on to enjoy sexless marriages (Travis, 2010). In contrast to asexuality, individuals who have sexual desire but intentionally refrain from acting on it are practicing **celibacy**. There are two variations of celibacy. *Complete celibacy* refers to abstention from any kind of solitary or partnered sexual activity, whereas *partial celibacy* refers only to abstention from partnered acts, while still engaging in masturbation. Whereas asexuality

Table 9.1 Male and Female Sexual Behaviors across the Lifespan

Behavior	Age range															
	18–19		20–24		25–29		30–39		40–49		50–59		60–69		70+	
	M	F	M	F	M	F	M	F	M	F	M	F	M	F	M	F
Masturbated alone	81%	60%	83%	64%	84%	72%	80%	63%	76%	65%	72%	54%	61%	47%	46%	33%
Received oral sex from women	54%	4%	63%	9%	77%	3%	78%	5%	62%	2%	49%	1%	38%	1%	19%	2%
Received oral sex from men	6%	58%	6%	70%	5%	72%	6%	59%	6%	52%	8%	34%	3%	25%	2%	8%
Gave oral sex to women	51%	2%	55%	9%	74%	3%	69%	4%	57%	3%	44%	1%	34%	1%	24%	2%
Gave oral sex to men	4%	59%	7%	74%	5%	76%	5%	59%	7%	53%	8%	36%	3%	23%	3%	7%
Vaginal intercourse	53%	62%	63%	80%	86%	87%	85%	74%	74%	70%	58%	51%	54%	42%	43%	22%
Receptive penile–anal intercourse	4%	18%	5%	23%	4%	21%	3%	22%	4%	12%	5%	6%	1%	4%	2%	1%
Insertive penile–anal intercourse	6%		11%		27%		24%		21%		11%		6%		2%	

Note: M = male, F = female. Numbers represent the percentage of people reporting each behavior in the past year. Adapted from the National Survey of Sexual Health and Behavior (Herbenick et al., 2010).

is increasingly being viewed as a sexual orientation in the sense that it can be seen as an enduring characteristic of a person, celibacy is instead regarded as a form of sexual expression because it reflects a voluntary decision to forego certain types of sexual behavior for a period of time ranging from months to years.

Celibacy is practiced for various reasons, but it is perhaps most frequently associated with religion. For example, nuns and priests are usually required to take vows of celibacy, and many adolescents and adults abstain from sex before marriage because they believe it is the moral thing to do. However, there are a number of other reasons one might choose to become celibate, including a desire to focus on personal growth, physical and psychological health concerns, and having endured some bad sexual experiences (Siegel & Schrimshaw, 2003). Of course, not everyone becomes celibate by choice. *Involuntary celibacy* is a reality for some individuals when they lack access to a desired partner due to separation (e.g., military deployment), institutional restrictions (e.g., nursing homes may have rules that restrict sexual activity among patients), and other constraints (e.g., persons with physical and psychological disabilities may have caregivers who discourage or do not allow sex). Regardless of the reason, some people find that they benefit from the experience, while others find it challenging and lonely.

Sexual Fantasy

One of the most common forms of sexual expression occurs entirely within the brain: fantasizing. **Sexual fantasies** have been defined as "any mental imagery that is sexually arousing or erotic to the individual. A sexual fantasy can be an elaborate story, or it can be a fleeting thought of some romantic or sexual activity. It can involve bizarre imagery, or it can be quite realistic. It can involve memories of past events, or it can be a completely imaginary experience" (Leitenberg & Henning, 1995, p. 470). Sexual fantasies are thus very diverse in nature, ranging from mild to wild.

The vast majority of people fantasize. In fact, studies have revealed that more than 95% of men and women have fantasized at least once in their lives (Davidson, 1985; Pelletier & Herold, 1988). That said, men tend to fantasize more frequently than women, and the sexes have different fantasy content. For a discussion of some of the ways that male and female fantasies differ and how sexual orientation factors into this, see the Digging Deeper 9.1 box.

Sexual fantasies serve a number of functions, including enhancement of sexual arousal, compensation for a less than ideal sexual situation, and reduced sexual anxiety (McCauley & Swann, 1980). Others may fantasize in order to express hidden desires (e.g., for culturally taboo activities) or to break free of traditional gender role expectations. Our fantasies may also serve a self-protective function. For example, consider a study in which participants were primed to feel either attachment security or anxiety by subliminally exposing them to photos of either (1) a mother looking at and caressing her child (security prime) or (2) a mother who had turned her back on a crying child (insecurity prime; Birnbaum, Simpson, Weisberg, Barnea, & Assulin-Simhon, 2012). Afterward, participants wrote down one of their sexual fantasies. Participants who were primed to feel insecure and anxious reported more fantasy content that involved distancing the self from one's partner (i.e., emotionless sex) than participants who received the security prime. This suggests that among persons who are feeling situational anxiety or are chronically insecure, the nature of their fantasies may shift so as to

Figure 9.1   Sexual fantasies are very common in both men and women and serve a number of different purposes. ©Yuri Arcurs/123RF.COM.

Digging Deeper 9.1   How Do Men's and Women's Sexual Fantasies Differ?

"Hot tub filled with whipped cream, pudding, and multiple blondes"
"We're out for a drive in the country and it starts to rain. We pull into the driveway at home and my partner pulls me into the barn, where we make love on a bale of hay as the rain continues outside."

Can you guess which of the above fantasies was written by a man and which was written by a woman? If you guessed a man wrote about the hot tub and a woman wrote the romantic farm story, you would be right. When it comes to sexual fantasies, is it usually this easy to categorize which fantasies belong to which sex? Are men's and women's fantasies really that different?

Research has found that fantasy content differs in several ways between the sexes, and those differences frequently align with modern stereotypes (Zurbriggen & Yost, 2004). First, *men's sexual fantasies are more sexually explicit than women's on average*. That is, not only are men's fantasies more focused on the sexual act itself, but they frequently include mention of specific body parts (including pieces of their own and their partner's anatomy). Second, *women's fantasies contain more in the way of emotional and romantic content than do men's*. Women frequently describe the setting of their sexual encounter in detail (e.g., on the beach

Figure 9.2   The content of men's and women's sexual fantasies differs, and often in a way that is consistent with gender role stereotypes. Image Copyright altafulla, 2013. Used under license from Shutterstock.com.

Figure 9.3   Image Copyright zhu difeng, 2013. Used under license from Shutterstock.com.

or under the stars), as well as the "prelude" or build-up to sex (e.g., drinking champagne at a candlelight dinner before adjourning to the bedroom).

Third, men are more likely than women to fantasize about having several sexual partners at the same time (e.g., threesomes, "fourgys," and more). Finally, the sexes also differ when it comes to fantasizing about dominance and submission. *While men are equally likely to fantasize about being dominant and submissive, women seem to fantasize more about being submissive than dominant.*

How does sexual orientation play into all of this? Do gays and lesbians have different fantasy content than their heterosexual counterparts? Most research on this topic suggests that the only reliable difference between the fantasies of gay and heterosexual men and between lesbian and heterosexual women is the sex of the person(s) they are fantasizing about (Leitenberg & Henning, 1995). Thus, the same sex differences in fantasy content observed among heterosexuals also emerge when you compare gay men to lesbians.

In short, the fantasy worlds that occupy men's and women's minds are quite distinct and, while there is always a vast amount of individual variability, there appears to be at least a hint of truth to some of the gender stereotypes that exist regarding fantasy content.

Note: Reprinted with permission from *The Psychology of Human Sexuality* blog (www.lehmiller.com).

protect the self from further feelings of rejection. In other words, when we are feeling anxious, our fantasies may contain less content that could potentially result in further harm to our self-esteem (e.g., feelings of dependence on one's partner).

Sexual fantasies are generally regarded as a healthy aspect of human sexuality. Indeed, people who fantasize more often tend to report being more sexually satisfied (Leitenberg & Henning, 1995). That said, people are sometimes concerned about the content of their fantasies. In particular, students have frequently asked me whether it is normal to fantasize about (1) being "forced" to have sex, and (2) imagining sex with someone other than your current partner. As it turns out, both of these are very common fantasies and they do not signify anything pathological about the individual or the relationship. With respect to forced sex (i.e., "rape") fantasies, studies indicate that 31 to 57% of women report having them (Critelli & Bivona, 2008); however, this should not be taken to mean that 31 to 57% of women want to be sexually assaulted. This research simply tells us that many women find the *thought* (not the reality) of some type of forced sex to be arousing, and it is important to emphasize that the amount and type of force desired varies, as does the nature of the resistance (for many women, arousal comes from providing token resistance). Thus, "rape fantasies" generally do not resemble a rape, if for no other reason than that the woman remains in control – a feature that is absent in actual rape. Although it was once thought that only victims of sexual assault fantasized about forced sex, research has found that this is not the case (Gold, Balzano, & Stamey, 1991). Where do these fantasies come from? It appears that forced sex fantasies are simply a product of greater openness to sexual experience (Bivona, Critelli, & Clark, 2012). The idea is that women with more positive feelings about sex have more fantasies, and that as the frequency of fantasizing increases, so does the range of fantasy content. Thus, forced sex fantasies are not a reflection of past experience or a product of unhealthy attitudes toward sex. With respect to fantasies about cheating, research indicates that 98% of men and 80% of women in relationships have fantasized about someone other than their current romantic partner, and these fantasies become more common the longer a relationship goes on (Leitenberg & Hicks, 2001). Thus, cheating fantasies appear to be normative and do not mean that someone actually wants to cheat or has plans to do so. If such fantasies signified trouble, then almost all of us would be headed for breakup!

Of course, this is not to say that all sexual fantasies are inherently good. There are certainly some cases where the desire for a specific sexual activity could be dangerous. For more on the darker aspects of sexual fantasy, check out the Your Sexuality 9.1 box.

Masturbation

Sexual fantasies go hand-in-hand with a variety of sexual behaviors, especially masturbation. **Masturbation** refers to all solo forms of self-stimulation focusing on the genitals. Masturbation practices vary widely depending upon the individual's body and personal preferences. For instance, masturbation among women may involve manipulation of the clitoris and labia, stimulation of the breasts, or vaginal penetration with a sex toy. To learn more about sex toys and how they came to be so popular among women, check out the Digging Deeper 9.2 box. Among men, masturbation most frequently involves using one or both hands to stimulate the penis. Of course, men sometimes utilize sex toys too (e.g., masturbation sleeves, butt-plugs, etc.). Across individuals of all sexes, masturbation habits vary in terms of the motion, speed, and amount of pressure applied, as well as whether they incorporate pornography (e.g., erotic images, videos, or stories).

Your Sexuality 9.1   The Dark Side of Sexual Fantasy

Having sexual fantasies is generally considered a sign of a healthy sex life (Leitenberg & Henning, 1995). However, there is wide variability in terms of what people fantasize about. Although most fantasies are relatively harmless, some are potentially problematic and even dangerous to others. For instance, if a man develops an obsession with a very idiosyncratic fantasy that is incompatible with his partner's desires, it could negatively impact the relationship. In addition, to the extent that someone fantasizes about an activity that is harmful to another person (e.g., sexually assaulting children or adults), there may be a risk of other people eventually getting hurt.

Unfortunately, however, determining which fantasies are acceptable and which are unacceptable is not as clear-cut as it sounds. For instance, the fantasy most common among people who identify as *feeders* is that their partner will gain an excessive amount of weight, sometimes to the point where that person becomes physically immobile and requires a caretaker. Such individuals often find complete dependency on someone else to be sexually arousing. Is this a healthy or an unhealthy fantasy? What about a heterosexual man who only fantasizes about having sex with married women who are cheating on their husbands? In these scenarios, the subject of the fantasy is consensual sex, but somebody ends up getting hurt. The question therefore becomes this: at what point does a sexual fantasy cross the line? And who should be the one to draw this line?

Are there certain fantasies that you think are potentially problematic? What should someone do if they have a sexual fantasy that is potentially harmful?

Digging Deeper 9.2   The History of Motorized Sex Toys

Believe it or not, human beings have been making sex toys since the Stone Age. Dildos, Ben Wa balls, and various other devices to aid in sexual pleasure have a surprisingly long (and quite interesting) history. However, out of all of the different sex toys ever created, one in particular stands out for having a most unique and "hysterical" backstory: the vibrator.

In the modern world, vibrators are a sex and masturbation aide utilized by men and women alike. However, the world's first vibrator was designed as a therapeutic device for doctors to use on their female patients who were diagnosed with **hysteria**. At one point in time, hysteria was among the most common medical disorders diagnosed in women, and included a wide range of symptoms from nervousness and insomnia to loss of appetite for sex with one's husband, to a "tendency to cause trouble for others" (Maines, 1998). The symptoms were so broad that almost any woman with any medical complaint could be diagnosed as hysterical. Although hysteria was originally thought to be the result of a woman's uterus "wandering" throughout her body and causing problems, later physicians viewed the disorder as a consequence of inadequate or insufficient sex.

For centuries, the primary treatment for hysteria was a "pelvic massage" culminating in "hysterical paroxysm" (i.e., orgasm; Maines, 1998). Massages of this nature were usually performed by doctors, who made a hefty profit practicing this "therapy," given that hysteria was so prevalent and required multiple treatments. In reality, all these doctors were doing was giving women the orgasms that their husbands did not (or could not) **and** taking the husbands' money for the privilege of doing so! The only problem was that these treatments became rather tedious because it can take some women a long time to reach orgasm (even with effective stimulation, an average woman may take up to 20 minutes) and the doctors were doing it by hand. The first vibrator was thus invented to cut down on the length of office visits, thereby allowing doctors to "treat" more patients.

As electricity started making its way into people's homes, the consumer market for vibrators grew rapidly. Not only could a personal vibrator save money on trips to the doctor's office, but it could also be utilized within the privacy of one's own home day or night. The demand for vibrators was so strong that motorized sex toys became just the fifth electric device approved for home use after the sewing machine, fan, teakettle, and toaster (Maines, 1998). Vibrators thus made their way into homes long before vacuum cleaners, electric irons, and television sets.

Figure 9.4 Sizes, and shapes, and colors, oh my! Image Copyright IVL, 2013. Used under license from Shutterstock.com.

Modern vibrators are battery operated (or solar powered, for the environmentally conscious), many are waterproof, and hundreds of variations exist to serve many different sexual purposes. Certain vibrators are optimized for clitoral stimulation, others for the G-spot, and yet others for the anus. Some vibrators are lifelike, others are pointy and ribbed, and some look like probes taken from an alien spaceship. And, of course, vibrators come in all different sizes, shapes, and colors and are made for people of all genders and sexualities. However, please keep in mind that if you incorporate vibrators or other sex toys into partnered sex, those toys need to be properly cleaned before sharing to reduce the risk of transmitting sexual and other infections.

As you can see, the history and evolution of vibrators is a fascinating subject. If you want to know more, check out *The Technology of Orgasm* by Rachael Maines (1998).

Note: Reprinted with permission from *The Psychology of Human Sexuality* blog (www.lehmiller.com).

Table 9.2	Frequency of Masturbation by Age and Gender Groups							
	Age							
	18–19	*20–24*	*25–29*	*30–39*	*40–49*	*50–59*	*60–69*	*70+*
Men								
In the last month	61.1%	62.8%	68.6%	66.4%	60.1%	55.7%	42.3%	27.9%
Lifetime	86.1%	91.8%	94.3%	93.4%	92%	89.2%	90.2%	80.4%
Women								
In the last month	26%	43.7%	51.7%	38.6%	38.5%	28.3%	21.5%	11.5%
Lifetime	66%	76.8%	84.6%	80.3%	78%	77.2%	72%	58.3%

Note: Adapted from the National Survey of Sexual Health and Behavior (Herbenick et al., 2010).

Most people masturbate. For instance, as seen in Table 9.1, the NSSHB revealed that a majority of men and women across all age groups reported masturbating before. The percentage of masturbators is higher today than it was in the original Kinsey reports as well as the NHSLS; however, it is not clear whether this reflects a true increase in masturbation, or simply an increase in comfort admitting to this behavior. Although masturbation is something that most people have done, there are some important sex differences in this practice. Specifically, research indicates that men are more likely to masturbate than women, and also that men do it with greater frequency (see Table 9.2). Despite these differences, the NHSLS found that men and women masturbate for similar reasons, including tension relief, pleasure, relaxation, and the unavailability of a sexual partner. Research in the US finds that masturbation practices also vary according to age, education level, and race (Laumann, Gagnon, Michael, & Michaels, 1994). Specifically, being younger (i.e., under age 49), having a higher level of education, and being White are associated with a greater likelihood of masturbating compared to being older (i.e., over age 50), having less education, and being African American.

Concerns About Masturbation
Masturbation has been a source of moral and medical concern for centuries. Historically, penis-in-vagina intercourse within the context of a heterosexual marriage was seen as the only "valid" form of sex by many world religions. Because masturbation provides pleasure without the possibility of procreation, it was long condemned as a sinful activity. However, this view of masturbation began to change in the eighteenth century with a movement that is best described as *the medicalization of sex*. During this time period, masturbation, homosexuality, and other sexual activities that had traditionally been seen as immoral came to be viewed largely as health problems and diseases.

For instance, in the 1700s, Swiss physician Samuel Auguste Tissot wrote extensively about the physical and psychological health damage that accompanies masturbation. In Tissot's view, semen was an "essential oil" that the body cannot function properly without. He argued that excessive masturbation could therefore lead to everything from blindness to insanity. These beliefs about the

Figure 9.5 John Harvey Kellogg warned the public of the (now-debunked) physical and psychological heath dangers of masturbation. Image Source: Library of Congress, Prints & Photographs Division, [LC-DIG-ggbain-15047].

dire consequences of masturbation persisted for centuries after and led to many inventive attempts to "cure" the masturbation pandemic. One supposed cure was dietary modification. It was thought that being a vegetarian, eating bland foods, and getting frequent exercise would curb the desire to masturbate. To that end, the Reverend Sylvester Graham invented the original graham cracker and Dr. John Harvey Kellogg invented to original cornflake. Yes, you read that right – cornflakes and graham crackers were originally designed for the purpose of stopping chronic masturbators. I bet you will never look at the cereal aisle in the grocery store the same way again! Of course, keep in mind that the original formulations of graham crackers and cornflakes were very bland, and barely resemble the sweetened versions you see on supermarket shelves today, which do not claim to have any anti-masturbatory properties. At any rate, Kellogg and Graham were both strong believers that masturbation was a source of both physical and psychological ailments ranging from acne to epilepsy to insanity and, therefore, required a cure.

When the nutritional solution did not work, the means for stopping masturbation became more extreme. For instance, in his book *Plain Facts for Old and Young*, Kellogg (1881) recommended that young boys be circumcised without anesthetic, because the pain of the procedure would serve as a deterrent to future masturbation. Another procedure he recommended for boys was to pull the foreskin over the glans and suture it together so as to prevent erections. For girls, Kellogg recommended applying carbolic acid to the clitoris in order to reduce "abnormal excitement."

As if that were not enough, a number of other masturbation "remedies" emerged, which included genital cages (a sort of chastity belt that could only be removed by the person who held the key), spermatorrhoea rings (which sort of looked like modern "cock rings," but with an extra, inner layer of sharp metal teeth that would dig into the penis should the wearer get an erection), as well as the spermatic truss (a device that involved stretching the penis out and strapping it to a short pole in order to make an erection impossible). However, my personal favorite is what I call "the bell-ringer," a device patented in 1899 that would ring a bell any time the wearer's penis started to swell, effectively alerting everyone in town that an erection was nearby. Rather than try to physically prevent erections, this device was designed to curb them through shame and embarrassment.

As it turns out, all of the longstanding health concerns about masturbation have been completely unsubstantiated by modern research, which means that all of these radical attempts to stop people from pleasuring themselves have been for naught. In fact, research suggests that, if anything, masturbation is associated with *enhanced* physical and psychological health. As just a few examples, masturbating frequently is linked to higher self-esteem among women (Hurlbert & Whittaker, 1991) and a lower risk of prostate cancer among men (Giles et al., 2003). There is simply no truth to the idea that masturbation will make you go blind, crazy, or grow hair on your palms. On a side note, there is also no evidence that masturbation is harmful to people's romantic and sexual relationships, which has also been a major concern about self-pleasure. For instance, some research has found that people in relationships masturbate more than singles (Laumann et al., 1994), suggesting that masturbation may complement an active sex life rather than supplant partnered sex. As a result of these and other findings, most modern medical and psychological associations around the world have adopted the view that masturbation is a normal part of sexual experience and is not something that requires treatment.

Partnered Sexual Behaviors

At this point, we will shift our focus to some of the most common partnered sexual activities, including kissing, sexual touching, oral sex, anal sex, and vaginal intercourse. This is not meant to be an exhaustive list of all possible sexual behaviors, just those that are most frequently observed. I should also clarify that "partnered" does not necessarily mean just two people, because some individuals enjoy these activities in the context of groups. We will also consider the nature of same-sex behavior and correct some of the most common misconceptions about the sex lives of gay men and lesbians. Sexual behavior variations (i.e., uncommon forms of sexual expression) will be addressed separately in this book in chapter 13.

When do people start engaging in partnered sexual activities? That depends upon the specific activities and cultural backgrounds in question. For example, one study of US college students found that, on average, men and women reported having their first kiss around age 15 and their first act of sexual intercourse around age 17 (Regan, Durvasula, Howell, Ureno, & Rea, 2004). Other research is consistent with these numbers, although men usually become sexually active at a slightly younger age. How does cultural background factor into the equation? Regan and colleagues found that White and African American participants tended to have their first kiss and first sex at a younger age than those who were Latino(a) or Asian American. The largest difference was seen between African and Asian Americans. Specifically, African Americans reported their first kiss at age 14.8 and first sex at age 16.3, whereas Asian Americans had their first kiss at age 17.6 and first sex at 18.85.

As noted at the beginning of this chapter, once partnered sexual activity begins, it often continues through the rest of our lives. In fact, it is not uncommon for men and women to stay sexually active into their 70s and 80s. However, a number of factors are related to continued sexual activity, including good health (both physical and psychological), having a positive view of sex and one's own sexuality, not to mention access to a partner (DeLamater, 2012). It is also worth noting that even in cases where older adults' health has declined or they have acquired physical disabilities or chronic illnesses, sex often continues to be an important part of their lives.

Kissing

Kissing is an activity that people frequently associate with sex, and this makes sense. The mouth is an erogenous zone endowed with many nerve endings, which means kissing can be very pleasurable. In Western society, kissing is one of the most common and socially accepted sexual behaviors; however, it is not universally practiced throughout the world. In fact, in some cultures (such as the Thonga of South Africa), kissing is viewed as a disgusting activity (Gregersen, 1996). In places where kissing is deemed acceptable, it often becomes an individual's first and, for some, most memorable sexual experience.

Although most people only distinguish between two types of kissing, the closed-mouth kiss of affection and the open-mouthed kiss of passion, kissing can take many different forms. In fact, the *Kama Sutra* denotes 17 different types of kisses that vary in terms of whether they

Figure 9.6   For some individuals, kissing is one of the most pleasurable sexual activities there is. Image Copyright Alexandru Chiriac, 2013. Used under license from Shutterstock.com.

permit tongue action, the amount of pressure and force applied, and so on. Because there are so many different manners of kissing and we each have our own preference when it comes to what feels good, it is inevitable that we will think of some people as "bad kissers" and others as "good kissers."

Touching

As discussed in chapter 4, touch is the predominant sexual sense in most people. As a result, it should not be a surprise to learn that touching is often an integral part of sexual activity. In fact, the role of touch in sexual arousal and pleasure was considered so vital by Masters and Johnson that they recommended it as part of almost every sex therapy routine (we will return to this idea in chapter 12). Sexual touching usually focuses on primary and secondary erogenous zones; however, almost any part of the body can be involved, because nerve endings are present throughout our skin. It is important to note that sexual pleasure can be derived from touch even if the genitals are not directly stimulated. What matters most is the individual's personal preferences and how the touch is interpreted, which means that it is important to communicate with your partner about what does and does not feel good.

One of the most common forms of sexual touching is **tribadism**, which refers to the act of rubbing one's genitals on the body of a sexual partner. This could mean rubbing the genitals together, or rubbing them against other parts of the body. Tribadism is most commonly used to describe vulva-to-vulva contact between two women (known colloquially as "scissoring," because it involves interlocking the legs of the partners like two pairs of scissors; Hite, 2003).

Figure 9.7   Touch can be a sensual experience even if it is not focused on the genitals. Image Copyright Dewayne Flowers, 2013. Used under license from Shutterstock.com.

Oral Sex

Stimulation of the genitals with the mouth has become extremely common over the past century. As evidence of the current prevalence of this behavior, both the NSSHB and the NHSLS have reported that approximately three-quarters of all adults have engaged in oral sex within the past year (Herbenick et al., 2010; Laumann et al., 1994). As you can see in Table 9.1, oral sex practices vary with age, with younger folks being the most likely to do it; however, even among older adults, oral sex still occurs with some frequency. There are also educational and racial differences in the practice of oral sex. Being college-educated and White are linked to a greater likelihood of having ever practiced oral sex compared to having a high school education (or less) and being African American or Hispanic (Laumann et al., 1994). It is also important to note that within some religions and some parts of the world (e.g., Sub-Saharan Africa), oral sex is seen as an unnatural and unclean activity and is not practiced widely.

The general term used to describe stimulation of the vulva by a partner's mouth is **cunnilingus**, while the term used to describe oral stimulation of the penis is **fellatio**. Oral sex is a behavior practiced by people of all genders and sexualities, and it can take many forms. For instance, oral sex varies in terms of whether it is performed individually vs. simultaneously in the so-called *sixty-nine* position. In addition, the area of focus may differ (e.g., fellatio sometimes includes oral stimulation of the scrotum), as does movement, speed, pressure, and use of the hands (e.g., a finger or two may be used for vaginal insertion during cunnilingus). If applicable, couples also vary in terms of how they prefer to deal with ejaculate. Some find ejaculation inside the mouth to be exciting, while others dislike it. As always, it is best to communicate with your partner about your preferences and it is important to recognize that when your partner reveals personal likes and dislikes, it should not be construed as an attack on you. Everyone's bodies and brains are different, which means that the sexual techniques that brought you compliments in a previous relationship may not necessarily draw praise from all future sexual partners. Thus, it is wise not to assume you know what your partner will enjoy or that your partner will automatically know what you want. When it comes to sex, communicate early and often.

Not surprisingly, many men and women find that oral stimulation alone is enough to bring them to orgasm. In fact, about one in ten men and one in five women report that oral sex is their preferred route to climax (Janus & Janus, 1993). Despite the large number of people who practice and enjoy oral sex, there is a lot of misinformation out there about this activity. Perhaps the biggest misconception is that oral sex is a "safe" activity with little to no risk of disease transmission. However, as we will discuss in chapter 11, there are multiple infections that can be spread through this activity, which means it is important to take appropriate precautions no matter what kind of sex you are having.

Vaginal Intercourse

Among heterosexual adults, vaginal intercourse (also known as **coitus**) is the most common form of partnered sexual activity (see Table 9.1) and it is most frequently practiced among those who are younger, married, and more highly educated (Laumann et al., 1994). As with all of the other behaviors we have discussed up until this point, vaginal intercourse is an activity that can take many forms. For one thing, a multitude of sexual positions are possible. The four most basic positions are man-on-top (i.e., "missionary"), woman-on-top, side-by-side, and rear-entry (i.e., "doggy style"). People obviously vary in their position preferences, and those preferences can change over time (e.g., during pregnancy, certain positions can become impossible or uncomfortable). In general, research shows that men tend to prefer woman-on-top, while women tend to prefer man-on-top (Elliot & Brantley, 1997). We do not know why that is, but I take it as evidence that most people are lazy in bed. That, or perhaps a lot of us just like to give up control.

One of the most common things students ask about in my human sexuality course is the "best" position for vaginal intercourse, usually meaning the position that provides the greatest likelihood of female orgasm. Research has found that the **coital alignment technique (CAT)** significantly increases the odds of both female orgasm and simultaneous orgasm during heterosexual intercourse (Pierce, 2000). The CAT is a modified "missionary" position in which the male partner leans further forward to the point where the base of his penis comes into contact with his partner's clitoris. Instead of thrusting in and out, the partners "grind" back and forth to maintain the penile–clitoral connection. This is a very coordinated set of body movements that takes some practice to master, but many people find that the results are worth the effort.

Beyond position selection, partners also vary in terms of what they do with their hands (e.g., providing breast and/or clitoral stimulation), whether they keep their eyes open or closed, whether they require an artificial lubricant, and so on. There are also cross-cultural differences in the practice of vaginal intercourse, such as the common preference for **dry sex** in Sub-Saharan Africa. Dry sex (not to be confused with "dry humping," or non-penetrative sex) is a form of intercourse accompanied by removal of a woman's natural vaginal lubrication (Sandala et al., 1995). Lubrication is removed or minimized by wiping the vagina out or by placing leaves or chemicals inside the vagina. The goal is to increase friction during sex, thereby providing more pleasure to the male partner; however, this behavior may also stem from a cultural view that female wetness is a sign of promiscuity. Regardless of the reason, the practice is painful for women and may increase the risk of contracting infections by causing trauma to the vaginal lining.

Anal Sex

Although anal sex tends to be among the least commonly reported partnered sexual behaviors (see Table 9.1), it is certainly not rare and, like oral sex, has been on the increase in recent years. For instance, according to the NSSHB, as many as one in four or one in five US adults in their 20s and 30s report having practiced this behavior in the past year (Herbenick et al., 2010). Lifetime prevalence estimates are even higher. For instance, the 2006–2008 National Survey of Family Growth found that about one-third of women and almost half of all men surveyed had attempted anal sex at least once before (Chandra, Mosher, & Copen, 2011). However, there are age, education, and racial differences in this practice (Laumann et al., 1994). Similar to masturbation and oral sex, anal sex is more common among those who are younger and more highly educated. With respect to race, White and African American men are equally likely to reported having ever tried it; however, African American women are about half as likely as White women to report having had anal sex in their lifetime.

Anal sex is an activity that produces divided opinions. Some people find it repulsive, while others find it thoroughly arousing. Although anal sex is most commonly associated with gay men, it is also practiced frequently among heterosexuals. Given the prevalence of anal sex observed in survey studies and the fact that heterosexuals vastly outnumber gay men, the reality is that most of the people who practice anal sex in this world are straight couples, a fact that many people find surprising.

When most people hear the term "anal sex," they tend to think about penile-anal penetration. However, this is not the only way that the anus can be involved in sexual activity. Some people may insert a finger or sex toy into the anus during masturbation or partnered sex. Others orally stimulate the anus, a practice known as **anilingus** (colloquially referred to as "rimming").

There are a few special health concerns that merit mention in our discussion of anal stimulation. First, the rectum is a rather delicate structure and does not produce its own lubrication, unlike the vagina. As a result, a generous amount of a safe, non-irritating lubricant should be used, in addition to gentle, slow penetration. This applies regardless of whether a penis or a sex toy is being inserted. If inserting a sex toy, please ensure that the base is significantly larger than the top so that it does not accidentally enter all of the way and become stuck. I have heard many a story from my friends in medicine who have encountered emergency room patients with devices lodged in their rectums. Perhaps the most interesting case I ever heard about was a man who had set his cellular phone to vibrate, wrapped it inside a condom, and inserted it into his anus before proceeding to call himself repeatedly from another phone (this gives new meaning to the terms "butt-dialing" and "booty call," right?). Unfortunately for him, however, his phone made for a poor sex toy. It became irretrievable after going in too far and had to be removed in the middle of the night by a very talented and slightly amused surgeon.

In addition, it is important to note that anal sex carries the highest risk of disease transmission out of all of the sexual activities we have discussed above (for more on this, see chapter 11). To reduce risk, condoms should be worn during penile-anal penetration and, during anilingus, *dental dams* should be used to limit transmission of intestinal infections. On a side note, a practice known as ATM ("ass-to-mouth") is becoming increasingly common in pornography and involves taking the penis directly from a person's anus and putting it in someone's mouth without cleansing the penis in between. This is an extremely risky activity and is not recommended because of the very high risk of transmitting infections.

Same-Sex Behaviors

The sex lives of gays and lesbians are strikingly similar to those of heterosexuals in most regards. The one exception, of course, is the lack of penile–vaginal intercourse. Nonetheless, there are numerous stereotypes about what non-heterosexual individuals do when it comes to sex. For instance, perhaps the most prevalent sex stereotype targeting lesbians is the notion of "lesbian bed death," or the idea that sexual activity drops off dramatically in long-term female couples, a result some have argued stems from the fact that there is no man around to initiate sex (see Schwartz & Blumstein, 1983). Although the sex lives of some lesbian couples eventually slow down, the idea that this is somehow a universal phenomenon is a myth and many psychologists have been critical of the data used to support the notion of "lesbian bed death" (Jasenza, 2000). The reality is that many lesbian couples maintain long-term, sexually satisfying relationships. Within these relationships, the most common sexual behaviors tend to be oral sex and tribadism.

What about gay men? There is a widespread belief that anal intercourse is the primary sexual behavior practiced by gay men. However, this could not be further from the truth. As it turns out, oral sex and mutual masturbation are far more common. See the Digging Deeper 9.3 box for more on what the sex lives of gay men are actually like.

There is less research into the sexual behaviors of bisexually identified individuals, but existing work suggests that, like persons of other sexual orientations, they also have a wide sexual repertoire. For example, in a study of bisexual men in the Midwestern US, researchers found that the vast majority (>75%) reported having practiced vaginal intercourse, given and received oral sex with male and female partners, engaged in mutual masturbation with male and female partners,

Figure 9.8   Despite the widespread stereotype of "lesbian bed death," many female same-sex couples lead very active and satisfying sex lives. ©Rikke Breiting/123RF.COM.

Digging Deeper 9.3   Do Gay Men's Sex Lives Match Up With the Stereotypes?

There are several common stereotypes about the sex lives of gay men. One of the most prevalent is that anal sex is the primary (if not only) sexual activity that gay men practice. Another is that sex in public places (e.g., in parks, à la George Michael) is a common occurrence. And yet one more is that gay men mostly have sex with anonymous partners. Is there any truth to these widespread stereotypes? According to research, the answer is *no*.

Rosenberger and colleagues (2011) examined the sexual behaviors of a national US online sample of nearly 25,000 men who have sex with men (86% of whom identified as gay). Participants were asked to describe the details of their most recent sexual event with a male partner. Results indicated that gay men have a diverse sexual repertoire, with over 1,300 unique combinations of sexual behavior reported. Most participants (63.2%) reported engaging in somewhere between five and nine different sexual activities during their most recent sexual encounter.

The single most commonly reported behavior was kissing on the mouth (74.5%), followed closely by oral sex (72.7%) and mutual masturbation (68.4%). Contrary to popular belief, only about one-third of men in the sample reported engaging in anal sex (37.2%). This tells us that the common assumption that "gay sex" is necessarily anal sex is inaccurate.

In terms of the context of sexual behavior, only a very small minority of participants reported that their sexual activity took place in what would be considered a public setting (3.1%) – the vast majority had sex in their own home or in their partner's home (77.7%). In

Figure 9.9 Contrary to popular belief, kissing on the mouth is the most frequently reported sexual behavior among men who have sex with men. ©Yuri Arcurs/123RF.COM.

addition, 37% reported that sex occurred with a boyfriend or dating partner, and 17% indicated a friend. Thus, for the majority of the men in this study, their most recent partner was well known to them and was not anonymous.

While it is certainly true that *some* gay men have anonymous anal sex in public places, this is not necessarily what all or even most gay men do. The results of this research thus seem to counteract many common stereotypes about the sex lives of gay men. In addition, these findings suggest that doctors and public health professionals should not make too many assumptions about the sexual behaviors of men who have sex with men; rather, we need to take into account the wide individual variability that exists.

Note: Reprinted with permission from *The Psychology of Human Sexuality* blog (www.lehmiller.com).

and practiced some form of anal sex (Dodge et al., 2013). Notably, bisexual men were much more likely to have anal sex with male partners compared to female partners, and they were far more likely to be the insertive partner rather than the receptive partner during such activities; however, a small number of bisexual men reported that their only experience being the receptive partner during anal intercourse occurred with women (e.g., being penetrated with a strap-on dildo, known colloquially as "pegging"). Thus, the sexual practices of bisexuals are incredibly diverse.

Frequency and Benefits of Sex and Orgasm

One of the most common concerns people have about their own sex lives is whether they are having "enough" sex. As a result, students taking this course often ask what a "normal" frequency of sexual activity is. As discussed in chapter 2, however, we cannot look to a single number to represent normalcy; rather, we need to consider a range of responses. The reason for this is because people have preferences for different amounts and types of sexual activity. For instance, some older married couples may be content having sex just one per year on their anniversary, whereas some younger couples may not be content unless they are having sex most days of the week. Thus, the "correct" amount of sex is the amount that makes you and your partner(s) happy. As a result, it is usually not productive to worry whether you "should" be doing it more; rather, the question is whether you are satisfied with the amount of sex you are having.

With that said, to give you a general sense of frequency, Table 9.3 presents selected results from the NHSLS. As you can see, most people reported having sex somewhere between a few times per month and two or three times per week. However, sexual frequency depends upon a variety of factors. For instance, sexual activity tends to be higher among younger adults (under age 40) and among people who are married.

On a side note, research suggests that there may be some physical and psychological health benefits of being sexually active on at least a semi-frequent basis. For instance, a study of male rats that were randomly assigned to sex deprivation (i.e., just one act of sex over the course of the study) or daily sex for two weeks revealed that the more sexually active rats exhibited greater neuron growth (a key factor in mental agility) and lower circulating levels of stress hormones (Leuner, Glasper, & Gould, 2010). In addition, research on humans has found that people who have recently fallen in love have higher levels of nerve growth factor in their blood (Emanuele et al., 2005). Together, these results suggest the intriguing possibility that sex may help maintain and possibly enhance cognitive functioning.

In addition, sex may promote better physical health and longevity. As some evidence of this, an experimental study in which men's blood was tested immediately after masturbating to orgasm or after refraining from sexual activity revealed that orgasm was linked to enhanced immune system functioning, including an increase in natural killer cells (Haake et al., 2004). Could frequent immune boosts following orgasm potentially help you to live longer? A study of men from the United Kingdom found that participants with the highest orgasmic frequency had a 50% lower risk of death than those men who had did not have as many orgasms (Davey Smith, Frankel, & Yarnell, 1997).

Table 9.3	Frequency of Sexual Activity in the Past Year among Adults Age 18–59				
	Never	*A few times during the year*	*A few times each month*	*2–3 times per week*	*4+ times per week*
Men	9.8%	17.6%	35.5%	29.5%	7.7%
Women	13.6%	16.1%	37.2%	26.3%	6.7%

Note: Adapted with permission from Laumann, Gagnon, Michael, and Michaels (1994).

Figure 9.10   Frequent sex increases the growth rate of neurons in rats. Are creatures that have more frequent sex smarter? ©Cathy Keifer/123RF.COM.

Sexual Behavior in Psychological Perspective

As we close out this chapter, we will further explore the role of psychology on sexual behavior. In chapter 1, we mentioned a few psychological influences in detail, including personality traits (e.g., erotophilia, sociosexuality, and sensation seeking), classical and operant conditioning, observational learning, and evolved tendencies. However, beyond these factors, there are a number of other variables psychologists have identified that can affect how and when we express our sexuality. In this section, we will consider the roles of self-regulation (i.e., self-control), attachment style, and mortality salience.

Self-Regulation

According to the Strength Model of Self-Control (Baumeister, Vohs, & Tice, 2007), our willpower is a limited resource. In other words, our ability to exert self-control is finite. You can think of self-control as being akin to a muscle in the sense that drawing upon your willpower repeatedly in a short period of time will deplete your strength, thereby making it harder to exert self-control again in the near future. Psychologists have documented evidence of this time and again in a variety of settings. For example, when people's self-control abilities have been weakened, they have less ability to resist the temptation to consume alcohol, eat sugary foods, and spend money impulsively (see Baumeister et al., 2007). Does self-regulatory failure also have implications for our sex lives? It would appear so.

Before we get into the findings, it is worth pointing out that there is a difference in *trait* vs. *state* self-control. **Trait self-control** refers to your overall, chronic level of self-control. It is a simple fact of life that some people just have bigger self-control reserves than others. For instance, you probably

Figure 9.11 When our self-control resources are low, we may become more susceptible to cheating on a romantic partner. Image Copyright Kzenon, 2013. Used under license from Shutterstock.com.

know some people who are very good at sticking to diets, and others who constantly fail at them. Part of the reason for this is because self-control is, to some extent, a psychological trait that we can possess in larger or smaller quantities. **State self-control** refers to your self-control abilities *at a specific moment*, taking into account situational factors. State self-control therefore fluctuates moment to moment and can go up or down depending upon how much willpower you have exerted recently.

With regard to trait self-control, research on adolescents has found that lower overall levels of self-control longitudinally predict pursuit of riskier sexual behaviors (e.g., Raffaelli & Crockett, 2003). Thus, being chronically low on self-control may predispose individuals to forego condoms, have larger numbers of partners, and engage in other behaviors that increase their risk of infection transmission. Likewise, research has demonstrated that lower levels of trait self-control are associated with more temptation to cheat on one's current romantic partner. For instance, a study of romantically involved, heterosexual male participants seated in a waiting room with an attractive female confederate revealed that the men with lower levels of trait self-control engaged in more flirting with the confederate than men who possessed greater willpower (Pronk, Karremans, & Wigboldus, 2011). With regard to state self-control, we discussed a study by Gailliot and Baumeister (2007) in chapter 2 in which they found that when participants' self-regulatory abilities were temporarily weakened, participants subsequently engaged in more extensive sexual activities with their current romantic partner. In two other studies, Gailliot and Baumeister found that when participants' self-control abilities were temporarily depleted, they reported a greater likelihood of cheating on their partner and had a stronger tendency to unscramble letter sets (e.g., N I S E P) as sex words (PENIS) instead of non-sex words (SPINE). Thus, both our trait and state levels of self-control appear to influence our sexual thoughts and behaviors.

Attachment Style

As described in chapter 8, each of us has our own *attachment style*, which can be thought of as one's general approach to developing and maintaining relationships with other people (Hazan & Shaver, 1987). To refresh your memory, people can be securely attached (i.e., they have an easy time getting close to others), anxiously attached (i.e., they fear that their partners may leave), or avoidantly attached (i.e., they are uncomfortable with intimacy). Research has found that these attachment styles are associated with different sexual behaviors, as well as different overall levels of sexual functioning.

Specifically, a review of 15 studies in this area by Stefanou and McCabe (2012) revealed that higher levels of anxious attachment were associated with a greater frequency of sex and the pursuit of sex as a means of getting closer to one's partner. Additionally, higher levels of avoidant attachment were linked to a lower frequency of sexual activity and pursuing sex for nonromantic reasons (e.g., to enhance one's own status or to manipulate a partner). Moreover, both anxious and avoidant attachment were linked to lower levels of sexual satisfaction and a higher number of sexual problems (e.g., difficulty achieving orgasm). Other research has found that patterns of attachment also predict safe-sex practices. For example, high levels of attachment anxiety are associated with lower levels of condom use (Strachman & Impett, 2009), perhaps because anxious individuals feel as though they have less power to negotiate condom use out of fear that their partner will leave. Thus, our attachment style may lead us to view sex very differently, which may ultimately influence the frequency with which we engage in certain behaviors as well as the quality and safety of the sex that we have.

Mortality Salience

One additional psychological factor that can affect sexual behavior is **mortality salience**, which refers to human beings' conscious or unconscious recognition that we will eventually die. According to Terror Management Theory (Solomon, Greenberg, & Pyszczynski, 1991), when we are reminded of our own mortality, we subconsciously alter our attitudes and behaviors in order to help us cope with the "terrifying" prospect of our eventual death. If you have ever taken a social psychology course, you have probably learned that these coping mechanisms focus on embracing cultural worldviews and enhancing self-esteem; however, what you may not have learned is that changes in sexual attitudes and behavior may be an important part of coping efforts for some people.

Consider a series of studies conducted by Landau and colleagues (2006) in which participants were primed with mortality salience (i.e., the prospect of death was brought to mind by asking participants to write a brief essay about what will happen to their body when they physically die). Their research consistently found that mortality salience primes *reduced* heterosexual men's interest in sexy and alluring women; however, mortality salience did not diminish their interest in women who appeared more "wholesome" (i.e., women who were dressed more conservatively). Landau and colleagues argue that, for some men, "the experience of raw sexual attraction… transforms the individual from something unique and special to an impulsive, animalistic, material, and finite piece of biological protoplasm" (p. 132). In other words, sexy women may remind men of their creaturely instincts and impulses. As a result, when a man is already feeling threatened (e.g., as a result of a mortality salience prime), he may seek to distance himself from and perhaps even derogate sexy women as a way of helping him feel better about himself.

However, mortality salience does not lead everyone to distance themselves from sex. In fact, for some people, the opposite effect emerges. For example, interest in sex *increases* after a mortality salience prime among people who have positive body image (Goldenberg et al., 2000). What this suggests is that for people who are more comfortable with their physical appearance, the body itself and bodily activities like sex come to represent an important source of self-esteem. For such individuals, sex may be an appropriate way of dealing with the prospect of one's own mortality by reducing feelings of anxiety. Research has also found that mortality salience primes make people with a low fear of intimacy more willing to have risky sex (i.e., having sex with a new partner without protection; Taubman-Ben-Ari, 2004). Again, this suggests that for people who are more comfortable with physical intimacy, reminders of death may spur sexual behavior. Thus, the specific effects of mortality salience fundamentally depend upon how we feel about ourselves and about sex in general.

As you can see, a variety of dispositional (e.g., trait self-control, attachment style) and situational factors (e.g., state self-control, mortality salience) may affect the likelihood that an individual will engage in sexual behavior. Because there are so many factors that can promote or inhibit sexuality, it makes understanding both the causes and treatments of sexual problems incredibly complex, an issue we will return to in chapter 12.

Key Terms

celibacy	cunnilingus	dry sex
sexual fantasies	fellatio	anilingus
masturbation	coitus	trait self-control
hysteria	coital alignment technique	state self-control
tribadism	(CAT)	mortality salience

Discussion Questions: What is Your Perspective on Sex?

* What (if anything) were you told about masturbation while you were growing up? What does the information you received (or failed to receive) suggest about modern society's attitudes toward self-pleasure?
* Several studies have suggested that people who have sex and reach orgasm more frequently tend to be healthier. Do you think this is primarily because sex is good for you, or because healthy people are just more capable of sex and tend to "do it" more often?
* Out of all of the different psychological influences on sexual behavior we have considered thus far, which ones do you think best explain your own sexual attitudes and behaviors?

References

Baumeister, R.F., Vohs, K.D., & Tice, D.M. (2007). The strength model of self-control. *Current Directions in Psychological Science, 16*, 351–355. DOI:10.1111/j.1467-8721.2007.00534.x.

Birnbaum, G. E., Simpson, J. A., Weisberg, Y. J., Barnea, E., & Assulin-Simhon, Z. (2012). Is it my overactive imagination? The effects of contextually activated attachment insecurity on sexual fantasies. *Journal of Social and Personal Relationships, 29*, 1131–1152. DOI:10.1177/0265407512452978.

Bivona, J.M., Critelli, J.W., & Clark, M.J. (2012). Women's rape fantasies: An empirical evaluation of the major explanations. *Archives of Sexual Behavior, 41*, 1107–1119. DOI:10.1007/s10508-012-9934-6.

Blumstein, P.W., & Schwartz, P. (1983). *American couples: Money, work, and sex*. New York: William Morrow.

Bogaert, A.F. (2013). The demography of asexuality. In A. Baumle (Ed.), *International handbook on the demography of sexuality* (pp. 275–288). New York: Springer.

Chandra, A., Mosher, W.D., & Copen, C. (2011). Sexual behavior, sexual attraction, and sexual identity in the United States: Data from the 2006–2008 National Survey of Family Growth. *National Health Statistics Reports, 36*, 1–36.

Critelli, J.W., & Bivona, J.M. (2008). Women's erotic rape fantasies: An evaluation of theory and research. *Journal of Sex Research, 45*, 57–70. DOI:10.1080/00224490701808191 .

Davey Smith, G., Frankel, S., & Yarnell, J. (1997). Sex and death: Are they related? Findings from the Caerphilly Cohort Study. *British Medical Journal, 315*, 1641–1644. DOI:10.1136/bmj.315.7123.1641.

Davidson, J. (1985). The utilization of sexual fantasies by sexually experienced university students. *Journal of American College Health, 34*, 24–32. DOI:10.1080/07448481.1985.9939614.

DeLamater, J. (2012). Sexual expression in later life: A review and synthesis. *Journal of Sex Research, 49*, 125–141. DOI:10.1080/00224499.2011.603168.

Dodge, B., Schnarrs, P.W., Reece, M., Martinez, O., Goncalves, G., Malebranche, D., … & Fortenberry, J.D. (2013). Sexual behaviors and experiences among behaviorally bisexual men in the midwestern United States. *Archives of Sexual Behavior, 42*, 247–256. DOI:10.1007/s10508-011-9878-2.

Elliot, L., & Brantley, C. (1997). *Sex on campus: The Details guide to the real sex lives of college students*. New York: Random House.

Emanuele, E., Politi, P., Bianchi, M., Minoretti, P., Bertona, M., & Geroldi, D. (2005). Raised plasma nerve growth factor levels associated with early-stage romantic love. *Psychoneuroendocrinology, 20*, 1–7. DOI:10.1016/j.psyneuen.2005.09.002.

Gailliot, M.T., & Baumeister, R.F. (2007). Self-regulation and sexual restraint: Dispositionally and temporarily poor self-regulatory abilities contribute to failures at restraining sexual behavior. *Personality and Social Psychology Bulletin, 33*, 173–186. DOI:10.1177/0146167206293472.

Giles, G.G., Severi, G., English, D.R., McCredie, M.R.E., Borland, R., Boyle, P., & Hopper, J.L. (2003). Sexual factors and prostate cancer. *British Journal of Urology International, 92*, 211–216. DOI:10.1046/j.1464-410X.2003.04319.x.

Gold, S.R., Balzano, B.F., & Stamey, R. (1991). Two studies of females' sexual force fantasies. *Journal of Sex Education & Therapy, 17*, 15–26.

Goldenberg, J.L., McCoy, S.K., Pyszczynski, T., Greenberg, J., & Solomon, S. (2000). The body as a source of self-esteem: The effect of mortality salience on identification with one's body, interest in sex, and appearance monitoring. *Journal of Personality and Social Psychology, 79*, 118–130. DOI:10.1037/0022-3514.79.1.118.

Gregersen, E. (1996). *The world of human sexuality: Behaviors, customs, & beliefs*. New York: Irvington.

Haake, P., Krueger, T.H., Goebel, M.U., Heberling, K.M., Hartmann, U., & Schedlowski, M. (2004). Effects of sexual arousal on lymphocyte subset circulation and cytokine production in man. *Neuroimmunomodulation, 11*, 293–298. DOI:10.1159/000079409.

Hazan, C., & Shaver, P. (1987). Romantic love conceptualized as an attachment process. *Journal of Personality and Social Psychology, 52*, 511–524. DOI:10.1037/0022-3514.52.3.511.

Herbenick, D., Reece, M., Schick, V., Sanders, S. A., Dodge, B., & Fortenberry, J.D. (2010). Sexual behavior in the United States: Results from a national probability sample of men and women ages 14–94. *Journal of Sexual Medicine, 7*(Suppl. 5), 255–265. DOI:10.1111/j.1743-6109.2010.02012.x.

Hite, S. (2003). *The Hite Report: A national study of female sexuality*. New York: Seven Stories.

Hurlbert, D.F., & Whittaker, K.E. (1991). The role of masturbation in marital and sexual satisfaction: A comparative study of female masturbators and nonmasturbators. *Journal of Sex Education & Therapy, 17*, 272–282.

Janus, S., & Janus, C. (1993). *The Janus report on sexual behavior*. New York: John Wiley & Sons.

Jasenza, S. (2000). Lesbian sexuality post-Stonewall to post-modernism: Putting the `lesbian bed death' concept to bed. *Journal of Sex Education & Therapy, 25*, 59–69.

Kellogg, J. H. (1881). *Plain facts for old and young*. Burlington, IA: Segner & Condit.

Landau, M.J., Goldenberg, J.L., Greenberg, J., Gillath, O., Solomon, S., Cox, C., Martens, A., & Pyszczynski, T. (2006). The siren's call: Terror management and the threat of men's sexual attraction to women. *Journal of Personality and Social Psychology, 90,* 129–146. DOI:10.1037/0022-3514.90.1.129.

Laumann, E.O., Gagnon, J., Michael, R., & Michaels, S. (1994). *The social organization of sexuality: Sexual practices in the United States.* Chicago: University of Chicago Press.

Leitenberg, H., & Henning, K. (1995). Sexual fantasy. *Psychological Bulletin, 117,* 469–496. DOI:10.1037/0033-2909.117.3.469.

Leitenberg, H., & Hicks, T.V. (2001). Sexual fantasies about one's partner versus someone else: Gender differences in incidence and frequency. *Journal of Sex Research, 38,* 43–50. DOI:10.1080/00224490109552069.

Leuner, B., Glasper, E.R., & Gould, E. (2010). Sexual experience promotes adult neurogenesis in the hippocampus despite an initial elevation in stress hormones. *PLoS ONE 5*(7): e11597. DOI:10.1371/journal.pone.0011597.

Maines, R.P. (1998). *The technology of orgasm: "Hysteria", the vibrator, and women's sexual satisfaction.* Baltimore, MD: The Johns Hopkins University Press.

McCauley, C., & Swann, C. (1980). Sex differences in the frequency and functions of fantasies during sexual activity. *Journal of Research in Personality, 14,* 400–411. DOI:10.1016/0092-6566(80)90022-7.

Pelletier, L.A., & Herold, E.S. (1988). The relationship of age, sex guilt, and sexual experience with female sexual fantasies. *Journal of Sex Research, 24,* 250–256. DOI:10.1080/00224498809551420.

Pierce, A.P. (2000). The coital alignment technique (CAT): An overview of studies. *Journal of Sex & Marital Therapy, 26,* 257–268. DOI:10.1080/00926230050084650.

Pronk, T.M., Karremans, J.C., & Wigboldus, D.H.J. (2011). How can you resist? Executive control helps romantically involved individuals to stay faithful. *Journal of Personality and Social Psychology, 100,* 827–837. DOI:10.1037/a0021993.

Raffaelli, M., & Crockett, L.J. (2003). Sexual risk taking in adolescence: The role of self-regulation and attraction to risk. *Developmental Psychology, 39,* 1036–1046. DOI:10.1037/0012-1649.39.6.1036.

Regan, P. C., Durvasula, R., Howell, L., Ureno, O., & Rea, M. (2004). Gender, ethnicity, and the developmental timing of first sexual and romantic experiences. *Social Behavior and Personality: An international journal, 32,* 667–676.

Rosenberger, J.G., Reece, M., Schick, V., Herbenick, D., Novak, D.S. Van Der Pol, B., & Fortenberry, J.D. (2011). Sexual behaviors and situational characteristics of most recent male-partnered sexual event among gay and bisexually identified men in the United States. *Journal of Sexual Medicine, 8,* 3040–3050. DOI:10.1111/j.1743–6109.2011.02438.x.

Sandala, L., Lurie, P., Sunkutu, M.R., Chani, E.M., Hudes, E.S., & Hearst, N. (1995). 'Dry sex' and HIV infection among women attending a sexually transmitted diseases clinic in Lusaka, Zambia. *AIDS, 9,* S61.

Siegel, K., & Schrimshaw, E.W. (2003). Reasons for adopting celibacy among older men and women living with HIV/AIDS. *Journal of Sex Research, 40,* 189–200. DOI:10.1080/00224490309552180.

Solomon, S., Greenberg, J., & Pyszczynski, T. (1991). A terror management theory of social behavior: The psychological functions of self-esteem and cultural worldviews. *Advances in Experimental Social Psychology, 24,* 93–159. DOI:10.1016/S0065-2601(08)60328-7.

Stefanou, C., & McCabe, M.P. (2012). Adult attachment and sexual functioning: A review of past research. *Journal of Sexual Medicine, 9,* 2499–2507. DOI:10.1111/j.1743-6109.2012.02843.x.

Strachman, A., & Impett, E.A. (2009). Attachment orientations and daily condom use in dating relationships. *Journal of Sex Research, 46,* 319–329. DOI:10.1080/00224490802691801.

Taubman-Ben-Ari, O. (2004). Intimacy and risk sexual behaviour – What does it have to do with death? *Death Studies, 28,* 865–887. DOI:10.1080/07481180490490988.

Travis, M. (2010). Asexuality. In M. Stombler, D.M. Baunach, E.O. Burgess, D. Donnelly, W. Simonds, & E.J. Windsor (Eds.), *Sex matters: The sexuality & society reader* (3rd ed.). Boston, MA; Allyn & Bacon.

Zurbriggen, E.L., & Yost, M.R. (2004). Power, desire, and pleasure in sexual fantasies. *Journal of Sex Research, 41,* 288–300. DOI:10.1080/00224490409552236.

10

Sex Education, Contraception, and Pregnancy

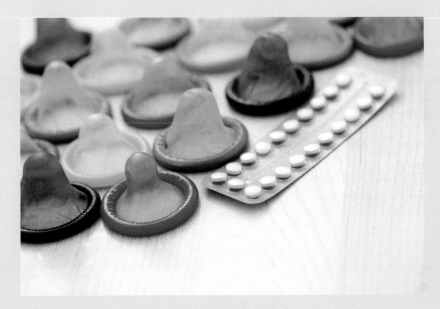

©Monika Adamczyk/123RF.COM.

Chapter Outline

- Introduction   256
- Sex Education   256
- Contraception   261
  - History   262
  - Types of Contraceptives   262
  - Choosing the Right Contraceptive   270
- Pregnancy   272
  - The Psychology of Trying to Have a Baby   272
  - Psychological Changes During Pregnancy and After Birth   273
  - Abortion   274

The Psychology of Human Sexuality, First Edition. Justin J. Lehmiller.
© 2014 John Wiley & Sons, Ltd. Published 2014 by John Wiley & Sons, Ltd.

Introduction

When and where did you first learn about sex? There is a surprising amount of variability in how people answer this question. Some people learned from a sex education course taught in middle or high school, whereas others learned from parents, friends, books, Wikipedia, or perhaps even pornography. Obviously, each of these sources could provide *very* different information, and even among those who learned from their school, there can be a staggering difference in content from one curriculum to the next. This wide range of experience tells us that children and adolescents are not getting standardized information about sex, and this is part of the reason unintended pregnancy, abortion, and sexually transmitted infections (STIs) are as common as they are. One goal of this chapter is to shed some light on the nature of sex education in the twenty-first century and to examine how different types of programs impact adolescents' and adults' sexual attitudes and behaviors.

In addition, we will consider the topics of contraception and pregnancy. Our discussion of contraception will provide a review of some of the most common forms of birth control on the market today and consider some of the unique benefits and drawbacks of each. In my experience, far too many college students tend to think that condoms and birth control pills are their only options when it comes to pregnancy prevention, and research has found that there are many misunderstandings about just how effective different forms of birth control really are (Eisenberg et al., 2012). There are also some little-known psychological side effects of hormonal birth control worth considering.

We will finish this chapter by discussing pregnancy. In particular, we will focus on the psychological effects associated with trying to get pregnant, as well as psychological changes that occur during pregnancy and after birth for both partners. We will also address the topic of abortion, including the most common reasons for ending a pregnancy and the psychological effects abortion can have on women and men.

Sex Education

Despite the fact that the vast majority of parents believe their children should receive a fairly thorough sex education, a surprising number of kids fail to get it (NPR, 2004). The problem is that many parents feel too embarrassed to talk to their kids about sex (Walker, 2001), so they palm the responsibility off onto the schools. That would not necessarily be a bad thing if the schools were providing kids with the information they need, but it turns out that many school-based sex education programs are teaching insufficient and, in some cases, incorrect information (Committee on Government Reform, 2004). As a result, kids simply are not learning what they should. Many of them end up turning to their peers and porn for answers; however, those sources tend to impart less than reliable information (see chapter 14 for more on this). The end result is that far too many adolescents embark on their first sexual experience with a profound lack of knowledge about sex and the human body, which helps to explain why there are so many unintended teen pregnancies and why young people have the highest rates of STI acquisition (in fact, young people aged 15–24 make up about half of all new STI cases in the US each year; CDC, 2012a).

Adolescents in the United States have higher rates of unintended pregnancy and STIs compared to other industrialized nations, including France, Germany, the Netherlands, and Australia

Figure 10.1   Sex education courses often contain insufficient and, in some cases, inaccurate information about sex and sexuality. ©Marek Uliasz/123RF.COM.

(Alford & Hauser, 2011; Weaver, Smith, & Kippax, 2005). In the US, the current birth rate for teenage women aged 15–19 is 34.3 per 1,000, with a public cost of nearly $11 billion each year (Hamilton & Ventura, 2012). These sexual health disparities are not a result of US teens being more sexually active; rather, what appears to be going on is that US teens are less likely to use condoms and other forms of contraception than their counterparts in other Western countries (Alford & Hauser, 2011).

Why are US teens less likely to use condoms and contraception? Although there are many factors contributing to this (including cultural differences in the acceptability of teenage sexual activity and access to condoms), a major element in this equation is inadequate sex education. As some evidence of this, let us look at a study of US women who have had an unintended pregnancy and were asked why they did not use contraception to try and prevent it. As seen in Table 10.1, nearly half of all women surveyed said they "did not think they could get pregnant" (Mosher & Jones, 2010). If that many women do not understand when pregnancy can occur, it is clear that we simply are not teaching people enough about sex or about their bodies.

In the US, a culture war has been waged over the past few decades over the content that should be covered in school-based sexual education. This has resulted in three different methods of teaching adolescents about sex. First is the **abstinence-only approach**, in which the focus is teaching kids to abstain from sex. Information on obtaining and using contraception and condoms is not provided. Second is **abstinence-plus**, where kids are still taught that abstinence is the best policy, but they are provided with information on contraception and condoms so that students who decide to have sex are prepared. Third is **comprehensive sex education**, in which abstinence is not emphasized as the primary goal. Instead, students are provided with a wide range of information and the focus is developing responsible decision-making skills when it comes to sexual activity. Advocates of the abstinence-only approach argue that providing too much information promotes teenage sex, whereas advocates of the more inclusive approaches argue that some teens will have sex no matter what they are told, and

Table 10.1   Reasons Women Failed to Use Contraception Before an Unintended Pregnancy

Reason	Percentage of women reporting that reason
Did not think you could get pregnant	43.9%
Did not really mind getting pregnant	22.8%
Concerned about side effects of birth control	16.2%
Did not expect to have sex	14.1%
Male partner did not want to use contraception	9.6%
Male partner did not want you to use contraception	7.3%

Note: Women could select more than one answer. Data obtained from Mosher & Jones (2010).

Your Sexuality 10.1   What Should School-Based Sex Education Look Like?

Experiences with school-based sex education vary widely, ranging from awkward to awesome. Think for a moment about what your experience was like (if any). Do you think you learned what you needed to know? Using your own experiences as a guide, imagine that you have the opportunity to design a sex education course that your own child might take. How would your course deal with the following issues?

- At what age or grade would your course begin?
- Would students be separated by sex, or would everyone learn together?
- Would your course be mandatory or would attendance be optional depending upon the desires of the other children's parents?
- Would abstinence be the ultimate goal of your course? Why or why not?
- After the course, would students have the opportunity to access condoms and/or birth control for free and without their parents' knowledge?

they need to learn how to protect themselves. What do you think about these different approaches? Weigh in with your opinion by checking out the Your Sexuality 10.1 box.

US survey studies find that parental support for abstinence-only education is relatively low (15%); instead, most parents support abstinence-plus (46%) or comprehensive education (36%; NPR, 2004). Despite the fact that support for abstinence-only education is low, it is widely taught, and advocates of this approach have had great success in attracting federal funding for such programs. In fact, a survey of principals in middle and high schools found that 30% of US schools were teaching abstinence-only (NPR, 2004). The US is unique among Western countries in having this high prevalence of abstinence-based education. However, abstinence-only programs do not appear to be particularly effective in achieving their goals and may have the counterintuitive effect of exacerbating the sexual health issues facing teenagers.

For instance, a study of 1,719 teenagers in the US examined the link between type of sex education received and sexual health outcomes (Kohler, Manhart, & Lafferty, 2008). Results indicated that, compared to comprehensive sex education, abstinence-only did nothing to reduce rates of sexual activity, teenage pregnancy, and STIs. In fact, this study found that students who received comprehensive sex education had a 50% *lower* risk of teenage pregnancy than students who received abstinence-only! Several other studies have reported similar effects. For example, research has found that in US states where abstinence-only sex education is more widespread, teenage pregnancy rates are the highest (Stanger-Hall & Hall, 2011).

Thus, it does not appear to be the case that providing comprehensive sex education encourages students to have sex or to attempt riskier behaviors; rather, it is a lack of information that tends to be problematic. Some have argued that the abstinence-only approach may also be potentially harmful in the sense that it ignores the needs of certain groups. For instance, we know that most teenagers are sexually active and that the average age of first intercourse in the US is 17, with some starting much sooner than that (CDC, 2012b). Failing to provide information about condoms and contraception therefore does an active disservice to teens who eventually become sexually active. Abstinence-only programs also frequently ignore the sexual health needs of gay, lesbian, bisexual, and transgendered youth by leaving sexual orientation and gender identity out of their programs entirely and by promoting sexual intercourse within heterosexual marriage as the ideal. Moreover, a study by the US Department of Health and Human Services found that more than 80% of abstinence-only programs contained scientific errors, taught false information, and promoted gender stereotypes (Committee on Government Reform, 2004). For example, some programs falsely claimed that HIV is spread via sweat and tears, which we will see is not true in chapter 11. Others claimed that condoms are not effective at preventing the spread of STIs, and that women need "financial support" while men need "admiration."

In addition to the fact that some abstinence programs teach students incorrect information, these programs may also leave students with the impression that safe sex and pleasurable sex are at odds with one another. By using scare tactics (e.g., STIs) as a way of motivating students to practice safe sex, these programs imply that condoms and pleasure just are not compatible. This association is further reinforced by the popular media, which usually depicts sex as highly pleasurable, while completely avoiding the topic of safety. Sex education programs might be well-served by reconceptualizing safe sex in pleasurable terms because if we can make safe sex seem more desirable to students, they may be more inclined to practice it. To that end, several sex education organizations have begun a mission of promoting pleasurable safe sex by using techniques such as eroticizing the use of condoms (e.g., learning how to make the application of a condom sensual), teaching couples how to have better sex, and helping people to improve their sexual communication (Philpott, Knerr, & Boydell, 2006).

Thus, to best address the sexual health needs of teenagers, school-based sex education must go beyond talking only about abstinence and the dangers of sexual activity. However, changing what schools are teaching will not resolve all of the issues. Parents also need to play a more active role in their children's sex education because schools cannot teach everything and kids need a safe and reliable resource to go to when they have questions. For some practical suggestions on increasing sexual communication between parents and their children, see the Digging Deeper 10.1 box.

Digging Deeper 10.1   When and How Should You
Talk to Your Kids About Sex in the Age of
Internet Porn?

How are adolescents learning about sex today? By pointing, clicking, and streaming through an endless supply of Internet pornography (Bowater, 2011). Online porn is now the default form of sex education for a growing number of kids because they are not getting the information they need elsewhere. Many of us find this prospect kind of scary. Although it is unlikely that you can prevent your children from searching for porn, what you can do is teach them about sex in a responsible way so that porn does not become their "how-to" guide for sex and relationships.

When it comes to teaching kids about sex, most parents do not know what they should say, how they should say it, or when it should happen. As a result, many parents do not talk about sex at all, or they do not address it in a serious way. This is a shame because, by a wide margin, teenagers report that their parents are the most influential figures in their lives when it comes to making decisions about sex, and most teens report that they would have an easier time postponing sexual activity if they could talk more to their parents about sex (Albert, 2010). So when should you have "the talk" and what should you say?

Figure 10.2   Talking to kids about sex can be an awkward and embarrassing experience for some parents, but it is important to not let that stop the conversation. Image Copyright Golden Pixels LLC, 2013. Used under license from Shutterstock.com.

1. *Initiate the talk about sex early*. Too many parents want to wait until their kids are older or until the time seems "right." However, the longer you wait, the less likely it is that the talk will happen, or if it does, it may be too little, too late. Admittedly, it is more difficult

with boys than it is with girls to determine the "right" age, because girls' menstruation provides a natural segue into talking about sexual development. However, consider that some kids are searching for online porn as early as age 6 (Dima, 2013)! With that in mind, it tells us that both boys and girls need a relatively early lesson with age-appropriate content.

2. *Find out when and what your kids are learning about sex in school, and be prepared to fill in the gaps.* Consider attending the sex education program your kids will be exposed to or speak with your child's teacher about what will be covered. You do not want to assume that your kids are getting all of the knowledge they need. Just consider that about one-third of teenage boys and girls report receiving no formal instruction regarding contraceptive use in school (Martinez, Abma, & Copen, 2010). You need to know what the school is providing so that you can supplement it and answer questions.

3. *Recognize that uncertainty and embarrassment are typical reactions for any parent in this situation.* Please do not avoid having the talk because you do not know how or because your parents never had the talk with you. Few people know what they are supposed to say in this situation, and there is not one "correct" way to do it. You may find the talk embarrassing, but if you are worried that you will not have the right words or be able to describe things well enough, bring out some pictures and books to help, or try to tie the conversation in with things that you see together on television.

4. *Do not leave all of the hot-button and serious issues off of the table.* The talk that you have about sex should include more than just the mechanics of how babies are made, because your kid wants (and needs) to know more than just the basics. Topics such as sexual orientation, masturbation, oral sex, and sexual assault should all be addressed too. You might think that teaching your kids how to avoid pregnancy is the only goal here, but keep in mind that vaginal intercourse is just one of many sexual activities teenagers might pursue and that not all children are heterosexual.

5. *Keep the conversation going and be sure to talk about relationships too.* Finally, keep in mind that "the talk" is not a one-time thing. This is an ongoing conversation. New questions are bound to come up and it is impossible to teach someone everything in the span of one conversation. Also, remember that your talks should not focus exclusively on sex – it is important to talk about relationships too. Developing healthy relationships is something most of us learn by trial and error. Sex, love, and intimacy go together, so try to relate these to one another over the course of your talks.

Note: Reprinted with permission from *The Psychology of Human Sexuality* blog (www.lehmiller.com).

Contraception

Although contraception is often discussed in the context of sex education, the focus is usually on condoms and birth control pills. In reality, however, there are dozens of methods and techniques that can help reduce the odds of pregnancy resulting from sexual activity. Before we detail these methods, let us begin with a brief history of birth control because I think it will give you a greater appreciation of both the sheer number of methods available today and their ease of use.

History

The concept of birth control is not new. In fact, we can trace the origins of fertility regulation back to the ancient Greeks and Egyptians. For example, one of the earliest known contraceptives was a diaphragm made out of crocodile excrement mixed with honey that Egyptian women would insert into the vaginal canal to block passage of sperm (Jutte, 2008). Why crocodile dung? I do not know, but suffice it to say, this was probably not the best idea. Other creative (and more sanitary) techniques emerged over time, such as jumping up and down or squatting and sneezing after sex as ways of expelling semen from the vagina. However, as you might imagine, these were not particularly effective methods either, and were probably rooted more in superstition than anything else.

In the 1500s, condoms made their debut (Youssef, 1993). The earliest condoms were either made of linen or animal intestines. It is not clear how effective those early condoms were, but it is possible that they had at least some efficacy, given both their popularity and the fact that condoms made from animal intestines are still produced and sold today (marketed as "skin" or "natural skin" condoms). Despite the fact that condoms were first developed centuries ago, they did not become cheap and widely available until recently. Mass production of condoms did not occur until the 1800s when vulcanized rubber was invented; however, those condoms were as thick as the tires on a bike and (obviously) were not particularly appealing or pleasurable. When latex rubber condoms were developed about a century later, the fit and feel of condoms was forever altered and they really caught on.

It is important to note that contraceptives, including condoms, were illegal in many parts of the world for much of recent history. In fact, in the United States, it was not until 1965 that the Supreme Court made a landmark ruling in *Griswold vs. Connecticut* that marital couples had a right to privacy that extended to the use of contraceptive devices. This means that just a few decades ago, people in some US states could not necessarily even get condoms if they wanted to, and were still forced to turn to homemade contraceptive remedies, including (I hate to say it) Coca-Cola douches. Just so you know, while Coca-Cola does indeed have spermicidal qualities, lab tests have found that Diet Coke is superior (Umpierre, 1985). That said, soda is not an effective contraceptive and is not recommended for such purposes because flushing the vagina with your favorite carbonated beverage can cause vaginal infections or, even worse, embolisms (i.e., air bubbles in the bloodstream that can block the flow of blood). In addition, sperm travel far too quickly for any type of post-sex douche to have significant contraceptive effects.

Fortunately, women and their partners have a multitude of far more effective and less scary options for birth control in the modern world due to scientific advances. In the following section, we will consider the major classes of contraceptives legally available and their unique strengths and weaknesses.

Types of Contraceptives

Behavioral Methods
The goal of behavioral methods of birth control is to prevent or reduce the odds of pregnancy by altering one's behaviors. The major advantage of this class of methods is that they are easy on your wallet and pose no health risks (unlike hormonal contraceptives). However, these behaviors are

challenging to implement perfectly because they require excellent relationship communication and because, as we noted in chapter 9, people have a limited ability to exert self-control. The major behavioral methods include abstinence, outercourse, withdrawal, and fertility awareness.

The strict definition of **abstinence** would be zero genital contact, but some people interpret this differently. For instance, consider the results of a study of 298 Canadian college students who were asked to determine whether each of 17 different behaviors were allowed according to their own personal definition of abstinence (Byers, Henderson, & Hobson, 2008). Results indicated that there was not 100% agreement on any behavior. Most participants felt that behaviors such as kissing (92.2%) and oral contact with the breasts (77.4%) were permissible during abstinence, and very few thought that penile–vaginal intercourse (6.8% without orgasm, 7.5% with orgasm) and penile–anal intercourse (11.1% without orgasm, 8.1% with orgasm) were permissible. Participants were more split on whether genital touching (59.2% without orgasm, 48.6% with orgasm) and oral sex were acceptable (43.7% without orgasm, 39.1% with orgasm). As you can see, there is no universal definition of abstinence, so it can be hard to know exactly what someone means when they say they are "abstinent." That said, if one's definition prohibits penile–vaginal intercourse, abstinence is the only guaranteed way of preventing pregnancy because it would not allow semen to come into contact with the female reproductive tract.

Outercourse refers to any type of sexual activity other than penile–vaginal intercourse. Thus, outercourse may mean very different things to different people, but the basic goal (similar to abstinence) is preventing sperm from entering the vagina. This will virtually guarantee pregnancy prevention, assuming that nothing slips and goes where it is not supposed to go during sexual activity.

Withdrawal, also known as *coitus interruptus* and "pull and pray," refers to removing the penis from the vagina prior to ejaculation. This method provides *some* protection from pregnancy, but is not perfect because (1) the pre-ejaculate secreted by the Cowper's glands has the potential to contain active sperm (as discussed in chapter 3) and, perhaps more importantly, (2) some guys are not particularly good at judging when they are going to ejaculate. How effective is withdrawal? For this and the other contraceptive methods that follow, we will discuss effectiveness in terms of both perfect use and typical use. For purposes of this book, **perfect use** will tell you the percentage of women who will *not* get pregnant over the course of a year if they utilized a given method consistently and never made a mistake. However, perfect use is rarely achieved in the real world, so you should pay more attention to **typical use** rates, which provide the same information, but account for human error. With that said, withdrawal is 96% effective with perfect use, but only 78% effective with typical use (Trussel, 2011). Thus, while withdrawal is better than nothing, it is not something you can bank on in practice. To compare perfect and typical use rates for all forms of contraception covered in this chapter, see Table 10.2.

Fertility awareness refers to a class of methods that attempt to inform women when they are most likely to be fertile so that they can temporarily abstain from vaginal intercourse or use barriers. There are many possibilities here, including the *standard days method*, which involves plotting the menstrual cycle on a calendar to determine which days are likely "safer" to have sex, and the *symptothermal method*, which involves checking for biological indicators of ovulation (e.g., cervical mucus consistency and body temperature). When a woman is ovulating, the consistency of her cervical mucus resembles egg whites, and her body temperature immediately after awakening in the morning will be slightly elevated. Overall, effectiveness rates for fertility awareness methods are similar to withdrawal (see Table 10.2), but biological methods tend to be more effective than the calendar method.

Table 10.2 Typical and Perfect Use Effectiveness Rates for Various Contraceptives

Method	Effectiveness rates	
	Typical use	*Perfect use*
No method	15%	15%
Spermicide	72%	82%
Fertility awareness methods	76%	95–99.6%
Withdrawal	78%	96%
Female condom	79%	95%
Male condom	82%	98%
Diaphragm	88%	94%
Oral contraceptives (combined & progestin-only)	91%	99.7%
Contraceptive patch	91%	99.7%
Vaginal ring	91%	99.7%
Depo-Provera	94%	99.8%
IUD	99.2–99.8%	99.4–99.8%
Contraceptive implant	99.95%	99.95%
Female sterilization	99.5%	99.5%
Male sterilization	99.85%	99.9%

Note: Numbers indicate the percentage of women who will *not* become pregnant after one year of use. Adapted from Trussel, J. (2011). Contraceptive failure in the United States. *Contraception, 83*, 397–404, with permission from Elsevier.

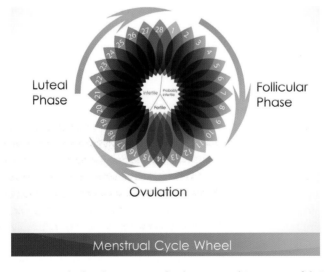

Figure 10.3 Fertility awareness methods utilize a variety of techniques to advise women of their fertile periods, during which time they will either abstain from sex or use barriers. ©Gunita Reine/123RF.COM.

Barrier Methods

The purpose of barrier methods is to prevent sperm from reaching the uterus during penile–vaginal intercourse. These methods are good for people who do not have sex on a regular basis because they do not need to be practiced every day in order to be successful. However, partners have to use them every time *and* use them correctly to avert unintended pregnancy. This class of methods includes male and female condoms, spermicides, and cervical barriers (i.e., diaphragms and cervical caps).

Male condoms consist of a thin latex (or polyurethane, for people with latex allergies) sheath that covers an erect penis during sexual activity. Condoms are one of the most popular methods of birth control in use today (Mosher & Jones, 2010) and offer a major advantage over other contraceptives in that they also provide some protection against STIs. With perfect use, condoms are 98% effective at preventing pregnancy, but when you factor in human error, that drops to 82% (Trussel, 2011). Why? A review of 50 condom use studies revealed 14 common errors people make when using condoms (Sanders et al., 2012). In some studies, up to 51% of participants reported putting a condom on *after intercourse had already started*, up to 45% reported removing a condom *before intercourse was over*, and nearly half reported condom application errors that increase the likelihood of breakage, such as failing to leave space at the tip to collect semen or failing to squeeze air from the tip while putting the condom on. Other errors included failing to withdraw promptly after ejaculation (which can allow semen to leak out of the condom), using latex-incompatible lubricants (e.g., oil-based), and (I wish I did not have to say this) re-using the same condom multiple times. Is it any wonder typical use rates are as low as they are?

Female condoms are a polyurethane pouch that lines the interior of the vagina. The penis is then inserted through a ring that sits outside of the vaginal opening. On a side note, although these are called "female" condoms, they are sometimes used by men who have sex with men during anal sex for STI protection. Female condoms are not as widely used as male condoms (and, in fact, it can be difficult to even find them in some places), but some women opt for them because they prefer female-controlled methods of contraception and/or because the external ring may provide some degree of clitoral stimulation during sex. Effectiveness rates are similar to male condoms, but slightly lower overall (see Table 10.2).

Spermicides are chemicals that are placed inside the vagina that attempt to kill or disable sperm for a certain period of time. Although spermicides come in many different forms (i.e., foams, creams,

Figure 10.4 Female condoms are less well-known and utilized than male condoms; however, both are desirable in that they provide at least some protection from STIs. Image Copyright nito, 2013. Used under license from Shutterstock.com.

jellies, and suppositories), they all have about the same effectiveness rate. With perfect use it is 82% and with typical use, 72%. Because of the relatively low effectiveness rate even with perfect use, spermicides are perhaps best coupled with other methods of birth control, such as condoms and diaphragms.

Cervical barriers are devices that obstruct sperm from entering the cervix. These devices include the *diaphragm* and *cervical cap*. The only difference between the two is that the diaphragm is larger and covers the upper portion of the vaginal wall as well. Before insertion, cervical barriers are usually lined with a spermicide to provide additional protection. After sex, the diaphragm must remain in place for at least six hours to prevent live sperm entering the cervix. On the plus side, one of these devices can last up to a year or longer with regular use, but it must be inserted prior to each sex act and requires that the woman is *very* comfortable with her own body. Diaphragms are 96% effective with perfect use, and 88% effective with typical use (Trussel, 2011).

Hormonal Methods

Hormonal forms of birth control have the effect of temporarily reducing female fertility. They accomplish this through a combination of three factors: (1) preventing ovulation, (2) thickening the cervical mucus in order to make it more difficult for sperm to enter the uterus, and (3) altering the uterine lining to make it impossible for a fertilized egg to implant (Kiley & Hammond, 2007). The main advantages of these methods over others are increased effectiveness and the establishment of a predictable menstrual cycle. The main disadvantages are hormone-related health risks, the potential for medication interactions, possible weight gain, and sexual side effects (e.g., reduced sexual interest and arousal); however, the side effects vary widely depending upon which specific contraceptive is being used and each woman's unique body chemistry.

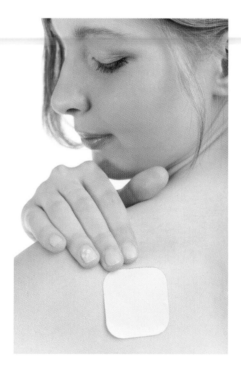

Figure 10.5   Combined hormonal methods of contraception come in a variety of forms and dosages to meet women's needs, such as the contraceptive patch. ©Tomasz Trojanowski/123RF.COM.

There are two main types of hormonal methods: combined (i.e., joint administration of estrogen and progestin) and progestin-only. The **combined hormone methods** can take many forms, including "the pill," the contraceptive patch, and the vaginal ring. The way these methods differ is in terms of how the hormones are administered and the required "maintenance." With "the pill," hormones are administered orally with one pill each day. With the patch, hormones are absorbed through the skin via a patch that is replaced weekly. With the ring, hormones are absorbed through the vaginal tissues via a ring that is replaced once per month. One other important difference between these methods is that, unlike the patch and ring, "the pill" comes in dozens of different formulations, meaning it is easier to find an oral contraceptive to match a given woman's body chemistry. It is partly for this reason that "the pill" remains one of the most commonly used methods of birth control (for some sense of the most popular forms of contraception among women in the United States, see Figure 10.7). Effectiveness rates for all three of these methods are identical: 91% with typical use and 99.7% with perfect use (Trussel, 2011).

For women who cannot take estrogen for health reasons (i.e., women who smoke or are at high risk of heart disease), several **progestin-only methods** of birth control are available, including the progestin-only pill, the hormonal injection, the hormonal intrauterine device (IUD), the contraceptive implant, and emergency contraception. Compared to the combined methods, the progestin-only methods (other than the pill) typically cost more money up front (if they are not covered by insurance), but this is balanced out by much longer-lasting protection. Side effects are similar to the combined hormone methods, but irregular bleeding is more likely to occur.

While the progestin-only pill is similar to the combined pill in terms of how it works and its effectiveness, the other methods work quite differently. The hormonal injection (Depo-Provera – see chapter 4 for other uses of this drug) is administered once every three months and provides very long-lasting fertility reduction. In fact, it can take nearly a year for fertility to resume once injections are stopped, compared to just a few weeks for oral contraceptives. That said, one unique risk to the hormone injection is the potential for bone density loss; however, such effects appear to be reversible when injections are discontinued (Scholes, LaCroix, Ichikawa, Barlow, & Ott, 2005). The hormonal IUD is a small, plastic device shaped like a "T" that is inserted into the uterus by a physician. It lasts the longest of all contraceptives currently on the market (it can prevent pregnancy for up to five years!) and is so highly effective that it is sometimes referred to as "reversible sterilization" (MacIsaac & Espey, 2007). The contraceptive implant is a tiny plastic rod that is surgically

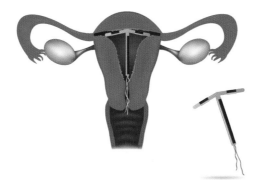

Figure 10.6 An IUD sits inside the uterus like this and can remain in place and effective for up to five years. ©Gunita Reine / 123RF.COM.

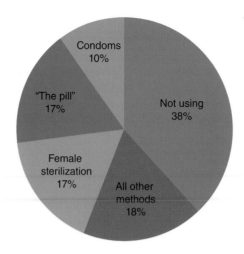

Figure 10.7   This chart depicts contraceptive use patterns among US women ages 15–44. About 62% of women of childbearing age actively use some form of contraception. Source: Mosher & Jones (2010).

implanted into the upper arm. The implant secretes hormones for several years and provides long-lasting effects. All three of these methods (injection, IUD, and implant) are highly effective with both typical and perfect use (see Table 10.2). For women who want a long-lasting and highly effective contraceptive but are concerned about hormonal side effects, there is also an IUD made of copper. It works equally well because copper ions act as a spermicide inside of the uterus.

One additional progestin-only method is **emergency contraception** (EC), a hormone pill that is meant to prevent pregnancy after an instance of unprotected intercourse (e.g., as a result of a broken condom or a sexual assault). These pills may be taken up to five days after unprotected sex and they work by preventing a fertilized egg from implanting in the uterus. Please note that if implantation has already occurred, EC will not affect it. In other words, EC will not cause an abortion, which is one of the most common misconceptions about how this drug works. How effective is EC? The label for *Plan B* (one of the most popular forms of EC) cites an 89% reduction in likelihood of becoming pregnant if taken according to instructions. In the US, EC is currently legally available to women and girls ages 15 and older and can be purchased over the counter (i.e., without a prescription). In the event that EC is difficult or impossible to access (e.g., if your local pharmacy chooses not to keep it in stock or it is not affordable), it is possible to mimic the effects of EC by ingesting a hefty dose of combined hormone birth control pills; however, it is important to consult with a health care provider to determine the correct dosage.

Psychological effects of hormonal contraception.   Most women realize that being on a hormonal contraceptive means putting up with a few side effects, such as weight gain, mood changes, or nausea. However, one side effect you almost never hear about is the fact that hormonal methods of birth control may alter women's sexual behaviors and the types of men that heterosexual women are attracted to. Before we get into specifics, please note from chapter 3 that there are four phases of the menstrual cycle, with ovulation being the fertile period (i.e., the point with the highest probability of conception). During ovulation, several hormones are released that prep the body for a potential pregnancy; however, in addition to causing changes in the reproductive tract, these hormones affect the female brain, thereby modifying female sexual preferences and behaviors in several ways.

First, when women are near ovulation, their grooming habits and clothing choices change, seemingly in an effort to appear more attractive. As support for this idea, research has found that participants can pick out photographs of women taken while they were ovulating compared to photos taken during other phases of the menstrual cycle because ovulating women appear to go for "nicer" and "more fashionable" outfits that show more skin (Haselton, Mortezaie, Pillsworth, Bleske-Rechek, & Frederick, 2007). In addition, in a study where women engaged in online clothing shopping at different stages of the menstrual cycle, researchers found that ovulating women put a greater percentage of sexy items in their shopping carts than nonovulating women (Durante, Griskevicius, Hill, Perilloux, & Li, 2011). Also, if you recall from chapter 4, ovulating strippers earned higher tips than strippers who were using hormonal contraceptives (Miller, Tybur, & Jordan, 2007), another finding that suggests women's behaviors may change throughout the menstrual cycle. Other research has found that when women are ovulating, the pitch of their voice (Bryant & Haselton, 2009), their body movements (Fink, Hugill, Lange, 2012), and their bodily scent change in ways that increase their attractiveness to men (Havlíček, Dvořáková, Bartoš, & Flegr, 2006). Such findings raise legitimate questions about the oft-cited notion in many biology textbooks that human females have "concealed ovulation."

Second, heterosexual women are attracted to different types of men during ovulation. Specifically, ovulating women show an exaggerated preference for short-term sexual relationships with guys who have masculine faces, hot bodies, and lots of confidence (think Channing Tatum, Hugh Jackman, and other guys who have been named "Sexiest Man Alive") compared to women at other stages of their cycle (Gangestad, Thornhill, & Garver-Apgar, 2005). This preference is not just visual either. During ovulation, women prefer men who have deeper voices (Puts, 2005), as well as the bodily scents of "manlier" men (Gangestad & Thornhill, 1998). Evolutionary psychologists have reasoned that this is because masculine guys offer the best genetic material for making babies because masculine features are supposedly a sign of a strong immune system (Gangestad & Buss, 1993). The idea is that masculine features are a product of high testosterone, but testosterone actually suppresses the immune system. Thus, for a hypermasculine man to survive this immunosuppression, he has to have very strong, disease-resisting genes to begin with. If that is the case, then why is masculinity not universally preferred across the menstrual cycle? Perhaps because women see masculine men as less reliable partners who are more likely to cheat (e.g., O'Connor, Re, & Feinberg, 2011). Masculine men are therefore only seen as good sexual partners during those periods where his genetic benefits can be conferred to a woman's offspring; women's preference for these men declines when no such reproductive benefits are possible.

So what happens when women take hormonal contraceptives? These ovulatory shifts in mating preferences and behaviors get wiped out. For one thing, these women do not show the same cyclical sexual desire for masculine men. Also, in the study of exotic dancers, women who were on "the pill" did not see an increase in tips at any point during the month, suggesting that they did not alter their style of dress and behavior in the same way as naturally-cycling women (Miller et al., 2007). Perhaps even more fascinating is research demonstrating that women taking oral contraceptives seem to pick more reliable partners and have longer-lasting relationships than their naturally-cycling counterparts, perhaps because women on "the pill" show a more stable preference for a certain type of guy (Roberts et al., 2012). One caveat to this research is that most work looking at how hormonal contraceptives are related to female sexual behavior has focused on the combined hormone pill. While it is likely that all hormonal contraceptives would have similar psychological effects, that has not yet been systematically studied.

Figure 10.8   Heterosexual women report greater attraction to masculine men like Channing Tatum when they are ovulating compared to other stages of the menstrual cycle. Image Copyright s_bukley, 2013. Used under license from Shutterstock.com.

Other Methods

There are several other methods of birth control available, including male and female sterilization. Sterilization is the most common form of birth control in the United States and throughout the world (see Figure 10.6). Female sterilization is known as **tubal ligation** and involves clamping or severing the fallopian tubes so that any eggs released cannot come into contact with sperm, thus making fertilization impossible. Male sterilization (i.e., **vasectomy**) involves severing or sealing the vas deferens so that sperm can no longer become part of the seminal fluid. Both procedures are considered permanent and although it may be possible to have them surgically reversed, it is not guaranteed. Sterilization is virtually 100% effective at preventing pregnancy (Trussel, 2011).

Most of the methods of birth control covered in this chapter involve regulating female fertility in some way. Aside from vasectomies, are there any other ways of biologically regulating male fertility? Some scientists think so. See the Digging Deeper 10.2 box for more on this growing area of research.

Choosing the Right Contraceptive

There are lots of decisions to be made when it comes to choosing a contraceptive, and what is right for one woman and her relationship may not necessarily be right for others. Certainly, effectiveness is one important consideration, but you also need to look at potential side effects, convenience, and individual comfort. It is also vital to take into account how much protection you want

Figure 10.9 Sterilization involves severing the fallopian tubes (female) or vas deferens (male) in order to eliminate the possibility of conception. Image Copyright Graeme Dawes, 2013. Used under license from Shutterstock.com.

Digging Deeper 10.2 How Close Are We to Having a Male Version of "The Pill?"

It is a simple biological fact that regulating female fertility is less complicated than regulating male fertility. Just think about it: is it easier to try and stop one egg per month from being released, or to try and stop up to a half billion sperm from being released *per ejaculation*? Despite this challenge, some scientists have been hard at work trying to create the male equivalent of "the pill" and their research has yielded some promising new developments.

For the past few decades, there have only been two options for guys who want to ensure they do not accidentally get a woman pregnant: use a condom or get a vasectomy. Unfortunately, these options represent two extreme ends of the spectrum. Condoms must be used correctly and consistently each time, and some guys complain of dulled sexual sensation. Vasectomies eliminate these concerns because after surgery, there are no special precautions to take and no loss in sensation. The downside of vasectomies is that they are expensive and are not guaranteed to be reversible. Thus, if a guy thinks he might want to father future children, he is probably better off sticking with condoms. Is there any way to get the best of both worlds? Is there something that neither reduces sexual sensation nor runs the risk of creating permanent infertility?

Two procedures may have such potential. One is something reported in the media as the "testicular zap," in which a specialized ultrasound is performed on the testicles. A study testing this on rats found that two 15-minute ultrasounds administered two days apart had the effect of significantly reducing sperm count (Tsuruta et al., 2012). It is yet to be determined whether this would have the same effect in humans and how often it would need to be performed, but this technique is promising for its noninvasive nature.

The other procedure involves injecting a polymer into the vas deferens. This polymer stays in place and disables sperm as they pass by. It is known as Reversible Inhibition of Sperm Under Guidance (RISUG; Sharma, Chaudhury, Jagannathan, & Guha, 2001). Despite the rather unfortunate name and acronym, it sounds more pleasant than the testicular "zap." This procedure does not affect sperm production; rather, it serves to immobilize sperm before they can exit the body. It is supposedly reversible by flushing the polymer out of the vas deferens. RISUG is currently undergoing clinical trials.

Before those of you with scrotums get excited about being zapped and injected, I should warn you that we are a way off from either of these methods becoming widespread around the globe. We do not have enough evidence of the effectiveness of these procedures and their potential long-term side effects to start performing them routinely. For the time being, you will probably want to keep that condom drawer fully stocked.

Note: Reprinted with permission from *The Psychology of Human Sexuality* blog (www.lehmiller.com).

from STIs, because aside from strict abstinence, condoms (both male and female) are the only method that can reduce risk from a wide range of infections. Your best bet is to consult with a health care provider about your concerns and current physical condition and to communicate with your partner about your goals and sexual health needs.

Pregnancy

We will round out this chapter with a brief discussion of pregnancy. As mentioned above, the menstrual cycle exerts profound effects on female psychology at different stages. Perhaps not surprisingly, the hormonal changes that occur during and after pregnancy can have a range of psychological effects as well. We begin by addressing the psychological changes associated with trying to get pregnant before moving on to the changes that occur after a child has been conceived.

The Psychology of Trying to Have a Baby

The act of trying to get pregnant can be both exciting and stressful. The nature of the experience is dependent upon how long the couple has been trying, how much pressure the partners put on one another, and whether there are any fertility issues present. The more that sex starts to become a rigidly structured chore, the more performance pressure there is, and the longer a couple tries to get pregnant unsuccessfully, the more stressful things end up being. Stress effects are particularly pronounced among couples in which one or both partners are facing fertility problems (Oddens, den Tonkelaar, & Nieuwenhuyse, 1999). The prevalence of infertility varies across countries, but the estimated median prevalence is 9% (Boivin, Bunting, Collins, & Nygren, 2007). This means that about one in ten couples will have difficulty conceiving within a year. Infertility is something that can affect both men and women. As a result, it is important for both partners to be checked. It should be noted that infertility is not just a stressor faced by heterosexual couples; same-sex couples who are trying to have their own biological children may grapple with this as well. Having a baby is equally stressful regardless of the sex and sexuality of the parents involved and the way that the child is being conceived.

Figure 10.10 Trying to have a child and the transition to parenthood are stressful events for people of all sexes and sexualities—not just for heterosexual couples. ©Maria Dubova / 123RF.COM.

Of course, it is important to note that not all pregnancies are planned. Whereas a planned pregnancy usually results in feelings of joy and relief, unintentional pregnancies can have a much wider range of effects. Some people may be very pleased by the surprise, while others have a difficult time adapting to it. In general, unplanned pregnancies are more likely to result in the parents feeling stressed and powerless regarding the changes that are about to occur (Clinton & Kelber, 1993).

Psychological Changes During Pregnancy and After Birth

There are many stereotypes about pregnant women perpetuated by the popular media, with one of the most common being that pregnant women are unstable and irrational, exhibiting wild mood swings. In reality, however, the psychological effects of pregnancy vary, and it is not just pregnant women who experience psychological changes – their partners do as well.

One of the more common changes is depression. In fact, in the industrialized world, rates of female depression vary from 7 to 15% during pregnancy and are about 10% *postpartum* (i.e., after pregnancy; O'Keane, & Marsh, 2007). Why does this affect so many women? For one thing, the act of being pregnant and raising a new child is demanding both physically and psychologically. However, there are direct biological effects of pregnancy as well, because pregnancy-related hormone changes affect the portions of the brain that regulate mood (O'Keane & Marsh, 2007). The risk of depression is particularly pronounced in women with a past history of mood disorders. It is important to note that pregnancy-related depression can also occur in nonpregnant partners. For instance, research has found that about 10% of fathers experience depression during either the prenatal or postpartum periods (Paulson & Bazemore, 2010).

Changes in sexual interest and behavior are also common during pregnancy. For instance, up to half of women in survey studies report worrying that sex while pregnant will harm their baby (vod Sydow, 1999). Specifically, many women who have male partners are concerned that their child will be traumatized or "poked" during vaginal intercourse. As a result, this may decrease the frequency of sexual activity and reduce enjoyment for both partners, which can create stress and relationship turmoil. However, you will be glad to know that vaginal intercourse during pregnancy is generally safe as long as both partners are in good health and the pregnancy is not high-risk. In fact, research has found that the majority of heterosexual couples have sex up until the seventh month, and about one-third report having sex up until the ninth month (vod Sydow, 1999); however, different intercourse positions may be necessary later in the pregnancy to make the woman more comfortable.

Finally, major psychological changes often arise when problems are encountered during the pregnancy. For instance, the discovery that the fetus possesses a major birth defect can be highly distressing to the parents. The same goes for very premature births in which functional development is not yet complete. In addition, some pregnancies end spontaneously in *miscarriage*. In fact, it is estimated that 15–20% of pregnancies end in miscarriage (American College of Obstetricians and Gynecologists, 2011). Although most miscarriages occur early on, and may not necessarily even be detected in some cases (i.e., when it occurs before the pregnancy is known), miscarriages sometimes happen much later on. In such cases, the effect can be psychologically devastating for the parents. Research suggests that clinically significant depression and anxiety are common among women following a miscarriage, as are feelings of guilt (Frost & Condon, 1996). Although most research has focused on the psychological effects on mothers, miscarriage can also result in emotional disturbances for partners and surviving children.

Abortion

When a pregnancy is unwanted, an elective abortion is sometimes pursued. **Abortion** is a catch-all term for a number of different medical procedures capable of ending a pregnancy. Abortions that occur within the first few weeks of pregnancy can be accomplished with medications, whereas later abortions require more involved surgical procedures. No matter when or what methods are utilized, allowing women the option to voluntarily end a pregnancy is controversial. Some people believe it should never happen, others believe it should only happen under certain circumstances, and some believe it should always be a viable option. The purpose of this section is not to wade into that debate, but rather to address why abortions are sometimes sought, their psychological effects, and what can be done to reduce the number of unintended pregnancies so that fewer women find themselves in the position of having to make this difficult decision.

Women cite multiple reasons for pursuing abortions. For instance, a study of 671 women from the southern US revealed that the most commonly cited reasons were as follows (note that women could indicate more than one reason): not being able to afford a child (48.2%), not being ready for children (39.9%), not wanting additional children (35.8%), being in an unstable relationship (21.8%), being too young for kids (25.1%), and having personal health problems (9.5%; Santelli, Speizer, Avery, & Kendall, 2006). Based upon these reasons, it is clear that almost all of these women were seeking abortions because their pregnancies were unintended.

How do women feel after having an abortion? A separate study of 442 women who were followed for two years after undergoing the procedure revealed that the majority (72%) were satisfied with their decision and a similar number reported that they would have done the same thing again (Major et al., 2000). That said, this study also revealed that 20% of the women experienced at least one episode of clinical depression after the procedure, and 1% met the criteria for post-traumatic stress disorder or PTSD (for more on the nature of PTSD, see chapter 14). Experiencing depression prior to the pregnancy was a very strong predictor of experiencing depression after the abortion. Thus, although the vast majority of women who get abortions do not regret doing so, some women are unhappy with the outcome. Less research exists on men's psychological reactions to their partner's abortions, but existing studies paint a similar picture: most men report being satisfied with their partner's decision to have an abortion, but some report pain and sadness afterward (Kero & Lalos, 2004).

Given that so many abortions are pursued as a result of unplanned and unwanted pregnancies, it would seem logical to assume that with better sex education and greater access to effective contraception, we could dramatically reduce the abortion rate, an outcome that most people would probably see as a good thing. Consider that fewer abortions would mean that public health clinics would have more resources available for addressing other urgent sexual health needs (e.g., STI screenings), and fewer women would be faced with a decision that can be incredibly difficult and stressful. So is this possible? Research suggests that it is. Peipert, Madden, Allsworth, and Secura (2012), recruited 9,256 US women at high risk of unwanted pregnancy to participate in a longitudinal study. All participants were given free contraceptive counseling and received their choice of birth control. Most women opted for either the IUD or contraceptive implant. Results revealed that study participants evidenced significantly lower rates of teen pregnancy and abortion compared to the national average. For instance, across the three years of the study, the abortion rate among participants fluctuated between 4.4 and 7.5 per 1,000 women, while the national rate stood at 19.6 per 1,000. These findings suggest that reducing teen pregnancy and abortions can be effectively achieved through better education and access to free contraceptives. Such efforts would likely have the added benefit of dramatically reducing rates of STIs, the topic we turn to in the next chapter.

Key Terms

abstinence-only approach	perfect use	combined hormone
abstinence-plus	typical use	methods
comprehensive sex	fertility awareness	progestin-only methods
education	male condoms	emergency contraception
abstinence	female condoms	tubal ligation
outercourse	spermicides	vasectomy
withdrawal	cervical barriers	abortion

Discussion Questions: What is Your Perspective on Sex?

- Parents have mixed feelings about the discussion of masturbation, homosexuality, and abortion in school-based sex education courses. Do you think these topics should be addressed? Why or why not?
- How do you define "abstinence?" What sexual behaviors can someone engage in and still be considered "abstinent?"
- Do the psychological effects of hormonal contraceptives make you think any differently about this form of birth control? Do you think women should be aware that this type of birth control could potentially alter their behaviors and the partners they are attracted to?

References

Albert, B. (2010). With one voice 2010: America's adults and teens sound off about teen pregnancy. *The National Campaign to Prevent Teen and Unplanned Pregnancy*. Retrieved from http://www.thenationalcampaign.org/resources/pdf/pubs/wov_2010.pdf (accessed September 5, 2013).

Alford, S., & Hauser, D. (2011). Adolescent sexual health in Europe and the US. Retrieved from http://www.advocatesforyouth.org/component/content/article/419-adolescent-sexual-health-in-europe-and-the-us (accessed September 5, 2013).

American College of Obstetricians and Gynecologists (2011). Early pregnancy loss: Miscarriage and molar pregnancy. Retrieved from http://www.acog.org/~/media/For%20Patients/faq090.pdf?dmc=1&ts=20130603T2022576459 (accessed September 5, 2013).

Boivin, J., Bunting, L., Collins, J.A., & Nygren, K.G. (2007). International estimates of infertility prevalence and treatment-seeking: Potential need and demand for infertility medical care. *Human Reproduction, 22*, 1506–1512. DOI:10.1093/humrep/dem046.

Bowater, D. (2011). Pornography is replacing sex education. *Daily Telegraph*. Retrieved from http://www.telegraph.co.uk/education/educationnews/8961010/Pornography-is-replacing-sex-education.html (accessed September 5, 2013).

Bryant, G.A., & Haselton, M.G. (2009). Vocal cues of ovulation in human females. *Biology Letters, 5*(1), 12–15. DOI:10.1098/rsbl.2008.0507.

Byers, E.S., Henderson, J., & Hobson, K.M. (2009). University students' definitions of sexual abstinence and having sex. *Archives of Sexual Behavior, 38*, 665–674. DOI:10.1007/s10508-007-9289-6.

CDC (2012a). Sexual risk behavior: HIV, STD, & teen pregnancy prevention. Retrieved from http://www.cdc.gov/HealthyYouth/sexualbehaviors/ (accessed September 5, 2013).

CDC (2012b). *Key statistics from the National Survey of Family Growth*. Retrieved from http://www.cdc.gov/nchs/nsfg/key_statistics.htm (accessed September 5, 2013).

Clinton, J.F., & Kelber, S.T. (1993). Stress and coping in fathers of newborns: Comparisons of planned versus unplanned pregnancy. *International Journal of Nursing Studies, 30*, 437–443. DOI:10.1016/0020-7489(93)90053-W.

Committee on Government Reform (2004). *The content of federally funded abstinence-only education programs*. Retrieved from http://spot.colorado.edu/~tooley/HenryWaxman.pdf (accessed September 5, 2013).

Dima, B. (2013). Case study: Kids & online threats. Retrieved from http://www.bitdefender.com/media/materials/white-papers/en/Bitdefender-CaseStudy-Kids.pdf (accessed September 5, 2013).

Durante, K.M., Griskevicius, V., Hill, S.E., Perilloux, C., & Li, N.P. (2011). Ovulation, female competition, and product choice: Hormonal influences on consumer behavior. *Journal of Consumer Research, 37*, 921–934. DOI:10.1086/656575.

Eisenberg, D.L., Secura, G.M, Madden, T.E., Allsworth, J.E., Zhao, Q., & Piepert, J.F. (2012). Knowledge of contraceptive effectiveness. *American Journal of Obstetrics and Gynecology, 206*, 479.e1–e9. DOI:10.1016/j.ajog.2012.04.012.

Fink, B., Hugill, N., & Lange, B.P. (2012). Women's body movements are a potential cue to ovulation. *Personality and Individual Differences, 53*, 759–763. DOI:10.1016/j.paid.2012.06.005.

Frost, M. & Condon, J.T. (1996). The psychological sequelae of miscarriage: A critical review of the literature. *Australian and New Zealand Journal of Psychiatry, 30*, 54–62.

Gangestad, S.W., & Buss, D.M. (1993). Pathogen prevalence and human mate preferences. *Ethology & Sociobiology, 14*, 89–96. DOI:10.1016/0162-3095(93)90009-7.

Gangestad, S.W., & Thornhill, R. (1998). Menstrual cycle variation in women's preferences for the scent of symmetrical men. *Proceedings of the Royal Society of London. Series B: Biological Sciences, 265*, 927–933. DOI:10.1098/rspb.1998.0380.

Gangestad, S.W., Thornhill, R., & Garver-Apgar, C.E. (2005). Adaptations to ovulation: Implications for sexual and social behavior. *Current Directions in Psychological Science, 14*, 312–316. DOI:10.1111/j.0963-7214.2005.00388.x.

Hamilton, B.E., & Ventura, S.J. (2012). Birth rates for U.S. teenagers reach historic lows for all age and ethnic groups. NCHS Data Brief, *89*. Retrieved from http://www.cdc.gov/nchs/data/databriefs/db89.htm (accessed September 5, 2013).

Haselton, M.G., Mortezaie, M., Pillsworth, E.G., Bleske-Rechek, A., & Frederick, D.A. (2007) Ovulatory shifts in human female ornamentation: Near ovulation, women dress to impress. *Hormones and Behavior, 51*, 40–45. DOI:10.1016/j.yhbeh.2006.07.007.

Havlíček, J., Dvořáková, R., Bartoš, L., & Flegr, J. (2006). Non-Advertized does not Mean Concealed: Body Odour Changes across the Human Menstrual Cycle. *Ethology, 112*(1), 81–90. DOI:10.1111/j.1439-0310.2006.01125.x.

Jutte, R. (2008). *Contraception: A history.* Cambridge, UK: Polity Press.

Kero, A., & Lalos, A. (2004). Reactions and reflections in men, 4 and 12 months post-abortion. *Journal of Psychosomatic Obstetrics & Gynecology, 25*, 135–143. DOI:10.1080/01674820400000463.

Kiley, J., & Hammond, C. (2007). Combined oral contraceptives: A comprehensive review. *Clinical Obstetrics and Gynecology, 50*, 868–877. DOI:10.1097/GRF.0b013e318159c06a.

Kohler, P.K., Manhart, L.E., & Lafferty, W.E. (2008). Abstinence-only and comprehensive sex education and the initiation of sexual activity and teen pregnancy. *Journal of Adolescent Health, 42*, 344–351. DOI:10.1016/j.jadohealth.2007.08.026.

MacIsaac, L., & Espey, E. (2007). Intrauterine contraception: The pendulum swings back. *Obstetrics and Gynecology Clinics of North America, 34*, 91–111. DOI:10.1016/j.ogc.2007.02.004.

Major, B., Cozzarelli, C., Cooper, M., Zubek, J., Richards, C., Wilhite, M., & Gramzow, R.H. (2000). Psychological responses of women after first-trimester abortion. *Archives of General Psychiatry, 57*, 777–784. DOI:10.1001/archpsyc.57.8.777.

Martinez, G., Abma, J., & Copen, C. (2010). Educating teenagers about sex in the United States. NCHS Data Brief, *44*. Retrieved from http://www.cdc.gov/nchs/data/databriefs/db44.pdf (accessed September 5, 2013).

Miller, G., Tybur, J. M., & Jordan, B.D. (2007). Ovulatory cycle effects on tip earnings by lap dancers: Economic evidence for human estrus? *Evolution and Human Behavior, 28*, 375–381. DOI:10.1016/j.evolhumbehav.2007.06.002.

Mosher, W.D., & Jones, J. (2010). Use of contraception in the United States: 1982–2008. National Center for Health Statistics. Vital and Health Statistics, 23(29). Retrieved from http://www.cdc.gov/nchs/data/series/sr_23/sr23_029.pdf (accessed September 5, 2013).

NPR (2004). *Sex education in America: An NPR/Kaiser/Kennedy School poll.* Retrieved from http://www.npr.org/templates/story/story.php?storyId=1622610 (accessed September 5, 2013).

O'Connor, J.J.M., Re, D.E., & Feinberg, D.R. (2011). Voice pitch influences perceptions of sexual infidelity. *Evolutionary Psychology, 9*, 64–78.

Oddens, B.J., den Tonkelaar, I., & Nieuwenhuyse, H. (1999). Psychosocial experiences in women facing fertility problems—a comparative survey. *Human Reproduction, 14*, 255–261. DOI:10.1093/humrep/14.1.255.

O'Keane, V., & Marsh, M.S. (2007). Depression during pregnancy. *British Medical Journal, 334*, 1003–1005. DOI:10.1136/bmj.39189.662581.55.

Paulson, J.F., & Bazemore, S.D. (2010). Prenatal and postpartum depression in fathers and its association with maternal depression: A meta-analysis. *JAMA: Journal of the American Medical Association, 303*, 1961–1969. DOI:10.1001/jama.2010.605.

Peipert, J.F., Madden, T., Allsworth, J.E., & Secura, G.M. (2012in press). Preventing unintended pregnancies by providing no-cost contraception. *Obstetrics & Gynecology, 120*, 1291–1297. DOI:10.1097/AOG.0b013e318273eb56.

Philpott, A., Knerr, W., & Boydell, V. (2006). Pleasure and prevention: when good sex is safer sex. *Reproductive Health Matters, 14*, 23–31.

Puts, D.A. (2005). Mating context and menstrual phase affect women's preferences for male voice pitch. *Evolution and Human Behavior, 26*, 388–397. DOI:10.1016/j.evolhumbehav.2005.03.001.

Roberts, C.S., Klapilova, K., Little, A.C., Burriss, R.P., Jones, B.C., DeBruine, L.M., Petrie, M., & Havlíček, J. (2012). Relationship satisfaction and outcome in women who meet their partner while using oral contraception. *Proceedings of the Royal Society B, 279*, 1430–1436. DOI:10.1098/rspb.2011.1647.

Sanders, S.A., Yarber, W.L., Kaufman, E.L., Crosby, R.A., Graham, C.A., & Milhausen, R.R. (2012). Condom use errors and problems: A global view. *Sexual Health*, *9*, 81–95. DOI:10.1071/SH11095.

Santelli, J.S., Speizer, I.S., Avery, A., & Kendall, C. (2006). An exploration of the dimensions of pregnancy intentions among women choosing to terminate or to initiate prenatal care in New Orleans, Louisiana. *American Journal of Public Health*, *96*, 2009–2015. DOI:10.2105/AJPH.2005.064584.

Scholes, D., LaCroix, A.Z., Ichikawa, L.E., Barlow, W.E., & Ott, S.M. (2005). Change in bone mineral density among adolescent women using and discontinuing depot medroxyprogesterone acetate contraception. *Archives of Pediatrics & Adolescent Medicine*, *159*, 139–144. DOI:10.1001/archpedi.159.2.139.

Sharma, U., Chaudhury, K., Jagannathan, N.R., & Guha, S.K. (2001). A proton NMR study of the effect of a new intravasal injectable male contraceptive RISUG on seminal plasma metabolites. *Reproduction*, *122*, 431–436.

Stanger-Hall, K.F., Hall, D.W. (2011). Abstinence-only education and teen pregnancy rates: Why we need comprehensive sex education in the U.S. *PLoS ONE* 6(10): e24658. DOI:10.1371/journal.pone.0024658.

Trussel, J. (2011). Contraceptive failure in the United States. *Contraception*, *83*, 397–404. DOI:10.1016/j.contraception.2011.01.021

Tsuruta, J.K., Dayton, P.A., Gallippi, C.M., O'Rand, M.G., Streicker, M.A., Gessner, R.C., … Sokal, D.C. (2012). Therapeutic ultrasound as a potential male contraceptive: Power, frequency and temperature required to deplete rat testes of meiotic cells and epididymides of sperm determined using a commercially available system. *Reproductive Biology and Endocrinology*, *10*(7). DOI:10.1186/1477-7827-10-7.

Umpierre, S.A. (1985). Effect of Coke on sperm motility. *New England Journal of Medicine*, *21*, 1351. DOI:10.1056/NEJM198511213132111.

vod Sydow, K. (1999). Sexuality during pregnancy and after childbirth: A metacontent analysis of 59 studies. *Journal of Psychosomatic Research*, *47*, 27–49. DOI:10.1016/S0022-3999(98)00106-8.

Walker, J.L. (2001). A qualitative study of parents' experiences of providing sex education for their children: The implications for health education. *Health Education Journal*, *60*, 132–146. DOI:10.1177/001789690106000205.

Weaver, H., Smith, G., & Kippax, S. (2005). School-based sex education policies and indicators of sexual health among young people: a comparison of the Netherlands, France, Australia and the United States. *Sex Education*, *5*, 171–188. DOI:10.1080/14681810500038889.

Youssef, H. (1993). The history of the condom. *Journal of the Royal Society of Medicine*, *86*, 226–228.

11

Sexually Transmitted Infections and Safer-Sex Practices

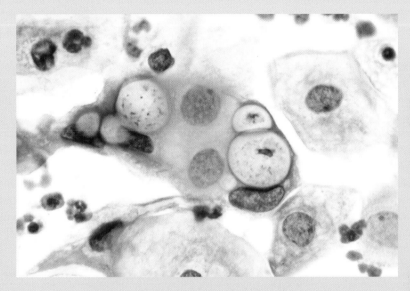

Source: Dr. Lance Liotta Laboratory, via National Cancer Institute Visuals Online.

Chapter Outline

- Introduction   280
- Sexually Transmitted Infections   280
  - Bacterial Infections   281
  - Viral Infections   284
  - Other Infections   289
- Factors That Increase the Spread of STIs   290
  - Biological   290
  - Psychological   291
  - Social and Environmental   292
- The Psychological Impact of STIs   293
  - Implications for Romantic and Sexual Relationships   295
- Preventing Infection   296

The Psychology of Human Sexuality, First Edition. Justin J. Lehmiller.
© 2014 John Wiley & Sons, Ltd. Published 2014 by John Wiley & Sons, Ltd.

Introduction

Although sex has many positive features associated with it (e.g., pleasure, intimacy), there is also a dark side to sexual activity. In this chapter, we will begin to explore this dark side by considering the various infections that can be spread through sexual contact. The reason for discussing this topic is not to discourage you from being sexually active or to make you feel scared or anxious about having sex in the future; rather, the goal is simply to ensure that you have a complete picture when it comes to sex so that you can make informed decisions and take appropriate precautions. In addition, there are a lot of myths and misconceptions about sexual infections and how they are spread that are worth correcting (e.g., some people think that oral sex poses no disease risk, while others think that HIV can be spread through sweat).

We will begin by describing the most commonly encountered sexually transmitted infections (STIs). We will talk about how these infections are transmitted, their prevalence, and their potential effects. This biological background is necessary for understanding the psychological and relational implications of having an STI, a topic we will address later in the chapter. We will also consider biological, psychological, and social factors that contribute to the prevalence of STIs, and explore the steps that you can take to prevent infection in your own sex life.

Before we move on, please note that we will use the term STI throughout this chapter instead of sexually transmitted disease (STD), a term some of you may be more familiar with. The reason for this is because STI is broader and more inclusive in that it refers to any case in which an infection is present in an individual, regardless of whether symptoms exist. In contrast, STDs only refer to cases in which there is an infection causing symptoms. Thus, not all STIs are STDs, but all STDs had to be STIs first. In addition, not all STIs will go on to become STDs (e.g., only some cases of the human papilloma virus or HPV will go on to produce symptoms).

Sexually Transmitted Infections

In the United States alone, there are approximately 19 million new cases of STIs each year and about $17 billion in associated health care costs, which makes this a major public health issue (CDC, 2011a). Young people are disproportionately affected by the STI epidemic, with persons aged 15–24 comprising approximately half of all new diagnoses. Although STIs are certainly a concern for people across all stages of the lifespan (e.g., consider that STI outbreaks are being documented among nursing home patients with increasing frequency; Jameson, 2011), it is clear that STIs are something the college crowd should be especially worried about.

Of course, STIs are a global concern and the US represents only a small portion of the total number of infections worldwide. As some evidence of this, see Table 11.1, which presents incidence and prevalence data on three of the most common curable STIs throughout world regions. This table also reveals that the highest prevalence rates of these particular STIs are in Africa, North and South America, and the Western Pacific Region (e.g., China, Japan, Australia); prevalence rates are substantially lower in South-East Asia (e.g., India) and the Mediterranean (e.g., Iran, Pakistan). Incidence and prevalence rates for incurable STIs, such as HIV, also vary considerably across cultures. For instance, 4.9% of the population has HIV in Sub-Saharan Africa, compared to 0.6% in North America and 0.2% in Western and Central Europe (Kaiser Family Foundation, 2012).

Region	Number of new cases in 2008 (incidence)	Number of adults ages 15–49	Prevalence
Africa	32.8 million	384.4 million	8.5%
North and South America	40.2 million	476.9 million	8.4%
South-east Asia	35.6 million	945.2 million	3.8%
European region	24.2 million	450.8 million	5.4%
Mediterranean region	6.9 million	309.6 million	2.2%
Western Pacific region	82.5 million	986.7 million	8.4%

Table 11.1 Incidence and Prevalence of Selected Curable STIs across World Regions

Note: This table only presents data on three curable STIs: syphilis, gonorrhea, and chlamydia. Data obtained from World Health Organization (2008).

Table 11.2 CDC Screening Recommendations for STIs

Sexually active women age 25 and younger should have a yearly chlamydia test. Older women who have new sexual partners should be tested annually as well.

Women who have multiple partners or who live in communities with high rates of gonorrhea should receive an annual gonorrhea screening.

All pregnant women should be screened for HIV, syphilis, chlamydia, and hepatitis B. At-risk pregnant women should also be screened for gonorrhea.

All sexually active men who have sex with men (MSM) should be screened annually for gonorrhea, syphilis, chlamydia, and HIV. MSM with multiple partners or who use drugs should be screened every 3 to 6 months.

Sexually active heterosexual men should be screened according to risk, meaning annual STI screenings should occur for men at high risk (e.g., men with multiple partners or who have inconsistent condom use).

Source: CDC (2011a).

Below, we will review the most common STIs and provide some basic information about each. Given the nature of this book, we will not go into great depth about how each disease affects the body and its clinical presentation. However, if you would like more detailed information, you are encouraged to check out the Centers for Disease Control and Prevention website (cdc.gov), which contains a massive database of sexual health information and statistics. If you would like to get tested for STIs, the CDC also has a helpful online tool (hivtest.cdc.gov) for finding local resources. For current CDC screening recommendations, see Table 11.2.

Bacterial Infections

The three most well-known sexual infections caused by bacterial agents are chlamydia, gonorrhea, and syphilis. Each of these infections is spread primarily through sexual contact, which includes oral, anal, and vaginal sex. **Chlamydia** is the most prevalent of the bacterial STIs. In the US there are approximately

1.4 million new cases each year, and 70% of these infections occur among persons under the age of 24 (CDC, 2011a). Although chlamydia infections are relatively easily cured through an antibiotic regimen, the unfortunate reality is that chlamydia infections are not always caught because symptoms are often minimal and, in some cases, completely nonexistent. The danger in this is that, if left untreated, chlamydia can cause a range of problems, including premature birth among pregnant women, blindness (in cases where the bacteria come into contact with the eye), and both male and female infertility. It is estimated that up to 24,000 US women become infertile each year as a result of undiagnosed and untreated STIs like chlamydia (CDC, 2011a). In addition to these risks, untreated chlamydia can impair sexual pleasure and ability to reach orgasm. For more on this, see the Digging Deeper 11.1 box.

Digging Deeper 11.1   Do Sexually Transmitted Infections Affect Women's Ability to Orgasm?

The short answer is *yes*. The long answer is that there are both physical and psychological reasons STIs affect female orgasm.

Let us cover physical causes first. One of the most well-known factors that affects women's ability to reach orgasm during sex is *dyspareunia* (Butcher, 1999). This is a clinical term that refers to any type of genital pain experienced during sexual activity (see chapter 12 for more on this). When sex is painful, it is likely to be attempted less frequently and for shorter durations. In severe cases, sex may be avoided entirely. Many factors can cause female dyspareunia, including STIs such as chlamydia and gonorrhea. If a woman has one of these infections and is not treated for it, she may develop **pelvic inflammatory disease (PID)**. This occurs when the initial infection spreads from the vagina or cervix to other reproductive organs, such as the uterus and fallopian tubes. Because chlamydia and gonorrhea infections often produce few or no early symptoms in women, many women do not realize they have an STI until the infection has advanced to PID. If you are a woman who is experiencing pain during intercourse, it is advisable to see a physician to determine the exact cause. This is important not only for improving your sex life and potentially restoring ability to orgasm, but also because if PID is the cause, it can potentially result in infertility if left untreated for too long.

With regard to psychological factors, having an STI can evoke a number of emotional responses that interfere with both sexual arousal and orgasm. Sexual scientists have known for a long time that negative emotions and feelings are strongly related to sexual problems (Nobre & Pinto-Gouveia, 2006), and STIs are just one of many factors that can negatively affect one's mood state. For instance, a woman with herpes or HPV may experience a loss of sexual pleasure because she is afraid of or distracted by the thought of passing the infection to her partner. Likewise, emotions that frequently accompany being diagnosed with an STI are shame and guilt, which may not only lead one to shy away from sexual activity, but also to enjoy it less. Some people may also be so fearful of contracting STIs that they have a hard time relaxing and getting into the moment during sexual activity.

Thus, STIs can reduce a woman's ability to reach orgasm both biologically and psychologically. Although we focused primarily on how STIs affect women here, similar effects sometimes occur in men and can create the same types of sexual difficulties for them.

Note: Reprinted with permission from *The Psychology of Human Sexuality* blog (www.lehmiller.com).

SHE MAY LOOK CLEAN—BUT

PICK-UPS
"GOOD TIME" GIRLS
PROSTITUTES

SPREAD SYPHILIS AND GONORRHEA

You can't beat the Axis if you get VD

Figure 11.1   Historically, the US government sought to alert servicemen about the dangers of STIs during times of war. Source: US National Library of Medicine.

Gonorrhea ("the clap") is one of the oldest known STIs and, historically, has been a major problem during times of war due to large numbers of servicemen utilizing prostitutes. As some evidence of this, during World War II, the US government created a series of posters warning military members against visiting prostitutes because "you can't beat the Axis" if you have gonorrhea (see Figure 11.1). In fact, it was this fear of losing eligible servicemen to STIs that prompted the US government to outlaw prostitution. That said, while gonorrhea used to be one of the more prevalent STIs, the infection rate has dropped dramatically since the 1970s. There are approximately 320,000 new cases of it each year in the US, with 62% occurring among individuals under age 24 (CDC, 2011a). Like chlamydia, symptoms of gonorrhea are often minimal, which means many infected individuals do not realize they have it and fail to get tested. If left untreated, the infection can cause infertility in both men and women. Although gonorrhea used to be easy to treat with a massive dose of penicillin, antibiotic-resistant strains of this bacterium have popped up in recent years, making gonorrhea more difficult to manage (Unemo & Nicolas, 2012). Public health officials are concerned that gonorrhea may eventually become an untreatable "superbug" because it has developed resistance to almost all known antibiotics and, at the same time, drug manufacturers have very few new antibiotics in the pipeline, in large part because they are relatively unprofitable to produce at this time.

Despite being very well-known as an STI, **syphilis** is a far less common bacterial infection than both gonorrhea and chlamydia, with about 14,000 new cases diagnosed each year in the US (CDC, 2011a). Rates have declined dramatically over the past half-century; however, there has been a recent, dramatic uptick in cases among men who have sex with men (MSM). In fact, whereas 7% of cases of syphilis could be attributed to MSM in 2000, the proportion jumped to 67% in 2010 (CDC, 2011b)! Syphilis tends to have more noticeable symptoms of infection than the other bacterial STIs. Symptoms vary depending upon the stage of the disease, with the most prominent being a *chancre* or painless sore at the site of infection during *primary syphilis* (the earliest stage) and a rash on the hands or feet during *secondary syphilis*. As you learned in chapter 2 in our discussion of the Tuskegee Syphilis Study, untreated syphilis can be devastating and deadly the longer it goes on, with the potential for insanity, paralysis, and heart failure to occur. Syphilis is generally treatable with penicillin, although the dose required depends upon how far the disease has progressed.

Viral Infections

Some STIs are caused by viruses instead of bacteria, and these tend to be the most worrisome because, unlike bacterial STIs, we cannot cure viral STIs. As a result, viral infections are much more prevalent and far more difficult to eradicate. The most common viral STI (and also the most common sexual infection in general) is the **human papilloma virus (HPV)**, which infects at least 6 million people in the US each year (CDC, 2012a). HPV is spread through sexual activity and skin-to-skin contact. It is possible to spread HPV even when practicing safe sex because the virus can sit on portions of the skin that are not protected by condoms. Most people who have HPV do not realize it because there are dozens of different strains of the virus and only a few of them cause obvious symptoms, most notably, *genital warts*.

HPV has increasingly troubled the medical community due to research indicating that advanced infections are linked to an increased risk of cancer in the cervix, anus, and throat (Gillison, Chaturvedi, & Lowy, 2008). Although there is no cure for HPV, there is a vaccine (Gardasil) that has been approved for use in both men and women between the ages of 9 and 26 that can protect against the highest-risk strains of the virus (i.e., those linked to genital warts and cancers). Efforts to mandate this vaccine for adolescents in the US have been met with fierce resistance from certain political and religious groups, with some arguing that such vaccines will effectively license children to be promiscuous as adults. However, research on girls who have received this vaccine has found that they do not have more sexual partners than girls who do not get the vaccine (Bednarczyk et al., 2012). What do you think about adolescents receiving vaccines for sexual infections? Weigh in with your perspective in the Your Sexuality 11.1 box.

Herpes is another common viral STI that is characterized by painful blisters on or around the genitals, anus, and/or mouth. There are two strains of the virus that are of particular interest to sexual health researchers: Herpes simplex virus type 1 (HSV-1) and Herpes simplex virus type 2 (HSV-2). HSV-1 is typically linked to oral lesions (often referred to as "cold sores" or "fever blisters"), whereas HSV-2 is typically linked to genital area lesions; however, these viral strains can "cross over" and potentially cause sores in either area. It is estimated that 16.2% of individuals in the United States aged 14–49 have a genital HSV-2 infection, and a far higher number are thought to have the oral HSV-1 infection (CDC, 2012b).

Herpes is highly contagious and easily transmitted from one person to the next through sexual activity, skin-to-skin contact, and kissing. Part of the reason herpes is so prevalent is because the infection can be spread even when no obvious symptoms are present. Like HPV, herpes can be

> ### Your Sexuality 11.1   Should STI Vaccinations Be Mandated For Adolescents?
>
> As soon as the HPV vaccine Gardasil hit the market, several US states took the initiative to mandate the vaccine for adolescents or at least make a concerted effort to inform the public about the benefits of it. Although such legislation has been introduced in 41 states since 2006, only about half of them have enacted anything (National Conference of State Legislatures, 2012). Legislation has stalled in so many states partly because of cost and safety concerns, but also as a result of moral objections. Many political and religious groups feel it is wrong to require an adolescent to be vaccinated for a disease that is transmitted through sexual contact because they feel it presumes a certain level of promiscuity and fear that it may instill a false sense of security that ultimately licenses adolescents to engage in riskier sexual behavior. Some also argue that a mandatory vaccine infringes upon religious freedoms and individual choice. The counterarguments are that most people become sexually active as teenagers, you only need to have one partner in order to contract an STI, and this vaccine has the potential to prevent against some of the most devastating cancers.
>
> Are there any other arguments you can think of for or against mandatory STI vaccinations? Which set of arguments do you find most persuasive and why? What type of legislation (if any) would you want your government to support?

transmitted even when wearing a condom, because the virus may reside on areas of the skin that condoms do not protect. Herpes is experienced differently across individuals, with some persons experiencing regular flare-ups of symptoms, and others experiencing them rarely or never. We do not fully understand why, but some psychological factors have been implicated in frequent symptom outbreaks, including depression, anxiety, and stress (Massad et al., 2011). For those who experience frequent outbreaks, antiviral drugs such as Valtrex can either be taken daily to suppress future outbreaks or episodically to lessen the severity of current symptoms.

Despite the annoyance and pain of occasional blisters, the only major complications of herpes infection are the potential to transfer the virus to the eye (resulting in *ocular herpes*) and to expose a newborn to it through vaginal delivery. Herpes and many other STIs (including chlamydia and gonorrhea) pose a very serious health risk to infants during childbirth owing to their underdeveloped immune systems, which makes it all the more important for women who are pregnant or hoping to become pregnant to be up front with their doctors about their sexual histories and to receive appropriate STI screenings.

The final viral infection we will cover is the **human immunodeficiency virus (HIV)**, a retrovirus that targets and destroys a certain type of lymphocyte (T4 helper cells). By doing so, the immune system becomes compromised and susceptible to *opportunistic infections* (i.e., infections that are not normally harmful, but that can be deadly to someone with poor immune functioning). When an individual already has HIV and that person's T4 cell count drops to a dangerously low level, the **acquired immune deficiency syndrome (AIDS)** is diagnosed. It is at this time that opportunistic infections are most likely to take hold.

In the US, the incidence of HIV is estimated at 50,000 new cases each year, with about 1.1 million citizens in total currently living with an HIV infection (CDC, 2012c). Historically and even

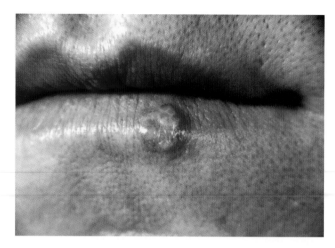

Figure 11.2   Many people fail to realize that "cold sores" and "fever blisters" are caused by the herpes virus and that they are highly contagious through kissing and oral sex. Source: CDC/Dr. Herrmann, via CDC Public Health Image Library.

today, most cases of HIV in the US have been attributable to MSM, with this group currently representing 63% of all new cases (CDC, 2012c). However, the nature of HIV/AIDS is dramatically different worldwide in terms of incidence, prevalence, and the groups most likely to be affected. For instance, in Sub-Saharan Africa, there are 1.9 million new cases per year and about 22.9 million individuals are currently infected (Avert, 2012). That effectively means that in parts of Africa, one in 20 adults is living with HIV/AIDS. The other major departure from US statistics is that, as opposed to disproportionate infection by gay men, most cases of HIV globally are attributable to heterosexuals, with men and women being equally impacted.

HIV is spread through sexual activity, including unprotected vaginal and anal intercourse, as well as other activities in which there is an exchange of cell-containing bodily fluids (e.g., childbirth, shared needles among injection drug users or people getting tattoos or body piercings). The greatest potential risk lies in exposure to the semen or blood of a person with a new or advanced infection because they tend to have the largest amounts of the virus in their system. Contrary to popular belief, there is virtually no risk of HIV infection from exposure to sweat, tears, or saliva, even though this has been taught in some sex education courses (see chapter 10). These bodily fluids contain only trace amounts of the virus, making transmission near impossible. For more common myths and misconceptions about HIV and other STIs, see the Digging Deeper 11.2 box.

Individuals infected with HIV may not realize it for months or potentially even years because there are few symptoms associated with the initial infection. In fact, it is estimated that as many as one in five infected individuals do not yet know they have it (CDC, 2012c), which is one important reason HIV continues to spread. Unfortunately, there remains no cure for HIV/AIDS; however, treatments have improved dramatically over the past two decades and people are able to live with the infection longer than ever before. Specifically, by taking daily *anti-retroviral drugs*, the progression of the disease slows considerably and the risk of passing the infection along to sexual partners decreases dramatically because the amount of the virus "free-floating" in bodily fluids drops to almost undetectable levels. In fact, in heterosexual relationships, the rate of HIV transmission in couples with discordant HIV status (i.e., cases where one partner has it and the other does not) is near zero when the HIV-positive partner's viral load is suppressed through drug therapy (Attia, Egger, Müller, Zwahlen, & Low, 2009). These drugs have also made it much less likely that pregnant

Figure 11.3 Out of all world regions, Africa is disproportionately affected by the HIV / AIDS epidemic. Image Copyright spirit of america, 2013. Used under license from Shutterstock.com.

Digging Deeper 11.2   Six Myths About Sexually Transmitted Infections Debunked

Although most people are sexually active, it is surprising how little some people know about sex. In particular, there are a multitude of myths and misconceptions about STIs. Below, we will review six of the most persistent false beliefs about sexual infections.

Myth #1: You can avoid STIs by having oral sex instead of vaginal or anal intercourse.   Do not believe this one for a second! Almost all STIs have the potential to be transmitted and contracted through oral sex. For instance, many people fail to realize that they can get chlamydia and gonorrhea infections of the throat. Likewise, a large number of people seemingly have no idea that "cold sores" are caused by the herpes virus, which means that if someone with this infection performs oral sex on you (particularly when they are experiencing on outbreak), they can potentially give you genital herpes. Also, keep in mind that "pubic lice" are not just for the pubic area. In fact, they can and will seize the opportunity to live in your moustache or beard if given the chance.

Myth #2: You can identify people with STIs by looking at them and/or inspecting their genitals.   Nope. Someone with an STI can look perfectly healthy and there may be nothing out of the ordinary with that person's genitals. The harsh reality of some STIs (such as HPV, HIV, and chlamydia) is that they often cause few to no symptoms initially, yet are still highly contagious.

Myth #3: You cannot get the same STI twice.   Just because you had gonorrhea once does not mean you will be inoculated against it or any other STIs in the future. In fact, you can get the same STI from the same partner over and over unless *both of you* get tested and treated.

Myth #4: People who use condoms cannot get STIs.   Although condoms provide *some* protection against STIs, they do not guarantee safety. Unless you are wearing a full-body condom, there is still the potential to transmit and contract herpes and HPV through skin contact. In addition, people make lots of mistakes using condoms, such as putting them on after sex has started or taking them off before sex is over, which undermines the protective benefits.

Figure 11.4   One of the most persistent myths about STIs is that condoms provide an absolute safety guarantee. ©Wavebreak Media Ltd/123RF.COM.

Myth #5: STIs can be transmitted through public toilet seats.   If you are having sex on top of a toilet, sure! Otherwise, it is pretty unlikely. In reality, many viruses and bacteria cannot live long outside of the human body, and even if you happened to sit in someone else's bodily fluids, infection can only occur if those fluids get inside your bloodstream or genital tract. So, unless you have a lot of open cuts on your buttocks or enjoy dry humping toilet seats, the risk is pretty minimal.

Myth #6: Only sluts get STIs.   Many people think they are not at risk for contracting STIs because they do not have "that many" sexual partners. However, you only need to have one partner to potentially get an STI, and it can happen the very first time you have sex.

   STIs are a risk that anyone who is sexually active must recognize. However, you can minimize your chances of contracting an infection and experiencing long-term negative effects by understanding the nature of STIs, taking the appropriate precautions, and getting into the habit of regular screenings.

Note: Reprinted with permission from *The Psychology of Human Sexuality* blog (www.lehmiller.com).

women with HIV will pass the virus along to their children during birth (European Collaborative Study, 2005).

   Although a cure for HIV is still a long way off, researchers are making progress in developing methods that can reduce one's risk of contracting the virus. One of the most promising preventive measures at this point involves administering anti-retroviral drugs to persons at high risk of contracting the virus. A longitudinal study of MSM found that among those men who took anti-retroviral drugs reliably their risk of contracting HIV dropped by 73% (Grant et al., 2010)! Although this may sound great, it is hardly the panacea we have been searching for because not only do such drugs carry serious side effects, but they can cost anywhere from $10,000–$20,000 *per person, per year* to administer. Fortunately, a number of other studies and clinical trials are underway, which gives us hope that a safer and more cost-effective alternative will eventually emerge. Of course, some of you may point out that condoms are far cheaper and already easy to access; however, as we will discuss later in this chapter, some people fail to use condoms because they are a perceived barrier to pleasure and/or do not fit well, and people make a lot of mistakes when it comes to proper condom use. Thus, if we want to make condoms a bigger part of this solution, we need to redesign them so that they are more pleasurable and easier to use.

Other Infections

The above discussion should not be taken to mean that there are only six possible STIs. The fact of the matter is that there are many other infections that can be spread through sexual contact, including parasites (i.e., pubic lice and scabies), hepatitis, and trichomoniasis. Consideration of the nature and causes of every possible STI is beyond the scope of this chapter; however, please be aware that the CDC website (cdc.gov) contains a wealth of information on all possible infections, including common signs, symptoms, and treatment courses.

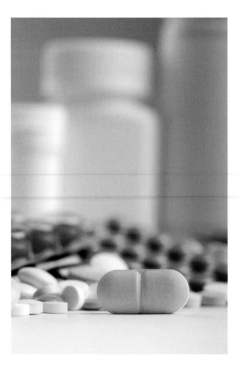

Figure 11.5   Anti-retroviral drug therapy significantly reduces the risk of HIV transmission during sexual activity and childbirth, and may potentially serve as a preventive agent for HIV-negative individuals who are at high risk of contracting the virus. © Nomadsoul1 / 123RF.COM.

Factors That Increase the Spread of STIs

Now that you know something about the most common sexual infections and how they are spread, let us look at some of the factors that contribute to the high prevalence of STIs. As you will see below, these factors are biopsychosocial in nature.

Biological

The biological nature of certain STIs makes them very easy to spread. For instance, as previously mentioned, many STIs exhibit few or no initial symptoms, including chlamydia, gonorrhea, HPV, and HIV. Consequently, many infected individuals are unaware of their status and may unknowingly and unintentionally pass along their infection to other sexual partners. Thus, even if you and your partner(s) feel completely normal, it is important to take appropriate precautions and get regular STI screenings because people can still be highly contagious even if they are not actively exhibiting any disease symptoms.

In addition, the nature of certain STIs not only makes them very easy to transmit, but they can increase your susceptibility to contracting other infections. For instance, both herpes and syphilis are known to create open sores on or around the genitals. Those sores make it very easy for infectious agents to readily enter and exit the body. Thus, someone with herpes or a syphilis chancre would be especially prone to contracting other STIs and spreading their infections to other partners.

Psychological

There are a multitude of psychological factors that promote the spread of sexual infections. First, among heterosexual couples, the use of birth control pills and other hormonal contraceptives can lull the partners into a false sense of security. By removing fear of unwanted pregnancy from the equation, many couples feel "protected" and therefore stop using condoms (Williams, Kimble, Covell, & Weiss, 1992). However, as discussed in chapter 10, hormonal contraceptives provide no protection against STIs whatsoever. Also, as discussed in chapter 8, sexual infidelity is surprisingly common. Thus, stopping condom use because pregnancy risk has been averted leaves the door open to infection unless both partners have been tested and maintain monogamy.

Second, there is a lot of social stigma and shame associated with getting tested for STIs, because getting screened for infections may imply that you have done something wrong. In addition, getting tested can potentially create an awkward scenario in which your current and/or former partners need to be contacted and informed of your results. Consequently, many individuals do not get tested out of fear that they will be judged by others or because they want to avoid embarrassment. Just consider that among men who have never received an HIV test, 59% of them reported that they did not get screened because they feared the potential social consequences (Stall et al., 1996). Obviously, this failure to get tested can lead to infections going undiagnosed and allow them to spread further; however, now that in-home HIV testing (e.g., OraQuick) is a reality, testing stigma may become less of a barrier.

Third, if you have ever taken a health psychology course, you have probably learned that people express **unrealistic optimism** about their own health (Weinstein, 1987). In other words, people think that they are unlikely to encounter health problems (such as STIs) in the future. This may lead some people to forego protection or to use protection inconsistently because they think "it won't happen to me" or "only sluts get sexually transmitted diseases." However, as discussed in the Digging Deeper 11.2 box, STIs are an issue that every sexually active person must be cognizant of.

Fourth, being committed to a sexual partner can lead you to view that partner as "safe" or as not representing a risk to your health (Gerrard, Gibbons, & Bushman, 1996). In some ways, this makes sense. As commitment to a relationship grows, we come to trust our partners more and become less concerned that they will lie to us or cheat, which may reduce the feeling that condoms or other forms of protection are needed. However, we know that people in monogamous relationships often cheat and, when they do, they frequently fail to use protection with those partners *and* typically do not disclose such encounters to their primary partner (Conley, Moors, Ziegler, & Karathanasis, 2012). Thus, while being committed is almost universally thought of as a good thing, commitment does carry some potential STI risks.

Fifth, the stereotypes we hold about certain people can increase our STI risk. In particular, the widespread stereotype that attractive people are healthier can potentially undermine safer-sex behaviors with some partners. For instance, research has found that participants rate attractive individuals as posing less STI risk (Agocha & Cooper, 1999) and report that they would be less likely to use a condom with an attractive partner (Kelaher, Ross, Drury, & Clarkson, 1994). In reality, however, if attractive people are more highly desired, then they probably have more opportunities for sex. To the extent that this translates to a higher number of sexual partners, there could be an *increased* STI risk associated with highly attractive individuals.

Finally, personality characteristics and attitudes toward condoms may predispose individuals to engage in behaviors that increase STI risk. For instance, persons with more erotophilic personalities and those who perceive condoms as a barrier to sexual pleasure are more likely to report

Figure 11.6 As people become more committed to one another, safe-sex practices tend to drop off; however, that can create risk if one of the partners ends up cheating. ©Yuri Arcurs/123RF.COM.

having unprotected sex (Crosby, Salazar, DiClemente & Yarber, 2004). Likewise, having a sensation-seeking personality is linked to reporting sex without condoms in risky situations, cheating on one's partner, and contracting more STIs (Ripa, Hansen, Mortensen, Sanders, & Reinisch, 2001). In addition, having an unrestricted sociosexual orientation is associated with risky sexual behaviors, such as unprotected sex (Seal & Agostinelli, 1994).

Social and Environmental

There are also some social factors implicated in the spread of STIs, such as alcohol use in social settings. Research has found that there is indeed a link between alcohol consumption and risky sexual behaviors (e.g., failure to use condoms or to discuss STI history with a new partner); however, the nature of this relationship is complicated (Cooper, 2006). In certain situations, alcohol may increase risky behavior, but in other cases, it can inhibit such behavior. The nature of the situation and the individual's beliefs about the effects of alcohol (known in psychological terms as **expectancy effects**) are important considerations. For instance, individuals who believe that consuming alcohol will disinhibit them tend to show greater levels of disinhibition when drinking alcohol than people with other expectancies. Thus, there is not a simple and straightforward link between alcohol and risky sex because alcohol affects people in different ways; suffice it to say that, at least in *some* cases, alcohol increases STI risk.

Social norms also play a role in the spread of STIs because sex remains a taboo topic of discussion in many cultures (Baxter & Wilmot, 1985). For instance, imagine you are out on a first date and you are asked the following questions: "How many people have you slept with? Have you ever had an STI? Do you practice safe-sex?" Some people would be offended or embarrassed by these questions and would not know how to react. As a result, these questions are not asked as often as they should be, and many people go on to have sex with partners with whom they have not exchanged meaningful sexual histories. It is ironic that modern society has somehow deemed talking about sex "more personal" than actually having sex. Related to this, research on men who have sex with men (MSM) has found that disclosure of HIV status is less likely to occur when meeting partners in person compared to meeting partners online (Grov, Hirshfield, Remien, Humberstone, & Chiasson, 2013). This may be because the anonymity provided by Internet communications allows people to talk about issues that might be too uncomfortable to discuss in person.

Despite the fact that online hookup websites appear to enhance sexual communication, many scientists have expressed concern that such sites are a risk factor for STIs because they facilitate the obtainment of multiple partners very quickly. Indeed, there is some research indicating that MSM who meet their partners online tend to report more STIs than those who meet partners offline (Evans, Wiggins, Mercer, Bolding, & Elford, 2007). However, is this because the technology promotes greater sexual activity, or because those who are more sexually active are just more likely to use the technology? Research supports the latter explanation, and indicates that MSM who use the Internet for casual sex have greater numbers of partners to begin with and are often pursuing partners online and offline simultaneously (Jenness et al., 2010). Thus, the link between the Internet and STI risk is not quite as simple and straightforward as some have suggested.

Poor communication between doctors and patients can also contribute to the spread of STIs. For example, does your doctor feel comfortable asking you about your sex life? Research has found that only about one in four doctors ask patients about STIs during routine checkups (Tao, Irwin, & Kassler, 2000)! By the same token, do you feel comfortable talking to your physician about your sex life? Many of us do not, which means there is a reluctance to discuss sex on both sides of the table. As a result, STIs often go undiagnosed and untreated even in the doctor's office. Further contributing to this problem is the fact that doctors frequently stereotype their patients based upon marital status, assuming that married folks are being faithful to their partners and therefore do not have the same sexual health concerns as their single counterparts. However, as discussed in chapter 8 in our section on infidelity, this is a bad assumption.

Finally, it is also important to note that the majority of condoms manufactured today come in a "standard" length and width, with the assumption being that condoms are "one size fits all." However, research finds that men with larger penises report that the average condom is too tight and, more importantly, these well-endowed men are more likely to have engaged in unprotected sex recently (Grov, Well, & Parsons, 2013). Thus, it appears that men who are unable to find condoms that fit well are less likely to take sexual precautions.

The Psychological Impact of STIs

Some STIs are curable and, once the infection has passed, there are no lingering aftereffects. However, other STIs (e.g., herpes, HPV, and HIV) are for life. Once you have it, there is no getting rid of it. As a result, chronic STIs can have a devastating psychological effect. Regular flare-ups of symptoms and/or the act of taking a daily medication may serve as constant reminders of one's disease status and potentially evoke feelings of guilt, shame, embarrassment, or anxiety. The psychological effects are even more severe for persons with HIV, who frequently report feelings of

Figure 11.7   Both doctors and patients express some reluctance to talking about sex during medical visits, which creates many missed opportunities for STI detection and diagnosis. ©Andres Rodriguez/123RF.COM.

victimization, constant mortality salience, and a fear of becoming dependent upon other people as the disease progresses (Watstein & Chandler, 1998). These psychological effects are compounded by the persistent social stigma surrounding STIs. For instance, there are a lot of myths about STIs that stoke unnecessary fear (e.g., in some US states, it is considered an act of "bioterrorism" for an HIV-positive individual to spit on someone else, even though it is virtually impossible for the infection to be transmitted in this way), and people who have STIs are often blamed for having contracted them because they are thought to have used poor judgment and/or to have engaged in immoral behavior (Sayles, Ryan, Silver, Sarkisian, & Cunningham, 2007).

Persons with STIs may respond to their diagnosis and cope with the resulting stress and stigma in a number of ways. For instance, among persons with HIV, anger and denial are common reactions to the initial diagnosis (Watstein & Chandler, 1998). In rare cases, such reactions may lead individuals to lash out by intentionally trying to infect others. At least in the case of HIV, intentional or reckless infection of another person is considered a criminal act in many parts of the world, and some individuals have been prosecuted for this. Fortunately, however, such behavior is uncommon. Other coping mechanisms include turning to alcohol and other substances as a means of psychological "escape" (McKirnan, Ostrow, & Hope, 1996). However, substance abuse can make mental health issues worse and potentially speed up the rate at which HIV infection progresses into AIDS (i.e., the rate at which one's T4 cell count drops).

Other individuals find more positive ways of coping. For instance, some people immerse themselves in supportive online communities (Reeves, 2000), while others engage in spiritual methods of coping or seek social support from family and friends (Vyavaharkar et al., 2007). Perhaps not surprisingly, people who adopt such approaches tend to experience better psychological adjustment and ultimately experience more positive outcomes.

Implications for Romantic and Sexual Relationships

In addition to feelings of stress and anxiety, persons with chronic STIs often feel as though they have reached the end of their sex and dating lives because they fear that others will not want to put themselves at risk by becoming intimate with someone who has an incurable infection. However, having a chronic STI does not necessarily mean that you must live a single and celibate life.

One option is to pursue a partner who has the same infection status as you (although this can be trickier than it sounds because there are multiple strains of some STIs. Thus, for example, having one strain of HPV does not make you immune from catching other strains of that virus, which may produce different symptoms and risks). The benefit of having the same infection as your partner is that neither of you will have to worry about passing anything on to the other person, which can increase sexual intimacy (Frost, Stirratt, & Ouellette, 2008). There are a growing number of websites and dating services such as PositiveSingles.com that seek to match partners with the same infection status. Such services have become increasingly popular owing to the fact that so many millions of people have chronic STIs and want to find partners who will not judge them based on their status and history and who will not be as concerned about potential infection risk.

However, you do not have to limit your dating pool in this way, and if you have already met someone you really like who does not share the same infection, things can still work out. In the modern world, it is increasingly possible for couples where the partners have discordant infection status to have happy and healthy sexual and romantic relationships. Of course, such relationships face a few important challenges. For one thing, there is likely to be some social stigma faced by infection-discordant couples. Just think about it – if you are HIV-negative but started dating

Figure 11.8　Several websites now offer persons with a positive infection status the chance to meet other partners of the same status. Source: PositiveSingles.com.

someone who is HIV-positive, how would your parents react? Many of them would probably not approve of the relationship out of concern for your health.

In addition to dealing with some potentially tricky social issues, such couples also need to figure out how to manage risk to the uninfected partner. In order to do so, couples must be willing to do a few things. First, the infected partner must be good about taking medications to manage symptoms. This would include daily anti-virals for persons with herpes and daily anti-retrovirals for persons with HIV. If the infected partner has HPV, it may be wise for the uninfected partner to get the HPV vaccine if they have not done so already. Second, condoms or other barriers should always be used during sexual activity to minimize risk of transmitting the infection. Finally, the couple members must have excellent communication. This includes disclosing infection status at the outset of the relationship, acknowledging and discussing anxieties about the potential risks, being cognizant about limiting sexual activity when infection risk is highest (e.g., during herpes outbreaks), and setting and respecting sexual limits and boundaries.

Preventing Infection

To close out this chapter, we will discuss steps you can take to reduce the likelihood of contracting STIs in your own sex life. This means practicing safer sex. Keep in mind that there really is no such thing as completely "safe" sex, meaning that there is always *some* risk associated with any sexual activity. Thus, there is only *safer* sex. Although risk can never be fully eliminated unless you practice strict abstinence or only engage in solitary activities, there are multiple things you can do to limit your chances of contracting and spreading STIs.

First and foremost, communicate with your partner about your sexual histories. Ask your partner about STIs and recent test results. At the same time, be prepared to answer those questions about yourself. This means that if you have an STI, be honest and upfront about it. Think about it this way – is this the kind of thing you would want someone to lie to you about? And would you really be OK with intentionally passing along an infection to an unsuspecting person, especially with your knowledge of the potential physical and psychological consequences of STIs? Discussing your status with a new partner can be tough, and one of the biggest inhibitors when it comes to disclosing STI status is fear of rejection. In fact, this is probably why up to a third of persons with HIV (Sullivan, 2005) and herpes (Green et al., 2003) report failure to disclose their status to their regular sex partners! However, keep in mind that honesty and mutual respect are vital to having a satisfying sexual relationship, and if you ever hope for a romance to develop with someone, lying is unlikely to lay the foundation for a successful long-term relationship.

Second, get regular STI tests so that you can know your own status and provide you partner(s) with reliable information. Also, if you start a monogamous relationship with someone, it is advisable for each partner to get an STI test early in the relationship to reduce the risk that one of you will spread an infection to the other, especially if you and your partner are at a point where you are considering stopping condom use. If financial costs are a concern, be advised that if you are a university student, you can usually get STI tests free of charge through your school's health center and, no, your parents will not find out that you were tested or be sent a copy of the results. If you are not affiliated with a university, many communities have free STI clinics that you can find with a quick online search.

Third, use of barriers during oral, anal, and vaginal sex is advisable because they will limit the possibility of another person's bodily fluids entering your bloodstream or genital tract. This means

Table 11.3	Guidelines for Proper Condom Use

Check packaging for expiration dates, holes, and tears. Throw away expired condoms and punctured packages.

Store your condoms somewhere cool and dry. Ideally, this would be your nightstand. Wallets and glove compartments are not good places to store condoms for prolonged periods of time.

Put condoms on before beginning sexual activity, and keep them on until it is over. Engaging in "dipping" (i.e., inserting a bare penis into the vagina or anus before putting the condom on) or removing the condom prior to ejaculation still permits an exchange of infectious organisms.

Use lubrication with condoms, and select a lubricant that explicitly notes on the bottle that it is compatible with latex condoms.

If you put on the condom inside out, throw it away and put on a different one. If you reuse the same condom, you can still expose your partner to infections.

Do not unroll the condom or blow it up like a balloon before using it. It may sound like fun, but you will weaken the condom by doing so.

Squeeze the tip of the condom when unrolling it down the shaft of the penis to leave a space at the end for catching ejaculate.

Remove the penis promptly after ejaculation. If the penis remains inside the other person while the erection subsides, ejaculate can leak out of the condom.

Remember that condoms are made for one-time only use!

using male or female condoms for intercourse. However, be sure to brush up on proper condom use before your next sexual encounter because, as mentioned in chapter 10, condom use errors are incredibly common (Sanders et al., 2012). See Table 11.3 for a list of suggestions that will help ensure consistent condom effectiveness. Also, if you are worried that using condoms will reduce genital sensitivity or impair your ability to reach orgasm, keep in mind that there are many different condoms on the market that vary in size, thickness, and material. As a result, you may need to do some experimenting to find the right one for you.

During intercourse, the use of artificial lubricants can help reduce the risk of internal tears to the vagina or rectum. A drop or two of lubricant on the inside of the condom may also help to enhance pleasure for the wearer – just do not put too much on the inside or the condom may slip off. Lubricants can be purchased at most drug stores, pharmacies, and sex shops, but be careful when selecting a lubricant to ensure that it is compatible with the type of condom you are using. In particular, avoid using oil-based lubricants with latex condoms because the oil can reduce condom efficacy. Thus, if you are in the habit of using items around the house as makeshift lubricants, it would be wise to avoid baby oil, vegetable oil, massage oil and other such products and instead get yourself a bottle of water-based or silicone-based lubricant from the store.

For oral sex, **dental dams** are worth considering. Dental dams are latex barriers that look kind of like a fruit roll-up (and, in fact, you can buy flavored ones that actually taste fruity). These barriers can be placed over the vulva for cunnilingus or over the anus for anilingus. Dental dams may be hard to find at your local drugstore, but they are readily available over the Internet and are often

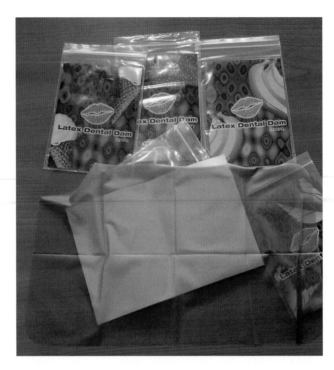

Figure 11.9   If you do not have access to a dental dam, remember that you can create one from an everyday latex condom. Source: inga (Own work) [CC-BY-SA-2.0 (http://creativecommons.org/licenses/by/2.0/deed.en)], via Wikimedia Commons.

carried by Planned Parenthood and other STI clinics. If you cannot get your hands on a dental dam, you can make one very easily from an ordinary latex condom. All you need to do is cut off the tip of the condom, and then slit it down the side with a pair of scissors. Unroll and behold your homemade dental dam! Related to this suggestion, latex gloves can be used to prevent infection when the fingers are used to stimulate the vagina or anus.

It may also help to maintain a high level of personal cleanliness and hygiene. This means many things, including keeping fingernails short if fingers will be inserted inside the vagina or rectum so as to limit the possibility of creating internal tears. In addition, regularly flossing and brushing your teeth to prevent gum and oral diseases can reduce the odds of spreading and contracting infections during oral sex. That said, flossing should not occur just before or after sex, especially among persons who do not already have healthy gums because of the potential for bleeding to occur. Washing your own and your partner's hands and genitals before and after sex may offer a limited protective benefit as well, but cleanliness is not a substitute for condoms and barriers. If you do wash after sex, it is best to avoid vaginal or rectal *douching* (i.e., flushing with water) because that can increase infection risk by irritating internal membranes and pushing infectious organisms further inside the body.

Finally, use common sense and exercise good judgment. For instance, if you are having a symptom outbreak of an STI (e.g., herpes), avoid partnered sexual activity because those symptoms can increase risk for both you and your partner(s). Also, avoid sex with at-risk persons (e.g., someone you know or suspect to be an injection drug user or someone you know does not reliably use protection with other partners). And keep in mind that the more sexual partners you have, the more

indirect partners you accumulate. This means that when you have sex with someone, you are indirectly being exposed to every other sex partner that person has had. Obviously, the more direct and indirect partners you have, the greater the likelihood that you will be exposed to an STI. It is important to think about these things if you want to make your infection risk as low as possible.

Key Terms

chlamydia

pelvic inflammatory disease (PID)

gonorrhea

syphilis

human papilloma virus (HPV)

herpes

human immunodeficiency virus (HIV)

acquired immune deficiency syndrome (AIDS)

unrealistic optimism

expectancy effects

dental dams

indirect partners

Discussion Questions: What is Your Perspective on Sex?

- Have you ever been tested for an STI? What prompted you to do so? If you have never been tested, why?
- When is the "right" time in a relationship for partners to share their sexual histories and STI status?
- What biopsychosocial factors can you think of that promote the spread of STIs other than those already discussed in this chapter?

References

Agocha, V., & Cooper, M. (1999). Risk perceptions and safer-sex intentions: Does a partner's physical attractiveness undermine the use of risk-relevant information? *Personality and Social Psychology Bulletin, 25*, 746–759. DOI:10.1177/0146167299025006009.

Attia, S., Egger, M., Müller, M., Zwahlen, M., & Low, N. (2009). Sexual transmission of HIV according to viral load and antiretroviral therapy: Systematic review and meta-analysis. *AIDS, 23*, 1397–1404. DOI:10.1097/QAD.0b013e32832b7dca.

Avert (2012). *Worldwide HIV and AIDS statistics.* Retrieved from http://www.avert.org/worldstats.htm (accessed September 6, 2013).

Baxter, L.A., & Wilmot, W.W. (1985). Taboo topics in close relationships. *Journal of Social and Personal Relationships, 2*, 253–269. DOI:10.1177/0265407585023002.

Bednarczyk, R.A., Davis, R., Ault, K., Orenstein, W., & Omer, S.B. (2012). Sexual activity–related outcomes after human papillomavirus vaccination of 11-to 12-year-olds. *Pediatrics, 130*, 798–805. DOI:10.1542/peds.2012-1516.

Butcher, J. (1999). Female sexual problems II: Sexual pain and sexual fears. *British Medical Journal, 318*, 110–112.

CDC (2011a). *STD trends in the United States: 2011 National Data for Chlamydia, Gonorrhea, and Syphilis.* Retrieved from http://www.cdc.gov/std/stats11/trends-2011.pdf (accessed September 6, 2013).

CDC (2011b). *2010 Sexually transmitted disease surveillance: Syphilis.* Retrieved from http://www.cdc.gov/std/stats10/syphilis.htm (accessed September 6, 2013).

CDC (2012a). *Genital HPV information – Fact sheet*. Retrieved from http://www.cdc.gov/std/HPV/STDFact-HPV.htm (accessed September 6, 2013).

CDC (2012b). *Genital herpes – CDC fact sheet*. Retrieved from http://www.cdc.gov/std/herpes/stdfact-herpes.htm (accessed September 6, 2013).

CDC (2012c). *HIV in the United States: At a glance*. Retrieved from http://www.cdc.gov/hiv/resources/factsheets/us.htm (accessed September 6, 2013).

Conley, T.D, Moors, A.C, Ziegler, A., & Karathanasis, C. (2012). Unfaithful individuals are less likely to practice safer sex than openly nonmonogamous individuals. *Journal of Sexual Medicine, 9*, 1559–1565. DOI:10.1111/j.1743-6109.2012.02712.x.

Cooper, M.L. (2006). Does drinking promote risky sexual behavior? A complex answer to a simple question. *Current Directions in Psychological Science, 15*, 19–23. DOI:10.1111/j.0963-7214.2006.00385.x.

Crosby, R., Salazar, L.F., DiClemente, R.J., & Yarber, W.L. (2004). Correlates of having unprotected vaginal sex among detained adolescent females: An exploratory study of sexual factors. *Sexual Health, 1*, 151–155. DOI:10.1071/SH04005.

European Collaborative Study (2005). Mother-to-child transmission of HIV infection in the era of highly active antiretroviral therapy. *Clinical Infectious Diseases, 40*, 458–465. DOI:10.1086/427287.

Evans, A.R., Wiggins, R.D., Mercer, C.H., Bolding, G.J., & Elford, J. (2007). Men who have sex with men in Great Britain: Comparison of a self-selected internet sample with a national probability sample. *Sexually Transmitted Infections, 83*, 200–205. DOI:10.1136/sti.2006.023283.

Frost, D.M., Stirratt, M.J., & Ouellette, S.C. (2008). Understanding why gay men seek HIV-seroconcordant partners: Intimacy and risk reduction motivations. *Culture, Health & Sexuality, 10*, 513–527. DOI:10.1080/13691050801905631.

Gerrard, M., Gibbons, F.X., & Bushman, B.J. (1996). Relation between perceived vulnerability to HIV and precautionary sexual behavior. *Psychological Bulletin, 119*, 390–409. DOI:10.1037/0033-2909.119.3.390.

Gillison, M.L., Chaturvedi, A.K., & Lowy, D.R. (2008). HPV prophylactic vaccines and the potential prevention of noncervical cancers in both men and women. *Cancer, 113*(10 Suppl.), 3036–3046. DOI:10.1002/cncr.23764.

Grant, R.M., Lama, J.R., Anderson, P.L., McMahan, V., Liu, A.Y., Vargas, L., … & Glidden, D.V. (2010). Preexposure chemoprophylaxis for HIV prevention in men who have sex with men. *New England Journal of Medicine, 363*, 2587–2599. DOI:10.1056/NEJMoa1011205.

Green, J., Ferrier, S., Kocsis, A., Shadrick, J., Ukoumunne, O.C., Murphy, S., & Hetherton, J. (2003). Determinants of disclosure of genital herpes to partners. *Sexually Transmitted Infections, 79*, 42–44. DOI:10.1136/sti.79.1.42.

Grov, C., Hirshfield, S., Remien, R.H., Humberstone, M., & Chiasson, M.A. (2013). Exploring the venue's role in risky sexual behavior among gay and bisexual men: An event-level analysis from a national online survey in the US. *Archives of Sexual Behavior, 42*, 291–302. DOI:10.1007/s10508-011-9854-x.

Grov, C., Well, B.E., & Parsons, J.T. (2013). Self-reported penis size and experiences with condoms among gay and bisexual men. *Archives of Sexual Behavior, 42*, 313–322. DOI:10.1007/s10508-012-9952-4.

Jameson, M. (2011). Seniors' sex lives are up – And so are STD cases. *Orlando Sentinel*. Retrieved from http://articles.orlandosentinel.com/2011-04-18/health/os-seniors-stds-rise-20110416_1_std-cases-syphilis-and-chlamydia-seniors (accessed September 6, 2013).

Jenness, S.M., Neaigus, A., Hagan, H., Wendel, T., Gelpi-Acosta, C., & Murrill, C.S. (2010). Reconsidering the internet as an HIV/STD risk for men who have sex with men. *AIDS and Behavior, 14*, 1353–1361. DOI:10.1007/s10461-010-9769-x.

Kaiser Family Foundation (2012). *The global HIV/AIDS epidemic: Fact sheet*. Retrieved from http://www.kff.org/hivaids/upload/3030-17.pdf.

Kelaher, M., Ross, M.W., Drury, M., & Clarkson, A. (1994). Dominant situational determinants of sexual risk behaviour in gay men. *AIDS, 8*, 101–105. DOI:10.1097/00002030-199401000-00015.

Massad, L.S., Agniel, D., Minkoff, H., Watts, D.H., D'Souza, G., Levine, A.M., … & Weber, K. (2011). Impact of stress and depression on the frequency of squamous intraepithelial lesions. *Journal of Lower Genital Tract Disease, 15*, 42–47. DOI:10.1097/LGT.0b013e3181e66a82.

McKirnan, D.J., Ostrow, D.G., & Hope, B.B. (1996). Sex, drugs and escape: A psychological model of HIV-risk sexual behaviours. *AIDS Care, 8*, 655–669. DOI:10.1080/09540129650125371.

National Conference of State Legislators (2012). *HPV vaccine.* Retrieved from http://www.ncsl.org/issues-research/health/hpv-vaccine-state-legislation-and-statutes.aspx.

Nobre, P.J., & Pinto-Gouveia, J. (2006). Emotions during sexual activity: Differences between sexually functional and dysfunctional men and women. *Archives of Sexual Behavior, 35*, 491–499. DOI:10.1007/s10508-006-9047-1.

Reeves, P.M. (2000). Coping in cyberspace: The impact of Internet use on the ability of HIV-positive individuals to deal with their illness. *Journal of Health Communication, 5*, 47–59. DOI:10.1080/10810730050019555.

Ripa, C.P.L., Hansen, H.S., Mortensen, E.L., Sanders, S.A., & Reinisch, J.M. (2001). A Danish version of the Sensation Seeking Scale and its relation to a broad spectrum of behavioral and psychological characteristics. *Personality and Individual Differences, 30*, 1371–1386. DOI:10.1016/S0191-8869(00)00119-7.

Sanders, S.A., Yarber, W.L., Kaufman, E.L., Crosby, R.A., Graham, C.A., & Milhausen, R.R. (2012). Condom use errors and problems: A global view. *Sexual Health, 9*, 81–95. DOI:10.1071/SH11095.

Sayles, J.N., Ryan, G.W., Silver, J.S., Sarkisian, C.A., & Cunningham, W.E. (2007). Experiences of social stigma and implications for healthcare among a diverse population of HIV positive adults. *Journal of Urban Health, 84*, 814–828. DOI:10.1007/s11524-007-9220-4.

Seal, D.W., & Agostinelli, G. (1994). Individual differences associated with high-risk sexual behaviour: Implications for intervention programmes. *AIDS Care, 6*, 393–397. DOI:10.1080/09540129408258653.

Stall, R., Hoff, C., Coates, T.J., Paul, J., Phillips, K.A., Ekstrand, M., … & Diaz, R. (1996). Decisions to get HIV tested and to accept antiretroviral therapies among gay/bisexual men: Implications for secondary prevention efforts. *Journal of Acquired Immune Deficiency Syndromes, 11*, 151–160.

Sullivan, K.M. (2005). Male self-disclosure of HIV-positive serostatus to sex partners: A review of the literature. *Journal of the Association of Nurses in AIDS Care, 16*, 33–47. DOI:10.1016/j.jana.2005.09.005.

Tao, G., Irwin, K.L., & Kassler, W.J. (2000). Missed opportunities to assess sexually transmitted diseases in US adults during routine medical checkups. *American Journal of Preventive Medicine, 18*, 109–114. DOI:10.1016/S0749-3797(99)00139-7.

Unemo, M., & Nicholas, R.A. (2012). Emergence of multidrug-resistant, extensively drug-resistant and untreatable gonorrhea. *Future Microbiology, 7*, 1401–1422. DOI:10.2217/fmb.12.117.

Vyavaharkar, M., Moneyham, L., Tavakoli, A., Phillips, K.D., Murdaugh, C., Jackson, K., & Meding, G. (2007). Social support, coping, and medication adherence among HIV-positive women with depression living in rural areas of the southeastern United States. *AIDS Patient Care and STDs, 21*, 667–680. DOI:10.1089/apc.2006.0131.

Watstein, S.B., & Chandler, K. (1998). *The AIDS dictionary.* New York: Facts on File.

Weinstein, N.D. (1987). Unrealistic optimism about susceptibility to health problems: Conclusions from a community-wide sample. *Journal of Behavioral Medicine, 10*, 481–500. DOI:10.1007/BF00846146.

Williams, S.S., Kimble, D.L., Covell, N.H., & Weiss, L.H. (1992). College students use implicit personality theory instead of safer sex. *Journal of Applied Social Psychology, 22*, 921–933. DOI:10.1111/j.1559-1816.1992.tb00934.x.

World Health Organization (2008). *Global incidence and prevalence of selected curable sexually transmitted infections - 2008.* Retrieved from http://apps.who.int/iris/bitstream/10665/75181/1/9789241503839_eng.pdf.

12

Sexual Dysfunction and Sex Therapy

©iStockphoto.com/diane39.

Chapter Outline

- Introduction   303
- Causes of Sex Difficulties   303
  - Biological   303
  - Psychological   304
  - Social   306
- Types of Sexual Dysfunction   308
  - Desire Problems   308
  - Arousal Problems   311
  - Orgasm Problems   311
  - Pain Disorders   312
- Sex Therapy   313
  - Schools of Thought   313
  - Specific Treatments   318
- Tips For Avoiding Sexual Difficulties   324

The Psychology of Human Sexuality, First Edition. Justin J. Lehmiller.
© 2014 John Wiley & Sons, Ltd. Published 2014 by John Wiley & Sons, Ltd.

Introduction

[Sexual health is] a state of physical, emotional, mental and social well-being in relation to sexuality; it is not merely the absence of disease, dysfunction or infirmity. Sexual health requires a positive and respectful approach to sexuality and sexual relationships, as well as the possibility of having pleasurable and safe sexual experiences, free of coercion, discrimination and violence. For sexual health to be attained and maintained, the sexual rights of all persons must be respected, protected and fulfilled.

World Health Organization (2012)

The above definition of sexual health will serve to guide our discussion in the final three chapters of this book as we turn to the topics of sexual difficulties and their resolution (in this chapter) and sexual coercion and violence (in Chapters 13 and 14). As this definition makes clear, sexual health has biopsychosocial roots, which is why we will begin this chapter by discussing the biological, psychological, and social factors that contribute to sexual dysfunction. Following that, we will detail the most common sexual difficulties encountered in modern times and discuss their prevalence. The latter half of this chapter will delve into the topic of sex therapy, including coverage of the various schools of thought in treating sex difficulties and some of the most common therapeutic techniques. As you might imagine, given the myriad factors that can generate sexual problems, there is not one simple or singular approach to solving them. We will end the chapter with practical advice and suggestions for avoiding sexual difficulties in your own life.

Causes of Sex Difficulties

When we talk about **sexual dysfunction** or sex difficulties, we are only talking about cases in which a specific sexual issue persistently emerges (i.e., it is not a one-time thing) and creates distress at either the level of the individual or of the relationship. To clarify the importance of this definition, consider someone who lacks sexual desire. Would you say that this person has a problem? Many people would say yes; however, keep in mind that some people are asexual. For asexual individuals, their lack of desire is not personally distressing and they can go on to lead perfectly satisfying and normal lives without sex. Thus, we must take care when labeling certain sexual attitudes and behaviors as inherently "dysfunctional" or "pathological" because subjective perceptions matter and our goal should not be to create problems where none exist.

It is also important to keep in mind that the *absence* of sexual dysfunction does not necessarily mean that someone is sexually healthy and satisfied. It is entirely possible to be free from sexual problems, but to have less than satisfying sexual experiences (Basson et al., 2003). As some of you may have found in your own life, simply having functional genitalia is not a guarantee of great sex. With that said, let us address the biopsychosocial factors that can contribute to sexual problems.

Biological

There are numerous biological factors that can impair sexual function or cause pain during sex, including the natural aging process, chronic illnesses, physical disabilities, sexually transmitted infections (STIs), and drugs. As we get older, most of us will experience decreases in sexual functioning because our bodies and hormone levels change. In addition, the older we get, the more likely we are to develop chronic illnesses. These include diseases of the cardiovascular and nervous systems, which are especially likely to interfere with sexual functioning. For instance, diabetes (a disease that progressively damages blood vessels and inhibits effective blood circulation) is a major contributor to male erectile dysfunction (Johannes et al., 2000). Diabetes can also contribute to female sexual difficulties by reducing blood flow to the clitoris and vagina (Giraldi & Kristensen, 2010). In addition, multiple sclerosis (a disease that damages nerve fibers throughout the central nervous system, thereby disrupting nerve impulses) often produces changes in genital sensitivity and may impact ability to reach orgasm (Basson et al., 2010).

Various cancers are also linked to sexual problems, although it is sometimes the cancer treatment that is more damaging to one's sexuality than the cancer itself. For instance, surgical treatment for cancers of the breast, penis, and testicles tend to change the body in very noticeable ways and often create body image issues. Likewise, surgery for prostate cancer often results in erectile and ejaculatory difficulties (Vale, 2000), a fact that is not surprising given the important role of the prostate in male sexual functioning discussed in chapter 3.

With respect to disabilities, spinal cord injuries are linked to erectile and ejaculatory difficulties in men and often impair the ability to orgasm in women (Basson et al., 2010). Contrary to popular belief, however, permanent sexual difficulties such as these do not necessarily diminish sexual desire or make it impossible to have a satisfying sex life. Redefining what sex is and/or creating secondary erogenous zones (see chapter 4) can help persons with physical disabilities develop and maintain sexual relationships.

As discussed in chapter 11, untreated STIs such as chlamydia and gonorrhea can turn into pelvic inflammatory disease in women, a condition that can lead to painful intercourse and impair ability to orgasm. In addition, a number of drugs and medications have negative sexual side effects. As discussed in previous chapters, antidepressants (namely SSRIs) tend to delay orgasm in men and women because they keep serotonin in the brain longer. Other psychiatric medications such as antipsychotics and tranquilizers also have neurological effects that can inhibit ability to reach orgasm. Some blood pressure and allergy medications have been reported to have negative sexual effects as well. Finally, as discussed in chapter 4, alcohol, tobacco, and other drugs can not only create episodic sexual problems, but long-term use of these substances can generate chronic sexual dysfunction. For instance, chronic alcoholism is linked to problems with sexual desire, arousal, and orgasm (Segraves & Balon, 2003). Likewise, men who smoke for years are at increased risk of having erectile difficulties due to tobacco's damaging effects on the body's blood vessels. In addition, chronic use of cocaine, opiates, and other such drugs can inhibit sexual arousal and response (Segraves & Balon, 2003).

Psychological

Some of the most common psychological causes of sexual dysfunction include distraction, previous learning experiences, beliefs about sexual difficulties, body image, and mental illness. First, distraction often takes the form of **spectatoring** (Masters & Johnson, 1970), which involves over-thinking or over-analyzing one's own sexual performance while having sex. You can think of spectatoring as the act of becoming a spectator to your own sexual activity by mentally stepping out of the moment and evaluating how you are doing (e.g., Are you pleasing your partner? Could you be

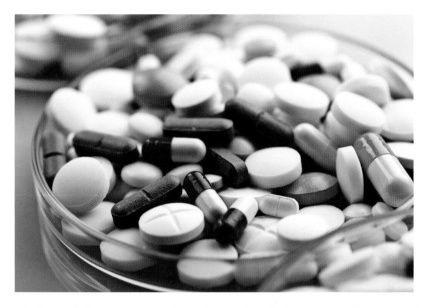

Figure 12.1 Both prescription and non-prescription drugs and medications can contribute to sexual problems. ©Sebastian Duda/123RF.COM.

doing a better job?). Over-thinking your sexual performance may create anxiety that reduces arousal and likelihood of orgasm.

Second, past learning experiences have important implications for our sexual functioning. For instance, people who grew up learning that sex is a shameful or sinful activity and women who have been taught to think that they should not enjoy sex may end up thinking about these things during the act, thereby dulling sexual response and pleasure. Likewise, people who have experienced traumatic sexual events in the past, such as rape, sexual assault, or childhood sexual abuse may feel an aversion to sex or have post-traumatic stress, which can make sex thoroughly unenjoyable and perhaps impossible. In fact, a history of sexual abuse is often uncovered during sex therapy for both women and men (McCarthy, 1990).

Third, our beliefs about sexual dysfunction are linked to our experiences with sexual problems. For example, research has found that, at least among women, the more prevalent they believe sexual difficulties to be, the lower their own sexual functioning is (Chang, Klein, & Gorzalka, 2013). These beliefs about higher prevalence may lead to monitoring oneself for sexual problems or simply produce more anxiety and worry that one will develop a problem.

Fourth, poor body image and a lack of knowledge regarding your own body can contribute to sexual problems. As discussed in Chapter 3, many women and men are dissatisfied with the size and shape of their chest and genitals. This can create distress and anxiety that ultimately leads people with poor body image to avoid sexual activity altogether (La Rocque & Cioe, 2011). Alternatively, they may only have sex under very limited circumstances (e.g., at night with all of the lights off or only while wearing a shirt). These restrictions have the added effect of reducing sexual spontaneity and frequency. Also, when such persons do have sex, they may be preoccupied with how they look or what their partner is thinking. With respect to sexual knowledge, a lack of familiarity with one's own genital anatomy, particularly among women, is sometimes implicated in orgasmic difficulties.

Figure 12.2   Spectatoring and other distractions during sex can make it difficult to maintain arousal and reach orgasm. ©ostill/123RF.COM.

Finally, mental illness (irrespective of whether one is receiving pharmacological treatment) is linked to sexual dysfunction, but not always in the same way. For instance, affective disorders are sometimes associated with low libido (as in the case of major depression), and other times with hypersexuality (as in the case of bipolar disorder, at least when people are in the manic phase; Dell'Osso et al., 2009). Additionally, psychotic disorders such as schizophrenia are associated with several forms of sexual dysfunction. Certain mental disabilities are linked to sexual difficulties too; however, less is known about this because sexuality and sexual behavior are typically ignored for this population. Many societies deem the mentally disabled unable to provide sexual consent and, in some cases, these individuals may be institutionalized. Thus, sexual difficulties among the mentally disabled have gone unstudied and unaddressed because these individuals are often denied a sex life altogether.

On a side note, sometimes it is difficult to separate out biological causes from psychological causes of sex difficulties because they frequently go hand-in-hand. For instance, coronary heart disease is linked to erectile dysfunction (Johannes et al., 2000). Part of this linkage is a result of general cardiovascular problems, but it is also the case that having a heart attack makes people anxious about future sexual activity because they are afraid of getting "too worked up." Thus, a given sexual dysfunction can have more than one cause, with biological and psychological factors often being intimately intertwined.

Social

Last but not least, there are several social variables than can generate sexual difficulties. First, ineffective communication about sex both in and out of the bedroom is correlated with lower sexual satisfaction (Babin, 2013). This makes sense because if you fail to tell you partner what you like or what feels good, then you may not receive the stimulation you need in order to maintain arousal and to reach orgasm. Second, relationship problems such as unresolved conflict and anger often reduce desire for partnered sexual activity (Brotto, 2010a), which has a tendency to breed further relationship problems. Third, the way the partners in a relationship view sex can affect partners' performance and satisfaction. For example, as noted in chapter 10, couples who are actively trying to have a baby sometimes put too much performance pressure on one another, which may create anxiety and arousal problems. Also, couples who turn sex into a chore or duty, or whose sex lives become very routine (e.g., a couple who only has sex on Tuesdays and only in the missionary position) may risk reducing their enjoyment. Lastly, cultural and religious factors are extremely important to take into account because they may dictate certain prohibitions when it comes to seeking out and experiencing pleasure from sex. For example, it is well known that East Asian cultures tend to have more conservative attitudes toward sex than European cultures. Research finds that persons of East Asian descent tend to report lower sexual desire and functioning than their European counterparts, at least partly because they report feeling more guilt about pursuing and enjoying sexual activity (Brotto, Woo, & Gorzalka, 2012).

As the above discussion makes clear, sexual dysfunction is a biopsychosocial phenomenon. For even more information on the biopsychosocial factors associated with sexual dysfunction, see Table 12.1. One theory that attempts to integrate all of these influences is the **dual control model** (Bancroft, Graham, Janssen, & Sanders, 2009). The idea behind this model is that underlying sexual arousal and behavior are two important brain mechanisms: an excitatory system and an inhibitory system. Activation of the excitatory system promotes sexual arousal and activity, whereas activation of the inhibitory system suppresses it. Having two separate systems is thought to be adaptive. For instance, the excitatory system is important for ensuring that reproduction happens, whereas the inhibitory system may be useful for helping to maintain harmonious interpersonal relationships by suppressing the impulse to have sex with our friends' romantic partners.

Table 12.1   Factors Associated with Risk of Sexual Dysfunction in the National Health and Social Life Survey

Emotional problems and stress were correlated with experiencing arousal and desire disorders in both men and women, as well as painful intercourse in women.

In men, poor physical health was linked to greater risk for premature ejaculation, erectile dysfunction, and low sexual desire. In women, poor health was only linked to painful sex.

Being sexually touched before puberty was linked to arousal disorders in both men and women, as well as desire disorders and premature ejaculation in men.

Women who were previous victims of sexual assault were more likely to experience arousal disorders. Men who reported having forced themselves on a woman before were more likely to experience erectile dysfunction.

Having previously had an STI was associated with lower sexual desire among women.

Having had an abortion was unrelated to female sexual dysfunction.

Masturbation frequency was unrelated to sexual difficulties in both men and women.

Source: Laumann, Paik, & Rosen (1999).

It is theorized that both systems are influenced by biopsychosocial factors. For example, some people may be biologically "hardwired" to have one system be more active than the other. At the same time, however, activation of these systems is also affected by our previous learning experiences (e.g., have your previous sexual experiences been rewarding or punishing?) and by cultural factors (e.g., does your culture believe that sexual responses should be controlled and hidden away?).

When one system becomes disproportionately active, no matter whether it is a result of biological, psychological, or social factors, sexual difficulties are more likely to occur. For example, higher excitatory activity may lead to compulsive and risky sexual behavior or premature orgasm, whereas higher inhibitory activity may lead to difficulties with sexual desire or with becoming and staying aroused. As you can see, the dual control model may be useful for understanding the origins of a wide range of sexual dysfunctions.

Types of Sexual Dysfunction

At this point, we will turn to a discussion of specific sexual difficulties. Research on sexual difficulties has historically been heterosexist and made the assumption that everyone fits into the gender binary. As some evidence of this, many of the diagnostic criteria for sexual difficulties emphasize problems with penile–vaginal intercourse and there is typically little, if any coverage of sexual problems among individuals who are transgendered. However, anyone can experience sexual dysfunction, regardless of their sexual orientation, gender identity, or specific sexual practices. As a result, we will attempt to describe sexual difficulties here at a broader level than you might see elsewhere, without making too many assumptions about people's sexual identities and practices.

Below, we will describe sexual dysfunction according to four distinct classes: problems with desire, arousal, orgasm, and painful intercourse. Please note that the problems identified can be issues people have had for their entire lives (a *primary dysfunction*), or issues that appeared out of the blue one day after a period of healthy sexual functioning (a *secondary dysfunction*). Also, it is important to recognize that these dysfunctions may only occur with one partner or during one type of sexual activity (a *situational dysfunction*), or they may occur with all partners and all sexual acts (a *global dysfunction*).

Desire Problems

The most common difficulties pertaining to sexual desire are **female sexual interest/arousal disorder (SIAD)** and **male hypoactive sexual desire disorder (HSDD)**, both of which are characterized by absent or reduced sexual fantasies and thoughts, a lack of desire for sexual activity, and personal distress resulting from these symptoms. The HSDD label used to apply to both men and women, but in the DSM-5, this label is technically now applicable only to men, and the new category of SIAD was created for women. SIAD is much broader than a lack of sexual desire and also includes reduced or absent excitement during sexual activity, reduced genital sensations during sex, as well as a lack of *responsive desire* (i.e., desire that sets in after sexual activity has started; Brotto, 2010a). Because female sexual desire and arousal difficulties are frequently comorbid (i.e., they co-occur) and can be difficult to distinguish, two previous diagnostic categories (female HSDD and *female sexual arousal disorder*) were combined into one in the latest version of the DSM.

Low sexual desire is the most common form of female sexual dysfunction, and it tends to be more common among women than men (for information on the prevalence of various sexual dysfunctions at different life stages in men and women, see Table 12.2). Of course, keep in mind that a lack of sexual desire is not necessarily pathological (e.g., as in the case of asexuals). Also, it is perfectly normal for sexually active people to experience fluctuations in desire throughout their lives (e.g., desire may temporarily decrease during times of significant stress). SIAD and HSDD are only considered disorders when they are both *persistent* and *personally distressing*. In cases where one partner has less sexual desire than the other and it generates relationship difficulties, this is known as a **sexual desire discrepancy** and is considered a couple-level problem, not the fault of one individual. Contrary to popular belief, sometimes men are the low-desire partners and sometimes women are the high-desire partners in different-sex relationships; however, it is important to note that desire discrepancies can also affect same-sex couples.

Another desire difficulty is **sexual aversion disorder**, which refers to an aversion to any type of partnered sexual activity (Brotto, 2010b). The aversion can take many forms, ranging from fear to disgust. In severe cases, just the thought of sexual activity may be enough to generate a panic attack. We do not have good data on the prevalence of this disorder, but it is thought to be extremely rare. In fact, this diagnostic category was so infrequently used by clinicians that it was dropped from the DSM-5.

What about the opposite of low sexual desire? **Compulsive sexual behavior**, also known as hypersexuality, refers to cases where people have "excessive" sexual desire and engage in very high amounts of sexual behavior. This can take the form of non-stop pornography use, a large number of anonymous sexual encounters, and/or an obsessive preoccupation with all things sex. The popular media often refers to this pattern of behavior as "sexual addiction"; however, despite all you have heard about this "addiction" and all of the celebrities who have entered "sex rehab," compulsive sexual behavior was not recognized as a disorder in the DSM-5, at least partly because there is a lack of research on this topic and a lack of agreement about what constitutes "too much" when it comes to sexual behavior. That said, there is a listing for *excessive sexual drive* in the International Classification of Diseases (ICD) published by the World Health Organization. This diagnosis is subdivided into *satyriasis* (for men) and *nymphomania* (for women), with those names derived from the most sexually active creatures in Greek mythology (i.e., satyrs and nymphs). However, the notion of sexual "addiction" remains controversial. What do you think about it? Weigh in with your perspective in the Your Sexuality 12.1 box.

Table 12.2	Prevalence of Various Forms of Sexual Dysfunction Across Different Life Stages						
	Lack of sexual desire		Difficulty reaching orgasm		Pain during sex	Vaginal lubrication difficulty	Erectile difficulties	Premature orgasm
Age	Men	Women	Men	Women	Women	Women	Men	Men
18–29	14	32	7	26	21	19	7	30
30–39	13	32	7	28	15	18	9	32
40–49	15	30	9	22	13	21	11	28
50–59	17	27	9	23	8	27	18	31

Source: Laumann, Paik, & Rosen (1999)

Your Sexuality 12.1 Is Sexual "Addiction" Real?

Figure 12.3 Golfer Tiger Woods is just one of many male celebrities who have sought treatment for "sexual addiction" in recent years after it was revealed that he was having an affair. Image Copyright photogolfer, 2013. Used under license from Shutterstock.com.

Tiger Woods. David Duchovny. Jesse James. Russell Brand. The list of male celebrities who have checked into treatment facilities to deal with sexual "addiction" seems to grow by the day. However, each case follows a seemingly predictable pattern in that the addiction only comes to light after the guy is caught cheating on his drop-dead gorgeous wife. This has led many in the media to question whether sexual addiction is a real thing, or if it is just a way for rich and powerful men to absolve themselves from personal responsibility when caught with their pants down. Adding fuel to the fire is the fact that the American Psychiatric Association opted not to include compulsive sexual behavior as a diagnosis in the DSM-5. That said, a number of therapists have publically stated that they frequently deal with clients presenting with sexual behaviors that are out of control, and you can easily locate numerous case reports of compulsive sexual behavior with a quick PsycINFO search. In addition, given that extremely low sexual desire and arousal is a diagnostic category in the DSM, it seems odd that the opposite end of the spectrum is unaddressed.

Without a diagnosis in the DSM, therapists have a hard time determining what is and is not "excessive" when it comes to sexual behavior and clients may be unable to get insurance coverage for treatment, which is too expensive for the average person to pay out of pocket. Taking all of this into account, what do you think? Can someone truly be "addicted" to sex? If so, how is it similar to or different from other addictions? Should a diagnosis of excessive sexual behavior appear in the next version of the DSM?

Arousal Problems

Sexual arousal difficulties fall into two categories: (1) problems becoming or staying aroused and (2) problems with persistent and uncontrollable arousal. In biological women, chronic difficulty becoming aroused is given the SIAD label discussed above, whereas uncontrollable arousal is known as **persistent genital arousal disorder** (sometimes called "restless genital syndrome"). SIAD may be diagnosed when effective stimulation reliably fails to produce vaginal lubrication and other physical signs of arousal and/or when such stimulation produces physical but not psychological arousal (Graham, 2010a). In contrast, persistent genital arousal disorder, a relatively new and rare diagnosis, involves uncontrollable sexual arousal that occurs spontaneously, without being preceded by sexual desire or activity (Leiblum, Brown, Wan, & Rawlinson, 2005). In such cases, arousal can last for days at a time with orgasms providing only temporary relief. Some of you might be thinking to yourself, "What's so bad about that?" Let me assure you it is not as pleasurable as you are imagining. People with this disorder report that constant arousal is physically uncomfortable and significantly impairs concentration, making it difficult to lead a normal life and to carry out very ordinary tasks. Physical causes have been implicated in both of these disorders, although research has suggested that psychological and relationship factors can sometimes play a role in SIAD (Graham, 2010a).

In biological men, difficulty becoming aroused is known as **erectile disorder** (ED), while uncontrollable arousal is known as **priapism**. ED, also commonly known as *erectile dysfunction* or *impotence*, refers to a persistent inability to develop or maintain an erection sufficient for sexual performance. This is one of the most common forms of sexual dysfunction in men, especially as they get older (see Table 12.2). ED can have physical or psychological causes and, depending upon the origin, the treatment is very different. In contrast, priapism ("permanent erection") is defined as an erection that simply will not go away on its own. More specifically, it is an erection lasting longer than four hours. Such erections are painful and should be viewed as a medical emergency because, if left untreated, it can severely damage the penile tissues and eventually cause ED. Most cases of priapism are caused by medications or physical conditions and are not a result of having a high sex drive.

Orgasm Problems

There are two types of orgasm problems: finishing too quickly or not at all. Although both problems can occur in men and women, men are more likely to have the problem of reaching orgasm too soon and women are more likely to have the problem of never reaching orgasm. **Premature orgasm** (also referred to as *premature ejaculation* or *early ejaculation* in men) occurs when an individual consistently reaches orgasm before it is desired. In such cases, orgasm occurs rapidly and sometimes prior to any sexual penetration. In men, it may even occur before a full erection is reached. However, pinpointing the exact moment when an orgasm becomes "premature" is dicey. Although the DSM-5 technically defines male premature ejaculation as occurring within one minute, I would argue that it is probably best not to define it in terms of seconds, minutes, or number of thrusts and instead focus on how the orgasm is subjectively perceived (i.e., Is the timing of it distressing? Does the individual avoid sexual intimacy because of it?). Although most people associate this problem with men, it has been documented among some women as well (Carvalho et al., 2011). Premature orgasm can have both physical and psychological roots, but some researchers have proposed that (at least among men) it may not be a dysfunction at all and instead may reflect an adaptive advantage. The idea is that because the male orgasm is essential to reproduction, having it occur faster will maximize the likelihood of conception by reducing the odds that the sexual act will be interrupted before completion (Hong, 1984). An alternative explanation is that some boys may condition themselves to ejaculate rapidly during adolescence to reduce the risk of being caught in the act. Given the prevalence of male premature orgasm (see Table 12.2), some have argued that adaptive and psychosocial explanations like these make sense and that perhaps we are unnecessarily pathologizing early ejaculation by classifying it as a disorder.

In contrast, **orgasmic disorder** (also known as *anorgasmia*) is the term used to refer to women who have either an inability to achieve orgasm or a greatly delayed orgasm during sexual activity. Orgasmic disorder is common (see Table 12.2) and involves delayed or absent orgasm, and/or reduced orgasmic intensity. In some cases, the inability to orgasm represents a lifelong pattern of behavior, whereas for others, it is situational (e.g., they may be able to reach orgasm through masturbation but not with a partner; Graham, 2010b). Psychological factors are often at play, but female anorgasmia may also have physical roots (e.g., untreated STIs, spinal cord injury) and, in some cases, may result solely from insufficient stimulation. Please note that heterosexual women who cannot reach orgasm as a result of vaginal intercourse alone but can reach orgasm in other ways (e.g., through clitoral stimulation) are not considered to have a dysfunction.

In the DSM-5, orgasmic disorder is technically termed **delayed ejaculation** when it affects biological men, and it is far less common than both premature ejaculation and ED (see Table 12.2). In most cases, it involves a man whose ability to ejaculate is either significantly delayed or frequently absent during intercourse, but functions normally during masturbation and other activities (Segraves, 2010). In this scenario, there is often a psychological explanation (e.g., such men may have a preference for other sexual activities over intercourse); however, in cases where a man's ability to orgasm is lost completely, there are usually medical reasons (e.g., prostate cancer, spinal cord injury).

As mentioned in chapter 5, orgasmic difficulties are also an issue faced by postoperative transsexuals, largely because sex reassignment surgery may disrupt the body's original sensory pathways (Lief & Hubschman, 1993). However, male-to-female transsexuals usually face more difficulties after surgery than female-to-male transsexuals.

Pain Disorders

The final class of sexual dysfunction we will consider is disorders that involve pain. The two main forms of sexual pain in men (both of which are relatively rare) are **phimosis**, a condition in which an uncircumcised man's foreskin is too tight and makes erections painful, and **Peyronie's disease**, a condition in which a build-up of scar tissue around the cavernous bodies results in a severe curvature of the penis and makes intercourse difficult and painful. STIs, smegma, and urinary infections can also lead men to experience physical pain during sex.

In women, painful sex is far more common (see Table 12.2) and has many possible causes (Butcher, 1999). When women experience pain in anticipation of or during vaginal intercourse, or when vaginal penetration is difficult, it is known as **genito-pelvic pain/penetration disorder (GPD)**. In the DSM-5, GPD represents the merging of two previous diagnostic categories: dyspareunia and vaginismus. These categories were merged because they frequently co-occurred and were hard for clinicians to distinguish.

Dyspareunia referred to any type of pelvic or genital pain that occurred during sexual arousal or activity. As noted in chapter 11, STIs are one such reason, but other possible contributors include infections of the Bartholin's glands, yeast infections, smegma accumulation under the clitoral hood, as well as vaginal scars and tears (from childbirth, an episiotomy, prior sexual assault, etc.). Other potential causes include inadequate lubrication, irritation from spermicides, and allergies to latex condoms. Psychological factors may also play a role in both developing and maintaining painful sex. For example, eye-tracking research has revealed that when women with dyspareunia are shown erotic imagery, they spend less time looking at the sexual aspects of the scene and more time looking at the background and contextual features compared to women with no sexual difficulties (Lykins, Meana, & Minimi, 2010). This suggests that women with dyspareunia are either distracted from sexual stimuli, or they seek to avoid it. Of course, it is unclear to what extent distraction and avoidance may be a cause or a consequence of painful sex, but this pattern of responding to sexual stimuli could help painful sex persist once it starts.

Vaginismus referred to a situation in which the lower third of the vagina exhibits sudden and severe contractions during any attempt at vaginal penetration, thereby making intercourse difficult and painful (Butcher, 1999). This may coincide with the very first attempt at vaginal penetration, or develop at some later point in life. Such contractions are completely involuntary and not only inhibit intercourse, but also gynecological exams and the insertion of tampons. Vaginismus usually represents a conditioned response, and often stems from a chronic history of painful sex. Vaginismus may also develop in response to chronic relationship problems, or past experiences with sexual coercion or assault.

Sex Therapy

Now that you have an understanding of some of the most common sexual difficulties and their causes, we will turn our attention to the resolution of those difficulties. We begin by considering the major schools of thought when it comes to sex therapy, because there is not just one way of approaching a given sexual problem.

Schools of Thought

The Behavioral Approach

First is **behavioral therapy**, an approach pioneered by Masters and Johnson (1970). Their view was that sexual dysfunction can often be explained by basic principles of psychological learning theory, namely, punishment and reinforcement. If the behaviorism movement has taught us anything, it is that we can often learn new associations to replace those that are maladaptive. Thus, the goal of Masters and Johnson's therapy was to change the way that people approach sex and to recondition the client to feel pleasure rather than stress in sexual situations.

In order to accomplish this, sex therapists must get their clients to stop perseverating on what they are "supposed" to achieve each time they have sex (i.e., orgasm) and, instead, relax. In other words, we need to remove the fear of failure in the bedroom that all too often becomes a self-fulfilling prophecy. One way of achieving this is for couples to do something that sounds coun-

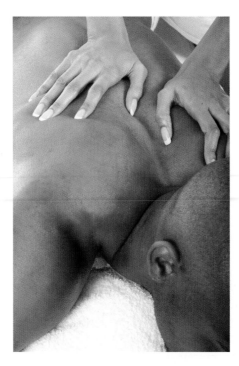

Figure 12.4   Sensate focus exercises focus on promoting relaxation, communication, and intimacy. These exercises alone are often enough to resolve sexual difficulties. Image Copyright Dewayne Flowers 2013. Used under license from Shutterstock.com.

terintuitive: temporarily stop having sex. Couples will then slowly work their way back into it through a series of **sensate focus techniques**. Sensate focus can be thought of as a gradual reconditioning process in which individuals ultimately come to associate sexual arousal and activity with relaxation and pleasure instead of anxiety. The way this works is that the partners will start out slow, with no demands placed upon each other, and progressively build up sexual intensity as they learn to let go of sexual fears and distractions. For instance, in the early stages of sensate focus, couple members may be instructed to take turns touching or massaging each other without focusing on the breasts or genitals and to simply enjoy the feeling of one another's bodies. Next, partners may be instructed to guide the other person's hand over their own body to demonstrate what they find pleasurable. In the days and weeks ahead, genital touch and the desired forms of sexual activity are reintroduced. During these later stages, couples are instructed to continue telling each other what feels good and not to view orgasm as the ultimate goal. These exercises are based on the notion that both touch and communication are vital aspects of healthy sexuality.

Sensate focus techniques are often combined with sex education because many cases of sexual dysfunction can be attributed to a lack of knowledge about the human body (your own and/or your partner's). One such combined approach is the **PLISSIT model of sex therapy**, developed by psychologist Jack Annon (1976). PLISSIT is an acronym that stands for *Permission*, *Limited Information*, Specific *Suggestions*, and *Intensive Therapy*. The idea behind this model is that most people experiencing sexual dysfunction do not need major therapy; instead, most clients just need a little reassurance (permission), an anatomy lesson (limited information), or some new sexual strategies or advice such as sensate focus (specific suggestions). Most cases do not require the final step of intensive therapy.

How well does behavioral therapy work? Masters and Johnson (1970) reported a 20% failure rate overall, which many people interpreted as meaning that their methods were successful 80% of the time. However, it appears that the 80% of non-failures represented a mix of partial and complete successes, so it cannot necessarily be inferred that 80% of the problems were completely resolved (Zilbergeld & Evans, 1980). As it turns out, it is more problematic than it might seem to define "success" in sex therapy. For example, consider a client with premature orgasm who was previously only able to last one minute, but was able to last an extra 30 seconds by the end of therapy. Is that a successful outcome? Some would say yes, but others might disagree. Despite significant variation in definitions and rates of success across disorders, there is no dispute that behavioral therapy can generate improvement for a variety of sexual dysfunctions.

On a side note, it is worth mentioning that while Masters and Johnson's sex therapy research was originally validated on heterosexual clients, they found that administering the same type of sex therapy to same-sex couples was about equally effective (Masters & Johnson, 1979).

The Cognitive-Behavioral Approach

Cognitive-behavioral sex therapy (CBST) builds upon the behavioral approach by combining it with theories of cognition. Instead of simply instructing clients to alter their behaviors, CBST goes further by looking at the thoughts and feelings underlying our behaviors. Thus, in CBST, a client will be involved in some type of "talk therapy" in which a psychologist will attempt to identify the thoughts that generate anxiety that, in turn, create sexual problems. Ultimately, the goal is to reshape thought patterns to make them more positive. Such an approach would be most applicable to clients who have problems with spectatoring or who have distressing thoughts that pop into their minds during sexual activity. CBST is reasonably effective; again, however, success rates vary across disorders and with definitions of "success" (McCabe, 2001).

Other Approaches

Beyond behavioral therapy and CBST, there are several other approaches to treating sexual dysfunction, including sex surrogacy and pharmacotherapy. **Sex surrogacy** involves cases where a therapist provides clients with substitute or "practice" partners in order to reach desired therapeutic outcomes. As you might imagine, this is highly controversial. For more on sex surrogacy, see the Digging Deeper 12.1 box.

Pharmacotherapy involves the treatment of sexual difficulties with medicinal drugs. Only psychiatrists (who are medical doctors by training) can practice the full range of pharmacotherapy because, even in the few locales that allow prescription privileges for psychologists, the types of drugs they are permitted to prescribe are limited in scope. The number of medications with a demonstrated therapeutic effect on sexual dysfunction is growing rapidly. This list includes hormonal therapy (testosterone supplementation for low desire in men and women, as well as estrogen replacement in post-menopausal women with arousal problems), Viagra (for treating erectile dysfunction), SSRIs (for premature orgasm), and Botox (for

Digging Deeper 12.1   Sex Surrogacy: The "Hands-On" Approach to Sex Therapy

The best therapy for a man suffering impotence… may be a therapist-supplied "other woman" who embodies patience. Actual patience with a willing woman is crucial.

Quote from the November 1, 1969 San Francisco Chronicle
(as cited in Apfelbaum, 1977, p. 239)

Some within the sexual health community have argued that the best way to resolve a sexual difficulty is to practice with a substitute partner who is knowledgeable and experienced. This idea first catapulted into the spotlight in the 1970s when Masters and Johnson publicly advocated for at least some usage of so-called "surrogate" partners in the practice of sex therapy. As part of their pioneering research, Masters and Johnson recruited female volunteers to serve as sex surrogates for single men who were experiencing sexual difficulties and achieved a very high rate of success in treating erectile dysfunction. However, this approach was greeted with a great deal of skepticism and concern by both the broader community of sex therapists and the general public alike. So what is the status of sex surrogate therapy today?

Figure 12.5   In the 2012 film *The Sessions*, Helen Hunt portrayed a sex surrogate who helped a disabled man discover his sexual potential. The film is based on a true story and offers an eye-opening look at the field of sex surrogacy. Image Copyright Featureflash, 2013. Used under license from Shutterstock.com.

We do not know a lot about the nature of modern sex surrogacy from a research standpoint because this therapy continues to remain outside the mainstream; however, we know that it is practiced and, according to the International Professional Surrogates Association, follows many of the basic principles outlined by Masters and Johnson (1970). For instance, Masters and Johnson advocated that surrogates should be *supplied by the sex therapist* (i.e., the therapist should not double as the substitute partner). The therapist and surrogate are thus two separate parts of the therapeutic team. In addition, Masters and Johnson argued that surrogates should basically be anonymous to the client and not share information that could lead them to be personally identified later on.

Who are these sex surrogates? Research suggests that they represent a diverse group of people, including men and women and people of all sexual orientations (although it appears that most surrogates are college-educated, heterosexual women; Noonan, 1984). In addition, these therapists do more than just provide a sexual service to their clients. They also spend time providing emotional support, building social skills, and teaching the client how to relax (Noonan, 1984). The few studies that exist suggest that surrogates can be highly effective in treating both male and female sexual difficulties ranging from erectile and ejaculatory problems (Dauw, 1988) to vaginismus (Ben-Zion, Rothschild, Chudakov, & Aloni, 2007).

Questions about the ethicality and legality of this practice remain. The major psychiatric and psychological societies consider it unethical for a therapist of any sort to have sexual contact with a client, whether it has a therapeutic goal or not. It is easy to understand the ethical concerns here because there is a power discrepancy, the potential for abuse and exploitation, and the possibility of therapeutic harm if unreciprocated feelings develop. Also, legally speaking, many have likened surrogacy to prostitution (i.e., an exchange of money for sexual services). Thus, the practice of sex surrogacy continues to be as controversial as when it was first introduced, and the debate over it is unlikely to go away any time soon.

Note: Reprinted with permission from *The Psychology of Human Sexuality* blog (www.lehmiller.com).

vaginismus). We will explain the effects of these drugs shortly, but suffice it to say, more and more people are receiving medication instead of working with a therapist to deal with their sexual difficulties.

The growth of pharmacotherapy has been controversial, with some arguing that drug manufacturers and physicians are increasingly ignoring the biopsychosocial nature of sexual dysfunction and valuing physical treatments over psychotherapy (e.g., Bancroft, 2002). The concern is that because drug treatments can be administered quickly, are highly profitable, and are preferred by some patients who seek convenience, they are on their way to becoming the first line of defense, even in cases where psychological treatments or couples therapy would be more appropriate. As a result, we may be fundamentally altering the nature of sex therapy away from an emphasis on the couple (as we saw in the Masters and Johnson approach) and toward the individual. Certainly, drugs have a place in sex therapy, and nobody is advocating that we get rid of them entirely – just that we do not overuse them and completely forget that the modern sex therapy movement was founded on the premise that many sexual problems can be alleviated simply by enhancing relationship intimacy and communication.

Critiques and Controversies

As mentioned above, there are some ongoing controversies in the field of sex therapy about how we should define therapeutic "success" and how large a role pharmacotherapy should play. In addition, there is a more general controversy about how we should define a sexual "disorder" or "dysfunction" in the first place, and when treatment is appropriate. For one thing, it is important to remember that what is "normal" and "abnormal" when it comes to sex is culturally relative. For instance, while people in the US may view a lack of sexual desire as problematic for a woman, some African and Middle-Eastern cultures may see this as normative and acceptable. In addition, some cultures may see sexual problems as having supernatural rather than organic or psychological causes, which means their approach to dealing with sexual difficulties will be quite different.

Related to this point, psychiatrist Thomas Szasz (1990) has argued that having diagnoses based upon patterns of behavior is completely arbitrary because what represents a sexual "problem" for one individual may be a desired outcome for another person. Thus, the whole notion of sexual "dysfunction" is a social creation in his view. To illustrate his point, why do we consider it problematic when someone has difficulties becoming aroused or typically reaches orgasm in under a minute, yet we do not call it dysfunctional when someone dislikes kissing or does not enjoy giving and/or receiving oral sex? Are we just selectively imposing sexual illnesses on certain people?

All of this is not to deny the existence of sexual difficulties; rather, it is to reiterate the point made at the beginning of this chapter that we need to recognize the role of subjective perception when it comes to diagnosing and treating sexual problems. Specifically, we should be reserving the "dysfunction" label only for cases in which the behavior is causing personal distress or harming the individual's ability to establish or maintain the intimate relationship desired.

Specific Treatments

At this point, we will address some of the specific therapeutic treatments that have been developed for sexual difficulties.

Treating Desire Problems

Desire dysfunctions tend to be the most difficult to treat and typically have the lowest success rates of all sexual disorders. However, there are multiple treatment options to consider, and it may take more than one attempt to achieve resolution. One possibility is behavioral therapy or CBST, because low desire and desire discrepancies sometimes stem from relationship problems (Graham, 2010a). Thus, enhancing intimacy and communication through sensate focus or other techniques may help. Beyond this, pharmacotherapy is another possibility. As discussed in chapter 4, testosterone is a hormone that is linked to higher levels of sexual desire. Among both men and women, testosterone supplementation has increasingly been used to treat desire difficulties with some degree of success (Bhasin, Enzlin, Coviello, & Basson, 2007).

Treating Arousal Problems

In women, difficulties becoming aroused can be treated with CBST if psychological or relationship factors are the root of the issue. If there are physical causes, hormone therapy is an option. In particular, estrogen replacement in post-menopausal women can enhance vaginal lubrication. Alternatively, artificial lubricants can be used with fewer side effects. Another option for increasing arousal is the *EROS Clitoral Therapy Device*, which you can think of as the female equivalent of the penis pump. EROS works by drawing more blood into the clitoris through a small, motorized suction device, thereby increasing genital sensation and sensitivity. Unfortunately, because persistent genital arousal disorder has only recently been identified and is relatively rare, research on possible treatments for this problem is very limited.

In men, persistent arousal (i.e., priapism) can be treated by drawing the blood out of the penile tissues. This can be accomplished with medications that constrict blood vessels in the penis, thereby forcing more blood out, or by manually removing blood with a needle. Ouch. In contrast, ED can be treated with CBST, drugs, pumps, or surgery. Before determining the appropriate treatment, a physician would need to assess whether the cause is biological or psychological. This can be determined by testing whether the patient is still getting erections during his sleep. Males naturally get four to five erections per night as they move in and out of different sleep cycles, which is why they often wake up with "morning wood" (on a side note, women get the same number of clitoral erections at night too, which means women technically get morning wood too; Siegel, 2005). By encircling the base of the penis with a thin paper ring, men can easily see whether they are still getting sleep erections based upon whether that ring breaks during the night. If it does, psychotherapy would be the appropriate treatment. If not, some type of mechanical device (i.e., a penis pump, which draws blood in through a vacuum mechanism) or medical therapy would be warranted.

Of the medical options, drug treatment with Viagra (or its sister medications Cialis and Levitra) would be the least invasive. All of these drugs are chemically similar and work by creating the capacity for an erection. Specifically, these medications dilate the blood vessels leading to the penis, which allows more blood to flow in during sexual stimulation. Contrary to popular belief, these drugs do not produce automatic erections (erotic stimulation is required) and their effects are not immediate (they may take up to two hours to work). Most men with ED respond well to these drugs, but research suggests that their effectiveness is amplified when combined with couple's sex therapy that focuses on improving communication and intimacy (Aubin et al., 2009). However, it is important to be aware that one of the potential side effects of ED drugs is priapism.

The more involved option would be a penile implant, which is only considered if all other options have failed or are unsatisfactory because implants require destroying the cavernous bodies of the penis, thereby making it impossible to achieve a natural erection afterward. One type of implant involves placing inflatable tubes inside the cavernous bodies that are attached to a fluid-filled reservoir inside the abdomen and a pumping mechanism implanted in the scrotum. When an erection is desired, the scrotal pump is pressed until the penis is fully inflated by the fluid from the reservoir. A release valve is also implanted in the scrotum so that the erection can be deflated when it is not needed. Alternatively, rather than a pump, a pair of semi-rigid rods may be implanted inside the cavernous bodies. The penis can then be bent upward when an erection is desired, and

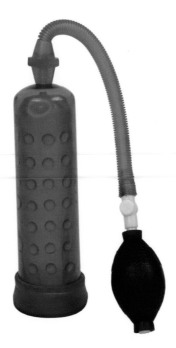

Figure 12.6   One option for treating erectile dysfunction is a penis pump, which draws blood into the penis through vacuum pressure. A constriction band at the base of the penis serves to trap blood in the penis, thereby maintaining an erection for the duration of sexual activity. Image Copyright CTR Photos 2013. Used under license from Shutterstock.com.

Figure 12.7   Upon its release in the late 1990s, Viagra quickly became the fastest-selling prescription drug of all time and continues to be a popular ED treatment to this day. ©Daniel Korzeniewski/123RF.COM.

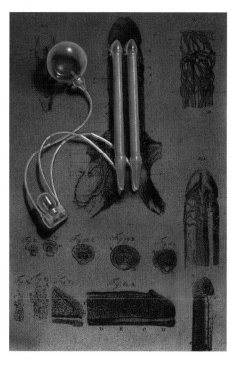

Figure 12.8 One type of penile implant involves placing inflatable cylinders inside the cavernous bodies, which are attached to a fluid-filled reservoir in the pelvic cavity and a pumping mechanism placed inside the scrotum. © 2008 Sharon Ellis.

bent back down afterward. Most men (85–86%) who receive an implant tend to be satisfied with the results (Cortés-González & Glina, 2009); however, be aware that implants cannot restore lost sensation or orgasm capacity.

Treating Orgasm Problems

As mentioned above, premature orgasm is an issue that can affect both men and women; however, it is substantially more common among men. To learn about the most common treatments for this sexual issue, check out the Digging Deeper 12.2 box. Although this box focuses on treatment for male premature orgasm, it is likely that many of these same techniques could be adapted to treat premature orgasm in women, although that has yet to be empirically studied.

Resolution of inhibited or delayed orgasm requires looking at whether the underlying cause is physical or psychological. Behavioral therapy and CBST may be useful if relationship conflict, anxiety, or distraction is the root of the problem. As part of a behavioral treatment program, clients may be instructed to get to know their own body better (e.g., getting comfortable with masturbation and exploring different stimulation techniques to determine what feels best) or to communicate more with their partner about what they enjoy. Kegel exercises (as discussed in chapter 3) may also be recommended because they tend to enhance genital sensitivity and may increase the likelihood of orgasm.

Of course, these techniques may not be effective if there is an underlying physiological cause. For instance, we know that SSRIs often cause delayed orgasm. Persons taking these drugs may

Digging Deeper 12.2   How Long Should Sex Last and
How Can I Last Longer in Bed?

These are some of the most common questions among men seeking sex therapy. In terms of how long sex "should" last, a survey of sex therapists indicated that an "adequate" intercourse session lasts anywhere from 3 to 7 minutes, while a "desirable" one lasts 7 to 13 minutes (Corty & Guardiani, 2008). However, what matters more is not how many minutes or hours you spend making love, but whether the time you spend is enough to satisfy both you *and* your partner. If your sexual sessions typically only last two minutes, but both of you are content with that, there is no problem. In contrast, if one of you finishes much sooner than the other and this is creating distress or anxiety for either of you, then you may have a serious issue. Thus, judgments of what constitutes "adequate" or "desirable" sex depend upon how both partners feel about it.

If a man finds that he is consistently finishing sooner than he or his partner would like, he may have premature orgasm; however, this can be treated relatively easily and the success rates are very high. Perhaps the most commonly prescribed treatment is the **stop–start technique** (a therapy originally developed, appropriately enough, by a urologist named Dr. Semans). This technique involves continuing sexual activity to the point where orgasm is about to happen, then stopping everything until the feeling goes away. Once it does, stimulation resumes, but stops again the next time the feeling arises. Going through this cycle of starting and stopping stimulation typically produces better ejaculatory control. Related to this is something known as the **squeeze technique**, which also involves continuing sex until the point of an impending orgasm, but then squeezing the head or base of the penis to prevent ejaculation. Again, once the sensations subside, stimulation resumes until another squeeze is necessary.

If those techniques do not work, there are at least three other options. First, you could purchase a desensitizing spray or cream (e.g., Promescent), or a condom lined with a numbing agent on the inside. This should dull sexual sensations, thereby allowing you to last longer. Just be careful that you do not end up numbing your partner if you use these products! Second, you could try Kegel exercises (as discussed in chapter 3), which can help increase ejaculatory control. The other possibility would be to talk to a doctor about taking a small dose of an SSRI like Prozac. SSRIs have been used to treat depression for years, but they often produce sexual side effects, including delayed orgasm. Some men with premature orgasm have successfully resolved it simply by taking these drugs even though they were not clinically depressed (Kaufman, Rosen, Mudumbi, & Tesfaye, 2009).

Premature orgasm is a common sexual issue for which there are numerous well-established treatment options. If you encounter this issue in your own life, it is highly likely that you can resolve it with one or more of the methods described above.

Note: Reprinted with permission from *The Psychology of Human Sexuality* blog (www.lehmiller.com).

need to work with their physician to reduce the dosage, switch to a non-SSRI antidepressant (e.g., buproprion, which affects dopamine reuptake instead), or consider taking an additional drug to counteract the effect (case studies have suggested that Viagra can work for this purpose; Ashton, 1999). Treatment courses would obviously be quite different if another physical factor (e.g., chronic illness, injury, substance use) were contributing to orgasmic difficulties.

Treating Pain Problems

Finally, let us consider treatment options for painful sex. For phimosis, circumcision and superincision/dorsal slit (both discussed in chapter 3) can alleviate the tightness of the foreskin; however, recent research has found that application of topical steroids can expand the foreskin and are about as effective as surgery at resolving symptoms (Esposito Centonze, Alicchio, Savanelli, & Settimi, 2008). For Peyronie's disease, anti-inflammatory medication and physical therapy may be enough to manage the pain for some men, but in severe cases, surgery may be necessary to correct the penile curvature.

Treating GPD in women requires figuring out the source of the pain, with treatment courses differing widely depending upon whether it is the result of an infection, trauma, irritation, or vaginal dryness. When GPD represents vaginismus, there are at least two possible treatment courses. One involves the use of dilators, which are cylinders of varying sizes that can be inserted into the vagina. The goal with dilators is to gradually desensitize the vaginal muscles to different degrees of penetration, not to increase the size of the vaginal opening. A newer (and somewhat surprising) treatment possibility for vaginismus is Botox. Many of you are familiar with Botox as a drug injected into the face to prevent or reduce the appearance of wrinkles by temporarily paralyzing certain muscles. Physicians have discovered that by paralyzing the vaginal muscles with Botox, the involuntary contractions that characterize vaginismus no longer occur, which makes intercourse possible (Pacik, 2011). By the time the Botox wears off and the muscles regain their ability to contract (a process that can take several months), the learned association that caused vaginismus usually disappears.

Figure 12.9   Botox has a number of unexpected but potentially useful applications including an ability to prevent facial wrinkles, stop excess sweating, and treat vaginismus. ©Vitaly Valua/123RF.COM.

Tips For Avoiding Sexual Difficulties

We will round out this chapter by offering practical advice to reduce the risk of encountering future difficulties in your own sex life. First and foremost, communicate with your partner both verbally and nonverbally during sex. Make it clear to your partner what you like, either by explicitly saying it, demonstrating it, or moaning with delight when it happens. Both verbal and nonverbal sexual communication are positively correlated with sexual satisfaction (Babin, 2013). Also, be specific in your communication and do not be afraid to use sexual terms. Research finds that men and women who use more sexual terms in their communication tend to be more satisfied and report feeling closer to their partners (Hess & Coffelt, 2012). The specific terms used appear to make a difference, though. For example, among women, there is no correlation between using clinical terminology (e.g., labia, fellatio, copulate) and relationship satisfaction; in contrast, using slang (e.g., pussy, blow job, screw) is positively correlated with satisfaction in women. Let me be clear: this does not mean that everyone should start talking dirty in order to improve their relationships. Rather, the important thing is to find the right set of terminology for you and your partner that feels comfortable and conveys the point.

Second, follow the advice of Masters and Johnson and do not look at sex as an activity in which you are "supposed" to achieve something. Sex is an activity that should be relaxing and pleasurable, not a high-pressure job. Related to this, recognize that your body will not always function the way you want it to (e.g., sometimes men will not be able to "get it up" and sometimes women will not be able to reach orgasm); however, do not let this destroy your evening or your relationship. "Failure to launch" will happen to almost everyone at least once, but the key is not to perseverate on it because that can plant the seed for a future self-fulfilling prophecy.

Lastly, take care of yourself physically and psychologically. As you have seen throughout this chapter, sexual well-being is intimately intertwined with the health of both your brain and body. Alcohol use, smoking, obesity, stress, anxiety, and a multitude of other factors have the potential to impair sexual functioning. Thus, in order to have a healthy sex life, you need to be in good shape mentally and physically.

In the event that you encounter a sex difficulty, do not be ashamed or embarrassed to seek help. Sexual problems are very common. To locate a sex therapist, check out the American Association of Sex Educators, Counselors, and Therapists website (aasect.org) to gather some leads. Be sure to check out the therapist's credentials and training and make sure your desired therapist has a degree in psychiatry, psychology, counseling, or social work from an accredited university and is licensed to practice. When you visit the therapist, be sure to keep your expectations in check. Sex therapy is sometimes uncomfortable and the solutions are not necessarily immediate, but if you stick with it, the rewards can be immense.

Key Terms

sexual dysfunction
spectatoring
dual control model
female sexual interest/arousal
 disorder (SIAD)

male hypoactive sexual desire
 disorder (HSDD)
sexual desire discrepancy
sexual aversion disorder
compulsive sexual behavior

persistent genital arousal
 disorder
erectile disorder (ED)
priapism
premature orgasm

orgasmic disorder	dyspareunia	cognitive-behavioral sex
delayed ejaculation	vaginismus	therapy (CBST)
phimosis	behavioral therapy	sex surrogacy
Peyronie's disease	sensate focus techniques	pharmacotherapy
genito-pelvic pain/	PLISSIT model of sex	stop–start technique
penetration disorder (GPD)	therapy	squeeze technique

Discussion Questions: What is Your Perspective on Sex?

- In your view, is sex surrogacy an ethical and appropriate form of sex therapy?
- What do you make of the criticisms of sex therapy by Thomas Szasz and others, who have argued that sexual "dysfunction" is an arbitrary social creation? Is all sexual dysfunction in the eye of the beholder, or are there certain sexual attitudes and behaviors that are clear disorders?
- What do you see as the benefits and costs of the medicalization of sexual disorders (i.e., the quest to treat dysfunction with medication and surgery rather than psychotherapy)?

References

Annon, J.S. (1976). The PLISSIT model: a proposed conceptual scheme for the behavioral treatment of sexual problems. *Journal of Sex Education and Therapy, 2*(1), 1–15.

Apfelbaum, B. (1977). The myth of the surrogate. *Journal of Sex Research, 13,* 238–249. DOI:10.1080/00224497709550981

Ashton, A.K. (1999). Sildenafil treatment of paroxetine-induced anorgasmia in a woman. *American Journal of Psychiatry, 156,* 800.

Aubin, S., Heiman, J.R., Berger, R.E., Murallo, A.V., & Yung-Wen, L. (2009). Comparing Sildenafil Alone vs. Sildenafil plus brief couple sex therapy on erectile dysfunction and couples' sexual and marital quality of life: A pilot study. *Journal of Sex & Marital Therapy, 35,* 122–143. DOI:10.1080/00926230802712319.

Babin, E.A. (2013). An examination of predictors of nonverbal and verbal communication of pleasure during sex and sexual satisfaction. *Journal of Social and Personal Relationships, 30,* 270–292. DOI:10.1177/0265407512454523.

Bancroft, J. (2002). The medicalization of female sexual dysfunction: The need for caution. *Archives of Sexual Behavior, 31,* 451–455. DOI:10.1023/A:1019800426980.

Bancroft, J., Graham, C.A., Janssen, E., & Sanders, S.A. (2009). The dual control model: Current status and future directions. *Journal of Sex Research, 46,* 121–142. DOI:10.1080/00224490902747222.

Basson, R., Rees, P., Wang, R., Montejo, A., & Incrocci, L. (2010). Sexual function in chronic illness. *Journal of Sexual Medicine, 7*(1, Pt 2), 374–388. DOI:10.1111/j.1743-6109.2009.01621.x.

Basson, R.R., Leiblum, S.S., Brotto, L.L., Derogatis, L.L., Fourcroy, J.J., Fugl-Meyer, K.K., … Schultz, W. (2003). Definitions of women's sexual dysfunction reconsidered: Advocating expansion and revision. *Journal of Psychosomatic Obstetrics & Gynecology, 24,* 221–229. DOI:10.3109/01674820309074686.

Ben-Zion, I., Rothschild, S., Chudakov, B., & Aloni, R. (2007). Surrogate versus couple therapy in vaginismus. *Journal of Sexual Medicine, 4,* 728–733. DOI:10.1111/j.1743-6109.2007.00452.x.

Bhasin, S., Enzlin, P., Coviello, A., & Basson, R. (2007). Sexual dysfunction in men and women with endocrine disorders. *The Lancet, 369,* 597–611. DOI:10.1016/S0140-6736(07)60280-3.

Brotto, L.A. (2010a). The DSM diagnostic criteria for hypoactive sexual desire disorder in women. *Archives of Sexual Behavior, 39,* 221–239. DOI:10.1007/s10508-009-9543-1.

Brotto, L.A. (2010b). The DSM diagnostic criteria for sexual aversion disorder. *Archives of Sexual Behavior*, *39*, 271–277. DOI:10.1007/s10508-009-9534-2.

Brotto, L.A., Woo, J.S., & Gorzalka, B.B. (2012). Differences in sexual guilt and desire in East Asian and Euro-Canadian men. *Journal of Sex Research*, *49*, 594–602. DOI:10.1080/00224499.2011.618956.

Butcher, J. (1999). Female sexual problems II: Sexual pain and sexual fears. *British Medical Journal*, *318*, 110–112.

Carvalho, S., Moreira, A., Rosado, M., Correia, D., Maia, D., & Pimentel, P. (2011). Female premature orgasm: Does this exist? *Sexologies*, *20*, 215–220. DOI:10.1016/j.sexol.2011.08.008.

Chang, S.C., Klein, C., & Gorzalka, B.B. (2013). Perceived prevalence and definitions of sexual dysfunction as predictors of sexual function and satisfaction. *Journal of Sex Research*, *50*, 502–512. DOI:10.1080/0022 4499.2012.661488.

Chu, N.V., & Edelman, S.V. (2001). Diabetes and erectile dysfunction. *Clinical Diabetes*, *19*, 45–47. DOI:10.2337/diaclin.19.1.45.

Cortés-González, J.R., & Glina, S. (2009). Have phosphodiesterase-5 inhibitors changed the indications for penile implants? *British Journal of Urology International*, *103*, 1518–1521. DOI:10.1111/j.1464-410X.2009.08356.x.

Corty, E.W., & Guardiani, J.M. (2008). Canadian and American sex therapists' perceptions of normal and abnormal ejaculatory latencies: How long should intercourse last? *Journal of Sexual Medicine*, *5*, 1251–1256. DOI:10.1111/j.1743-6109.2008.00797.x.

Dauw, D.C. (1988). Evaluating the effectiveness of the SECS' surrogate-assisted sex therapy model. *Journal of Sex Research*, *24*, 269–275. DOI:10.1080/00224498809551423.

Dell'Osso, L., Carmassi, C., Carlini, M., Rucci, P., Torri, P., Cesari, D., … Maggi, M. (2009). Sexual dysfunctions and suicidality in patients with bipolar disorder and unipolar depression. *Journal of Sexual Medicine*, *6*, 3063–3070. DOI:10.1111/j.1743-6109.2009.01455.x.

Esposito, C., Centonze, A., Alicchio, F., Savanelli, A., & Settimi, A. (2008). Topical steroid application versus circumcision in pediatric patients with phimosis: A prospective randomized placebo controlled clinical trial. *World Journal of Urology*, *26*, 187–190. DOI:10.1007/s00345-007-0231-2.

Giraldi, A., & Kristensen, E. (2010). Sexual dysfunction in women with diabetes mellitus. *Journal of Sex Research*, *47*, 199–211. DOI:10.1080/00224491003632834.

Graham, C.A. (2010a). The DSM diagnostic criteria for female sexual arousal disorder. *Archives of Sexual Behavior*, *39*, 240–255. DOI:10.1007/s10508-009-9535-1.

Graham, C.A. (2010b). The DSM diagnostic criteria for female orgasmic disorder. *Archives of Sexual Behavior*, *39*, 256–270. DOI:10.1007/s10508-009-9542-2.

Hess, J.A., & Coffelt, T.A. (2012). Verbal communication about sex in marriage: Patterns of language use and its connection with relational outcomes. *Journal of Sex Research*, *49*, 603–612. DOI:10.1080/002244 99.2011.619282.

Hong, L.K. (1984). Survival of the fastest: On the origin of premature ejaculation. *Journal of Sex Research*, *20*, 109–122. DOI:10.1080/00224498409551212.

Johannes, C.B., Araujo, A.B., Feldman, H.A., Derby, C.A., Kleinman, K.P., & McKinlay, J.B. (2000). Incidence of erectile dysfunction in men 40 to 69 years old: Longitudinal results from the Massachusetts male aging study. *Journal of Urology*, *163*, 460. DOI:10.1097/00005392-200002000-00015.

Kaufman, J., Rosen, R., Mudumbi, R., & Tesfaye, F. (2009). Treatment benefit of dapoxetine for premature ejaculation: Results from a placebo-controlled phase III trial. *British Journal of Urology International*, *103*, 651–658. DOI:10.1111/j.1464-410X.2008.08165.x.

La Rocque, C.L., & Cioe, J. (2011). An evaluation of the relationship between body image and sexual avoidance. *Journal of Sex Research*, *48*, 397–408. DOI:10.1080/00224499.2010.499522.

Laumann, E.O., Paik, A., & Rosen, R.C. (1999). Sexual dysfunction in the United States. *The Journal of the American Medical Association*, *281*, 537–544. DOI:10.1001/jama.281.6.537.

Leiblum, S., Brown, C., Wan, J., & Rawlinson, L. (2005). Persistent sexual arousal syndrome: A descriptive study. *Journal of Sexual Medicine*, *2*, 331–337. DOI:10.1111/j.1743-6109.2005.20357.x.

Lief, H.I., & Hubschman, L. (1993). Orgasm in the postoperative transsexual. *Archives of Sexual Behavior*, *22*, 145–155. DOI:10.1007/BF01542363.

Lykins, A.D., Meana, M., & Minimi, J. (2010). Visual attention to erotic images in women reporting pain with intercourse. *Journal of Sex Research*, 48, 43–52. DOI:10.1080/00224490903556374.

Masters, W., & Johnson, V. (1970). *Human sexual inadequacy*. Boston: Little, Brown.

Masters, W., & Johnson, V. (1979). *Homosexuality in perspective*. Boston: Little, Brown.

McCabe, M.P. (2001). Evaluation of a cognitive behavior therapy program for people with sexual dysfunction. *Journal of Sex & Marital Therapy*, 27, 259–271. DOI:10.1080/009262301750257119.

McCarthy, B.W. (1990). Treating sexual dysfunction associated with prior sexual trauma. *Journal of Sex & Marital Therapy*, 16, 142–146. DOI:10.1080/00926239008405260.

Noonan, R.J. (1984). *Sex surrogates: A clarification of their functions* (Master's thesis). Retrieved from http://www.sexquest.com/surrogat.htm (accessed September 6, 2013).

Pacik, P.T. (2011). Vaginismus: Review of current concepts and treatment using Botox injections, bupivacaine injections, and progressive dilation with the patient under anesthesia. *Aesthetic Plastic Surgery*, 35, 1160–1164. DOI:10.1007/s00266-011-9737-5.

Segraves, R.T. (2010). Considerations for a better definition of male orgasmic disorder in DSM V. *Journal of Sexual Medicine*, 7(2, Pt 1), 690–695. DOI:10.1111/j.1743-6109.2009.01683.x.

Segraves, R.T., & Balon, R. (2003). *Sexual pharmacology: Fast facts*. New York: Norton.

Siegel, J.M. (2005). REM sleep. *Principles and practice of sleep medicine*, 4, 120–135.

Szasz, T.S. (1990). *Sex by prescription: The startling truth about today's sex therapy*. Syracuse, NY: Syracuse University Press.

Vale, J. (2000). Erectile dysfunction following radical therapy for prostate cancer. *Radiotherapy and Oncology*, 57, 301–305. DOI:10.1016/S0167-8140(00)00293-0.

World Health Organization (2012). *Gender and human rights*. Retrieved from http://www.who.int/reproductivehealth/topics/gender_rights/sexual_health/en/ (accessed September 6, 2013).

Zilbergeld, B., & Evans, M. (1980). The inadequacy of Masters and Johnson. *Psychology Today*, 14(3), 29–43.

13

Variations in Sexual Behavior

©Eugene Sergeev/123RF.COM.

Chapter Outline

- Introduction   329
- What are Paraphilias?   329
- Types of Paraphilias   331
  - Fetishism   331
  - Transvestism   335
  - Sadomasochism   336
  - Voyeurism   338
  - Exhibitionism   339
  - Pedophilia   341
  - Other Paraphilias   341
- Treatment of Paraphilic Disorders   345
  - Medical Therapies   346
  - Psychological Therapies   346
  - Social Skills Training   347
  - Effectiveness   347

The Psychology of Human Sexuality, First Edition. Justin J. Lehmiller.
© 2014 John Wiley & Sons, Ltd. Published 2014 by John Wiley & Sons, Ltd.

Introduction

After puberty… [my interest in horses] became more sexual… One night [when 19 years old] there was a horse standing in a narrow ditch… She was a mare, and it suddenly struck me I might be able to straddle the ditch and have sex with her. I had had many sexual encounters with human females so I knew what went where… I pressed the head of my penis against her vulva, started thrusting, and suddenly slid in. The sensation is hard to describe, incredibly warm, almost a shock to the senses, culminating in a very strong orgasm.

Male zoophile describing his first sexual encounter (as cited in
Williams & Weinberg, 2003, p. 528)

For most people, having sex with a horse probably falls beyond the boundaries of what they would consider "normal" sexual activity. As a result, many of you probably reacted to the above quote with shock, revulsion, or perhaps even anger. While sex with animals is indeed an unusual sexual interest, it is just one of many sexual variations documented by psychologists that may evoke such responses. For instance, we know that some people like to expose their genitals to strangers on the subway, others like to asphyxiate themselves just before reaching orgasm, and a few are turned on by the prospect of having sex with a corpse. Thus, when we consider the full range of human sexual expression, we see that it is far broader than was discussed in chapter 9. The purpose of the current chapter is to explore sexual interests and practices that are out of the ordinary and, in some cases, are harmful to the persons involved and/or their partners. Specifically, we will explore **paraphilias**, or patterns of sexual attraction and behavior that deviate from social and cultural norms. We begin by describing the nature of paraphilias. Following that, we will discuss some of the most common types, and finish by considering treatment options in cases where it is warranted.

What are Paraphilias?

The word *paraphilia* is often translated as "beyond typical love" or "abnormal love." However, this leads to the obvious question of how we define words like "normal" and "typical" when it comes to sexual behavior. There is no clear answer to this question because, as we have discussed previously in this book, judgments of sexual normalcy are culturally relative. For instance, in the Western world, the general consensus of the medical and psychological communities is that homosexuality is not a disorder and that it represents a normal variation in sexual behavior. However, in some parts of Africa and the Middle East, homosexuality continues to be seen as an illness and a "crime against nature." Likewise, consider that the age of sexual consent in some countries is a low as 12 and as high as 21 in others (Avert, 2012). As you can see from these examples, the same sexual act involving the same people may be viewed in a very different light depending upon where it takes place, which means that the criteria for establishing what constitutes typical and atypical sexual behavior may differ dramatically across cultures and societies. In other words, the types of behaviors that would be classified as paraphilic can differ depending upon how a given culture views sex (e.g., is sex seen as something that is primarily practiced for pleasure, or is sex inextricably linked to the goal of procreation?).

When discussing paraphilias, it is useful to distinguish between having a *paraphilia* and having a *paraphilic disorder* (Blanchard, 2010a). Historically, psychologists and psychiatrists have viewed virtually all paraphilias as disordered behavior; in the DSM-5, however, a distinction has been made between unusual sexual interests that are relatively harmless and those that are actively harmful. Thus, we can think of a paraphilia as simply representing an unusual sexual interest that does not necessarily require any type of treatment. In contrast, a paraphilic disorder represents an unusual sexual interest that is personally distressing to the individual (e.g., perhaps it interferes with one's ability to establish a satisfying sexual or romantic relationship) and/or involves victimization of others. In addition, paraphilic disorders represent persistent patterns of behavior (according to the DSM-5, the urges or behaviors must last longer than 6 months). The paraphilia/paraphilic disorder distinction makes it clear that it is possible for someone to have sexual interests outside of the mainstream, yet still be psychologically healthy; non-normative sexual interests are usually only pathological to the extent that some harm results from them.

Where do paraphilias come from? Like all other sexual attitudes and behaviors, they have biopsychosocial roots. For instance, it is theorized that certain hormones (e.g., testosterone) and neurotransmitters (e.g., serotonin) are linked to paraphilic interests (Kafka, 1997). As support for this idea, research has found that by providing medications that alter the balance of these chemicals in the body, it is possible to reduce paraphilic desires (more on this at the end of the chapter). In addition, psychological learning theory (i.e., classical and operant conditioning) has been implicated in the development of several paraphilias, which explains why so many sex therapists attempt behavioral therapy as a means of treating paraphilic disorders. Social factors also play a role, with research indicating that poor interpersonal skills are linked to many paraphilias (Emmers-Sommer et al., 2004). This suggests that when people are unable to find partners with whom to explore normative sexual behaviors, they may end up gravitating toward unusual forms of sexual gratification.

Another factor that may play a role in the development of paraphilias is the finding that sexual arousal overrides our disgust impulses. That is, when we are highly aroused, some things that we would normally consider gross do not seem quite as offensive and, instead, may be perceived as pleasurable. As support for this idea, consider a novel study by Borg and Jong (2012) in which heterosexual women were randomly assigned to watch either (1) a sexually arousing film, (2) an arousing but nonsexual film (i.e., people skydiving and rock climbing), or (3) a neutral and non-arousing video. Afterward, participants were asked to perform a series of disgusting tasks (e.g., they were asked to place their hand in a bowl of condoms that appeared to have been used and feel each one). The women who were sexually aroused were most willing to attempt the disgusting tasks and felt the least disgusted afterward compared to the other groups of women. These findings may help to explain how some people first come to incorporate seemingly disgusting things into their sex lives. If high levels of arousal alter our perceptions and open the door to trying things we might normally stay away from, that could lay the basis for developing all kinds of unusual interests.

It is worth noting that almost all paraphilias are more common among men than they are among women. This is not a small sex difference either. For example, a national survey from Sweden found that, compared to women, men were about twice as likely to have exposed their genitals to a stranger and about three times as likely to have spied on other people having sex (Långström & Seto, 2006). We do not know exactly why this is the case, but as discussed in chapter 6, it may have something to do with women's supposedly greater erotic plasticity. To the extent that men's sexuality is indeed more "fixed" and women's is more "flexible," it could explain why men are more likely to become oriented on a specific sexual interest and why it is more difficult to treat paraphilic disorders in men.

Types of Paraphilias

Paraphilias are generally grouped into two broad categories: those that are *noncoercive and nonvictimizing* (i.e., paraphilias that involve only the self or that include consenting adults) and those that are *coercive and victimizing* (i.e., paraphilias that involve nonconsensual sexual activity with adults or children). Fetishism, transvestism, and sadomasochism as usually lumped into the noncoercive camp, while voyeurism, exhibitionism, telephone scatologia, pedophilia, necrophilia, and zoophilia are usually lumped into the coercive camp. Below, we detail each of these sexual interests. For a brief summary of each paraphilia, see Table 13.1.

Fetishism

Fetishism occurs when a person experiences intense sexual arousal in response to either a nonhuman object, a non-genital body part, or a bodily secretion (Kafka, 2010). You may be wondering whether you have a fetish because you get turned on by certain parts of the body (e.g., nice legs, big biceps) or by seeing other people wearing certain articles of clothing (e.g., skimpy underwear, high heels); however, what distinguishes a "turn-on" from a fetish is that someone with a fetish tends to obsess over the fetish object and focus exclusively on it. The object eventually becomes a

Table 13.1 Types of Paraphilias	
Paraphilia	*Source of sexual arousal*
Fetishism	A nonhuman object, body part, or bodily secretion
Transvestism	Dressing up as a member of the other sex or seeing oneself as a member of the other sex
Masochism	Receiving pain
Sadism	Giving pain to others
Voyeurism	Spying on unsuspecting others who are undressing or having sex
Exhibitionism	Exposing one's genitals to unsuspecting others
Telephone Scatologia	Placing obscene telephone calls
Pedophilia	Prepubescent children
Necrophilia	Corpses or human bones
Zoophilia	Nonhuman animals

Figure 13.1 Feet and toes are among the most common fetish objects. Image Copyright Lisa F. Young 2013. Used under license from Shutterstock.com.

Digging Deeper 13.1 Why Do People Have Fetishes?

Given that fetishes can run the gamut from the conventional (e.g., silk panties and leather boots) to the unusual (e.g., dirt and cars), it is perhaps no surprise that the most common question people have about fetishes is how they develop in the first place. There are several schools of thought on this issue, but the explanation that has received the most attention suggests that fetishes develop from learned associations. In other words, we are talking about conditioned behaviors, or cases in which people have learned an association between a certain object and sexual pleasure. To illustrate this point, consider this example reported in a research article of a man describing his first encounter with a fetish object:

> I was home alone and saw my uncle's new penny loafers. I went over and started smelling the fresh new leather scent and kissing and licking them. It turned me on so much that I actually ejaculated my first load into my pants and have been turned on [by them] ever since. (Weinberg, Williams, & Calhan, 1995, p. 22)

In this case, the presentation of a novel object (leather loafers) created arousal in the individual, which he psychologically interpreted as being sexual in nature. It appears that this single event was so powerful that it instilled in him a lifelong sexual association with this object. Of course, not all fetishes develop so quickly. Some people might require repeated pairings of the

Figure 13.2 Rachman (1966) classically conditioned a mild boot fetish in a group of male participants, thereby providing a clear demonstration of the role of learning in the development of paraphilias. Image Copyright Karkas 2013. Used under license from Shutterstock.com.

object with pleasure to develop such an association. However, you get the idea from this example: fetishism is something that we seem to acquire through experience and learning.

A related way fetishes can develop is through *classical conditioning*. To the extent that a specific object repeatedly appears just before we experience sexual arousal, we may eventually come to see that object as a cue for sexual arousal in the future such that every time we see that object, we get turned on. This idea was demonstrated in a fascinating experiment conducted in the 1960s in which heterosexual male participants were hooked up to a penile strain gauge to measure their arousal (Rachman, 1966). Participants were then shown images of boots (a non-arousing stimulus to most heterosexual guys), immediately followed by images of sexy naked women (an arousing stimulus to most heterosexual guys). After repeatedly showing boots followed by nudes, the men eventually started showing arousal in response to the boots alone! Thus, the experimenter successfully conditioned a mild boot fetish into the participants. A more recent study replicated this effect using an image of a jar of pennies (something that is not sexual at all) instead of boots, which goes to show that you can develop a fetish for almost anything (Plaud & Martini, 1999).

Learning theory thus provides a rather simple and intuitive explanation for the origin of fetishes. While it is not the only possible theory regarding why fetishism exists, it has the strongest body of research supporting it and suggests that all fetishes, regardless of how unusual they are, may potentially develop as a result of the same underlying process.

Note: Reprinted with permission from *The Psychology of Human Sexuality* blog (www.lehmiller.com).

Table 13.2	Prevalence of Selected Fetishes among Members of Online Fetish Communities
Bodily fetishes	
Fetish	*Percentage of group members with that fetish*
Feet and/or toes	47%
Bodily fluids (e.g., blood, urine)	9%
Hair	7%
Muscles	5%
Tattoos and piercings	4%
Oral area (mouth, lips, and/or teeth)	2%
Fingernails or toenails	Less than 1%
Body odors	Less than 1%
Object fetishes	
Fetish	*Percentage of group members with that fetish*
Stockings, skirts, and other objects worn on the legs	33%
Footwear	32%
Underwear	12%
Stethoscopes	1%
Diapers	Less than 1%
Catheters (i.e., tubes inserted into the urethra to draw urine out of the bladder)	Less than 1%

Data Source: Scorolli et al. (2007).

sexual necessity, such that the individual may not be able to become aroused and/or reach orgasm without it. People can develop fetishes for nearly anything, but to get a sense of some of the most and least common fetishes, check out Table 13.2.

Fetishism has been described as a "multi-sensory sexual outlet" (Kafka, 2010), meaning that a fetish object may produce arousal because the individual likes the way it looks, tastes, smells, or feels. In addition, it is common for fetishes to occur in clusters (e.g., the same individual may have a fetish for both a body part and an object) and to overlap with other paraphilias, particularly transvestism and sadomasochism (Kafka, 2010). For information on how fetishes develop, consult the Digging Deeper 13.1 box.

Many people with fetishes do not meet the criteria for *fetishistic disorder* because they do not necessarily experience any personal distress or impairment (Scorolli et al., 2007). Fetishists can often develop satisfying sexual and romantic relationships and find partners who enjoy their fetish behavior or do not mind it. Treatment is generally only warranted in cases where the fetish interferes with one's ability to maintain a relationship, leads the individual to engage in criminal behavior such as burglary (indeed, fetishists sometimes steal the objects of their desire; Kafka, 2010), or causes some other type of distress.

Transvestism

Transvestism is characterized by cross-dressing for purposes of sexual arousal (i.e., dressing up as a member of the other sex because it is a turn-on). Please recall from chapter 5 that transvestism is not the same as transsexualism, nor is it the same as performing in drag. Although cross-dressing may occur in all of these cases, it is done for entirely different reasons. Transvestism used to be viewed as a subtype of fetishism. In fact, in earlier editions of the DSM, it was referred to as *transvestic fetishism* (in contrast, it is referred to as "transvestic disorder" in the DSM-5). However, this label was inappropriately narrow because while there are indeed some transvestites for whom this behavior is a type of fetish (i.e., they are aroused by the feeling of the other sex's clothing), there are other transvestites who become aroused by seeing themselves as a member of the other sex (Blanchard, 2010b).

There is a popular stereotype that most (if not all) transvestites are gay men. However, this could not be further from the truth. For instance, in a survey of over 1,000 male transvestites, 87% identified as heterosexual and 83% were currently married or had been married before (Doctor & Prince, 1997). It is for this reason that the DSM criteria for transvestic disorder limits the diagnosis only to heterosexual men. Transvestism is almost unheard of in women, and when it occurs in gay

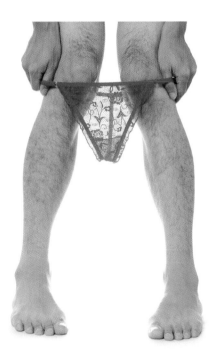

Figure 13.3 Transvestites dress as members of the other sex because they receive sexual arousal from it, not because they truly want to become members of the other sex. Image Copyright joesayhello 2013. Used under license from Shutterstock.com.

men it rarely becomes clinically significant. We do not know exactly how transvestism develops, but individuals' first experience with it tends to occur very early in life (often before age 10; Doctor & Prince, 1997) and it is theorized to have roots similar to fetishism (i.e., conditioning and reinforcement).

Some cross-dressers dislike the term "transvestite" and its clinical implications and prefer the label of "cross-dresser" instead. In addition, many within this community find the diagnosis of "transvestic disorder" offensive because they feel that it unnecessarily pathologizes the behavior of cross-dressing. Our use of these terms in this textbook is not meant to be hurtful or stigmatizing, but rather to be scientifically accurate and to use the language that you would see in the DSM and in journal articles. That said, it is important to emphasize that cross-dressing does not inherently represent disordered behavior. The current view in the mental health community is that the "transvestite" label is simply used to describe a behavior and does not imply any type of disorder. Like all other paraphilias, the DSM only categorizes transvestism as a "disorder" when it causes significant personal distress or impairment.

Sadomasochism

Sadomasochism is the umbrella term used to refer to a class of sexual activities in which sexual arousal is derived from either giving or receiving pain. In popular culture, the acronym BDSM (which stands for bondage, discipline, dominance, submissions, sadism, and masochism) is often used to describe such behaviors. Psychologists generally make a distinction between **masochists**, who derive sexual gratification from *receiving* physical or psychological pain (Krueger, 2010a), and **sadists**, who derive sexual gratification from *inflicting* physical or psychological pain on others (Krueger, 2010b). Individuals who engage in one of these behaviors do not necessarily engage in the other.

There are a number of public misconceptions about BDSM. First, research indicates that BDSM practices are relatively common, with survey studies indicating that somewhere between 10% and 15% of the population has had at least some experience with sadomasochistic activities (e.g., Janus & Janus, 1993). Thus, it is not as rare as people think. Second, although masochists may enjoy the experience of pain during sexual activity, they do not find all forms of pain to be pleasurable and arousing. For instance, a masochist with a stubbed toe will find the experience to be just as unpleasant as anyone else. Third, most people tend to associate BDSM with very extreme activities and torture devices, perhaps because in media depictions of BDSM, people who are into pain almost invariably have a medieval dungeon in their basement. However, for most BDSM practitioners, the preference is for mild or perhaps even symbolic pain that stays within mutually agreeable limits. In fact, "safe, sane, and consensual" is the mantra of most in the BDSM community. Consistent with that idea, the most commonly reported BDSM activities involve bondage, light flagellation (i.e., whipping or flogging), blindfolds, and gags—activities that are not particularly violent and pose a low risk of danger (Sandnabba, Santtila, Alison, & Nordling, 2002). The more extreme and potentially harmful activities (e.g., cutting, electric shocks) are practiced by a few people, and a small number of deaths have been linked to such behaviors over the years (perhaps most commonly with *asphyxiophilia*, a behavior that overlaps with masochism and involves receiving sexual arousal from oxygen deprivation; Krueger, 2010a). However, such cases are quite rare.

Fourth, many people assume that BDSM is pathological because sadism and masochism are listed in the DSM and because media depictions of the BDSM community (e.g., Christian Grey, the main character in the popular book *Fifty Shades of Grey*) promote the stereotype that people

Figure 13.4   Contrary to popular belief, most people who practice BDSM prefer to give or receive only very mild forms of pain. Image Copyright Doug Stevens 2013. Used under license from Shutterstock.com.

who associate pain with sex are victims of childhood abuse who have developed psychological problems as adults. In reality, however, people who practice BDSM are no more likely to be psychologically disturbed than anyone else. In fact, research has found that BDSM is *not* linked to having been a victim of childhood sexual abuse nor is it associated with higher levels of psychological distress in adulthood (Richters, de Visser, Rissel, Grulich, & Smith, 2008). It is also important to note that *sexual masochism disorder* is only diagnosed when fantasizing about or receiving pain causes psychological distress (Krueger, 2010a) and *sexual sadism disorder* is only diagnosed when sadistic urges or behaviors cause distress or are inflicted on a nonconsenting person (Krueger, 2010b).

There are many possible explanations for the emergence of sadomasochistic desires. One possibility is that they may stem from a sensation-seeking personality, in which riskier or more thrilling activities are required in order to achieve arousal. As some support for this idea, research has found an association between sensation seeking and sexual sadism (Aluja, 2007). Learning theory and conditioning processes represent another possibility (e.g., children who are punished for masturbating may come to psychologically associate pleasure and pain over time). Finally, it has also been proposed that masochism may represent an escape from high self-awareness (Baumeister, 1988). In other words, masochistic activities may allow you to "lose yourself" in the moment because either your focus shifts to the physical sensations you are having, or you start to see yourself as an object rather than a person during the experience. Another way to think about this is that the experience of pain may help to block out anxieties and insecurities that impede sexual pleasure by redirecting your attention away from the self.

Voyeurism

Voyeurism refers to the act of experiencing sexual arousal from fantasizing about or viewing an unsuspecting person(s) who is naked or having sex (Långström, 2010). This appears to be one of the most common sexual behavior variations, despite the fact that it is illegal in many cultures and can potentially get you in a lot of trouble, resulting in anything from financial penalties, to jail time, to mandatory sex offender registration. To give you some idea of prevalence, a nationally representative survey in Sweden revealed that 12% of male adults and 4% of female adults reported having spied on another person having sex at least once and derived sexual arousal from it (Långström & Seto, 2006).

Given the immense popularity of pornography, strip clubs, and reality television shows (some of which go so far as to include cameras in bedrooms and bathrooms), it would appear that at least some degree of voyeurism is socially accepted. However, it is worth noting that people who appear in professionally produced porn, dance at strip clubs, or appear on reality TV fully realize that other people will be watching them, so if you enjoy watching these things, it does not necessarily make you a true voyeur.

Another defining feature of voyeurism is repeating the behavior over time. For example, one study of men undergoing treatment for voyeurism found that, on average, they reported having spied upon 470 people (Abel & Rouleau, 1990)! It is important to note that this study only looked at voyeurs who had been caught in the act, and was based upon retrospective recall of past events, which means there are some concerns about the reliability and validity of the numbers. For voyeurs who are better at concealing their behavior, the number of voyeuristic acts committed over the course of a lifetime may be far higher than anyone ever suspected.

Figure 13.5   As the name "peeping tom" implies, most voyeurs are men who become aroused by watching unsuspecting persons undress or have sex. Image Copyright Zurijeta 2013. Used under license from Shutterstock.com.

Voyeuristic disorder is only diagnosed to the extent that the individual is distressed by their voyeuristic urges and/or acts upon them with a nonconsenting person (Långström, 2010). People may act upon these urges in a variety of ways and settings. For instance, voyeurism may take place in public, such as in a department store dressing room or a restroom, or it can take place in one's own home (e.g., by spying on people who are using your bedroom or bathroom to undress or have sex). Voyeurism may or may not include photographing or filming the unsuspecting person(s) with a hidden camera. On a side note, it is important to recognize that filming yourself having sex with another person can get you charged with voyeurism under the law and lead to major criminal consequences if your partner has not consented to appearing on film.

Like many other paraphilias, voyeuristic urges and behaviors often begin at a young age (early teenage years or sooner). Although we do not know where voyeurism comes from, research has found that it is correlated with reports of psychological problems, substance use, as well as having a higher sex drive and higher overall levels of sexual activity (Långström & Seto, 2006). Thus, one potential explanation is that biological factors create a predisposition (e.g., an unusually high sex drive) that, combined with certain psychosocial factors (e.g., poor social skills and/or a lack of a socially appropriate sexual outlet), may plant the seed for developing voyeuristic tendencies or other unusual sexual interests (e.g., exhibitionism). Operant conditioning may provide another possible explanation in the sense that if spying on others is incredibly rewarding the first time (e.g., if it is accompanied by a particularly powerful orgasm), the behavior is likely to occur again in the future.

Voyeurism can be psychologically harmful to its victims, particularly in cases where someone is filmed and that video is uploaded to the Internet. Voyeurs will sometimes sell their videos to websites for financial gain. Unfortunately, if it is unknown who filmed the video and/or the video is hosted on a foreign website, victims may have little recourse. Related to this, it is becoming increasingly common for people who have been dumped to try and get back at their partner by posting their partner's sex videos or nude pictures on "revenge porn" sites (Chang, 2013). The combined betrayal by a former loved one and the resulting embarrassment can be particularly devastating for the victim. However, people who attempt to exact revenge through such means often fail to realize that they may be breaking *video voyeurism* laws. What this means is that even if your partner originally consented to having those pictures taken, publishing those pictures without your partner's consent can potentially get you in major legal trouble.

Exhibitionism

Revealing one's genitals in public, often referred to as "indecent exposure," is illegal in many countries; however, there is wide cross-cultural variability in terms of what type of exposure is considered "indecent." For instance, throughout most of the United States, it is illegal to expose one's genitals or a woman's nipples in public regardless of the reason behind it (with the exception of breastfeeding a child), and such behavior can be subject to jail sentences and/or required sex offender registration. This means you may want to check local laws before streaking across campus as part of a fraternity or sorority stunt! In contrast, in parts of Europe, attitudes toward public nudity are somewhat more relaxed, at least with regard to nudity that does not have a sexual purpose (e.g., sunbathing in the park or on a beach). Such behavior is typically only considered problematic to the extent that an individual uses nudity to harass others.

Although people commonly apply the label of "exhibitionist" to everyone who publicly exposes themselves, psychologists reserve the term only for those persons who expose their genitals (or fantasize about exposing their genitals) to an unsuspecting stranger (Långström, 2010). Thus, the

Figure 13.6   What turns the exhibitionist on is the shocked reaction of an unsuspecting stranger. Exposing oneself to willing others is not of particular interest to the true exhibitionist. Image Copyright Gemenacom 2013. Used under license from Shutterstock.com.

true exhibitionist engages in socially inappropriate nudity. What exhibitionists find arousing is the shocked reaction of others, and it is this reaction that exhibitionists tend to think about when pleasuring themselves or having sex.

Research suggests that **exhibitionism** is much more common among men than women. For instance, in the aforementioned national survey from Sweden, 4.1% of men and 2.1% of women reported having exposed themselves to a stranger at least once and received arousal from it (Långström & Seto, 2006). However, such behavior is far more likely to be labeled problematic and punished under the law when committed by a man – an example of a reverse double standard. Think about it this way: how would a heterosexual man likely react to a female flasher? How would a heterosexual woman likely react to a male flasher? Would one be more likely to call the police than the other?

Exhibitionistic disorder is only diagnosed when an individual experiences distress or impairment resulting from these urges or acts upon these urges with a nonconsenting person (Långström, 2010). The nonconsenting person should rightfully be thought of as a *victim* in this case because some people find the experience traumatizing and experience concern for their personal safety.

The profile of a typical exhibitionist is similar in many ways to the typical voyeur, with the first experience occurring early in life. In addition, both behaviors are associated with psychological problems, substance use, and hypersexuality (Långström & Seto, 2006). Exhibitionists frequently exhibit social skills deficits as well (Emmers-Sommer et al., 2004), a factor that could potentially contribute to the development of this paraphilia due to difficulties establishing healthy sexual and romantic relationships. It is also worth noting that exhibitionism and voyeurism frequently overlap (meaning an individual who has one of these interests often has the other), which is another reason to suspect common roots.

Telephone Scatologia
Telephone scatologia, or the practice of making obscene telephone calls to an unsuspecting stranger, is considered a subtype of exhibitionism (Dalby, 1988). The goal is to induce a shocked reaction in the recipient, because that is what the caller finds arousing. Telephone scatologists are often young and share many of the same characteristics as the typical exhibitionist. Repeat calls are often made to the same individual, which can lead to feelings of sexual harassment and concerns about being stalked among victims.

Pedophilia

Pedophilia is characterized as a sexual attraction toward prepubescent children and, generally speaking, tends to be the most socially abhorred of all paraphilias. According to the DSM-5, *pedophilic disorder* is diagnosed when an individual of at least 16 years of age either acts upon the urge to have sex with a prepubescent child (usually age 13 or younger) or experiences psychological distress related to such urges. In addition, the individual must be at least 5 years older than the target of their arousal. Despite being subject to much criticism for being vague (e.g., What constitutes "acting on" a pedophilic urge? Is it still pedophilia if the victim is very young but has started puberty?), the diagnostic criteria were not changed during the most recent revision of the DSM. The only change that was made was to rename the diagnosis from pedophilia to pedophilic disorder.

Although it was not always the case, psychologists have increasingly come to recognize that not all pedophiles are child molesters and not all child molesters are pedophiles (Blanchard, 2010a). In other words, not all pedophiles will seek out sexual contact with a child, and not everyone who sexually molests a child has a sexual preference for children. Thus, although most people use the terms "pedophile" and "child molester" interchangeably, it is useful to distinguish between the two of them by using (1) *pedophilia* in reference to a pattern of sexual attraction to children and (2) *child molestation* in reference to specific sexual actions taken against children. Such a distinction avoids implying that all child sexual abuse stems from the same motive (and, indeed, it does not; see chapter 14).

Most pedophiles are heterosexual, married men (de Silva, 1999) and it is estimated that pedophiles make up somewhere around 4% of the population (Cloud, 2003). For years, it was thought that pedophilia had primarily psychological roots and stemmed from past personal experience with childhood sexual victimization. Consistent with this idea, most pedophiles report having been sexually abused themselves as children (de Silva, 1999). However, recent research suggests that there may be a biological or biosocial basis. For instance, pedophiles are three times as likely to be left-handed or ambidextrous relative to the general population, and they typically possess below average IQs (Blanchard et al., 2007). These findings suggest that pedophilia may potentially be traced to prenatal hormone exposure or some developmental variation that either alters brain function or creates a predisposition that is brought out through environmental factors.

Child sexual abuse is a serious issue that can have devastating consequences for victims and their families. We will address the prevalence and effects of such abuse in the following chapter.

Other Paraphilias

The paraphilias discussed above are the ones that have received the most research attention and are addressed at length in the DSM. However, there are a multitude of other, less common sexual variations that have been documented. In this section, we will discuss necrophilia and zoophilia. For a brief sampling of a few other paraphilic interests, visit the Digging Deeper 13.2 box.

Digging Deeper 13.2   A Top 10 List of Unusual Sexual Behaviors

An enormous number of paraphilias have been identified, with one source putting the total at 547 (Aggrawal, 2009)! Of course, many of these behaviors are exceedingly rare and most of them have not received enough research attention to merit mention in the DSM. With that in mind, let us take a look at ten of the most interesting, but lesser known paraphilias.

10.   Paraphilic infantilism: Sexual arousal is derived from dressing up like a baby or being treated like one. This may or may not overlap with diaper fetishism, in which a person receives sexual pleasure from wearing or using diapers.

9.   Formicophilia: Sexual arousal is derived from having insects (e.g., ants) crawl all over your body and/or genitals. Some people enjoy the sensation of insect bites during this activity.

8.   Troilism/Cuckoldism: Sexual pleasure is derived from seeing one's partner engage in sexual activity with another person, or from knowing that one's partner is having an affair.

7.   Abasiophilia: Sexual arousal is derived from either viewing or sexually interacting with a person who has limited mobility, such as an individual wearing a cast or using crutches.

6.   Omorashi: Sexual pleasure is derived from either having a full bladder, or watching someone else with a full bladder wet themselves. This is separate from urophilia, in which a person experiences arousal in response to urinating on someone else or being urinated upon.

Figure 13.7   Frotteurists derive sexual arousal from rubbing up against unsuspecting strangers in crowded places. ©Ahmet Ihsan Ariturk/123RF.COM.

5. Frotteurism: Sexual arousal is derived from rubbing up against a nonconsenting person in a public place (e.g., on a subway or at a bar). Compared to the others on this list, frotteurism is somewhat more common and appears in the DSM.

4. Bug chasing: Sexual arousal is derived from having sex with (or fantasizing about having sex with) someone who is HIV-positive. Some of these individuals hope to catch the infection in the process.

3. Symphorophilia: Sexual pleasure is derived from watching a disaster occur, such as a car accident or fire.

2. Sacofricosis: Sexual arousal is derived from cutting a hole inside the pocket of one's pants in order to masturbate in public without anybody realizing that it is happening.

1. Vorarephilia: Sexual arousal is derived from the thought of eating another person or being eaten by someone else. Most vorarephiles just fantasize about the act, but some actually go through with it. Case in point: a few years back, a 43-year-old German man solicited a younger guy online who wanted to be eaten (literally). I do not know the full extent of their relationship other than that they kissed and dined on the young man's penis together before he bled to death (Harding, 2003).

Note: Reprinted with permission from *The Psychology of Human Sexuality* blog (www.lehmiller.com).

Necrophilia

Necrophilia is a very rare sexual variation that involves an erotic attraction to dead bodies. When cases of this behavior are discovered, they often make international headlines due to their highly unusual nature. For instance, in 2012, a Swedish woman was arrested for "violating the peace of the dead" after it was discovered that she had a large collection of human bones in her home that she filmed herself using as sex toys (France-Presse, 2012). This case received a lot of attention not only because it involved a woman (studies have found that 95% of necrophiles are men; Rosman & Resnick, 1989) but also because the focus was on skeletons (most cases of necrophilia I have read about involve a recently deceased corpse).

You are probably wondering why anyone would want to have sex with a dead body. What the research indicates is that the single most common reason given by necrophiles is a desire for a partner who will not put up resistance or reject one's advances (Rosman & Resnick, 1989). This suggests that interpersonal difficulties may precede necrophilic behavior in many cases. However, other reported motivations include wanting to "reconnect" sexually with a partner who has passed away and not having a current living partner.

To fulfill their desires, some necrophiles work in morgues so that they can access bodies, or they may convince a live partner to "play dead." In contrast, other necrophiles will commit murder so that they can have sex with the body afterward (Rosman & Resnick, 1989). *Homicidal necrophiles* are those who kill as a means of fulfilling their desire for sex with a corpse. In contrast, *pseudonecrophilic killers* are those who prefer live partners, but will still have sex with someone they have killed, perhaps because violating their victim in this way further increases their feelings of power and enhances their self-esteem.

Necrophilia is considered an extremely deviant behavior because of its nonconsensual nature and the fact that homicidal tendencies sometimes accompany it. However, it is a difficult behavior

Figure 13.8 Necrophiles often work in settings where they can easily access corpses. Homicidal necrophiles may kill in order to have access to a dead body, but such behavior is quite rare. ©Imagehit International Ltd/123RF.COM.

to identify and prevent because the victims cannot report it and because research has found that most necrophiles (aside from the murderous ones, of course) do not meet clinical criteria for psychosis and typically lead relatively normal lives in most other ways (Rosman & Resnick, 1989).

Zoophilia

Contrary to popular belief, the term **zoophilia** does not mean "love of the zoo"; rather, it refers to a true love of animals. And I mean "love" as in the passionate and erotic kind. Zoophilia is generally classified as a coercive and victimizing paraphilia because it is presumed that animals cannot consent to sex with humans. However, zoophiles argue otherwise. In fact, in a study of 114 men who have had sex with animals, most participants expressed concern for the well-being of their animal partners and felt that it was important to obtain consent before having sex with them (Williams & Weinberg, 2003). In the words of some of the participants themselves:

> My relationship with animals is a loving one in which sex is an extension of that love as it is with humans, and I do not have sex with a horse unless it consents. (p. 526) Although I do get an erection when interacting sexually with a stallion, my first priority is always the animal's pleasure, erection, and personal affection toward me. (p. 526)

Most participants in this study made a distinction between *zoophiles* (i.e., those who are concerned for the animal's health, safety, and pleasure) and *bestialists* (i.e., those who care only about their own sexual pleasure), and the majority (93%) identified with the zoophile label. Dogs (63%) and horses (29%) were the most common animal partners reported, but some participants indicated experience with sheep, cats, cows, dolphins, and chickens. Most of the men (58%) indicated being

Your Sexuality 13.1   Perspectives on Zoophilia

Most people would label someone who has sex with animals a "pervert." It is usually argued that because animals cannot consent, it is an act of cruelty to have sex with them. As a result, many countries around the world have instituted bans on zoophilia and bestiality. At the same time, however, the countries that ban these practices typically permit and make exceptions for animal husbandry (i.e., breeding of animals for food or other purposes). Animal husbandry takes many forms, but humans often play a very active role in the breeding. For instance, when artificially inseminating a female pig, breeders sometimes sexually stimulate the pig with their hands because that has been found to increase fertility rates (Roach, 2008). In fact, I have even seen an instructional video on how to stimulate a sow for such purposes and, let me tell you, it was a very "hands on" encounter. What is interesting about this is the fact that the issue of consent almost never arises when it comes to the subject of breeding. In response to this, many zoophiles have argued that it is hypocritical to suggest that zoophilia is morally wrong because animals cannot consent to sex, while simultaneously condoning forced sexual stimulation of animals for breeding purposes (*Spiegel*, 2012). Where do you stand on this issue? Can animals consent to sexual contact with humans? Is sexual stimulation of an animal acceptable under certain circumstances, but not others?

bisexual with respect to the desired sex of their partner and, on average, participants reported having had eight animal partners, with whom they most commonly engaged in vaginal and oral sex.

The prevalence and origin of zoophilia is not well understood. Kinsey found that about 8% of the men in his research had some previous sexual experience with an animal, and this number was much higher among men who grew up or lived on farms (Kinsey, Pomeroy, & Martin, 1948); however, his numbers are likely an overestimate due to the nonrepresentative nature of his sample. Most zoophiles report starting this behavior at a young age (early teens) and indicate various motivations, including desire for sexual pleasure and affection, lack of interest in human sex, and not being attractive or popular enough to find a human partner (Williams & Weinberg, 2003). As with the other paraphilias discussed above, operant conditioning could serve as one viable explanation for zoophilia, such that if the first encounter with an animal is extremely pleasurable (e.g., as described in the chapter-opening quote), the individual will likely seek to repeat it.

What are your thoughts on zoophilia? Check out the arguments raised in the Your Sexuality 13.1 box and weigh in with your perspective.

Treatment of Paraphilic Disorders

It should be clear from the above discussion that not every unusual sexual interest is a problem or disorder that requires treatment. Indeed, therapeutic intervention is only warranted for paraphilic interests that cause subjective distress or impairment to the individual or that cause physical or psychological harm to others. Several therapeutic approaches have been developed, each based on a different theoretical perspective.

Medical Therapies

Some scientists have proposed biological explanations for paraphilias, suggesting that unusual sexual interests stem from variations in hormone and/or neurotransmitter levels. As a result, many treatments have been developed in an attempt to alter the composition of individuals' body chemicals with the goal of changing unwanted or socially undesirable sexual behaviors. Historically, the primary medical treatment for men with unusual or dangerous sexual interests was surgical castration (i.e., removal of the testes). In the past, not only was castration used on persons with paraphilias like those described in this chapter, but it was also applied to any individuals who expressed sexual behaviors that were considered "deviant" at the time, including persons who engaged in same-sex activity. Today, however, surgical castration is generally regarded as cruel and unusual punishment and is not forced upon sexual offenders like it once was. However, in some countries, sex offenders have the option of selecting surgical castration in exchange for reduced prison sentences (Sealey, 2012).

In modern times, *chemical castration* (previously introduced in chapter 4) has become more normative. Chemical castration involves administering drugs such as Depo-Provera in order to block the body's ability to produce testosterone. Research has found that such drugs can be effective at reducing deviant sexual urges among convicted sex offenders; however, it is difficult to get individuals to continue with these drug programs on a voluntary basis, owing to the fact that people find their paraphilic desires pleasurable and because there are side effects. There is also a high rate of reoffending among those who stop treatment (Miner & Coleman, 2001). Chemical castration is not free from controversy either, given that it is not always effective, and some have argued that it is cruel and unusual.

One other medical approach involves the use of antidepressants, particularly SSRIs like Prozac. Such drugs are potentially useful for two reasons. For one thing, there is the arousal-inhibiting effect of serotonin previously discussed in chapter 4. However, the other reason SSRIs may be helpful is because these drugs have been found to reduce compulsive behavior in obsessive-compulsive disorder (OCD). Some have argued that paraphilic urges are like compulsions in many ways and perhaps represent a variant of OCD, which may be why the same drug can be used to treat both disorders. Consistent with this idea, case studies have found that paraphilic urges often decline among patients on SSRIs. However, the use of these drugs on their own is generally only recommended for those seeking treatment for nonviolent paraphilias where the risk of reoffending is low (Guay, 2009). When the risk of reoffending is higher, combined treatment consisting of SSRIs and anti-androgen drugs is recommended.

Psychological Therapies

Medical therapies are effective in treating some paraphilias, but the best outcomes typically occur when drug treatment is combined with a psychological intervention (Guay, 2009). This is especially true in cases where there are multiple victims, sexual violence, and a past history of failed treatments.

Most psychological therapies are cognitive-behavioral in nature. One of the most common is **orgasmic reconditioning** (Marquis, 1970). In this therapy, the client is instructed to masturbate to a paraphilic fantasy (e.g., spying on a neighbor who is undressing) until the brink of orgasm, at which point the client is asked to think about a more socially appropriate fantasy (e.g., watching a stripper or exotic dancer). After a few attempts, the client will start introducing the new fantasy earlier and earlier into masturbation. This therapy is based upon classical conditioning principles, with the idea being that the pairing of masturbation with an appropriate stimulus will ultimately lead the appropriate stimulus to become arousing in and of itself.

An alternative approach is **aversive conditioning**, where the goal is to psychologically pair the paraphilic desire with something unpleasant or punishing. In an earlier time and place, this may have involved using a truly painful punishment, such as electric shocks. In the modern world, however, it would probably be more likely to involve administration of nausea-inducing drugs, exposure to unpleasant photographs, or offensive odors. There is also a somewhat milder variant of aversive conditioning known as **covert sensitization**, in which paraphilic desires are paired with unpleasant thoughts, such as being put in jail or socially ridiculed (Maletzky, 1980).

One other variation on aversive conditioning is **masturbatory satiation** (Abel et al., 1984). In this approach, the client is instructed to masturbate to orgasm (if at all possible) while thinking of a socially appropriate stimulus. Upon climaxing, however, the client is instructed to start thinking about their paraphilic desire. In men, the continued masturbation is likely to be unpleasant and their refractory period is likely to make a second orgasm difficult. The idea is that such behavior will enhance the pleasure associated with the socially appropriate fantasy and decrease it for the paraphilic urges.

Social Skills Training

One final approach to treating paraphilic disorders involves enhancing the client's social interaction skills and abilities (Graves, Openshaw, & Adams, 1992). As mentioned above, social skills deficits are associated with certain paraphilias, including exhibitionism. It may be the case that persons who have difficulty developing and maintaining sexual and romantic relationships gravitate toward unusual forms of sexual fulfillment because they lack a socially appropriate outlet.

Social skills training has many elements and may involve addressing social fears, coping with rejection, developing conversational skills, and learning how to express intimacy appropriately. Sex surrogates (discussed in the previous chapter) are sometimes used in this training and may serve as mock dates for the client. These "dates" may involve going out to dinner and practicing typical dating conversation, and potentially practicing sexual intimacy afterward.

Effectiveness

Although each of the above therapeutic approaches has shown promise, the results have left a bit to be desired. For instance, a meta-analysis of 80 studies revealed a 37% reduction in the re-offense rate for persons with paraphilias who received some treatment versus those who received none (Schmucker & Losel, 2008). Although that is a substantial reduction, it is far from perfect. Treatment efficacy also varied considerably across paraphilias, with the meta-analysis revealing better success for exhibitionism and less for pedophilia. Moreover, research has found that treatment tends to be far more successful when it is sought voluntarily than when it is mandated, and the unfortunate reality is that most sex offenders do not spontaneously seek treatment on their own. These problems, combined with the damaging effects caused by sexual victimization (a topic we will consider in the next chapter), make it clear that the search for effective treatments for paraphilic disorders will remain an urgent area of sexuality research for years to come.

Key Terms

paraphilias

fetishism

transvestism

sadomasochism

masochists

sadists

voyeurism

exhibitionism

telephone scatologia

pedophilia

necrophilia

zoophilia

orgasmic
  reconditioning

aversive conditioning

covert sensitization

masturbatory
  satiation

Discussion Questions: What is Your Perspective on Sex?

- BDSM practices range from mild to wild. Although most people engage in relatively mild activities, should people be permitted to carry out their desires no matter what? Is there a line that can be crossed and, if so, where do you draw that line?
- Do you agree with the perspective that paraphilias are largely learned behaviors and that more appropriate sexual desires can be learned? Why or why not?
- For individuals with paraphilias who are convicted of sex crimes, should they be required to undergo treatment? If so, what type of treatment do you think is most appropriate?

References

Abel, G.G., Becker, J.V., Cunningham-Rathner, J., Rouleau, J.L., Kaplan, M., & Reich, J. (1984). *The treatment of child molesters*. Atlanta, GA: Behavioral Medicine Institute of Atlanta.

Abel, G.G., & Rouleau, J.L. (1990). The nature and extent of sexual assault. In W. L. Marshall, D. R. Laws, & H. E. Barbaree (Eds.), *Handbook of sexual assault: Issues, theories, and treatment of the offender* (pp. 9–22). New York: Plenum Press.

Aggrawal, A. (2009). *Forensic and medico-legal aspects of sexual crimes and unusual sexual practices*. Boca Raton, FL: CRC Press.

Aluja, A., Cuevas, L., García, L.F., & García, O. (2007). Zuckerman's personality model predicts MCMI-III personality disorders. *Personality and Individual Differences, 42,* 1311–1321. DOI:10.1016/j.paid.2006.10.009.

Avert (2012). *Worldwide ages of consent*. Retrieved from http://www.avert.org/age-of-consent.htm (accessed September 7, 2013).

Baumeister, R.F. (1988). Masochism as escape from self. *Journal of Sex Research, 25,* 28–59. DOI:10.1080/00224498809551444.

Blanchard, R. (2010a). The DSM diagnostic criteria for pedophilia. *Archives of Sexual Behavior, 39,* 304–316. DOI:10.1007/s10508-009-9536-0.

Blanchard, R. (2010b). The DSM diagnostic criteria for transvestic fetishism. *Archives of Sexual Behavior, 39,* 363–372. DOI:10.1007/s10508-009-9541-3.

Blanchard, R., Kolla, N.J., Cantor, J.M., Klassen, P.E., Dickey, R., Kuban, M.E., & Blak, T. (2007). IQ, handedness, and pedophilia in adult male patients stratified by referral source. *Sexual Abuse: Journal of Research and Treatment, 19,* 285–309. DOI:10.1177/107906320701900307.

Borg, C., & de Jong, P. J. (2012). Feelings of disgust and disgust-induced avoidance weaken following induced sexual arousal in women. *PLoS ONE 7*(9): e44111. DOI:10.1371/journal.pone.0044111.

Chang, J. (2013). Dozens of women join 'revenge porn' class action lawsuit against Texxxan.com. *ABC News*. Retrieved from http://abcnews.go.com/Technology/dozens-women-join-revenge-porn-class-action-lawsuit/story?id=18369797 (accessed September 7, 2013).

Cloud, J. (2003). Pedophilia. *Time magazine*. Retrieved from http://www.time.com/time/magazine/article/0,9171,232584-1,00.html (accessed September 7, 2013).

Dalby, J. (1988). Is telephone scatologia a variant of exhibitionism? *International Journal of Offender Therapy and Comparative Criminology, 32*, 45–49. DOI:10.1177/0306624X8803200106.

De Silva, W.P. (1999). Sexual variations. *British Medical Journal, 318*, 654–656.

Doctor, R., & Prince, V. (1997). Transvestism: A survey of 1,032 cross-dressers. *Archives of Sexual Behavior, 26*, 589–605. DOI:10.1023/A:1024572209266.

Emmers-Sommer, T.M., Allen, M., Bourhis, J., Sahlstein, E., Laskowski, K., Falato, W. L., & … Cashman, L. (2004). A meta-analysis of the relationship between social skills and sexual offenders. *Communication Reports, 17*, 1–10. DOI:10.1080/08934210409389369.

France-Presse, A. (2012). Swedish woman arrested for using human skeleton for sex. *The Raw Story*. Retrieved from http://www.rawstory.com/rs/2012/11/20/swedish-woman-arrested-for-using-human-skeleton-for-sex/ (accessed September 7, 2013).

Graves, R., Openshaw, D.K., & Adams, G.R. (1992). Adolescent sex offenders and social skills training. *International Journal of Offender Therapy and Comparative Criminology, 36*, 139–153. DOI:10.1177/0306624X9203600206.

Guay, D.P. (2009). Drug treatment of paraphilic and nonparaphilic sexual disorders. *Clinical Therapeutics: The International Peer-Reviewed Journal of Drug Therapy, 31*, 1–31. DOI:10.1016/j.clinthera.2009.01.009.

Harding, L. (2003). Victim of cannibal agreed to be eaten. *The Guardian*. Retrieved from http://www.guardian.co.uk/world/2003/dec/04/germany.lukeharding (accessed September 7, 2013).

Janus, S., and Janus, C. *The Janus Report on Sexual Behavior*. 1993. New York: John Wiley & Sons.

Kafka, M.P. (1997). A monoamine hypothesis for the pathophysiology of paraphilic disorders. *Archives of Sexual Behavior, 26*, 343–358. DOI:10.1023/A:1024535201089.

Kafka, M.P. (2010). The DSM diagnostic criteria for fetishism. *Archives of Sexual Behavior, 39*, 357–362. DOI:10.1007/s10508-009-9558-7.

Kinsey, A., Pomeroy, W.B., & Martin, C.E. (1948). *Sexual behavior in the human male*. Philadelphia: Saunders.

Krueger, R.B. (2010a). The DSM diagnostic criteria for sexual masochism. *Archives of Sexual Behavior, 39*, 346–356. DOI:10.1007/s10508-010-9613-4.

Krueger, R.B. (2010b). The DSM diagnostic criteria for sexual sadism. *Archives of Sexual Behavior, 39*, 325–345. DOI:10.1007/s10508-009-9586-3.

Långström, N. (2010). The DSM diagnostic criteria for exhibitionism, voyeurism, and frotteurism. *Archives of Sexual Behavior, 39*, 317–324. DOI:10.1007/s10508-009-9577-4.

Långström, N., & Seto, M.C. (2006). Exhibitionistic and voyeuristic behavior in a Swedish national population survey. *Archives of Sexual Behavior, 35*, 427–435. DOI:10.1007/s10508-006-9042-6.

Maletzky, B.M. (1980). Self-reported vs. court referred sexually deviant patients: Success with assisted covert sensitization. *Behavior Therapy, 11*, 306–314. DOI:10.1016/S0005-7894(80)80048-7.

Marquis, J. (1970). Orgasmic reconditioning: Changing sexual object choice through controlling masturbation fantasies. *Journal of Behavior Therapy and Experimental Psychiatry, 1*, 263–271. DOI:10.1016/0005-7916(70)90050-9.

Miner, M.H., & Coleman, E. (2001). Advances in sex offender treatment and challenges for the future. *Journal of Psychology & Human Sexuality, 13*, 5–24. DOI:10.1300/J056v13n03_02.

Plaud J.J., & Martini, J.R. (1999). The respondent conditioning of male sexual arousal. *Behavior Modification, 23*, 254–268. DOI:10.1177/0145445599232004.

Rachman, S. (1966). Sexual fetishism: An experimental analogue. *Psychological Record, 16*, 293–296.

Richters, J., de Visser, R.O., Rissel, C.E., Grulich, A.E., & Smith, A.A. (2008). Demographic and psychosocial features of participants in bondage and discipline, 'sadomasochism' or dominance and submission (BDSM): Data from a national survey. *Journal of Sexual Medicine, 5*, 1660–1668. DOI:10.1111/j.1743-6109.2008.00795.x.

Roach, M. (2008). *Bonk: The curious coupling of science and sex*. New York: Norton.

Rosman, J.P., & Resnick, P.J. (1989). Sexual attraction to corpses: A psychiatric review of necrophilia. *Bulletin of the American Academy of Psychiatry and Law, 17*, 153–163.

Sandnabba, N.K., Santtila, P., Alison, L., & Nordling, N. (2002). Demographics, sexual behaviour, family background and abuse experiences of practitioners of sadomasochistic sex: A review of recent research. *Sexual and Relationship Therapy, 17*, 39–54. DOI:10.1080/14681990220108018.

Schmucker, M., & Losel, F. (2008). Does sexual offender treatment work? A systematic review of outcome evaluations. *Psicothema, 20*, 10–19.

Scorolli, C., Ghirlanda, S., Enquist, M., Zattoni, S., & Jannini, E.A. (2007). Relative prevalence of different fetishes. *International Journal of Impotence Research, 19*, 432–437.

Sealey, G. (2012). Some sex offenders opt for castration. *ABC News*. Retrieved from http://abcnews.go.com/US/story?id=93947&page=1#.T8aQolI8WSp (accessed August 31, 2013).

Spiegel (2012). Evolution: Germany to ban sex with animals. Retrieved from http://www.spiegel.de/international/zeitgeist/germany-plans-to-outlaw-sex-with-animals-a-869402.html (accessed September 7, 2013).

Weinberg, M.S., Williams, C.J., & Calhan, C. (1995). "If the shoe fits…": Exploring male homosexual foot fetishism. *Journal of Sex Research, 32*, 17–27. DOI:10.1080/00224499509551770.

Williams, C.J., & Weinberg, M.S. (2003). Zoophilia in men: A study of sexual interest in animals. *Archives of Sexual Behavior, 32*, 523–535. DOI:10.1023/A:1026085410617.

14

Sex Laws, Sexual Victimization, and the Sexual Marketplace

©Jan van der Hoeven 2013. Used under license from Shutterstock.com.

Chapter Outline

- Introduction 352
- A Brief History of Sex Laws 352
- Sexual Coercion and Violence 354
  - Sexual Assault 354
  - Child Sexual Abuse 357
  - Sexual Harassment 358
- The Sexual Marketplace 360
  - Prostitution 360
  - Sex Trafficking 364
  - Pornography 365

The Psychology of Human Sexuality, First Edition. Justin J. Lehmiller.
© 2014 John Wiley & Sons, Ltd. Published 2014 by John Wiley & Sons, Ltd.

Introduction

For centuries, cultures and societies around the world have imposed religious and legal restrictions on human sexual activity. Sex laws exist in the modern world, but their nature has changed dramatically. In this chapter, we will review some of the most common legally regulated sexual activities. While there is general consensus that some of these activities should be against the law (e.g., sexual assault and child sexual abuse), there is controversy surrounding other acts. For instance, public opinion is more divided over whether prostitution should be legal, as well as the extent to which pornography should be subject to regulation (e.g., should porn actors be required to wear condoms in order to reduce the spread of STIs?). Because the sexual marketplace has long been an area of contention, we will provide expanded coverage of this topic toward the end of the chapter. To begin, let us briefly review the history of sex laws.

A Brief History of Sex Laws

In the days of the Ancient Greeks and Romans, there were few formally established limits when it came to sex. Homosexuality and bisexuality were common, as were orgies and group sex. In addition, some people practiced pederasty and other sexual activities that would be considered taboo by today's standards. However, all of this changed with the rise of Christianity and the view that penile–vaginal intercourse within marriage for the purpose of procreation is the only "valid" form of sexual activity. This forever altered how societies around the world approached and regulated sex. Indeed, throughout much of modern history, any type of sex that conflicted with the sex-for-procreation view (e.g., same-sex activity, oral and anal sex, adultery) has been illegal, with violators subject to severe penalties. Moreover, sex before marriage, cohabitation, contraception, and so many other things that we take for granted today were banned at one time or another for the same reason. These are just the tip of the iceberg when it comes to governments telling people what they can and cannot do in the bedroom. For a summary of some of the more unusual sex laws ever passed, check out the Digging Deeper 14.1 box.

Today, sexual activity continues to be regulated to at least some extent in most societies as a result of various religious and cultural legacies. In the Western world, laws regulating sexual behavior between consenting adults have been loosened considerably in recent years (e.g., in the 2003 case of *Lawrence v. Texas*, the US Supreme Court ruled that so-called "sodomy laws" prohibiting oral and anal sex among consenting adults can no longer be enforced); however, restrictions on such behaviors remain in place in other countries (e.g., Malaysia, Zimbabwe). That said, there appears to be some cross-cultural agreement that sexual victimization, prostitution, and the distribution of sexually explicit materials should be regulated. Nonetheless, there is substantial variability in how the laws are written, the penalties they carry, and their likelihood of being enforced. For instance, while rape is banned in most modern societies, the way "rape" is defined can be wildly different. Although we will discuss rape in more detail below, consider that *spousal rape* does not exist from a legal standpoint in some countries, such as India (Denyer, 2013). Some cultures hold the belief that women cannot deny sex to the men they are married to, which effectively means that, within marriage, rape cannot technically happen. In contrast, most Western countries have sexual assault laws that explicitly address spousal rape, and those laws were enacted decades ago. Exploring all of the variation in sex laws throughout the world is

Digging Deeper 14.1　A Top 10 List of Wacky Sex Laws

For centuries, governments have gone to great lengths to regulate people's sex lives. Below are ten of the most interesting sex laws I have ever heard of. As you will see, some of the laws are even stranger when you think about what they *do not* say. I cannot necessarily vouch for the current status of these laws or whether they can still be enforced. All I can tell you is that they have appeared in multiple news stories over the years.

Figure 14.1　Many cultures and societies regulate the sexual behavior of consenting adults, which has resulted in some truly surprising sex laws. ©Atthidej Nimmanhaemin / 123RF.COM.

10. Texas law prohibits the sale of dildos and makes it illegal for anyone to own more than six sex toys.
9. In Utah, you are not allowed to marry your first cousin until you reach the age of 65.
8. In Minnesota it is illegal for any man to have sexual intercourse with a live fish. *Editor's note: But a dead fish is OK? And women are free to have sex with aquatic creatures as they please?*
7. In Florida, it is illegal for men to wear strapless gowns in public.
6. In the United States, there is no federal law banning necrophilia (i.e., sex with corpses), and only 21 states have enacted laws prohibiting it.
5. In Idaho, public displays of affection are illegal if they last more than 18 minutes.
4. In Maryland, it is illegal to sell condoms from vending machines… except in places where alcoholic beverages are sold on the premises. *Editor's note: Because sober people do not need condoms?*

3. In Connersville, Wisconsin, it is illegal for a man to fire a gun when his female partner reaches orgasm.
2. In the state of Florida, having sex with a porcupine is illegal. *Editor's note: Is sexual abuse of porcupines so rampant that there had to be a law specifically about it?*
1. An old California law prohibited either partner from orgasming before the other during foreplay. *Editor's note: I know at least a few people who would not be opposed to this law coming back!*

Note: Reprinted with permission from *The Psychology of Human Sexuality* blog (www.lehmiller.com).

beyond the scope of this book; however, as you read about sexual regulations in this chapter, keep in mind that huge cultural variation exists in terms of which acts are criminalized and how they are punished.

Sexual Coercion and Violence

In this section, we will consider three forms of sexual coercion and violence that are legally banned in many modern cultures and societies: sexual assault, child sexual abuse, and sexual harassment.

Sexual Assault

For purposes of this textbook, **sexual assault** is defined as any event in which a person is touched in a sexual way against that person's will or made to perform a nonconsensual sex act by one or more other persons. This definition is intentionally broad and means that a person of *any* gender or sexuality can be assaulted and, further, that sexual assault can take *any* form, from groping to oral, anal, and vaginal sex. I make no distinction between sexual assault and rape here, although a distinction certainly exists in many legal codes. In discussing rape, I do not find it productive to include any qualifying terms in front of it, as politicians frequently do. For example, in US politics, the term "forcible rape" is often used in discussions on Capitol Hill (Bronner, 2012). Regardless of the intent behind the usage of terms like this, they are unnecessary (e.g., rape is, by definition, sex that is forced upon a nonconsenting partner) and they have the effect of implying that some rapes are more "legitimate" than others.

Although we are adopting this broad definition, legal definitions of rape and sexual assault vary, as noted above in our discussion of spousal rape. As additional evidence of this, until 2013, India's legal code defined rape only as nonconsensual penetration of a woman; anything less (e.g., groping) was considered an attempt to "outrage [a woman's] modesty" and was almost never prosecuted (Denyer, 2013). In contrast, groping a nonconsenting woman has been illegal in the United States and Europe for some time and is considered a form of sexual battery or assault. Fortunately, India's law was recently expanded, but only after widespread public outrage in response to a few horrific high-profile gang rapes that captured international attention. In addition to variations in which acts "count" as rape, laws also vary in terms of who can be a victim. For example, within the United States, some states' definitions are written such that only women can be victims of

Table 14.1 Number of Sexual Assaults in the US

	Year		
	2002	2010	2011
Total population (ages 12+)	231,589,260	255,961,940	257,542,240
Number of sexual assaults	349,810	268,570	243,800
Percentage of victimizations reported to police	55%	49%	27%

Source: Truman & Planty (2012)

rape. These variations are largely a function of outdated, patriarchal legal codes and they have the unfortunate effect of (1) perpetuating sexual assault myths (e.g., "only women can be raped"), (2) encouraging underreporting of sexual violence, and (3) minimizing victims' experiences.

Sexual assault is an all-too-common reality worldwide. In the United States alone, national survey data indicate that there are approximately 668 sexual assaults per day (Truman & Planty, 2012). As you can see in Table 14.1, the number of assaults has decreased somewhat in recent years, despite the size of the population increasing. Although this is a promising trend, it is worrisome that the percentage of assaults reported to the police appears to be declining. As seen in Table 14.1, most sexual assaults currently go unreported, which means that an unconscionably high number of perpetrators go unpunished and many victims fail to get the help they need. Unfortunately, it is difficult to compare rates of sexual assault across world countries given the differing legal definitions mentioned above. In countries where rape is defined very narrowly, it is quite possible that the number of assaults reported may appear low on paper, but could be much higher if a broader definition were applied.

Sexual assault can take many forms, and it is often given different names depending upon how the perpetrator knows the victim (e.g., stranger, acquaintance, date, spouse), the age of the victim (**statutory rape** is the term usually used to describe sexual assault against a minor), and when or where the act occurs (e.g., prison, wartime). One increasingly common form of rape involves furnishing the victim with alcohol, drugs, or both, as a means of rendering that person unconscious or incapable of providing consent (Schwartz, Milteer, & LeBeau, 2000). The drug **rohypnol** (known colloquially as "roofies") is a sedative commonly used for this purpose. It is 10 times more powerful than Valium, is fast acting (effects occur in under 20 minutes), and is cleared from the body quickly, making it extremely dangerous in the hands of a rapist.

Although persons of any gender and sexuality can commit and be victims of sexual assault, most reported sexual assaults involve a male perpetrator and a female victim. Also, contrary to popular belief, most sexual assaults involve an assailant who is known to the victim, such as a friend or romantic partner (Cowan, 2000).

The motivations for rape and sexual assault are complex and controversial. Many psychologists subscribe to the idea that rape is fundamentally about power and control and has little to do with sex. In fact, a number of popular textbooks and websites offer power/control as the sole explanation for rape. While there is *some* truth to this idea, research suggests that this is an overly broad generalization and that sexual motives do indeed contribute in many cases of rape. As some evidence of this, sex offenders frequently cite sexual gratification needs when asked about their reasons for committing sexual

Figure 14.2   Rohypnol ("roofies") tends to be the date rapist's drug of choice due to its fast-acting and powerful sedative effects. Image Copyright Monkey Business Images 2013. Used under license from Shutterstock.com.

assault (Mann & Hollin, 2007). Thus, it is perhaps most useful to think of rapists in terms of a typology based upon motive. For instance, Beech, Ward, and Fisher (2006) identified five motivations underlying men's sexual violence against women: (1) anger and resentment, (2) hostility toward women, (3) seeing women only as sex objects, (4) having an uncontrollable sex drive, and (5) feelings of entitlement. It is important not to try and oversimplify the causes of sexual assault because without fully understanding the reasons, we cannot hope to effectively prevent future assaults and rehabilitate offenders. This is an important point because many sex offenders (a meta-analysis puts this number at 13.4%; Hanson & Bussiere, 1998) go on to commit future sex crimes.

Sexual assault can have a devastating psychological impact on victims and their close social networks. This can include a range of emotions and cognitions, including depression and anxiety, anger at the assailant, feeling powerless, fear of future victimization, and possible shame or guilt (an unfortunate reality is that many victims wrongly feel that they bear some responsibility for the assault). Common rape myths (e.g., "she asked for it by dressing that way" and "she shouldn't have had so much to drink") can make these reactions even more severe because they incorrectly place blame on the victim instead of the perpetrator. Of course, the duration and severity of the emotional reaction varies considerably across persons. In some cases, **post-traumatic stress disorder (PTSD)** may result (Cloitre, Scarvalone, & Difede, 1997), in which there is a prolonged emotional reaction characterized by reliving the trauma through flashbacks and dreams, extreme anxiety and hypervigilance, social detachment, and insomnia. Although PTSD can have many causes (e.g., natural disaster, war), rape is one of the most common among

Figure 14.3   The aftermath of sexual assault includes a variety of negative emotional responses, with the potential for post-traumatic stress. ©Diego Cervo/123RF.COM.

women. Rape can also have sexual effects (e.g., vaginismus, erectile dysfunction) to the extent that the individual comes to associate sexual activity with anxiety. In cases where a sexual assault survivor has these prolonged reactions or difficulty moving on with life, professional counseling or psychotherapy may be useful.

Child Sexual Abuse

Thus far, we have primarily focused on sexual assault as it affects adults. Tragically, children can also be targets of sexually coercion and violence. **Child sexual abuse (CSA)** is the umbrella term used to describe any instance in which a child is sexually victimized by an adult. This definition is intentionally broad so as to encompass the widest possible range of victims and acts. Again, however, legal definitions vary across states and countries due to differences in age of consent. This means that what may be considered CSA in one culture may be viewed differently elsewhere (e.g., that same act may be classified as statutory rape or potentially as consensual sex).

CSA is often divided into two categories: abuse by relatives and nonrelatives. CSA perpetrated by someone related to the child (e.g., a parent or older sibling) is referred to as **incest**. CSA perpetrated by a nonrelative may be classified as *pedophilia* (if the abuse stems from a sexual attraction to children; see chapter 13) or as *child molestation* (a broader term used to describe any type of sexual abuse against a child by a nonrelative, regardless of motive). Most cases of CSA are attributable to pedophilia; however, sexual abuse of children has many contributing causes (Murray, 2000). For example, a teenager may abuse a younger child due to sexual curiosity and opportunity, not because of a primarily attraction to children. Alternatively, someone with a severe intellectual disability may commit CSA because that person does not fully comprehend what constitutes appropriate and inappropriate sexual behavior. Regardless of whether the abuser is sexually attracted to children, research indicates that sexual gratification needs are one of the most frequently cited reasons given by child molesters to explain their behavior (Mann & Hollin, 2007).

A review of the research on the perpetrators of CSA revealed that most acts of CSA are committed by men and often involve someone who is known to the victim, as we saw in the case of sexual assault more broadly (Murray, 2000). This review also revealed that pedophiles and child molesters may have heterosexual, homosexual, or bisexual orientations, although they tend to select female victims twice as often as male victims. In addition, most perpetrators report that they experienced CSA themselves and, in some cases, the abuse they commit reflects the abuse they previously experienced.

Students are often surprised to learn just how common CSA is. A meta-analysis of studies from 22 different countries put the prevalence of CSA (defined as experiencing any form of sexual victimization before age 18) at 7.9% among men and 19.7% among women (Pereda, Guilera, Forns, & Gomez-Benito, 2009). Exact statistics vary widely across studies and countries, as does the nature of the abuse; however, what is clear from this research is that CSA is a topic of worldwide concern that impacts a disturbingly high number of children.

CSA can have a range of psychological, sexual, and relational effects on its victims, effects that can reverberate for a lifetime. Psychologically, the same emotional disturbances reported by adult survivors of sexual assault often occur (e.g., depression, anger, guilt, shame), not to mention PTSD. These reactions are often exacerbated when family members or authorities fail to take the victim's abuse claims seriously. In addition, CSA is linked to engaging in risky behaviors (e.g., alcohol and drug abuse, having greater numbers of sexual partners), learning disabilities, frequent *dissociation* (i.e., blocking traumatic memories through psychological escape), as well as thinking about and attempting suicide (Jarvis & Copeland, 1997). CSA survivors may also have a difficult time establishing trust and intimacy with romantic partners and suffer from sexual performance problems (e.g., difficulties with arousal, orgasm, and/or pain during sex).

On a side note, several studies have found a correlation between CSA victimization and adult attraction to members of the same sex (e.g., Roberts, Glymour, & Koenen, 2012). On the basis of such findings, some have suggested that CSA may be a contributing factor to adult homosexuality and bisexuality (e.g., perhaps because childhood victimization creates a stigmatized identity that, in turn, makes it more likely that such individuals will adopt other stigmatized identities later in life); however, this explanation is controversial and far from conclusive. It could also be that the link between CSA and adult same-sex attraction is a function of youth revealing their attractions or displaying gender nonconforming behaviors early on, which predisposes them to abuse. It may also be that adults with same-sex attraction are just more willing to acknowledge and discuss early experiences with CSA. Although we do not fully understand why this association exists, it is clear that more research attention is warranted to address the origins of this disparity.

Sexual Harassment

A third type of sexual victimization we will consider is **sexual harassment**, which refers to unwanted verbal and/or physical sexual advances that occur in the workplace or in an academic environment. Sexual harassment can take one of two forms: (1) **quid pro quo**, which occurs when someone in a position of power offers some benefit or reward (e.g., a promotion or good grade) in exchange for sexual favors, and (2) **hostile environment**, which occurs when

Figure 14.4 Although many people think of the nature of sexual harassment as being cut and dried, such as unwanted physical touching, the reality is that harassment may constitute a wide range of verbal and physical acts. Image Copyright Ydefinitel 2013. Used under license from Shutterstock.com.

other people's words or actions of a sexual nature have the effect of creating a hostile or abusive environment for the victim. As these definitions make clear, several different activities could potentially be considered harassment, ranging from requests for sex to crude jokes to inappropriate touching. In addition, as with all of the other forms of sexual victimization we have considered in this chapter, persons of any sexual and gender identity can commit and be subject to sexual harassment; however, most cases of harassment tend to be perpetrated by men against women (Work Harassment, 2012). Also, like sexual assault, the motivations behind sexual harassment vary. Some may harass out of a desire for sex, a need to dominate or control others, negative stereotypes about the victims' sex or sexuality, or the perception that the victim is a competitive threat.

Sexual harassment of the quid pro quo variety is perhaps the easiest to spot when it happens. There is usually little ambiguity in a request for sex in exchange for preferential treatment. In contrast, the hostile environment type is often less obvious. The reason for this is because different persons may perceive the same sexual action in a very different manner. The key to determining when a given behavior crosses the line into sexual harassment is how that behavior is perceived by the victim. Harassment must be *unwanted* and it must make the victim feel offended or uncomfortable. Thus, if you are the victim of harassment, you will know it. However, making the case to the courts that sexual harassment occurred is another matter. Research indicates that workplace sexual harassment lawsuits are more likely to be decided in favor of the victim to the extent that the harassment was severe, there were witnesses or documentation that harassment occurred, and the victim notified management of the activity, but management failed to do anything about it (Terpstra & Baker, 1992). Thus, a man who tells a one-time crude joke in the break room but is reprimanded by the boss afterward would be unlikely to find himself in legal hot water. In contrast, a woman who repeatedly taunts a gay male co-worker over his sexuality in front of the rest of the staff would be more likely to face legal sanctions.

Prevalence estimates of sexual harassment vary across studies depending upon how sexual harassment is defined, the nature of the sample (i.e., random vs. convenience), and the environment (i.e., work vs. school vs. military); however, all studies indicate that it is reasonably common. A recent meta-analysis of various forms of work-related harassment revealed that 24% of women reported having experienced sexual harassment on the job, and that 58% reported having been on the receiving end of a potentially harassing behavior at work (Ilies, Hauserman, Schwochau, & Stibal, 2003). These statistics make it clear that the way harassment is measured (i.e., asking participants if they have ever experienced harassment vs. giving them a checklist of behaviors that psychologists think might constitute harassment) yields strikingly different estimates. Although this meta-analysis only focused on women, men can experience harassment too; however, they are less likely to be victims and, when victimized in this way, they are less likely to report it. For instance, of the 11,000–12-000 claims of sexual harassment reported to the United States' Equal Employment Opportunity Commission each year, about 16% are filed by men (EEOC, 2012).

Sexual harassment can have a wide range of negative effects on its victims. Psychological effects include depression, anxiety, and post-traumatic stress (Rederstorff, Buchanan, & Settles, 2007). As a result, it is perhaps not surprising that harassment often interferes with victims' work and school performance. Not only does the quality of victims' work suffer, but they are also more prone to absences and, when it occurs in the workplace, victims often end up quitting their job (Willness, Steel, & Lee, 2007).

The Sexual Marketplace

At this point, we will shift our focus to the sale of sex, another aspect of sexuality regulated by law in many parts of the world. We begin by considering prostitution and sex trafficking, followed by an in-depth exploration of pornography.

Prostitution

Prostitution is most commonly defined as "trading sexual services for money." However, this definition is rather nebulous because it neither defines "sexual services" nor "money." For instance, what if the "services" do not include sexual penetration (e.g., consider an individual who is paid only to masturbate in front of another person)? Also, what if jewels or drugs exchange hands instead of money? Perhaps a more precise definition of a **prostitute** is a person who (1) makes an explicit agreement to perform a sexual act in exchange for some type of compensation and (2) is willing to offer this service to almost anyone who can afford it. Please keep in mind that the way we have defined prostitution here is not a legal definition. As with all other sexual activities regulated by law, the definition of prostitution varies across cultures.

Although persons of any sex, including transsexuals, can be prostitutes, the majority are female. As discussed in chapter 1, this may be because female sexuality is far more "valuable" than male sexuality from the standpoint that there is a lot of demand for casual sex among heterosexual men, but a limited supply of women who are willing to provide it (Baumeister & Vohs, 2004). Regardless of their sex, prostitutes generally fall into two classes: those who

Figure 14.5 When it comes to prostitution, women are most commonly the sellers and men the buyers; however, male prostitutes and female "johns" certainly exist. Image Copyright luckyraccoon 2013. Used under license from Shutterstock.com.

literally walk the streets (often referred to as *streetwalkers* if they are female and *hustlers* if they are male) and those who work as "escorts" (more frequently known as *call girls* and *gigolos* if they are female or male, respectively). Prostitutes who work the streets typically charge the least for their services and are the most likely to be arrested, owing to their heightened visibility. Streetwalkers often have a pimp who provides protection in exchange for a portion of their earnings; hustlers usually do not. Either way, these prostitutes are the most likely to have problems with drug abuse and an extensive history of STIs. In contrast, "escorts" are often contracted with an agency and tend to have a regular client list. They perform fewer sexual acts than those who work the streets and are able to charge a much higher rate, although the agency takes a portion of it for facilitating client visits. Escorts may also provide companionship and intimacy in addition to sex. Across all types of prostitutes, there is variation in terms of the limits they set on sex acts (e.g., some prostitutes may not kiss or have anal sex with clients), as well as their willingness to accept clients who are not of their desired sex (e.g., some prostitutes might identify as heterosexual, but are willing to be "gay for pay").

One additional variety of prostitute is the *brothel worker*, who is almost always female and lives and works inside a house with other prostitutes. Brothels are usually managed by a madam, who takes a portion of the workers' earnings in exchange for running the house and arranging client visits. In places where brothels are legal, there are often safeguards in effect to protect the health and safety of workers and their clients. For instance, brothels are permitted in a few counties in the US state of Nevada, and workers are required to use condoms with clients, as well as receive routine STI tests. In contrast, even though brothels are legal in the Netherlands, no STI tests are required for persons selling sex. A modern variant of the brothel is the *massage parlor*, a business that sometimes serves as a front for houses of prostitution in places where trading sex for money is illegal.

Figure 14.6   In the state of Nevada, brothels are legal in a couple of counties; however, several laws and regulations are in place to protect the health of the workers and their clients. ©Joerg Hackemann/123RF.COM.

What motivates people to enter prostitution? Most prostitutes do not wake up one morning and say, "Of all the careers I could possibly have, I think prostitution is the right one for me." Certainly, there are some prostitutes who enjoy what they do and find it to be exciting, but they are the exception rather than the rule (Kramer, 2004). The majority of prostitutes appear to enter the profession because they feel they have little other choice – they have simply fallen on hard times and need money. Indeed, the primary reason both male (Smith, Grov, Seal, & McCall, 2013) and female (Dalla, 2000) prostitutes report entering the profession is financial incentives. However, one interesting sex difference is that for female prostitutes, selling sex is usually their only means of earning money; in contrast, male prostitutes usually "turn tricks" as a side business (i.e., they often have a day job or other source of income). Of course, there are other reasons for becoming a prostitute. For some, it is a way to support a drug habit, and for others, it is because a person with power has coerced them. There is also research linking early childhood sexual victimization to becoming an adult sex worker, and this is especially true for women (Vanwesenbeeck, 2013). The exact role that this background factor plays is not at all clear, though.

Working as a prostitute carries a number of physical and psychological health risks. Survey studies of prostitutes reveal that most female escorts and streetwalkers find their work emotionally unpleasant and report feelings of anxiety, sadness, and shame (Kramer, 2004). As a result, most of these women report that they would exit their current lifestyle if they felt as though there were another option. Male prostitutes also report many negative reactions and discomfort with their work, as well as arousal difficulties when working with clients they do not find attractive (Smith et al., 2013). In order to cope with unpleasant working conditions, prostitutes may adopt strategies such as dissociating during sexual activity, reminding themselves of the money, and/or seeking social support from other sex workers.

Also, because prostitutes (particularly those who are female) are at a heightened risk of rape and violence from customers and pimps alike, it should not be surprising that a large number of prostitutes meet the diagnostic criteria for PTSD (Farley, 2004). In order to cope with this reality, many prostitutes report turning to drugs or alcohol as a way of psychologically distancing themselves from their work (Kramer, 2004); however, to the extent that this leads to addiction, it can make it all the more difficult for a prostitute to ultimately exit the profession. One other major health risk faced by prostitutes is STIs (Shannon & Csete, 2010). HIV, herpes, syphilis and a number of other infections occur at a very high rate among prostitutes. Of course, having a greater number of partners is a risk factor in and of itself, but compounding this is the fact that many prostitutes have an incentive to *not* practice safe sex because customers are often willing to pay extra for sex without condoms.

Although most research on prostitution has focused on the prostitutes themselves, there is a growing amount of work addressing the people who patronize them. Most customers of prostitutes (whether they are male, female, or transsexual) are men. There are certainly some women who visit prostitutes, but they are often seeking companionship in addition to sex, which is rare for male customers. Among the men who visit prostitutes, research indicates that they are not social or sexual deviants; instead, most are college educated and employed, and (surprisingly) nearly half are married (Monto, 2002).Why are these men visiting prostitutes? The most commonly reported sexual activity with a prostitute is fellatio, so the simple desire for a blowjob may be one reason; however, other motivations may include a desire for "uncomplicated" sex, the excitement of risky or illegal activity, and/or a low frequency of sex with a current relationship partner (Monto, 2002).

Although prostitution is illegal in many countries (including most of Africa, Asia, eastern Europe, and the US), many people have argued that it is in the interest of public health to legalize and regulate prostitution because it will keep sex workers and their clients safer. Do you agree? Check out the Your Sexuality 14.1 box and weigh in with your perspective.

Your Sexuality 14.1   Should Prostitution Be Legal?

Proponents of legalized prostitution argue that legalization will increase the health and safety of sex workers and their clients. If legalized, the profession as a whole could potentially be regulated, with requirements such as routine STI tests for workers and mandatory condom use (just like in the Nevada brothels). Moreover, by pulling the behavior out of the shadows, it may reduce the risk of sexual assault and violence against prostitutes. Another common argument in favor of legalization is that it will significantly reduce taxpayer spending (arrests and prosecutions are not a cheap date), while allowing the possibility of taxing the sale of sex. Thus, it could represent a big influx of money to the government. On the other hand, those who argue against legalizing prostitution frequently cite concerns that the sale of sex is morally wrong. In addition, it is sometimes argued that legalized prostitution could encourage more people to enter the profession, not to mention potentially increase rates of STIs. Where do you stand on this issue? What other arguments for or against legalized prostitution can you think of?

Sex Trafficking

Sex trafficking is related to prostitution in the sense that it involves an exchange of money for sexual services; however, these two concepts are not exactly synonymous. As defined by the United States Victims of Trafficking and Violence Protection Act of 2000, sex trafficking involves "the recruitment, harboring, transportation, provision, or obtaining of a person for the purpose of a commercial sex act." However, this definition does not fully describe the nature of this activity. It is important to add that sex trafficking includes "deception, fraud, coercion, force, or exploitation of the trafficked human by the trafficker" (Schauer & Wheaton, 2006; p. 148). Thus, sex trafficking occurs when one person sells another for sex, and the person being sold is exploited in the process (i.e., the victim is effectively a sex slave). This is one of the ways in which trafficking and prostitution differ: it is possible for someone to become a prostitute without being exploited (although it is important to note that many prostitutes are exploited by pimps and customers alike and have not sought out their profession by choice).

No one knows exactly how prevalent sex trafficking is, but there are estimated to be millions of victims and it is thought to be one of the three largest global criminal operations (Walker-Rodriguez & Hill, 2011). Sex trafficking is usually discussed as an international phenomenon, whereby vulnerable women and children from disadvantaged or unstable countries are smuggled into other countries where sex tourism is popular, such as Thailand, the Netherlands, and the US (of course, men can be victims too, but it is not nearly as common). Although transportation from one city or country to another is not required for trafficking to occur, it can make the impact on the victims even more severe when it happens because they may not speak the local language or have the resources to seek help.

Traffickers tend to prey upon those who are most desperate (e.g., persons who are homeless or jobless) and may initially entice their victims with promises of help, such as marriage or a high-paying job. Alternatively, some traffickers may kidnap victims or, in some cases, may purchase children from parents who feel that they cannot afford to raise them. The victims' identification and personal belongings are often held hostage by the traffickers, who may promise to give them back to the victim in exchange for some type of sex work (e.g., working in a brothel, performing in a strip club). Traffickers may also control their victims through fear and violence, or potentially through drug use (Estes & Weiner, 2001).

Repeated experiences with rape and other forms of violence result in a very severe psychological impact on victims. Studies of survivors of sex trafficking have found that the vast majority reported lingering symptoms of depression and anxiety. For example, in a study of women and adolescents who had previously been trafficked, Zimmerman and colleagues (2006) found that 95% reported feeling depressed, 76% felt hopeless about the future, 91% reported nervousness, and 85% reported fearfulness. Many of these victims met criteria for PTSD.

Many groups around the world are working to combat sex trafficking; however, not everyone agrees on the best approach. Some argue that legalizing prostitution would reduce the underground sex trafficking business by allowing those who want to purchase sex a legitimate means of doing so. Others argue that the goal should be educating and empowering women in order to prevent future victimization. Yet others argue that it is law enforcement that needs to change, because oftentimes it is the victim who winds up in jail on prostitution charges (and is effectively victimized twice) instead of the traffickers.

Pornography

Pornography refers to any type of sexually explicit material that has the intent of producing arousal in those who consume it. Does this definition mean that all depictions of sex are therefore *pornographic*? Not necessarily. Most sexual scientists distinguish between pornography and erotica, with **erotica** referring to depictions of sex that evoke themes of mutual attraction and usually incorporate some emotional component in addition to the sex act itself. That said, under the law, any distinction between pornography and erotica is usually nothing more than semantics because any explicit depictions of sex can potentially be deemed *obscene*.

In the United States, the First Amendment to the Constitution guarantees a right to freedom of speech; however, the courts have determined that this is not a limitless right, especially when it comes to the production and distribution of sexual materials. Specifically, in the case of *Miller v. California* (1973), the Supreme Court determined that when a work meets *all three* of the following criteria, it is considered obscene and can therefore be legally banned:

1. Whether the average person, applying contemporary community standards would find that the work, taken as a whole, appeals to prurient interest.
2. Whether the work depicts or describes, in a patently offensive way, sexual conduct specifically defined by the applicable state law.
3. Whether the work, taken as a whole, lacks serious literary, artistic, political, or scientific value.

Figure 14.7 Like pornography, erotica may depict explicit sexual activity. The difference is that erotica generally evokes themes of mutual consent, equality, and emotionality. Image Copyright vgstudio 2013. Used under license from Shutterstock.com.

In other words, when the material appears to be excessively focused on sex (i.e., "it appeals to the prurient interest"), depicts sex in an "offensive" way, and lacks social "value," it is subject to censorship, regardless of whether it is technically pornography or erotica. These criteria are intentionally subjective in that they allow each community to set its own standards, such that magazines and advertisements that might be legal in Las Vegas could be deemed illegal in rural Alabama. That said, the extent to which these criteria can be used to ban Internet pornography remains an unsettled area of law because online porn is much harder to regulate and restrict. The only type of online porn that law enforcement at the US federal and state levels routinely concern themselves with stopping is child pornography.

In addition to obscenity laws regulating distribution and access to certain types of porn, the law also governs how porn is produced. For instance, in the US, federal law (the Child Protection and Obscenity Enforcement Act) requires all porn producers to verify the age of any actors or actresses they film or photograph to ensure that no one under age 18 appears in porn. In addition, voters in the state of California approved a law in 2012 requiring porn actors in Los Angeles County (the porn capital of the US) to wear condoms during acts of vaginal and anal sex with the goal of reducing the spread of STIs among performers (Del Barco, 2013). Within the porn industry, this law stoked a large amount of controversy, and many producers have threatened to move their filming elsewhere rather than comply with the law, because it is seen as a violation of personal liberty.

Outside of the US, porn laws vary considerably. In some countries, pornography is outlawed altogether (e.g., Iran, Saudi Arabia, Sudan, China). In other countries, it is legal to possess pornography, but not to distribute it (e.g., India). In yet other countries, the distribution and possession of porn is legal, but certain types of pornography are prohibited (e.g., the United Kingdom has a law against "extreme pornography," which is defined as porn that depicts serious violence, necrophilia, or zoophilia).

The Psychological Profile of a Porn Star

Two of the most common questions students have about pornography are what motivates people to appear in porn, and whether porn stars are psychologically different from the average person. Money is typically the most common incentive (Griffith, Adams, Hart, & Mitchell, 2012), just as it is in prostitution. However, unlike prostitution, very few porn actors report being coerced or forced into this career (although that does occasionally happen, with one high-profile example being Linda Lovelace, the star of the infamous 1970s film *Deep Throat*). Beyond money, other common motives for entering porn include sex and the desire for attention or fame.

With respect to psychological health, public perceptions of porn stars suggest that they represent "damaged goods." Specifically, people believe porn stars come from dysfunctional family backgrounds and are more likely to be drug abusers and addicts (Evans-DeCicco & Cowan, 2001). However, research finds that this stereotype is not entirely true. In one study, researchers compared 177 women who had appeared in porn to a matched sample of women who had never been in any adult films (Griffith, Mitchell et al., 2013). The porn actresses, 67% of whom identified as bisexual, started having sex at a younger age (2 years earlier on average) and reported a greater number of lifetime sexual partners outside of their work than did the mostly heterosexual matched sample; however, there were no differences in reports of past experience with CSA. In addition, both groups of women reported relatively high levels of self-esteem; however, self-esteem was actually significantly *higher* among the porn actresses. The only place where the "damaged goods" hypothesis received support was in history of drug and alcohol abuse. Porn actresses were significantly more

Table 14.2   Comparing Porn Actresses to a Matched Sample of Women who have Never Been in Porn

Question	Porn actresses Mean (standard deviation)	Matched sample Mean (standard deviation)
Age of first sexual intercourse	15.12 (2.80)*	17.28 (2.32)*
Lifetime number of sex partners	74.76 (159.64)*	5.18 (5.56)*
Number of sex partners in the last year	9.64 (18.80)*	1.46 (2.32)*
Degree of concern about contracting an STI	8.30 (2.67)*	5.86 (3.62)*
Sexual satisfaction	14.07 (1.88)*	13.52 (2.04)*
Positive emotions	15.38 (2.94)*	14.45 (2.87)*
Negative emotions	8.51 (3.37)	8.93 (3.06)
Body Image	13.77 (2.02)	13.63 (1.94)

Note: Asterisks indicate statistically significant ($p < 0.05$) mean differences within rows. STI concern was rated on a scale from 1 to 10, with higher numbers indicating more concern. The last four categories were rated on a scale ranging from 4 to 20, with higher values indicating higher levels of that category. The large standard deviation for number of lifetime sexual partners among porn actresses suggests the presence of a few outliers; however, even when considering medians instead of means, porn actresses still had substantially more partners than did the matched sample (20 vs. 3, respectively). Data obtained from Griffith, Mitchell et al. (2013).

likely to report having had problems with drugs and alcohol, but by no means did these problems characterize *every* porn actress. For more information on how porn actresses differed from the matched sample, see Table 14.2.

A parallel study comparing men who work in porn to a matched sample of non-actors does not yet exist, but there is some data on male porn actors that suggests similar conclusions. Consider a study in which researchers asked 105 predominately heterosexual men who had worked in the adult film industry about their sexual history and psychological profile (Griffith, Hayworth, Adams, Mitchell, & Hart, 2013). The actors reported losing their virginity at age 15.5, which is about 1.5 years earlier than men in other studies (Sonfield, 2002). In addition, the actors reported an average number of sex partners off camera (170) that is much higher than the typical male average. For some reference point, consider that the NHSLS found that 67% of men reported having 10 or fewer sexual partners and 83% reported 20 or fewer (Laumann, Gagnon, Michael, & Michaels, 1994). It is also worth noting that the reported rate of child sexual abuse among the actors was 11%, which is only slightly higher than the global meta-analytic rate for men of 7.9% mentioned earlier (Pereda et al., 2009). Finally, porn actors reported levels of self-esteem that were closer to the top of the scale than the midpoint, suggesting that they felt very positively about themselves on average.

The results of these studies suggest that porn stars may be just as psychologically healthy as anyone else in many regards and, overall, they tend to have a very positive self-image. This stands in stark contrast to our above discussion of the psychological consequences of prostitution. There are several possible explanations for this difference. One is that there is a selection effect in the world of professionally produced porn that is not present in prostitution. Think of it this way:

Figure 14.8   Despite the widespread belief that porn stars represent "damaged goods," research suggests that porn actresses feel just as positively about themselves as other women. Image Copyright Juan Camilo Bernal 2013. Used under license from Shutterstock.com.

anyone who wants to become a prostitute can start walking the streets. However, only people with certain body types and personalities can make it into the porn world. In addition, consider the fact that porn stars generally get to have sex with other physically attractive persons, whereas prostitutes often report having sex with undesirable partners who sometimes make them feel disgusted and "dirty" (Smith et al., 2013).

Keep in mind that the above discussion largely pertains to those individuals who work in the big-budget adult film industry. In the modern world, anyone can technically become a porn star by filming their own masturbation or sex videos and uploading them to the Internet. The world of amateur porn has seen explosive growth in recent years and, in fact, some of the most popular porn sites these days are those that feature only "real people" having "real sex." What motivates someone to produce and distribute their own porn through one of these websites? Research on this topic is lacking, but it seems clear that many of the people doing it are not in pursuit of financial gain and, instead, derive some degree of sexual arousal from the knowledge that others are watching them and becoming aroused too. Thus, there may be an exhibitionistic quality (although not in the clinical sense) for many of these persons.

Who Uses Porn?

The adult film industry puts out about 11,000 videos on DVD annually (De Vries, 2009). Although that may sound like a lot, it is a paltry amount when compared to the amount of Internet porn produced. An analysis of just two popular porn sites (YouPorn and xHamster – and, no, I do not

Figure 14.9   Not only do more men report having utilized porn than women, but men also tend to use it on a much more frequent basis. Image Copyright jaymast 2013. Used under license from Shutterstock.com.

know why anyone would name a porn website after a rodent) revealed that 22,000 new videos are uploaded *per month* with an average length of 11 minutes each (Rowinski, 2012). Clearly, there is not going to be a shortage of porn any time soon!

So who is utilizing all of this pornography? Largely men. For instance, in a survey of college students at six different universities across the United States, almost nine in ten men reported using pornography, compared to only one in three women (Carroll et al., 2008). There was also a large sex difference in frequency of use, with 48.4% of men reporting weekly or daily porn use, compared to just 3.2% of women. This study also revealed that students who were more religious were less likely to use porn and that, among men, pornography use was unrelated to their relationship status (i.e., single guys were just as likely to use porn as guys in relationships). In contrast, among women, pornography use was higher among those in relationships than it was for those who were single.

In addition to a major sex difference in who uses porn and how often, there is also an important sex difference in what men and women focus on when they watch pornography. To learn more about what men and women pay attention to when they view porn, check out the Digging Deeper 14.2 box.

Across the sexes, one other factor that predicts both the extent to which people utilize pornography and become aroused by it is personality. Specifically, both men and women who score high on the personality traits of sensation seeking and erotophilia (see chapter 1 for definitions) report consuming more porn and say that they find porn to be more sexually arousing (Paul, 2009).

Digging Deeper 14.2   What Do Men and Women Focus on When They Watch Porn?

When people watch pornography, what is it that first captures their attention? Most of us would probably guess the actors' bodies and/or genitals, especially for male porn viewers. Although this would seem to make intuitive sense, is it really the case?

Rupp and Wallen (2007) assigned heterosexual male and female participants to view a series of sexually explicit images downloaded from the Internet. Each image consisted of a male-female couple engaged in either oral sex or intercourse. Before viewing the photos, each participant was fitted with a head mounted eye-tracking device that recorded the exact section of each image an individual was focused on at any given moment. Thus, not only could researchers measure what first captured people's attention, but they could also identify the areas participants spent the most time looking at.

Results indicated that the first thing to capture men's attention and the thing men spent the most time looking at was female faces. Of course, this was not the *only* thing men focused on – they also spent a good deal of time looking at genitals. However, it is interesting to note (and contrary to popular belief) that faces stood out so much to men. Why? Perhaps men want to know how excited and "into it" the woman really is.

What about female participants? What they focused on depended upon whether they were taking "the pill" or not. For *naturally cycling* women (i.e., women who were *not* taking hormonal contraceptives), the thing that first caught their eye and what they looked at most were genitals, followed by the female body. In contrast to men, naturally cycling women spent relatively little time looking at anyone's faces. For women who were taking oral contraceptives, they spent comparatively less time looking at the sexual features of the images. The first thing these women noticed and spent the most time viewing were contextual features of the situation (e.g., the actors' clothing and the background imagery). These women also spent a fair amount of time looking at female bodies and faces, but they spent less time looking at genitals than did naturally cycling women.

You are probably wondering two things about the female results: Why did the focus of women's attention depend upon their method of birth control, and why were heterosexual women looking at the female body more than the male body? We cannot answer either question definitively, but the researchers reason that this effect is driven by hormones. Birth control pills keep women's hormone levels relatively constant, whereas naturally cycling women experience natural fluctuations. This suggests that the amount of hormones in the body may affect how women perceive sexual stimuli. As for why heterosexual women seemed so interested in other women, it may be another sign that women have more erotic plasticity than men (see chapter 6). Of course, it may also be that women are more likely than men to compare themselves to the bodies they see on screen.

Based upon these findings, the logical conclusion seems to be that not everyone sees the same thing when they are looking at porn.

Note: Reprinted with permission from *The Psychology of Human Sexuality* blog (www.lehmiller.com).

Effects of Pornography Exposure

To round out our discussion of pornography, let us examine the potential effects of exposure to sexually explicit materials. Politicians frequently make claims about the inherent dangers of porn, such as 2012 US Republican Presidential contender Rick Santorum, whose campaign website stated:

> America is suffering a pandemic of harm from pornography. A wealth of research is now available demonstrating that pornography causes profound brain changes in both children and adults, resulting in widespread negative consequences… Pornography is toxic to marriages and relationships. It contributes to misogyny and violence against women. (Santorum, 2012)

Those are some pretty strong claims. Are they true? Let us examine each claim one by one and see what the science says. First, with regard to porn *causing* "profound brain changes," there is indeed some research suggesting that among persons who consume extremely large amount of porn, some signs of brain atrophy (i.e., wasting) are present (Hilton & Watts, 2011). However, this is correlational research, which means that it is impossible to make claims about causality. In addition, most of the heavy porn users in this research had histories of other problematic behaviors (e.g., substance abuse). As a result, it is just as plausible to argue that the brain changes were a product of something other than porn.

Second, is porn "toxic to marriages and relationships?" Research indicates that the surge in *Playboy* magazine readership that occurred in the 1960s and 1970s was correlated with an increase in the US divorce rate (Daines & Shumway, 2011). But did *Playboy* cause those divorces? Again, we cannot say. Perhaps this association is a product of the fact that the 60s and 70s represented the "sexual revolution" in America, and the increase in porn use and divorces both stemmed from that third variable. Likewise, there is a small, but statistically significant correlation between pornography consumption and extramarital sex (Wright, 2013); again, however, it is unclear whether porn causes cheating, or if this association is a function of both porn use and cheating being confounded with erotophilia, sensation seeking, or some other personality characteristic. Perhaps more compelling evidence that porn may affect relationships comes from a classic experiment in which heterosexual men were randomly assigned to view images of *Playboy* centerfolds or abstract art prior to reporting how they felt about their wives (Kenrick, Gutierres, & Goldberg, 1989). Results indicated that the men who saw sexy naked women reported less attraction to and less love for their spouses compared to the guys who viewed art instead (you can think of this as a *contrast effect*, a topic we discussed in chapter 7). However, because these effects were assessed immediately after exposure to the images, we cannot say whether we are talking about a temporary decrease in love and attraction, or whether this is a cumulative, long-term effect. There is some research indicating that when one partner in a relationship uses porn "excessively" such that there is a compulsive aspect to it, this behavior can indeed contribute to sexual and other problems within the relationship (Bridges, Bergner, & Hesson-McInnis, 2003). This tells us that porn can be "toxic" to some relationships, but this is likely only true in a relatively small number of cases in which one partner's porn use gets completely out of control or when partners have disagreements about what constitutes an appropriate amount and type of porn use.

Finally, does porn lead to "violence against women?" A meta-analysis of the research in this area concluded that there is no evidence of pornography consumption causing individuals to commit rape or sexual assault (Ferguson & Hartley, 2009). In fact, the reverse association has been documented. The last couple of decades have seen a dramatic increase in the amount of porn being consumed, but at the same time, the frequency of sexual assaults has *decreased* (see Table 14.1). That said, there is some research indicating that porn consumption is positively correlated with acceptance of violence against women (Hald, Malamuth, & Yuen, 2010); however, this association appears to be strongest for violent pornography and for men who have aggressive tendencies to begin with. Thus, for certain types of porn and for certain types of men, there may be reason for concern, but it would be wise to avoid generalizing this concern to *all* porn and *all* viewers.

In short, most of the political claims about the harm caused by pornography are, at best, misleading and, at worst, false. That said, there is at least one area in which porn can undeniably have a negative effect, and that is through observational learning. Through porn, people may walk away with inappropriate conclusions about what is "normal" in terms of the human body and sexual behavior. To learn about a few such misconceptions spread by pornography, see the Digging Deeper 14.3 box.

Digging Deeper 14.3   Five Misconceptions About Sex and the Human Body Spread By Porn

Although research has found that many claims about the inherent dangers of porn are without merit, this should not be taken to mean that watching porn is necessarily harmless. Pornography can give people false impressions about how their bodies are "supposed" to look and how sex is "supposed" to happen. Below are five of the biggest misconceptions about human sexuality spread by pornography. These misconceptions are most prevalent in professionally produced porn, and perhaps somewhat less so in the growing amateur porn world.

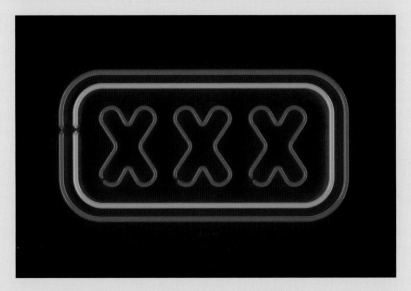

Figure 14.10   Frequent pornography viewing may result in distorted views about what is normal when it comes to sex and the appearance of the human body. ©Carsten Reisinger/123RF.COM.

Myth #1: All men have massive penises.   The guys who appear in porn videos (regardless of whether they are gay or straight) tend to have extra large penises, frequently in the range of 8 inches (20.3 cm) or more. In reality, the average erect penis is 5.3 inches (13.5 cm), and the vast majority of men fall in the range of 4.6 and 6.0 inches (11.7 and 15.2 cm, respectively; Lever, Frederick, & Peplau, 2006). Thus, the genitals you see in porn are far from average and it would be wise to avoid comparing yourself or your partners to them.

Myth #2: All women go bare "down there".   Porn videos give viewers the impression that all women are opting for the "full Brazilian" or "Hollywood wax" these days (i.e., complete removal of all hair in the genital region, including the buttocks). However, most women tend to keep at least some of their pubic hair and waxing is relatively rare (less than 10% of women do it, probably because it is costly and very painful; Herbenick, Schick, Reece, Sanders, & Fortenberry, 2010). In the real world, there is a diverse range of pubic hair styles and women's reasons for removal vary considerably.

Myth #3: Women can reach orgasm in any position.   Pornography gives the impression that women *always* reach orgasm and that they can do it no matter how they have sex. This is far from the case in reality, though. In fact, many women are unable to achieve orgasm through vaginal penetration alone and require other forms of stimulation (e.g., clitoral) in order to climax (Fugl-Meyer, Oberg, Lundberg, & Lewin, 2006). There is wide variability across women in terms of what "works" when it comes to orgasm, so do not conclude that there is something wrong with you if you cannot reach orgasm in the same way porn actresses do.

Myth #4: Everyone loves a dirty talker.   In between all of their moaning and groaning, porn performers usually interject dirty (and sometimes downright raunchy) dialogue. Preferences for dirty talk are highly variable outside of the porn world, however. Some people do like a little nasty language during sex, but there are others who find any talking at all to be a big turnoff. It is probably best to confirm your partner's preferences before you start narrating sex and calling your partner by the names you may have heard in porn.

Myth #5: Big penises bring women more pleasure.   A common theme in heterosexual porn videos is that the woman is "surprised" and delighted at the enormous size of her male companion's member ("It's just so… big!"). However, most women say that a larger penis does not increase their ability to reach orgasm (Costa, Miller, & Brody, 2012). There are certainly some women for whom a bigger member is preferred and may bring them more erotic pleasure, but this does not appear to be the case for most women.

I realize that there are a number of other misconceptions about sex spread by porn that I did not cover here (e.g., that sex is *only* about prolonged genital contact, that "good" sex is a matter of moving as fast and hard as you can), but those are stories for another day.

Note: Reprinted with permission from *The Psychology of Human Sexuality* blog (www.lehmiller.com).

Key Terms

sexual assault

statutory rape

Rohypnol

post-traumatic stress
    disorder (PTSD)

child sexual abuse (CSA)

incest

sexual harassment

quid pro quo

hostile environment

prostitute

sex trafficking

pornography

erotica

Discussion Questions: What is Your Perspective on Sex?

- Should any legal restrictions exist for sexual behaviors among consenting adults? Is it the government's job to regulate sexual behaviors that are potentially dangerous and/or unhealthy?
- In your own view, is pornography use acceptable within the context of a romantic relationship? Would you be comfortable with your partner looking at porn?
- Are there any kinds of pornography (other than child porn) that you think should be legally restricted? Why or why not?

References

Baumeister, R.F., & Vohs, K.D. (2004). Sexual economics: Sex as female resource for social exchange in heterosexual interactions. *Personality and Social Psychology Review, 8*, 339–363. DOI:10.1207/s15327957pspr0804_2.

Beech, A.R., Ward, T., & Fisher, D. (2006). The identification of sexual and violent motivations in men who assault women: Implication for treatment. *Journal of Interpersonal Violence, 21*, 1635–1653. DOI:10.1177/0886260506294242.

Bridges, A.J., Bergner, R.M., & Hesson-McInnis, M. (2003). Romantic partners' use of pornography: Its significance for women. *Journal of Sex & Marital Therapy, 29*, 1–14. DOI:10.1080/713847097.

Bronner, E. (2012). *A candidate's stumble on a distressing crime.* Retrieved from http://www.nytimes.com/2012/08/24/us/definition-of-rape-is-shifting-rapidly.html?_r=0 (accessed September 7, 2013).

Carroll, J.S., Padilla-Walker, L.M., Nelson, L.J., Olson, C.D., Barry, C., & Madsen, S.D. (2008). Generation XXX: Pornography acceptance and use among emerging adults. *Journal of Adolescent Research, 23*, 6–30. DOI:10.1177/0743558407306348.

Cloitre, M., Scarvalone, P., & Difede, J. (1997). Posttraumatic stress disorder, self- and interpersonal dysfunction among sexually retraumatized women. *Journal of Traumatic Stress, 10*, 437–452.

Costa, R., Miller, G.F., & Brody, S. (2012). Women who prefer longer penises are more likely to have vaginal orgasms (but not clitoral orgasms): Implications for an evolutionary theory of vaginal orgasm. *Journal of Sexual Medicine, 9)*, 3079–3088. DOI:10.1111/j.1743-6109.2012.02917.x.

Cowan, G. (2000). Beliefs about the causes of four types of rape. *Sex Roles, 42*, 807–823. DOI:10.1023/A:1007042215614.

Daines, R.M., & Shumway, T. (2011). *Pornography and divorce.* Retrieved from http://marriottschool.net/emp/boyer/financeseminar/s11_12/Tyler%20Shumway%20F11.pdf (accessed September 7, 2013).

Dalla, R.L. (2000). Exposing the "pretty woman" myth: A qualitative examination of the lives of female streetwalking prostitutes. *Journal of Sex Research, 37*, 344–353. DOI:10.1080/00224490009552057.

De Vries, L. (2009). *Follow the porn*. Retrieved from http://www.cbsnews.com/2100-500156_162-1548040. html (accessed September 7, 2013).

Del Barco, M. (2013). *Porn industry turned off by L.A. mandate of condoms on set*. Retrieved from http://www. npr.org/2013/01/15/169423027/porn-industry-turned-off-by-l-a-mandate-for-condoms-on-set (accessed September 7, 2013).

Denyer, S. (2013). *India toughens laws on sexual assault following gang rape*. Retrieved from http://www.twincities. com/national/ci_22512764/india-toughens-laws-sexual-assault-following-gang-rape (accessed September 7, 2013).

EEOC (2012). *Sexual harassment charges*. Retrieved from http://www.eeoc.gov/eeoc/statistics/enforcement/ sexual_harassment.cfm (accessed September 7, 2013).

Estes, R.J., & Weiner, N.A. (2001). The commercial sexual exploitation of children in the U.S., Canada, and Mexico. Retrieved from http://www.sp2.upenn.edu/restes/CSEC_Files/Exec_Sum_020220.pdf (accessed September 7, 2013).

Evans-DeCicco, J.A., & Cowan, G. (2001). Attitudes toward pornography and the characteristics attributed to pornography actors. *Sex Roles, 44*, 351–361. DOI:10.1023/A:1010985817751.

Farley, M. (2004). "Bad for the body, bad for the heart": Prostitution harms women even if legalized or decriminalized. *Violence Against Women, 10*, 1087–1125.

Ferguson, C. J., & Hartley, R. D. (2009). The pleasure is momentary…the expense damnable? The influence of pornography on rape and sexual assault. *Aggression and Violent Behavior, 14*, 323–329. DOI:10.1016/ j.avb.2009.04.008.

Fugl-Meyer, K., Oberg, K., Lundberg, P., & Lewin, B. (2006). On orgasm, sexual techniques, and erotic perceptions in 18- to 74-year-old Swedish women. *Journal of Sexual Medicine, 3*, 56–68. DOI:10.1111/ j.1743-6109.2005.00170.x.

Griffith, J.D., Adams, L.T., Hart, C.L., & Mitchell, S. (2012).Why become a pornography actress? *International Journal of Sexual Health, 24*, 165–180. DOI:10.1080/19317611.2012.666514.

Griffith, J.D., Hayworth, M., Adams, L.T., Mitchell, S., & Hart, C.L. (2013).Characteristics of pornography film actors: Self-report versus perceptions of college students. *Archives of Sexual Behavior, 42*, 637–47. DOI:10.1007/s10508-012-0033-5.

Griffith, J.D., Mitchell, S., Hart, C.L., Adams, L.T., & Gu, L.L. (2013). Pornography actresses: An assessment of the damaged goods hypothesis. *Journal of Sex Research, 50*, 621–32. DOI:10.1080/002244 99.2012.719168.

Hald, G.M., Malamuth, N.M., & Yuen, C. (2010). Pornography and attitudes supporting violence against women: Revisiting the relationship in nonexperimental studies. *Aggressive Behavior, 36*, 14–20. DOI:10.1002/ab.20328.

Hanson, R.K., & Bussiere, M.T. (1998). Predicting relapse: A meta-analysis of sexual offender recidivism studies. *Journal of Consulting and Clinical Psychology, 66*, 348–362. DOI:10.1037/0022-006X.66.2.348.

Herbenick, D., Schick, V., Reece, M., Sanders, S., & Fortenberry, J.D. (2010). Pubic hair removal among women in the United States: Prevalence, methods, and characteristics. *Journal of Sexual Medicine, 7*, 3322–3330. DOI:10.1111/j.1743-6109.2010.01935.x.

Hilton Jr., D.L., & Watts, C. (2011). Pornography addiction: A neuroscience perspective. *Surgical Neurology International, 2*, 19. DOI:10.4103/2152-7806.76977.

Ilies, R., Hauserman, N., Schwochau, S., & Stibal, J. (2003). Reported incidence rates of work-related sexual harassment in the United States: Using meta-analysis to explain reported rate disparities. *Personnel Psychology, 56*, 607–631. DOI:10.1111/j.1744-6570.2003.tb00752.x.

Jarvis, T.J., & Copeland, J. (1997). Child sexual abuse as a predictor of psychiatric co-morbidity and its implications for drug and alcohol treatment. *Drug and Alcohol Dependence, 49*, 61–69. DOI:10.1016/ S0376-8716(97)00139-7.

Kenrick, D.T., Gutierres, S.E., & Goldberg, L.L. (1989). Influence of popular erotica on judgments of strangers and mates. *Journal of Experimental Social Psychology, 25*, 159–167. DOI:10.1016/0022-1031(89)90010-3.

Kramer, L.A. (2004). Emotional experiences of performing prostitution. *Journal of Trauma Practice, 2*, 186–197. DOI:10.1300/J189v02n03_10.

Laumann, E.O., Gagnon, J., Michael, R., & Michaels, S. (1994). *The social organization of sexuality: Sexual practices in the United States*. Chicago: University of Chicago Press.

Lever, J., Frederick, D.A., & Peplau, L.A. (2006). Does size matter? Men's and women's views on penis size across the lifespan. *Psychology of Men and Masculinity, 7*, 129–143. DOI:10.1037/1524-9220.7.3.129.

Mann, R.E., & Hollin, C.R. (2007). Sexual offenders' explanations for their offending. *Journal of Sexual Aggression, 13*, 3–9. DOI:0.1080/13552600701365621.

Monto, M.A. (2001). Prostitution and fellatio. *Journal of Sex Research, 38*, 140–145. DOI:10.1080/00224490109552081.

Murray, J.B. (2000). Psychological profile of pedophiles and child molesters. *Journal of Psychology: Interdisciplinary and Applied, 134*, 211–224. DOI:10.1080/00223980009600863.

Paul, B. (2009). Predicting Internet pornography use and arousal: The role of individual difference variables. *Journal of Sex Research, 46*, 344–357. DOI:10.1080/00224490902754152.

Pereda, N., Guilera, G., Forns, M., & Gómez-Benito, J. (2009). The prevalence of child sexual abuse in community and student samples: A meta-analysis. *Clinical Psychology Review, 29*, 328–338. DOI:10.1016/j.cpr.2009.02.007.

Rederstorff, J.C., Buchanan, N.T., & Settles, I.H. (2007). The moderating roles of race and gender-role attitudes in the relationship between sexual harassment and psychological well-being. *Psychology of Women Quarterly, 31*, 50–61. DOI:10.1111/j.1471-6402.2007.00330.x.

Roberts, A.L., Glymour, M.M., & Koenen, K.C. (2013). Does maltreatment in childhood affect sexual orientation in adulthood? *Archives of Sexual Behavior, 42*, 161–171. DOI:10.1007/s10508-012-0021-9.

Rowinski, D. (2012). *1.2 million years of porn watched since 2006, on just 2 tube sites*. Retrieved from http://readwrite.com/2012/12/18/12-million-years-of-porn-watched-since-2006-on-just-2-tube-sites (accessed September 7, 2013).

Rupp, H.A., & Wallen, K. (2007). Sex differences in viewing sexual stimuli: An eye-tracking study in men and women. *Hormones and Behavior, 51*, 524–533. DOI:10.1016/j.yhbeh.2007.01.008.

Santorum, R. (2012). *Enforcing laws against illegal pornography*. Retrieved from http://www.icyte.com/system/snapshots/fs1/c/b/c/4/cbc4e9acde4db6410e4b6814f69ad30e21feb1a1/index.html (accessed September 7, 2013).

Schauer, E. J., & Wheaton, E. M. (2006). Sex trafficking into the United States: A literature review. *Criminal Justice Review, 31*, 146–169. DOI:10.1177/0734016806290136.

Schwartz, R.H., Milteer, R., & LeBeau, M.A. (2000). Drug-facilitated sexual assault ('date rape'). *Southern Medical Journal, 93*, 558.

Shannon, K., & Csete, J. (2010). Violence, condom negotiation, and HIV/STI risk among sex workers. *JAMA: the journal of the American Medical Association, 304*, 573–574. DOI:10.1001/jama.2010.1090.

Smith, M.D., Grov, C., Seal, D.W., & McCall, P. (2013). A social-cognitive analysis of how young men become involved in male escorting. *Journal of Sex Research, 50*, 1–10. DOI:10.1080/00224499.2012.681402.

Sonfield, A. (2002). Looking at men's sexual and reproductive health needs. *The Guttmacher Report on Public Policy, 5*(2). Retrieved from http://www.guttmacher.org/pubs/tgr/05/2/gr050207.html (accessed September 7, 2013).

Terpstra, D.E., & Baker, D.D. (1992). Outcomes of federal court decisions on sexual harassment. *The Academy of Management Journal, 35*, 181–190. DOI:10.2307/256505.

Truman, J.L., & Planty, M. (2012). Criminal victimization, 2011. *Bureau of Justice Statistics*, NCJ239437.

Vanwesenbeeck, I. (2013). Prostitution push and pull: Male and female perspectives. *Journal of Sex Research, 50*, 11–16. DOI:10.1080/00224499.2012.696285.

Walker-Rodriguez, A., & Hill, R. (2011). Human sex trafficking. *FBI Law Enforcement Bulletin*. Retrieved from http://www.fbi.gov/stats-services/publications/law-enforcement-bulletin/march_2011/human_sex_trafficking (accessed September 7, 2013).

Willness, C.R., Steel, P., & Lee, K. (2007). A meta-analysis of the antecedents and consequences of workplace sexual harassment. *Personnel Psychology, 60*, 127–162. DOI:10.1111/j.1744-6570.2007.00067.x.

Work Harassment (2012). *Sexual harassment in the workplace*. Retrieved from http://www.workharassment.net/index.php/sexual-harassment-in-the-workplace.html (accessed September 7, 2013).

Wright, P.J. (2013). U.S. males and pornography, 1973–2010: Consumption, predictors, correlates. *Journal of Sex Research, 50*, 60–71. DOI:10.1080/00224499.2011.628132.

Zimmerman, C., Hossain, M., Yun, K., Roche, B., Morison, L., & Watts, C. (2006). *Stolen smiles: A summary report on the physical and psychological health consequences of women and adolescents trafficked in Europe*. London: London School of Hygiene & Tropical Medicine.

Epilogue

Throughout this book, I hope you have come to learn about and appreciate the inherent diversity and complexity that exists in human sexual behavior. I did my best to present you with a wide range of sexual attitudes, behaviors, and theories with the hope that readers would come to the realization that this world contains more than just heterosexual men and women who engage in penile–vaginal intercourse. However, it is important to recognize that this book only scratches the surface when it comes to sexual diversity. There are so many cultural and societal variations that I could have easily filled a thousand more pages.

I also hope that you have come to see sex and sexuality as products of biological, psychological, and social factors. As a psychology textbook, I have tried to make it clear that your brain really is your largest sex organ and that your memories, thoughts, and emotions are paramount to healthy sexual functioning. At the same time, however, I hope you now see that in order to truly understand where our sexuality and sexual behaviors come from, you need to look at more than just psychological factors.

Moreover, I hope that you have come to a better understanding of your own body and what it means to be sexually "normal." I hope you have also become a more informed consumer of sex research and advertisements and that you will no longer fall prey to misleading media headlines and sexual gimmicks advertised in magazines, the Internet, and on late-night television.

Above all else, I hope you see this book at just the beginning of your sex education and not the end. Human sexuality is a huge field and it is impossible to cover everything in the span of a single course or book. So go out and keep learning about sex. I guarantee that you will be fascinated, and that you will have a lot of fun doing it!

The Psychology of Human Sexuality, First Edition. Justin J. Lehmiller.
© 2014 John Wiley & Sons, Ltd. Published 2014 by John Wiley & Sons, Ltd.

Glossary

5-alpha-reductase deficiency (5αRD): A sex variation that occurs when a biological male fetus is unable to convert testosterone into dihydrotestosterone (DHT) due to insufficient levels of the 5-alpha reductase enzyme

abortion: A medical procedure capable of ending a pregnancy.

abstinence: The strict definition is zero genital contact, but personal definitions vary widely.

abstinence-only approach: A form of sex education that focuses on teaching kids to abstain from sex. Information on obtaining and using contraception and condoms is not provided.

abstinence-plus: A form of sex education that promotes abstinence, but provides accurate information on obtaining and using contraception and condoms.

acquired immune deficiency syndrome (AIDS): The diagnosis given to someone with HIV whose T4 cell count has dropped to a dangerously low level and is seriously immunocompromised.

amenorrhea: The absence of menstruation.

anaphrodisiacs: Substances that decrease sexual desire and behavior.

androgen insensitivity syndrome (AIS): A sex variation that occurs when a biological male fetus is insensitive to the production of its own androgens.

anilingus: Oral stimulation of the anus. Also known as "rimming."

aphrodisiacs: Substances that increase sexual desire and behavior.

areola: The round, darkened area that surrounds the nipple.

arranged marriage: When two sets of parents join their children for pragmatic reasons.

asexuality: Having no interest in partnered sexual activity.

assortative mating: The tendency for people to match with partners who are similar to them on a variety of dimensions.

attachment style: A unique pattern of approaching and developing relationships with others.

aversive conditioning: A therapy that involves psychologically pairing a paraphilic desire with something unpleasant or punishing.

Bartholin's glands: Glands near the vaginal opening that secrete a drop or two of fluid prior to orgasm. Thought to create a genital scent.

The Psychology of Human Sexuality, First Edition. Justin J. Lehmiller.
© 2014 John Wiley & Sons, Ltd. Published 2014 by John Wiley & Sons, Ltd.

behavioral therapy: Sex therapy based upon the principle that we can learn new associations to replace those that are maladaptive.

The Big Five: A set of five factors that any personality can supposedly be boiled down to: openness to experience, conscientiousness, extraversion, agreeableness, and neuroticism.

biopsychosocial perspective: The view that health and behavior stem from the interaction of biological, psychological, and social factors.

biphobia: Prejudice specific to bisexuals.

bogus pipeline technique: A social psychological technique in which participants are hooked up to a lie-detector machine and falsely convinced that it can detect whether they are telling the truth. Commonly used as a means of ensuring greater honesty in responding.

case report: The study of one participant or a small group of participants in great depth and detail.

castration: Surgical removal of the testes.

cavernous bodies: Two cylinders of erectile tissue that run along the upper portion of the penis.

celibacy: When individuals with sexual desire intentionally refrain from acting on it.

cerebral cortex: The outer layer of the brain that controls our thoughts, memories, imagination, and use of language.

cervical barriers: Devices that obstruct sperm from entering the cervix

cervix: The lower end of the uterus.

chemical castration: The administration of anti-androgen drugs so as to block the production of testosterone.

child sexual abuse (CSA): Any instance in which a child is sexually victimized by an adult.

chlamydia: The most prevalent bacterial STI. Often produces minimal symptoms, but can lead to infertility if left untreated.

chromosomal sex: The specific combination of sex chromosomes contained within one's genes.

circumcision: Surgical removal of the penile foreskin.

classical conditioning: A form of learning in which repeated pairings of stimuli result in a neutral stimulus becoming a cue for a specific behavior.

clitoris: A female genital structure that contains erectile tissue and is composed of a glans, shaft, and crura. Its only known function is to provide sexual pleasure.

cognitive-behavioral sex therapy (CBST): An extension of behavioral therapy in which the therapist also considers the thoughts and feelings underlying the patient's behaviors.

coital alignment technique (CAT): A modified missionary (i.e., man-on-top) position in which the base of the penis and the clitoris stay in constant contact through a coordinated rocking or grinding motion.

coitus: Another term for penile-vaginal intercourse.

combined hormone methods: Joint administration of estrogen and progestin to prevent pregnancy.

commitment: The cognitive component of Sternberg's Triangular Theory of Love.

companionate love: A strong emotional attachment and commitment to another person based on full knowledge and appreciation of another person's character.

comparison level: The standard by which we evaluate our relationship outcomes.

comprehensive sex education: A form of sex education that does not promote abstinence and focuses instead on providing information and developing responsible decision-making skills.

compulsive sexual behavior: Cases where people have "excessive" sexual desire and engage in very high amounts of sexual behavior.

confidentiality: An ethical requirement that involves protecting the privacy of research participants.

congenital adrenal hyperplasia (CAH): A sex variation that occurs when a person's adrenal glands produce excessive amounts of androgens starting before birth.

consensual nonmonogamy: An explicit agreement with one's partner that the pursuit of other sexual and/or romantic relationships is acceptable.

consummate love: The ideal form of love in which passion, intimacy, and commitment are present simultaneously.

contrast effect: The idea that perceptions of average can be thrown off by the presence of a few outliers.

convenience samples: The persons who are most readily accessible for research purposes.

correlation: The degree to which two variables are statistically associated.

covert sensitization: A therapy in which paraphilic desires are paired with unpleasant thoughts. A variant of aversive conditioning.

Cowper's glands: During sexual arousal, these glands release a small amount of pre-ejaculate that alkalinizes the urethra.

cremaster muscle: A muscle that helps regulate testicular temperature by moving the testes closer or further from the body.

cross-dressing: The act of wearing clothing that is typically associated with the other sex.

cunnilingus: Oral stimulation of the vulva.

debriefing: The act of telling participants the true purpose of the research and informing them of any deception that took place after the study is over.

deception: Intentionally withholding information or misleading participants in a research study.

delayed ejaculation: The technical term for orgasmic disorder in men, involving a persistent pattern of delayed or absent ejaculation during sexual activity.

dental dams: Latex barriers that can be placed over the vulva for cunnilingus or over the anus for anilingus.

dhat: Semen loss anxiety found among men in certain Eastern cultures.

direct observation: A method of inquiry in which researchers watch subjects and record what they observe

dopamine: A neurotransmitter linked to increases in sexual arousal and behavior.

dry sex: A form of intercourse accompanied by removal of a woman's natural vaginal lubrication

dual control model: The theory that humans have excitatory and inhibitory brain systems that control sexual arousal and behavior.

dysmenorrhea: Painful menstruation caused by overproduction of prostaglandins or a pre-existing medical condition.

dyspareunia: Any type of pelvic or genital pain that occurs during sexual arousal or activity.

ego: The portion of the personality that keeps the id in check. Operates under the reality principle, trying to satisfy the id and avoid self-destruction.

emergency contraception: A hormone pill that is meant to prevent pregnancy after an instance of unprotected intercourse.

endometriosis: A condition in which a woman has endometrial cells outside of her uterus.

epididymis: A structure that sits behind each testicle in which sperm maturation occurs.

erectile disorder (ED): A persistent inability to develop or maintain an erection sufficient for sexual performance.

erotic plasticity: The degree to which a person's sex drive and sexual behavior is "flexible" and responsive to cultural and situational pressures.

erotica: Depictions of sex that evoke themes of mutual attraction that usually incorporate some emotional component in addition to the sex act itself.

erotophilia: A tendency to exhibit strong, positive emotions and attitudes toward sex.

erotophobia: A tendency to exhibit strong, negative emotions and attitudes toward sex.

evolutionary psychology: The study of psychological traits as evolved adaptations.

exchange theories: The idea that how we feel about a given relationship depends upon the type of outcomes we receive in return for what we have put into the relationship.

excitement: The start of sexual arousal and the first phase of the Masters and Johnson sexual response cycle.

exhibitionism: A paraphilia in which individuals expose their genitals (or fantasize about exposing their genitals) to unsuspecting strangers.

exotic becomes erotic: Bem's theory that feelings of difference from our peers evokes physiological arousal that later transforms into sexual arousal.

expectancy effects: The idea that our beliefs about how something will affect us can ultimately shape our experiences.

experiment: A research method in which one variable is manipulated in order to see what effect this has on a measurable outcome.

fallopian tube: A structure that carries eggs from the ovaries to the uterus.

fellatio: Oral stimulation of the penis.

female condoms: A polyurethane pouch that lines the interior of the vagina during sexual activity.

female copulatory vocalizations: The sounds that women make during sex.

female genital cutting: A procedure in which a woman's external genital structures are permanently damaged or removed without medical necessity.

female sexual interest/arousal disorder (SIAD): Among women, absent or reduced sexual fantasies and desire for sex, and/or reduced excitement and genital sensations during sexual activity.

fertility awareness: A class of birth control methods that attempt to inform women of when they are most likely to be fertile so that they can temporarily abstain from vaginal intercourse or use barriers.

fetishism: A paraphilia in which a person experiences intense sexual arousal in response to either a nonhuman object or a specific body part or secretion.

foreskin: The loose and retractable layer of skin that serves as a sheath for the head of the penis

friends with benefits: Persons who have a non-romantic, sexual relationship in addition to a friendship.

gay affirmative therapy: A therapeutic approach that involves getting patients to accept their sexuality, not to change their identity, pattern of attraction, or behavior.

gender: A psychosocial term that refers to the psychological, cultural, and social characteristics that we think of as belonging to men and women.

gender dysphoria: Unhappiness and discomfort that stems from a mismatch between one's physical sex and one's psychological gender identity.

gender identity: An individual's own psychological perception of being male or female.

gender roles: A set of cultural norms or rules that dictate how people of a specific sex "should" behave.

gender stereotypes: Overgeneralized beliefs about the qualities and characteristics of men and women.

genito-pelvic pain/penetration disorder (GPD): A condition in which a woman experiences pain in anticipation of or during vaginal intercourse, or when vaginal penetration is difficult.

gonadal sex: The specific gonads (i.e., ovaries vs. testes) present within one's body.

gonorrhea: A bacterial STI formerly known as "the clap." Like chlamydia, it often produces minimal symptoms and can lead to infertility if left untreated.

Grafenberg spot: A highly sensitive portion of the vagina. Scientists are debating whether it is a distinct anatomic site, or the internal portion of the clitoris.

herpes: A highly contagious viral STI characterized by painful blisters around the genitals, anus, or mouth.

heterosexism: The assumption that everyone is heterosexual and that attraction to the other sex is normative.

homophobia: Prejudice specific to gays and lesbians.

hookups: One-time sexual encounters among persons who do not know each other on a deep level.

hormonal sex: The major class of hormones released by one's gonads (i.e., androgens or estrogens).

hostile environment: A form of sexual harassment that occurs when other people's words or actions of a sexual nature have the effect of creating a hostile or abusive environment around the victim.

human immunodeficiency virus (HIV): A retrovirus that targets and destroys T4 helper cells, thereby weakening the immune system.

human papilloma virus (HPV): The most common viral STI. Spread by skin-to-skin contact and linked to genital warts, as well as cancers of the cervix, throat, and anus.

hymen: A thin piece of tissue that covers the introitus.

hypogonadism: A physical condition in which testosterone production is diminished

hypothalamus: A portion of the limbic system that plays an important role in regulating sexual behavior.

hysteria: A debunked medical diagnosis for a condition in which a woman's uterus was thought to be "wandering" throughout her body.

id: The most basic part of personality. Houses the libido and operates under the pleasure principle.

incest: Child sexual abuse perpetrated by someone related to the child. This term is often used more generally to describe any sexual activity among blood relatives, regardless of whether it is consensual.

incidence: The rate at which new cases of a problem or disease occur.

indirect partners: Sexual partners you are indirectly exposed to through sexual contact with others.

informed consent: The act of informing participants at the outset of a study of any potential risks and rewards, thereby enabling them to make a truly informed decision.

intersexed: A person who possesses both male and female biological traits.

interstitial cells: Cells within the testes that produce sex hormones.

intimacy: The emotional component of Sternberg's Triangular Theory of Love.

introitus: The vaginal opening.

investments: Everything we have put into our relationship over time that would be lost or decreased in value were the relationship to end.

Kinsey Scale: A sexual orientation continuum that ranges from 0 (exclusive heterosexual attraction and behavior) to 6 (exclusive homosexual attraction and behavior).

Klinefelter's syndrome: A sex variation that occurs when a Y-carrying sperm fertilizes an egg that possesses two X chromosomes.

koro: Fear that the penis is retracting inside the body. Typically found among men in southeast Asia.

labia majora: The outer lips. Encases the genital structures beneath the mons.

labia minora: The inner lips. Protects the vaginal and urethral openings.

libido: The Freudian term for sex drive.

limbic system: A set of structures deep within the brain that includes the hypothalamus, amygdala, and hippocampus. Sometimes referred to as the brain's "pleasure center."

lordosis: A sexual posture that occurs naturally in female rats in which the back curves upward to assist in copulation.

love: A special set of cognitions, emotions, and behaviors observed in an intimate relationship.

male condoms: A thin latex or polyurethane sheath that covers an erect penis during sexual activity.

male hypoactive sexual desire disorder (HSDD): Among men, absent or reduced sexual fantasies and desire for sex.

masochists: Persons who derive sexual gratification from receiving physical or psychological pain.

masturbation: Solo forms of self-stimulation focusing on the genitals.

masturbatory satiation: A therapy in which the client is instructed to masturbate to orgasm while thinking of a socially appropriate stimulus. After orgasm, the client is instructed to start thinking about the paraphilic desire. A variant of aversive conditioning.

mean: The average value of all of the scores in a dataset.

median: The middle score (i.e., 50th percentile) in a dataset.

menstruation: The shedding of the endometrial lining of the uterus when pregnancy has not occurred.

mere exposure effect: The more familiar we become with a given stimulus, the more we tend to like it.

metoidioplasty: A type of sex reassignment surgery in which the clitoris is turned into an erectile phallus.

minimal risk: A classification for research studies that are unlikely to cause more harm to someone than they might ordinarily experience in their everyday life.

misattribution of physiological arousal: When the true source of arousal is ambiguous, we may incorrectly label the cause.

monosexism: The belief that exclusive attraction to one sex is the norm.

mons veneris: A pad of fatty tissue that cushions the internal genital structures and is typically covered in hair.

mortality salience: Human beings' conscious or unconscious recognition that we will eventually die.

myotonia: Voluntary and involuntary tensing and contracting of muscles.

necrophilia: A very rare sexual variation that involves an erotic attraction to dead bodies.

need to belong: A near universal human desire to develop and maintain social ties.

negging: Pointing out something negative about another person as a means of catching that person's attention.

nipple: The structure through which maternal milk is released at the center of the areola.

nonconsensual nonmonogamy: Cases in which a romantic partner violates a spoken or unspoken agreement to be sexually exclusive.

nonresponse: The idea that not everyone contacted will want to participate in a given research study.

oophorectomy: Surgical removal of the ovaries.

open relationships: Partners have a relational "home base," but also the ability to pursue other intimate relationships simultaneously.

operant conditioning: A form of learning based on principles of reinforcement and punishment.

orgasm: The peak of sexual arousal during which the muscles around the genitals make a series of brief, rhythmic contractions.

orgasmic disorder: An inability to achieve orgasm or a greatly delayed orgasm during sexual activity.

orgasmic platform: The increased swelling of the outer third of the vagina

orgasmic reconditioning: A therapy in which the client is instructed to masturbate to the paraphilic desire until the brink of orgasm, at which point the client is asked to think about a more socially appropriate fantasy.

outercourse: Any type of sexual activity other than penile-vaginal intercourse.

ovaries: The female gonads.

ovulation: The portion of the menstrual cycle during which a mature egg is released from an ovary.

oxytocin: A neuropeptide hormone manufactured in the brain and released during physical intimacy that plays a role in bonding.

pansexuality: Attraction to members of all sexes and gender identities.

paraphilias: Patterns of sexual attraction and behavior that deviate from social and cultural norms.

parental investment: The amount of effort required to produce a child who carries your own genetic material.

passion: The motivational component of Sternberg's Triangular Theory of Love.

passionate love: An all-consuming physiological and psychological state characterized by obsessive preoccupation, intense sexual attraction, and excitement.

paternity uncertainty: The idea that a man cannot easily tell whether a pregnant women is carrying his child.

pederasty: An ancient Greek practice in which an older man educated and mentored a male adolescent, who would have sex with him in return.

pedophilia: A paraphilia characterized by sexual attraction toward prepubescent children.

pelvic inflammatory disease (PID): A chlamydia or gonorrhea infection that has spread to the upper reproductive tract causing pain and, potentially, infertility.

penile strain gauge: A device for measuring sexual arousal through changes in penile circumference.

perfect use: The percentage of women who will not get pregnant over the course of a year if a given contraceptive method is utilized consistently and no mistakes are made.

perineum: An area of skin that runs between the introitus and the anus.

persistent genital arousal disorder: Uncontrollable sexual arousal that occurs spontaneously, without being preceded by sexual desire or activity.

personality psychology: The study of relatively stable, intrapsychic factors that generate consistent patterns of behavior

Peyronie's disease: A build-up of scar tissue around the cavernous bodies that results in a severe curvature of the penis and makes intercourse difficult and painful.

phalloplasty: A form of sex reassignment surgery in which skin is taken from other parts of the body and transplanted to the genital area to create a functional penis. This term is also used to describe several forms of penile augmentation surgery.

pharmacotherapy: The treatment of sexual difficulties with medicinal drugs.

pheromones: Chemicals secreted by the body that play a role in sexual communication.

phimosis: When an uncircumcised man's foreskin is too tight and makes erections painful.

physical attractiveness: The degree to which we perceive another person as beautiful or handsome.

placebo effect: The idea that when people strongly believe that a treatment will have an effect on them, it often does, even though the treatment is biologically inert.

plateau: An extension of the excitement phase in which vasocongestion and myotonia become more pronounced.

PLISSIT model of sex therapy: An acronym that stands for Permission, Limited Information, Specific Suggestions, and Intensive Therapy.

polyamory: The practice of having multiple sexual and/or romantic partners simultaneously with an emphasis on building intimate relationships.

polygamy: A form of marriage featuring multiple spouses.

polymorphously perverse: The Freudian notion that humans can derive sexual pleasure from almost anything.

pornography: Any type of sexually explicit material that has the intent of producing arousal in those who consume it.

post-traumatic stress disorder (PTSD): A prolonged emotional reaction to trauma characterized by distressing flashbacks and dreams, extreme anxiety and hyper-vigilance, social detachment, and insomnia.

premature orgasm: When an individual consistently reaches orgasm before it is desired.

premenstrual dysphoric disorder (PMDD): A controversial DSM diagnosis that describes particularly severe cases of PMS.

premenstrual syndrome (PMS): The general term that encompasses all of the emotional changes and physical discomfort a woman might experience prior to getting her period

prepuce: Also known as the clitoral hood. Akin to the foreskin that covers the glans of the penis.

prevalence: The total number of people who are currently afflicted with a given problem or disease.

priapism: An erection that will not go away on its own. In medical terms, it is an erection lasting longer than four hours.

primary erogenous zones: Portions of the body where nerve endings are present in large quantities.

progestin-only methods: Administration of progestin only to prevent pregnancy.

propinquity effect: The closer two people are, the greater the odds that they will meet and an attraction will develop between them.

prostate gland: Produces alkaline secretions that aid in sperm survival. Sometimes referred to as the "male G-spot."

prostitute: A person who makes an explicit agreement to perform a sexual act in exchange for some type of compensation and is willing to offer this service to almost anyone who can afford it.

quality of alternatives: One's perception of the desirability of other potential partners and relationship states.

quid pro quo: A form of sexual harassment in which someone in a position of power offers a benefit or reward in exchange for sexual favors.

random selection: A sampling procedure in which participants are recruited at random from the target population

reactivity: The idea that research participants sometimes alter their behavior when they know others are watching

refractory period: The period of time after an orgasm during which no additional orgasms are possible. Usually only experienced by men.

reparative therapy: The use of operant conditioning principles to change someone's sexual orientation, usually from homosexual to heterosexual.

resolution: The return of the genitals to their nonaroused state and the final phase of the Masters and Johnson sexual response cycle.

rohypnol: A powerful sedative commonly used as a means of facilitating rape.

sadists: Persons who derive sexual gratification from inflicting physical or psychological pain on others.

sadomasochism: A class of sexual activities in which sexual arousal is derived from either giving or receiving pain.

satisfaction: One's subjective evaluation of a relationship.

secondary erogenous zones: Regions of the body that have taken on sexual significance as a result of conditioning.

self-expansion theory: A theory that posits human beings have a fundamental need to "expand" or grow the self over time.

self-fulfilling prophecy: When others' expectations elicit and reinforce certain behavior, effectively making a stereotype come true.

self-selection: The idea that persons who volunteer to participate in research studies are different from the rest of the population.

semen: The accumulated secretions of the vas deferens, seminal vesicles, and prostate.

seminal vesicles: Two small glands that empty into the ejaculatory duct and produce the bulk of the seminal fluid.

seminiferous tubules: A series of tightly coiled tubes in which sperm production occurs.

sensate focus techniques: A gradual reconditioning process in which individuals come to associate sexual arousal and activity with relaxation and pleasure instead of anxiety.

sensation seeking: A general tendency to pursue risky and thrilling activities.

serial monogamists: Persons who pursue a pattern of entering and exiting sexually exclusive relationships.

serotonin: A neurotransmitter linked to decreases in sexual arousal and behavior.

sex: A biological term used to categorize whether someone is genetically male or female.

sex reassignment surgery: A surgical procedure in which a transsexual person's body is adjusted to match that person's gender identity.

sex surrogacy: An approach in which a sex therapist provides a client with a substitute or "practice" partner in order to reach a desired therapeutic outcome.

sex trafficking: A type of slavery in which victims are bought and sold for sexual purposes.

sexology: The scientific study of sex.

sexual assault: Any event in which a person is touched in a sexual way against that person's will or made to perform a non-consensual sex act by one or more other persons.

sexual aversion disorder: An aversion to any type of partnered sexual activity.

sexual communal strength: The willingness to satisfy your partner's sexual needs, even when they do not necessarily align with your own personal desires.

sexual desire discrepancy: A case where one partner has less sexual desire than the other and it generates relationship difficulties.

sexual dysfunction: Specific sexual issues that repeatedly emerge and create distress at either the level of the individual or of the relationship.

sexual fantasies: Mental imagery that an individual perceives as sexually arousing.

sexual fluidity: The ability to adapt sexual and romantic attraction toward a specific person instead of an overall gender category.

sexual harassment: Unwanted verbal and/or physical sexual advances that occur in the workplace or in an academic environment.

sexual orientation: The unique pattern of sexual and romantic desire, behavior, and identity each person expresses.

sexual prejudice: All forms of prejudice that stem from an individual's actual or perceived sexual orientation.

sexual strategies theory: The idea that men and women have developed different mating strategies as a function of differing levels of parental investment.

singlism: Prejudice against singles.

social comparison theory: This theory posits that we are driven to obtain accurate evaluations of the self and that one way of doing so is by comparing our attitudes and beliefs to those of others.

social or observational learning: Learning that occurs by watching others' activities.

socially desirable responding: The tendency for research subjects to present themselves in the most favorable light possible

sociocultural perspective: Acknowledges that biological and evolved factors play some role in contributing to sex differences, but specifies that such differences are primarily a function of the social structure.

sociosexuality: The degree to which commitment and an emotional connection to one's partner are necessary precursors to sexual activity. Those with a restricted sociosexual orientation require commitment and intimacy, while those with an unrestricted orientation do not.

spectatoring: A form of distraction that involves overthinking or overanalyzing one's own sexual performance while having sex.

spermicides: Chemicals that are placed inside the vagina that attempt to kill or disable sperm for a certain period of time.

spongy body: A cylinder of erectile tissue that encases the urethra and expands to form the glans.

squeeze technique: A treatment for premature ejaculation that involves squeezing the head or base of the penis to prevent ejaculation during an impending orgasm.

state self-control: One's self-control abilities at a specific moment.

statutory rape: Sexual assault against a minor.

stonewalling: Appearing indifferent or showing no emotional response to a partner's concerns.

stop–start technique: A treatment for premature ejaculation that involves repeatedly starting and stopping sexual stimulation of the penis as a means of producing better ejaculatory control.

superego: The portion of the personality representing the conscience. Tries to persuade the ego to do what is moral.

superincision: A lengthwise slit in the upper portion of the foreskin. Also known as a dorsal slit.

survey research: A research method in which people are asked to report on their own sexual attitudes and practices.

swinging: A sexual practice in which married couples temporarily swap partners.

syphilis: A less common bacterial STI that often produces noticeable symptoms and can be deadly if left untreated.

telephone scatologia: A paraphilia that involves making obscene telephone calls to unsuspecting strangers. Often considered a subtype of exhibitionism.

testes: The male gonads.

testosterone: A steroid hormone secreted by both the gonads and the adrenal glands that affects sexual behavior.

trait self-control: One's overall, chronic level of self-control.

transgender: Someone whose behaviors or physical appearance is not consistent with societal gender roles.

transphobia: Prejudice against transsexuals.

transsexual: Someone whose gender identity does not match that person's biological sex.

transvestism: A paraphilia characterized by cross-dressing for purposes of sexual arousal.

tribadism: The act of rubbing one's genitals on the body of a sexual partner.

tubal ligation: Clamping or severing the fallopian tubes so that any eggs released cannot come into contact with sperm.

Turner's syndrome: A sex variation in which an individual is born with a single X chromosome.

two-spirit: A Native American phenomenon in which both male and female spirits are presumed to occupy a single person's body.

typical use: Accounting for human error, the percentage of women who will not get pregnant over the course of a year while using a given contraceptive method.

unrealistic optimism: The tendency to think that one is unlikely to encounter health problems in the future.

uterus: A muscular organ that protects and nourishes a developing fetus. Also known as the womb.

vagina: A canal that extends from the introitus to the uterus that changes in size during sexual arousal and childbirth.

vaginal photoplethysmograph: A device for measuring sexual arousal via changes in vaginal blood volume as determined by a photocell that captures reflected light.

vaginismus: A conditioned response in which the lower third of the vagina exhibits sudden and severe contractions during any attempt at vaginal penetration.

vaginoplasty: A form of sex reassignment surgery that involves removing the penis and scrotum and reusing the skin to create a functional vagina with labia.

vas deferens: The tube that carries sperm from the epididymis to the ejaculatory duct.

vasectomy: Severing or sealing the vas deferens so that sperm can no longer become part of the seminal fluid.

vasocongestion: An increase in blood flow to bodily tissues.

vestibular bulbs: A set of erectile tissue that expands in size during sexual arousal extending the vulva outward.

vomeronasal organ (VNO): The portion of the olfactory (i.e., smell) system that processes pheromones.

voyeurism: A paraphilia that involves experiencing sexual arousal from fantasizing about or viewing an unsuspecting person(s) who is naked or having sex.

vulva: All of the external female genital structures.

withdrawal: Removing the penis from the vagina prior to ejaculation as a means of pregnancy prevention.

zoophilia: A sexual variation characterized by an erotic attraction to non-human animals.

Index

5-alpha-reductase deficiency (5αRD), 121, 125

abortion: defined, 274; emergency contraception and, 268; psychological reactions to, 274–275; reasons for, 274; sexual dysfunction and, 307

abstinence, 257–259, 263

abstinence-only approach to sex education, 257–259

abstinence-plus approach to sex education, 257–259

acquired immune deficiency syndrome (AIDS), *see* AIDS (acquired immune deficiency syndrome)

adolescents: contraceptive use, 257; HPV vaccination, 284–285; media influences on, 14–15, 129–130; self-control, 250; sexting, 7; sexual victimization, 364; STI rates, 256; transgender issues, 134

adrenal glands, 97

adultery, *see* nonconsensual nonmonogamy

Africa: dry sex, 244; female genital cutting, 70, 73, 78; HIV/AIDS, 60, 286; kissing, 241; views on female virginity, 70, 72; views on homosexuality, 159

African Americans: age of first sex, 240; anal sex, 244; kissing, 240; marriage length, 220; masturbation, 238; oral sex, 243

age: bodily concerns and, 75, 78; resolution of sexual response and, 108; sexual behavior and, 230–231, 241; sexual dysfunction and, 303–304; sexual prejudice and, 160; testosterone production and replacement, 98–99

age of sexual consent, 357

aggression, 14, 137–138

AIDS (acquired immune deficiency syndrome); defined, 285; NHSLS and, 36–37; prevalence, 286; prevention, 289; psychological impact, 293–294

alcohol: aphrodisiac, 102; beer goggles, 180; coping mechanism, 294, 363; expectancy effects, 102–103, 292; hookups, 199–201; sexual dysfunction and, 304; sexual victimization and, 355, 358

alloparenting hypothesis, 152

amenorrhea, 80

amygdala, 41, 88–89, 150

amyl nitrate, *see* poppers

anal sex: anal intercourse, 244–245; anilingus, 244–245; bisexual men, 247; female condoms, 265; gay men, 246–247; prevalence of, 231; sex laws, 352

anaphrodisiacs, 100, 103

androgens, *see* testosterone

Androgen Insensitivity Syndrome (AIS), 122–125

androgynous, 136

anilingus, 6, 244–245, 297

animals, *see* zoophilia

anorgasmia, *see* orgasmic disorder

antidepressants, 90, 304, 321–322, 346

antipsychotic drugs, 90, 304

antiviral drugs, 285

anti-retroviral drugs, 286

anxiety, performance, 305, 307

aphrodisiacs, 5, 100–103

The Psychology of Human Sexuality, First Edition. Justin J. Lehmiller.
© 2014 John Wiley & Sons, Ltd. Published 2014 by John Wiley & Sons, Ltd.

areola, 75–76, 104

arousal problems, 311, 319–21

arranged marriage, 4, 206, 214

asexuality, 136, 146, 199, 230–232

Asia: aphrodisiacs, 101; attitudes toward sex, 307; koro, 66; STI prevalence, 280–281; third gender, 4; views on homosexuality, 159

Asian Americans: age of first intercourse, 240; kissing, 240; marriage length, 220

asphyxiophilia, 336

assault, sexual, *see* sexual victimization

assortative mating, 177–179

attachment anxiety, 224, 251

attachment style, 221, 223, 251

attractiveness, 173, 177, 180, 182–184, 188

aversive conditioning, 13, 347

bacterial infections, 281–284

baculum, 57

barrier methods of birth control, 265–266

Bartholin's glands, 71, 312

bed nucleus of the stria terminalis (BNST), 118–119

behavioral therapy, 313–315 318, 321, 330

behaviorism, 11, 28, 314

bestiality, *see* zoophilia

Big Five personality factors, 16–17, 137

bigendered, 136

biopsychosocial perspective, 21–23

biphobia, 158–159

birth control, *see* contraception

birth control pills, *see* oral contraceptives

bisexuality: defined, 145; Freudian theory, 149; myths, 164–167; prejudice, 158–159; prevalence, 147–148; sexual behaviors, 245–246; sexual fluidity, 154–155

body image, 56, 64, 252, 304–305

bogus pipeline technique, 189

Botox, 323

brain: pornography exposure, 371; prenatal hormone effects, 118–119; sex differences, 118–119; sexual arousal, 76, 88–90; sexual orientation, 149–150; transsexual research, 119; *see also* fMRI

breakup, 7, 216, 224

breasts, 45, 75–78, 81

breast augmentation, 77–78, 133

breast cancer, 81

breast self-exam, 81–82

brothels, 361–364

bulbourethral glands, *see* Cowper's glands

case report, 10, 32, 42

castration, 4, 98–99, 118, 346

casual sex, *see* friends with benefits; hookups

cavernous bodies, 59, 66, 312, 319–321

celibacy, 155, 199, 230–232

cerebral cortex, 89–90

cervical barriers, 266

cervical cancer, 80–81

cervical cap, 266

cervix, 74, 76, 81, 266, 284

cheating, *see* nonconsensual nonmonogamy

chemical castration, 99, 346

child molestation, 341, 357

Child Protection and Obscenity Enforcement Act, 366

child sexual abuse (CSA); defined, 357; perpetrators, 341, 358; prevalence, 358, 367; psychological impact, 358; types, 357–358

children: gender nonconformity, 152–154, 358; media influences on, 7, 14–15, 129–130; social influences on, 126–128; teaching about sex, 256–261; transsexual issues, 134; *see also* adolescents; child sexual abuse

China: aphrodisiacs, 101; attitudes toward sex, 5; national sex surveys, 38; pornography, 366; STIs, 280–281; views on marriage, 214

chlamydia, 281–285, 287–288, 290, 304

Christianity, 4–5, 135, 352

chromosomal sex, 117–118

chronic illness, 241, 303–304, 322

cilia, 75

circumcision, female, 70–71

circumcision, male, 58, 60, 123, 323

classical conditioning, 11, 93, 177, 333, 347

clitoral hood, 68, 72, 312

clitoridectomy, 69–70

clitoris: anatomy, 69–70; female genital cutting, 70–71; Freudian view, 10; G-spot, relation to, 74; in gender reassignment surgery, 133–134; orgasm, 69–70, 76; sexual arousal, 104, 318

cock rings, 40, 67, 239

cognitive-behavioral sex therapy (CBST), 315, 318–319

cohabitation, 178, 214–216, 220, 352

coital alignment technique (CAT), 244

coitus, 231, 243–244, 263–266

collectivist cultures, 214–215

college students: age of first intercourse, 240; as research subjects, 33–34, 49; attitudes toward cheating, 222–223; definitions of abstinence, 263; friends with benefits, 200–201; hookups, 200; pornography use, 369

combined hormone methods, 267–269

commitment: as a risk factor for STIs, 291; in the Investment Model, 208–211; in the Triangular Theory, 206–207

communication, 138, 216; *see also* sexual communication

companionate love, 205

comparison level, 208

comparison level for alternatives, 208

comprehensive sex education, 257–259

compulsive sexual behavior, 309–310

condoms: errors in use, 265, 297; female condoms, 265; how to use, 297; lubricant compatibility, 297; male condoms, 265; relation to penis size, 293; *see also* contraception

confidentiality, 51

confounding, 42, 371

Confucianism, 5

congenital adrenal hyperplasia (CAH), 7, 121, 125, 189–190

consensual nonmonogamy: definition and types, 211–214; relationship satisfaction, 214; sexual health implications, 214

consummate love, 206–207

contraception: barrier methods, 265–266; behavioral methods, 262–264; history, 262; hormonal methods, 266–270; new directions, 271–272; psychological implications of use, 268–269; *see also* tubal ligation; vasectomy

contraceptive implant, 264, 267–268

contraceptive patch, 264, 267

contrast effect, 183, 371

convenience samples, 33

corona, 58

correlation, 42, 44–45

covert sensitization, 347

Cowper's glands, 63, 263

cremaster muscle, 62

cross-dressing, *see* transvestism

cryptorchidism, 62

cuckold, 223, 342

cunnilingus, 203, 243, 297; *see also* oral sex

debriefing, 50–51

deception, 48, 50

Deep Throat (film), 366

delayed ejaculation, 312

dental dams, 297–298

dependent variable, 32, 42–43

Depo-Provera: anaphrodisiac, 103; chemical castration, 99, 346; contraceptive, 264, 267

depression: during and after pregnancy, 273–274; link to low testosterone, 98–99; link to sexual dysfunction, 306; relation to abortion, 274–275; *see also* SSRI

desire problems, 308–310, 318–319

desire stage, Kaplan's model, 108

dhat, 66

Diamond, Lisa, 154, 166

Diamond, Milton, 124

diaphragm, 262, 264, 266

dildos, *see* sex toys

direct observation, 32, 38–41

dirty talk, 11–12, 96, 373

disabilities, 91, 232, 304, 306

distraction, *see* spectatoring

divorce, 215–216, 220, 222, 371

dopamine, 90, 103, 182, 322

double-barreled questions, 35

douching, 81, 262, 298

drag kings and queens, 136

drugs: effects on sexual arousal and response, 102–103, 304; pharmacotherapy, 315–317; treatment of paraphilic disorders, 346–347; treatment of sex offenders, 99, 346–347; *see also* aphrodisiacs; anaphrodisiacs; medicalization of sex

dry sex, 244

DSM (*Diagnostic and Statistical Manual of Mental Disorders*): gender identity, 132; homosexuality, 13, 162–163; paraphilias, 330, 335–336, 341–343; premenstrual syndromes, 80; sexual dysfunctions, 308–312

dual control model, 307–308

dysmenorrhea, 80

dyspareunia, 282, 313

Ecstasy (drug), 102

ectopic pregnancy, 74

ego, 8–9

eHarmony, 178

ejaculation: during oral sex, 243; in men, 64, 104; in women, 73; *see also* delayed ejaculation; premature orgasm

ejaculatory duct, 62–63

Electra complex, 10

emergency contraception, 268

endometriosis, 80

endometrium, 74

epididymis, 62, 66

episiotomy, 72

erectile disorder/erectile dysfunction (ED): defined, 311; prevalence, 309; treatments, 318–321

erection, 57, 102–104, 239–240; *see also* erectile disorder; Peyronie's disease

Eros Clitoral Therapy Device, 318

erotic plasticity, 92, 139, 155–158, 331, 370

Erotic Stimulus Pathway Theory, 110

erotica, 365–366

erotophilia, 16, 18, 291–292, 369

erotophobia, 16, 18

estrogen, 75, 97, 118, 133, 319; *see also* combined hormone methods

evolutionary psychology, 19–21, 186–188

evolutionary theory: attraction, 186–188; breasts, 75; critiques and alternative perspectives, 188–192; description, 19–21, 186–188; genitalia, 62–64; jealousy, 221; orgasm, 105–106; ovulation, 268–269; polygamy, 213; sexual orientation, 151–152

exchange theories, 15–16, 208

excitement, 104, 108–110

exhibitionist, 39, 331, 339–341, 347

exotic becomes erotic, 152–154

expectancy effects, 102–103, 292

experiment, 42–43

faking orgasms, 106–107

fallopian tube, 75, 80, 270–271

fantasies, *see* sexual fantasy

fascinum, 57

feeders, 236

feeling thermometer, 159

fellatio, 243, 363

female condoms, 265

female copulatory vocalizations, 96

female genital cutting, 70–71, 73, 78

female sexual arousal disorder, 308

female sexual interest/arousal disorder (SIAD), 308, 311

females: attitudes toward sex, 138–139; bodily concerns, 77–79; breast and genital health issues, 78–82; mate preferences, 183–191; orgasm, 68–69, 73–74, 76, 105–108; sexual anatomy, 68–76; sexual dysfunction, 308–313; sexual response, 103–108

fertility, 56, 67, 75, 152, 262; *see also* contraception; infertility

fertility awareness, 263–264

fetishism, 139, 157, 331–335

field of eligibles, 185

Fifty Shades of Grey (book), 336–337

fimbriae, 74

finger length ratios, in relation to sexual orientation, 150

fMRI (functional magnetic resonance imaging), 41, 76, 89

food, *see* aphrodisiacs

foreskin, 58, 60, 68

frequency of sexual activity, 230, 248, 251, 363

Freud, Sigmund, 8–9, 29, 42, 149

friends with benefits, 200–202, 206

frotteurism, 343

functional magnetic resonance imaging (fMRI), *see* fMRI

game-playing, 207–209

Gardasil, 284–285

gay, *see* homosexuality

gay affirmative therapy, 164

gaydar, 150, 165

gender: biological influences, 117–125; defined, 117; psychosocial influences, 126–130; variations in gender expression, 130–136; *see also* sex differences; transgender

gender conformity and nonconformity, 152–153

gender differe nces, *see* sex differences

gender dysphoria, 130, 132

gender identity, 56, 117–130, 259; *see also* transgender

gender identity disorder, 132

gender roles: cohabitating relationships and, 215; defined, 117; psychosocial influences on, 126–130; religion and, 4; same-sex relationships and, 165; sexual fantasy and, 232

gender stereotypes, 117, 127, 129, 259

genderqueer, 136

genital echo theory, 75

genitals: female genital concerns, 75–79; female genital health issues, 79–81; male genital concerns, 64–66; male genital health issues, 66–67

genital warts, 284

genito-pelvic pain/penetration disorder (GPD), 312, 323

glans, clitoral, 69

glans, penile, 62, 64, 67

gonads, *see* ovaries; testes

gonadal sex, 117–118

gonorrhea, 281–285, 287–288, 290, 304

Gottman, John, 216

Grafenberg spot (G-spot): amplification, 78; controversy, 73; described, 73

Graham, Sylvester, 239

Griswold v Connecticut, 262

hate crimes, 161–162

herpes, 282, 284–288, 290, 296, 363

heterosexism, 158

heterosexual, 145–146

hippocampus, 88

HIV (human immunodeficiency virus); circumcision and, 60; defined, 285; disclosure of infection status, 291, 293; discordant status couples, 295–296; prevalence, 166–167, 280, 285–286; prevention, 286–289; psychological impact, 293–294; screening recommendations, 281; transmission, 286, 290

homophobia, 135, 158–161

homosexuality: biological theories of, 149–151; biopsychosocial theories of, 152–155; defined, 145–146; evolutionary theories of, 151–152; gay and lesbian relationships, 185, 211–212; myths about, 165–167; prevalence of, 146–148; sexual behaviors, 234, 245–247; *see also* homophobia; heterosexism

Hooker, Evelyn, 163

hookups, 199–203

hormonal contraceptives: combined hormone methods, 267; progestin-only methods, 267–268; psychological implications of, 268–269

hormonal sex, 118

hormones and sexual behavior, 97–100, 118, 182, 268–269; *see also* sex therapy; sexual dysfunction

hostile environment, 358–359

human immunodeficiency virus (HIV), *see* HIV

human papilloma virus (HPV), 60, 80–81, 284–285, 288, 295–296

Human Sexual Response (book), 31, 39

Humphreys, Laud, 46–47

hymen, 71–72

hymenoplasty, 72

hypersexuality, *see* compulsive sexual behavior

hypogonadism, 98

hypothalamus, 41, 88–89, 119, 149

hysterectomy, 133

hysteria, 236

id, 8–9

incest, 3–4, 357

incidence, 44

indecent exposure, *see* exhbitionism

independent variable, 32, 42–43

India: arranged marriage, 214–215; third gender, 135; sex laws, 352, 354, 366; STIs, 280

indirect partners, 298–299

individualist cultures, 214

infertility, 80, 272, 282–283

infibulation, 70

infidelity, *see* nonconsensual nonmonogamy

informed consent, 48, 50

intercourse, *see* coitus; anal sex

Internet: online dating and hookups, 178, 185, 293; pornography, 260–261, 366; research tool, 34; sexual expression, 7; STI risk, 293

interracial relationships, 5, 178–179, 185

interreligious relationships, 178–179, 185

intersexed, 56, 80, 120–125, 135

interstitial cells, 62

intimacy (in the Triangular Theory), 206–207

intrauterine device (IUD), 264, 267–268, 275

introitus, 71–73

Investment Model, 208–211

investments, 210

Islam, 4–5, 60

jealousy, 221

Johnson, Virginia, 28, 30–31, 39–40

Kama Sutra (book), 241–242

Kaplan, Helen Singer, 108–110

Kegel exercises, female, 72–73

Kegel exercises, male, 62, 322

Kellogg, John Harvey, 239

Kinsey, Alfred, 28–30, 36; *see also*, Kinsey Scale; Kinsey's research findings

Kinsey Scale, 145–146

Kinsey's research findings: experience with prostitutes, 36; homosexuality, 36, 146; masturbation, 36; zoophilia, 345

kissing, 4, 241–242, 246–247, 263, 284–286

Klinefelter's syndrome, 120–121

koro, 66

labia majora, 68

labia minora, 68

labial reduction surgery, 68, 71, 78

Lawrence v Texas, 352

leading questions, 35
Lee, John, 207
lesbian, *see* homosexuality
libido, 8; *see also* sex drive
limbic system, 41, 88–89, 119
lordosis, 118
love: companionate love, 205; defined, 203–204;
    passionate love, 204; Triangular Theory,
    206–207; *see also* love styles
love styles, 207–209
Loving v Virginia, 179
lubricants, 73, 97, 244–245, 297, 318

male condoms, 264–265; *see also* condoms
male hypoactive sexual desire disorder (HSDD),
    308–309
males: attitudes toward sex, 138–139; genital health
    concerns, 64–66; genital health issues, 66–67;
    mate preferences, 183–191; orgasm, 104–108;
    sexual anatomy, 58–63; sexual dysfunction,
    308–313; sexual response, 103–108
mammary glands, 75–76
mammography, 81
marijuana, 102–103
marriage: interracial and interreligious, 179; length
    of, 220; marital privilege, 198–199; same-sex,
    159, 211–212; vs. cohabitation, 214–216; *see
    also* arranged marriage; polygamy; spousal
    rape; swinging
masochism, 331, 336–337
mastectomy, 133
Masters, William, 28, 30–31, 39–40
Masters and Johnson model of sexual response, *see*
    sexual response cycle
masturbation: defined, 235; frequency of, 238;
    myths and sociocultural concerns, 66, 70,
    238–240; reasons for, 238; sex differences in,
    138, 238; *see also* sex toys
masturbatory satiation, 347
mate choice hypothesis, 106
MDMA, *see* Ecstasy (drug)
mean, 44
meatus, 58, 71
media influences on sex, 5–7, 14–15, 259, 336–337;
    see also social/observational learning
median, 44
medicalization of sex, 29, 238
men, *see* males
Men are from Mars, Women are from Venus (book), 137

menarche, 80
menopause, 80, 99
menstrual cycle, 79–80; *see also* ovulation
menstrual cycle problems, 80
menstrual synchrony, 94
menstruation, 79–80
mere exposure effect, 177
metoidioplasty, 133–134
Miller v California, 365
minimal risk, 49
misattribution of physiological arousal, 181
miscarriage, 274
Money, John, 123
monogamy, 3, 166, 211–214, 224
monosexism, 158
mons veneris, 68, 73
mortality salience, 251–252
mother-to-child transmission of HIV, 286, 289
multiple orgasms, 106
Muslims, 4–5, 60
myometrium, 74
myotonia, 104

National Health and Social Life Survey (NHSLS);
    interreligious relationships, 179;
    masturbation, 238; methods of survey,
    36–37; number of partners, 367; oral sex,
    243; sexual frequency, 248
National Survey of Sexual Health and Behavior
    (NSSHB): anal sex, 244; masturbation, 238;
    methods of survey, 37–38; oral sex, 243;
    selected findings, 38; sexual activities across
    the lifespan, 230–231
necrophilia, 331, 343–344
need to belong, 197
negging, 174
neurotransmitters: paraphilias and, 330; sexual
    arousal and, 90; sexual attraction and,
    182, 184
nipple, 75–76, 90–91, 104, 106, 339
nonconsensual nonmonogamy, 222–224
nonresponse, 34
nymphomania, 309

obscene telephone calls, *see* telephone scatologia
Oedipus complex, 10
online research, *see* Internet
oophorectomy, 99
open relationships, 213–214

operant conditioning, 9, 11–13, 330, 339

opportunistic infections, 285

oral contraceptives, 95, 264, 267, 370

oral herpes, 284–286

oral sex: defined, 243; definitions of abstinence and, 263; in same-sex relationships, 245–246; prevalence, 231; safer-sex practices and, 287, 297–298

orgasm: fake orgasms, 106–107; female orgasm, 68–69, 73–74, 76, 105–108; health benefits of, 248; in the Erotic Stimulus Pathway Theory, 110; in Kaplan's model, 108; in Masters and Johnson model, 104–105; male orgasm, 104–108; relationship type and, 202–203; sex differences in, 106–108; theories of, 105–106; *see also* orgasm problems

orgasm problems, 311–312, 321–322

orgasmic disorder, 312

orgasmic platform, 104

orgasmic reconditioning, 346–347

outercourse, 263

ova, 75

ovaries, 75

ovulation, 75, 79–80, 95–96, 187, 268–269; *see also* contraception; fertility awareness

oxytocin, 58, 99–100, 102–103, 182

pain: sexual pleasure and, 331, 336–337; sexual problems and, 59–60, 282, 309, 312–313; treatment of sexual pain, 323; *see also* dysmenorrhea; dyspareunia; sexually transmitted infections

pansexuality, 146

Pap test, 81

paraphilias: definition and characteristics, 329–331; exhibitionism, 339–340; fetishism, 331–335; masochism, 336–337; necrophilia, 343–344; pedophilia, 341, 357–358; sadism, 336–337; telephone scatologia, 341; transvestism, 130–132, 335–336; treatment of, 345–347; voyeurism, 338–339; zoophilia, 344–345

paraphilic disorder, 330

parental investment, 20–21, 139, 186

parents and parenting: influence on gender identity, 126–127; intersex issues, 123–124; pregnancy and childbirth, 272–275; sexual orientation and, 160–161, 166; views on sex education, 256, 258, 260–261

passion (in the Triangular Theory), 206–207

passionate love, 204

paternity uncertainty, 221

pederasty, 4, 352

pedophilia, 341, 357–358

pegging, 247

pelvic floor muscles, 72

pelvic inflammatory disease (PID), 282, 304,

penile strain gauge, 40, 92, 164, 166, 333

penis: anatomy, 58–64; concerns, 64–66; health issues, 66–67; size, 59, 64–66; social attitudes, 56–57

perfect use, 263–264

performance anxiety, 305, 307

perimetrium, 74

perineum, 64, 72, 90

persistent genital arousal disorder, 311, 319

personality psychology, 16–19

Peyronie's disease, 59, 312, 323

phalloplasty, 64, 134

pharmacotherapy, 315, 317–318

pheromones, 93–96, 182

phimosis, 60, 312, 323

physical attractiveness, 91, 177, 182–187

physiological arousal, 41, 152–153, 180–182

pick-up lines, 174–176

placebo effect, 100–101

Plan B, 268

plateau, 104, 108–110

Playboy (magazine), 68, 183, 371

pleasure principle, 8

PLISSIT model of sex therapy, 314

polyamory, 213–214

polygamy, 213

polymorphously perverse, 149

poppers, 102

pornography: actor characteristics, 366–368; defined, 365; effects of pornography exposure, 15, 245, 371–373; the law and, 365–366; sex education and, 260–261; user characteristics, 368–369; *see also* revenge porn; social/observational learning

positions, sexual, *see* sexual positions

postpartum depression, 273

posttraumatic stress disorder (PTSD), 274, 356, 358, 363–364

pregnancy: abortion, 274–275; adolescent, 256–257, 275; intercourse during, 274; miscarriage, 274; psychology of, 272–274; *see also* infertility; postpartum depression

premature orgasm, 311–312, 321–322

premenstrual dysphoric disorder (PMDD), 80
premenstrual syndrome (PMS), 80
preoptic area (POA), 89, 118–119
prepuce, 58, 68–70
prevalence, 44
priapism, 311, 319
primary erogenous zones, 90–91
progestin-only methods, 267–268
prolactin, 106
propinquity effect, 177, 181, 184–185
prostaglandins, 80
prostate gland, 63, 105
prostitution: defined, 360; motivations, 362; patrons, 363; psychological impact of, 362–363; types of prostitutes, 360–361
provocation, 137
Prozac, *see* SSRI (selective serotonin reuptake inhibitor)
puberty-blocking drugs, 132, 134
pubic hair, 59, 67–68, 373
pudendum, 67

quality of alternatives, 208, 210
questionnaire research, 34–38
quid pro quo, 358

race: anal sex and, 244; divorce and, 220; masturbation and, 238; oral sex and, 243; penis size and, 59; *see also* interracial relationships
random assignment, 42
random selection, 33
rape, *see* sexual victimization
rape fantasy, 235
reactivity, 39
reality principle, 8
Reed, David, 110
refractory period, 106, 347
reinforcement, 9, 11–12, 174, 313
religion and sexuality, 4–5, 60, 128, 159–161, 232, 369; *see also* interreligious relationships
reparative therapy, 13, 160, 164
research methods: ethical issues, 45–51; experimental methods, 42–43; nonexperimental methods, 34–42; sampling issues, 32–33; statistical issues, 44–45; technologies, 40–41
responsive desire, 308
resolution, 108
revenge porn, 7, 339

Reversible Inhibition of Sperm Under Guidance (RISUG), 271–272
The Rocky Horror Picture Show (film), 131–132
rohypnol (roofies), 355
root, penile, 58

sadism, 331, 336–337
sadomasochism, 336–337
sample, 32–33
satisfaction: as a component of the Investment Model, 208, 210; with breast size, 75, 77; with penis size, 65; with relationship, 178, 218, 224; with sex, 60, 64–65, 134, 202–203, 251; *see also* sexual communication
satyriasis, 309
scarcity, 180
scrotum, 59–63, 66, 243, 319
secondary erogenous zones, 91, 242, 304
secondary sex characteristics, 75, 124, 132, 134
self-control: state self-control, 250; strength model of, 43, 249–250; trait self-control, 249
self-expansion theory, 218–219
self-fulfilling prophecy, 102, 127–128, 178, 324
self-selection, 32, 35, 39
semen, 4, 58, 63–64, 66, 97
seminal vesicles, 63, 105
seminiferous tubules, 62
sensate focus techniques, 314–315, 318
sensation seeking, 16–17, 337, 369, 371
senses: hearing, 96; smell, 92–96; taste, 96–97; touch, 90–91; vision, 91–92
serial monogamists, 202–203, 214
serotonin, 90, 103, 304, 330
sex: chromosomal sex, 117–118; defined, 117; gonadal sex, 117–118; hormonal sex, 118; *see also* anal sex; coitus; oral sex
Sex and the City (TV show), 6, 164, 198
Sex at Dawn (book), 21, 192
sex differences: arousal, 92; attraction, 20–21, 172, 183–192; hookups, 200; orgasm, 106–108; paraphilias, 330; pornography use, 369–370; psychology, 137–138; sexual attitudes, 138–139; sexual orientation, 155–158
sex drive, 139, 156, 166, 217, 339, 356; *see also* libido
sex education: approaches, 257–258; outcomes, 259; public views, 258
sex flush, 104
sex reassignment surgery, 132–134, 312
sex surrogacy, 315–317

sex therapy: behavioral approach, 313–315; cognitive-behavioral therapy, 315; critiques, 317–318; treating arousal problems, 319–321; treating desire problems, 318–319; treating orgasm problems, 321–322; treating pain problems, 323; *see also* pharmacotherapy; PLISSIT model; sex surrogacy

sex toys, 67, 235–237, 353

sex trafficking, 364

sexology, 28

sexting, 7

sexual abuse, *see* sexual victimization

sexual addiction, *see* compulsive sexual behavior

sexual arousal: brain and, 88–90; hormones and, 97–100; senses and, 90–97; substances, 100–103; technology for measuring, 40–41

sexual assault, *see* sexual victimization

sexual aversion disorder, 309

sexual behaviors: anal sex, 244–245; celibacy, 230–232; coitus, 243–244; kissing, 241–242; masturbation, 235–240; oral sex, 243; same-sex, 245–247; sexual fantasy, 232–236; sexual touching, 242; *see also* paraphilias

sexual communal strength, 217–218

sexual communication, 203, 217, 259, 293, 324

sexual desire discrepancy, 309

sexual double standard, 78–79, 92, 139

sexual dysfunction: arousal problems, 311; avoiding sexual difficulties, 324; causes, 303–308; desire problems, 308–310; orgasm problems, 311–312; pain problems, 312–313; statistics, 309

sexual fantasy: controversial fantasies, 235–236; defined, 232; functions, 232, 235; sex differences, 233–234

sexual fluidity, 154–155, 166

sexual harassment, 358–360

sexual orientation: defined, 145–146; measurement and prevalence, 146–148; myths, 164–167; prejudice and social attitudes, 158–162; same-sex relationships, 211; sex differences in, 155–158; theories of, 149–155; *see also* asexuality; bisexuality; homosexuality

sexual positions, 4, 243–244, 373

sexual prejudice, 158–162

sexual response cycle: excitement, 104; orgasm, 104–108; plateau, 104; resolution, 108

sexual strategies theory, 20

sexual touching, 242, 263, 313–314, 359

sexual victimization: child sexual abuse, 357–358; psychological impact, 356–358, 360, 364; sexual assault and rape, 354–357; sexual harassment, 358–360; sex trafficking, 364

sexually transmitted infections (STIs); bacterial infections, 281–284; myths, 287–289; other infections, 289; prevention efforts, 296–299; psychological impact, 293–296; risk factors, 290–293; statistics, 280–281; viral infections, 284–289

shaft, clitoral, 68

shaft, penile, 58, 62, 64, 66

similarity, 177–179, 185

singles: prejudice against, 197–199; sexual activity and satisfaction, 202–203; types of sexual relationships, 199–202

singlism, 199

Skene's glands, 73

Smegma, 58, 66, 68, 81, 312

social comparison theory, 177–178

social disapproval, 220–221

social or observational learning, 9, 12–15, 75, 372

social skills training, 347

socially desirable responding, 35, 39

sociocultural perspective, 139, 189–191

sociosexuality, 18–19, 182, 292

spectatoring, 304–306, 314

sperm, 58, 62–64, 73, 105, 117; *see also* contraception

spermarche, 62

spermatic cord, 59, 62

spermicides, 265–266, 313

spinal cord injury, 91, 304, 312

spongy body, 59

spousal rape, 352

squeeze technique, 322

SSRI (selective serotonin reuptake inhibitor), 90, 103, 304, 319–322, 346

standard days method, 263

statutory rape, 355, 357

stereotype threat, 128

sterilization, 264, 268, 270

sternberg, Robert, 206

stonewalling, 216

stop–start technique, 322

sunna, 69–70

superego, 8–9

superincision, 58, 322

survey research, 34–38

swinging, 213–214

symptothermal method, 263

syphilis, 60, 281, 284, 290, 363; *see also* Tuskegee Syphilis Study

Szasz, Thomas, 318

talking, *see* communication; sexual communication

Taoism, 5

target population, 32–33

Tearoom Trade Study, 46–48

technology and sex research, 40–41

telephone scatologia, 331, 341

television, 5–6, 129–130, 202, 338

terror management theory, 251–252

testes, 62, 66, 97–98, 117–125

testosterone: prenatal exposure effects, 119, 150–151; role in sexual behavior, 97–99; testosterone replacement therapy, 98–99, 318; *see also* castration; chemical castration

theory of gender neutrality, 123–124

threesome, 213, 234

Tissot, Samuel Auguste, 238–239

tobacco, 304

touching, sexual, *see* sexual touching

transgender, 117, 130–136, 259

transphobia, 135

transsexual, 116, 119, 130–135, 312

transvestism, 131–132, 135–136, 331, 335–336

Triangular Theory, 206–207

tribadism, 242, 245

Triphasic Model of Sexual Response, 108–110

tubal ligation, 270

Turner's syndrome, 120–121, 125

Tuskegee Syphilis Study, 47–48, 284

two-spirit, 135

typical use, 263

United States: contraceptive laws and use, 262, 268; pornography, 365–366; sex education, 256–259; sex laws, 352–355; STIs, 280

unrealistic optimism, 291

urethra, 62, 133–134, 334

urethral opening, *see* meatus

uterus, 73–74, 78–79, 104–105, 236, 267–268

vagina: anatomy, 71–74; concerns, 78; health issues, 80; orgasm, 68–69; sexual arousal and response, 104–106

vaginal intercourse, *see* coitus

vaginal photoplethysmograph, 40, 92

vaginal ring, 264, 267

vaginismus, 312–313, 317, 322, 357

vaginoplasty, 133

vas deferens, 62–63, 105, 270–272

vasectomy, 270–272

vasocongestion, 104

vestibular bulbs, 73

Viagra, 37, 102–103, 319–320, 322

vibrators, *see* sex toys

video voyeurism, 339

violent pornography, 372

viral infections, 284–289

vomeronasal organ (VNO), 93–94

voyeurism, 331, 338–339

vulva: anatomy, 68–72; appearance concerns, 78; social attitudes, 67–68

Watson, John, 28–29

withdrawal, 263–264

women, *see* females

X-chromosome, 117, 120–121

Y-chromosome, 117

zoophilia, 331, 344–345, 366